Frommer's®

Greek Islands

7th Edition

by John S. Bowman, Sherry Marker, & Peter Kerasiotis

with cruise coverage by Heidi Sarna

LINDENHURST MEMORIAL LIBRARY
LINDENHURST, NEW YORK 11757

D1113575

John Wiley & Sons, Inc.

Published by:
JOHN WILEY & SONS, INC.
111 River St.
Hoboken, NJ 07030-5774

Copyright © 2012 John Wiley & Sons, Inc., Hoboken, New Jersey. All rights reserved. No part of this publication may be reproduced, stored in a retrieval system or transmitted in any form or by any means, electronic, mechanical, photocopying, recording, scanning or otherwise, except as permitted under Sections
107 or 108 of the 1976 United States Copyright Act, without either the prior written permission of the
Publisher, or authorization through payment of the appropriate per-copy fee to the Copyright Clearance
Center, 222 Rosewood Drive, Danvers, MA 01923, 978/750-8400, fax 978/646-8600. Requests to the
Publisher for permission should be addressed to the Permissions Department, John Wiley & Sons, Inc., 111
River Street, Hoboken, NJ 07030, 201/748-6011, fax 201/748-6008, or online at http://www.wiley.com/go/
permissions.

Wiley and the Wiley logo are trademarks or registered trademarks of John Wiley & Sons, Inc. Frommer's
is a trademark or registered trademark of Arthur Frommer. Used under license. All other trademarks are
the property of their respective owners. John Wiley & Sons, Inc., is not associated with any product or
vendor mentioned in this book.

ISBN 978-1-118-09602-4 (paper); ISBN 978-1-118-22354-3 (ebk); ISBN 978-1-118-24576-7 (ebk);
ISBN 978-1-118-23693-2 (ebk)

Editor: Michael Kelly, with Maureen Clarke
Production Editor: Michael Brumitt
Cartographer: Roberta Stockwell
Photo Editor: Richard Fox
Production by Wiley Indianapolis Composition Services

Front Cover Photo: Shipwreck Beach on Zakynthos (Zante) in the Ionians ©SIME / eStock Photo

Back Cover Photo: Temple of the Acropolis of Rhodes ©SIME / eStock Photo

For information on our other products and services or to obtain technical support, please contact our
Customer Care Department within the U.S. at 877/762-2974, outside the U.S. at 317/572-3993 or fax
317/572-4002.

Wiley also publishes its books in a variety of electronic formats. Some content that appears in print may
not be available in electronic formats.

Manufactured in the United States of America

5   4   3   2   1

CONTENTS

LIST OF MAPS

ABOUT THE AUTHORS

John S. Bowman has been a freelance writer and editor for more than 45 years. He specializes in nonfiction ranging from archaeology to zoology, baseball to biography. He first visited Greece in 1956 and has traveled and lived there over the years. He is the author of numerous guides to various regions in Greece; for several decades, his *Travellers' Guide to Crete* was the premier guide to that island. He currently resides in Northampton, Massachusetts.

Sherry Marker majored in classical Greek at Harvard, studied archaeology at the American School of Classical Studies in Athens, and did graduate work in ancient history at the University of California at Berkeley. The author of a number of guides to Greece, she has also written for the *New York Times, Travel + Leisure,* and *Hampshire Life.* When not in Greece, she lives in Massachusetts and London.

Peter Kerasiotis, a native Athenian, currently lives in New York City where he works as a web developer and editor. A newcomer to Frommer's, he hopes to continue a career of travel- and screenwriting.

Heidi Sarna is a freelance writer who has crisscrossed the world by ship for nearly 20 years, often with her twin sons and lucky husband in tow. Coauthor of *Frommer's Cruises & Ports of Call from US and Canadian Homeports* and *Frommer's Singapore Day by Day,* she has also contributed to several other guidebooks and writes regular travel columns for Frommers. com and *Porthole* magazine. She's written for many magazines, newspapers, and websites, including CNN.com, the *International Herald Tribune, Condé Nast Traveller, Brides,* the *Straits Times, Expat Living,* and *Travel Weekly.*

HOW TO CONTACT US

In researching this book, we discovered many wonderful places—hotels, restaurants, shops, and more. We're sure you'll find others. Please tell us about them, so we can share the information with your fellow travelers in upcoming editions. If you were disappointed with a recommendation, we'd love to know that, too. Please write to:

Frommer's Greek Islands, 7th Edition
John Wiley & Sons, Inc. • 111 River St. • Hoboken, NJ 07030-5774
frommersfeedback@wiley.com

ADVISORY & DISCLAIMER

Travel information can change quickly and unexpectedly, and we strongly advise you to confirm important details locally before traveling, including information on visas, health and safety, traffic and transport, accommodation, shopping and eating out. We also encourage you to stay alert while traveling and to remain aware of your surroundings. Avoid civil disturbances, and keep a close eye on cameras, purses, wallets and other valuables.

While we have endeavored to ensure that the information contained within this guide is accurate and up-to-date at the time of publication, we make no representations or warranties with respect to the accuracy or completeness of the contents of this work and specifically disclaim all warranties, including without limitation warranties of fitness for a particular purpose. We accept no responsibility or liability for any inaccuracy or errors or omissions, or for any inconvenience, loss, damage, costs or expenses of any nature whatsoever incurred or suffered by anyone as a result of any advice or information contained in this guide.

The inclusion of a company, organization or Website in this guide as a service provider and/or potential source of further information does not mean that we endorse them or the information they provide. Be aware that information provided through some Websites may be unreliable and can change without notice. Neither the publisher or author shall be liable for any damages arising herefrom.

FROMMER'S STAR RATINGS, ICONS & ABBREVIATIONS

Every hotel, restaurant, and attraction listing in this guide has been ranked for quality, value, service, amenities, and special features using a **star-rating system.** In country, state, and regional guides, we also rate towns and regions to help you narrow down your choices and budget your time accordingly. Hotels and restaurants are rated on a scale of zero (recommended) to three stars (exceptional). Attractions, shopping, nightlife, towns, and regions are rated according to the following scale: zero stars (recommended), one star (highly recommended), two stars (very highly recommended), and three stars (must-see).

In addition to the star-rating system, we also use **seven feature icons** that point you to the great deals, in-the-know advice, and unique experiences that separate travelers from tourists. Throughout the book, look for:

special finds—those places only insiders know about

fun facts—details that make travelers more informed and their trips more fun

kids—best bets for kids and advice for the whole family

special moments—those experiences that memories are made of

overrated—places or experiences not worth your time or money

insider tips—great ways to save time and money

great values—where to get the best deals

The following **abbreviations** are used for credit cards:

AE	American Express	V	Visa
DC	Diners Club	MC	MasterCard

TRAVEL RESOURCES AT FROMMERS.COM

Frommer's travel resources don't end with this guide. Frommer's website, **www.frommers. com**, has travel information on more than 4,000 destinations. We update features regularly, giving you access to the most current trip-planning information and the best airfare, lodging, and car-rental bargains. You can also listen to podcasts, connect with other Frommers. com members through our active-reader forums, share your travel photos, read blogs from guidebook editors and fellow travelers, and much more.

THE BEST OF THE GREEK ISLANDS

G reece is, of course, the land of ancient sites and architectural treasures—the Acropolis in Athens, the amphitheater of Epidaurus, and the reconstructed palace at Knossos among the best known. But Greece is much more: It offers age-old spectacular natural sights, for instance—from Santorini's caldera to the gray pinnacles of rock of the Meteora—and modern diversions ranging from elegant museums to luxury resorts.

It can be bewildering to plan your trip with so many options vying for your attention. Take us along and we'll do the work for you. We've traveled the country extensively and have chosen the very best that Greece has to offer. We've explored the archaeological sites, visited the museums, inspected the hotels, reviewed the tavernas and ouzeries, and scoped out the beaches. Here's what we consider the best of the best.

THE best ISLANDS

- **Hydra** (Saronic Gulf Islands): Old-timers keep waiting for Hydra, with its handsome stone mansions overlooking a picture-postcard harbor, to be spoiled. After all, even before Mykonos and Santorini, Hydra was one of the first Greek islands to be "discovered." So far, so good: Donkeys still outnumber motorcycles, and the day-trippers who blitz through the appealing harborside shops leave at twilight. That means that except in August you can almost always find the table you want at one of Hydra's pleasant small restaurants. See chapter 6.
- **Crete:** Whether for its rugged mountains or its countless beaches, its ancient remains or its ultramodern hotels, its layered history or its intense people, Crete cannot be denied. It is not just a distinctive Greek island—it is a world unto itself. See chapter 7.
- **Santorini** (Cyclades): This is undoubtedly one of the most spectacular islands in the world. The streets of **Fira** and **Ia** are carved into the face of a high cliff, overlooking the circular caldera left by an ancient volcanic eruption and now filled with the deep-blue waters of the Aegean. The site of **Akrotiri** offers a unique glimpse into life in a Minoan city, frozen in time by the eruption 3,600 years ago. Be sure to find out if this spectacular site, which was partly closed to the public at press

Greece

BULGARIA

THRACE

Drama

Xanthi

Komotini

Kavala

Alexandroupolis

Sea of Marmara

Thasos

Samothraki

Mt. Athos

Limnos

EUROPE

AEGEAN SEA

GREECE

Alonissos

Lesvos
(Mitilini)

SPORADES

Skyros

NORTHEASTERN
AEGEAN ISLANDS

TURKEY

Kimi

EVVIA

Izmir

Karystos

Andros

Samos

Sounion

Kea

Tinos

Ikaria

Siros

Mykonos

Patmos

Delos

Serifos

Paros

Naxos

Donoussa

Kalimnos

Antiparos

Sifnos

Kos

CYCLADES

Ios

Amorgos

Milos

Folegandros

Simi

Anafi

DODECANESE

Santorini

Rhodes

To Crete
(approx. 235 miles
from Piraeus)

Sea of Crete

Karpathos

3

time, has completely reopened when you visit. Add to this the Fira nightlife scene, and you'll see why this is one of the most popular (and overcrowded) summer vacation spots in the Aegean. See chapter 8.

o **Sifnos** (Cyclades): Sifnos is a green island of ravines, mountaintops, and pristine beaches. Sifnos is small enough that a hardy walker can explore the entire island on foot, following well-maintained foot and donkey paths from church to church and village to village. From a distance, the villages look alike, with clusters of small, whitewashed flat-roofed houses. Up close, each village turns out to have its own very distinct character. In the capital, **Apollonia,** houses are cheek by jowl, with tiny gardens. Just out of Apollonia, two villages could not be more different: **Artemona** has startling neoclassical mansions and **Ex Ambela** has low houses with unusually large gardens. The village of **Kastro** (castle), on its seaside rock, is the medieval locus of the island, whereas **Platis Yialos** is a bustling beach resort. Don't visit in August, when the island is mobbed with vacationing Athenians. See chapter 8.

o **Siros** (Cyclades): This tiny island has it all: a vivacious, cosmopolitan capital town; thriving beach resorts; and a starkly beautiful region of farming communities, archaeological remains, and remote beaches to the north. Siros is also one of the centers of *rembetika,* a form of Greek traditional music with roots in Asia Minor. The "Fragosiriani," a classic known throughout Greece, was composed by the Siriot Markos Vamvakaris, and you're sure to hear its simple and infectious rhythms many times during your stay here. See chapter 8.

o **Tinos** (Cyclades): The island often called the "Lourdes of Greece," because of the church, **Panagia Evangelistria** (Our Lady of Good Tidings) with its healing icon, also has Venetian dovecotes; farm fields set off with handsome stone boundary walls; fine sand beaches; and Pirgos, the village of marble with a superb Museum of Marble Crafts. See chapter 8.

o **Rhodes** (Dodecanese): The island of Rhodes has everything a visitor could want—dazzling ancient and medieval ruins, great food, spectacular beaches, and some of the hottest nightlife outside of Athens—the one drawback being that everyone knows it. See chapter 9.

o **Hios** (Northeastern Aegean): You'd think that an island with such gorgeous beaches, exquisite medieval towns, and remarkable scenery wouldn't remain a secret for long. Despite the qualities that attract a small group of devotees year after year, Hios remains surprisingly quiet. If you like the idea of getting away from the tour buses, being alone on a beach to rival any in the Cyclades, and exploring towns that preserve the contours of medieval life, Hios is for you. Local hospitality hasn't worn thin here, as it has on many of the more heavily toured islands. See chapter 10.

o **Skyros** (Sporades): Winding roads and remote beaches, one main town and a few villages, some ancient legends and 20th-century tales: Skyros's charms remain perhaps the most elusive of the four northern Sporades. But though the island remains a bit difficult to access and not overstocked with touristy amenities, Skyros also offers both a living local culture and some natural wildness. See chapter 11.

o **Corfu** (Ionian Islands): With lush vegetation, some still-undeveloped interior and unspoiled coast, ancient sites and a 19th-century presence, a dash of Italy and a dose of the cosmopolitan, Corfu is a Greek island like no other. Tourism may be rampant, but Corfu's attractions have survived worse. See chapter 12.

THE best TRAVEL EXPERIENCES

- **Making Haste Slowly:** Give yourself time to sit in a seaside taverna and watch the fishing boats come and go. If you visit Greece in the spring, take the time to smell the flowers; the fields are covered with poppies, daisies, and other blooms. Even in Athens, you'll see hardy species growing through the cracks in concrete sidewalks—or better yet, visit Athens's Ancient Agora, which will be carpeted with a dazzling variety of wildflowers. See chapter 5.

- **Island-Hopping in the Cyclades:** Though the Cyclades are bound by unmistakable family resemblance, each island has a unique personality. Distances between islands are small, making travel by ferry logistically straightforward (at least in principle). Whether you are traveling in the off season, when you do not need hotel reservations, or in high season, when hotel reservations are a must, we suggest that you prepare to be flexible—which is a tactful way of preparing you for the unexpected in island boat schedules. See chapter 8.

- **Leaving the Beaten Path:** Leave the main routes and major attractions behind, and make your own discoveries of landscape, villages, or activities. For instance, seek out an out-of-the-way church or monastery—you may be rewarded by a moving encounter with the church and its caretaker. When you visit the Cycladic Islands, consider a base on Tinos or Siros. Both are popular with Greeks but attract hardly any foreigners. See chapter 8.

- **Exploring the Naturalists' Greece:** There is a Greece beyond the columns and cafes—a land of rugged terrain and wildflowers and birds and other natural phenomena. Sign up for a special tour (see chapter 2) or go it alone with one of the several beautifully illustrated handbooks available, such as Oleg Polunin's *Flowers of Greece and the Balkans* (Oxford University Press) or Paul Sterry's *Birds of the Mediterranean* (Yale University Press). And don't forget your binoculars!

- **Sunrise, Sunset, Siesta:** Get up a little earlier than usual to see the sun rise (preferably from the Aegean, illuminating the islands). Then watch it sink over the mountains (anywhere in Greece, but try not to miss the sunsets that change the Ionian Sea from the deepest blue to a fiery red). And, between sunrise and sunset, don't forget to have a siesta—most Greeks do, especially in the summer.

THE best OF ANCIENT GREECE

- **The Acropolis** (Athens): No matter how many photographs you've seen, nothing can prepare you for watching the light change the colors of the marble buildings, still standing after thousands of years, from honey to rose to deep red to stark white. If the crowds get you down, think about how crowded the Acropolis was during religious festivals in antiquity. See p. 135.

- **Palace of Knossos** (Crete): A seemingly unending maze of rooms and levels, stairways and corridors, in addition to frescoed walls—this is the Minoan Palace of Knossos. It can be packed at peak hours, but it still exerts its power if you enter in the spirit of the labyrinth. King Minos ruled over the richest and most powerful of Minoan cities and, according to legend, his daughter Ariadne helped Theseus kill the Minotaur in the labyrinth and escape. See p. 198.

- **Delos** (Cyclades): This tiny isle, just 3.2km (2 miles) offshore of Mykonos, was considered by the ancient Greeks to be both the geographical and spiritual center of the Cyclades; many considered this the holiest sanctuary in all of Greece. The extensive remains here testify to the island's former splendor. From Mount Kinthos (really just a hill, but the island's highest point), you can see many of the Cyclades most days; on a very clear day, you can see the entire archipelago. The 3 hours allotted by excursion boats from Mykonos or Tinos are hardly sufficient to explore this vast archaeological treasure. See chapter 8.

THE best OF BYZANTINE & MEDIEVAL GREECE

- **Church of Panagia Kera** (Kritsa, Crete): Even if Byzantine art seems a bit stilted and remote, this striking chapel in the foothills of eastern Crete will reward you with its unexpected intimacy. The 14th- and 15th-century frescoes are not only stunning but depict many familiar biblical stories. See p. 231.
- **A Profusion of Byzantine Churches in the Cyclades:** The fertile countryside of the island of Naxos is dotted by well-preserved Byzantine chapels. Parikia, the capital of Paros, has the Byzantine-era cathedral of **Panagia Ekatondapiliani.** Santorini boasts the 11th- to 12th-century **Church of the Panagia** in the hamlet of Gonias Episkopi. See chapter 8.
- **Nea Moni** (Hios, Northeastern Aegean): Once home to 1,000 monks, this 11th-century monastery high in the interior mountains of Hios is now inhabited by only a handful of monks and nuns. Try to catch one of the excellent tours sometimes offered by the monks. The mosaics in the cathedral dome are works of extraordinary power and beauty; even in the half obscurity of the nave, they radiate a brilliant gold. Check out the small museum, and take some time to explore the monastery grounds. See p. 391.

THE best BEACHES

- **Chrissi Akti** and **Santa Maria** (Paros, Cyclades): Energetic beach lovers head to Santa Maria and Chrissi Akti for superb windsurfing; the less energetic will have plenty of action to watch, beachside cafes and restaurants, and lots of lovely sand and surf. See p. 272.
- **Porto** and **Kolimbithres** (Tinos, Cyclades): Two long sand beaches, both with umbrellas, cafes, and restaurants. You can walk to Porto from Tinos town, but why bother? There's excellent bus service in summer. If you take the bus to Kolimbithres, you get to see a good deal of the island as a bonus en route. And when the wind is down, the water at Kolimbithres is unusually silky. If you're travelling with small children, head for Kolimbithres; the water is usually both calm and shallow quite a way out. See p. 320.
- **Paradise** (Mykonos, Cyclades): Paradise is the quintessential party beach, known for wild revelry that continues through the night. An extensive complex built on the beach includes a bar, taverna, changing rooms, and souvenir shops. This is a place to see and be seen, a place to show off muscles laboriously acquired during the long winter months. See p. 295.
- **Vroulidia** (Hios, Northeastern Aegean): White sand, a cliff-rimmed cove, and a remote location at the southern tip of the island of Hios combine to make this one

of the most exquisite small beaches in the Northeastern Aegean. The rocky coast concealed many cove beaches similar to this one, and they rarely become crowded. See p. 392.

- **Lalaria Beach** (Skiathos, Sporades): This gleaming, white-pebble beach boasts vivid aquamarine water and white limestone cliffs with natural arches cut into them by the elements. Admittedly, Skiathos's famous Koukounaries Beach offers a more pleasant sandy beach and is more accessible and thus more popular, but Lalaria rewards one with its gorgeous and pristine environment. See p. 411.
- **Myrtos** (Kefalonia, Ionian Islands): Although remote enough to require you come with your own wheels, this isolated sand-pebble beach has long charmed countless visitors. It does lack shade and it offers limited refreshments—perhaps bring a picnic—but the setting makes up for these deficiencies. See p. 450.

THE best PLACES TO GET AWAY FROM IT ALL

- **National and Zappeion Gardens** (Athens): It's all too easy to overlook this oasis of calm and cool in the heart of Athens. You'll discover shady benches, a small cafe, the excellent Aegli/Cibus cafe and restaurant in the adjacent Zappeion Gardens, and lots of opportunities to enjoy watching Greek families out for a stroll. Keep an eye out for the balloon sellers on weekends. See p. 135.
- **Mount Likavitos, aka Mount Lycabettus** (Athens): Walk up Likavitos at dawn and enjoy the sunrise over the hills that surround Athens. Come back for a spectacular sunset, with the city laid under your feet like a sparkling map, the sounds of its ferocious traffic pleasantly distant. See p. 101.
- **Milia** (Crete): Here is a true retreat from not only the hustle and bustle of mass tourism but of most modern distractions: a once-abandoned village off in the mountains of western Crete where you live in a renovated stone house and spend your days hiking, enjoying the wildlife, eating simple meals, and just plain relaxing. See p. 210.
- **Folegandros** (Cyclades): Most visitors to Greece once sailed past the formidable Folegandros cliffs en route from the mainland to Santorini and other islands; they'd catch a glimpse of the whitewashed kastro walls perched 300m (984 ft.) above the sea. The beauty of Hora, the fine beaches, and the great walking trails are no longer secrets, but if you arrive during the off season, Folegandros still offers a restful retreat. Largely free of the commercialism that has engulfed so many Aegean isles, Folegandros is now appearing on insider lists as *the* new place to visit. See p. 253.
- **The Road Not Taken:** Don't fret if you take a wrong turn in Greece, whether it is on a street in Athens or a road on some island. Go with it! This may be the highlight of your trip—the Athenian shop-owner who shows you pictures of his aunt's family in Chicago when you stop to ask for directions; the *yiayia* (granny) next to you on that boat that you caught after the boat you wanted to catch had left; the schoolchild who quizzes you about why you came to Greece when you bump into him at an ancient site; the little village you chance upon because you stumbled onto the road you did not mean to take.

THE best MUSEUMS

- **Acropolis Museum** (Athens): Athens's newest high-profile museum is also its most stunning. This impressive five-story building handsomely displays the riches that adorned the Acropolis in its heyday: stunning sculptures, statues, free-standing objects, and 36 of the original 115 frieze panels that remain in Greece. On the lower levels, visitors can peer through glass panels at the ongoing excavations of an ancient Athenian neighborhood and an early Christian settlement. See p. 144

○ **National Archaeological Museum** (Athens): This stunning collection has it all: superb red- and black-figured vases, bronze statues, Mycenaean gold, marble reliefs of gods and goddesses, and the hauntingly beautiful frescoes from Akrotiri, the Minoan site on the island of Santorini. See p. 146.

○ **Museum of Popular Greek Musical Instruments** (Athens): Life-size photos of musicians beside their actual instruments and recordings of traditional Greek music make this one of the country's most charming museums. On our last visit, an elderly Greek gentleman listened to some music, transcribed it, stepped into the courtyard, and played it on his own violin. See p. 146.

○ **Archaeological Museum of Iraklion** (Crete): Few museums in the world can boast of holding virtually all the important remains of a major culture. This museum can do just that with its Minoan collection, including superb frescoes from Knossos, elegant bronze and stone figurines, and exquisite gold jewelry. The museum also contains Neolithic, Archaic Greek, and Roman finds from throughout Crete. See p. 196.

○ **Archaeological Museum of Chania** (Crete): Let's hear it for a truly engaging provincial museum, not one full of masterworks but rather of representative works from thousands of years, a collection that lets us see how many people experienced their different worlds. All this, in a former Italian Renaissance church that feels like and is a special place. See p. 209.

THE best RESORTS & HOTELS

○ **AVA Hotel & Suites** (Athens, p. 92): Excellent location, clean and spacious grounds and a highly personable and helpful staff, the AVA has stolen our hearts. This no-smoking hotel is in actuality 46 self-contained apartments all equipped with their own kitchenettes and balconies—several of them (on the higher floors) are quite large and feature jaw-dropping city and Acropolis views. See p. 107.

○ **Grande Bretagne** (Athens, p. 92): Back for a return engagement and better than ever, Athens's premier hotel still overlooks the best view in town if you have the right room: Syntagma Square, the Houses of Parliament, and, in case you wondered, the Acropolis. See p. 114.

○ **Lato Boutique Hotel** (Iraklion, Crete; p. 193): There may be grander and more luxurious hotels in Crete, but few can beat the Lato's attractions: a central location, modern facilities, views over a busy harbor, and perhaps most important, the always helpful staff. With its newly renovated bathrooms, Wi-Fi throughout, and a superb restaurant attached, this modestly-sized hotel can now stand with the best. See p. 201.

○ **Doma** (Chania, Crete; p. 206): A former neoclassical mansion east of downtown, the Doma has been converted into a comfortable and charming hotel, furnished with the proprietor's family heirlooms. Although it's not for those seeking the most luxurious amenities, its atmosphere appeals. See p. 212.

○ **ASTRA Suites** (Santorini, Cyclades; p. 235): This location looks like a miniature whitewashed village—and has spectacular views over Santorini's caldera. The sunsets here are not to be believed, the staff is incredibly helpful, and the village of Imerovigli itself offers an escape from the tourist madness that overwhelms the island each summer. This is a spot to get married at—or celebrate any special occasion. See p. 248.

○ **Anemomilos Apartments** (Folegandros, Cyclades; p. 253) and **Castro Hotel** (Folegandros, Cyclades; p. 253): The small island of Folegandros has two of the nicest hotels in the Cyclades, both with terrific cliff-top locations. The Anemomilos has all the creature comforts, traditional decor, and a good location, with a pool and sea views that seem to stretch forever. The Castro, built into the walls of the 12th-century Venetian castle that encircles the village, has lots of character; it closed for a complete renovation in 2011, but promises to be back in 2012. See p. 256.

○ **Hotel Dina** (Paros, Cyclades; p. 266): This cozy little eight-room hotel combines traditional Greek hospitality with up-to-date comforts. Step from busy Market Street into the Dina's courtyard and you can feel yourself relax as you inhale the aromas of gardenias, roses, and pine trees. Every detail is lovely, from the soft pastels of the rooms to the prints of island scenes on the walls. Several rooms have balconies, with a view of a picture-postcard church dome.

○ **S. Nikolis Hotel and Apartments** (Rhodes, Dodecanese; p. 332): This small hotel in the Old Town of Rhodes combines such modern amenities as Wi-Fi and Jacuzzis with the experience of living in a renovated centuries-old Venetian mansion. The decor and furnishings maintain the sense that you are indeed in a special place and the proprietors' warm hospitality enhances this feeling. See p. 342.

○ **Hotel Nireus** (Simi, Dodecanese; p. 353): Perfect island, perfect location, unpretentious and tasteful. The views from the sea-facing rooms, framed by the fluid swirls of the wrought-iron balcony, define the spell of this little gem of an island. You'll never regret one more night on Simi, and here's the place to spend it. See p. 356.

○ **White Rocks Hotel & Bungalows** (Kefalonia, Ionian Islands; p. 445): For those who appreciate understated elegance, a shady retreat from all that sunshine, a private beach, and quiet but attentive service, this hotel, a couple of miles outside Argostoli, can be paradise. See p. 448.

THE best RESTAURANTS

○ **Varoulko** (Athens; p. 92): Near Athens's wildest nightlife district, Gazi, with a menu that adds tasty meat dishes to its signature seafood, Varoulko continues to win plaudits. Everything here is so good that many Athenians believe chef/owner Lefteris Lazarou serves not only the finest seafood in Athens, but some of the best food in all of Greece. See p. 126.

○ **Spondi** (Athens; p. 92): *Athinorama,* the weekly review of the Athenian scene, has chosen Spondi several years running (2001–07, 2011) as the best place in town. Exceptional cuisine, setting (a beautiful 19th-c. town house with a stone courtyard covered with bougainvillea) and service, this winner of two Michelin stars for exceptional dining (2002, 2008) is justly considered by many to be the finest restaurant in all of Greece. See p. 130.

○ **Brillant Gourmet** (Iraklion, Crete; p. 193): Since its opening in 2007, this restaurant positioned itself as the most stylish restaurant on Crete, with food and wine to match its decor. Admittedly, it's a restaurant for special occasions, but it's worth inventing one for yourself during your trip to Greece. See p. 202.

- **Well of the Turk** (Chania, Crete); p. 206): Set back in a quiet square in Chania's old Venetian quarter, this restaurant offers both a delightful ambience and a novel selection of dishes. The proprietress and her staff make dining here a special experience. See p. 215.
- **Selene** (Santorini, Cyclades; p. 235): The best restaurant on an island with lots of good places to eat, Selene is one of the finest restaurants in all Greece. The reason: Owner George Haziyannakis constantly experiments with local produce to turn out innovative versions of traditional dishes. Inside, the dining room is elegant, while the terrace has a wonderful view over the caldera. See p. 252.
- **Petrino** (Kos, Dodecanese; p. 358): When royalty comes to Kos, this is where they dine. Housed in an exquisitely restored, two-story, century-old stone (*petrino*) private residence, this is hands down the most elegant taverna in Kos, with cuisine to match. This is what Greek home cooking would be if your mother were part divine. See p. 365.
- **Venetian Well** (Corfu, Ionian Islands; p. 430): A bit severe in its setting at the edge of a small enclosed square in Corfu town, with no attempt at the picturesque, this restaurant gets by on its more esoteric, international, and delicate menu. It's for those seeking a break from the standard Greek scene. See p. 440.

THE best NIGHTLIFE

- **Theater under the Stars** (Athens): If you can, take in a performance of whatever is on at Odeion of Herodes Atticus theater in Athens. You'll be sitting where people have sat for thousands of years to enjoy a play beneath Greece's night sky. See chapter 5.
- **Mykonos** (Cyclades): Mykonos isn't the only island town in Greece with nightlife that continues through the morning, but it was the first and still offers the most abundant, varied scene in the Aegean. Year-round, the town's narrow, labyrinthine streets play host to a remarkably diverse crowd—Mykonos's unlimited ability to reinvent itself has assured it of continued popularity. Spring and fall tend to be more sober and sophisticated, whereas the 3 months of summer are reserved for unrestrained revelry. See chapter 8.
- **Rhodes** (Dodecanese): From cafes to casinos, Rhodes has not only the reputation but also the stuff to back it up. A good nightlife scene is ultimately a matter of who shows up—and this, too, is where Rhodes stands out. It's the place to be seen, and if nobody seems to be looking, you can always watch. See chapter 9.
- **Skiathos** (Sporades): With as many as 50,000 visitors packing this island during the high season, the many nightspots in Skiathos town are often jammed with the mostly younger set. If you don't like the music at one club, cross the street. See chapter 11.
- **Corfu** (Ionian Islands): If raucous nightspots are what you look for on a holiday, Corfu offers probably the largest concentration in Greece. Most of these are beach resorts frequented by young foreigners. More sedate locales can be found in Corfu town. Put simply, Corfu hosts a variety of music, dancing, and "socializing" opportunities. See chapter 12.

THE best SHOPPING

- **Traditional Arts & Crafts:** So many places in Greece pride themselves on their needlework that it is hard to single out even a few, but among those few is Crete, Rhodes, and Skyros. Two places in Athens deserve mention: **The Center of Hellenic Tradition** (59 Mitropoleos and 36 Pandrossou) and the **National Welfare Organization** (6 Ipatias and Apollonos). The center offers ceramics, woodcarvings, prints—and one of the finest views of the Acropolis in Athens. The National Welfare Organization contains hand-loomed rugs and silk embroidery done by village women, as well as excellent copperwork and ceramics.

- **Leatherwork:** Both Rhodes and Crete feature local leatherwork, from sandals to handbags, from belts to jackets. Pay attention to quality.

- **Jewelry:** It now seems that half of Greece's retail stores sell jewelry, so shop around. Much of it is really no different than what can be found in cities all over the world, but Athens does have major, internationally known jewelers such as LALAoUNIS and Zolotas. Try Chania, Crete, for sophisticated local artisans' work. Islands such as Hydra, Mykonos, Paros, Santorini, Skiathos, and Rhodes have scores of stores appealing to the tourist trade, many with the work of local jewelers.

- **Ceramics:** As with needlework, pots and ceramics of all kinds are to be found throughout Greece. Some of the more traditional may be found on Hios, Crete, Mitilini, Sifnos, and Skopelos.

- **Wood:** Corfu seems to be the center of olive-wood products—carving boards, bowls, and utensils. Rethymnon, Crete, also has a selection. The islands of Paros, Syros, Hios, and Mitilini also boast wood-carving traditions.

- **Icons, Ecclesiastical Books & Religious Items:** On the streets around the Greek Orthodox Cathedral (Metropolitan) in Athens, you'll find many shops selling votive offerings, candles, and reproductions of icons. Many of the most important religious shrines, such as Panagia Evangelistria on Tinos, and many convents and monasteries, including most of the Meteora monasteries, sell reproductions of icons and other religious items. On Crete, the Petrakis couple in Elounda paints internationally sought traditional icons.

- **Museum Reproductions:** Fine replicas of many famous museum pieces may be purchased at the Archaeological, Byzantine, Benaki, Goulandris, and LALAoUNIS museums in Athens; and at official archaeological service stores in Rhodes Old Town and in Chania and Rethymnon, Crete. Even small museums often have excellent shops.

- **Books:** Whether you're looking for books about Greece or books for vacation reading, in Athens the places to go are **Eleftheroudakis, Compendium, Ifognomon,** and **Kaufman.** Chania boasts the **Notos Bookstore,** with its superb selection of Crete-related books.

GREEK ISLANDS IN DEPTH

2

by Sherry Marker & Peter Kerasiotis

There are some things that are true throughout Greece, from the big cities to the smallest islands. Look up at the crowded apartment buildings that line so many streets in Athens, and you'll probably see pots of basil on most balconies. Travel through the famous isles of Greece and almost every whitewashed island house has at least one pot of basil on its doorstep. No wonder that the 19th-century Greek politician Ion Dragoumis said, "A pot of basil may symbolize the soul of a people better than a play of Aeschylus."

In fact, the pot of basil, lovingly clipped to a perfect sphere, may be the only item in Greece that outnumbers the cellphone *(kineto)*. The 10-million-plus Greek citizens have at least 11 million cellphones, with many adults wielding at least one for business and another for personal calls. On May Day, I watched Greek families out in the countryside gather wildflowers to make traditional May Day wreaths, stopping only to dance age-old circle dances—all the while snapping photos of each other and sending them to distant friends on their ubiquitous cellphones. The wreaths, the dances, many of the words the dancers spoke, would all have been familiar to the ancient Greeks. Only the cellphones were new.

Most Greeks are besotted with all that is new; in fact, a common greeting is *Ti nea?* ("What's new?"). Still, most Greeks are fiercely proud of precisely those longtime attractions that attract visitors: Greece's mind-boggling physical beauty and its glorious past. In the islands, many visitors want to see the acres of antiquities on the little island of Delos; have their picture taken by the Portara, the famous ancient temple door on Naxos; and visit the shrine of Asklepion on Kos. Not to see some ancient remains while visiting the isles of Greece would be, as Aeschylus himself might have said, tragic.

As for Greece's physical beauty, it is so stunning that it traps almost everyone into spouting clichés. Palamas, the poet who wrote the words to the Olympic Hymn, was reduced to saying of his homeland, "Here, sky is everywhere." Of course, Palamas was right: the Greek sky, the Greek light, the Greek sea, are all justly famous. This is especially obvious on the islands. Just how many islands there are depends on what you call an island, an islet, or a large rock. Consequently, estimates of the number of Greek islands range from 1,200 to about 6,000. In any event, almost all of the approximately 200 inhabited islands are ready and waiting to welcome visitors; witness the fact that more than half of all the hotels in Greece are on islands. Each year, more and more Greek hotels aspire to be boutique hotels, with Wi-Fi, spas, cocktails by the pools (fresh and saltwater), and restaurants serving sushi as well as souvlaki.

On the islands and on the mainland, throughout the Greek countryside, picture-postcard scenes are around every corner. Shepherds still urge flocks of goats and sheep along mountain slopes, and fishermen still mend nets by their caiques. In Greece's two largest cities, Athens and Thessaloniki (where cars seem to outnumber residents), the islands make their presence known in neighborhood street markets that sell cheese from flocks of sheep that graze on distant island mountains, and fish caught far out to sea. When the island boats dock at Piraeus in the morning, even fresh bread from many islands is rushed to the main market in Athens for islanders unhappy with bread made anyplace but on their home island.

If this sounds romantic and enticing, it is. But it's a good idea to remember that the Greek love of the new includes a startling ability to adjust to the unexpected. Everything—absolutely everything—in Greece is subject to change. The boat that you board in Athens's port of Piraeus, to visit the island of Tinos, may steam past Tinos to Mykonos, and then wander back to Tinos via several unscheduled stops at unidentified islands. Ask anyone on board—including the captain—why this happened and you'll see the most Greek of all gestures: the face and shoulder shrug. Then you'll probably hear the most Greek of all remarks: *Etsi einai e zoe*, which literally means "That's life," but might better be translated as "Whatchya gonna do?" With luck, you'll learn the Greek shrug, and come to accept—even enjoy—the unpredictable as an essential part of life in Greece.

Recently, the unpredictable has become almost the only thing that is predictable in Greece. Greece's massive debts—and the government's unpopular attempts to restructure the economy, involving tax hikes and salary and pension reductions—led in 2010 and 2011 to strikes and demonstrations. At press time, serious questions remain as to how Greece will solve its problems. Tourism—which makes up from 15% to 20% of Greece's annual income—was significantly down, as word of strikes, closing museums and archaeological sites, and disrupted travel persuaded many potential visitors to go elsewhere. Most Greeks are deeply concerned about the future, deeply worried at the decline in tourism, and deeply convinced that they will weather this storm as they have weathered so many other storms since the dawn of history. More than ever, Greeks are eager to welcome the visitors who come to see the glories of ancient Greece and enjoy the pleasures of Greece today.

GREECE TODAY

In 2007, the notoriously expensive, yet successful 2004 Olympic Summer Games appeared to be paying off. Athens, now a radically different city, with state-of-the-art infrastructure and glowing worldwide reviews of its homecoming Games, was witnessing a 20% increase in tourism for the third year in a row. During the same year, Greece saw nearly 20 million visitors to its mainland and islands, putting Greece, for the first time, in the top-10 list of most-visited tourist destinations. For a country whose tourism industry accounts for 15% of its total GDP, that was great news. Despite growing inflation, some government scandals, and an illegal migrant population that was swelling dangerously out of control, things appeared to have been on the right track for Greece to continue experiencing unprecedented growth.

However, 2008 and 2009 were not good years for Greece. Autumn of 2008 saw Greece's economy collapse, along with the global economy; inflation continued to grow, even though salaries had remained frozen at pre-euro levels, and unemployment crept up to 9.2%. The illegal immigrant population had become a problem by the end of 2008, with their numbers rising to more than two million, causing more strain on an already collapsed economy. The end of 2008 saw civic unrest in the streets of the country's capital and other major cities, the likes of which had not been seen in decades. Some protests turned violent and costly, prompted by the fatal police shooting of a teenager in the Athens bohemian district of Exarchia. By 2009, most Greeks had lost faith in the conservative government ruling the country, a government elected on the promise to sweep the country clean of all the scandals of the previous ruling party, only to create an avalanche of scandals all their own. To make matters worse, during August 2009, forest fires ravaged the northeastern fringes of Athens, destroying 50% of the capital's much-needed forest land, olive groves, and farms, and adding to the devastation of the fires that plagued much of mainland Greece in 2007. The weakened global economy also meant fewer tourists for the first time in many years. Many Greeks are feeling the pinch of these hard economic times, as Greece's two major sectors—agriculture and tourism—remain troubled.

Yet not all news is bad. The economy appears to be bouncing back; unemployment and inflation are falling. Greece's purchasing power–adjusted GDP per capita is the world's 28th highest, with an estimated average per-capita income comparable to that of other European Union (E.U.) countries, such as Germany, France, and Italy. And Athens continues to be in the midst of an impressive urban-renewal stage—new and ambitious art centers and projects continue to spring up almost monthly, along with an expanding Metro system and new cutting-edge hotels and restaurants. The results have inspired the rest of the country to follow suit, from smaller cities to the most remote of islands. The recently opened New Acropolis Museum, a stunning museum with breathtaking treasures not seen in nearly 200 years, was a much-needed boost for a country that was beginning to lose its Olympic afterglow to the harsh realities of the times. Greece today is also adjusting to its new face. The recent immigrant communities from the Balkans, Africa, and Asia mixed with E.U. immigrants and retirees have suddenly made Greece a multicultural society. All in all, the mood in Greece remains festive and cautiously optimistic after a rather harsh year. Most Greeks believe the country has gone through much worse in its long and turbulent history and remain optimistic that better times are just around the corner.

LOOKING BACK AT GREECE

Greece has a very long history, indeed. Here is a brief introduction to some of the main periods in Greek history, along with some suggestions as to where you can see some of Greece's most memorable monuments. We use the term "Greece" throughout, even though today's country did not come into being until the 19th century. Still, long before that, the people who lived here regarded themselves as unified by a common language and many shared traditions and beliefs. We know more about what occurred on the mainland than on the islands for much of Greece's history due to the better preservation of records there and the fact that for much of antiquity, the major powers were on the mainland. In relative modern times, the history of Greece has been dominated by a series of Athenocentric governments, with the islands often feeling distinctly ignored. That said, each island has its own rich history, and you can start boning up by buying a guide when you arrive at your chosen island. These little guides, often written by local school teachers or archaeologists, are an invaluable source of island history for visitors.

STONE AGE   Greeks were delighted when a Neanderthal skull, found in 1960 in the Petralona cave in Chalkidiki, Macedonia, pushed their long history back as far as 700,000 B.C. There are plenty of signs of human habitation in Greece from the more recent Paleolithic (ca. 7000 B.C.) and Neolithic (ca. 6000–3000 B.C.) eras, and you can walk the narrow streets of astonishingly well-preserved Neolithic sites at Lerna, and in the Argolid and Dimini and Sesklo, in Thessaly. The archaeological museums in Thessaloniki and Volos are two places that bring daily life in Greece's oldest civilizations to life, with displays of useful pottery and tools, and ornamental necklaces and rings. Some of the oldest-known representational sculpture in Greece comes from this period, often being small, well-endowed clay figurines of women. Some believe that these figures represent a mother goddess, who was honored before Zeus and the Olympians became popular.

BRONZE AGE   In Greece, the Bronze Age seems to have lasted from around 3000 B.C. to 1500 B.C. By around 3000 B.C., people in much of Greece seem to have learned how to craft bronze; this meant that they no longer had to fashion weapons and tools out of stone and obsidian, but could make the sharp knives, swords, and heavy shields now seen in so many Greek museums. What the Bronze Age inhabitants of Greece *thought* is more mysterious, in the absence of written records, which were rare except for lists of the pots, pans, shields, and swords kept in palaces. Archaeologists and historians have identified three different civilizations or cultures that flourished in different parts of Greece during the Bronze Age: Cycladic, Minoan, and Mycenaean. Historians think that all these civilizations spoke a form of Greek. Only the Mycenaeans seem to have used early forms of writing, Linear B

DATELINE

700,000– Human remains, including a
160,000. Neanderthal skull, suggest long
B.C habitation of Petralona Cave,
Chalkidiki peninsula.

40,000 B.C. Signs of human habitation appear in several caves in the Louros Valley, Epirus.

7000– People begin to live together in
3000 B.C. small villages, such as Sesklo and Dimini, in Thessaly, and Lerna, in the Argolid.

4000 B.C. Neolithic settlement on Athens Acropolis.

3000 B.C. Waves of invaders from Anatolia (today's Turkey) introduce bronze working and an early form of Greek to Crete, the Cyclades, and the mainland, beginning the Bronze Age. Possibly the first-known "palace" in Greece is built at Lerna, Argolid.

1700 B.C. A massive earthquake on Crete destroys the great Minoan palaces at Knossos and Phaestos. Undeterred, Minoans rebuild even more luxurious digs.

1600– The Mycenaean civilization rises
1100 B.C. and abruptly collapses, sending Greece into centuries of strife and

continues

and Linear A, to keep inventories. No one seems to have used writing to send a note, or write a poem.

The Cycladic civilization takes its name from the Cycladic islands where it flourished. Although architectural remains are sparse, you can see elegant Cycladic figurines, crafted from island marble, at the National Archaeological Museum in Athens, the Goulandris Museum in Athens, and the Archaeological Museum on Naxos. Unfortunately, even the world's leading experts on Cycladic figurines are not sure whether the figurines were representations of deities or people. Almost everyone is startled by how "modern" these spare figurines are. The Minoan civilization was centered at the Palace of Knossos, on Crete, but fanned out to nearby islands and onto the mainland. Visitors to Crete can visit the Palace of Knossos, while visitors to Santorini will have to wait until the Minoan town of Akrotiri, currently undergoing restoration, reopens. Alas, the protective roof over Akrotiri's partially excavated site collapsed in 2005, and it has been closed since then.

Much of Santorini was destroyed in 1500 B.C., in an unimaginably powerful earthquake that also destroyed settlements on Minoan Crete, 63 nautical miles away, and led to its decline. On mainland Greece, the Mycenaean civilization, named after its center at Mycenae in the Peloponnese, flourished during many of these same years. The extensive remains of Mycenae, with its defense walls, palace, and enormous beehive tombs, demonstrate the architectural skill and political power of the Mycenaeans. The National Archaeological Museum in Athens is a showcase for the famous gold of Mycenae, whereas the Archaeological Museum at Mycenae itself tries to reconstruct how people there lived, and to suggest what they may have believed and how they may have worshipped. Mycenae's museum also reminds us of that city's maritime empire, which may have extended from the Black Sea to the Atlantic. In the *Iliad,* Homer commemorated the Greek expedition to recapture the beautiful Helen, which was led by Mycenae's best-known king, Agamemnon. The *Iliad* ends with the fall of Troy to the Greeks; Mycenae's own decline seems to have begun not long after, and is sometimes blamed on the mysterious invaders known as the Dorians.

cultural isolation. The Dorian invasion from the north contributes to instability.

1450 B.C. A volcanic eruption on Santorini (Thira)—one of the most violent on record—buries ancient Akrotiri, causes destruction as far away as Crete, and helps speed Minoan decline.

1000– 600 B.C. Glints of Greece's resurrection appear in the form of city-states. Homer and Hesiod initiate the first great age of Greek poetry. The use of written Greek spreads.

776 B.C. The first Olympic Games are held.

700– 500 B.C. Black figure pottery spreads throughout Greece from Corinth; red figure ware spreads from Athens. Geometric statues of *kouroi* (youths) and *korai* (maidens) are widely produced. Athens and most Greek city-states ruled by tyrants.

525– 485 B.C. The birth of "Athenian democracy," under Cleisthenes. The great playwrights, Aeschylus, Sophocles, and Euripides, are born. Classical sculpture in marble and bronze flourishes.

THE GEOMETRIC & ARCHAIC PERIODS These two terms are both used to describe Greece during the years from around 1000 B.C. until the dawn of the classical era, around 500 B.C. The Geometric period takes its name from the figured pottery that started to be made around 800 B.C., on which bodies are often shown as simple triangles, and borders are created from rows of meanders and crosshatchings. The Archaic period is used for the period, beginning around 700 B.C., when the first monumental human sculpture was made in Greece. The National Archaeological Museum in Athens has superb collections of both geometric pottery and archaic sculpture. After the decline of the Mycenaeans in mainland Greece, things were a bit murky for several hundred years—hardly surprising, as we have no contemporary written sources of this period. Gradually, it seems that people living on mainland Greece, and in the islands, began to live in the sort of towns we would recognize today, rather than in small, scattered settlements. Many of the cities that are still prominent in Greece today developed during this period: Athens and Sparta, Argos and Corinth among them.

There are substantial remains on many of the Cycladic islands from this period, although many of the most important temples and shrines on Delos, Naxos, Tinos, and other islands were later chopped up and used to build new buildings. Almost every church in the Cyclades has at least one column, one foundation stone, built into it. The church of the Panagia, on Sifnos, for example, has a column from the Temple of Apollo in its courtyard. And on Naxos, the two massive figures of unfinished statues of *kouroi* (youths) are testament to that island's importance in the Archaic period, as is the sphinx Naxos sent to Apollo's shrine at Delphi (now on view at the museum). The treasury that the little island of Sifnos built at Delphi in the 6th century B.C. is another reminder of that island's wealth and importance during this time.

The growth of independent city-states—many ruled by powerful tyrants—was important, as was the spread of trade and invention of coinage, but the emergence of writing, using an early, but still recognizable form of the Greek alphabet, was even more important. The city-states were fiercely independent. This is a serious understatement: Each city-state had not only its own dialect, but also its own calendar,

490–480 B.C. The First and Second Persian wars. Xerxes, emperor of Persia, invades Greece, burning Athens and the Acropolis. Greeks get revenge on land, at Marathon and Plataea, and at sea, near Salamis and Mycale.

461–429 B.C. Under its leader, Pericles, Athens begins to rebuild the Parthenon and ornament it with the sculptures now known as the Parthenon (or Elgin) Marbles.

431–404 B.C. Peloponnesian War leads to the fall of Athens and its empire. From 430 to 428, the Great Plague kills thousands, including Pericles.

399 B.C. Socrates is tried for heresy and sentenced to death. Given the chance to escape, he declines and drinks hemlock potion. Plato immortalizes him in *The Apology* and other philosophical dialogues.

338 B.C. At the Battle of Chaironeia, Philip of Macedon defeats the Greek armies and unifies Greece under Macedonian rule.

336–323 B.C. Philip's son, Alexander the Great, establishes reign over a kingdom that stretches as far as Egypt and India.

continues

system of weights and measures, and important deities. Still, when the Persians from adjacent Asia Minor invaded Greece in 490 and 480 B.C., many of the Greeks—led by Athens and Sparta—stood together and turned back the Persians. You can read about the conflict in Herodotus, visit the battlefields of Marathon and Thermopylae, and see the bust of the Spartan hero, Leonidas, in the Archaeological Museum at Sparta. If Persia had conquered Greece, our history of Greece might well end now, before the classical era and the birth of Greek democracy.

THE CLASSICAL ERA Brief and glorious, the classical era lasted from the 5th century to the rise of Philip of Macedon, in the mid–4th century. For many of the Greek islands, this was a period of being conquered, first by Athens and then by Philip. This is when Pericles led Athens and when the Parthenon—and virtually every other ancient Greek monument, statue, and vase most of us are familiar with—was created. This is when Greek democracy was born in Athens: All male citizens, but no women, resident aliens, or slaves, could vote. Very quickly, Athenian democracy morphed into an aggressive empire, which "liberated" Greek city-states in Asia Minor from Persia—and then turned those Greek cities into Athenian client states. Athens next turned to taking over many of the Greek islands and turning them into client states. Greece's other major power, Sparta, saw its own influence threatened, and Athens and Sparta fought on and off from 431 to 404 B.C., by which time Athens had exhausted its resources and surrendered to Sparta. The historian Thucydides wrote an account of these Peloponnesian Wars. For the next 50 or so years, Athens, Sparta, and Thebes alternately united and fought with each other. This left all three cities weakened and unable to stop Philip of Macedon, when he moved south to conquer Greece.

THE HELLENISTIC ERA The Hellenistic era is usually said to run from the 4th to the late 1st centuries B.C. and to include the rise of Philip of Macedon, the triumphs of his son Alexander the Great, and the several centuries of rule by Alexander's heirs and successors. As during the classical era, most of the Greek islands found themselves paying tribute first to Philip, then to Alexander and his successors. Philip of Macedon conquered Greece in 338 B.C. and died only 2 years later. During his

---

323 B.C. Worn out by a host of dissipations, Alexander dies in Babylon. His successors squabble among themselves, squandering great parts of his empire.

146 B.C. After a series of wars, Rome crushes Greece, renaming the northern parts Macedonia, the southern and central parts Achaea.

1ST & 2ND CENTURIES A.D. New Testament is written in Greek dialect, the *koine*. Local author, John of Patmos, gets the last word, in Revelation.

A.D. 328 Roman emperor Constantine the Great moves his capital to Byzantium (Constantinople), initiating the focus on the East that results in the Byzantine Empire.

476 Rome falls to the Goths; Greece is no longer a world power in any sphere, political or cultural.

1204 Fourth Crusade (led by the Western powers) sacks Constantinople and divides up much of the Byzantine Empire.

1453 Constantinople falls to Sultan Mehmet II, initiating more than 350 years of Turkish domination brief reign, Philip endowed a number of quite spectacular buildings at important Greek sanctuaries, including the Philippeion at Olympia, which he modestly named after himself. The royal tombs at Vergina, with their gold ornaments and frescoes, are lasting proof of Macedon's wealth. Alexander became King of Macedon when he was only 23 and marched from his base camp at Dion all the way to India, conquering everything in his path. At that point, his soldiers virtually turned him around and pointed him back toward Macedonia. Alexander died under mysterious circumstances (Poison? Too much wine?) en route home in 334 B.C., leaving behind the vast empire that he had conquered, but not had time to organize and administer. Alexander's leading generals divided up his empire, and declared themselves not just rulers but, in many cases, divine rulers. Alexander's conquests, which included much of Asia Minor and Egypt, made the Greek language the administrative and spoken language of much of the world. Within Greece itself, powerful new cities, such as Thessaloniki, were founded. Old cities, such as Athens, were revivified and ornamented with magnificent new civic buildings, such as the 2nd-century-B.C. Stoa of Attalos, which contained shops and offices. Today, this Hellenistic building, restored by American archaeologists in the 20th century, is the most conspicuous building in the Athenian Agora.

THE ROMAN CONQUEST   Along with most of Europe, North Africa, and Asia Minor, Greece was ruled by Rome from the 2nd century B.C. to the 3rd century A.D. As part of their eastward expansion, the Romans conquered Macedon in 168 B.C. and turned the once-powerful kingdom into the Roman province of Macedonia. In 147 B.C., Rome grabbed most of the rest of Greece and called it the province of Achaea. During this period, the island of Delos, formerly most important as a Greek shrine to Apollo, became the center of the Roman slave market. Many slaves who worked there remained when they won their freedom, and worked in the port and marketplace.

Still, the Romans honored the Greeks for their literature and art, and a tour of Greece was the equivalent of a gap year for many well-born Roman youths. As occupations go, the Roman occupation was benign and the Greeks participated in what has become known as the Pax Romana, the several centuries of general peace and

continues

calm in the Roman Empire. By the late 3rd century A.D. the Roman Empire was so vast that it was divided into eastern and western empires, each with its own emperor. One lasting legacy of the Roman occupation: the sprawling bath complexes that are often the most visible remain at many ancient Greek sites, from Dion in Macedonia to Corinth in the Peloponnese. An elegant Roman villa with fine mosaics has been unearthed on Kos, where Roman baths were later converted into a Christian church. And almost every museum in even the smallest island has at least one dusty bust of a Roman emperor on display, a reminder of the long Roman occupation.

THE BYZANTINE EMPIRE   In various forms, in various countries, the Byzantine Empire lasted from the 4th to the 15th century. In A.D. 328, the Roman emperor Constantine the Great took control of the entire empire, moved its capital from Rome to the Greek city of Byzantium on the Bosphoros, and renamed his capital Constantinople (Constantine's city). This move effectively remade the Roman Empire (which included Greece), and firmly based it in the east. In another bold move—his deathbed conversion to Christianity—Constantine changed the religious character of his vast empire. The monasteries of Mount Athos and the Meteora of Osios Loukas, in Central Greece; the icons on view in the Byzantine museums in Athens and Thessaloniki; and the countless chapels in use everywhere in Greece today all speak to Christianity's deep and lasting influence. It took a new people, the Ottoman Turks, to overturn the Byzantine Empire; in Greece, most people privately continued to speak the Greek language and remained devout Orthodox Christians. The official end of the empire came when Constantinople fell to the Turks, led by Mehmed the Conqueror, on Tuesday, May 29, 1453; to this day, Tuesday is considered an unlucky day in Greece.

There are two places in the islands where Byzantine monuments are especially rich: the Cycladic islands of Naxos and Crete. The Byzantine churches on Naxos and Crete are a lasting testament to the presence of that empire across the Aegean.

THE OCCUPATION(S) & INDEPENDENCE   The Greeks celebrate Independence Day on March 25. On that day in 1821, Bishop Germanos of Patras raised a blue and white flag at the monastery of Agia Lavra near Patras and the struggle for

1919 Greece occupies Izmir; Mustafa Kemal (Atatürk) rises through ranks of military to champion Turkish nationalism.	**1936–44** Dictator George Metaxas takes over, modeling his Greece on the examples of Mussolini and Hitler.
1923 The Greco-Turkish War ends in disaster for Greece, with a compulsory exchange of populations between Greece and Turkey. Greece takes in more than a million Greek refugees from Turkey.	**1940–41** Italy invades Greece, followed by more-determined German forces.
	1944 Greece is liberated; civil war soon breaks out in Athens and the north.
	1949 Civil war ends.
	1952 Greek women gain the right to vote.
1924–28 Greece declares itself a republic, but political upheaval leads to 11 military coups.	**1967–73** A military coup; King Constantine goes into exile; Operation Prometheus establishes military junta known as "the Colonels"; civil liberties are suspended.

Greek independence officially began. Fighting was concentrated on the mainland, with skirmishes on the islands. In 1827, the so-called Great Powers (primarily the English, French, Italians, and Russians) finally backed Greek independence. In 1832, those same Great Powers declared that Greece was to be an independent country, ruled by a king, and dispatched a Bavarian princelet, Otto, to be King of the Hellenes. This put an end to the long period of occupation (1453–1832), when Greece was ruled by a bewildering and often overlapping series of foreign powers: Venetians and Franks from the West, and Turks from the East. The Turkish occupation was especially brutal in the islands closest to Turkey, which Turkey wished to claim. In 1822, there was a bloody massacre of the Greek inhabitants of Chios.

Today, the considerable Catholic population of many Cycladic islands (specifically Tinos and Naxos) is a testament to the days when the Venetians ruled these islands. Castles and fortresses, in Tinos and Naxos, on Crete and Rhodes, are imposing reminders of the Venetians. Another reminder: today's roofless Parthenon. In 1687, a shell lobbed by the Venetians hit the Parthenon, which the Turks were using as a storehouse for gunpowder. Throughout Greece, almost every village has at least one monument to the War of Independence, and every island museum has old prints showing famous battles. Athens's Benaki Museum has superb displays of paintings, flags, costumes, and weapons documenting the struggle for Greek independence.

GREECE SINCE INDEPENDENCE By the end of the 19th century, Greece's capital was in Athens, but most of today's country was still held by the Turks and Italians. This was especially true of the Greek islands, where the occupations lasted much longer than on the mainland. The port of Ermoulis, capital of both the island of Syros and the Cyclades, received a great influx of refugees from Turkey and from the Greek islands off the coast of Turkey during the revolution. The great Greek leader from Crete, Eleftherios Venizelos (after whom Athens International Airport is named) led Greece in the Balkan Wars of 1912–13. When the wars were done, Greece had increased its territory by two-thirds, and included much of Epirus, Macedonia, and Thrace, in the north; and the large islands of Samos, Chios, and Crete. At the end of World War I, Greece invaded Turkey in an attempt to reclaim

Performances of certain classical dramas, especially *Electra,* are forbidden as subversive.

1974 Turkey invades Cyprus; junta collapses; democratic republic established when referendum abolishes the monarchy.

1981 Greece joins EC (Common Market); PASOK victory brings leftist Andreas Papandreou to power.

1989 Papandreou government collapses under corruption charges.

1993 After a 3-year hiatus, PASOK and Papandreou are victorious at the polls.

1996 Papandreou resigns and is succeeded by Costas Simitis.

1997 Athens is selected as the site for the 2004 Olympic Games.

1998 The European Council begins entry negotiations with Cyprus, with a view toward its inclusion in the European Union.

1999 The growth rate of the Greek economy remains strong for a fourth consecutive year, surpassing most of its European partners, and the minister of finance speaks of a "new Greece."

continues

Constantinople and much of Aegean Turkey. Initially, the invasion went well, but the Turks, led by their future leader Mustafa Kemal (Atatürk), rallied and pushed the Greeks back to the sea. There, in 1922, in Smyrna (Izmir) and other seaside towns, the Greeks were slaughtered, in what is still referred to in Greece as "the Catastrophe." In the Treaty of Lausanne, Greece and Turkey agreed to an exchange of populations. The boundaries of mainland Greece were fixed more or less as they are today. Some 1.5 million Greek who lived in Turkey had to move to Greece, and about 500,000 Turks were sent from Greece to Turkey. Many spoke little or none of their ancestral language, and most were regarded with intense hostility in their new homelands. Thessaloniki, which doubled in size in less than a year, bore the brunt of the Greek population exchange. To this day, Greece is dotted with towns with such names as Nea Smyrni and Nea Chios (New Smyrna and New Chios), reminders of this forced migration. A small Greek Muslim population still lives in Greece, primarily in Thrace.

Whatever stability and prosperity Greece gained after the population exchange of the 1920s was seriously undercut by the harsh German and Italian occupations during World War II. The resistance to occupation was especially fierce on the island of Crete. Both there and on many islands in the Cyclades, a number of British troops who were not able to be evacuated were sheltered by Greek families at great personal risk.

The famines of 1941 and 1942 were particularly harsh; in Athens, carts went around the city each morning to collect the corpses of those who had died in the night. A bitter Civil War (1944–49), between pro- and anticommunist forces, further weakened Greece. Recovery began slowly—assisted by the Marshall Plan—and did not take hold until well into the 1960s. This was especially true in the islands, where recovery was slow and poverty was endemic. In the 1960s, Greece was discovered by travelers from Western Europe and North America who fell in love with the unspoiled—and very cheap—country, especially the islands of Mykonos and Hydra.

During the 1960s, a right wing junta of army officers, nicknamed the Colonels, seized power (1967), ended the monarchy, and were eventually themselves toppled,

2000–02 The Pan-Hellenic Socialist Movement, led by Costas Simitis, wins a third term. Greece applies to become the 12th member of the Eurozone in 2001, exchanging the millennia-old drachma for the euro in 2002. The Olympic flame is lit at Olympia for the 2000 Summer Games in Sydney, as Athens awaits its turn in 2004.

2004 Conservative Kostis Karamanlis elected prime minister. Greece erupts in joy when the national team wins the European Soccer Championship shortly before the 2004 Olympic Games are held in Athens.

2006–09 Widespread summer forest fires, many set by property developers, devour vast stretches of the Greek countryside, the Peloponnese and Attica, many islands, and around Thessaloniki. Karamanlis reelected to a second term, but then defeated by PASOK's George Papandreou in October 2009.

2009–11 As the world economy declines, and the Greek debt to the EEC (Common Market) grows, tourism to Greece drops steeply, adversely affecting the already vexed Greek economy.

when democracy was restored in 1974. In the years since then, Greek voters have alternated between favoring two parties: the conservative New Democracy and the left-wing PASOK. For much of the time, New Democracy has been led by various members of the powerful Caramanlis family, while PASOK has been led by a series of Papandreous. In 1981, Greece was accepted into the European Union (Common Market) and began a period of initial prosperity (jump-started by EEC funding), followed by steady inflation. The euphoria of 2004, when Greece won the European Soccer Championship and hosted the wildly successful Athens Olympic Summer Games, lasted a year and then fizzled, as did plans to turn the Olympic village into low-income housing. Soon, Greece, along with its Common Market neighbors, was trying to cope with the problems of illegal immigration, rising prices, an increasingly fragile ecosystem, and the economic recession that began to affect much of the world in 2008.

In 2009, tourism—which brings in more than 15% of Greece's GDP—declined steeply in Greece. This was felt especially in the Greek islands, many of which are heavily dependent on tourism. Many holiday makers stayed home, while many others headed for Turkey—where prices for food and lodging are cheaper, service is often superior, and the strikes that so often close museums and monuments in Greece are unknown.

GREECE'S ART & ARCHITECTURE

Many of the buildings we know best—from football stadiums to shopping malls—have Greek origins. The simple Greek megaron gave birth to the temple and the basilica, the two building forms that many civic and religious shrines still embody. The Greek temple, with its pedimental facade, lives on in civic buildings, palaces, and ostentatious private homes throughout the world. Football and soccer are played in oval stadiums, the spectators now sitting on seats more comfortable than the stone slabs or dirt slopes they sat on in ancient Greek stadiums. Most theaters are now indoors, not outdoors, but the layout of stage, wings, and orchestra goes back to Greek theaters. The prototypes of shopping malls, with their side-by-side multiplicity of shops, can be found in almost every ancient Greek city. In fact, the confusing mixture of shops and civic buildings, private homes and public parks, is one that most ancient Greeks knew very well. And, whenever we can look inside those ancient buildings, we see

Kylix Krater. Amphora.

pots and pans in varying shapes, many of which are familiar today (round, lidded casseroles and long-handled frying pans, to name just two of the most common). Many elegant homes still emulate the frescoed walls and pitched red-tile roofs of classical Greek antiquity. In short, Greece was not just the "cradle of democracy," but the nursery of much of Western art and architecture. The portrait

Loutrophoros. Hydria. Lekythos.

Greek pediments and column types.

busts and statues of heroes that ornament almost every European city have their origins in ancient Greece. Both the elaborate vaulted funerary monuments and the simple stone grave markers of today can be found throughout ancient Greece. Much of Greek art and architecture was dedicated to one or more of the Greek gods, many of whose names are unfamiliar today. The feature below has a handy list of the better-known Greek gods and goddesses and some illustrations of some of the well-known elements of Greek art and architecture.

THE GODS & GODDESSES

As you travel around Greece, you'll notice that many of the monuments you see were dedicated to one or another of the Greek gods. For the ancient Greeks, the world was full of divine forces, most of which were thought to be immortal. Death, sleep, love, fate, memory, laughter, panic, rage, day, night, justice, victory—all of the timeless, elusive forces confronted by humans—were named and numbered among the gods and goddesses with whom the Greeks shared their universe. The most powerful of the gods lived with Zeus on Mount Olympus and were known as the Olympians. To make these forces more familiar and approachable, the Greeks (like every other ancient people) imagined their gods to be somehow like themselves. They were male and female, young and old, beautiful and deformed, gracious and withholding, lustful and virginal, sweet and fierce.

Principal Olympian Gods & Goddesses

GREEK NAME	LATIN NAME	DESCRIPTION
Zeus	Jupiter	Son of Kronos and Rhea, high god, ruler of Olympus. Thunderous sky god, wielding bolts of lightning. Patron-enforcer of the rites and laws of hospitality.
Hera	Juno	Daughter of Kronos and Rhea, queen of the sky. Sister and wife of Zeus. Patroness of marriage.
Demeter	Ceres	Daughter of Kronos and Rhea, sister of Hera and Zeus. Giver of grain and fecundity. Goddess of the mysteries of Eleusis.
Poseidon	Neptune	Son of Kronos and Rhea, brother of Zeus and Hera. Ruler of the seas. Earth-shaking god of earthquakes.
Hestia	Vesta	Daughter of Kronos and Rhea, sister of Hera and Zeus. Guardian of the hearth fire and of the home.
Hephaestos	Vulcan	Son of Hera, produced by her parthenogenetically. Lord of volcanoes and of fire. Himself a smith, the patron of crafts employing fire (metalworking and pottery).
Ares	Mars	Son of Zeus and Hera. The most hated of the gods. God of war and strife.
Hermes	Mercury	Son of Zeus and an Arcadian mountain nymph. Protector of thresholds and crossroads. Messenger-god, patron of commerce and eloquence. Companion-guide of souls en route to the underworld.
Apollo	Phoebus	Son of Zeus and Leto. Patron-god of the light of day, and of the creative genius of poetry and music. The god of divination and prophecy.
Artemis	Diana	Daughter of Zeus and Leto. Mistress of animals and of the hunt. Chaste guardian of young girls.
Athena	Minerva	Daughter of Zeus and Metis, born in full armor from the head of Zeus. Patroness of wisdom and of war. Patron-goddess of the city-state of Athens.
Dionysos	Dionysus	Son of Zeus and Semele, born from the thigh of his father. God of revel, revelation, wine, and drama.
Aphrodite	Venus	Born from the bright sea foam off the coast of Cyprus. Fusion of Minoan tree goddess and Near Eastern goddess of love and war. Daughter of Zeus. Patroness of love.

As told by the ancient poets, the "Lives of the Olympians" has elements of an eternal soap opera. Sometimes generous, courageous, and insightful, the gods are also notoriously petty, quarrelsome, spiteful, vain, frivolous, and insensitive. And how could it be otherwise with the Olympians? Not made to pay the ultimate price of death, they need not know the ultimate cost of life. Fed on *ambrosia* ("not mortal") and *nektar* ("overcoming death"), they cannot go hungry, much less perish. When life is endless, everything is reversible.

EATING & DRINKING IN GREECE

Recently in a Peloponnesian village, we eavesdropped on the customers of a local establishment. If we had not known some Greek, we would have thought that the gaggle of grandmotherly women were having a fierce argument. Voices were raised and disapproving fingers were shaken by speaker after speaker. What was the topic? That day's lunch, what to have, and how best to prepare it. The women were comparing, in minute detail, the way each would prepare her stuffed eggplant, her chicken stew, or her bean soup. Voices were raised over the precise amount of dill to use, the variety of onion best suited for the stew, and whether the season's first tomatoes were worthy of taking their place in a salad, or still to be used only for sauce. Greeks may not live to eat, but they certainly take what they eat, and how it is prepared, very seriously. Whereas many non-Greeks go out to a restaurant in the hopes of getting something different from home cooking, in Greece it is always high praise to say that a restaurant's food is "spitiko" (homemade). Here are some tips on places to eat in Greece and what to eat there.

What we say here is as true of the islands as the mainland, although wherever you go in Greece, you will find some local dishes, including the huge omelets of Tinos, the chickpea soup of Sifnos, and the citron liqueur of Naxos. Best not to praise the food of one island too highly when you are on another island: Each island is convinced that its cuisine is the most "authentic." One enormous change in island cuisine is a result of the vastly improved transportation between many of the Greek islands, which allows fresh produce to be brought into the islands all year, so you may find yourself eating a salad on Sifnos, with lettuce flown in from Crete. The growth of small Chinese communities on many islands means that you'll find Chinese shops and restaurants in the most unexpected spots. And the great number of expats who settle in the islands means that you'll find French food on Paros, Spanish and German food on Naxos, and just about everything on Mykonos and Santorini.

MEALS & DINING CUSTOMS There's a variety of different categories of places to eat and drink in Greece, and although you may find many of the same dishes and drinks in different kinds of establishments, it's useful to know what's out there. Almost every village has at least one *kafeneion* (coffeehouse), and usually two. It would take a team of anthropologists working with a team of sociologists to figure out how most Greeks choose their favorite local kafeneion. When I asked a friend why she always went to the kafeneion in the main square in our village, she replied vaguely that she could not remember why, but thought it had to do with a disagreement a friend of hers had had several decades earlier with the owner of the other kafeneion. Often clients choose their kafeneion based on political ideology or profession (whether white or blue collar). Families, and women on their own, usually sit at tables outside. Indoors, the kafeneion is still an almost exclusively male establishment and often functions as a clubhouse. Men stop by, play a hand of cards or a game of *tabli* (backgammon), and nurse a coffee or ouzo for hours. Greeks almost never drink without eating something, if only some chunks of feta cheese, a few olives, and perhaps some cucumber and tomato slices. This is an especially wise custom, especially when drinking fiery and potent ouzo, which turns a deceptively milky hue when diluted with water.

An *ouzeria* is usually quite similar to a kafeneion, but with the emphasis more squarely on ouzo, and the food often a bit heartier, including grilled sausage or octopus. Thessaloniki is famous for its ouzerias, which are often filled wall to wall with both the beautiful people and the passersby. It is perfectly possible, and usually very satisfying, to make a full meal from a selection of *mezedes* (appetizers) at an ouzeria.

Two recent additions to the scene include the *fastfooddadiko* and the lounge bar. The fastfooddadiko, as its name suggests, serves up snacks, to go or to munch at the counter. Souvlaki joints, on the other hand, usually stick to souvlaki and gyro, with or without pita bread. The lounge bar, an offspring of the disco, is usually a cafe with elaborate decor (mirrors, reflecting globes, massive flatscreen TVs), where full meals may be served and whiskey usually flows. The important thing at the lounge bar is to see and be seen and to survive the assault of the amplified music.

Restaurants serving full meals fall into a number of categories: a *psistaria* usually specializes in grilled meat, sometimes the *koukouretsi* (entrails) that are especially popular in Larissa and Lamia, while a *psarotaverna* serves mainly fish. As for the *estiatorio*, we're still trying to figure out the real difference between a *taverna* and an estiatorio. In theory, the taverna is more down home, the estiatorio more prone to certain refinements. At both, as at an ouzeria, you can make a full meal from *mezedes.*

There was a time when you could usually tell which was which by checking to see if the tablecloth was paper or cloth, but now, many chic places are deliberately casual and use paper cloths, while many simple places have a paper cloth on top of a cloth cover. Still, a taverna is usually a bit less formal, with less choice on the menu, than an estiatorio. Both usually have *magireio,* vegetable or meat stews, prepared in advance, usually tastier at lunch than in the evening, by which time they have been sitting around for a while. (Of course, some dishes, such as the vegetable stew called *briam,* often benefit from this process, with the flavors getting extra time to mingle.)

Many Greek restaurants, whatever tablecloth they may use, do not serve dessert, and Greeks often troop off after a meal to a pastry shop (the tongue-twisting *zacharopolasteion*). In recent years, many tavernas and estiatoria have started to serve a free dessert, ranging from simple apple slices with honey and cinnamon to elaborate ice cream confections topped with sparklers. Cafes and coffee shops usually serve light snacks, and some people head to them for dessert.

A few suggestions that may come in handy wherever you eat: Greeks usually tend to skip breakfast, or have a light snack in midmorning. Consequently, staying in a hotel that offers breakfast is not a bad idea, and will save you searching out a place that serves some approximation of a familiar breakfast. Greeks make lunch their big meal of the day, and eat it between 2 and 3pm. Especially in summer, Greeks often head to a cafe for some ice cream around 8pm. Dinner is often a light meal, seldom earlier than 9pm, but when Greeks do go out to dinner, they usually don't think of eating before 10pm. If you want to be sure of a table, try for the off hours—and be prepared to have the place to yourself and other foreigners. Menus are usually in Greek and English but, if not, just ask for help from your waiter, who is probably fluent in restaurant English. He may take you into the kitchen to eye what's available. Often, the printed menu has little bearing on what is available, and it never hurts to ask what's special that day. As to water, if you want tap water, not bottled, ask for it from the *vrisi* (tap). If you want the house wine, ask what their own wine is (*to diko sas krasi*), lest you be guided to much more expensive bottled wine.

Service is included in the bill, but it is customary to leave your waiter another 10% at a simple place, 15% at a fancy place. Some Greeks do and some do not tip in family-owned and -operated places. If you go out with Greek friends, prepare to go late and stay late and to put up a losing fight for the bill. Greeks frown on bill-splitting; usually, one person is host, and that is that. And if you are invited to a Greek home for a meal, assume that everything will run hours late and that you will be offered an unimaginable amount of food. This is especially true on holidays, especially Easter, when families spend most of their time preparing and eating roast lamb and all the fixings from the time that the Holy Saturday service ends at midnight until sunset on Easter day. Another thing: Greeks do not waste food. The traditional *margeritsa* soup that breaks the Lenten fast includes the entrails of the lamb that makes up the Easter dinner. Easter is *the* big feast day of the year, with feasting continuing on Easter Monday. The week after Easter, most newspapers carry supplements on "How to Lose the Weight You Gained at Easter."

THE CUISINE   Although all fresh ingredients are vital, excellent olive oil is the one essential in Greek cuisine. Ineptly translated menus often offer "oilies," the vegetable stew that you may know better as briam, or ratatouille. The seriousness of the forest fires that swept so much of Greece in 2007 struck home when there were reports that Greece would have to do the unthinkable and import olive oil. Greeks consume more olive oil than any other nation (some 30L per person per year) and they want that oil to be not just Greek, but from specific regions, preferably from specific groves. A friend of ours who has a home on Sifnos knows the individual nicknames of the olive trees her neighbor gives her oil from. In recent years, there has been a burst of interest in organic and virgin olive oil, and you'll probably see shops in major tourist destinations, such as Mykonos and Santorini, that sell varieties of olive oil from around Greece, as well as olive oil products such as soaps, shampoos, and lotions.

Cheese is the other staple of the Greek diet. Some visitors to Greece leave thinking that feta is the only Greek cheese. They are wrong. Although a slab of feta, usually sprinkled with oregano, tops most Greek salads, there's a wide variety of cheeses. Most Greek cheeses, such as feta, are made from sheep or goat's milk. Creamy *mizithra* is more delicate than feta, best when eaten fresh and soft, but useful when cured and grated on pasta. *Kefalotyri* and *graviera* are popular favorites, slightly bland, but with enough tang to be interesting. Every island you visit will have its own version of these cheeses, and at least one that is distinctive to the island.

Until recently, the standard Greek snack was a handful of olives, a chunk of bread, and a slab of cheese. Now, alas, potato chips are in the ascendency, as is childhood obesity. Still, fresh Greek fruit and vegetables in season are top-notch and still make up a major part of the Greek diet. The first zucchini, peas, and green beans of the season are eagerly anticipated. Unfortunately, the widespread proliferation of hot-house gardening means that more and more fruit is picked before it has ripened. And, like the fruit in supermarkets almost everywhere else, more and more Greek peaches and apricots, melons and pears, look beautiful, but taste, well, tasteless.

With oil, cheese, and fresh produce very popular throughout Greece, it's often said that there are few regional differences in Greek cuisine. While it is true that you can sit down to *mousaka* (veal in red sauce) or stuffed eggplant anywhere in Greece, each region is fiercely proud of its own version of the national favorites. The *revithadha* (chickpea) soup of Sifnos is famous throughout Greece, as are the almond cookies of

Andros and Naufpaktos. *Loukoumi* from Syros—to me indistinguishable from any other chewy piece of what the unwary visitor calls Turkish delight—is prized above all other *loukoumi*. The spread of supermarkets now means that you can get *loukoumi* from Syros in supermarkets throughout Greece. Still, bringing home a souvenir box of *loukoumi* from Syros for the neighbors is as popular here as bringing home maple syrup from Vermont (the same bottle one could get at the local supermarket) is in the United States.

WINE   The Greek wine that almost every visitor to Greece has heard of is the one that almost no foreigner loves: retsina. It's the pine resin that's added to the brew to preserve the wine that gives the pungent taste. Most retsina is either white or rosé, and most non-Greeks like theirs good and cold. Many villagers in Crete still make their own retsina, and you should be able to get some "real" retsina if you visit there. In recent years, the Greek wine industry has taken off, with Santorini's Boutari vintages and the island's prized white Assyrtiko wines becoming well known outside Greece. From the mainland, reds from the Naoussa area of Macedonia and Nemea in the Peloponnese are excellent, as are whites from Macedonia. And keep in mind that it's always a good idea to ask if the restaurant has a house or a local wine. Virtually every island has its own reds and whites. Another thing to keep in mind: There's a wide variety of sweet Greek dessert wines. If you like sweet wines, you are in luck. If not, by all means avoid *mavrodaphne,* vinsanto—and don't even think about trying the syrupy Greek fruit liqueurs! For more about Greek wines, check out the website http://greekwineworld.net, or get a copy of Nico Manessis's *The Illustrated Greek Wine Book* (Olive Press).

WHEN TO GO

Just about everyone agrees that the best time to visit is Greece is spring and early summer (mid-Apr to mid-June) or autumn (Sept to mid-Oct). This way, you'll avoid the summer high season, with its inflated prices, hordes of tourists, and high temperatures (heat waves of 100°F/40°C and up are routine). In fact, unless you *really* like scorching heat, crowds, and overbooked planes, ferry boats, and hotels, August in Greece, especially in the islands, is to be avoided. In the spring, you'll see more wild flowers than you could have imagined—and swim in a colder sea than you had hoped for. In the autumn, you will enjoy golden days with still-warm seas to swim in. One drawback: In off-season, there are fewer boats and flights to the islands, where some shops, hotels, and restaurants do not open until June and then close in October.

Something else to keep in mind if you are coming to Greece in the spring: During Easter week, virtually every hotel room outside of Athens is booked well in advance by city Greeks who head to the country to celebrate Greece's most important holiday. Many sites and museums are closed Good Friday, Easter Saturday, and Easter Sunday, while many shops close on Good Friday and Easter Saturday. And when St. George's Day (usually celebrated on Apr 23) falls in Lent, it is celebrated on the Monday after Easter Sunday, which just prolongs the Easter break. Also, the Feast of the Virgin on 15 August is an enormous holiday, especially on Tinos and Paros, but also on virtually every other Greek island and across the mainland.

WEATHER   Keep in mind that winters can be very harsh on the islands and spring can be plagued by high winds and rain. We've been visiting Greece since the 1960s and for the last decade, we've spent about half the year in Greece, most of it in a village in the Peloponnese, south of Athens. The one thing we can swear to is that the weather throughout Greece is getting less predictable every year. When Greeks talk about the weather, increasingly they say that everything is *"ano kato"* (upside down). Villages where snow was almost unknown had blizzards in the winter of 2010–11. Areas where February always meant steady rain saw hardly a drop all month. One thing that everyone agrees on: The winters are colder—sometimes drier, sometimes wetter, sometimes with unusual bursts of warm weather, but, all in all, increasingly colder. Summers, on the other hand, are just plain hotter (and usually drier) than even 10 years ago. Even though our temperature charts below reflect some sound statistics, don't be surprised if you find deviations from it when you visit Greece. You'll find more on the weather patterns in different regions of Greece in each chapter of the guide.

Average Monthly Temperatures & Precipitation

Athens	JAN	FEB	MAR	APR	MAY	JUNE	JULY	AUG	SEPT	OCT	NOV	DEC
Temp (°F)	50	50	54	59	67	75	81	81	75	67	59	53
Temp (°C)	10	10	12	15	19	24	27	27	24	19	15	12
Precip. (in.)	1.9	1.6	1.6	0.9	0.7	0.3	0.2	0.3	0.4	2.1	2.2	2.4
Iraklion	JAN	FEB	MAR	APR	MAY	JUNE	JULY	AUG	SEPT	OCT	NOV	DEC
Temp (°F)	53	54	56	61	66	73	77	77	73	68	62	56
Temp (°C)	12	12	13	16	19	23	25	25	23	20	17	13
Precip. (in.)	3.7	2.6	1.9	1.1	0.6	0.1	–	–	0.7	2.3	2.6	3.5

HOLIDAYS Every day in Greece is sacred to one or more saints. That means that every day, at least one saint (and everyone named for that saint) is being celebrated. Tiny chapels that are used only once a year are opened for a church service followed by all-day wining and dining. If you're lucky, you'll stumble on one of these celebrations. For information on national holidays, check out chapter 13, which also has a detailed calendar of important events that take place each year in Greece. For an exhaustive list of events beyond those listed there, check http://events.frommers. com, where you'll find a searchable, up-to-the-minute roster of what's happening in cities all over the world.

THE LAY OF THE LAND

Even though you may be visiting only Athens and the islands, here's a sense of the lay of the land in the islands and beyond to mainland Greece itself. The thing that is most startling about Greece is that this small country—about the size of the American state of Alabama—is so astonishingly diverse. This is especially true of the Greek islands, a world unto themselves, with each island its own little universe. Travel through the islands and you're bound to be informed at least once that when God finished creating the universe, he had a pile of stones left, so he threw them into the sea and created the Greek islands. And from the marble and limestone that make up the islands, the islanders have made their flat-slabbed stone paths, the winding walls that girdle their property and enclose their flocks, their thick-walled stone houses, and even the whimsical dovecots that cluster on many island hills. The islands are like delicious chocolates: One is never enough, each has its distinct pleasures, yet all are clearly related. But as you'll find out, if you sail, for example, from rocky little Folegandros to barren Hydra, to terraced Tinos and gentle Paros, and then on to Crete, with its snow-topped mountains, each island is very distinctive. A few islands—Poros and Zakynthos, for example—have landscapes very similar to the mainland they once formed part of. Other islands—notably the Cyclades—are abrupt and mountainous, with small but surprisingly fertile valleys and plains. As for Crete, it has everything, from long sandy beaches to snow-topped mountains.

All of Greece is a southern extension of the Balkan mountain range, albeit one with some 8,500km (5,280 miles) of largely serrated and irregular mainland coastline, and 7,500km (4,660 miles) of island coastlines. No place in Greece is more than 100km (62 miles) from the sea. In addition to the startling variety of landscapes within a few miles almost anywhere in Greece, there are some real regional differences. In the north, the mountains of Macedonia and Epirus are close cousins to the Alps, the rivers are broad and deep, and the forests are home to the last brown bears and most of the wild boars in Greece.

With the possible exception of the flat, often dusty, plains of Thrace and Thessaly, there is no part of Greece where you can drive very long without seeing something that takes your breath away. And even Thrace and Thessaly have the cliffs of the Meteora and the vast stretches of wetlands that make Greece a birder's paradise. As for Attica, Athens has almost devoured the gentle plain that once produced the grapes for almost all of Greece's pungent retsina wine. The mountains that flank Athens—Hymettos, Parnes, and Pentelicon—seldom turn the violet hues that the ancient poets described. In fact, the ring of mountains is now often blamed for trapping Athens's nasty summer *nefos* (smog) within the city. Many days, the Acropolis of Pindar's "violet-crowned Athens" is barely visible through the beige smog. It's often a relief to leave Athens behind and head, for example, to mountain villages such as Delphi and Arachova, on the Parnassos range. That said, the ski industry is busily covering much of Parnassos with chalets, ski lifts, and boutique hotels. Still, the sweeping views down from Parnassos to the Gulf of Corinth and the Peloponnese remain virtually unchanged. And we'd be remiss to not mention the beauties of the Peloponnese, which really does have it all: the Parnon and Tayegetus mountain ranges, the lush valleys of Arcadia, crescent sand beaches tucked below seaside cliffs, and a tantalizing sprinkle of off-shore islands.

RESPONSIBLE TRAVEL

Greece has a population of about 11.2 million. Astonishingly, between 10 million and 14 million tourists visit Greece annually. Each year, visitors use a veritable Niagara of water, whether by flushing hotel toilets; standing under long, restorative showers; or chugging down bottles of iced water. And of late, several water-hungry golf courses have been built in Greece, a country in which until recently the only broad swath of green grass was the lawn of the American Embassy in Athens.

Along with most of the rest of the world, Greece has not rushed to expect responsible travel from either themselves or their foreign visitors. Greeks are loathe to be told what to do and that includes being told where to park or how to recycle. As one of us was trying to inch precisely between the lines marking off a small parking space in a municipal parking lot in the Peloponnese, a car zipped ahead and parked lengthwise across two parking places, blocking the exit for two already properly parked cars. We've seen families ostentatiously dump beer cans and plastic bottles mere feet from recycling containers—just to demonstrate that no one could tell them what to do. Add to this all those foreign visitors, many of whom have no idea of the severe water shortages that perpetually plague Greece, and you begin to get an idea of how important it is for all of us to travel responsibly in Greece. Here are some hints on how to protect Greece's natural resources and make the Greeks you meet hope you come back again.

HELPING TO CREATE A SUSTAINABLE GREECE Be sure that any match, cigarette, or flammable material that you dispose of is completely out. Summer forest fires consume thousands of acres of Greek forests every year.

Few Greek hotels post requests that visitors conserve water and reuse bath towels because almost all hotels are afraid of antagonizing visitors. It's up to us visitors to keep that in mind everywhere you go, but especially the islands, which perpetually face severe water shortages.

Be sure to turn off all lights and the air-conditioning in your hotel room when you go out. I know more than one small island hotel that has resorted to disconnecting its air conditioners and pretending all season that they are "temporarily" out of order. "What can I do?" one proprietor asked me. "If the tourists can use the air conditioners, they leave them on high while they are out sightseeing all day."

Finally, if you want to help create a greener Greece, you can make a contribution to the Plant Your Roots in Greece foundation, which will use your money to help reforest the denuded hills of Greece. For information, check out the website **www. plantyourrootsingreece.org**. And to help preserve Greek wildlife, the Hellenic Wildlife Hospital (HWH) on Aegina treats wounded and injured wildlife, including many of the sea turtles that are injured each year by jet skis.

BEING A WELCOME GUEST IN GREECE **Dress Codes** Most Greeks wear bathing suits only on the beach and do not go into restaurants, cafes, or shops without putting something over their swimsuits. Also, most Greeks consider bare feet off the beach seriously odd and quite rude. And almost no Greek man would go into a church in shorts and virtually no Greek woman would go into church in a sleeveless top or shorts. That said, slacks for women are now acceptable almost everywhere, except in the most traditional churches and monasteries.

Hello & Goodbye Most encounters between Greeks begin and end with ritual phrases. Very few Greeks go into a bakery and say "Loaf of bread, please," and then pay and leave. Almost all begin with a greeting. "Kali mera" (good day) is always acceptable, but on Monday, you'll hear "kali ebdomada" (good week) and on the first of the month "kalo mena" (good month). Sprinkle your requests on how to find the Acropolis or where to buy a bus ticket with "sas para kalo" (excuse me, please) and "eucharisto" (thanks), and you'll help to make Greeks reconsider all those things they've come to believe about rude tourists. And on that topic, although most Greeks are happy to have their photo taken, always ask first, unless you have a superb telephoto lens. Finally, if you are traveling with your beloved pet dog, remember that most Greeks do not regard dogs as house pets, but as unclean outdoor watchdogs. Except in chic city cafes, don't sit down with your dog without asking permission.

TOURS

Until recently, virtually all tours of mainland Greece focused on classical antiquities and leavened the serious sightseeing with some shopping and an afternoon or two at the beach. Gradually, most tour groups added a visit to Medieval Mistra in the Peloponnese or the monasteries of the Meteora in Thessaly. Today, there's a wide variety of tours, special-interest trips, classes and workshops available, focusing on everything from antiquities to wine tasting. A number of cruises concentrate on the Greek islands (see chapter 4, "Cruising the Greek Islands"). In addition, there are a number of organized possibilities for volunteerism, whether on excavations or on farms. Here are some suggestions.

Academic Trips & Language Classes

Want to arrive in Greece knowing how to say more than "Sorry, I don't speak Greek"? Check out the Dartmouth College Rassias Center (© **603/646-2922;** http://rassias. dartmouth.edu) language program in modern Greek. This very popular, very successful 10-day total-immersion session should have you arriving ready to amaze and delight Greeks with your command of their glorious and tricky language. If you can't go to the Rassias Center but find yourself staying on in Greece and wanting to learn the language, the **Athens Centre,** 48 Archimidous, Mets, 11636 Athens (© **210/ 7012-268;** www.athenscentre.gr), has been around since 1969 and offers modern Greek classes year-round.

Many colleges offer tours of Greece, led by scholars at the institution sponsoring the tour. Most of these tours are serious but very comfortable—and not cheap. Some of these tours are open only to graduates of the institution; others welcome all comers, so you'll probably want to check out a few university and college websites to find what interests you.

Archaeological Tours, 271 Madison Ave., Ste. 904, New York, NY 10016 (© **866/740-5130;** www.archaeologicaltrs.com), offers tours led by expert guides; typical tours might be to classical Greek sites or to Cyprus, Crete, and Santorini. **FreeGate Tourism,** 585 Stewart Ave., Ste. 560, Garden City, NY 11530 (© **888/ 373-3428;** www.freegatetours.com), also specializes in guided trips in Greece.

The **Aegean Center for the Fine Arts** (© **22840/23-287;** www.aegeancenter. org), based on the island of Paros, offers courses in painting, photography, music, creative writing, and modern Greek. Most of the students are college-age Americans; the instructors are Greek, American, and international.

The American-run **Island Center for the Arts** (© **617/623-6538;** www.island center.org) conducts classes in painting, photography, and Greek culture on the island of Skopelos between June and September. As it is affiliated with the Massachusetts College of Art, some educational institutions grant credits for its courses.

Adventure & Wellness Trips

Trekking Hellas (© **210/331-0323;** www.trekking.gr) offers white-water rafting excursions in the Peloponnese and northern Greece. Although plenty of beginners (including many macho Greek guys) do go on these trips, most foreign participants have had some previous experience. Trekking Hellas also organizes hiking tours (see "Walking Tours," below).

Skyros Center (© **01983/86-55-66;** www.skyros.com) offers yoga and holistic holidays (as well as writing holidays and singles holidays) on the island of Skyros. It is a British operation with a year-round office on the Isle of Wight, and is best contacted via e-mail (office@skyros.com).

Limnisa (Creative Holidays by the Sea; © **01424/71-83-68;** www.limnisa.com) is also based in the U.K., and offers silent retreats, writing retreats, and workshops by the sea near Methana, in the east Peloponnese, near the island of Poros.

Eumelia (© **213/036-9814;** www.eumelia.com;), in the Peloponnese south of Sparta, has five rental houses, a staff of three, and never more than 25 guests on its organic farm outside the hamlet of Gouves. Eumelia (the name means "melody") focuses on both agritourism and the manufacture and sale of organic produce (olive oil, herbs, and so on). There are frequent workshops and seminars (2011 had a "raw vegan cooking seminar"). Eumelia aims for "100% self-sufficiency" and all its buildings are built with great attention to environmental issues—and have TV and Internet access. Prices are very reasonable: 120 € for two people sharing a two-bedroom cottage.

Food & Wine Trips

If you're heading for Santorini and want to learn about Greek cuisine, the island's best restaurant, **Selene** (✆ **228/602-2249;** www.selene.gr), offers cooking classes with the most varied and fresh local ingredients each summer. Aglaia Kremezi (**www. aglaiakremezi.com**), an American-educated Greek authority on Greek food, and her husband, Costas Moraitis, run a cooking school on the island of Kea. And Nikki Rose (**www.cookingincrete.com**), a Cretan-American professional chef, operates seminars on Crete that combine some travel with cooking lessons and investigations of Crete's diet.

Want to mix seeing where the Olympic Games began with some cooking, creative writing, or painting? Check out the website of the **Hotel Pelops** (www.hotelpelops. gr), where co-owner Susanna Spiliopoulou offers 3- and 4-day workshops a short walk from the pine groves of ancient Olympia.

Guided Tours

Organized and guided **bus tours** focusing on the glories of ancient Greece are widely available, and many are the granddaddies of organized travel in Greece. Escorted tours are structured group tours, with a group leader. The price usually includes everything from airfare to hotels, meals, tours, admission costs, and local transportation. Single travelers are usually hit with a "single supplement" to the base price for package vacations and cruises, while the price of a single room is almost always well over half that for a double.

CHAT Tours, founded in 1953, is the oldest and most experienced provider of a wide selection of bus tours led by highly articulate guides. Its main office is at 9 Xenofontos, Athens 10557 (✆ **210/323-0827;** www.chattours.gr). Recently, a close friend went on a CHAT tour and thought the pace was just about right, although she could have used a bit more free time. Be sure to ask how many will be on your tour, as a large group usually results in a more regimented and much less personal tour.

Another long-standing Greek tour organizer is **Homeric Tours** (✆ **800/223-5570;** www.homerictours.com). Such tours fall into the "moderate" category in pricing and accommodations, and carry the risk of all charter flights—that is, delays. They offer some variety—often these tours provide local guides, and often they include short cruises as part of the entire stay.

A more upscale agency is **TrueGreece** (✆ **800/817-7098** in North America, 203/026-1176 in the U.K., or 210/612-0656 in Greece; www.truegreece.com), which says it is an "innovative luxury vacation travel company" and escorts small groups on customized and more intimate tours to selected destinations.

For more information on escorted general-interest tours, including questions to ask before booking your trip, see www.frommers.com/planning.

Volunteer & Working Opportunities

Many Greek Orthodox churches in the U.S. and the U.K. can offer suggestions for volunteer work in Greece, although many opportunities assume a fluency in Greek. **GoGreece.about.com** lists many volunteer possibilities in Greece, including chances to help sea turtles on Zakynthos or donkeys on Corfu. The **National Marine Park of Zakynthos** (www.nmp-zak.org) also accepts volunteers. Other possibilities include the **World Wide Opportunities on Organic Farms** (www. wwoof.org) organization offers possibilities for volunteers in several locations in Greece, including Mount Pelion.

On Chios, **Masticulture and Ecotourism Activities** (www.masticulture.com) has a range of tours and activities, letting visitors participate in the mastic and wine harvests and learn about local pottery, cooking, and customs.

Walking Tours

Trekking Hellas (see "Adventure & Wellness Trips," above) is the best-known outfit offering guided hiking tours of the Greek mainland, Crete, and several Cycladic islands. If you don't want to be with a group, but do want some pointers, Trekking Hellas will help you plan an itinerary and book you places to stay along the way.

In the United States, **Appalachian Mountain Club,** 5 Joy St., Boston, MA 02108 (© **800/372-1758;** www.outdoors.org), often organizes hiking tours in Greece. **EcoGreece,** P.O. Box 2614, Rancho Palo Verdes, CA 90275 (© **877/838-7748;** www.ecogreece.com), conducts tours in Greece centered around activities such as hiking, sailing, diving, and horseback riding.

SUGGESTED GREEK ISLAND ITINERARIES

3

Greece is so small—almost precisely the size of the state of Alabama—that you might think it's easy to see most of the country in a relatively short visit. There are two reasons why that's not true and they are the same two reasons that make travel here so beautiful: the mountains and the sea. Greece's mountainous terrain almost always makes mainland travel take much longer than you'd expected when you just figured out the distance on your map. As to island travel, often you can see your next island destination from the island you are on, only to find out that getting there requires an infuriatingly time-consuming, roundabout sea journey with either nerve-wrenchingly tight connections or unwanted—sometimes totally unscheduled—stopovers on other islands. Still, with advance planning, some good luck, and a willingness to be flexible, you can see what you set out to see. And don't be surprised if your most lasting memories are of unexpected sights and unanticipated delights en route to your planned destinations.

If you'd like a little less of the unexpected on your Greek holiday, you might want to sign up for one of the standard cruises that stop at several of the major islands and often take in mainland highlights such as Delphi and Olympia. (Such cruises are described in detail in chapter 4.)

On most itineraries, you'll take a mixture of buses, trains, cars, ships, and planes. Here's something to keep in mind: Strikes often make travel in Greece very tricky when airports close and buses and ferry boats stop running. When everything works, travel by bus and ferry is terrific—and a great way to meet Greeks. Driving your own car is much more isolating, but frees you from worry about most strikes (even gas stations, after all, can close because of strikes). If you choose to drive, you'll find out that most Greeks drive with hair-raising flair, passing on the right, using sidewalks as extra lanes, and almost never signaling before turning. And, yes, the traffic accident rate in Greece is one of the highest in the world.

Because these itineraries include islands, they work best in the summer, May through September. Off-season, the weather is not dependable, many hotels and restaurants close, and airline and ferry schedules to some of these places become extremely limited. Of course, in summer, you can travel more easily from island to island, but you may find yourself sleeping rough unless you have a reservation. Off-season, you can luxuriate in the natural rhythm of uncrowded island villages, but you may find the best restaurants are closed.

Speaking of seasonal schedules and closings, Greece often keeps to its own—frequently mysterious—schedule. On any given day, a museum or archaeological site may be closed without notice. Call in advance to make sure that a destination will be open while you're traveling, and double-check your reservations, especially during special occasions such as Greek Easter week and the August 15 Assumption of the Virgin. Just as in western Europe and the U.S. at Christmas, overbooking is not unknown here on major holidays. If you can, avoid the most crowded travel times. And now, as you set off for Greece, *Kalo taxidi!* (Have a good trip!)

THE GREEK ISLANDS IN 1 WEEK

Ideally, everyone should have a whole summer for Greece. But let's face it, most people leave home on a Friday evening and then fly back to work the next Sunday. That's 8 full days on the ground. We've included 2 weekends, but any 8 days will work. This itinerary is for those interested in sampling the distinctive "historical" Greece. Mold this to your needs. You can always drop a museum or site and take time to relax on a beach. However, this particular itinerary involves a fair amount of moving about and checking in and out of hotels: Maximum Greek Islands in a minimum of time.

Day 1: Athens & the Acropolis

Arrive in Athens and get settled in your hotel. Then walk to the **Acropolis** ★★★ (p. 135) to see the **Parthenon,** arguably the world's number-one destination. Be sure to make time for the **New Acropolis Museum** ★★★ (art-course sculptures) and the **Theater of Dionysos** ★ (ground zero of Greek drama). For a modest dinner in a lovely spot, head to **Platanos Taverna** ★★ (p. 121) or another of the restaurants in the Plaka (p. 120).

Day 2: Athens & Santorini

Check out the gold masks, jewelry, sculptures, and other highlights at the **National Archaeological Museum** ★★★ (p. 146). Then head to the **Ancient Agora** ★★ (p. 141) to experience the more down-to-earth ancient Athens. Imagine the individuals' lives when you visit the ancient **Kerameikos Cemetery** ★ (p. 142). Any cafe nearby will do for a cool drink. Then hit the museum trail again (p. 142). Plan to lunch at **Oraia Ellada,** in the Plaka (p. 129). Explore **Syntagma Square** (p. 135). Take the evening flight or overnight ferry to Santorini. Get a taxi to Oia (Ia) and, after checking in at a hotel there, try **Skala** for dinner (p. 252).

Days 3 & 4: Santorini & Folegandros

Ancient Akrotiri ★★★ has been intermittently open since the protective roof over the site collapsed in 2005, but you must try to see it if it's open (p. 240). Spend the rest of the day at Kamari, with its black sand and pebble beach, and no end of cafes for snacks. Have lunch on the beach at **Camille Stefani** ★ (p. 251). Later, take in the restored mansion as you dine formally at **Restaurant-Bar 1800** ★ (p. 252), in Oia. On Day 4, look for the ancient cave houses hollowed into the solidified ash (p. 243), before taking the 2-hour-plus ferry ride to **Folegandros.** Get a taxi or bus to **Hora** ★, Folegandros's capital. It's one of

The Greek Islands in 1 Week

the most beautiful Cycladic villages, and it's largely built inside the walls of a 12th-century Venetian castle. Cars—and motorcycles—are banned from Hora. It's easy to laze away the rest of the day at one of the cafes or restaurants in the perfect little *plateia* (square) shaded by almond trees. End the day with a swim at **Angali** beach before dinner. Then settle into your room at the very charming **Anemomilos Apartments** ★★, with its spectacular view out to sea, or at the **Castro Hotel** ★★, built into a Venetian castle.

Days 5 & 6: Crete

Go early to visit **Knossos** ★★★ (p. 198), and then see the snake goddesses and rich Minoan artifacts at the **Archaeological Museum** ★★★ (p. 196). After lunch and a siesta, take the walking tour of Iraklion (p. 198) before treating yourself to a superb meal at the **Brillant Gourmet** (p. 202). Spend Day 6 touring **Chania** ★★ (by rental car, public transportation, or escorted tour), with its relatively intact Venetian-Turkish old town (p. 206); or **Phaestos** ★★, the second-most ambitious Minoan palace (p. 205). Expect to be on the road for 5 hours round-trip for each. Eat lunch at the restaurant at the Phaestos site; or, if you didn't take that trip, eat along Chania's harbor at the **Amphora** (p. 215). By early evening, return to Iraklion.

Day 7: Athens & the Temple of Poseidon

Take an early morning flight back to Athens. If you're up to another excursion, continue on to the **Temple of Poseidon,** at Sounion (p. 149). Stay for a swim and the sunset before heading back to Athens. If you want to admire the Acropolis while you eat, try a rooftop table at **Strofi's** ★ (p. 134). Then, either collapse or do as the Greeks do and head off for the cafes (see "Athens After Dark," p. 151).

Day 8: Flight Home

Go to the airport and fly home.

THE GREEK ISLANDS IN 2 WEEKS

From the must-see ancient monuments (the Acropolis in Athens, the stadium in Olympia, and the site of the Delphic Oracle on the slopes of Mount Parnassus) to the famous isles (Mykonos, with its snow-white houses and trendy all-night bars, and volcanic Santorini, with its amazing harbor and sheer cliffs) to less famous places that not all visitors know about when they come to Greece (but fall in love with when they discover them)—we're going to show you how to see all this—and also keep some time for discoveries of your own. Here's how to do it in 2 weeks.

Day 1: Athens & the Archaeological Parkway

Settle into your hotel, then go for a get-acquainted walk along **The Archaeological Park,** which runs from Syntagma Square around the **Acropolis** ★★★, past the **Agora** ★★, and into the **Plaka,** the heart of old—and touristy—Athens (p. 135). Do what the Athenians do and stop for cappuccino, pastries, cheese, or yogurt at **Oraia Ellada** ★★ (p. 129), a Plaka shop with a restaurant that offers a drop-dead gorgeous Acropolis view. Browse through the old and new Greek folk art before continuing your walk. (If you get really tired, hop the Metro back to your hotel.) For lunch, sit under the plane tree as you enjoy roast lamb at **Platanos Taverna** ★★ (p. 121), one of the nicest old-time "authentic" tavernas. Feeling revived? Stop at the little **Museum of Popular Greek Musical Instruments** ★★ (p. 146), just a few feet away. Listen to Greek music and enjoy the peaceful garden. The slumbering tortoises there may remind you that it's siesta time. Go to your hotel for a nap before you head out again for a nighttime stroll back to the Acropolis (even if it's closed) and dinner. If you're hungry, have a bite at one of the many fast-food cafeterias on Syntagma Square. Point to what you want and leave your phrase book in your pocket.

Day 2: Museums & Mount Likavitos

Visit the **National Archaeological Museum** ★★★ to see art-course sculptures, gold, and other incredible artifacts (p. 146). Then head to the Acropolis, but first grab a snack at one of the kiosks on the slopes. Spend the rest of the day enjoying Athens's sprawling **National Gardens** (p. 135) and watching Greek families. Then have dinner at nearby **Aegli** ★★ (p. 129). Or ride the cable car up **Mount Likavitos** (p. 101) before dinner at **To Kafeneio** ★★ (p. 132). Located in Kolonaki, the restaurant near the mountain is a great place to enjoy the bustle of Athens's most fashionable neighborhood.

Day 3: Mykonos & Paradise

By plane or ship, go to Mykonos. Settle into your hotel, then take a bus to one of the beaches outside town—**Paradise** ★ (p. 295) attracts partiers who love loud beach-bar music with their sun and sand, while **Ornos** is a quieter beach preferred by families (p. 295). Buy something for lunch on the beach. Back in town, get lost in the town's winding streets; end up at **Caprice** in "Little Venice" for a dry martini and good people-watching (p. 309). Before dinner, walk to Mykonos's famous three waterside windmills to take in the view back across the harbor. You'll see Little Venice's bars, perched vertiginously over the sea. The fish is fresh at **Kounelas** ★ on the harbor (p. 306), where you'll vie for a table with locals.

Day 4: Mykonos & Delos

Take an early excursion boat from Mykonos to **Delos** ★★★ (p. 311) and spend several hours admiring the acres of marble ruins. There's a little snack bar by the museum, but you'll probably do better bringing your own food from Mykonos and picnicking in a patch of shade cast by the ancient monuments. When you get back to Mykonos, tarry in its excellent shops, which include some of the best jewelers in Greece. Be sure to stop at the LALAoUNIS shop here (p. 299). For dinner, sample the *mezedes* and grilled fish (or meat) at the **Sea Satin Market** ★, past the windmills at Kato Myli, overlooking the sea (p. 308).

Day 5: Santorini & Akrotiri

Head to Santorini next, by plane or ship (p. 235). If you go by ship, you'll sail into the deep harbor with its high cliffs streaked with lava from the volcanic eruption that tore the island in half around 1450 B.C.—this is one of the world's great travel experiences. Check into your hotel and rent a car or sign up for a tour of the ancient site of **Akrotiri** ★★★, often called the "Pompeii of Greece" (p. 236). Then take in the **Boutari Winery,** where your tour includes enough snacks and samples of local wines for a light lunch (p. 241). In the evening, do what everyone does in Fira, Santorini's capital: Wander down the narrow streets before having drinks and dinner. For an inventive, memorable meal in a beautiful setting, make reservations at one of the best restaurants in all of Greece, **Selene** ★★★ (p. 252), now in the village of Pyrgos.

Day 6: Ancient Thira & Kamari

Explore the island by car, tour, or the excellent local bus system. See the dramatic cliff-top site of **Ancient Thira** ★★ (p. 240). Then head down to the famous black-sand beach at Kamari for a swim, and lunch at **Camille Stefani taverna** ★, a longtime favorite (p. 251). Back in Fira, see the fantastic reproductions of the beautiful Minoan wall paintings of Akrotiri, in the **Thira Foundation** ★ (p. 241). If you're here in season, watch the sunset from the village of **Imerovigli** (p. 247). Try **Katina's** ★, an excellent fish place in Ammoudi, the minuscule port of little Oia (Ia; p. 252).

Day 7: Folegandros

Take the ferry from bustling Santorini to the little island of **Folegandros** (p. 253), one of the last "undiscovered" Cycladic islands. Explore the capital

The Greek Islands in 2 Weeks

town of **Hora,** much of which is built into the walls of a Venetian fortress (p. 255). Swim at Livadaki or Ambeli beach (p. 254), and then relax over dinner at one of the little tavernas clustered around the main square in Hora (p. 255). Stay either in the **Castro Hotel** (p. 256), built into the walls of the Venetian castle, or in the **Anemomilos** (p. 256), just outside town, with its own swimming pool and a drop-dead view out to sea.

Day 8: Folegandros to Tinos

Catch a ferry from Folegandros to **Tinos** (p. 314). Some days, this may involve changing ferries at Santorini, Sifnos, or Mykonos; you'll experience the hustle and bustle of the harbor front. While at sea, laze the day away watching the islands come and go on the horizon. Bring a picnic with you: the food on most island boats is as undistinguished as the scenery is beautiful. When you arrive at Tinos, if you want to be in the heart of things, stay at the harbor-front **Oceanis Hotel** (p. 322). If you want to be on the beach, get a room at the **Tinos Beach Hotel** (p. 323), just outside Tinos town. If you arrive late on Tinos, don't worry: the waterfront restaurants and cafes stay open almost all night (p. 324).

Day 9: Exploring Tinos

Head uphill in the cool and quiet of the morning to the **Cathedral of the Panagia Evangelistria** (p. 317). You may encounter a family bringing a baby to be baptized at this important shrine. Be sure to take in the cluster of small museums in the Cathedral precincts before strolling back downhill to stop in the **Archaeological Museum** (p. 326). Then head out into the lush Tinian countryside to take in some of its sparkling white villages, with their bubbling springs and ornate **dovecotes** (p. 315). **Pirgos** (p. 319) is one of the loveliest villages, and lunch at one of the cafes on its shaded square is memorable (p. 319). If you want lunch by the sea, keep going to the beach at Panormos (p. 320), as yet undeveloped, but not for long. In the evening, explore the shops in Tinos town before eating a seriously good meal at **Metaxi Mas** (p. 323) or **Palaia Pallada** (p. 324). Most tourists on Tinos are Greek, and they know and love their food.

Day 10: Paros

There are frequent boats from Tinos to **Paros** (p. 266), and it's easy to sail over to spend a few hours or a full day on Paros, whose profusion of shops, boutiques, and restaurants have earned it the nickname of the "poor man's Mykonos." The island's capitol, **Parikia,** has its own handsome fortress, a lovingly restored Byzantine church, the **Ekatondapiliani,** which, according to local legend, has 100 doors (p. 270). If you're here in June, be sure to take in the **Valley of the Petaloudes** (Butterflies; p. 271), an easy excursion by bus or car from Parikia. Then catch a ferry back to Tinos for the night.

Day 11: Tinos to Siros

Take the ferry to **Siros** (p. 324) to experience an island unlike the other Cyclades. Yes, Siros has some of the typical shining white, cubelike Cycladic houses, especially in **Ano Siros,** the oldest part of Siros's capitol, **Ermoupolis** (p. 327). Ermoupolis also has the most handsome city hall in the Cyclades—and an opera house modeled on Milan's La Scala. This was the most important and prosperous Cycladic island in the 19th century; and you can learn all about the shipbuilding that made Siros famous around the world at Ermoupolis's superb **Industrial Museum** (p. 327). That said, you may find it so pleasant to watch the world go by from one of the cafes or tavernas in Ermoupolis's main square, the spacious Plateia Miaoulis, that you don't budge for hours.

Day 12: Siros to Crete

Take the interisland ferry from Siros to Crete (depending on the day of the week, you may have to take it on Day 11) and, on arriving at **Iraklion,** go straight from the dock to the **Lato Boutique Hotel** ★ (p. 201), where I recommend spending the next 2 nights. After you check in, head for either the great Minoan **Palace of Knossos** ★★★ (p. 198) or the **Archaeological Museum** ★★★ (p. 196): opinions differ as to whether one is best viewed before the other but they definitely complement each other. (Both stay open fairly late in high season.) Get away from the crowds by walking down to the harbor or out around the great **Venetian walls** ★ (p. 198); if you are up for it, take our complete "stroll around the city" (p. 198). Have a refreshing drink on the Lion Fountain Square, but take your meals at the **Pantheon** (p. 204) for an "indigenous" experience or **Loukoulos** ★ for something more cosmopolitan (p. 203).

Day 13: Crete

Rent a car for the day, or sign on with a tourist-agency excursion. Archaeological buffs will appreciate **Phaestos** ★★ (p. 205), the second great Minoan Palace; include stops at **Gortyna** ★ (with its extraordinary law code; p. 205) and, if time permits, **Matala** ★, with its seaside caves (p. 205). Bring a picnic for your midday meal. But city types might head along the coast to **Rethymnon** and/or **Chania** (reachable by frequent public transport), both with Old Towns that are filled with Venetian and Turkish structures (and lots of shops). If you've chosen the latter, plan to eat at the **Well of the Turk** in Chania ★ (p. 215), before heading back to Iraklion. Those taking the other trip will be ready for a final meal in Iraklion; consider the basic **Ippocampus** (p. 203).

Day 14: To Athens

Fly back to Athens. End your trip with a final stroll beneath the Acropolis.

THE GREEK ISLANDS WITH A FAMILY

This itinerary works well for families with kids between 7 and 15 years old. We tried to balance the adults' reasons for coming all the way to Greece (seeing unique sites) with the children's desires (swimming in hotel pools). As for food? The varied Greek menu should provide something for everyone's taste. And for better or worse, fast food is increasingly available all over Greece. Heat, especially in high season, should be a concern for travelers of all ages. Stay out of the midday sun, especially on the beach. Most forms of transportation offer reduced rates for kids 11 and under, as do most hotels, museums, and archaeological sites. We also recognize that children wilt faster than adults do while traveling.

Days 1 & 2: Athens

After you arrive in Athens, settle in to offset jet lag. Cool off by getting a day pass to the **Athens Hilton pool** (p. 117). By late afternoon, stroll over to the **Acropolis** ★★★ (p. 135). Before and after dinner, walk around the **Plaka/ Monastiraki** district (p. 150). On Day 2, visit the **National Archaeological Museum** ★★★ (p. 146)—forget the vases and go straight to the gold objects and the statues. Have lunch at the museum's outdoor cafe; or head to the National Gardens, with its cool paths, small zoo, and outdoor dining (p. 135). Later, take in the changing of the guard at the **Tomb of the Unknown Soldier,** on Syntagma Square. After a rest at your hotel, ride the cable car up Mount Likavitos, and treat yourself to a traditional Greek dinner.

Day 3: Crete

Take a morning flight to **Iraklion.** Hit the lovely beach soon after checking into the **Candia Maris Resort and Spa** ★ (p. 202); it's right out the door. The kids can also play basketball, tennis, or minigolf here. Dine at the hotel or, if you are up to it, go into Iraklion for an early dinner at **Ippocampus** (p. 203). The kids should love the fried zucchini and potato slices. You'll like the seafood.

The Greek Islands with a Family

Day 4: Knossos & Water City

Your hotel can arrange a visit to the Minoan **Palace of Knossos** ★★★ (p. 198), one of the great archaeological sites of the world. Kids will appreciate its sheer complexity. Reward them with time back at the hotel's beach or a visit to **Water City,** a water park at Kokkini Hani. That night, try dinner at the **Pantheon** (p. 204), in Iraklion's famous "Dirty Alley"—no longer "dirty," but still atmospheric.

Day 5: Matala

In a rental car, drive to the caves and bluff-enclosed cove beach at **Matala** ★, once a major hippie destination (p. 205). Hang out here, and be sure to bring a picnic lunch.

Day 6: Santorini

Take the ferry to Santorini (a 5-hr. trip). Check in at a hotel at **Kamari,** if you prefer a beach (p. 244), or at **Oia (Ia),** if you prefer a spectacular view (p. 242). In the evening, dine on the terrace overlooking the caldera at **Koukoumavlos** ★★

(p. 251), in Fira town. Try the yogurt panna cotta with pistachios, honey, and sour cherries for dessert.

Days 7 & 8: Akrotiri & Fira

On **Day 7,** if it's open, visit the unique excavated ancient city (nicknamed the "Pompeii of Greece") at **Akrotiri** ★★★: Even jaded kids will be impressed by the three-story, 3,500-year-old houses (p. 240). Then snorkel (or relax) by the beach at **Kamari** (p. 244), or take in the sights of **Fira** town (p. 246). For **Day 8,** wake up in time to take the excursion to the volcanic islet in the caldera—it will probably be your only chance ever to walk on an emerging volcano (p. 243). You should also have time to take the cable car from Fira town down to the shore and then come back up by donkey (p. 238) before flying to Athens in the early evening.

Day 9: Flight Home

Take a taxi to the airport, and fly home.

IN THE FOOTSTEPS OF THE APOSTLE PAUL

This itinerary is designed not just for Christians, but for anyone interested in a major chapter of early Western history. The Apostle Paul visited a number of Greek sites linked to the New Testament and the earliest years of Christianity. Paul visited territories belonging to modern Greece on at least three different journeys—and most of the places still bear the same names. These visits are accounted for in the Book of Acts, in the Bible; we recommend reading the section beforehand—perhaps even taking along a copy of the New Testament. Due to the exigencies of modern travel and time, we can't plot a trip that follows Paul's exact itinerary, just highlights.

Days 1 & 2: Athens

Refer to **Day 1** and the Athens part of **Day 2** in "The Greek Islands in 1 Week," earlier in this chapter. Include a walk to the hill opposite the Acropolis known as the **Pnyx** (p. 148); this was the meeting place of the Aereopagus (the Athenian Assembly), which Paul addressed on his first journey to Greece. Also, when you visit the **Ancient Agora** ★★ (p. 141), imagine Paul conversing with the people of Athens here.

Days 3 & 4: Rhodes & Lindos

Fly from Athens to **Rhodes** ★★ (p. 332). For local color, try the **S. Nikolis Hotel** ★★ (p. 342). The Old Town of Rhodes is the oldest inhabited medieval town in Europe (p. 337). Don't miss the **Street of the Knights** ★★, a 600m-long (1,968-ft.) cobblestone street from the early 16th century. Take up Paul's journey by spending the day at picturesque **Lindos** (p. 348), where Paul is said to have landed. Explore the **Acropolis** ★ and the Byzantine **Church of the Panagia** ★ (p. 317). Have lunch at **Mavrikos** ★ (p. 350), for a French twist on Greek food. Back in Rhodes Town, try for a garden table at the **Romeo** ★ restaurant (p. 346).

Days 5 & 6: Patmos

On **Day 5,** set out for **Patmos** ★ (p. 367), either by ferry direct from Rhodes or by plane to Kos, and take the ferry from there to Patmos. If you arrive at Kos at lunchtime, try the **Platanos** ★ (p. 422); if already on Patmos, go to **Pantelis** (p. 373), in the port town Skala. Check in at either **Skala Hotel** or **Blue Bay** ★ (p. 371). You can wander through town. Patmos has 30-plus churches. Nothing remains on Patmos to testify to Paul's visit, but a must-see for Christians is the **Cave of the Apocalypse** ★, where John the Divine is said to have written the Book of Revelation (p. 369). Everyone will want to visit the nearby **Monastery of St. John** ★, built to withstand pirates (ca. 1090). It contains frescoes from the 12th century (p. 370). While at the monastery, lunch at the **Vagelis** (p. 373) and take in the view. In the evening, dine at the restaurant in the **Skala Hotel** (p. 372).

Day 7: Patmos to Crete

You'll spend most of the day returning to Rhodes by ferry and then flying on to **Iraklion,** Crete (p. 193). You can't go wrong with the **Lato Boutique Hotel** ★ or at the **Loukoulos** ★, with its delicious Greek/Italian fare. Try to get a patio table (p. 203). Paul never made it to Iraklion, of course, but you can visit the **Church of Ayios Titos,** patron saint of the island because Paul named him leader of the first Christian community.

Day 8: Iraklion

Take a day off from Paul in recognition of this island's unique heritage. To fully explore Crete would take many weeks, what with its Minoan, Roman, Byzantine, Venetian, Turkish, and 19th-century remains. Your hotel can arrange for you to visit the Minoan **Palace of Knossos** ★★★ (p. 198), one of the great archaeological sites of the world. And don't miss the **Archaeological Museum** ★★★ (p. 196). You can lunch at one of the many **tavernas** across from the entrance to Knossos, or return to town and try the **Ippocampus** (p. 203). After a siesta, take the walking tour of Iraklion (p. 198), before treating yourself to a gourmet dinner at the **Brillant Gourmet Restaurant** ★★ (p. 202).

Day 9: Gortyna

Travelers focused on following Paul will definitely want to rent a car and take a day trip to visit **Gortyna.** There you'll see the ruins of the **Basilica of Ayios Titos** (p. 205); in the New Testament, this is the "Titus" appointed by Paul to head the Christian community of Crete (and still the patron saint of the island). The palace of **Phaestos** ★★ and the caves and beach at **Matala** ★ are definitely worthy detours (p. 205). You can lunch at Phaestos itself or at one of the many restaurants at Matala. In the evening, back in Iraklion, dine outdoors at the **Pantheon** (p. 204) in "Dirty Alley."

Day 10: Fair Havens or Chania

Those truly dedicated to tracking down Paul could ask a travel agency to arrange for a trip to **Kaloi Limines** on the south coast, said to be the "Fair Havens," where Paul put in to escape a storm. Others may decide to visit **Chania** ★★, Crete's second-biggest city (p. 206). After checking in to your hotel and exploring some of the Old Town, take lunch at the **Amphora,** on the harbor (p. 215). Continue your exploration of the town, as described on p. 210, and be sure to

In the Footsteps of the Apostle Paul

set aside time for a visit to the **Archaeological Museum** ★. That evening, take dinner at the **Well of the Turk** ★ (p. 215) before driving back to your hotel in Iraklion (although you could overnight in Chania and fly out of its airport; make such arrangements well in advance).

Days 11 & 12: Athens & Ancient Corinth

Fly back to the Athens airport in time to rent a car to drive to Corinth. **Ancient Corinth** ★★ is one of the major sites of ancient Greece, with numerous Roman remains that date from the time of Paul's visit. In particular, ask to see the Roman bema, or rostrum, said to be on the site where the Roman governor Gallio defended Paul. In addition to the link to Paul, the area stands on its own with a 6th-century Temple of Apollo and wide, marble-paved roads. It's easiest to eat lunch at one of the many restaurants adjacent to the site. Back in Athens, in the evening, treat yourself to dinner and people-watching at **Aegli** ★★, in the Zappeion Gardens (p. 129).

Day 13: Flight Home

Take a taxi to the airport and fly home.

CRUISING THE GREEK ISLANDS

by Heidi Sarna

4

There are few truly perfect cruise ship destinations in the world, and the Greek isles are one of them. Who can argue with jagged islands crowned by white-washed villages and harbors of stunning blue sea lapping up against charming beaches and ancient city walls? The sea approach to places like Santorini and Rhodes is really hard to beat. Cruising in Greece is all about gorgeous scenery, ancient historic sites, delicious Mediterranean food, and lots of local culture. You don't have to worry about ferry schedules, driving a car, or changing hotel rooms. You get on the ship, you unpack once, and the vessel is your floating hotel. It's your familiar retreat after a long day of touring or a place to kick back and bask in the Greek sun. Among the most beautiful regions to cruise in all the world, the seas are relatively calm and the islands are individual in character, offering travelers a satisfying mix of local culture, stunning scenery, and ancient and medieval ruins to explore.

Most Greek island itineraries highlight the region's history with optional guided **shore excursions** that take in the major sights, spicing up the vacation brew with other, less history-minded excursions such as visits to beaches, meals at local restaurants, and fishing or sailing excursions.

Of course, you can choose to get off the ship at each port of call and head off on your own to explore the sights, hit the beach, or check out the local color at the nearest taverna. Solo is often the best way to go.

If cruising sounds like a good deal to you, fares can be low due to the worldwide economic downturn (though you may find the airfare to Europe can be high). The region has many cruising options. You can go ultraluxe on a small, yachtlike ship like the *SeaDream I* or übercasual on the *easyCruise Life*. You can choose a classic vessel or a modern megaship. You can choose from cruise lines making new inroads into Greece; other companies build on their current offerings and add new ports.

THE RIGHT CRUISE FOR YOU

In choosing your cruise, you need to think about what you want to see and at what level of comfort you want to see it.

We recommend you first decide **what you want to see.** Are you looking to visit the most popular islands—Mykonos, Santorini, and Rhodes—or are you interested in places off the beaten path? Whichever it is, you'll want to make sure your itinerary allows you enough time to experience the place or places that take your fancy. Some ships visit a port and spend the full day, while others visit two ports in 1 day, which limits your sightseeing time in each (but gives you more overall visits to different places).

Many Greek islands cruises either begin or end their itineraries elsewhere, often Venice or Istanbul, so you'll have to consider which embarkation and disembarkation points in making your decision.

Greece is also visited by ships as part of European itineraries where Greece is one of several countries visited. Most cruise lines like to give their passengers a bit of variety, which means the Greek isles itinerary you're considering might include a day in Alexandria, Egypt, or Dubrovnik, Croatia. This chapter focuses on cruises that spend the better part of the itinerary in Greece and Turkey, but there are lots of other options for Mediterranean cruises that include some Greek ports among a more varied lineup.

You'll also want to think about **what you want out of the cruise experience.** Is the purpose of your cruise to see as much as you can of the islands, or to relax by the ship's pool? And what level of comfort, entertainment, onboard activities, and so forth do you require? Some ships spend a day or more at sea, meaning they don't visit a port at all that day, and while some experienced cruisers enjoy those days the most, treasuring the opportunity they offer for real relaxation, they won't do you much good if your goal is seeing as much of Greece as you can.

Next, consider **how long you want to spend** cruising the islands—3 days, a week, 2 weeks? If you have the time, you may want to consider a **cruisetour,** which combines a cruise to the islands with a guided tour of important sights on the mainland. This is made easy in Greece with some lines offering cruises of only 3 or 4 days, which you can combine with a land tour into a 1-week vacation, and 1-week cruises you can combine with a land tour to make a 2-week vacation.

Also consider **when you want to cruise.** Most of the action on the islands takes place in the warmer months, late May through October; traveling in early spring and late fall has its own special charms, including the fact it allows you to avoid the tourist crush (although some visitor facilities may be closed in the off season) and the hottest months (in July and Aug, temperatures can reach 100°F/38°C). For the record, August is the month the islands are most crowded with vacationers (expect beaches, bars, and discos to be either lively or packed, depending on your point of view). April and November are the rainiest months. May and October are relatively problem-free, making them particularly nice times to sail in Greece.

Choosing Your Ship

The onboard experience changes dramatically depending on how many people and amenities you can fit onto your ship. You can choose anything from a 16-deck, 3,000-passenger ship with a three-story restaurant, ice-skating rink, and minigolf course, to a yachtlike ship for 100 or 200 people where the idea of entertainment is an open sun deck, a novel, and an attendant who drops by periodically with a glass of champagne and some jumbo shrimp. Which you choose has a lot to do with your personality and vacation goals.

MEGASHIPS & LARGE SHIPS   Cruises aboard these vessels focus as much on onboard activities as they do on their destination. They are floating resorts—sometimes glitzy—offering American-style luxury and amenities along with attentive service.

These ships, which tend to be newer, feature Las Vegas–style shows, lavish casinos, big spas and gyms, plenty of bars and restaurants, extravagant meals, and lots of daytime activities from water slides and mini golf to goofy pool-side contests. You or your children can take part in games, contests, cooking lessons, wine tastings, and sports tournaments—although generally few ethnic Greek activities are offered.

CLASSIC & MIDSIZE SHIPS   Ships in this category include older, classic vessels as well as newer ships. Destination is more a focus than on the bigger ships, and itineraries may be very busy, with the ship visiting an island a day, or sometimes two. This leaves little time for onboard daytime activities, although some will be offered. In the Greek market, some of these ships feature Greek crews and cuisine, and service tends to be a big area of focus. Because some of these ships are often sold heavily in the European markets, you may hear many languages spoken onboard. The ships offer a variety of bars and lounges, at least one swimming pool and a small casino, a spa and gym, and plenty of open deck space. Entertainment is generally offered in a main show lounge; some ships show films in their cinemas. Some of the ships in this category fall in the luxury camp and offer upscale restaurants, modern spas and cabins with lavish touches, and big, private balconies; other ships are older and definitely more modest.

SMALL & YACHTLIKE SHIPS   These tend to offer a more relaxed pace and may seek itineraries that focus on smaller, alternative ports, which they can get into because of their small size and shallow draft (the amount of ship that rides beneath the waterline). They may offer "soft-adventure" cruise experiences focused on nature- and outdoor-oriented activities; or they may offer an experience more like that of a luxury yacht. Some feature Greek crews and Greek cuisine. On these small ships, there will typically be more interaction with fellow passengers than on larger ships—there's fewer faces to keep track of. There will be fewer entertainment options compared with the big ships, and there may or may not be a swimming pool, casino, spa, or gym. Both cabins and public rooms range from small and serviceable to large and luxurious, depending on the ship. Some ships are fully engine-powered while others are sailing vessels (though these sails are typically more for show than for power).

In addition to the small ships we mention in depth later in this chapter, you may want to look into even smaller yachts, especially if you're seeking a charter or a truly private yachtlike experience. We'll explore this option later in the chapter.

CALCULATING THE COST

Cruises in the Greek islands range from 3 nights to 2 weeks, with starting prices per day ranging from around $100 to more than $800 per person, double occupancy, and going up from there. These days, you can almost always get a rate that's substantially **less than brochure and/or cruise-line website prices.** Like new-car sticker prices, brochure rates are notoriously inflated, so that's why we've listed rates here from a pair of real travel agents, Sherrie and Charlie Funk, owners of Just Cruisin' Plus (✆ **800/888-0922**; www.jcp.travel). Depending on economic conditions and the age-old tenets of supply and demand, you may get a good price, as well as a shot at the best cabins, if you book early; alternatively, if you're flexible with the cabin category you might be able to get a good price if you wait until the last minute, when the lines are trying to top up their sailings (cruise ships almost always sail full).

Travel agencies and Web-based agencies, as opposed to booking directly through the cruise lines, will typically offer the best overall deal (see "Booking Your Cruise," below). Depending on demand, you may snag a two-for-one deal or free airfare or onboard credits or hotel stays. No matter what price you end up paying, rates include three meals a day (with a couple of exceptions, which we've noted in the ship reviews later), accommodations, most of the onboard activities and entertainment, and, if you book your airfare through the cruise line, a transfer from the airport to the ship. Some rates even include airfare (the inclusion of airfare is more common on European cruises than Caribbean cruises), and in rare cases the fare may include tips, shore excursions, and/or pre- and/or post-cruise hotel stays. Some cruises are packaged as cruise tours, meaning the price includes both hotel stays and land tours. With the exception of a handful of high-end lines, don't expect alcoholic beverages to be included in the rates; almost never included are charges for spa and beauty treatments, Internet access, shore excursions, and tips for the crew.

Port charges can run anywhere from around $60 to upward of $500 per person, depending on the length of your cruise and which ports you visit. These charges will be part of your total cruise fare, but be aware when you're pricing your cruise that although some lines include these charges in the initial base price, some do not. Government taxes and fees are usually excluded from the base rate but will be assessed when your final payment is due.

Cruise prices are based on two people sharing a cabin. Most lines have **single supplement** prices for solo passengers who want their own cabin. The "supplement," in this case, goes to the cruise line as their compensation for not getting two passenger fares for the cabin. At the opposite end, most lines offer highly discounted rates for a third or fourth person sharing a cabin with two full-fare passengers.

Seniors may be able to get extra savings on their cruise. Some lines will take 5% off the top for those 55 and over, and the senior rate applies even if the second person in the cabin is younger. Membership in groups such as AARP is not required, but such membership may bring additional savings.

If your package does not include **airfare,** you might want to consider booking air transportation through the cruise line. While the rates offered by the lines may or may not be as low as you can find on your own, booking through the line allows the cruise company to keep track of you if, for instance, your flight is delayed. In this case, the ship may be able to wait for you, and if it can't wait, it will arrange transportation for you to the next port of call. The cruise lines also negotiate special deals with hotels at port cities if you want to come in a few days before your cruise or stay after it.

In the past several years whenever the price of oil surges, some lines add a **fuel surcharge** on to your tab, which typically ranges from $5 to $10 per person, per day. Be sure to ask when you book.

BOOKING YOUR CRUISE

Today, everybody has a website, and the difference between so-called **Web-based cruise sellers** and more **traditional travel agencies** is that the former rely on their sites for most of their actual bookings, while the latter use theirs as advertising space to promote their offerings and do most of their actual business in person or over the phone. As far as cruise prices go, there's no absolutely quantifiable difference between the live travel agents and Internet-based cruise sellers. Sometimes one or the other, due to them buying or reserving cabins in bulk, can offer you perks like free onboard credits, a bottle of champagne or cabin upgrades. Though there are some loopholes, these days the major cruise lines tout a level playing field, where everybody gets the same price and agents aren't allowed to advertise discounted rates.

In deciding how to book your cruise, consider the value of your time, and your level of experience as a cruiser and as an Internet user. Most websites give you a menu of ships and itineraries to select from, plus a basic search capability that takes into account destination, price, length of trip, and date; some sites aid your search with sophisticated options such as interactive deck plans and ship reviews. If you've cruised before and know what you want, no problem. If, on the other hand, you have limited experience with cruising or with booking on the Web, or your time could be better used elsewhere, it may be better to go through a traditional agent (such as Just Cruisin' Plus, who supplied the rates for this book), who can help you wade through the choices and answer your questions, from which cabins have their views obstructed by lifeboats to information on dining, tuxedo rentals, onboard kids programs, and cuisine.

A travel agent can also help you book airfare to and from the ship, and hotels and sightseeing trips before or after your cruise. No matter which way you wind up booking your cruise, you may want to first check out the cruise-line websites and browse the Internet for ship reviews, virtual tours, chats, and industry news.

To find an agent, rely on referrals from trusted friends and colleagues. Some agents (such as Just Cruisin' Plus), really know the business—they travel themselves to sample what they sell and can reel off the differences between cabins on Deck 7 and Deck 8 down to where the towel racks are placed—while others are not much more than order-takers. Start looking as soon as you can, which can result in early booking rates and the best cabin choices.

Choosing a Cabin

One of your biggest decisions is what type of cabin you need. Will you be happy with a slightly cramped space without a window (the most budget-minded choice); a cabin with a private balcony; or a suite with a dining room, hot tub, and a personal butler?

Obviously, price will determine your choice. If you don't plan to spend time in your cabin except to sleep, shower, and change clothes, an **inside cabin** (one without a porthole or window) might do just fine. If you get claustrophobic; or if you insist on sunshine first thing in the morning; or if you intend to hole up in your cabin for extended periods, pay a bit more and take an **outside cabin,** which have windows— or pay a bit more and take one with a **private balcony,** where you can open the door and feel the sea breezes. On smaller or older ships, your choice might be limited to inside and outside cabins, some with the old-style porthole windows. Newer ships will have balconies on the majority of cabins, making them more affordable than ever.

One concern if you do go the window route is **obstructed views.** This isn't an issue with newer ships because the lifeboats are housed on the decks containing the public spaces like restaurants and lounges; the passenger cabins are either above or below those decks. But check to make sure none of the cabins in the category you've selected have windows that directly face lifeboats or other objects that may block your view of the clear blue sea. You can determine this by looking at a diagram of the ship (included in the cruise brochure or found online) or by consulting with your travel agent.

Most ships offer cabins for two with private bathroom and shower. (Bathtubs are considered a luxury on most ships and are usually offered only in the most expensive cabins.) These days, most ships have a double bed, or twin beds that may be convertible to a queen. Other variations are cabins with bunk beds (referred to as "upper and lower berths"), cabins designed for three or four people, and connecting cabins for families. Many lines, including Oceania, Holland America, and Regent feature fluffy mattresses and soft down duvets.

Cabin amenities vary by line, and often include TVs (with a closed system of programmed movies and features and the occasional news channel), DVD players, hair dryers, safes, and mini-refrigerators. If any of these are must-haves, let your agent know. Cruise lines tend to one-up their amenities pretty often, so it's possible your cabin may have a flat-panel LCD TV, a powerful hair dryer, brand-name toiletries, and fresh flowers or fruit awaiting you on arrival.

Usually the higher on the ship the cabin is located, the more expensive it is. But upper decks also tend to be rockier in rough seas than the middle or lower parts of the ship, a factor to consider if you're prone to seasickness.

The **size of a cabin** is determined by square feet. Keep in mind that ship cabins are generally smaller than the equivalent hotel rooms you'd find on land. As a rough guide, 11 sq. m (120 sq. ft.) is low end and cramped, 17 sq. m (180 sq. ft.) is mid-range and fairly roomy, and 23 sq. m (250 sq. ft.) and larger is suite-size and very comfortable.

If noise bothers you, pick a cabin far from the engine room and nowhere near the disco.

Mealtimes: Early, Late, or Anytime

Dining on cruise ships has undergone a revolution in the past decade or so. Traditionally, guests ate in the large dining room, at the same time and at the same table every night. Today, you can still dine the traditional way—many ships offer that as the default preference (if not the only preference). But there are several variations on the mealtime theme now, from complete open seating to separate restaurants specializing in seafood or steaks to proper en suite dining.

For traditional dining, because most ship dining rooms are not large enough to accommodate all passengers at one dinner seating, dining times and tables are assigned. When you book your trip, you will also indicate your preferred mealtime. Early, or "main," seating is usually at 6 or 6:30pm, late seating at 8 or 8:30pm. Lines catering to a majority of European clientele may offer seatings an hour or so later than these. Some of the bigger lines offer four staggered seatings, which gives you more choice and eliminates some of the crowding at the dining room door.

There are advantages to both times. **Early seating** is usually less crowded, and it's the preferred time for families and older passengers who want to get to bed early. Since the waiters know that the second wave is coming, they may be rushed. On the other hand, early diners get first dibs on nighttime entertainment venues, and might be hungry enough in a few hours to take advantage of a midnight buffet. **Late seating** allows time for a nap or late spa appointment before dinner, especially if you're returning to the ship from a full day in port. Service is slower paced, and you can linger with after-dinner drinks, then catch the late show at 10pm.

When choosing a mealtime, you also need to consider **table size** (on most ships, you can request to be at a table for 2, 4, 8, 10, or 12), though sometimes it's tough to snag a table for two since they're usually in great demand. On the other hand, many cruisers appreciate the fun that comes from sitting around a big table and talking up your adventures of the day. Most dining rooms are **nonsmoking,** so there's generally no need to request a smoking or nonsmoking table. You can request a different table when you get onboard, too.

If your ship has **open-seating** arrangements, you can dine at any hour the restaurant is open. You also choose your dinner partners, or you can ask the maitre d' to sit you with other guests. Open seating can feel more casual and less regimented. Open seating arrangements are typically offered on the smaller and/or most upscale lines, although now some of the majors offer this option as well. The pioneer in the big-ship category is Norwegian Cruise Line, which now builds its ships with up to 10 different restaurants. Princess Cruises, Celebrity Cruises, and Holland America Line, for example, have a hybrid dining policy: Passengers choose whether they want the traditional seating or the open plan, and then show up at the restaurants accordingly.

Most ships now also have at least one or two restaurants separate—in location, cuisine, and atmosphere—from the main dining room. These so-called **specialty restaurants** or **alternative restaurants** are open seating, so you can choose your dinnertime and dining companions. If you'd like to try an evening or two at these restaurants, make reservations in advance. A per-person cover charge, typically in the $20 to $30 range, often applies, so you should check in advance.

On most ships, **breakfast** and **lunch** are open seating. Most vessels also have buffet restaurants, where you can have both meals at any time during open hours.

Inform the cruise line at the time you make your reservations if you have any **special dietary requests.** Kosher menus, vegetarian, low fat, low salt, low carb, "spa," and sugar-free are some of the options available.

Deposits, Cancellations & Extras

After you've made your decision about what ship you will vacation on, you will be required to put down a deposit if you're booking 2 or more months in advance (with the remaining fare usually paid no later than 2 months in advance of your departure date); or you must pay the entire fare if you're booking within 60 or 70 days of your sailing date.

Note: Cruise lines have varying policies regarding cancellations, and it's important to look at the fine print in the brochure or agency website to make sure you understand the policy. Most lines allow you to cancel for a full refund on your deposit and payment any time up to about 70 days before the sailing, after which you have to pay a penalty (a few lines charge an administrative fee if you cancel your cruise less than 120 days before departure, and some levy a cancellation fee once the deposit is made regardless of the sailing date). If you cancel at the last minute, you likely will lose the entire fare you paid, unless you bought trip cancellation or interruption insurance.

An agent will discuss with you optional **airline arrangements** offered by the lines, **transfers** from the airport to the pier, and any pre- or post-cruise **hotel or tour programs.** Some lines also let you purchase **shore excursions** in advance (for more on shore excursions, see the section later in this chapter). And you may also be able to prebook certain onboard spa services.

If you are not booking airfare through the cruise line, make sure to allow several hours between the plane's arrival and the time you must board the ship. To reduce anxiety, it may be best to fly in the day before and spend the night in a hotel.

CRUISE PREPARATION PRACTICALITIES

About 1 month before your cruise and no later than 1 week before, you should receive your **cruise documents,** including your airline tickets (if you purchased them from the cruise line), a boarding document with your cabin number and sometimes dining choices on it, boarding forms to fill out, luggage tags, and your prearranged bus-transfer vouchers and hotel vouchers (if applicable). Some lines offer some or all of these documents and forms online. You'll save time checking in at the cruise terminal if you've filled out your boarding documents online.

There will also be information about **shore excursions** and additional material detailing things you need to know before you sail. Most lines also list excursions on their websites and allow you to book shore excursions in advance of your sailing online, which will give you first dibs at popular offerings that may sell out later.

Read all of this pretrip information carefully. Make sure your cabin category and dining preferences are what you requested, and that your flight and arrival times are what you were told. If there are problems, call your agent immediately. Make sure there is enough time so you can arrive at the port no later than an hour before departure.

You will be required to have a passport for your trip (see chapter 13 for more on this). If you are flying into Istanbul, you will also be required to have a Turkish visa, which can be easily obtained upon arrival at Istanbul airport for about $20.

Confirm your flight 3 days before departure. Also, before you leave for the airport, tie the tags provided by the cruise line onto your luggage and fill in your boarding cards. This will save you time when you arrive at the ship.

Cash Matters

You already paid for a good portion of your vacation when you paid for your cruise, but you will still need a credit card or traveler's checks to handle your **onboard expenses** such as bar drinks, dry cleaning and laundry, e-mail, spa services, salon services, photos taken by the ship's photographer, babysitting, wine at dinner, souvenirs, shore excursions, specialty restaurant charges, and tips (see below for more on tipping). On most lines, you'll use your cabin key card as a charge card. Prepare to spend at least $200 and easily $600 to $800 per person on a weeklong cruise for "extras"—or more, depending on how much you drink, shop, love massages, and spend in the casino, and how many shore excursions you purchase during the cruise.

Some ships (but not all) will take a personal check for onboard expenses. If you want to pay in cash or by traveler's check, you will be asked to leave a deposit. Some ships have ATMs if you need to get cash while aboard, and some (but not all) offer currency-exchange services.

We suggest you keep careful track of your onboard expenses to avoid an unpleasant surprise at the end of your cruise. You can get this information at the purser's office or guest-relations desk.

You will want to have some cash in hand when going ashore for expenses, including taxis, snacks or meals, drinks, small purchases, and tips for guides.

Packing

Generally, ships describe their **daily recommended evening attire** as casual, informal, and formal, prompting many people to think they'll have to bring a steamer trunk full of clothes. Not true; you can probably get along with about half of what you think you need. Almost all ships offer laundry and dry-cleaning services, and some have coin-operated self-serve laundries, so you have the option of packing less and having your clothes cleaned midway through your trip.

During the day, the onboard style is casual, but keep in mind that some ships do not allow swimsuits or tank tops in the dining room. If your ship operates under the "traditional" dress codes, you can expect two formal dinners and two informal nights during a 5- to 7-day cruise, with the rest casual (or more typical these days, 1 or 2 formal nights and all the rest casual). There will usually be proportionally more formal nights on longer cruises.

The daily bulletin delivered to your cabin each day will advise you of the proper dress code for the evening. **Formal** means a tux or dark suit with tie for men and a cocktail dress, long dress, gown, or dressy pantsuit for women. **Informal** is a jacket with or without a tie, and dress slacks or a light suit for men and a dress, skirt with blouse, or pants outfit for women. **Casual** means different things to different people. Typically it means a sports shirt or open dress shirt with slacks for men; women can wear skirts, dresses, or pants outfits. Jeans and shorts are usually frowned upon.

Check your cruise documents to determine the number of formal nights (if any) during your cruise. Men who don't own a tuxedo might be able to rent one in advance through the cruise line's preferred supplier (who delivers the tux to the ship). Information on this service often is sent with your cruise documents. Also, some cruises offer **theme nights,** so you may want to check your cruise documents to see if there are any you'll want to bring special clothes for. (For instance, Greek Night means everyone wears blue and white—the Greek national colors.)

Having said all this about formal and informal, you might not even need to know about it: A few lines, especially the smaller, more casual ships, have an all-casual policy, meaning slacks and sundresses at night are as dressy as you need to be; others are "formal-optional," which gives you the option of dressing up (or not). If you're one of those people who refuses to wear a tie on vacation, consider that many lines also offer a casual alternative during formal evenings, such as dining in the buffet restaurant or in your cabin.

If you want to bring the crown jewels, be careful. If you're not wearing them, leave them either in your in-room safe (if there is one) or with the purser.

In general, during the day in Greece you're best off packing loose and comfortable cotton or other lightweight fabrics. You'll also want to pack a swimsuit, a sun hat, sunglasses, and plenty of sunscreen—the Greek sun can be intense. Adjust your wardrobe depending on when you plan to travel. Even if you're traveling in August, though, you should bring a sweater, as you'll be in and out of air-conditioning. And don't forget an umbrella.

For shore excursions, comfortable walking shoes are a must, as some excursions involve walking on stone or marble. Also, some tours may visit religious sites that have a "no shorts or bare shoulders" policy, so it's best to bring something to cover up with. (If you're taking the tour through the cruise line, you'll be advised of this before you go.)

If you plan on bringing your own hair dryer, electric razor, curling iron, or other electrical device, check out the ship's electric current in advance. An adapter may be required. Because of the risk of fire, items like irons are prohibited; ask your cabin steward about pressing services or bring a portable steamer.

EMBARKATION

Check-in is usually 2 to 3 hours before sailing. You will not be able to board the ship before the scheduled embarkation time. You have up until a half-hour (on some ships it's 1 hr.) before sailing to embark.

At check-in, your boarding documents will be checked and your passport will likely be taken for immigration processing. You will get it back sometime during the cruise. (Make a photocopy and carry that as backup.) Depending on the cruise line, you may establish your **onboard credit account** at this point by presenting a major credit card or making a deposit in cash or traveler's checks. On other ships you need to go to the purser's office onboard to establish your account.

You may be given your **dining-room table assignment** in advance of your sailing (on your tickets) or as you check in, or find a card with your table number waiting for you in your stateroom. If you do not receive an assignment by the time you get to your stateroom, you will be directed to a maitre d's desk. This is also the place to make any changes if your assignment does not meet with your approval.

Once you're aboard, a crew member will show you to your cabin and, on the smaller high-end lines, will probably offer to carry your hand luggage. No tip is required for this service, though feel free to slip the steward a few bucks if you're feeling generous.

In your cabin, you will find a **daily program** detailing the day's events, mealtimes, and so forth, as well as important information on the ship's **safety procedures** and possibly its **deck plan.** Deck plans and directional signs are posted around the ship, generally at main stairways and elevators.

Tip: If you plan to use the ship's **spa services,** it's best to stop by as soon as you board the ship to make appointments so you can get your preferred times. (The best times, particularly the slots during the days at sea, go fast, and some popular treatments sell out.) Ditto dropping by the **shore excursions desk** if you plan to purchase an excursion. Even better, some lines allow you to prebook shore excursions or spa treatments online before you board the ship.

Note: The ship's casino and shops are always closed when the ship is in port, and the fresh- or saltwater swimming pool(s) could be covered.

Some lines offer **escorted tours** of the public rooms to get you acquainted with the ship. Check the daily program in your cabin for details.

Lifeboat/Safety Drill

Ships are required by law to conduct safety drills the first day out. Most do this either right before the ship sails or shortly thereafter. At the start of the drill, the ship will broadcast its emergency signal. You will then be required to return to your cabin (if you're not there), grab your **life jacket** (which you're shown as soon as you arrive in your cabin), and report to your assigned muster station—outside along the promenade deck, or in a lounge or other public room. A notice on the back of your cabin door will list the procedures and advise you as to your assigned **muster station** and how to get there. You will also find directions to the muster station in the hallway. You will be alerted as to the time of the drill in both the daily program and in repeated public announcements (and probably by your cabin steward as well). If you hide out in your cabin to avoid the drill, you'll likely get a knock by the cabin steward reminding you to please join the others.

DEALING WITH seasickness

If you suffer from seasickness, plan on packing **Bonine** or **Dramamine** in case your ship encounters rough seas. Keep in mind that with both these medications, it is recommended you not drink alcohol; Dramamine in particular can make you drowsy. Both can be bought over the counter. Ships stock supplies onboard, either at the purser's office, at the medical center, or in the gift shop.

Another option is the **Transderm patch,** available by prescription only, which goes behind your ear and time-releases medication. The patch can be worn for up to 3 days, but it comes with all sorts of side-effect warnings. Some people have had success in curbing seasickness with **ginger capsules** available at health-food stores. If you prefer not to ingest anything, you might try the **acupressure wristbands** available at most pharmacies. When set in the proper spot on the wrist, they effectively ease seasickness, although if the seas are particularly rough they may have to be supplemented with medication.

If you're **traveling with children,** make sure your cabin is equipped with special children's life jackets. If not, alert your steward.

END-OF-CRUISE PROCEDURES

Your shipboard account will close in the wee hours before departure, but prior to that time you will receive a preliminary bill in your cabin. If you are settling your account with your credit card, you don't have to do anything except make sure all the charges are correct. If there is a problem, report it to the purser's office.

If you are paying by cash or traveler's check, you will be asked to settle your account either during the day or night before you leave the ship. This will require a trip to the purser's office. A final invoice will be delivered to your room before departure.

Tips

You can bet you'll find tipping suggestions in your cabin on the last day of your cruise. These are only suggestions, but since service personnel make most (or all) of their salaries through tips, we don't recommend tipping less—unless, of course, bad service warrants it. (On some very upscale lines, acceptance of tips is strictly forbidden.)

Most cruise lines now **automatically add gratuities** to your shipboard account; and other lines will add gratuities to your bill on a request basis. It typically adds up to about $12 per person, per day. This takes a little of the personal touch out of tipping, but then again, you don't have to worry about running around with envelopes of cash on the last night of your vacation. Check with your cruise line to see if they offer automatic tipping. If you prefer to tip the crew in person or in cash, your ship should be able to cancel the automatic tips. There's also nothing wrong with tipping your cabin steward or waiter on top of the automatic tips.

If you do decide to tip the crew on your own, the cruise line will provide suggested minimums. Generally, each passenger should usually tip his or her cabin steward and waiter about $4 per day each, and the assistant waiter about $2. That minimum comes to about $70 for a 7-day cruise. You are, of course, free to tip more. On some

European ships, the suggested minimums are even less. The reason: Europeans aren't as used to tipping as Americans. On some ships you are encouraged to tip the maitre d' and headwaiter. You may also encounter cases where tips are pooled: You hand over a suggested amount and it's up to the crew to divide it among themselves. Bar bills often automatically include a 15% tip, but if the wine steward, for instance, has served you exceptionally well, you can slip him or her a bill, too. If you have spa or beauty treatments, you can tip that person at the time of the service (though make sure a tip wasn't already automatically added on to the bill before you write one in).

Don't tip the captain or other officers. They're professional, salaried employees.

The porters who carry your bags at the pier will expect a tip.

Packing Up

Because of the number of bags being handled, big ships require guests to pack the night before departure and leave their bags in the hallway, usually by midnight. (Be sure they're tagged with the cruise line's luggage tags, which are color-coded to indicate deck number and disembarkation order.) The bags will be picked up overnight and removed from the ship before passengers are allowed to disembark. (Don't pack bottles or other breakables; luggage is often thrown from bin to bin as it's being off-loaded.) You'll see them again in the cruise terminal, where they'll most likely be arranged by deck number. *Reminder:* When you're packing that last night, be sure to leave at least one extra change of clothing, as well as necessary toiletries, in the cabin with you.

Tip: Pack all your purchases in one suitcase. This way you can easily retrieve them if you're stopped at Customs.

LARGE & MIDSIZE SHIPS

In this section, we describe the ships offering cruises with predominantly Greek islands itineraries; that is, itineraries where at least half of the port calls are in Greece and Turkey. We've broken the offerings up into two categories, based on ship size: Mega- and midsize ships (more than 400 passengers), and small and yachtlike vessels (anywhere from 40 passengers to 400).

The lines are listed alphabetically within each category. Working with travel agents Sherrie and Charlie Funk, owners of Just Cruisin' Plus (© 800/888-0922; www.jcp. travel), we present a sample of the *actual prices* people are paying for cruises aboard all the ships in this chapter (as opposed to the often-inflated **brochure** or cruise-line website fares). We priced summer 2012 cruises in June 2011, and fares are based on two people sharing a cabin, unless otherwise noted. With a few exceptions, most of these rates were quoted in U.S. dollars.

The **itineraries** we list are also for the 2012 season unless otherwise noted. Both prices and itineraries are subject to change.

We've listed the **sizes of ships** in two ways: **passenger capacity** and **gross registered tons (GRTs).** Rather than describing actual weight, the latter is a measure of interior space used to produce revenue on a vessel. One GRT equals 100 cubic feet of enclosed, revenue-generating space.

Note that we've listed Athens as a port of call for many cruises, but in most cases you'll actually be calling in **Piraeus,** the port city for Athens. Other popular embarkation ports include Istanbul, Turkey; Venice, Italy; and Civitavecchia, Italy, about an hour's drive from Rome.

AZAMARA CLUB CRUISES

1050 Caribbean Way, Miami, FL 33132. ℰ **877/999-9553.** www.azamaracruises.com.

Azamara and its two midsize gems, *Azamara Journey* (built in 2000; 710 passengers, 30,277 GRTs) and sister *Azamara Quest* (built in 2000; 710 passengers, 30,277 GRTs), were originally built for now-defunct Renaissance Cruises. The twins straddle the mainstream and luxury segments of the cruise biz—somewhere between Celebrity and Crystal or Regent, though closer to the luxury end and geared to adults (there are is no formal kids programming). Fares include complimentary house wines at lunch and dinner, free gratuities, free specialty coffees and bottled wines, and a good number of overnights in port and high-end excursions. The mood is casually elegant. On the Pool Deck, enjoy a quiet jazz trio and a harpist plays in the cafe, and overall, service is tops, from the butlers who attend to all cabins to little touches such as the cold towels offered at the gangway after a hot day in port. Dining feels high end and is open seating at the ships' three restaurants for optimal flexibility. Activities run from the usual (bingo, napkin folding, team trivia) to the unusual, including poetry reading/writing get-togethers and seminars on etiquette and art. Evenings, catch a cabaret, comedy or magic act, or enjoy a late-night movie or drinks and conversation.

Azamara Club Cruises Itineraries & Rates

SHIP	ITINERARY
Azamara Quest	**Seven-day round-trip Athens** cruise calls at Ephesus/Kusadasi (Turkey), Kos, Rhodes, Santorini, Chania, Nafplion. July 8. **Rates:** From $1,999.
	Seven-day Athens to Istanbul cruise calls at Hydra, Santorini, Mykonos (overnight), Patmos, Lesbos, Istanbul (overnight). July 15. **Rates:** From $1,999.
	Eleven-day Athens to Venice cruise calls at Ephesus/Kusadasi (Turkey), Mykonos, Santorini, Chania, Olympia/Katakolon, Corfu, Kotor (Montenegro), Dubrovnik (Croatia), Hvar (Croatia), Venice (overnight). Aug 1. **Rates:** From $2,899.
Azamara Journey	**Eleven-day Rome (Civitavecchia, Italy) to Athens** cruise calls at Sorrento (Italy, overnight), Capri (Italy, overnight), Amalfi (Italy), Taormina (Sicily, Italy), Siracusa (Sicily, Italy), Santorini, Ephesus/Kusadasi (Turkey), Mykonos, Athens (overnight). October 4. **Rates:** From $2,699.
	Eleven-day round-trip Athens cruise calls at Nazareth/Galilee (Haifa, Israel), Jerusalem/Tel Aviv (Ashdod, Israel, overnight). Cairo/Giza (Alexandria, Egypt, overnight), Rhodes, Ephesus/Kusadasi (Turkey), Mykonos. October 15. **Rates:** From $2,699.
	Ten-day Athens to Sokhna (Egypt) cruise calls at Ephesus/Kusadasi (Turkey), Kos, Rhodes, Paphos, Nazareth/Galilee (Haifa, Israel), Jerusalem/Tel Aviv (Ashdod, Israel, overnight), Cairo/Giza (Alexandria, Egypt), Suez Canal. October 26. **Rates:** From $2,299.

CELEBRITY CRUISES

1050 Caribbean Way, Miami, FL 33132. ℰ **800/437-3111.** www.celebrity.com.

Celebrity's got some of the industry's most stylish and chic ships, vessels that successfully marry innovation (from real grass lawns up on deck to glass-blowing studios, art collections, and craft beer bars) with gorgeous design, all for a decent price. Considered a premium U.S. operator (along with Holland America and Princess), Celebrity offers eastern Mediterranean itineraries that, for the most part, operate on *Equinox* (built in 2009; 2,850 passengers; 122,000 GRTs) and newer sister *Silhouette* (built in 2011; 2,850 passengers; 122,000 GRTs). The pair are part of the line's newest and biggest class of ship; a sophisticated mix of ultramodern and classic, spacious, and sleek, but not superflashy. Both are outfitted in muted woods, beiges, and artistically applied bold color accents. The ships have panoramic ocean views on nearly every cabin, and most staterooms have a veranda. The ships have plenty of spots in which to relax, including the lawn, spa, elegant bars and lounges, or the Oasis pool, with its retractable roof. If you're splurging, book a Sky Suite on Deck 12 for their extra large, 17-sq.-m (179-sq.-ft.) balconies. The *Constellation* (built in 2002; 1,950 passengers; 91,000 GRTs) is a smaller but equally attractive ship, recently renovated and it now offers a new **Tuscan Grille** steakhouse, martini bar, bistro and a martini bar with a permafrost bar top. Also, don't miss a gourmet meal in the **Ocean Liners** restaurant, a classic alternative dining venue that boasts artifacts from a variety of historic liners.

Service and cuisine are key with Celebrity. Little luxuries include chilled towels when you return from a day of port exploration and once per cruise, complimentary sorbets at poolside. The line, long known for its culinary focus, offers several specialty restaurants on its ships as well as a main dining room where you can choose to dine in the traditional early or late paradigm, or take advantage of a flexible program, where you can make a reservation for the time that suits your party best.

Celebrity Cruises Itineraries & Rates

SHIP	ITINERARY
Celebrity Silhouette	**Thirteen-day Rome (Civitavecchia, Italy) to Venice** cruise calls at Naples/Capri (Sorrento, Italy), Catania (Sicily, Italy), Valletta (Malta), Mykonos, Athens, Ephesus/Kusadasi (Turkey), Rhodes, Santorini, Chania, Venice (Italy, overnight). May 5, July 17. **Rates:** From $1,749.
	Twelve-day Rome (Civitavecchia, Italy) to Venice cruise calls at Naples/Capri (Sorrento, Italy), Catania (Sicily, Italy), Mykonos, Athens, Ephesus/Kusadasi (Turkey), Rhodes, Santorini, Chania, Venice (Italy, overnight). June 12. **Rates:** From $1,849.
Celebrity Equinox	**Ten-day round-trip Rome (Civitavecchia, Italy)** cruise calls at Messina (Sicily, Italy), Athena, Ephesus/Kusadasi (Turkey), Rhodes, Santorini, Mykonos, Naples/Capri (Sorrento, Italy). May 11. **Rates:** From $1,299.
	Ten-day round-trip Rome (Civitavecchia, Italy) cruise calls at Chania, Santorini, Athens, Rhodes, Ephesus/Kusadasi (Turkey), Mykonos, Naples/Capri (Sorrento, Italy). June 1, June 22; July 13; August 3, August 24; September 14; October 5, October 26; November 16 **Rates:** From $1,119.
Celebrity Constellation	**Twelve-day round-trip Istanbul** cruise calls at Istanbul (Turkey, overnight), Ephesus/Kusadasi (Turkey), Marmaris (Turkey), Rhodes, Bodrum (Turkey), Rhodes, Mykonos, Athens, Santorini, Chania. September 19. **Rates:** From $1,459.
	Twelve-day round-trip Istanbul cruise calls at Istanbul (Turkey, overnight), Ephesus/Kusadasi (Turkey), Bodrum (Turkey), Marmaris (Turkey), Rhodes, Santorini, Athens, Mykonos, Chania. October 1, October 13. **Rates:** From $1,279.

COSTA CRUISE LINES

Venture Corporate Center II, 200 S. Park Rd., Hollywood, FL 33021. © **877/88-COSTA** (882-6782). www.costacruises.com.

Fun and full of passion, Costa is an Italian line tracing its origins from 1860 and the Italian olive-oil business. Today it's among the most modern lines out there. These days Costa is owned by Carnival Corporation, parent of Carnival Cruise Lines, and you may recognize the colorful, flamboyant interiors. Many of both lines' ships were designed by interior designer Joe Farcus. However, aboard a Costa ship, Italy shows through in nearly everything, from the food to the Italian-speaking crew (although many are not from Italy), to the mostly Italian entertainers.

The line's ships represent one of the newer fleets in the industry, sporting blue-and-yellow smokestacks emblazoned with a huge letter C. And the fleet is growing fast: the past decade has seen seven new ships. The product is popular in the U.S./ Caribbean market but is not designed strictly for a North American audience, and therein lies the charm. In Europe, the ships attract a good share of Italian and French passengers, so don't be surprised if your tablemates speak limited English.

Entertainment includes Italian cooking and language classes. The line also offers an activities program for kids and teens.

Costa Classica (built in 1991; 1,308 passengers; 53,000 GRTs) is a downright cozy breath of fresh air in the mega world of giant ships, with public rooms and decks inspired by and named after iconic elements of Italian heritage.

Costa Deliziosa (built in 2009; 2,260 passengers; 92,000 GRTs) is an exciting ship with avant-garde style interiors incorporating marble, wood, mother-of-pearl, Murano glass and lots of art. High-tech features include a 4-D cinema, in-line skating track, golf simulator with putting green, and a Grand Prix race-car simulator.

Costa Fortuna (built in 2004; 2,720 passengers; 105,000 GRTs) is a glitzy, modern cruise vessel that offers cabins with balconies; multiple bars, lounges, and eateries; swimming pools; a large kids' play area; and a themed decor—in this case, the great Italian ocean liners of yore. Public rooms are named after legendary Italian ships, such as the Rex Theater and the Restaurant Michelangelo. Check out the miniature fleet of Costa ships affixed to the ceiling of the bar in *Fortuna*'s atrium.

Costa Magica (built in 2004; 2,672 passengers; 102,587 GRTs) is the sister ship with similar appointments.

Costa Mediterranea (built in 2003; 2,114 passengers; 85,619 GRTs) was designed to reflect Italy's 17th- and 18th-century *palazzi* and castles, and it does feel palatial.

Costa Pacifica (built in 2009; 3,000 passengers; 114,147 GRTs) manages to be elegant and opulent without going over the top. It offers an abundance of bars and lounges all with a musical theme. Some unusual amenities include a music studio, Grand Prix simulator, and Virtual World that offers PlayStation games.

Costa Romantica (built in 1993; 1,356 passengers; 53,000 GRTs) is the sister ship of Costa Classica with similar appointments.

Costa Serena (built in 2007; 2,930 passengers; 114,500 GRTs), a sister of the *Pacifica,* is flamboyant with a fun space-age design that's whimsically merged with every architectural theme in the book, then candy coated with a hodgepodge of rainbow hues that make Antoni Gaudi seem conservative.

Costa Cruises Itineraries & Rates

SHIP	ITINERARY
Costa Classica	**Seven-day round-trip Trieste** cruise calls at Ancona (Italy), Mykonos, Athens, Corfu, Dubrovnik (Croatia). May 19, May 26; June 2, June 9, June 16, June 23, June 30; July 7, July 14, July 21, July 28; August 4, August 11, August 18, August 25; September 1, September 8, September 15, September 22, September 29; October 6, October 13, October 20, October 27; November 3, November 10, November 17. **Rates:** From $649.
Costa Deliziosa	**Eight-day round-trip Civitavecchia (Italy)** cruise calls at Savona (Italy), Olympia/Katakolon, Athens, Valletta (Malta), Tunis (Tunisia). December 20. **Rates:** From $959.
	Eight-day round-trip Savona (Italy) cruise calls at Olympia/Katakolon, Athens, Valletta (Malta), Tunis (Tunisia), Rome (Civitavecchia, Italy). December 21. **Rates:** From $879.
	Eight-day round-trip Civitavecchia (Italy) cruise calls at Savona (Italy), Naples/Capri (Italy), Tunis (Tunisia), Olympia/Katakolon, Athens. December 28. **Rates:** From $1,139.
	Eight-day round-trip Savona (Italy) cruise calls at Naples/Capri (Italy), Tunis (Tunisia), Olympia/Katakolon, Athens. December 29. **Rates:** From $1,099

SHIP	ITINERARY
Costa Fortuna	**Ten-day round-trip Savona (Italy)** cruise calls at Naples/Capri (Italy), Messina (Sicily, Italy), Cairo/Giza (Alexandria, Egypt), Limassol (Cyprus), Marmaris (Turkey), Santorini, Olympia/Katakolon). September 12, September 22; October 2, October 12, October 22; November 1, November 11. **Rates:** From $1,029.
Costa Magica	**Ten-day round-trip Marseille (France)** cruise calls at Florence/Pisa (Livorno, Italy), Palermo (Sicily, Italy), Athens, Izmis (Turkey), Rhodes, Valletta (Malta). April 21; May 1, May 11; September 13, September 23; October 3, October 13, October 23; November 2. **Rates:** From $1,299.
Costa Mediterranea	**Eleven-day round-trip Civitavecchia (Italy)** cruise calls at Olympia/Katakolon, Athens, Izmir (Turkey), Jerusalem/Tel Aviv (Ashdod, Israel), Cairo (Port Said, Egypt), Cairo/Giza (Alexandria, Egypt). April 3; May 30; July 15; August 6, August 28; October 24; November 15. **Rates:** From $979.
	Thirteen-day round-trip Rome (Civitavecchia, Italy) cruise calls at Savona (Italy), Olympia/Katakolon, Mykonos, Izmir (Turkey), Constanta (Romania), Odessa (Ukraine), Yalta (Ukraine), Athens. May 17. **Rates:** From $1,999.
	Eleven-day round-trip Rome (Civitavecchia, Italy) cruise calls at Savona (Italy), Olympia/Katakolon, Athens, Izmir (Turkey), Rhodes, Limassol (Cyprus), Cairo/Giza (Alexandria, Egypt). June 10. **Rates:** From $1,699.
	Eleven-day round-trip Savona (Italy) cruise calls at Olympia/Katakolon, Athens, Izmir (Turkey), Jerusalem/Tel Aviv (Ashdod, Israel), Cairo (Port Said, Egypt), Cairo/Giza (Alexandria, Egypt), Rome (Civitavecchia, Italy). April 4; May 31; July 16; August 6. **Rates:** From $1,259.
	Thirteen-day round-trip Savona (Italy) cruise calls at Olympia/Katakolon, Mykonos, Izmir (Turkey), Istanbul (Turkey), Constanta (Romania), Odessa (Ukraine), Yalta (Ukraine), Athens, Rome (Civitavecchia, Italy). May 18; July 3; September 9. **Rates:** From $1,969.
	Eleven-day round-trip Savona (Italy) cruise calls at Olympia/Katakolon, Athens, Izmir (Turkey), Rhodes, Limassol (Cyprus), Cairo/Giza (Alexandria, Egypt), Rome (Civitivecchia, Italy). June 11; September 22. **Rates:** From $1,579.
Costa Pacifica	**Eleven-day round-trip Savona (Italy)** cruise calls at Olympia/Katakolon, Athens, Izmir (Turkey), Jerusalem/Tel Aviv (Ashdod, Israel), Cairo (Port Said, Egypt), Rome (Civitavecchia, Italy). March 28; April 19, April 30; October 4, October 15, October 26; November 6, November 17. **Rates:** From $1,239.
	Eleven-day round-trip Savona (Italy) cruise calls at Olympia/Katakolon, Athens, Izmir (Turkey), Nazareth/Galilee (Haifa, Israel), Cairo (Port Said, Egypt), Cairo/Giza (Alexandria, Egypt), Rome (Civitavecchia, Italy). April 8; September 12, September 23. **Rates:** From $1,279.
	Eleven-day round-trip Rome (Civitavecchia, Italy) cruise calls at Savona (Italy), Olympia/Katakolon, Athens, Izmir (Turkey), Jerusalem/Tel Aviv (Ashdod, Israel), Cairo (Port Said, Egypt), Cairo/Giza (Alexandria, Egypt). April 18, April 29; October 3, October 14, October 25; November 5, November 16. **Rates:** From $1,239.
	Eleven-day round-trip Rome (Civitavecchia, Italy) cruise calls at Savona (Italy), Olympia/Katakolon, Athens, Izmir (Turkey), Nazareth/Galilee (Haifa, Israel), Cairo (Port Said, Egypt), Cairo/Giza (Alexandria, Egypt). April 7; September 22. **Rates:** From $1,279.
Costa Romantica	**Eleven-day round-trip Venice (Italy)** cruise calls at Bari (Italy), Olympia/Katakolon, Santorini, Izmir (Turkey), Istanbul (Turkey, overnight), Volos, Athens, Split (Croatia). April 15; May 15; June 21; July 25; August 28; October 1. **Rates:** From $1,599.
	Twelve-day round-trip Venice (Italy) cruise calls at Bari (Italy), Olympia/Katakolon, Athens, Yalta (Ukraine), Odessa (Ukraine), Constanta (Romania), Istanbul (Turkey), Corfu, Split (Croatia). May 29; July 13; August 16; September 19. **Rates:** From $2,019.

continues

SHIP	ITINERARY
Costa Serena	**Eleven-day round-trip Civitavecchia (Italy)** cruise calls at Savona (Italy), Olympia/Katakolon, Jerusalem/Tel Aviv (Ashdod, Israel), Nazareth/Galilee (Haifa, Israel), Izmir (Turkey), Athens. January 7. **Rates:** From $869.
	Eleven-day round-trip Civitavecchia (Italy) cruise calls at Savona (Italy), Olympia/Katakolon, Athens, Izmir (Turkey), Jerusalem/Tel Aviv (Ashdod, Israel), Cairo (Port Said, Egypt), Cairo/Giza (Alexandria, Egypt). February 23; March 5, March 16. **Rates:** From $1,079.
	Eleven-day round-trip Savona (Italy) cruise calls at Olympia/Katakolon, Jerusalem/Tel Aviv (Ashdod, Israel), Nazareth/Galilee (Haifa, Israel), Izmir (Turkey), Athens, Rome (Civitavecchia, Italy). January 8. **Rates:** From $919.
	Eleven-day round-trip Savona (Italy) cruise calls at Olympia/Katakolon, Athens, Izmir (Turkey), Jerusalem/Tel Aviv (Ashdod, Israel), Cairo (Port Said, Egypt), Cairo/Giza (Alexandria, Egypt), Rome (Civitavecchia, Italy). February 13. **Rates:** From $1,019.
	Eleven-day round-trip Savona (Italy) cruise calls at Olympia/Katakolon, Nazareth/Galilee (Haifa, Israel), Jerusalem/Tel Aviv (Ashdod, Israel), Izmir (Turkey), Athens, Rome (Civitavecchia, Italy). March 6. **Rates:** From $1,199.

4 CRYSTAL CRUISES

2049 Century Park E., Ste. 1400, Los Angeles, CA 90067. ✆ **310/785-9300.** www.crystalcruises.com.

Crystal offers a cultured, elegant atmosphere and unobtrusive service aboard its pair of midsize ships that afford passengers the best of everything—space and intimacy. Its parent company, NYK, is a Japanese firm, the cruise line itself is based in Los Angeles, and you can see a kind of upscale, tranquil, and elegant California–influenced design to these ships, especially in the feng shui–designed spas, the Japanese cuisine (chef Nobu Matsuhisa of Nobu restaurant fame designed the menus in the ship's sushi restaurants), and some of the more modern interior looks of the *Crystal Serenity* (built in 2003; 1,080 passengers, 68,000 GRTs).

This operator offers luxury, but on a slightly larger scale than lines such as Silversea and Seabourn—and beginning in spring 2012, Crystal will begin including all alcoholic beverages in its fares as well as soft drinks. The line still preserves a traditional, two-seating dining pattern in its main restaurant and does formal nights. Crystal has invested heavily in education and enrichment. During the daytimes, passengers can take a financial planning class or pick up a new recipe or two. Cabins are spacious; the ship's upper-level penthouse suites (especially the top-of-the-line Crystal Penthouses) are top-notch.

Crystal Cruises Itineraries & Rates

SHIP	ITINERARY
Crystal Serenity	**Seven-day Civitavecchia (Italy) to Athens** cruise calls at Sorrento (Italy, overnight), Taormina (Sicily, Italy), Bodrum (Turkey), Mykonos. June 5. **Rates:** From $3,470.
	Seven-day Athens to Venice (Italy) cruise calls at Ephesus/Kusadasi (Turkey), Santorini, Corfu, Dubrovnik (Croatia), Venice (Italy, overnight). June 12. **Rates:** From $3,450.
	Twelve-day Istanbul (Turkey) to Monte Carlo (Monaco) cruise calls at Istanbul (overnight), Mykonos, Athens, Nafplion, Taormina (Sicily, Italy), Sorrento (Italy, overnight), Rome (Civitavecchia, Italy), Monte Carlo (overnight). July 1. **Rates:** From $5,946.
	Twelve-day Athens to Istanbul (Turkey) cruise overnights in Athens and calls at Nafplion, Mykonos, Samos, Odessa (Ukraine, overnight), Yalta (Ukraine), Sochi (Russia), Istanbul (overnight). September 6. **Rates:** From $6,210.

Twelve-day Istanbul (Turkey) to Venice (Italy) cruise overnights in Istanbul and calls at Mykonos, Athens, Nafplion, Corfu, Kotor (Montenegro), Zadar (Croatia), Venice (overnight). September 18. **Rates:** From $5,418.

Twelve-day Venice (Italy) to Athens cruise overnights in Venice and calls at Ravenna (Italy), Kotor (Montenegro), Corfu (Greece), Mykonos, Istanbul (Turkey, overnight), Athens (overnight). September 30. **Rates:** From $4,541.

Twelve-day Athens to Venice (Italy) cruise calls at Santorini, Jerusalem/Tel Aviv (Ashdod, Israel, overnight), Cairo/Giza (Alexandria, Egypt, overnight), Corfu, Dubrovnik (Croatia), Venice (overnight). October 12. **Rates:** From $5,418.

Twelve-day Venice (Italy) to Istanbul (Turkey) cruise overnights in Venice and calls at Dubrovnik (Croatia), Corfu, Cephalonia, Athens, Nafplion, Mykonos, Ephesus/Kusadasi (Turkey), Istanbul (overnight). October 24. **Rates:** From $4,541.

Twelve-day Barcelona (Spain) to **Athens** cruise overnights in Barcelona and calls at Catania (Sicily, Italy), Santorini, Rhodes, Limassol (Cyprus), Beirut (Lebanon), Damascus (Syria), Athens (overnight). December 9. **Rates:** From $7,255.

Fourteen-day Athens to Barcelona (Spain) cruise calls at Jerusalem/Tel Aviv (Ashdod, Israel, overnight), Cairo/Giza (Alexandria, Egypt, overnight), Valletta (Malta), Palermo (Sicily, Italy), Naples/Capri (Italy), Valencia (Spain), Barcelona (overnight). December 21. **Rates:** From $7,255.

HOLLAND AMERICA LINE

300 Elliott Ave. W., Seattle, WA 98119. ⓒ **877/SAIL-HAL** (724-5425). www.hollandamerica.com.

Holland America is a premium-level line that offers a more traditional cruise flavor onboard new, modern cruise ships. The line takes pride in its Dutch heritage—the tradition of naming its ships with a "dam" suffix goes back to 1883—and in offering good service in a refined setting: teak deck chairs around the promenade deck, classical music in the Explorers Lounge after dinner, formal nights, and a collection of art and artifacts from around the world. Still, Holland America stays on the top of current trends as well. As part of the line's "Signature of Excellence" program, over the past few years the fleet has been enhanced with a bunch of fresh amenities, from Culinary Arts centers where passengers can go for cooking classes to bigger-than-ever children's facilities, a specialty Pinnacle Grill restaurant on every ship, and big, comfortable Internet cafe-cum-lounges that encompass computers, the library, game room, and specialty coffee shop.

The ***Nieuw Amsterdam*** (built in 2010; 2,104 passengers; 86,000 GRTs) is the latest and greatest Holland America beauty and features private cabanas on upper pool decks, a culinary arts center offering interactive cooking demonstrations, and a coffeehouse complete with an extensive library.

The ***Noordam*** (built in 2006; 1,848 passengers; 85,000 GRTs) is extraordinarily spacious, with large standard cabins, glamorous two-level dining rooms, and distinctive specialty restaurants. The best of old and new, the ship's decor mixes classic wine reds, dark blues, and earth tones with just a hint of zany, such as the silver-framed benches on the elevator landings and in the **Pinnacle Grill** and **Pinnacle Bar.**

Holland America Itineraries & Rates

SHIP	ITINERARY
Nieuw Amsterdam	**Twelve-day round-trip Venice (Italy)** cruise overnights in Venice and calls at Kotor (Montenegro), Athens, Istanbul (Turkey, overnight), Mykonos, Ephesus/Kusadasi (Turkey), Santorini, Split (Croatia). April 30; June 5; July 18; August 23; October 5. **Rates:** From $1,799.

continues

SHIP	ITINERARY
Noordam	**Ten-day round-trip Rome (Civitavecchia, Italy)** cruise calls at Dubrovnik (Croatia), Corfu, Olympia/Katakolon, Santorini, Ephesus/Kusadasi (Turkey), Athens, Messina (Sicily, Italy). May 18; June 7, June 27; July 17; August 6, August 26; September 15; October 5. **Rates:** From $1,599.

LOUIS CRUISE LINES

8 Antoniou Ambatielou St., Piraeus, Greece. ℭ **210/458-3400.** www.louiscruises.com.

The Cyprus-based Louis Group has been in the passenger shipping business for more than 75 years, with its Louis Cruise Lines division dedicating two ships to the Greek islands in 2012 for shorter 3- to 7-night cruises out of Athens.

The **Louis Majesty** (built in 1992; 1,800 passengers; 40,876 GRTs) and the recently acquired **Cristal** (built in 1992; 1,278 passengers; 25,661 GRTs) are the line's main ships in Greece for 2012.

The bulk of Louis's fleet consists of older, more classic-style vessels that have been rebuilt and refurbished. The ships aren't as flashy or as new as the ones used by the major U.S.-based cruise lines, so you won't find state-of-the-art amenities or rows of balconies, though the *Cristal* is a newer, more modern vessel. However, these are cruises that concentrate on the destination: The itineraries are port intensive, and the ships will sometimes visit more than one island in a day. Embarkations are somewhat flexible, as Louis permits cruisers to pick up the ships in Mykonos, or disembark early in order to stay a few days on Santorini or Crete. Its ships fly the Greek flag, and its officers are Greek, but Louis also is increasingly designing its ships, cuisine, and entertainment to appeal to an American market: 60% to 65% of its clientele is North American.

Tragedy struck in 2007 when Louis ship the **Sea Diamond** sank after scraping its side on a volcanic reef in Santorini; all passengers were evacuated except for two, who were reported missing and whose bodies were never found. The company, however, has continued its commitment to the Greece market, spending $49 million to acquire the *Cristal* as a replacement to the *Sea Diamond* and maintaining a two- or three-ship deployment to the region.

Louis Cruises Itineraries & Rates

SHIP	ITINERARY
Louis Majesty	**Three-day round-trip Athens** cruise calls at Istanbul (Turkey), Izmir (Turkey). March 16, March 23, March 30. **Rates:** From $429.
	Four-day round-trip Athens cruise calls at Mykonos, Ephesus/Kusadasi (Turkey), Patmos, Santorini. April 6, April 13, April 20, April 27; May 4, May 11, May 18, May 25; June 1, June 8, June 15, June 22, June 29; July 6, July 13, July 20, July 27; August 3, August 10, August 17, August 24, August 31; September 7, September 14, September 21, September 28; October 5, October 12, October 19, October 26. **Rates:** From $446.
	Four-day round-trip Athens cruise calls at Mykonos, Ephesus/Kusadasi (Turkey), Patmos, Rhodes, Crete, Santorini. March 19, March 26; April 2, April 9, April 16, April 23, April 30; May 7, May 14, May 21, May 28; June 4, June 11, June 18, June 25; July 2, July 9, July 15, July 23, July 30; August 6, August 13, August 20, August 27; September 3, September 10, September 17, September 24; October 1, October 8, October 15, October 22, October 29. **Rates:** From $639.

SHIP	ITINERARY
Louis Cristal	**Seven-day round-trip Athens** cruise calls at Istanbul (Turkey, overnight), Izmir (Turkey), Patmos, Mykonos, Rhodes, Heraklion, Santorini. March 30; April 6, April 13, April 20, April 27; May 4, May 11, May 18, May 25; June 1, June 8, June 15, June 22, June 29; July 6, July 13, July 20, July 27; August 3, August 10, August 17, August 24, August 31; September 7, September 14, September 21, September 28; October 5, October 12, October 19, October 26. **Rates:** From $1,223.
	Three-day round-trip Athens cruise calls at Istanbul (Turkey), Izmir (Turkey). November 2. **Rates:** From $429.
	Four-day round-trip Athens cruise calls at Mykonos, Ephesus/Kusadasi (Turkey), Patmos, Rhodes, Heraklion, Santorini. November 5. **Rates:** From $639.

MSC CRUISES

6750 N. Andrews Ave., Fort Lauderdale, FL 33309. ☏ **800/666-9333.** www.msccruises.com.

MSC Cruises, a line with Italian heritage and a subsidiary of shipping giant Mediterranean Shipping Co., is one of the fastest-growing cruise lines. A few years ago MSC was an up-and-coming player, mixing a fleet of older, classic style ships with mostly midsize vessels. These days the line is adding megaships to its fleet that compete on size and amenities with the biggest cruise companies, has made a big push into the U.S. market, and has established itself in the contemporary cruise market.

The line's "classic Italian cruising," focuses on service and on playing up its Italian ambience—Italian actress Sophia Loren is the godmother to four MSC Cruises ships. The line is trying to "Americanize" some aspects of the voyages in order to make the Continental vibe seem more familiar to U.S. passengers, such as offering coffee along with dessert (instead of afterward) and adding more items to the breakfast buffet. Still, the passenger mix is more international than many other lines. Itineraries are port-intensive, and the onboard experience friendly and fun.

The **MSC Magnifica** (built in 2010; 2,550 passengers; 89,600 GRTs) and sister **MSC Musica** (built in 2006; 2,550 passengers; 89,600 GRTs) are a good example of where MSC Cruises has been heading, hardware-wise: They've got room for a minigolf course, a sushi bar, an Internet cafe, a solarium, yoga classes, a wine bar, and a children's playroom in addition to all the usual activities you'll find on ships (a casino, gym, sauna, and so on). Nearly 830 of the 1,275 suites and cabins have private balconies. The **MSC Armonia** (built in 2001; 1,566 passengers; 58,625 GRTs) is a bit older and offers fewer amenities.

MSC Cruises Itineraries & Rates

SHIP	ITINERARY
MSC Musica	**Seven-day round-trip Venice** cruise calls at Bari (Italy), Corfu, Athens, overnights in Mykonos, Katakolon, Dubrovnik (Croatia). *Musica* cruises are offered weekly departing on Saturdays. April 4 through October 3. **Rates:** From $999.
MSC Armonia	**Seven-day round-trip Venice (Italy)** cruise calls at Ancona (Italy), Corfu, Santorini, Athens, Argostoli, Kotor (Montenegro). May 11, May 18, May 25; June 1, June 8, June 15, June 22, June 29; July 6, July 13, July 20, July 27; August 3, August 10, August 17, August 24, August 31; September 7, September 14, September 21, September 28; October 5. **Rates:** From $619.
	Seven-day round-trip Ancona (Italy) cruise calls at Corfu, Santorini, Athens, Argostoli, Kotor (Montenegro), Venice (Italy). May 12, May 19, May 26; June 2, June 9, June 16. June 23, June 30; July 7, July 14, July 21, July 28; August 4, August 11, August 18, August 25; September 1, September 8, September 15, September 22, September 29. **Rates:** From $799.

continues

SHIP	ITINERARY
MSC Magnifica	**Nine-day round-trip Venice (Italy)** cruise calls at Bari (Italy), Rhodes, Nazareth/ Galilee (Haifa, Israel, overnight), Athens. January 5, January 14, January 23; February 17, February 26; March 6, March 15. **Rates:** From $799.
	Nine-day round-trip Bari (Italy) cruise calls at Rhodes, Nazareth/Galilee (Haifa, Israel, overnight), Athens, Venice. January 6, January 15; February 18; March 7. **Rates:** From $799.

NORWEGIAN CRUISE LINE

7665 Corporate Center Dr. Miami, FL 33126. ✆ **866/625-1166.** www.ncl.com.

Many mega–cruise lines operate with dinner seatings at set times and offer an alternative restaurant or two for a change of pace. Not so NCL; this company pushed the envelope a few years ago with a concept called Freestyle Dining: Pick one of several restaurants and make a reservation for dinner or stroll in whenever, just as you would at a shore-side restaurant. NCL started building its ships to take advantage of the Freestyle concept, and the result is a fleet of new ships that offer about 10 restaurant choices. Another difference: no required formal nights.

The **Norwegian Jade** (built in 2007; 2,380 passengers; 93,558 GRTs) is among the fleet's newest ships and among the most fun megaships today, offering a supersocial atmosphere, creative decor, and onboard music and pop culture references tailored to folks in their 20s and on up to those in their 50s. The **Bliss Ultra Lounge** juxtaposes bordello decor with a four-lane, Day-Glo bowling alley, while the nightclubs and atriums feature furniture out of *Alice in Wonderland*. The Jade's Garden Villas spread out up to an astonishing 500 sq. m (5,350 sq. ft.), and feature private gardens, multiple bedrooms with mind-blowing bathrooms, living rooms, full kitchens, and private butler service.

Norwegian Cruises Itineraries & Rates

SHIP	ITINERARY
Norwegian Jade	**Fourteen-day round-trip Venice (Italy)** cruise calls at Corfu, Santorini, Mykonos, Olympia/Katakolon, Venice (Italy), Dubrovnik (Croatia), Athens, Izmir (Turkey), Split (Croatia). April 28; May 12, May 26; June 9, June 23; September 8, September 22. **Rates:** From $1,379.
	Fourteen-day round-trip Venice (Italy) cruise calls at Dubrovnik (Croatia), Athens, Izmir (Turkey), Split (Croatia), Venice, Corfu, Santorini, Mykonos, Olympia/Katakolon. May 5; June 2, June 16; July 7; September 1, September 15, September 29. **Rates:** From $1,429.
	Ten-day round-trip Rome (Civitavecchia, Italy) cruise calls at Olympia/Katakolon, Athens, Izmir (Turkey), Cairo/Giza (Alexandria, Egypt, overnight). October 31; November 21; December 12. **Rates:** From $709.

OCEANIA CRUISES

8300 NW 33rd St., Ste. 308, Miami, FL 33122. ✆ **800/531-5619.** www.oceaniacruises.com.

This cruise line has grown quickly since its 2003 debut. It now boasts three ships, and it has orders in for two new 1,260-passenger ships. The current vessels are identical in layout, and their sizes, at 680 passengers each, make them cozy and intimate but able to stock a lot of amenities like multiple restaurants and big spas. Oceania straddles the line between the small luxury players and the larger, though less pricey, premium cruise lines. It tries to offer a reasonably priced yet intimate, casual, upscale experience.

Four ships hit the Greek Isles. The brand new *Marina* (built in 2011; 1,258 passengers; 65,000 GRTs) and sister *Riviera* (built in 2012; 1,258 passengers; 65,000 GRTs) are the line's newest and greatest, at twice the size of the *Regatta* and *Nautica* (built in 1998–2000; 684 passengers; 30,277 GRTs). The emphasis on all four of these ships is on casual, so you won't need to dress up (or even bring a tie or fancy dress). On Marina and Riviera, almost all of the cabins have balconies, while a good number also boast them on the older two ships. Public rooms, too, are of the big-but-not-too-big mold, and there are nice touches throughout the ships like teak decks and DVD players in the cabins. Private cabanas at the very top of the ship can be reserved for the day or for the whole cruise, and come with a dedicated attendant and food and beverage services. Alternative restaurants include the Polo steakhouse and Toscana Italian trattoria (plus two more, an Asian and a French venue, on the newer ships), fine complements to the main restaurant.

Oceania Cruises Itineraries & Rates

SHIP	ITINERARY
Marina	**Ten-day Venice (Italy) to Athens** cruise overnights in Venice and calls at Dubrovnik (Croatia), Kotor (Montenegro), Corfu, Monemvasia, Crete, Santorini, Ephesus/Kusadasi (Turkey), Delos, Mykonos. April 22. **Rates:** From $2,699.
	Ten-day Athens to Barcelona (Spain) cruise calls at Santorini, Ephesus/Kusadasi (Turkey), Taormina (Sicily, Italy), Amalfi (Italy), Rome (Civitavecchia, Italy), Florence/Pisa (Livorno, Italy, overnight), Marseille (France). May 2. **Rates:** From $2,549.
	Ten-day Istanbul (Turkey) to Athens cruise calls at Lesbos, Delos, Mykonos, Ephesus/Kusadasi (Turkey), Santorini, Marmaris (Turkey), Antalya (Turkey), Rhodes, Crete, Athens (overnight). October 12. **Rates:** From $2,949.
	Ten-day Athena to Istanbul (Turkey) cruise calls at Cairo/Giza (Alexandria, Egypt), Jerusalem/Tel Aviv (Ashdod, Israel), Nazareth/Galilee (Haifa, Israel), Limassol (Cyprus), Rhodes, Ephesus/Kusadasi (Turkey), Istanbul (overnight). October 22. **Rates:** From $2,749.
	Seven-day Istanbul (Turkey) to Athens cruise calls at Dikili (Turkey), Volos, Ephesus/Kusadasi (Turkey), Rhodes, Crete, Athens (overnight). November 1. **Rates:** From $2,199.
Nautica	**Ten-day Athens to Barcelona (Spain)** cruise calls at Santorini, Ephesus/Kusadasi (Turkey), Taormina (Sicily, Italy), Amalfi (Italy), Rome (Civitavecchia, Italy), Florence/Pisa (Livorno, Italy, overnight), Marseille (France). May 14. **Rates:** From $2,549.
	Ten-day Barcelona (Spain) to Athens cruise calls at Marseille (France), Florence/Pisa (Livorno, Italy, overnight), Rome (Civitavecchia, Italy), Amalfi (Italy), Taormina (Sicily, Italy), Ephesus/Kusadasi (Turkey), Santorini. October 26. **Rates:** From $2,749.
	Ten-day Athens to Istanbul (Turkey) cruise calls at Cairo/Giza (Alexandria, Egypt), Cairo (Port Said, Egypt), Jerusalem/Tel Aviv (Ashdod, Israel), Nazareth/Galilee (Haifa, Israel), Limassol (Cyprus), Rhodes, Ephesus/Kusadasi (Turkey), Istanbul (overnight). November 5. **Rates:** From $2,424.
Regatta	**Ten-day Barcelona (Spain) to Athens** cruise calls at Marseille (France), Florence/Pisa (Livorno, Italy, overnight), Rome (Civitavecchia, Italy), Amalfi (Italy), Taormina (Sicily, Italy), Ephesus/Kusadasi (Turkey), Santorini. June 25. **Rates:** From $2,999.
	Ten-day Istanbul (Turkey) to Athens cruise calls at Lesbos, Ephesus/Kusadasi (Turkey), Delos, Mykonos, Santorini, Rhodes, Crete, Monemvasia, Olympia/Katakolon, Athens (overnight). July 17. **Rates:** From $2,849.
	Twelve-day Athens to Istanbul (Turkey) cruise calls at Cairo/Giza (Alexandria, Egypt), Cairo (Port Said, Egypt), Jerusalem/Tel Aviv (Ashdod, Israel, overnight), Nazareth/Galilee (Haifa, Israel), Alanya (Turkey), Rhodes, Patmos, Ephesus/Kusadasi (Turkey), Istanbul (overnight). July 27. **Rates:** From $3,399.

continues

Twelve-day Istanbul (Turkey) to Athens cruise calls at Ephesus/Kusadasi (Turkey), Patmos, Rhodes, Alanya (Turkey), Limassol (Cyprus), Nazareth/Galilee (Haifa, Israel), Jerusalem/Tel Aviv (Ashdod, Israel, overnight), Cairo (Port Said, Egypt). August 30. **Rates:** From $3,399.

Ten-day Athens to Istanbul (Turkey) cruise calls at Nafplion, Olympia, Monemvasia, Crete, Rhodes, Santorini, Delos, Mykonos, Ephesus/Kusadasi (Turkey), Istanbul (overnight). September 11. **Rates:** From $3,199.

Twelve-day Athens to Istanbul (Turkey) cruise calls at Cairo/Giza (Alexandria, Egypt), Cairo (Port Said, Egypt), Jerusalem/Tel Aviv (Ashdod, Israel), Nazareth/Galilee (Haifa, Israel, overnight), Alanya (Turkey), Rhodes, Patmos, Ephesus/Kusadasi (Turkey), Istanbul (overnight). October 1. **Rates:** From $3,449.

Ten-day Istanbul (Turkey) to Rome (Civitavecchia, Italy) cruise calls at Ephesus/Kusadasi (Turkey), Santorini, Athens, Valletta (Malta), La Goulette (Tunisia), Trapani (Sicily, Italy), Sorrento (Italy, overnight). October 13. **Rates:** From $2,749.

Ten-day Rome (Civitavecchia, Italy) to Athens cruise calls at Monte Carlo (Monaco), Marseille (France), Florence/Pisa (Livorno, Italy, overnight), Sorrento (Italy), Messina (Sicily, Italy), Argostoli, Monemvasia, Ephesus/Kusadasi (Turkey). October 23. **Rates:** From $2,749.

Ten-day Athens to Barcelona (Spain) cruise call at Olympia/Katakolon, Messina (Sicily, Italy), Naples/Capri (Italy), Rome (Civitavecchia, Italy), Florence/Pisa (Livorno, Italy), Monte Carlo (Monaco), Marseille (France), Barcelona (overnight). November 2. **Rates:** From $2,424.

Riviera

Ten-day Barcelona (Spain) to Athens cruise calls at Marseille (France), Florence/Pisa (Livorno, Italy, overnight), Rome (Civitavecchia, Italy), Amalfi (Italy), Taormina (Sicily, Italy), Ephesus/Kusadasi (Turkey), Santorini. April 14. **Rates:** From $3,799.

Twelve-day Athens to Istanbul (Turkey) cruise calls at Santorini, Marmaris (Turkey), Nazareth/Galilee (Haifa, Israel), Jerusalem/Tel Aviv (Ashdod, Israel, overnight), Alanya (Turkey), Rhodes, Patmos, Ephesus/Kusadasi (Turkey), Istanbul (overnight). April 24. **Rates:** From $3,149.

Ten-day Istanbul (Turkey) to Venice (Italy) cruise calls at Lesbos, Sphesus/Kusadasi (Turkey), Mykonos, Athens, Argostoli, Corfu, Dubrovnik (Croatia), Split (Croatia), Venice (overnight). May 6. **Rates:** From $2,549.

Ten-day Venice (Italy) to Athens cruise overnights in Venice and calls at Dubrovnik (Croatia), Kotor (Montenegro), Corfu, Monemvasia, Crete, Santorini, Ephesus/Kusadasi (Turkey), Delos, Mykonos. May 16; October 4. **Rates:** From $2,799.

Ten-day Athens to Barcelona (Spain) cruise calls at Santorini, Ephesus/Kusadasi (Turkey), Taormina (Sicily, Italy), Rome (Civitavecchia, Italy), Florence/Pisa (Livorno, Italy, overnight), Marseille (France). May 26. **Rates:** From $2,549.

Ten-day Athens to Rome (Civitavecchia, Italy) cruise calls at Ephesus/Kusadasi (Turkey), Monemvasia, Argostoli, Messina (Sicily, Italy), Florence/Pisa (Livorno, Italy, overnight), Marseille (France), Monte Carlo (Monaco). October 14. **Rates:** From $2,749.

PRINCESS CRUISES

24844 Ave. Rockefeller, Santa Clarita, CA 91355. ☎ **800/PRINCESS** (774-6237). www.princess.com.

Forever connected to its *Love Boat* past, American premium line Princess has grown up and evolved into a multidestination, multimegaship line that blends California-style casual with elegance and sophistication. Still, the line keeps the theme of love alive, with special promotions at Valentine's Day and occasional appearances by "Captain Stubing" (actor Gavin MacLeod).

Princess's signature vessels, the Grand-class ships, were so ahead of their time when they debuted in 1998 that the design of sister ships isn't significantly changed. Though the vessels give an impression of immensity from the outside, inside they're well laid out, easy to navigate, and surprisingly cozy. The "cozy" aspect carries over to public rooms like the dimly lit **Explorer's Lounge** and **Wheelhouse Bar,** whose traditional accents recall a grander era of sea travel. In the elegant three-story atriums, classical string quartets perform on formal nights and during embarkation. Throw in good-size kid and teen zones and a plethora of show lounges, bars, and pools, and you've got ships that can keep you busy for a week, never mind the destination.

Crown Princess (built in 2006; 3,080 passengers; 113,000 GRTs) and *Ruby Princess* (built in 2008; 3,080 passengers; 113,000 GRTs) are slightly larger versions of the original Grand-class concept, with amenities including the Sanctuary, an adults-only, top-deck hideaway of cabanas, healthy snacks and soothing music, plus an international cafe, a wine and seafood bar, a piazza-style atrium with a street-cafe vibe, a giant movie screen on deck, and a steak and seafood restaurant. The newer *Ruby Princess* added some fresh experiences: a British pub at lunch on sea days (no charge), a range of cheeses to go with the wine and seafood snacks available in Vines, and the Ultimate Ship tour, a truly behind-the-scenes look at how a ship operates.

Ocean Princess (built in 1999; 680 passengers; 30,277 GRTs) and *Pacific Princess* (built in 1999; 680 passengers; 30,277 GRTs) are small, but comfortable ships. They're traditional, sedate and geared to adults, with an emphasis on intimate spaces—just like Princess's larger ships, but here it's the real thing. Like a European boutique hotel, they're decorated mostly in warm, dark woods and rich fabrics, and offer a small-scale, clubby feel that larger ships can only hope to mimic.

Princess Cruises Itineraries & Rates

SHIP	ITINERARY
Ruby Princess	**Twelve-day Barcelona (Spain) to Venice (Italy)** cruise calls at Monte Carlo (Monaco), Florence/Pisa (Livorno, Italy), Rome (Civitavecchia, Italy), Naples/Capri (Sorrento, Italy), Mykonos, Istanbul, Ephesus/Kusadasi (Turkey), Athens, Venice (overnight). May 30; June 23; July 17; August 10; September 3, September 27. **Rates:** From $1,990.
	Twelve-day Venice (Italy) to Barcelona (Spain) cruise overnights in Venice and calls at Athens, Ephesus/Kusadasi (Turkey), Istanbul (Turkey), Mykonos, Naples/Capri (Sorrento, Italy), Rome (Civitavecchia, Italy), Florence/Pisa (Livorno, Italy), Monte Carlo (Monaco). May 18; June 11; July 5, July 29; August 22; September 15. **Rates:** From $2,040.
Crown Princess	**Twelve-day Venice (Italy) to Rome (Civitavecchia, Italy)** cruise overnights in Venice and calls at Dubrovnik (Croatia), Corfu, Olympia/Katakolon, Athens, Mykonos, Ephesus/Kusadasi (Turkey), Rhodes, Santorini, Naples/Capri (Sorrento, Italy). May 24; June 17; July 11; August 4, August 28; September 21; October 15; November 8. **Rates:** From $1,790.
	Twelve-day Rome (Civitavecchia, Italy) to Venice (Italy) cruise calls at Monte Carlo (Monaco), Florence/Pisa (Livorno, Italy), Naples/Capri (Sorrento, Italy), Santorini, Athens, Mykonos, Olympia/Katakolon, Corfu, Split (Croatia), Venice (overnight). June 5, June 29; July 23; August 16; September 9; October 3. **Rates:** From $1,990.
	Twelve-day Rome (Civitavecchia, Italy) to Venice (Italy) cruise calls at Cairo/Giza (Alexandria, Egypt, overnight), Mykonos, Istanbul (Turkey), Ephesus/Kusadasi (Turkey), Athens, Venice (overnight). October 27. **Rates:** From $1,790.
	Twelve-day Rome (Civitavecchia, Italy) to Venice (Italy) Greek Isles cruise calls at Naples/Capri (Sorrento, Italy), Santorini, Rhodes, Ephesus/Kusadasi (Turkey), Mykonos, Athens, Olympia/Katakolon, Corfu, Dubrovnik (Croatia), Venice (overnight). November 20. **Rates:** From $1,690.
Ocean Princess	**Fourteen-day Barcelona (Spain) to Athens** cruise calls at Carcassonne (Sete, France), Portofino (Italy), Florence/Pisa (Livorno, Italy), La Goulette (Tunisia), Naples/Capri (Sorrento, Italy), Rome (Civitavecchia, Italy), Itea, Argostoli, Santorini, Ephesus/Kusadasi (Turkey), Crete. September 2. **Rates:** From $2,598.

continues

SHIP	ITINERARY

Twenty-one-day Barcelona (Spain to Athens) cruise calls at Carcassonne (Sete, France), Portofino (Italy), Florence/Pisa (Livorno, Italy), La Goulette (Tunisia), Naples/Capri (Sorrento, Italy), Rome (Civitavecchia, Italy), Itea, Argostoli, Santorini, Ephesus/Kusadasi (Turkey), Crete, Athens, Mykonos, Olympia/Katakolon, Corfu, Dubrovnik (Croatia), Korcula (Croatia). September 2. **Rates:** From $4,347.

Seven-day Rome (Civitavecchia, Italy) to Athens cruise calls at Itea, Argostoli, Santorini, Ephesus/Kusadasi (Turkey), Crete. September 9. **Rates:** From $1,399.

Fourteen-day Rome (Civitavecchia, Italy) to Venice (Italy) cruise calls at Itea, Argostoli, Santorini, Ephesus/Kusadasi (Turkey), Crete, Athens, Olympia/Katakolon, Corfu, Dubrovnik (Croatia), Korcula (Croatia). September 9. **Rates:** From $2,498.

Seven-day Athens to Venice (Italy) cruise calls at Mykonos, Olympia/Katakolon, Corfu, Dubrovnik (Croatia), Koper (Slovenia). September 16. **Rates:** From $1,299.

Seven-day Venice to Athens cruise calls at Koper (Slovenia), Dubrovnik (Croatia), Corfu, Olympia/Katakolon, Mykonos. September 23. **Rates:** From $1,299.

Fourteen-day Venice (Italy) to Rome (Civitavecchia, Italy) cruise calls at Koper (Slovenia), Dubrovnik (Croatia), Corfu, Olympia/Katakolon, Mykonos, Athens, Crete, Ephesus/Kusadasi (Turkey), Santorini, Argostoli, Itea. September 23. **Rates:** From $2,398.

Pacific Princess   **Seven-day Athens to Rome (Civitavecchia, Italy)** cruise calls at Crete, Ephesus/Kusadasi (Turkey), Santorini, Argostoli, Itea. September 30. **Rates:** From $1,299.

Twelve-day Venice (Italy) to Athens cruise calls in Split (Croatia), Istanbul (Turkey, overnight), Nesebur (Bulgaria), Constanta (Romania), Odessa (Ukraine), Yalta (Ukraine), Volos. June 29. **Rates:** From $3,090.

Twelve-day Athens to Rome (Civitavecchia, Italy) cruise calls at Patmos, Santorini, Ephesus/Kusadasi (Turkey), Nazareth/Galilee (Haifa, Israel), Jerusalem/Tel Aviv (Ashdod, Israel), Cairo (Port Said, Egypt), Cairo/Giza (Alexandria, Egypt), Naples/Capri (Sorrento, Italy). May 12; October 3, October 27; November 20. **Rates:** From $2,740.

Twelve-day Athens to Venice (Italy) cruise calls at Patmos, Ephesus/Kusadasi, Nazareth/Galilee (Haifa, Israel), Jerusalem/Tel Aviv (Ashdod, Israel), Cairo (Port Said, Egypt), Cairo/Giza (Alexandria, Egypt), Dubrovnik (Croatia), Ravenna (Italy). June 17; July 11; August 4. **Rates:** From $3,090.

Twelve-day Athens to Venice cruise calls at Volos, Yalta (Ukraine), Odessa (Ukraine), Constanta (Romania), Nesebur (Bulgaria), Istanbul (Turkey, overnight), Korcula (Croatia). August 28. **Rates:** From $2,940.

Twelve-day Rome to Athens cruise calls at Naples/Capri (Sorrento, Italy), Patmos, Ephesus/Kusadasi (Turkey), Nazareth/Galilee (Haifa, Israel), Jerusalem/Tel Aviv (Ashdod, Israel), Cairo (Port Said, Egypt), Cairo/Giza (Alexandria, Egypt), Santorini. September 23; October 15; November 8. **Rates:** From $2,840.

PULLMANTUR CRUISES

2 Mahonia St., Madrid, Spain 28043. ✆ **092-09-5512.** www.pullmantur.es.

Built for Celebrity Cruises, the **Zenith** (built in 1992; 1,500 passengers; 47,255 GRTs) is now a part of the Spain-based Pullmantur fleet, whose parent company is Royal Caribbean. The ship is a great midsize with attractive tiered decks at the stern and everything you'll need for a cozy cruise of the Greek Isles, from a kids playroom for ages 3 to 11 to an elegant, one-level oceanview dining room, gym, spa, and plenty of entertainment venues. Most guests will be European, the majority from Spain, with the languages spoken being Spanish, English, French, and Portuguese; prices onboard are in euros. Two seatings at dinner are offered, the early at 8pm and the late seating at 10:15pm. Fares include all meals and all alcoholic and soft drinks.

Pullmantur Cruises Itineraries & Rates

SHIP	ITINERARY
Zenith	**Seven-day round-trip Athens** cruise calls at Santorini, Marmaris (Turkey), Izmir (Turkey), Istanbul (Turkey), Mykonos. April 2, April 23; May 14; June 4, June 25; August 6, August 27. **Rates:** From $881.
	Seven-day Athens to Ravenna (Italy) cruise calls at Mykonos, Santorini, Olympia/Katakolon, Corfu, Dubrovnik (Croatia), Venice (Italy). April 9, April 30; May 21; June 11; July 2, July 23; August 13; September 3. **Rates:** From $642.
	Seven-day Ravenna (Italy) to Athens cruise calls at Venice (Italy), Dubrovnik (Croatia), Corfu, Olympia/Katakolon, Santorini, Mykonos. April 16; May 7, May 28; June 18; July 9, July 30; August 20; September 10. **Rates:** From $642.

REGENT SEVEN SEAS CRUISES

1000 Corporate Dr., Ste. 500, Fort Lauderdale, FL 33334. ✆ **800/285-1835.** www.rssc.com.

Founded by Radisson Hotels Worldwide in 1992, Regent Seven Seas Cruises is one of the cruise industry's ultraluxury cruise lines. The *Seven Seas Mariner* (built in 2001; 708 passengers; 50,000 GRTs) was the first all-suite, all-balcony ship, followed by sister *Seven Seas Voyager* (built in 2003; 708 passengers; 46,000 GRTs). On both, many cabins have sizeable suites and bathrooms with a tub (unusual on a cruise ship). The spacious ships have an abundance of art on the walls and the decor successfully combines classic furnishings with modern accents. The ship's size means it's easy to get around to the different restaurants and bars. Outdoor deck furniture has a South Beach feel, and alcoholic beverages as well as all soft drinks are included in the rates. The four restaurants onboard both ships (five if you count the Pool Grill) include **Signatures,** operated by Le Cordon Bleu of Paris.

Regent Seven Seas Cruises Itineraries & Rates

SHIP	ITINERARY
Seven Seas Voyager	**Seven-day Athens to Istanbul (Turkey)** cruise calls at Santorini, Ephesus/Kusadasi (Turkey), Rhodes, Mykonos, Kavala/Philippi, Istanbul (overnight). April 16. **Rates:** From $3,399.
	Ten-day Istanbul (Turkey) to Venice (Italy) cruise calls at Ephesus/Kusadasi (Turkey), Santorini, Athens, Olympia/Katakolon, Corfu, Kotor (Montenegro), Dubrovnik (Croatia), Ancona (Italy), Venice (overnight). April 23. **Rates:** From $5,599.
	Seven-day Istanbul (Turkey) to Athens cruise calls at Kavala/Philippi, Mykonos, Ephesus/Kusadasi (Turkey), Rhodes, Crete/Heraklion, Santorini. October 17. **Rates:** From $3,899.
	Seven-day Athena to Istanbul (Turkey) cruise calls at Crete/Heraklion, Santorini, Rhodes, Ephesus/Kusadasi (Turkey), Kavala/Philippi, Istanbul (overnight). October 24. **Rates:** From $3,899.
Seven Seas Mariner	**Ten-day Istanbul (Turkey) to Venice (Italy)** cruise calls at Mykonos, Ephesus/Kusadasi (Turkey), Santorini, Athens, Zakynthos, Corfu, Kotor (Montenegro), Dubrovnik (Croatia) Venice (overnight). May 10. **Rates:** From $4,999.
	Ten-day Rome (Italy) to Istanbul (Turkey) cruise calls at Sorrento (Italy), Trapani (Sicily, Italy), La Goulette (Tunisia), Valletta (Malta), Athens, Santorini, Ephesus/Kusadasi (Turkey), Istanbul (overnight). June 16. **Rates:** From $6,499.
	Seven-day Istanbul (Turkey) to Athens cruise calls at Kavala/Phillipi, Mykonos, Ephesus/Kusadasi (Turkey), Rhodes, Crete/Heraklion, Santorini. June 26; July 13; August 23. **Rates:** From $4,799.

continues

Seven-day Athens to Venice cruise calls at Ephesus/Kusadasi (Turkey), Santorini, Olympia/Katakolon, Corfu, Dubrovnik (Croatia), Venice (overnight). July 20; August 30. **Rates:** From $4,799.

Ten-day Barcelona (Spain) to Athens cruise calls at Marseille (France), Monte Carlo (Monaco), Florence/Pisa (Livorno, Italy), Rome (Civitavecchia, Italy), Taormina (Sicily, Italy), Santorini, Ephesus/Kusadasi (Turkey). September 26. **Rates:** From $5,999.

Fourteen-day Athens to Istanbul (Turkey) cruise calls at Rhodes, Alanya (Turkey), Limassol (Cyprus), Nazareth/Galilee (Haifa, Israel), Jerusalem/Tel Aviv (Ashdod, Israel, overnight) Cairo (Port Said, Egypt), Cairo/Giza (Alexandria, Egypt), Santorini, Ephesus/Kusadasi (Turkey), Patmos, Istanbul (overnight). October 6. **Rates:** From $8,399.

ROYAL CARIBBEAN INTERNATIONAL

1050 Caribbean Way, Miami, FL 33132. ℰ **877/202-1520** or 800/327-6700. www.rccl.com.

Heard about those megaships with the rock-climbing walls? Those are the vessels of Royal Caribbean International, which has made its unusual onboard features—ice-skating rinks and self-leveling billiards tables, for example—a benchmark for other cruise lines. Royal Caribbean sells a reasonably priced, big-ship, American-style experience. And they do it very well: The line's ships are consistent and well-run, and there are a lot of things to do, from wine tastings to climbing the ubiquitous rock wall. Royal Caribbean cultivates an active, fun image, most typified through advertising that urges would-be cruisers to "get out there."

The *Serenade of the Seas* (built in 2003; 2,100 passengers; 90,090 GRTs) is one of four Radiance-class ships, some of the most attractive vessels at sea. Sleek and spacious and a great size, the nine-story atrium is surrounded by glass for great views of the Greek Isles. The pleasing decor, a mix of dark-wood paneling, caramel-brown leathers, and deep-sea-blue fabrics and carpeting along with modern art and sculpture, is the backdrop for spaces like the **Viking Crown Lounge** up top to **Singapore Sling's** piano bar, **Champagne Bar** and many other attractive spaces. *Voyager of the Seas* (built in 1999; 3,114 passengers; 142,000 GRTs) was groundbreaking when it first launched, introducing amenities the world was shocked to see on a cruise ship, but that are now much more commonplace, from a full-sized ice-skating rink to an outdoor in-line skating track, minigolf, a full basketball court, and much more. The much smaller *Splendour of the Seas* (built in 1996; 1,802 passengers; 70,000 GRTs) is a Vision-class ship that can't hold a candle to her newer fleetmates, but if the price is right, amenities like the indoor-outdoor Solarium pool, nautically themed **Schooner Bar,** 18-hole mini golf course and the **Viking Crown Lounge** observatory-cum-disco will do just fine.

Royal Caribbean International Itineraries & Rates

SHIP	ITINERARY
Serenade of the Seas	**Twelve-day round-trip Barcelona (Spain)** cruise calls at Cannes (France), Florence/Pisa (Livorno, Italy), Rome (Civitavecchia, Italy), Athens, Ephesus/Kusadasi (Turkey), Santorini, Naples (Salerno, Italy). May 5, May 29; June 22; July 16; August 9; September 2. **Rates:** From $1,119.
	Twelve-day round-trip Barcelona (Spain) cruise calls at Cannes (France), Florence/Pisa (Livorno, Italy), Rome (Civitavecchia, Italy), Ephesus/Kusadasi (Turkey), Mykonos, Naples (Salerno, Italy). October 3. **Rates:** From $1,299.

	Twelve-day round-trip from Barcelona (Spain) cruise calls at Cannes (France), Florence/Pisa (Livorno, Italy), Athens, Ephesus/Kusadasi (Turkey), Chania, Naples (Salerno, Italy). October 27. **Rates:** From $1,099.
Splendor of the Seas	**Seven-day round-trip Venice (Italy)** cruise calls at Bari (Italy), Corfu, Mykonos, Athens, Dubrovnik (Croatia). May 19; June 2, June 16, June 30; July 28; August 11, August 25; September 8, September 22; October 6, October 20; November 3. **Rates:** From $549.
	Seven-day round-trip Bari (Italy) cruise calls at Corfu, Mykonos, Athens, Dubrovnik (Croatia), Venice (Italy). May 6, May 20; June 3, June 17; July 1, July 29; August 12, August 26; September 9, September 23; October 7, October 21; November 4. **Rates:** From $974.
	Eight-day round-trip Bari (Italy) cruise calls at Corfu, Santorini, Ephesus/Kusadasi (Turkey), Athens, Olympia/Katakolon, Venice (Italy). July 14. **Rates:** From $1,204.
Voyager of the Seas	**Ten-day round-trip Venice (Italy)** cruise calls at Dubrovnik (Croatia), Ephesus/Kusadasi (Turkey), Istanbul (Turkey, overnight), Athens, Chania. May 11; June 22; July 13; August 3, August 24; September 14; October 5. **Rates:** From $999.
	Eleven-day round-trip Venice (Italy) cruise calls at Dubrovnik (Croatia), Rhodes, Ephesus/Kusadasi (Turkey), Istanbul (Turkey, overnight), Athens, Chania. May 21; June 11; July 2, July 23; August 13; September 3, September 24. **Rates:** From $1,199.

SMALL & YACHTLIKE SHIPS
SEABOURN CRUISE LINE

6100 Blue Lagoon Dr., Ste. 400, Miami, FL 33126. ✆ **800/929-9391.** www.seabourn.com.

The top of the line in the cruise world, Seabourn excels in many areas, including food, service, itineraries, and a luxurious and refined environment. These cruises are pricey, and the customers who can afford them are well-traveled sophisticates used to being doted on.

Although the ambience can be casual during the day, it becomes decidedly more formal in the evening, although new dining options with modern cuisine and an "always informal" option at the restaurant at the top of the ship go a way to making it feel more casual. There's an open-bar policy (all alcoholic and soft drinks are included in the fare) and lots of open, teak decks, which make these ships very yachtlike. The ships are all-suite with marble bathrooms, walk-in closets, plush software, stocked mini bars, elegant fine dining and more.

Nighttime entertainment is low key, though cabaret nights with themes like 1950s rock 'n' roll can get the audience going.

Seabourn has three nearly identical ships, and a trio of new larger ships. The **Seabourn Legend** (built in 1992; 208 passengers; 10,000 GRTs) and **Seabourn Pride** (built in 1991; 208 passengers; 10,000 GRTs) dip into the Greek Isles, though the newer larger **Seabourn Odyssey** (built in 2009; 450 passengers; 32,000 GRTs) and **Seabourn Quest** (built in 2011; 450 passengers; 32,000 GRTs) offer many more Greek itineraries.

All cabins on the *Seabourn Legend* and *Pride* are outside suites, many with French balconies—sliding doors you can open to let in the ocean breezes (the ships were built before full balconies were all the rage). The other cabins have 1.5m-wide (5-ft.) picture windows, plenty big enough to make the room bright and airy. Owner's suites are plush and offer private verandas.

The *Seabourn Odyssey* and *Quest* boast verandas on 90% of all staterooms. There is a main open-eating restaurant, two alternative venues, plus a poolside grille. Enjoy a two-level state-of-the-art gym and spa, which includes a pair of spa villas.

Seabourn Cruises Itineraries & Rates

SHIP	ITINERARY
Seabourn Odyssey	**Seven-day Athens-to-Istanbul** cruise calls at Mylos, Rhodes, Patmos, Khylos, Kusadasi (Turkey). May 8; July 3; August 21. **Rates:** From $5,135.
	Seven-day Istanbul-to-Athens cruise calls at Dikili (Turkey), Kusadasi (Turkey), Bodrum (Turkey), Santorini, Mylos, Nafplion. May 15; July 10; 31; August 28. **Rates:** From $5,135.
	Seven-day Venice-to-Athens cruise calls at Sibenik (Croatia), Bari (Italy), Cephalonia, Katakolon, Gythion, Mykonos. May 29; June 26; August 14. **Rates:** From $5,530.
	Seven-day Athens-to-Istanbul, Istanbul-to-Athens and Venice-to-Athens, Athens-to-Venice cruises continue until October 23.
Seabourn Spirit	**Seven-day Civitavecchia-to-Athens** cruise calls at Sorrento (Italy), Lipari (Italy), Katakolon, Itea, Nafplion. May 8. **Rates:** From $4,260.

SEA CLOUD CRUISES

32-40 N. Dean St., Englewood, NJ 07631. ✆ **888/732-2568.** www.seacloud.com.

The flagship vessel *Sea Cloud* (built in 1931; 64 passengers; 2,532 GRTs) was built for heiress Marjorie Merriweather Post, who was involved in the design and construction of the sailing ship, planning the layout of the vessel down to where the antiques would be placed. At the time it was the largest sailing yacht to be built. The *Sea Cloud* served as a military support ship during World War II, was briefly owned by Dominican Republic dictator Rafael Trujillo, and sat tied up for 8 years before it was bought by a Hamburg-based group in the late 1970s and given a new, luxurious lease on life.

Guests can still see the care that Post originally put into it: fireplaces in the cabins, antiques, marble, and shining wood. In the owner's suite, guests sleep in a Louis XIV–style bed next to a decorative marble fireplace; the bathroom alone is 9 sq. m (97 sq. ft.). The Category 5 cabins, on the other hand, are upper-and-lower berths, but Sea Cloud points out that since the cabins open to the promenade deck guests can sleep with the doors open to let in the sea air. Sailing buffs will be happy to gaze up at the 3,973 sq. m (32,000 sq. ft.) of sail—it has 36 separate sails, from the flying jib to the mizzen royal to the jigger gaff.

Sea Cloud is often chartered by tour operators, who set their own itineraries for the ship; contact Sea Cloud for information on additional Greece cruises through tour operators. The company has a total of four vessels, including a river boat.

Sea Cloud Cruises Itineraries & Rates

SHIP	ITINERARY
Sea Cloud	**Seven-day round-trip Athens** cruise calls at Crete, Mylos, Naxos, Siros, Nafplion. May 31. **Rates:** From $4,515.
	Seven-day Athens-to-Istanbul cruise calls at Mylos, Siros, Patmos, Kusadasi (Turkey), Dikili (Turkey), Lesbos. June 7; July 9. **Rates:** From $4,515.
	Seven-day Athens-to-Istanbul cruise calls at Mylos, Santorini, Marmaris, Rhodes, Patmos, Kusadasi (Turkey). July 31. **Rates:** From $4,515.

SEADREAM YACHT CLUB

2601 S. Bayshore Dr., Penthouse 1B, Coconut Grove, FL 33133. ✆ **800/707-4911.** www.seadream yachtclub.com.

The owner and operator of SeaDream Yacht Club, Atle Brynestad, has a luxury-line pedigree as the founder of Seabourn Cruise Line. For more than 10 years, he has been carrying on the Seabourn tradition of luxury and elegance, on a smaller, more casual, yachtlike scale. SeaDream in 2001 purchased the *Sea Goddess I* and *Sea Goddess II* from Seabourn, and after renovations renamed them **SeaDream I** and **SeaDream II** (built in 1984; 116 passengers; 4,260 GRTs). Updated in 2009, the ships have all new bedding and one additional suite.

The company defines itself not as a cruise line but as an ultraluxury yacht company whose vessels journey to smaller, less-visited destinations. Guests are offered an unstructured, casually elegant vacation (no formal nights) with plenty of diversions. Toys carried aboard include jet skis and mountain bikes. You can dine outdoors or indoors; there are enough tables to accommodate all the passengers in one outdoor lunch seating. None of the cabins have private balconies, but the line often urges guests to treat the teak decks as one large veranda where you can sprawl on bed-size Balinese loungers. With advanced reservations, they will even make the beds up for you with a turn-down service so you can sleep under the stars. Another evening option is to meet for a drink at the **Top of the Yacht Bar**—SeaDream has an open-bar policy.

SeaDream Yacht Club Itineraries & Rates

SHIP	ITINERARY
SeaDream II	**Ten-day Venice (Italy) to Athens** cruise calls at Split (Croatia), Korcula (Croatia), Dubrovnik (Croatia, overnight), Kotor (Montenegro), Sarande (Albania), Delphi, Mykonos, Santorini, Hydra. May 30. **Rates:** From $6,999.
	Seven-day round-trip Athens cruise calls at Delos, Mykonos, Rhodes, Fethiye (Turkey), Gocek (Turkey), Bodrum (Turkey, overnight), Hydra. June 9. **Rates:** From $4,999.
	Seven-day round-trip Athens cruise calls at Hydra, Delphi, Olympia/Katakolon, Gythion, Elafonsios, Santorini. June 16. **Rates:** From $5,199.
	Seven-day Athens to Istanbul (Turkey) cruise calls at Hydra, Santorini, Paros Island, Patmos, Ephesus/Kusadasi (Turkey), Kepez (Turkey). June 23. **Rates:** From $5,199.
SeaDream I	**Seven-day Dubrovnik (Croatia) to Athens** cruise calls at Parga, Delphi, Hydra Patmos, Ephesus/Kusadasi (Turkey), Santorini. July 21. **Rates:** From $5,199.
	Seven-day Athens to Dubrovnik (Croatia) cruise calls at Hydra, Delphi, Parga, Sarande (Albania), Kotor (Montenegro), Kotor (Montenegro), Dubrovnik (overnight). July 28. **Rates:** From $5,199.
	Seven-day Rome (Civitavecchia, Italy) to Athens cruise calls at Capri (Italy), Sorrento (Italy, overnight), Taormina (Sicily, Italy), Fiskardho, Delphi, Hydra. August 25. **Rates:** From $5,199.
	Ten-day Athens to Istanbul (Turkey) cruise calls at Hydra, Santorini, Lindos, Antalya (Turkey), Bodrum (Turkey), Patmos, Ephesus/Kusadasi (Turkey), Kepez (Turkey), Istanbul (overnight). September 1. **Rates:** From $6,999.
	Seven-day Istanbul (Turkey) to Athens cruise calls at Kepez (Turkey), Ephesus/Kusadasi (Turkey), Patmos, Bodrum (Turkey), Rhodes, Santorini. September 22. **Rates:** From $6,199.
	Seven-day round-trip Athens cruise calls at Santorini, Lindos, Gocek (Turkey), Bodrum (Turkey), Agadir (Morocco), Hydra. September 29; October 6. **Rates:** From $4,999.

SILVERSEA CRUISES

110 E. Broward Blvd., Fort Lauderdale, FL 33301. ✆ **800/722-9055.** www.silversea.com.

The luxurious **Silver Wind** (built in 1995; 296 passengers; 16,800 GRTs) and newer and larger **Silver Spirit** (built in 2009; 540 passengers; 36,000 GRTs) carry their guests in splendor and elegance. Passengers are generally well traveled and used to the good life. Fares include all alcoholic and nonalcoholic beverages along with tips.

Aboard both the *Wind* and *Spirit*, all accommodations are outside suites with writing tables, sofas, walk-in closets, marble bathrooms, stocked minibars and all the amenities you'd expect of top-of-the-line ships. Throughout, both vessels allot more space to each passenger than most other ships. Dine on some of the best cuisine at sea in open-seating restaurants that allow you to dine when and with whom you desire. The larger Spirit boasts four restaurants, including **La Terrazza** for indoor or alfresco dining with breakfast and lunch buffets; **Le Champagne** for a six-course epicurean experience in an intimate atmosphere; **The Pool Grill** for lunch and dinner; the intimate **Seishin Restaurant** for a range of Asian fusion menu items, from Kobe beef and spider lobster to caviar and lots of sushi choices (per-person degustation menu cost is $40); and the **Stars Supper Club** where live music, dancing, and nightclub-style entertainment complement the innovative menus and provide a relaxed feeling.

Silversea Cruises Itineraries & Rates

SHIP	ITINERARY
Silver Wind	**Fourteen-day Barcelona (Spain) to Istanbul (Turkey)** cruise overnights in Barcelona and calls at Marseille (France), Monte Carlo (Monaco), Florence/Pisa (Livorno, Italy, overnight), Rome (Civitavecchia, Italy), Naples/Capri (Sorrento, Italy), Palermo (Sicily, Italy), Valletta (Malta), Crete, Athens. March 13 **Rates:** From $6,518.
	Ten-day Istanbul (Turkey) to Athens cruise calls at Canakkale (Turkey), Ephesus/Kusadasi (Turkey), Rhodes, Nazareth/Galilee (Haifa, Israel), Jerusalem/Tel Aviv (Ashdod, Israel), Cairo (Port Said, Egypt), Cairo/Giza (Alexandria, Egypt). March 27. **Rates:** From $4,678.
	Eleven-day Athens to Barcelona (Spain) cruise calls at Santorini, Valletta (Malta), Siracusa (Sicily, Italy), Palermo (Sicily, Italy), Cagliari (Sardinia, Italy), Alghero (Sardinia, Italy), Port Mahon (Menorca, Spain), Ibiza (Spain), Palma de Mallorca (Spain). April 6. **Rates:** From $5,158.
	Nine-day Istanbul (Turkey) to Athens cruise calls at Ephesus/Kusadasi (Turkey), Patmos, Rhodes, Crete, Santorini, Hydra, Mykonos. May 26. **Rates:** From $5,678.
	Nine-day Athens to Rome (Civitavecchia, Italy) cruise calls at Mylos, Zakynthos, Itea, Corfu, Gallipoli (Italy), Sorrento (Italy, overnight). June 4. **Rates:** From $5,678.
	Nine-day Istanbul (Turkey) to Athens cruise calls at Canakkale (Turkey), Ephesus/Kusadasi (Turkey), Damascus (Syria), Beirut (Lebanon), Limassol (Cyprus), Rhodes, Santorini. July 20. **Rates:** From $5,678.
	Nine-day Athens to Venice (Italy) cruise calls at Mykonos, Crete, Itea, Corfu, Kotor (Montenegro), Hvar (Croatia), Venice (overnight). July 29. **Rates:** From $5,678.
	Nine-day Venice (Italy) to Athens cruise overnights in Venice and calls at Zadar (Croatia), Dubrovnik (Croatia, overnight), Brindisi (Italy), Agrostoli, Monemvasia, Nafplion. August 25. **Rates:** From $5,678.
	Seven-day Athens to Istanbul (Turkey) cruise calls at Mykonos, Santorini, Crete, Rhodes, Ephesus/Kusadasi (Turkey). September 3. **Rates:** From $4,118.

Seven-day Istanbul (Turkey) to Athens cruise calls at Ephesus/Kusadasi (Turkey), Rhodes, Crete, Santorini, Mykonos. September 17. **Rates:** From $4,118.

Seven-day Athens to Venice (Italy) cruise calls at Monemvasia, Corfu, Kotor (Montenegro), Split (Croatia), Venice (overnight). September 24. **Rates:** From $4,118.

Nine-day Istanbul (Turkey) to Athens cruise calls at Canakkale (Turkey), Ephesus/Kusadasi (Turkey), Alanya (Turkey), Antalya (Turkey), Rhodes, Mykonos, Patmos. October 10. **Rates:** From $5,318.

Twelve-day Istanbul (Turkey) to Athens cruise calls at Ephesus/Kusadasi (Turkey), Rhodes, Limassol (Cyprus), Nazareth/Galilee (Haifa, Israel), Jerusalem/Tel Aviv (Ashdod, Israel), Cairo (Port Said, Egypt), Cairo/Giza (Alexandria, Egypt), Crete, Nafplion. October 31. **Rates:** From $6,438.

Silver Spirit

Seven-day Athens to Istanbul (Turkey) cruise overnights in Athens and calls at Crete, Rhodes, Ephesus/Kusadasi (Turkey), Mykonos. October 1. **Rates:** From $5,318.

Seven-day Istanbul (Turkey) to Athens cruise calls at Ephesus/Kusadasi (Turkey), Rhodes, Crete, Santorini, Mykonos. June 25; August 13; October 8. **Rates:** From $5,318.

Seven-day Athens to Venice (Italy) cruise calls at Monemvasia, Corfu, Kotor (Montenegro), Split (Croatia), Venice (overnight). July 2; August 20. **Rates:** From $5,318.

Seven-day Venice (Italy) to Athens cruise overnights in Venice and calls at Hvar (Croatia), Corfu, Itea, Olympia/Katakolon, Monemvasia. September 24. **Rates:** From $4,958.

Seven-day Athens to Rome (Civitavecchia, Italy) cruise calls at Monemvasia, Valletta (Malta), Catania (Sicily, Italy), Palermo (Sicily, Italy), Sorrento (Italy). October 15. **Rates:** From $4,958.

STAR CLIPPERS

7200 NW 19th St., Ste. 206, Miami, FL 33126. ✆ **800/442-0550.** www.starclippers.com.

Star Clipper (built in 1991; 170 passengers; 2,298 GRTs) is the name of the handsome old-timey vessel this three-ship line, named Star Clippers, is sending to Greece in 2012. It's a replica of the big 19th-century clipper sailing ships (or barkentines) that once circled the globe. Its tall square rigs carry enormous sails, are glorious to look at, and are a particular thrill for history buffs. And on this ship, the 3,345 sq. m (36,000 sq. ft.) of billowing sails are more than window dressing. The *Star Clipper* was constructed using original drawings and specifications of a leading 19th-century naval architect, but updated with modern touches so that today it is among the tallest (68m/226 ft.) and fastest clipper ships built.

The atmosphere onboard is akin to being on a private yacht rather than a mainstream cruise ship. It's active and casual in an L.L. Bean sort of way, and friendly too. Cabins are decorated with wood accents; the top categories have doors that open up directly onto the deck. There is one owner's suite. The public rooms include an open-seating dining room, and an Edwardian-style library with a Belle Epoque fireplace and bookshelf-lined walls. There are two small swimming pools. Local entertainment is sometimes brought aboard and movies might be shown, plus you can always count on silly contests and games at the deck bar as part of the after-dinner offerings. Other activities on the ship tend toward the nautical, such as visiting the bridge, observing the crew handle the sails, and participating in knot-tying classes. Or just padding around the decks and lying in a deck chair underneath the sails. When seas are calm you can lie in the rigging.

SHIP	ITINERARY
Star Clipper	**Seven-day round-trip Athens** cruise to the northern Greek islands calls at Camilimani (Turkey), Kusadasi (Turkey), Patmos, Amorgos, Mykonos and Monemvasia. Once a month or so between May and October. **Rates:** From $2,075.
	Seven-day round-trip Athens cruise to the southern Greek islands calls at Rhodes, Bodrum (Turkey), Daylan River (Turkey), Santorini, Hydra. Once a month or so between May and October. **Rates:** From $2,075.

SWAN HELLENIC CRUISES

Lynnem House, 1 Victoria Way, Burgess Hill, West Sussex, RH15 9NF. ℰ **800/257-5767** or 0844 871 4603. www.swanhellenic.com

This British company founded in 1954 excels in small-ship cruising and the *Minerva* (built in 1996; 320 passengers; 12,500 GRTs). The line appeals to those who really want to learn something about a destination. Escorted shore excursions are included in the fares (and so are all tips) and impressive guest lectures speak about the islands' history and culture. Called a "country house at sea," there are two open-seating restaurants, two bars, a cinema, swimming pool, gym, spa, beauty salon and beautiful tiered decks and teak promenade offering plenty of vantage points for sightseeing. For some down time, bring a book and your daydreams to the conservatory-style **Shackleton's Bar** with its cane chairs and potted palms.

Swan Hellenic Cruises Itineraries & Rates

SHIP	ITINERARY
Minerva	**Fourteen-day Sharm-El-Sheikh (Egypt) to Athens** cruise overnights in Sharm-El-Sheikh and calls at Sokhna (Egypt, overnight), Cairo/Giza (Alexandria, Egypt), Damascus (Syria), Latakia (Syria), Antalya (Turkey), Fethiye (Turkey), Santorini, Athens (overnight). April 11. **Rates:** From $3,199.
	Thirteen-day Athens to Rome (Civitavecchia, Italy) cruise overnights in Athens and calls at Itea, Olympia/Katakolon, Argostoli, Preveza, Kotor (Montenegro), Korcula (Croatia), Dubrovnik (Croatia), Palermo (Sicily, Italy), Rome (overnight). April 25. **Rates:** From $2,499.
	Fourteen-day Valletta (Malta) to Athens cruise overnights in Valletta and calls at Dubrovnik (Croatia, overnight), Korcula (Croatia), Split (Croatia), Trieste (Italy), Venice (Italy), Pula (Croatia), Kotor (Montenegro, overnight), Sarande (Albania), Itea, Athens (two overnights). August 15. **Rates:** From $3,999.
	Fourteen-day Athens to Istanbul (Turkey) cruise overnights in Athens and calls at Souda Bay, Gython, Nafplion, Delos, Mykonos (overnight), Paros Island, Chios, Symi, Fethiye (Turkey), Ephesus/Kusadasi (Turkey, overnight), Istanbul (overnight). August 29. **Rates:** From $3,899.
	Fourteen-day Izmir (Turkey) to Athens cruise overnights in Izmir and calls at Thessaloniki, Kavala/Philippi, Rhodes, Antalya (Turkey), Tasucu (Turkey), Latakia (Syria), Damascus (Syria), Limassol (Cyprus), Syros, Athens (overnight). September 26. **Rates:** From $4,199.

TRAVEL DYNAMICS INTERNATIONAL

132 E. 70th St., New York, NY 10021. ℰ **800/257-5767.** www.traveldynamicsinternational.com.

This operator of small ships offers a number of interesting itineraries that include Greek ports, and no wonder: The cofounders of Travel Dynamics are two Greek brothers from the island of Rhodes. The journeys are tailored to be unique, visiting some of the smaller and lesser known ports. Top-notch onboard educational programs complement the itineraries, and shore excursions are included in the cruise price. This line won't attract the budget-minded passenger or the folks who want to laze around. Itineraries are fast paced and educational. Each day has several components: a museum in the morning and an archaeological site in the afternoon, for example. The company's itineraries often include references to the nearby sites (Iraklion for Knossos or Gortyn, for example).

The cozy *Callisto* (built in 1992; 34 passengers; 499 tons) is adorned with rich fabrics, wood, polished brass, rare antiquities, and artwork, with cabins offering marble bathrooms, mini bars and fresh flowers. There's a swimming platform, hot tub and library as well. The larger *Corinthian II* (built in 1992; 114 passengers; 4,200 GRTs) also has luxe touches including marble bathrooms, minifridges, and private balconies. An outdoor bar and cafe accommodates alfresco diners. The ship also has a gym, salon, sun deck with hot tub, and Internet cafe.

Travel Dynamics International Itineraries & Rates

SHIP	ITINERARY
Corinthian II	**Ten-day Venice (Italy) to Limassol (Cyprus)** cruise overnights in Venice and calls at Zadar (Croatia), Dubrovnik (Croatia), Kotor (Montenegro), Corfu, Pylos, Rethymnon, Chania, Anamur Limani (Turkey), Tasucu (Turkey). April 27. **Rates:** From $8,295.
	Ten-day Limassla (Cyprus) to Istanbul (Turkey) cruise calls at Tasucu (Turkey), Antalya (Turkey), Marmaris (Turkey), Ephesus/Kusadasi (Turkey), Delos, Platamonas, Thessalonica (overnight), Canakkale (Turkey). May 17. **Rates:** From $7,995.
	Ten-day Istanbul (Turkey) to Athens cruise calls at Canakkale (Turkey), Nafplion, Pylos, Valletta (Malta), Trapani (Italy), Naples (Italy), Messina (Sicily, Italy), Ithaca. May 27. **Rates:** From $7,995.
	Eight-day Athens to Catania cruise calls at Argostoli, Lipari (Sicily, Italy), Sorrento (Italy), Agropoli (Italy), Palermo (Sicily, Italy), Marsala (Sicily, Italy), Siracusa (Sicily, Italy), Catania (Italy). June 6. **Rates:** From $7,795.
	Ten-day Rome (Civitavecchia, Italy) to Athens cruise overnights in Rome and calls at Salerno (Italy), Olympia/Katakolon, Rethymnon, Santorini, Rhodes, Ephesus/Kusadasi (Turkey), Athens (overnight). June 22; July 10. **Rates:** From $7,695.
	Ten-day Istanbul (Turkey) to Rome (Civitavecchia, Italy) cruise calls at Chios, Santorini, Rethymnon, Valletta (Malta), Marsala (Sicily, Italy), Cagliari (Sardinia, Italy), Alghero (Italy), Bonifacio (Corsica, France). July 28. **Rates:** From $7,995.
	Twelve-day Venice (Italy) to Istanbul (Turkey) cruise calls at Split (Croatia), Ploce (Croatia), Dubrovnik (Croatia), Kotor (Montenegro), Durres (Albania), Nafpaktos, Athens, Izmir (Turkey), Thessalonica, Constanta (Romania), Nessebur (Bulgaria). September 5. **Rates:** From $8,495.
	Ten-day Istanbul (Turkey) to Venice (Italy) cruise calls at Canakkale (Turkey), Ephesus/Kusadasi (Turkey), Rethymnon, Pylos, Siracusa (Sicily, Italy), Taranto (Italy), Vlore (Albania), Kotor (Montenegro), Dubrovnik (Croatia), Split (Croatia). September 17. **Rates:** From $7,985.
	Eleven-day Venice (Italy) to Athens cruise calls at Split (Croatia), Vlore (Albania), Taranto (Italy), Siracusa (Sicily, Italy), Gytheion, Agios Nikolaos, Fethiye (Turkey), Marmaris (Turkey), Bodrum (Turkey). September 27. **Rates:** From $8,495.
	Twelve-day round-trip Athens cruise overnights in Athens and calls at Santorini, Heraklion, Cairo/Port Said (Egypt), Jerusalem/Tel Aviv (Haifa, Israel), Limassol (Cyprus), Fethiye (Turkey), Marmaris (Turkey), Rhodes, Ephesus/Kusadasi (Turkey). October 7. **Rates:** From $9,395.
	Fourteen–day Athens to Casablanca (Morocco) cruise calls at Itea/Delphi, Saranda (Albania), Taranto (Italy), Calabria (Italy), Siracusa (Sicily, Italy), Valletta (Malta), Marsala (Italy), Tunis (Tunisia), Cagliari (Sardinia, Italy), Annaba (Algeria), Bejaia (Algeria), Tangier (Morocco). October 19. **Rates:** From $9,395.

continues

Callisto	**Nine-day round-trip Athens** cruise calls at Nafplion, Gytheion, Rethymnon, Santorini, Rhodes, Patmos, Ephesus/Kusadasi (Turkey), Delos. April 17; May 23. **Rates:** From $8,995.
	Nine-day round-trip Athens cruise calls at Milos, Rethymnon, Santorini, Rhodes, Didyma, Ephesus/Kusadasi (Turkey), Delos, Palea Epidavros. September 8, September 26. **Rates:** From $8,995.
	Nine-day round-trip Athens cruise calls at Ithaca, Parga, Preveza, Assos, Pylos, Kalamata, Nafplion. June 10. **Rates:** From $8,995.
	Nine-day round-trip Athens cruise calls at Folegandros, Amorgos, Nisyros, Patmos, Chios, Skopelos, Limni, Kea. June 28; July 7, July 16. **Rates:** From $8,995.
	Nine-day round-trip Athens cruise calls at Rethymnon, Chania, Aghia Galini (overnight), Ierapetra, Aghia Nicolaos, Heraklion, Santorini. August 3. **Rates:** From $8,995.
	Nine-day Kusadasi (Turkey) to Antalya (Turkey) cruise overnights in Ephesus/Kusadasi and calls at Bodrum (Turkey), Cnidos (Turkey), Symi, Rhodes, Ekincik (Turkey), Fethiye (Turkey), Castellorizo, Kekova (Turkey). October 15, October 24; November 2, November 11. **Rates:** From $8,995.

4 VARIETY CRUISES

494 Eighth Ave., 22nd Floor, New York, NY 10001. ℭ **800/319-7776.** www.varietycruises.com.

This line's Greek-flagged and -operated yachts might be just the ticket if you're looking for a casual, intimate experience with a more international flavor. Formerly known as Zeus Tours, the cruise portion of the company has been around since the mid-1960s when it chartered the yacht *Eleftherios;* it began scheduled weekly cruise service in 1973. Today, it divides its ships into three divisions. The more upmarket Variety Cruises division emphasizes a blend of cruising and yachting, relaxing, and exploring Greece's historical treasures. Ships in this fleet include the yacht *Harmony G* (built in 2001; 46 passengers; 490 GRTs).

There are sun decks but no pools except for the surrounding Mediterranean: passengers can swim off the side of the ship during swim stops. Fares include two meals a day, breakfast and then either lunch or dinner, depending on the itinerary, which gives guests the chance to eat and drink in port. There's no organized onboard entertainment per se, except for chatting with other guests in the saloon or while catching rays on deck. And with only a couple of dozen other guests, you'll probably get to know everyone within a day. Open-seating dinner helps with the mingling.

Variety Cruises Itineraries & Rates

SHIP	ITINERARY
Harmony G	**Seven-day round-trip Athens** cruise call at Nafplion/Mycenae, Gythion, Pylos, Olympia/Katakolon, Delphi. February 17, February 24; March 2, March 9, March 16, March 23; April 13. **Rates:** From $1,071.

VOYAGES TO ANTIQUITY

Frensham House, Headley Rd., Leatherhead, Surrey, KT22 8PT. ℭ **877/398-1460.** www.voyagesto antiquity.com.

The midsize ***Aegean Odyssey*** (built in 1973; 350 passengers; 11,563 GRTs) is a cozy boutique-style ship with classic lines and a retro feel. Built as a ferry, the ship was converted to a cruise ship in 1988 and extensively refurbished. Perfect for history buffs and class ship lovers, the *Aegean Odyssey* is an old-world gem, with two restaurants, six bars and lounges, a library, theater, Internet center, spa and beauty salon. Expert lecturers, often professors and historians, sail on board to educate guests about the region and fares include excursions; pre- and/or posthotel stays in Athens or Istanbul or Rome; all meals; free wine, beer or soft drinks with the evening meal; and tips. Voyages to Antiquity is geared to sophisticated travelers looking to be immersed in the destination and the focus is on education and learning.

Voyages to Antiquity Itineraries & Rates

SHIP	ITINERARY
Aegean Odyssey	**Fourteen-day Athens to Rome (Civitavecchia, Italy)** includes 2-night precruise hotel stay in Athens; cruise calls at Nauplia, Monemvasia, Heraklion, Rethimnon, Siracusa (Sicily, Italy), Valletta (Malta), Trapani (Sicily, Italy), Palermo (Sicily, Italy, overnight). March 19. **Rates:** From $3,795.
	Fifteen-day Venice (Italy) to Istanbul (Turkey) includes 2-night post-cruise hotel stay in Istanbul; cruise overnights in Venice and calls at Pula (Croatia), Split (Croatia, overnight), Korcula (Croatia), Dubrovnik (Croatia), Corfu, Monemvasia, Rethimnon, Santorini, Naxos, Lemnos. April 13. **Rates:** From $4,595.
	Fourteen-day Istanbul (Turkey) to Athens includes 2-night precruise hotel stay in Athens and 2-night post-cruise hotel stay in Istanbul; cruise calls at Lemnos, Mount Athos, Skiathos, Izmir (Turkey, overnight), Delos, Mykonos, Santorini, Rethimnon, Nauplia. April 23; August 25. **Rates:** From $4,450.
	Fifteen-day round-trip Athens included 2-night precruise hotel stay; cruise calls in Nauplia, Monemvasia, Rethimnon, Rhodes, Delos, Mykonos, Samos, Ephesus/Kusadasi (Turkey, overnight), Istanbul (Turkey, overnight), Mount Athos, Skiathos. May 2; September 3; October 16. **Rates:** From $4,695.
	Thirteen-day Athens to Venice (Italy) includes 2-night precruise hotel stay in Athens; cruise calls at Nauplia, Monemvasia, Olympia/Katakolon, Ithaca, Corfu, Sarande (Albanic), Dubrovnik (Croatia, overnight), Split (Croatia), Zadar (Croatia), Venice (overnight). May 14. **Rates:** From $4,250.
	Thirteen-day Venice (Italy) to Athens includes 2-night post-cruise hotel stay in Athens; cruise overnights in Venice and calls at Zadar (Croatia), Split (Croatia, overnight), Korcula (Croatia), Dubrovnik (Croatia), Corfu, Preveza, Olympia/Katakolon, Nauplia. June 23; October 7. **Rates:** From $4,250.
	Fourteen-day Athens to Istanbul (Turkey) includes 2-night precruise hotel stay in Athens and 2-night post-cruise hotel stay in Istanbul; cruise calls at Nauplia, Rethimnon, Santorini, Delos, Mykonos, Izmir (Turkey, overnight), Skiathos, Lemnos. July 1; September 15. **Rates:** From $4,450.
	Seventeen-day Istanbul (Turkey) to Rome (Civitavecchia, Italy) includes 2-night precruise hotel stay in Istanbul and 2-night post-cruise hotel stay in Rome; cruise calls at Lemnos, Izmir (Turkey), Delos, Mykonos, Athens, Nauplia, Taormina (Sicily, Italy), Palermo (Sicily, Italy, overnight), Sorrento (Italy, overnight). July 22. **Rates:** From $4,995.
	Seventeen-day Rome (Civitavecchia, Italy) to Istanbul (Turkey) includes 2-night precruise hotel stay in Rome and 2-night post-cruise hotel stay in Istanbul; cruise calls at Sorrento (Italy, overnight), Palermo (Sicily, Italy, overnight), Taormina (Sicily, Italy), Nauplia, Athens, Delos, Mykonos, Izmir (Turkey), Lemnos. August 13. **Rates:** From $4,995.
	Fifteen-day Istanbul (Turkey) to Venice (Italy) included 2-night precruise hotel stay in Istanbul; cruise calls at Mount Athos, Thessalonica, Volos, Patmos, Athens, Monemvasia; Preveza, Corfu, Dubrovnik (Croatia), Korcula (Croatia), Ravenna (Italy). September 24. **Rates:** From $4,750.
	Twelve-day Athens to Limassol (Cyprus) cruise overnights in Athens and calls at Nauplia, Santorini, Rethimnon, Heraklion, Rhodes, Fethiye (Turkey), Antalya (Turkey), Tasucu (Turkey). October 30. **Rates:** From $3,750.

BOOKING YOUR PRIVATE yacht CHARTER

CRUISING THE GREEK ISLANDS | **Small & Yachtlike Ships**

4

Do you imagine yourself cruising the Greek isles on a boat built for two? Or six? Maybe you fancy taking a more active role in itinerary planning? Do you love the idea of requesting that you cruise for a few hours and stop in a secluded cove for swimming? Or do you relish the thought of stepping off your 24m (80-ft.) sailing vessel in the marina and heading off to a nearby beachfront restaurant for dinner?

Greece is a great place for a private yacht charter. Altogether, there are about 6,000 isles and islands in Greek territory. You're as free as a bird; you can cruise to an island and stay as long as you like (as long as the captain says it's okay). And although yacht cruising can be expensive, it doesn't have to be. But there are a few things to keep in mind.

You could go through a travel agent who's familiar with yacht chartering, or you could find a **yacht charter broker.** Yacht charter brokers are a link between yacht owners and you—they're the ones who know the boats and the crew, the ones who will guide you through the process and take your booking. Charter brokers go to boat shows around the world to check up on yachts and companies and crew; they might have personally sailed within the area you want to go to (or know someone who has).

For more information about charter brokers, visit the **Charter Yacht Brokers** Association at **www.cyba.net**. The site has a page for prospective clients to request more information by describing their plans for a charter. Other associations for charter brokers include the **Mediterranean Yacht Brokers Association** and the **American Yacht Brokers Association.** The Greek Tourism Organization (www.gnto.gr) can also be a resource.

The yacht broker should ask questions and listen as you describe what you're looking for in a vacation. How many people are you traveling with? What are their ages—are there kids involved? Where are you interested in cruising, and when? Do you care more about visiting Greek towns and historic sites, or do you want to kick back on the boat and relax? Do you want to go ultraluxe, or are you on a tight budget? Do you want a power yacht, which is faster, or a sailing yacht, which burns less fuel? All these questions will help them plan the best route for you.

Here are a few tips:

○ Be reasonable in your **itinerary planning.** A yacht probably won't be able to get you comfortably from Athens to Mykonos to Rhodes and back in a week. Generally speaking, you'll want to stick to nearby groups of islands, such as the Ionian, Dodecanese, Cyclades, and Sporades. If you're sailing from Athens, the Saronic

WINDSTAR CRUISES

2101 Fourth Ave., Ste. 1150, Seattle, WA 98121. ℰ **87-STAR-SAIL** (877/827-7245). www.windstarcruises.com.

Although they look like sailing ships of yore, *Wind Star* and *Wind Spirit* (built in 1986 and 1988; 144 passengers; 5,350 GRTs) and their bigger sister *Wind Surf* (built in 1990; 312 passengers; 14,745 GRTs) are more like floating luxury hotels with the flair of sailing ships. These vessels feature top-notch service and cuisine, yet have a wonderful casual vibe. Million-dollar computers operate the sails, and stabilizers allow for a smooth ride.

Gulf and the Cyclades are close cruising areas. Many yachts are based in Athens, but sometimes you can have a yacht sent up to an island group, as long as you're willing to pay a relocation fee, plus fuel, in order to get it there.

○ Who's driving? There are two basic types of charters. **Crewed** means there's a crew onboard. How many crew depends on the size of the boat, as well as your own personal needs. You'll need a captain and maybe a cook, a hostess, and/or a guide. A **bareboat** charter means there's no crew, and you'll do the sailing or provide your own crew.

○ Champagne and caviar? Well, that's all part of the provisioning and the charter's costs. Different charters work differently. Some vessels work on a **half-board** basis; in other words, breakfast and lunch are included in the cost, under the assumption that passengers will want to venture off the boat for dinner and nightlife. Another way of determining costs is an **advance provisioning amount,** or APA. The APA is an amount of money paid upfront for costs associated with the charter, and it's on average about 30% of the base rate for the charter. The APA

could include fuel, crew costs, food and beverages, marina fees, Corinth Canal fees, and other extras. At the end of the cruise, the costs are tallied and the passenger either gets money back or has to pay a little more. In either case, crew gratuity is not included. Be sure to work out with your charter broker exactly what's included and what's not.

○ Party of eight (or more). You can rent a yacht for a cozy party of two, or bring a group of friends onboard—typically, the more people onboard the cheaper the cruise price works out per person. However, you're more limited in the choice of vessel once you go beyond 12 people. One solution for a big party: Charter two yachts and split the party (or if you have *lots* of friends, think about chartering one of the cruise ships listed in this chapter).

○ What vessel style? You can get a 12m (40-ft.) yacht or a 30m (100-ft.) yacht, in as modest or luxurious style as you can imagine (and afford). Another important consideration is whether you want a sleek, graceful sailing vessel or a modern, upscale power boat. Whatever you decide, there's probably a yacht out there that suits your style.

Windstar deploys its two smaller vessels, *Wind Spirit* and *Wind Star,* in the Greek islands. Casual, low-key elegance is the style. There's no set regime and no dress code above "resort casual." Most of the passengers are well heeled; the ships appeal to all ages except children. (There are no dedicated kids' facilities onboard the ships.)

The roomy outside cabins don't have balconies, but they do have large portholes. The top-level owner's cabins are slightly bigger. Refurbishments in 2009 include flatscreen TVs and DVD players; new mattresses, bedding, carpet, and curtains to the cabins; an expanded gym; and an updated spa.

A watersports platform at the stern allows for a variety of activities when the ships are docked. Entertainment is low key and sometimes includes local entertainers brought aboard at ports of call. Most of the onboard time revolves around the sun deck, plunge pool, and outdoor bar. The ships also have small casinos.

Windstar Cruises Itineraries & Rates

SHIP	ITINERARY
Wind Spirit	**Seven-day Rome (Civitavecchia, Italy) to Athens** cruise calls at Ischia (Italy), Lipari (Italy), Taormina (Sicily, Italy), Gythion, Monemvasia. April 28. **Rates:** From $2,496.
	Seven-day Athens to Istanbul (Turkey) cruise calls at Mykonos, Santorini, Rhodes, Bodrum (Turkey), Ephesus/Kusadasi (Turkey). May 5, May 19; June 2, June 16; July 14, July 28; August 25; September 8, September 22; October 6. **Rates:** From $2,949.
	Seven-day Istanbul (Turkey) to Athens cruise calls at Ephesus/Kusadasi (Turkey), Rhodes, Bodrum, Santorini, Mykonos. May 12, May 26; June 9, June 23; July 21; August 4; September 1, September 15, September 29; October 13. **Rates:** From $3,431.
	Seven-day Athens to Valletta (Malta) cruise calls at Gythion, Argostoli, Butrint National Park (Albania), Siracusa (Sicily, Italy), Gozo (Malta). June 30; August 11; October 20. **Rates:** From $2,948.
	Seven-day Valletta to Athens cruise calls at Gozo (Malta), Siracusa (Sicily, Italy), Butrint National Park (Albania), Argostoli, Gythion. July 7; August 18; October 27. **Rates:** From $3,091.
	Eight-day Athens to Rome (Civitavecchia, Italy) cruise calls at Monemvasia, Gythion, Taormina (Sicily, Italy), Lipari (Italy), Sorrento (Italy), Ischia (Italy). November 3. **Rates:** From $2,379.
Wind Star	**Seven-day Istanbul (Turkey) to Athens** cruise calls at Ephesus/Kusadasi (Turkey), Rhodes, Bodrum (Turkey), Santorini, Monemvasia. June 2, June 16, June 30; August 25; September 8, September 15, September 22, September 29; October 6, October 20. **Rates:** From $3,431.
	Seven-day Athens to Istanbul (Turkey) cruise calls at Mykonos, Santorini, Rhodes, Bodrum (Turkey), Ephesus/Kusadasi (Turkey). June 9, June 23; August 18; September 1, September 15, September 29; October 13. **Rates:** From $3,431.
	Eight-day Athens to Rome (Civitavecchia, Italy) cruise calls at Monemvasia, Gythion, Taormina (Sicily, Italy), Lipari (Italy), Sorrento (Italy), Ischia (Italy). July 7; October 27. **Rates:** From $2,756.
	Seven-day Rome (Civitavecchia, Italy) to Athens cruise calls at Ischia (Italy), Lipari (Italy), Taormina (Sicily, Italy), Gythion, Monemvasia. August 11. **Rates:** From $2,496.

BEST SHORE EXCURSIONS IN GREECE

Shore excursions are designed to help you make the most of your limited time in port by transporting you to sites of historical or cultural value, or of natural or artistic beauty. The tours are usually booked online in advance or on the first or second day of your cruise; are sold on a first-come, first-served basis; and are nonrefundable. Some lines—but not many—include shore excursions in their cruise fares.

Generally, shore excursions that take you beyond the port area are the ones most worth taking. You'll get professional commentary and avoid hassles with local transportation. In ports where the attractions are within walking distance of the pier, you may be best off touring on your own. In other cases, it may be more enjoyable to take a taxi to an attraction and skip the crowded bus tours; many lines offer private cars and vans for those who want to tour solo (or you can walk into the port and find a taxi, probably cheaper, on your own).

A few tips on choosing the best shore excursion for you, as you look through your cruise line's shore excursion information: See if the description includes sites of interest to you. Check the activity level of the tour: a "level 1" or "moderate" tour means minimal walking; a "level 3" or "strenuous" marker means you may be climbing steep steps or walking long distances—especially true in Greece, as some tours of sites and ruins require a lot of walking up steps or over uneven ground. And check the tour's length and price tag—the longer and/or more expensive the tour, in general, the more comprehensive it tends to be.

When touring in Greece, remember to wear comfortable walking shoes and bring a hat, sunscreen, and bottled water to combat the effects of the hot sun. Most lines offer bottled water for a fee as you disembark.

Also, keep in mind that some churches and other religious sites require modest attire, which means shoulders and knees should be covered.

Cruise lines tend to set shore excursion pricing and options closer to the sail date. We've included 2011 prices to give you a general idea of how much each tour will cost. Shore excursions are a revenue-generating area for the cruise lines, and the tours may be heavily promoted aboard the ship. They aren't always offered at bargain prices.

Below are selected shore excursion offerings at the major cruise ports. Keep in mind that not all the tours will be offered by every line, and prices will vary. The tour may also show up on different lines with a few variations and a different name. For more information on many of these ports, consult the relevant chapters in this book.

CORFU (KERKIRA)

See chapter 12 for complete sightseeing information.

The Achilleion & Paelokastritsa (4½ hr., $64): Visit the hilltop town of Paleokastritsa on the western side of Corfu, punctuated with olive, lemon, and cypress trees and bays and coves. Stop at the 13th-century Monastery of the Virgin Mary, on the edge of a promontory as well as Achilleion Palace, built in the late 19th century as the home of Empress Elizabeth of Austria. The palace, now owned by the Greek government, has been renovated and guests can visit the home and the gardens, which boast views of the island. The tour includes time for shopping in old Corfu Town before heading back to the ship.

4 X 4 Adventure (7 hr., $138): Get behind the wheel of a four-wheel-drive for this tour from the port (drivers must be 21 with a valid driver's license) across the island. Following a guide vehicle, you'll drive, caravan-style, along the coast and up the slopes of Pantokrator Mountain for panoramic views. Stop for sightseeing, beach visit and snacks.

Mountain Bike Expedition (4 hr., $149): Travel from the port by coach to the town of Dassia, where you'll pick up your bike. The bike tour starts with an uphill ride to Kato Korakiana, where you'll stop at a coffee shop. Bike through a narrow, paved alley to get to the town of St. Marcos, with stone houses and a Byzantine chapel. Stop here for a Greek snack and then bike downhill.

IRAKLION & AYIOS NIKOLAOS (CRETE)

See chapter 7 for complete sightseeing information.

Knossos & the Minotaur (3 hr., $75): Knossos was once the center of the prehistoric Minoan civilization; it is thought to be the basis for the mythological Minotaur's labyrinth. Today it is one of the great archaeological sites. What remains are portions of two major palaces, plus several restorations made between 2000 B.C. and 1250 B.C.; parts of the palace were rebuilt in the 20th century. Visit the excavation of the palace of King Minos; view the royal quarters, the throne room, and the queen's quarters, with its dolphin frescoes above the door. Other sites include the house of the high priest and the "small palace." Some tours include a visit to the archaeological museum, which includes artifacts from the Minoan civilization, or a stop in the town of Iraklion.

Windmills & Lassithi Plateau (4½ hr., $79): This tour takes participants up Mount Dikti to the Lassithi plateau. On the way you'll stop at the monastery of Kera, which houses Byzantine-era icons. The plateau boasts views of nearby mountains and the sailclothed windmills that irrigate the land. The tour includes about 2 hours of walking and standing, and there's considerable climbing involved. The tour includes a stop at a local restaurant.

ITEA (DELPHI)

The Mythology of Delphi (4 hr., $79): Delphi was the ancient home of the Oracle, where pilgrims came to ask questions of the Greek god Apollo. Visit the Sanctuary of Apollo to see the Temple of Apollo, where one of three Pythian priestesses gave voice to Apollo's oracles; the well-preserved amphitheater; and the Castalian Spring and the Sacred Way. Be sure to visit the museum as well. The tour includes time to shop in the village of Delphi.

KATAKOLON (OLYMPIA)

Ancient Olympia & Archaeological Museum (3 hr., $74): Visit the site of the original Olympic Games, held from 776 B.C. to A.D. 393 (and most recently used in the 2004 Olympics). View temples and altars, including the Temple of Zeus, which once housed the gold-and-ivory statue of Zeus that was one of the Seven Wonders of the Ancient World; and the original stadium, which could seat 20,000. Also included is the temple of Hera, the shrine of Pelops, the Treasuries, the gymnasium, and the Council House, where athletes took the Olympic Oath. You'll spend about an hour in the museum, viewing artifacts and sculpture and conclude the tour with a visit to the village of Olympia. Some tours feature a folkloric show or snacks in Katakolon.

MYKONOS & DELOS

See chapter 8 for complete sightseeing information.

A Visit to Delos (4 hr., $65): Delos is the small, uninhabited island just off the coast of Mykonos where, according to mythology, the gods Apollo and Artemis were born. The island was a religious center and a pilgrimage destination. Excavations have uncovered the city of Delos, and the tour explores the site, which includes marble lions, three temples dedicated to Apollo, the theater district, and the Sacred Lake, which dried up in 1926.

Historic Walking Tour of Mykonos (2½ hr., $55): A downhill walking tour of Mykonos town takes in the Archaeological Museum, the Maritime Museum, and Lena's Traditional House, which re-creates the home of a 19th-century Mykonos family.

A Day at the Beach (4 hr., $24): This tour transfer participants to one of Mykonos's public beaches, either Kalafatis Beach or Elia Beach, where you can rent a sun bed and an umbrella. Refreshments, snacks and watersports can also be purchased.

NAFPLION

Mycenae & Palamidi Castle (4 hr., $99): The area is rich with the remains of the ancient Mycenaean civilization. Drive by the ancient sites of Tiryns and come to the ruins of the ancient city of Mycenae, where excavation work begun in the 19th century eventually exposed the Lions Gate, the entrance to the city. Visit the Beehive Tomb, which gets its name from its shape. Take a shopping break at Fithia Village, then return to Nafplion and to the Palamidi Castle, which was built as a fortress by the Turks and Venetians (and later used as a prison). The castle offers views of the Argolic Gulf. *Note:* The path up consists of nearly 1,000 steps (buses can drive up to the gate).

PATMOS

See chapter 9 for complete sightseeing information.

St. John's Monastery & Cave of the Revelation (3 hr., $54): Depart the Port of Scala and travel by bus to the village of Chora and the 900-year-old, fortresslike Monastery of St. John, which overlooks the main harbor and is enclosed by fortified walls. You'll see the main church and the ecclesiastical treasures in the church and museum, including Byzantine icons, 6th-century Gospels, and frescoes in the chapel. Continue on by bus to the Cave of the Apocalypse. Niches in the wall mark the stone pillow and ledge used as a desk by St. John, said to have written the Book of Revelations here; a crack in the wall was said to have been made by the Voice of God. Refreshments are served in Scala. Visitors to the monastery must cover their shoulders; shorts are not allowed.

PIRAEUS/ATHENS

See chapter 5 for complete sightseeing information.

Athens & Cape Sounion (8 hr., $132): This tour visits the Acropolis, Athens's most prominent historical and architectural site, in the morning; after lunch, the tour continues to Cape Sounion (about a 1½–2 hr. drive from Athens), the most southern tip of the European landmass. Participants can explore the Temple of Poseidon, which is located at the top of a 60m (200-ft.) cliff and offers a panoramic view of the Saronic Gulf and the Cyclades.

Ancient Corinth and Canal Cruise (7 hr., $90): Drive past the coves of the Saronic Gulf to Isthmia, where you'll transit the Corinth Canal, a slim (30m/90-ft.-wide) waterway blasted through sheer rock in the 19th century. Explore ancient Corinth, including the Apollo Temple, Fountain of Glauke, Spring of Periander and the remains of 25-ft wide Lechaion Road. Lunch is included in the tour.

RHODES

See chapter 9 for complete sightseeing information.

Lindos Acropolis (4½ hr., $62): Travel through the scenic countryside to Lindos, an important city in ancient times. At Lindos, view the medieval walls, which were constructed by the Knights of St. John in the 14th century. Walk or take a donkey up to the ancient acropolis. Once you've reached the summit, visit the Doric Temple of Athena Lindia, built in 4th century B.C. The acropolis includes a double-winged portico, Byzantine church, and remains of the governor's quarters. The ruins are a backdrop for great views; souvenir shops can be found in the town of Lindos.

Filerimos Local Mezes & Wine Outing (3¾ hr., $63): Participants get a quick look at Rhodes Town before being driven to Filerimos, where hills are dotted with cypress, oaks, and pines. Visit Moni Filerimou and Lady of Filerimos, an Italian reconstruction of the Knights of St. John's 14th-century church, and ruins of the Temple of Athena. The tour continues to Kalithea Resort, where the thermal water was, according to story, once recommended by Hippocrates for its healing qualities; today the springs have dried up, but the area is known for swimming and scenery. There will be some time for shopping in Kalithea before you stop by a seaside taverna for local food and wine.

Walking Tour of Historic Rhodes (3½ hr., $52): Rhodes, which boasts one of the oldest inhabited medieval towns in Europe, is a great city for walking. This tour takes guests through the Old Town, a rambling collection of nearly 200 different, unnamed streets (thus a good place to have a guide). You'll see churches, the Jewish quarter, the Inns of the Knights, and other spots; you'll tour the rebuilt Palace of the Grand Masters and the Hospital of the Knights, now a museum. And you'll walk down the cobblestoned Street of the Knights, an old pathway leading from the Acropolis of Rhodes down to the port and lined with medieval towers and architecturally interesting facades.

SANTORINI (THIRA)

See chapter 8 for complete sightseeing information.

Santorini Volcano Hiking (3 hr., $70): Kameni, along the shores where volcanic rock has formed unique shapes. A half-hour hike up the crater of the volcano follows. Once you reach the crater you can rest and enjoy the views of Santorini and the caldera's cliffs. Then hike back down to the caique and sail to Palea Kemeni, a thermal spring. Here, sulfur pools can reach 98°F (36°C). There's a chance of swimming if time permits, so wear a bathing suit and bring a towel. The boat returns you to the port.

Village of Oia & Santorini Island (3½ hr., $72): Another whitewashed hilltop town is Oia, the town where so many postcard-perfect photos are taken of blue-domed, whitewashed buildings and the blue sea beyond. There are small cobblestone streets to explore; pop in at shops and cafes. A wine tasting is offered to tourgoers, as well as a walk to the cable car station at the top of Fira.

BEST SHORE EXCURSIONS IN TURKEY

The following Turkish ports of call are commonly visited on Greek itineraries. For more complete sightseeing information, pick up a copy of *Frommer's Turkey, Frommer's Turkey with Your Family,* or *Frommer's Istanbul* (all published by Wiley).

ISTANBUL

Grand Istanbul with Lunch in an Ottoman Home (9½ hr., $158): Includes the Hippodrome, once the largest chariot-race grounds of the Byzantine empire; Sultan Ahmet Mosque, also known as the Blue Mosque for its 21,000 blue Iznik tiles; the famous St. Sophia, once the largest church of the Christian world; the underground cistern, a reservoir held up by more than 300 Corinthian columns; and Topkapi Palace, the official residence of the Ottoman Sultans and home to treasures that include Spoonmaker's Diamond, one of the biggest diamonds in the world. Also visit the Grand Bazaar, with its 4,000 shops. In this version of the tour, stop for lunch in the gardens of an Ottoman house; other tours include lunch in a hotel, and/or a carpet-making demonstration.

The Blue Mosque, Hagia Sophia & the Bazaar (4 hr., $73): An example of an abbreviated tour of the previous one that visits the Blue Mosque, the Hippodrome, the Hagia Sophia, and the Grand Bazaar, as well as a carpet-making demonstration.

Scenic Bosphorus Cruise (4 hr., $59): A narrated cruise up the famous Bosphorus is a chance to view the city's most famous landmarks from the water. A visit to the Sadberk Hanim Museum is included, as well as a trip to the Grand Bazaar.

Magnificent Legacies with Visit to Spice Market (4 hr., $49): Start with a visit to the Suleymaniye Mosque, built by the architect Sinan. Continue to the Church of the Savior in Chora, now the Chora Museum, near the city's old Byzantine walls, which features mosaics and frescoes depicting biblical scenes. This tour also includes the underground cistern. At the end of the excursion you'll hit the famous spice market, where you can browse for all kinds of exotic items, from jewelry to spices and herbs.

KUSADASI

Ephesus, St. John's Basilica & Virgin Mary Shrine (7 hr., $112): This tour combines a visit to Ephesus with the House of the Virgin Mary, a chapel located in the valley of Bulbuldagi. Here is the site where the Virgin Mary is believed to have spent her last days. The site was officially sanctioned for pilgrimage in 1892. The tour also includes a visit to St. John's Basilica, another holy pilgrimage site. It is believed to be the site where St. John wrote the fourth book of the New Testament. A church at the site, now in ruins, was built by Justinian over a 2nd-century tomb believed to contain St. John the Apostle. This tour may also be offered as a full-day excursion, including lunch at a local restaurant and a visit to the museum of Ephesus.

Ephesus & Terraced Houses (4 hr.; $89): You'll see the Ephesus highlights on this tour, including the Celsus Library facade and Hadrian's Temple. You'll also view the Terrace Houses, a newly excavated area opposite Hadrian's Temple. The houses were once inhabited by Ephesus's rich and are decorated with mosaics and frescoes. The area can only be accessed by special permission, such as part of a shore excursion group.

Ruins of Miletus & Didyma (7½ hr., $89): This tour takes in the ruins that surround the region of Ephesus: Didyma, known for its Temple of Apollo; and Miletus, which includes the Bath of Faustina and a stadium built by the Greeks and expanded by the Romans to hold 15,000 spectators. A lunch at a restaurant in Didyma is included. Some tours also will include visits to Ephesus or the ancient village of Priene.

ATHENS

by Peter Kerasiotis with Sherry Marker

This is Athens: Exciting and exasperating, worldly and oh so hot, a city that attacks the senses and stirs the spirit as only the cradle of Western civilization can. Homeland to gods, goddesses, and some of history's greatest philosophers and athletes, Athens boasts glorious ancient temples such as the Acropolis and its iconic Parthenon, and beautiful beaches. Best of all, Athens has the Athenians, who welcome progress, feed on the latest trends and, true to their hedonistic roots, party with Olympian stamina.

THINGS TO DO   While you'll be itching to see the Acropolis, majestically crowned by the Parthenon, take a *siga, siga* (slowly, slowly) approach to sightseeing. Go on an architectural dig in the Acropolis Museum, explore the ancient Agora's marketplace, where democracy was born. For cool respite, head to the National Gardens and for gorgeous sunsets, perch on the peak of Lycabettus Mountain.

SHOPPING   Style-conscious Athenians browse for high-street fashion along pedestrian **Ermou** and for couture and designer jewelry in **Kolonaki** before brunch on Kolonaki Square. Skip the tourist kitsch in **Plaka** and **Monastiraki** in favor of poet/shoemaker **Stavros Melissonos'** handmade leather sandals. It's all early morning action in the 19th-century glass-and-steel **Central Market,** where stalls are laden with fresh fruit, nuts, and mounds of Aegean seafood.

NIGHTLIFE & ENTERTAINMENT   Athens is as hedonistic as its mythology suggests. **Psirri, Karitsi Square,** and **Panormou** street are pulsating districts; **Kolonaki** has fashionable bars, and born-again industrial zone **Gazi** is nightlife central. Summer means beach to Athenians—dress up for seafront cocktails and dancing in **Glyfada** and **Voula.**

RESTAURANTS & DINING   Whether it's creative Mediterranean cuisine in Michelin-starred **Spondi** or a take-out **souvlaki**—good food is taken for granted in Athens. Views of the Acropolis might distract you from the menu in **Plaka** and **Monastiraki,** where tavernas dish up Greek classics. Venture to the **Microlimano** harbor for fresh fish by the water's edge, and **Kolonaki's** trendy restaurants for a cosmopolitan feel.

ATHENS TODAY

Not too long ago, Athens used to be the city Greeks loved to hate. It had a reputation as expensive, polluted, and overcrowded, with more than five million inhabitants—over 40% of the country's population. Preparations

5

for the 2004 Olympics brought forth many changes, and the successful staging of the games imbued the ancient city and its residents with a newfound confidence that acted as a catalyst for more evolution. As they were in Barcelona, the Olympics were just what Athens needed to get its groove back. The city feels young again. Forever the city of 1,000 contradictions, Athens is one of the few ancient cities in the world where the cutting edge, the hip, and the modern can suddenly coexist so harmoniously with the classical.

Athens today is sophisticated and cosmopolitan but no matter how fascinating its current renaissance, keep in mind this is a city that has gone through countless transformations in its long and turbulent history. The city continues its urban renewal despite massive headaches. Athens saw its illegal migrant population swell to more than two million (in just 10 years), altering the demographics of several inner-city neighborhoods, spiking up petty crime, and creating an anti-immigrant sentiment just as the economy collapsed, the IMF moved in, and unemployment rose to over 16%.

The economic crisis and the government's austerity measures that have ushered in a recession, the constant fear of default and bankruptcy, and the persistent rumors of a return to the old currency, have darkened the mood in the usually festive metropolis. Athens is struggling to find its footing, but Europe's oldest city shows no signs of slowing down.

The dawn of the 21st century found the ancient city with a multitude of much-needed improvements: since the turn of the century, the city has created a vast new infrastructure; a sparkling and expanding new Metro, with immaculate stations, many of which display the artifacts found during its construction; a new international airport; miles of new roads; and a beltway that has eased the city's infamous traffic and has reduced the city's equally infamous smog.

The ancient sites have been linked together by a promenade, a sort of "boardwalk" around classical Athens, with antiquities on one side and modern-day sidewalk cafes, galleries, renovated mansions, and outdoor art installations on the other. All in all, 16km (10 miles) of downtown Athens's streets have been pedestrianized, transforming what had been one of the most pedestrian-unfriendly cities in the world into a more charming, accessible, and enjoyable city. The coastline has also been revived with a dizzying selection of cafes, restaurants, promenades, beaches, pedestrian shopping districts, and open-air nightclubs by the sea—accessible by a short tram ride from downtown.

The city's hotel scene has also gone through a renewal, with classic hotels restored to their former glory and boutique hotels continuing to pop up. The economic crisis might mean better deals can be found not only during the off-season, but year-round.

Greek cuisine continues its renaissance at the hands of talented new chefs, making Athens a haven for foodies; museums are being renovated and expanded, while several new and exceptional smaller museums have joined the impressive lineup. Galleries and art and exhibition centers continue to spring up—many housed in former warehouses and factories. The numerous industrial-to-art conversions have led to the rebirth of formerly run-down neighborhoods. Following the lead of Psirri and Thissio—two ancient neighborhoods once neglected, now the hippest downtown destinations—Gazi and Kerameikos have also risen from the ashes, going from gritty to urban chic.

As you explore Athens, try to make the city your own. Walk its streets; take in its scents; linger in its sidewalk cafes, courtyard gardens, squares, and rooftop terraces; take in a show in an ancient open-air theater, or an avant-garde performance, concert, or art exhibition at one of the new multipurpose arts complexes; enjoy a movie under the stars. Climb its mountains, swim in its waters, visit its ancient temples and Byzantine churches, try its food and its nightlife, and see as many museums as you can. Explore its ancient districts and its most modern ones, to witness an ancient city discovering its modern soul in front of your very eyes.

Take the bad in stride as well—long-term problems have been addressed, not eradicated. The smog does return from time to time (especially during heat waves) and traffic can still be fierce—so feel free to yell at the taxi driver who refuses to stop for you in a torrential rain or packs you into his taxi with many other passengers in the stifling summer heat; to mutter obscenities to yourself for getting stuck in traffic when you could have easily taken the Metro instead; and to throw up your hands in exasperation as a strike threatens to ruin your vacation—a glimpse of the floodlit Parthenon or a glass of wine on a rooftop, in an ancient quarter, or by the sea will have you back to your old self in no time.

Long after you have gone, you may feel a certain nostalgia. It is Athens, calling you back like a siren, as it has done to so many of us who have tried to leave. For anybody who has taken the time to truly get to know the city, you will find yourself longing to return. Exciting and exasperating, beautiful and gritty, ancient and modern, sultry and restless, seductive and unforgettable—welcome to my Athens.

ORIENTATION

Arriving & Departing

BY PLANE

The **Athens International Airport Eleftherios Venizelos** (© 210/353-0000; www.aia.gr), 27km (17 miles) northeast of Athens at Spata, is usually called "Venizelos" or "Spata," after the nearest town. Venizelos is a large, modern facility, with ample restrooms, interesting shops, and acceptable restaurants, but it is a serious slog from Athens; you no longer have the option of heading back into the city for a few extra hours of sightseeing if your flight is delayed, as visitors once did from the old airport. The airport has plenty to keep you busy, including a small museum with ruins found during the airport's construction and rotating art exhibits.

Neither the free brochures available around the airport, nor the airport's website can be relied on for accurate, up-to-date information. Here is a basic introduction to Athens's airport, based on information updated at press time.

ARRIVALS Most flights arrive at the main terminal, which has both an "A" and "B" area, but some flights—including most charter flights—arrive and depart from Spata's first of a projected cluster of satellite terminals. In addition, you may deplane down a steep flight of stairs onto the tarmac, where a bus will take you to the terminal. When planning what carry-on luggage to bring, remember that it can be quite a trek from your arrival point to the baggage claim area and Customs hall.

The baggage claim area has ATMs, telephones, restrooms, and luggage carts. Luggage carts cost 1€; if you see a cart attendant, he or she can make change for you. You can also use one of several free telephones in the baggage claim area to call for a porter.

If your suitcases do not greet you in the baggage claim area, proceed to a "baggage tracing" desk.

Signs in the baggage claim area indicate which route to use for Customs. Citizens of Common Market countries (EEC) do not have to go through Passport Control; citizens of non-EEC countries, such as the U.S. and Canada, must go through Passport Control.

If you are being met, you may want to rendezvous at the clearly marked Meeting Point (across from the Greek National Tourism Organization desk) between exits 2 and 3 in the main terminal Arrivals Hall.

The Pacific baggage storage (left luggage) facility is in the main terminal arrivals area; this service is officially open 24 hours a day and charges 2€ per piece per day.

Exits from the main terminal are signposted for taxi and bus connections into Athens.

GETTING INTO ATHENS   Getting into post-Olympics Athens is an entirely different experience than what it used to be. The airport is linked to the city with a six-lane expressway **(Attiki Odos),** Metro, buses, and taxis. Public transportation to and from the airport is excellent and advised (especially the Metro because buses can be slow and get stuck in traffic during rush hour once they enter the city).

By Metro   Line 3 of the Metro (**www.amel.gr;** 8€ one-way, 14€ round-trip—valid for 48 hr.; one-way fare for two people is 15€ and 20€ for three) is more convenient, less expensive, and faster than any other way of getting from the airport to downtown or vice versa. Unless you have a lot of luggage the Metro is an excellent, good-value option. Metro **line 3** serves the **city center** (where you can switch to the other lines at either Monastiraki or Syntagma stations) from the airport. The trip takes roughly 35 minutes and trains run every half-hour from 6:30am to 11:30pm. From the city to the airport (leaving from Syntagma and Monastiraki), trains run from 5:50am to 10:50pm. To get to Piraeus, switch at Monastiraki station to line 1; total travel time is about 1 hour. The airport ticket is valid for all forms of public transportation for 90 minutes; if you're approaching 90 minutes and are still in transit, simply revalidate your ticket by having it punched again. The Metro runs from 5:30am to midnight Sunday through Thursday and until 2am on Friday and Saturday.

By Suburban Railroad   The suburban railroad (**www.trainose.gr/en**) runs to and from the Larissa station, Doukissis Plakentias, with a connection to Metro line 1 at Nerantziotissa (at the Athens Mall in Marousi near the Athens Olympic Complex) and from the airport to the port of Piraeus. It might not be as convenient as line 3 to get downtown but it is more comfortable, not as crowded, and runs longer hours. Trains to the airport run from 4:30am to midnight, while the trains from the airport to the city run from 5am to 1:20am. The suburban railroad has the same pricing as the Metro; the only difference is that the return ticket is valid for a month. This is the best option to get from the airport to the port of Piraeus. Total travel time: 65 minutes.

By Bus   Buses (**www.oasa.gr**) are far slower than the Metro but they run 24 hours, and can reach areas the Metro does not, such as the coast. If you want to take a bus from the airport into central Athens, be prepared for what may be a long wait and a slow journey.

There are several bus lines running to and from destinations throughout the city. All buses depart from the designated area outside the Arrivals Hall of the main terminal building (doors 4 and 5). Bus service from the airport to Syntagma Square or to Piraeus costs about 5€. You can buy the ticket from a booth beside the bus stop or on the bus. Do *not* assume that the destination indicated on the front of the bus or on the sign at the bus stop is the actual destination of the bus. Always ask the driver where the bus is going. In theory, bus no. 95 (and, confusingly, sometimes bus no. 091) runs to Syntagma and Omonia squares before continuing to Piraeus every half-hour from 7am to 10pm (1€), and then every hour from about 10:15pm to 6:30am (5€).

By Taxi   The easiest way to get to town, you would assume, would be to take a taxi from the terminal. This is not as simple as it sounds: Greeks regard waiting in line with amusement, and getting a cab as a fiercely competitive sport. The City of Athens has created a **flat rate** from the airport to downtown Athens (Omonia Sq. and the Plaka/Makrigianni districts). Once you are in the taxi, make sure the meter is set on the correct tariff (tariff 1 is charged 5am–midnight; tariff 2 midnight–5am). For Omonoia, the price is 32€ (tariff 1); and 42€ (tariff 2); each rate **includes all additional charges** such as tolls and luggage. If you're heading for the Plaka/Makrigianni districts (at Hadrian's Gate), the rate is daytime 35€ and nighttime 50€. Depending on traffic, the cab ride can take under 30 minutes or well over an hour—something to remember when you return to the airport. Most likely you will not encounter any problems aside from city traffic. For more information check out the **Athens Taxi Info** site at **www.athenstaxi.info**. For other destinations, be sure to discuss your destination before getting into the taxi, either with an airline official or a policeman, to get the official flat rate price to your specific destination. If there's a problem with the taxi driver, you may threaten to call the police (℡ **100**).

By Car   Even though post-Olympics Athens is a radically different city—with the Metro, the railroad, and a new network of ring roads that have eased the city's notorious traffic—make no mistake, it is not an easy city to drive in, and if you're unfamiliar with the streets, it can be downright horrific. We recommend that you do not drive in Athens. If you still choose to drive into Athens, you'll pass through the region known as **Mesogeia** (the Inland). Until the new airport was built, this was one of the loveliest sections of Athens, with vineyards stretching for miles, sleepy country villages, and handsome chapels. Much of the area constituted the protected Attic Park; now, the once-protected wetlands and vineyards are being turned into new towns, subdevelopments, malls—and more roads. Numerous exits serve the most important areas of Athens.

If you plan to rent a car and head north or south, avoiding the city altogether, it's easier to do thanks to the new **National Highway.** If you're headed for Peloponnese, simply follow the signs for Elefsina. If you're headed toward northern Greece (including the city of Thessaloniki), get off at the Lamia exit.

DEPARTURES   If you are taking a taxi to the airport, ask the desk clerk at your hotel to reserve the car for you well in advance of your departure. Many taxis refuse to go to the airport, fearing that they will have a long wait before they get a return fare. Allow a minimum of an hour for the ride plus 2 hours for check-in for an international flight. Or, you can hop on Metro line 3 at Syntagma or Monastiraki, or take line 1 at Monastiraki and switch at Nerantziotissa for the suburban railroad.

For information on taxi fares to the airport, see above under "Getting into Athens."

For information on bus service to the airport from Syntagma, Ethniki Amyna, and Piraeus, see above under "Arrivals." For precise details on where to catch the airport bus from Athens to the airport, check with your hotel, the Greek National Tourism Organization, or—if you are very well organized and not too tired—at an information desk when you arrive at the airport.

The flight information screens should indicate where you check in and what departure gate to go to. Make sure that the information on your boarding pass agrees with the information on the flight information screen. There have been frequent complaints that adequate information on arrivals, departures, cancellations, delays, and gate changes is not always posted. Nonetheless, it is important to check these screens and ask at the information desks, as there are *no* flight announcements.

Last-minute changes in your departure gate are not unknown; arrive at your gate as early as possible. Your best chance of finding out about a change is at the original gate.

CONNECTING FLIGHTS   The airport authority advises you to allow a minimum of 45 minutes to make a flight connection; this should be adequate if you arrive and depart from the main terminal and do *not* have to clear Customs. Allow at least an hour (1½ hr. is even better) if you have to clear Customs or if you arrive or depart from the satellite terminal. At present, many charter flights use the satellite terminal.

AIRPORT FACILITIES   The airport has about 35 shops, ranging from chic boutiques to Travel Value to duty-free shops. There are 10 restaurants and cafes, including a food village with seven food "hubs" in the main departure lounge. A McDonald's overlooking the runways perches on the upper level of the main terminal building. As with airports around the world, both food and goods are overpriced, although the prices of books, newspapers, and magazines are reasonable.

Duty-free shops have different regulations for Intra-Schengen and Extra-Schengen passengers. In short, **Intra-Schengen** refers to flights **within the EEC; Extra-Schengen** refers to flights **outside the EEC.** If you are flying from Athens to a country outside the EEC, you may find it worthwhile to check out the duty-free prices on perfumes and spirits.

The **Greek National Tourism Organization** (abbreviated GNTO in English-speaking countries and EOT in Greece) has an information desk in the Arrivals Hall.

Hertz, Avis, and Alamo rental cars are available at the airport. *Note:* All these companies levy a steep surcharge (at least 10%) if you pick up your car at the airport rather than at their in-town offices.

Both short-term (3€ per hr.) and long-term (12€ per day) parking is available at the airport. Much of the long-term parking is a serious walk from the main terminal. If you have the proper change (unlikely), you can use a machine to pay for your ticket; otherwise, join the queue at the payment booth.

Useful telephone numbers at Athens International Airport include: Information ✆ 210/353-0000; Customs ✆ 210/353-2014; Police ✆ 210/663-5140; and First Aid ✆ 166 (from airport courtesy phones and information desks) and ✆ 210/353-9408 (from pay phones).

TRAVELING BETWEEN THE AIRPORT & PIRAEUS (PIREAS)   The suburban railroad takes 50 minutes to reach the port of Piraeus—it is the best option. Taking the Metro from the airport to Piraeus (1 hr.) requires a change at Monastiraki, so this is not recommended if you have a lot of luggage. The taxi flat rate from the airport to Piraeus is 35€ (5am–midnight) and 50€ (midnight–5am). It's important to know that boats to the islands leave from several *different* Piraeus harbors. Most ferryboats and hydrofoils (Flying Dolphins) for Aegina leave from the **Main Harbor.** Hydrofoils for other islands leave from **Marina Zea,** a vigorous half-hour walk from the Main Harbor. If you don't know which harbor your boat is departing from, tell your taxi driver your final destination and he can probably find out which harbor and even which pier you are leaving from.

In theory, buses leave the airport for Piraeus every hour (5€). The bus usually leaves passengers in Karaiskaki Square, several blocks from the harbor. The official daily schedule is as follows: **Spata-Piraeus** (E96): every 20 minutes from 5am to 7pm; every 30 minutes from 7pm to 8:30pm; every 40 minutes from 8:30pm to 5am.

Hotels near the Airport

Have an early flight out of Spata? You might consider spending the night before at **Hotel Avra** (✆ **22940/22-780;** www.hotelavra.gr), 30 to 45 minutes by taxi from the airport on the waterfront in the nearby port of Rafina. The Avra was remodeled in 2004 and has a decent restaurant (sometimes with live music). Or, you can stroll to one of Rafina's harborside restaurants and watch the fishing boats and ferries come and go as you enjoy fresh seafood. Doubles start at 100€. If you want to be at the airport itself for an early flight or late arrival, the 345-room **Sofitel Athens Airport Hotel** (✆ **210/681-0882;** www.sofitel.com) offers such creature comforts as its own restaurants, fitness club, and swimming pool. Rates are from 140€ to 220€ double.

AIRLINE OFFICES Most international carriers have ticket offices in or near Syntagma Square. Double check the location of your airline's Athens office before you leave, as these offices can move without warning. **Air Canada** is at 10 Othonos (✆ 210/322-3206). **American Airlines** is at 15 Panepistimiou (✆ 210/331-1045 or 210/331-1046). **British Airways** is at 1 Themistokleous, at 130 Leoforos Vouliagmenis, Glyfada (✆ 210/890-6666). **Delta Air Lines** is at 4 Othonos (✆ 800/4412-9506). **Lufthansa Airlines** is at 11 Leoforos Vas. Sofias (✆ 210/617-5200). **Qantas Airways** is at 2 Nikodimou (✆ 210/323-9063). **Swissair** is at 4 Othonos (✆ 210/323-5811). **Turkish Airlines** is at 19 Filellinon (✆ 210/324-6024).

Olympic, the national carrier, offers both international and domestic service and has offices just off Syntagma Square at 15 Filellinon (✆ 210/926-7555), at 6 Othonos (✆ 210/926-7444), and at 96 Leoforos Syngrou (✆ 210/926-7251 to -7254). The main reservations and information numbers are ✆ 210/966-6666 and 210/936-9111; the website is www.olympic-airways.com.

BY CAR

If you arrive by car from **Corinth** (to the southwest), the signs into Athens will direct you fairly clearly to Omonia Square, which you will enter from the west along Ayiou Konstantinou. In Omonia, signs *should* direct you on toward Syntagma Square and other points in central Athens (signs in Omonia disappear mysteriously). If you arrive from **Thessaloniki** (to the north), the signs pointing you into central Athens are few and far between. It is not a good idea to attempt this for the first time after dark. If this happens, your best bet is to look for the Acropolis and head toward it until you pick up signs for Omonia or Syntagma squares.

BY BUS

Before you start out on any bus trip, check with the **tourist police** (✆ **210/171**) or the **Greek National Tourism Organization (EOT)** office (✆ **210/870-0000;** www.visitgreece.gr) for current schedules and fares. As the Metro continues to open new stations, bus routes and fares are always changing. It's best to double-check all routes and to be prepared for fare increases. If possible, get someone to write down the name and address of your bus station in Greek; this will be a great help when you take a taxi or bus. Remember that many buses run both with and without a "0" prefix (024 and 24, for example).

There are two main stations for **KTEL,** the national bus company. **Terminal A,** 100 Kifissou (✆ **210/512-9233**), off the road out of Athens toward Corinth, handles buses to and from **the Peloponnese** and parts of **northern Greece.** A taxi here from Syntagma Square should cost 8€ to 16€; if traffic is light, the journey is less than 20 minutes, but it can take an hour. If you don't have much to carry, take public bus no. 051 to the terminal (.50€). It leaves from the corner of Zinonos and Menandrou, several blocks off Omonia Square; you can catch the same bus at the terminal for the trip into town.

Terminal B (© 210/831-7096) handles buses to and from **Central Greece** (including Delphi, Thebes, Evvia, and Meteora) and some destinations **to the north and east of Athens.** The GNTO, for reasons known best to itself, lists the address for Terminal B as 260 Liossion; this is where the bus for the terminal stops. To get to the terminal itself after you get off the bus, turn right onto Yousiou and you will see the terminal at the end of the street. Bus no. 024, which stops at Leoforos Amalias in front of the entrance to the National Gardens (a block south of Syntagma Sq.), will take you to and from the terminal for .80€. If you take this bus, tell the driver you want to get off at the bus terminal and then head right to Yousiou to reach the terminal. The **Mavromateon terminal** at Patission and Alexandras, a few hundred meters north of the Archaeological Museum, handles buses for most destinations in **Attica.**

BY TRAIN

Trains **from the south and west,** including Eurail connections via Patras, arrive at the **Peloponnese station** (**Stathmos Peloponnisou;** © 210/513-1601), about a mile northwest of Omonia Square on Sidirodromeon. Trains **from the north** arrive at **Larissa station** (**Stathmos Larissis;** © 210/529-8837), just across the tracks from the Peloponnese station on Deligianni. The Larissa station has both an exchange office (daily 8am–9:15pm) and luggage storage (daily 6:30am–9pm).

To get to the train stations, you can take the **Metro** to Larissa (line 2), close to both stations. A taxi from the center of town should cost about 10€. The Metro runs from Omonia, Syntagma, and Koukaki to the Larissa Metro station, which is near the train stations. The most central place to catch the Metro is the stop in front of the Parliament building on Syntagma Square.

You can purchase train tickets just before your journey at the train station (running the risk that all seats may be sold); at the Omonia Square ticket office, 1 Karolou (© 210/524-0647); at 17 Filellinon, off Syntagma Square (© 210/323-6747); or from most travel agents. Information (in theory in English) on timetables is available by dialing © **145** or 147.

BY BOAT

Piraeus, the main harbor of Athens's main seaport, 11km (7 miles) southwest of central Athens, is a 15-minute Metro ride from Monastiraki, Omonia, and Thissio Metro stations. The subway runs from about 5am to midnight and costs 1.40€. The far slower bus no. 040 runs from Piraeus to central Athens (with a stop at Filellinon, off Syntagma Sq.) every 15 minutes between 5am and 1am and hourly from 1am to

 Boat-to-Plane Connections

A word about making air connections after an island trip: It is unwise—even foolhardy—to allow anything less than 24 hours between your return to

Piraeus by island boat and your departure by air, as rough seas can significantly delay the trip.

5am for 1.20€. To get to Athens International Airport, you can take the X96 bus (5€), the Suburban Railroad (8€) or the metro which will require a change at Monastiraki station to line 3 (8€).

You may prefer to take a **taxi** to avoid what can be a long hike from your boat to the bus stop or subway terminal. Be prepared for serious bargaining. The normal fare on the meter from Piraeus to Syntagma should be about 15€ to 20€, but many drivers offer a flat fare, which can be as much as 30€. Pay it if you're desperate; or walk to a nearby street, hail another taxi, and insist that the meter be turned on.

If you arrive at Piraeus by hydrofoil (Flying Dolphin), you'll probably arrive at **Zea Marina** harbor, about a dozen blocks south across the peninsula from the main harbor. Even our Greek friends admit that getting a taxi from Zea Marina into Athens can involve a wait of an hour or more—and that drivers usually drive hard (and exorbitant) bargains. To avoid both the wait and big fare, you can walk up the hill from the hydrofoil station and catch bus no. 905 for 1.20€, which connects Zea to the Piraeus Metro (subway) station, where you can complete your journey into Athens. You must buy a ticket at the small stand near the bus stop or at a newsstand before boarding the bus. *Warning:* If you arrive late at night, you may not be able to do this, as both the newsstand and the ticket stand may be closed.

If you've disembarked at the port of **Rafina** (about an hour's bus ride east of Athens), you'll see a bus stop up the hill from the ferryboat pier. Inquire about the bus to Athens; it runs often and will take you within the hour to the **Areos Park bus terminal,** 29 Mavromateon, near the junction of Leoforos Alexandras and Patission. The Areos Park terminal is 1 block from the Victoria Square Metro stop and about 25 minutes by trolley from Syntagma Square. From the bus terminal, there are buses to Rafina every half-hour.

The port of **Lavrion** (℡ **22920/25-249**), 52km (32 miles) southeast of Athens, has taken over some of the itineraries from the port of Piraeus, including daily ferries and speedboats to Agios Efstratios, Alexandroupoli, Andros, Folegandros, Ios, Katapola, Kavala, Kea, Kythnos, Limnos, Milos, Mykonos, Naxos, Paros, Sikinos, Siros, and Tinos. The port's official website, www.oll.gr, is in Greek only, so check the GNTO site (see below) for more info. A taxi to Lavrio port from downtown Athens has a flat rate of 38€ (5am–midnight) and 55€ (midnight–5am). You can also get to the port by bus: Use the express lines of the interurban buses (KTEL) "Koropi station–Porto Rafti/Avlaki" or the urban buses of the area to reach the port. The price of the ticket is 5€. Also, there is a bus that can transfer you from the following Metro and suburban railway stations directly to the port: Pallini, Kantza, and Koropi.

Visitor Information

The **Greek National Tourism Organization** (**EOT** or **GNTO**) is at 7 Tsochas St., Ambelokipi (℡ **210/870-0000;** www.visitgreece.gr; Metro: Ambelokipi). The office is officially open Monday through Friday 8am to 3pm and is closed on weekends. The GNTO information desk office is at 26 Amalias (℡ **210/331-0392;** Metro: Syntagma; Mon–Fri 9am–7pm), across the street from the Gardens. There is also an information desk at the airport (℡ **210/345-0445**).

Information about Athens, free city maps, transportation schedules, hotel lists, and other booklets on many regions of Greece are available at the office in Greek, English, French, and German. The staff members often appear bored with their jobs and irritated by questions; be persistent.

Available 24 hours a day, the **tourist police** (✆ **210/171**) speak English as well as other languages, and will help you with problems or emergencies.

City Layout

As you begin to explore, you may find it helpful to look up to the **Acropolis,** west of Syntagma Square, and to **Mount Likavitos (Lycabettus),** to the northeast. From most parts of the city, you can see both the Acropolis and Likavitos, whose marble lower slopes give way to pine trees and a summit crowned with a small white church.

Think of central Athens as an almost perfect equilateral triangle, with its points at **Syntagma (Constitution) Square, Omonia (Harmony) Square,** and **Monastiraki (Little Monastery) Square,** near the **Acropolis.** The area bounded by Syntagma, Omonia, and Monastiraki squares is defined as the commercial center, from which cars are banned except for several cross streets. At one time **Omonia Square**—Athens's commercial hub—was considered the city center, but nowadays, most Greeks think of it as **Syntagma Square,** site of the House of Parliament. The two squares are connected by parallel streets, **Stadiou** and **Panepistimiou,** and where you will find the **Neoclassical University Trilogy.** (Panepistimiou is also known as Eleftheriou Venizelou.)

Flanking the Parliament building is one of Athens's most beautiful parks, the **National Gardens.** Right adjacent is the **Zappeio Hall and gardens,** another beautiful oasis in the center of the city. West of Syntagma Square, **Ermou** and **Mitropoleos** lead slightly downhill to **Monastiraki Square,** home of the city's famous flea market. From Monastiraki Square, **Athinas** leads north back to Omonia past the modern Central Market. The old warehouse district of **Psirri**—now the home of many chic galleries, cafes, and restaurants—is between Athinas and Ermou.

If you stand in Monastiraki Square and look south, you'll see the Acropolis. At its foot are the **Ancient Agora (Market)** and the **Plaka,** Athens's oldest neighborhood, many of whose street names honor Greek heroes from either classical antiquity or the Greek War of Independence. The twisting labyrinth of streets in the Plaka can challenge even the best navigators. Don't panic: The Plaka is small enough that you can't go far astray, and its side streets with small houses and neighborhood churches are so charming that you won't mind being lost. An excellent map may help (see "Street Maps," below). Also, many Athenians speak some English, and almost all are helpful to direction-seeking strangers—unless you happen to be the 10th person in as many minutes to ask where the Acropolis is when it is clearly visible.

FINDING AN ADDRESS   If possible, have the address you want written out in Greek so you can show it to your taxi driver, or ask for help from pedestrians. Most street signs are given both in Greek and a transliteration, which is a great help. Most taxi drivers carry a good Athens street guide and can usually find any destination. Increasingly, however, some Athenian cabbies are newcomers themselves to the capital and may have trouble with out-of-the-way addresses.

STREET MAPS   The free maps handed out at branches of the **Greek National Tourism Organization** have small print and poor-quality paper. You may prefer to stop at a newspaper kiosk or bookstore to pick up a copy of the Greek Archaeological Service's *Historical Map of Athens* (with maps of the Plaka and of the city center showing the major archaeological sites). The map costs about 4€.

GETTING AROUND
By Public Transportation
BY METRO

The **Metro** (**www.amel.gr**) runs from 5:30am to midnight Sunday through Thursday; on Friday and Saturday, trains run until 2am. All stations are wheelchair accessible. Stop at the Syntagma station or go to the GNTO for a system map. To travel on the Metro, buy your ticket at the station, validate it in the machines as you enter, and hang onto it until you get off. A single ticket costs 1.40€; a day pass costs 4€. Make sure you validate your ticket as you enter the waiting platform, or you'll risk a fine. Metro and bus tickets are interchangeable, except for bus E22, that heads to the coast.

Even if you do not use the Metro to get around Athens, you may want to take it from Omonia, Monastiraki, or Thissio to Piraeus to catch a boat to the islands. (Don't miss the spectacular view of the Acropolis as the subway goes aboveground by the Agora.) The harbor in Piraeus is a 5-minute walk from the Metro station. Take the footbridge from the Metro and you're there.

BY BUS & TROLLEY BUS

Although you can get almost everywhere you want in central Athens and the suburbs by bus or trolley, it can be confusing to figure out which bus to take. This is especially true now, when many bus routes change as new Metro stations open. Even if you know which bus to take, you may have to wait a long time until the bus appears—usually stuffed with passengers. Check out the **Athens Urban Transport Organisation** (📞 **185;** www.oasa.gr) for directions, timetables, route details, and maps.

If you find none of this daunting, tickets cost 1.20€ each (or 1.40€ to be combined with the Metro, trolley, and tram for up to 90 min.) and can be bought from *periptera* (kiosks) scattered throughout the city. The tickets are sold individually or in packets of 10. Tickets are good for rides anywhere on the system. **Be certain to validate** yours when you get on. *Tip:* Hold on to your ticket. Uniformed and plainclothes inspectors periodically check tickets and can levy a basic fine of 5€ or a more punitive fine of 30€ to 60€ on the spot.

If you're heading out of town and take a blue A-line bus to transfer to another blue A-line bus, your ticket will still be valid for the transfer.

In central Athens, minibus nos. 60 and 150 serve the commercial area free of charge.

Buses headed to farther points of Attica leave from **Mavromateon** on the western edge of Pedion tou Areos Park, at the western end of Leoforos Alexandras.

BY TRAM

Athens's **tram** (**www.tramsa.gr**) connects downtown to the city's coast. Though it may not be the fastest means of transport, it takes a scenic route once it hits the coast

Cultured Commuting

Allow extra time when you catch the Metro in central Athens: Three stations—**Syntagma Square, Monastiraki,** and **Acropolis**—handsomely display finds from the subway excavations in what amount to Athens's newest small museums. For more info, visit **www. amel.gr.**

and is handy for those wishing to visit the city's beaches and the coastline's attractions and nightlife. The tram runs on a 24-hour schedule Friday and Saturday and 5am to midnight Sunday through Thursday; tickets are 1.20€ (1.40€ if you wish to continue your journey with the Metro, bus, or trolley bus for up to 90 min.) and **must be validated** at the platform or inside the tram. Trams are comfortable and air-conditioned. A ride from Syntagma Square to the current last stop in seafront Voula is a little over an hour.

By Taxi

It's rumored that there are more than 15,000 taxis in Athens, but finding an empty one is not easy. Especially if you have travel connections to make, it's a good idea to reserve a radio taxi (see below). Fortunately, taxis are inexpensive, and most drivers are honest men trying to wrest a living by maneuvering through the city's endemic gridlock. However, some drivers, notably those working Piraeus, the airports, and popular tourist destinations, can't resist trying to overcharge obvious foreigners.

When you get into a taxi during the day and up until midnight, check the **meter.** Make sure it is **turned on** and set to 1 (the daytime rate) rather than 2 (the night rate). The meter will register 1€. The meter should be set on 2 (double fare) only between midnight and 5am *or* if you take a taxi outside the city limits; if you plan to do this, negotiate a flat rate in advance. The "1" meter rate is .32€ per kilometer. There's a surcharge of 1€ for service from a port or from a rail or bus station. Luggage costs .32€ per 10 kg (22 lb.). Taxis to and from the airport to downtown have a flat rate of 35€ (5am–midnight) and 50€ (midnight–5am), and 3.20€ from the airport. Don't be surprised if the driver picks up other passengers en route; he will work out everyone's share of the fare. The minimum fare is 2.80€. These prices will almost certainly be higher by the time you visit Greece.

If you suspect that you have been overcharged, ask for help at your hotel or destination before you pay the fare.

Your driver may find it difficult to understand your pronunciation of your destination; ask a hotel staff member to speak to the driver directly or write down the address so you can show it to the driver. Carry a business card from your hotel, so you can show it to the taxi driver on your return.

There are about 15 **radio taxi** companies in Athens; their phone numbers change often, so check the daily listing in "Your Guide" in the *Athens News.* Some established companies include **Athina** (© 210/921-7942), **Express** (© 210/993-4812), **Parthenon** (© 210/532-3300), and **Piraeus** (© 210/418-2333). If you're trying to make travel connections or are traveling during rush hour, a radio taxi is well worth the 2.80€ surcharge. Your hotel can call for you and make sure that the driver knows where you want to go. Most restaurants will call a taxi for you without charge.

The GNTO's pamphlet *Helpful Hints for Taxi Users* has information on taxi fares as well as a complaint form, which you can send to the **Ministry of Transport and Communication,** 13 Xenophondos, 10191 Athens. Replies to complaints should be forwarded to the *Guinness Book of World Records.*

By Car

In Athens, a car is far more trouble than convenience. The traffic is heavy, and finding a parking place is extremely difficult. Keep in mind that if you pick up your rental car at the airport, you may pay a hefty (sometimes daily) surcharge. Picking up a car in town involves struggling through Athens's traffic to get out of town. That said, we do have some suggestions to follow.

5

ATHENS | Getting Around

Alamo, Avis, Budget, Dollar, Hertz, and National all have offices at Athens International Airport.

Tip: Renting a car from abroad is invariably cheaper than negotiating for one on the spot in Athens. In fact, the savings in the rental rate usually make it worth your while to telephone or e-mail a major car-rental firm in the U.S. from Greece, if you haven't made arrangements to rent a car before you left your home country.

If you do decide to rent a car in Athens, you'll find many rental agencies south of Syntagma Square. Some of the better agencies include: **Athens Cars,** 10 Filellinon (© 210/323-3783 or 210/324-8870); **Autorental,** 11 Leoforos Syngrou (© 210/923-2514); **Avis,** 46–48 Leoforos Amalias (© 210/322-4951 to -4957); **Budget Rent a Car,** 8 Leoforos Syngrou (© 210/921-4771 to -4773); **Eurodollar Rent a Car,** 29 Leoforos Syngrou (© 210/922-9672 or 210/923-0548); **Hellascars,** 148 Leoforos Syngrou (© 210/923-5353 to -5359); **Hertz,** 12 Leoforos Syngrou (© 210/922-0102 to -0104) and 71 Leoforos Vas. Sofias (© 210/724-7071 or 210/722-7391); **Interrent-Europcar/Batek SA,** 4 Leoforos Syngrou (© 210/921-5789); and **Thrifty Hellas Rent a Car,** 24 Leoforos Syngrou (© 210/922-1211 to -1213). Prices for rentals range from 50€ to 100€ per day. *Warning:* Be sure to take full insurance and ask if the price you are quoted includes everything—taxes, drop-off fee, gasoline charges, and other fees.

On Foot

Since most of what you'll want to see and do in Athens is in the city center, it's easy to do most of your sightseeing on foot. Fortunately, Athens has created pedestrian zones in sections of the **Commercial Triangle** (the area bounded by Omonia, Syntagma, and Monastiraki squares), the **Plaka,** and **Kolonaki,** making strolling, window-shopping, and sightseeing infinitely more pleasant. **Dionissiou Areopagitou,** at the southern foot of the Acropolis, was also pedestrianized, with links to walkways past the Ancient Agora, Thissio, and Kerameikos. Still, don't relax completely, even on pedestrian streets: Athens's multitude of motorcyclists seldom respect the rules, and a red traffic light or stop sign is no guarantee that vehicles will stop for pedestrians.

Wheelchair users will find Athens challenging even though the 2004 Paralympics brought some improvements. For one, the Acropolis is finally wheelchair accessible. Ramps and platforms have been added to bus stops, railway stations, and ports, while Metro stations and sports venues are wheelchair accessible. Some central Athens streets, sites, and Metro stations have special sidewalks for the visually impaired, but making the rest of the city accessible will be quite a task. For more information contact the **Panhellenic Union of Paraplegic & Physically Challenged,** 3–5 Dimitsanis, Moschato (© **210/483-2564;** www.pasipka.gr).

[FastFACTS] ATHENS

ATMs Automated teller machines are increasingly common at banks throughout Athens. The **National Bank of Greece** operates a 24-hour ATM in Syntagma Square.

Banks Banks are generally open Monday through Thursday, 8am to 2pm and Friday 8am to 2:30pm. In summer, the exchange office at the **National Bank of Greece** in Syntagma Square (© **210/334-0015**) is open Monday through Thursday from 3:30 to 6:30pm, Friday from 3 to 6:30pm, Saturday from 9am to 3pm, and Sunday from 9am to 1pm. Other centrally located banks include **Citibank,** in Syntagma Square (☎ **210/322-7471**); **Bank of America,** 39 Panepistimiou (☎ **210/324-4975**); and **Barclays Bank,** 15 Voukourestiou (☎ **210/364-4311**). All banks are closed on the long list of Greek holidays. (See "When to Go," in chapter 2.) Most banks exchange currency at the rate set daily by the government. This rate is often more favorable than that offered at unofficial exchange bureaus. Still, a little comparison shopping is worthwhile. Some hotels offer better-than-official rates, though only for cash, as do some stores, usually when you are making a big purchase.

Business Hours Even Greeks get confused by their complicated, changeable business hours. In winter, shops are generally open Monday and Wednesday from 9am to 5pm; Tuesday, Thursday, and Friday from 10am to 7pm; and Saturday from 8:30am to 3:30pm. In summer, shops are generally open Monday, Wednesday, and Saturday from 8am to 3pm; and Tuesday, Thursday, and Friday from 8am to 2pm and 5:30 to 10pm. Most stores in central Athens, though, remain open all day.

Department stores and supermarkets are open 8am to 8pm Monday to Friday and 8am to 6pm Saturday.

Dentists & Doctors Embassies (see below) may have lists of dentists and doctors. Some English-speaking physicians advertise in the daily *Athens News.*

Embassies & Consulates **Australia,** 37 Leoforos Dimitriou Soutsou (☎ 210/870-4000); **Canada,** 4 Ioannou Yenadiou (☎ 210/727-3400 or 210/725-4011); **Ireland,** 7 Vas. Konstantinou (☎ 210/723-2771); **New Zealand,** Xenias 24, Ambelokipi (☎ 210/771-0112); **South Africa,** 60 Kifissias, Maroussi (☎ 210/680-6645); **United Kingdom,** 1 Ploutarchou (☎ 210/723-6211); **United States,** 91 Leoforos Vas. Sofias (☎ 210/721-2951, or 210/729-4301 for emergencies). Be sure to phone ahead before you go; most keep limited hours and are usually closed on their own national holidays as well as Greek ones.

Emergencies In an emergency, dial ☎ **100** for the **police** and ☎ **171** for the **tourist police.** Dial ☎ **199** to report a **fire** and ☎ **166** for an **ambulance** and the **hospital.** Athens has a **24-hour** line for foreigners, the **Visitor Emergency Assistance** at ☎ **112** in English and French. If you need an English-speaking doctor or dentist, try **SOS Doctor** (☎ **1016** or 210/361-7089). There are two medical hot lines for foreigners: ☎ **210/721-2951** (day) and 210/729-4301 (night) for U.S. citizens; and ☎ **210/723-6211** (day) and 210/723-7727 (night) for British citizens. The English-language *Athens News* (published Fri) lists some American- and British-trained doctors and hospitals offering emergency services. Most of the larger

hotels can call a doctor for you in an emergency.

KAT, the emergency hospital in Kifissia (☎ **210/801-4411** to -4419), and **Asklepion Voulas,** the emergency hospital in Voula (☎ **210/895-3416** to -3418), have emergency rooms open 24 hours a day. **Evangelismos,** a centrally located hospital below the Kolonaki district on 9 Vas. Sophias (☎ **210/722-0101**), usually has English-speaking staff on duty. If you need medical attention fast, don't waste time trying to call these hospitals: Just go. They will see to you as soon as possible.

In addition, each major hospital takes its turn each day being on emergency duty. A recorded message in Greek at ☎ **210/106** tells which hospital is open for emergency services and gives the telephone number.

Internet Access Internet cafes, where you can check and send e-mail, have proliferated in Athens almost as fast as cell-phones. Most midrange to top-end hotels have at least an "Internet corner," but for a current list of Athenian cybercafes, check out **www.athensinfoguide.com**. Also, there are several **Wi-Fi hot spots** across the city, such as Syntagma Square, Kotzia Square, Flisvos marina, and the Thission; the airport and several cafes also offer free Wi-Fi.

Luggage Storage & Lockers If you're coming back to stay, many hotels will store excess luggage while you travel. There are storage facilities at Athens International Airport, at the Metro stations in Piraeus and Monastiraki, and at the train stations.

Newspapers & Magazines The *Athens News* is published every Friday in English, with a weekend section listing events of interest; it's available at kiosks everywhere. Most central Athens newsstands also carry the *International Herald Tribune,* which has an English-language insert of highlights from the Greek daily *Kathimerini,* and *USA Today.* Local weeklies include the *Hellenic Times,* with entertainment listings, and *Athinorama* (in Greek), which has comprehensive listings of events. *Athens Best Of* (monthly) and *Now in Athens* (published every other month) have information on restaurants, shopping, museums, and galleries, and are available free in major hotels and sometimes from the Greek National Tourism Organization.

Pharmacies *Pharmakia,* identified by green crosses, are scattered throughout Athens. Hours are usually Monday through Friday, 8am to 2pm. In the evenings and on weekends, most are closed, but each posts a notice listing the location of pharmacies that are open or will open in an emergency. Newspapers such as the *Athens News* list the pharmacies open outside regular hours.

Police In an **emergency,** dial ⓒ **100.** For help dealing with a troublesome taxi driver, hotel staff, restaurant staff, or shop owner, stand your ground and call the **tourist police** at ⓒ **171.**

Post Offices The main post offices in central Athens are at 100 Eolou, south of Omonia Square; and in Syntagma Square, at the corner of 60 Mitropoleos. They are open Monday to Friday, 7:30am to 8pm, Saturday 7:30am to 2pm, and Sunday 9am to 1pm.

All post offices accept parcels, but the **Parcel Post Office** is at 4 Stadiou inside the arcade (ⓒ **210/322-8940**). It's open Monday through Friday from 7:30am to 8pm. It usually sells twine and cardboard shipping boxes. Parcels must remain open for inspection before you seal them at the post office.

You can receive correspondence in Athens c/o **American Express,** 2 Ermou, 10225 Athens, Greece (ⓒ **210/324-4975**), near the southwest corner of Syntagma Square, open Monday through Friday from 8:30am to 4pm and Saturday from 8:30am to 1:30pm. If you have an American Express card or traveler's checks, the service is free; otherwise, each article costs 2€.

Restrooms There are public restrooms in the underground station beneath Omonia and Syntagma squares and beneath Kolonaki Square, but you'll probably prefer a hotel or restaurant restroom. (Toilet paper is often not available, so carry tissue with you. Do not flush paper down the commode; use the receptacle provided.)

Safety Athens is among the safest capitals in Europe, and there are few reports of violent crimes. **Pickpocketing,** however, is not uncommon, especially in the Plaka and Omonia Square areas, on the Metro and buses, and in Piraeus. Unfortunately, it is a good idea to be wary of Gypsy children. We advise travelers to avoid the side streets of Omonia and Piraeus at night. As always, leave your passport and valuables in a security box at the hotel. Carry a photocopy of your passport, not the original.

Taxes A VAT (value-added tax) of between 4% and 18% is added onto everything you buy. Some shops will attempt to cheat you by quoting one price and then, when you hand over your credit card, they will add on a hefty VAT charge. Be wary. In theory, if you are not a member of a Common Market/E.U. country, you can get a refund on major purchases at the Athens airport when you leave Greece. In practice, you would have to arrive at the airport a day before your flight to get to the head of the line, do the paperwork, get a refund, and catch your flight.

Telephones Many public phones now accept only phone cards, available at newsstands and

Don't Count on Athens's ATMs

It is *not* a good idea to rely on ATMs in Athens, since the machines are often out of service when you need them most, particularly on holidays or during bank strikes. If your PIN includes letters, be sure that you know their numerical equivalent, as Greek ATMs do not have letters.

the **Telecommunications Organization of Greece (OTE)** offices in several denominations, currently starting at 3€. Most OTE offices and **Germanos** stores (including the one in the airport) sell cellphones and phone cards at reasonable prices; if you are in Greece for a month, you may find this a good option. Some kiosks still have metered phones; you pay what the meter records. The OTE office at 15 Stadiou, near Syntagma, is open 24 hours a day. The Omonia Square OTE, at 50 Athinas, and the Victoria Square OTE, at 85 Patission, are open Monday through Friday from 7am to 9pm, Saturday from 9am to 3pm, and Sunday from 9am to 2pm. Outside Athens, most OTEs are closed on weekends.

Tipping Athenian restaurants include a service charge in the bill, but many visitors add a 10% tip. Most Greeks do not give a percentage tip to taxi drivers, but often round up the fare; for example, you would round up a fare of 2.80€ to 3€.

WHERE TO STAY

Athens has a wide range of accommodations, from the luxurious and opulent landmarks such as the Grande Bretagne (dating from 1878), to designer chic boutique hotels, small pensions, and basic budget hotels and hostels. Nearly all hotels were renovated and updated with modern features and amenities at the very least in 2004, and new hotels appear all the time.

The Plaka

The **Plaka** district, below the Acropolis, is the most touristy—and picturesque—area of downtown Athens.

Best For: Travelers who want to be near the historic sites, to lose themselves in long walks around winding medieval streets and explore the city's oldest district.

Drawbacks: It's full of tourists—especially during high season.

EXPENSIVE

AVA Hotel & Suites ★★   With its excellent location, clean and spacious grounds and a personable and helpful staff, the AVA has stolen our hearts. This smoke-free

PRICE CATEGORIES

Very Expensive	250€ and up
Expensive	150€–250€
Moderate	80€–150€
Inexpensive	Under 80€

Athens Hotels

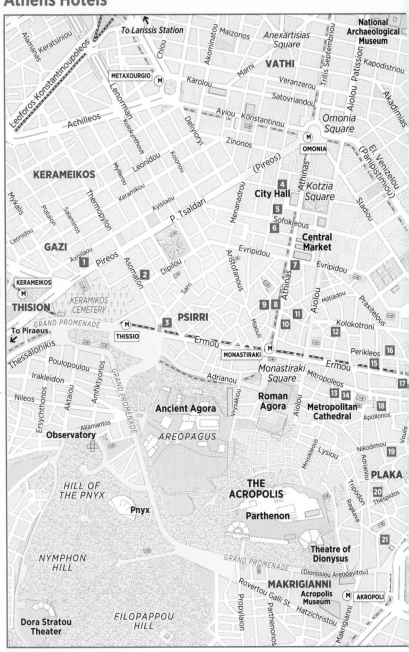

A for Athens **9**
Acropolis House Hotel **24**
Athens Center
  Square Hotel **7**
Athens Cypria **15**
Athens Lycabettus Hotel **30**
Athens Plaza (NJV) **27**
Attalos Hotel **8**
AVA Hotel & Suites **21**
Baby Grand Hotel **4**
Cecil Hotel **10**
Central Hotel **19**
Economy Hotel **5**

Electra Hotel **17**
Electra Palace **20**
Fresh Hotel **6**
Grande Bretagne **29**
Hermes Hotel **18**
Hilton Athens **33**
Hotel Achilleas **16**
Hotel Adonis **25**
Hotel Carolina **12**
Hotel Dioskouros
  (Dioskouros
  Guest House) **22**
Hotel Eridanus **1**

Hotel Plaka **13**
Hotel Tempi **11**
Jason Inn Hotel **2**
King George Palace **28**
Magna Grecia **14**
New Hotel **26**
Ochre & Brown **3**
Periscope **31**
St. George Lycabettus
  Hotel **32**
Student and Traveller's
  Inn **23**

WHAT YOU'LL really PAY

The prices quoted within this chapter are the hotel's rack rates, the maximum they can charge during the height of the season. Athens hotels have some of the lowest average room prices in Europe, so even during peak season you can often find good deals. Most hotels in town consider Easter through October high season; you can find discounts of 25% to 40% during low season. Interestingly enough, the opposite occurs with expensive and deluxe hotels downtown as upscale visitors tend to avoid Athens during the tourist rush of July and August, so you can find significant reductions in their prices during those 2 months. Deals can be found either by contacting the hotel directly, through online services such as **priceline.com** or

expedia.com, or through a reputable local travel agency. The recent economic woes in Greece have thrown the hotel industry off balance as well. Not long ago, you wouldn't have found a double in the Baby Grand Hotel (for the summer season) available for as low as 80€ and even lower online. Whether it's a sign of the bad economy or the plethora of options remains to be seen.

The best way to getting what you want is to contact the hotel directly and inform them of the prices you have found online and negotiate from there—most times they will match the online price.

Note: Quoted discount offers will seldom include breakfast, taxes, or resort fees.

hotel is actually 46 self-contained apartments all equipped with kitchenettes. The executive apartments and suites are preferable not only because they are spacious enough for four guests (perfect for a family) but because they have a living room and a large balcony with Acropolis views. The standard rooms are fine, spacious for two guests, with modern furnishings, polished wood floors, and nice-size bathrooms, but they only have a sitting room (not a separate living room) and their balconies are smaller.

9-11 Lysikratous, 10558 Athens. www.avahotel.gr. ⓒ **210/325-9000.** Fax 210/325-9001. 46 units. 180€ double; 400€ executive apt./suite. Rates include breakfast buffet. AE, DC, MC, V. Metro: Acropolis. **Amenities:** Breakfast room; concierge; room service. *In room:* A/C, TV, hair dryer, kitchenette, minibar, Wi-Fi.

MODERATE

Hotel Plaka ★★   This hotel is popular with Greeks, who prefer its modern conveniences to the old-fashioned charms of most other hotels in the area. It has a terrific location just off Syntagma Square. Most guest rooms have balconies; those on the fifth and sixth floors in the rear, where it's quieter, have views of the Plaka and the Acropolis (also visible from the roof-garden snack bar). Friends who stayed here recently were not charmed by the service, but enjoyed the location and the rooftop bar.

7 Mitropoleos and Kapnikareas, 10556 Athens. www.plakahotel.gr. ⓒ **210/322-2096.** Fax 210/322-2412. 67 units, 38 with shower only. 135€ double; 145€ triple. Rates include breakfast. AE, MC, V. Follow Mitropoleos out of Syntagma Sq. past cathedral and turn left onto Kapnikareas. **Amenities:** Bar; roof garden. *In room:* A/C, TV, hair dryer, minibar.

Magna Grecia ★★   Inside a beautiful 19th-century neoclassical building in a hard-to-beat location (right on Mitropoleos Sq.), this is easily one of the best hotels in the Plaka. You'll find high ceilings, French doors, and hardwood floors. All front rooms have sweeping Acropolis views, and there is a pleasant and relaxing **rooftop**

Hotels & Restaurants South of the Acropolis

HOTELS ■
Acropolis Hill Hotel **1**
Acropolis View Hotel **3**
Art Gallery Hotel **11**
Athens Gate Hotel **6**
Athens Studios **10**

Divani Palace Acropolis **12**
Herodion Hotel **5**
Hotel Hera **8**
Marble House Pension **14**
Royal Olympic Hotel **7**
Tony's Hotel **13**

RESTAURANTS ◆
Dionysos Zonar's **2**
Mani Mani **9**
Strofi Tavern **4**

bar as well (also with Acropolis views) that has so far gone by rather unnoticed by glamour-seeking Athenians. Rooms are named after Ionian and Aegean islands.

54 Mitropoleos, 10563 Plaka. www.magnagreciahotel.com. ✆ **210/324-0314.** Fax 210/324-0317. 12 units. 120€–145€ double; 180€ triple. AE, DC, MC, V. **Amenities:** Cafe/bar; rooftop garden; room service. *In room:* A/C, TV, DVD/CD/MP3 player, hair dryer, Internet.

INEXPENSIVE

Acropolis House Hotel ★ This small hotel in a handsomely restored 150-year-old villa retains many of its original architectural details. It offers a central location—just off Kidathineon in the heart of the Plaka, a 5-minute walk from Syntagma Square—and the charm of being on a quiet pedestrian side street. Room nos. 401 and 402 have good views and can be requested (but not guaranteed) when making a reservation. The newer wing, only 60 years old, isn't architecturally special; each unit's spartan bathroom is across the hall.

6-8 Kodrou, 10558 Athens. www.acropolishouse.gr. ✆ **210/322-2344.** Fax 210/324-4143. 19 units, 15 with bathroom. 70€ double without bathroom, 80€ double with bathroom; 104€ triple. 10€ surcharge for A/C. Rates include continental breakfast. V. Walk 2 blocks out of Syntagma Sq. on Mitropoleos and turn left on Voulis, which becomes Kodrou. *In room:* A/C, TV, Internet.

Hotel Dioskouros (aka Dioskouros Guest House)   As far as hostels go, this one is hard to beat. It's a small and intimate choice. There are no en suite bathrooms, but the place is clean and has a friendly staff, a peaceful garden, and an excellent location. Roughing it suddenly isn't so rough.

6 Pitakou, 10558 Plaka. www.hoteldioskouros.com. © **210/324-8165.** Fax 210/321-9991. 12 units, all with shared bathrooms. 50€–60€ double; 60€–80€ triple. AE, MC, V. Free parking. **Amenities:** Bar; cooking facilities (Oct–May); garden; Internet; TV area. *In room:* A/C.

Student and Traveller's Inn   On a quiet pedestrian street on the outskirts of the Plaka, the inn features a charming, casual look with four- and eight-bed dorm rooms with shared facilities, along with single, double, and triple rooms (some with en suite facilities) and a pleasant green courtyard, plus Internet access. What else do you need when you're young and on the go?

16 Kydathinaion, 10558 Athens. www.studenttravellersinn.com. © **210/324-4808.** Fax 210/321-0065. Private bathroom 65€ double, 78€ triple; shared bathroom 50€ single, 55€ double, 72€ triple. No credit cards. **Amenities:** Courtyard; Internet (shared terminals); vending machines; TV area. *In room:* A/C.

Monastiraki

The **Monastiraki** district is centrally located, close to all the sites, and busy 24 hours a day.

Best For: Travelers who want to be conveniently located but also in a "real" part of the city with all the frenzy, hustle and bustle of everyday city life. The area also has a large selection of inexpensive to moderate hotels to choose from.

Drawbacks: Surroundings get seedier the closer you get to Omonoia.

MODERATE
A for Athens ★ 🏨   This funky, hip, and modern arrival in Monastiraki has 35 rooms (apartments) with some of the best views in the city. The "Wide View" rooms (for one to three guests) all have windows facing bustling Monastiraki Square, the Plaka, and the Acropolis, and are spacious with modern decor, hardwood floors, and double-glazed windows. The "Comfy" rooms (for up to four guests) are just as nice, but face the backstreets of Psiri which are . . . well . . . not that pretty. The top floor **cafe** has some of the best city vistas around and has become a new favorite nighttime spot, particularly at sunset and after dark. The hotel has basic services but the rooms are spacious, bright, and immaculate; its location is super convenient and the views are awesome. It's a wonderful new arrival.

20 Miaouli St, 10552 Athens. www.aforathens.com. © **210/324-4244.** 35 units. 95€–150€ double. AE, MC, D, V. Metro: Monastiraki. *In room:* A/C, TV, hair dryer, minifridge.

Baby Grand Hotel ★ 🏨   The old Athens Grand Hotel underwent an extensive makeover in 2006 and reopened as Baby Grand, a "graffiti" hotel. Ten international artists were handpicked to decorate the 57 "graffiti" rooms with themes ranging from Japanese and Byzantine art to comic book art—check out the Spider-Man, Batman, and Smurfs rooms. The nongrafitti rooms are also spacious, comfortable, and contemporary. In the lobby, past the acid-green mirrors and the stainless-steel corridors, you will find the **Baby Grand Restaurant** with its reasonably priced menu and its glass floor that looks down to the pool.

65 Athinas and Lycourgou, 10551 Athens. www.classicalhotels.com. © **210/325-0900.** 76 units. 80€–120€ double; 165€ suite. Breakfast 10€. AE, DC, MC, V. Metro: Omonia/Monastiraki. **Amenities:** Restaurant/bar; gym; indoor pool; smoke-free rooms; spa; rooms for those w/limited mobility. *In room:* A/C, TV, hair dryer, minibar, Wi-Fi.

Fresh Hotel ★   What was once an undistinguished (well, ugly) hotel from the '70s has morphed into one of the coolest and most stylish designer hotels in the city. A black vertical fireplace in the reception area sets the tone for what is an ideal modern urban experience. The rooms aren't huge, but they are stylish and modern with many interesting choices, such as the armchairs that open into beds, blinds controlled from your bed, and funky colored glass dividers in the bathrooms. The **Magenta Restaurant** offers many healthy options during the day; on the ninth floor the **Air Lounge Bar** with its wooden deck and swimming pool has great city panoramas and good drinks. The only drawback is its location: a seedy street popular with the working girls at night.

26 Sofokleous and 2 Klisthenous, 10564 Athens. www.freshhotel.gr. ✆ **210/524-8511.** Fax 210/524-8517. 133 units. 110€–150€ double. AE, DC, MC, V. Parking 12€ per day. Metro: Omonia/Monastiraki. From Omonia Sq., head south along Athinas until you reach Sofokleus. From Monastiraki Sq., head north along Athinias until you reach Sofokleus. **Amenities:** Restaurant/bar; pool; minispa. *In room:* A/C, TV, hair dryer, Wi-Fi.

INEXPENSIVE

Hotel Tempi   If you believe that location is everything, consider the three-story Tempi, which faces the flower market by the Church of Ayia Irini (St. Irene) on a pedestrian street. The Tempi has simply furnished rooms (bed, table, chair), the mattresses are overdue for replacement, and the plumbing can be a problem—hot water is intermittent and the toilets can smell. But you can see the Acropolis from 10 of its balconied rooms (if you lean). This hotel is popular with students and other spartan travelers able to ignore the Tempi's drawbacks and focus on its location, rates, and handy communal kitchen facilities.

29 Eolou, 10551 Athens. www.tempihotel.gr. ✆ **210/321-3175.** Fax 210/325-4179. 24 units, 8 with bathroom. 64€ double with bathroom, 57€ (with shared bathroom); 78€ triple with bathroom. AE, MC, V. Metro: Monastiraki. *In room:* A/C, TV, Wi-Fi.

Psirri & Kerameikos

Psirri and **Kerameikos** are centrally located but a bit out of the tourist maelstrom and come alive as soon as the sun has set. **Gazi,** the undisputed king of downtown Athenian nightlife, is across the avenue from Kerameikos.

Best For: Travelers who want to be near some of the city's trendiest dining and nightlife options.

Drawbacks: Both areas are in the process of being gentrified. Outer pockets remain somewhat seedy.

EXPENSIVE

Hotel Eridanus ★   This very attractive boutique hotel (a former Athenian landmark house) feels and looks like an art gallery, with colors that alternate between shockingly bright and deeply soothing. The rooms have been tastefully furnished with modern designer touches, including funky furniture, luxurious dark green marble Indian bathrooms, original artwork, and huge beds. The well-known fish restaurant **Varoulko** next door is associated with the hotel. Some rooms have Acropolis views.

80 Piraeus, 10551 Athens. www.eridanus.gr. ✆ **210/520-5360.** 38 units. 195€ double; 285€ double deluxe with Acropolis views; 180€ junior suite. AE, MC, V. Free parking. Metro: Thissio/Kerameikos. **Amenities:** Restaurant; breakfast room; bar. *In room:* A/C, Internet TV, minibar, Wi-Fi.

Ochre & Brown ★★   This trendy, small boutique hotel in the heart of Psirri has found its niche for fashion-conscious and experienced travelers looking for style, highly personalized service, high-tech amenities, and a chic urban experience. Some rooms have Thissio views, but the finest room is the junior suite with Acropolis views from its terrace. Rooms have stylish furnishings, large work desks, Wi-Fi access, and marble bathrooms with glass-enclosed showers. The hotel's **lounge/bar** and **restaurant** have become one of the city's favorite haunts.

7 Leokoriou, 10554 Athens. www.ochreandbrown.com. © **210/331-2950.** Fax 210/331-2942. 17 units. 120€–192€ double; 208€ junior suite. AE, MC, V. Metro: Monastiraki/Thissio. **Amenities:** Restaurant; lounge bar. *In room:* A/C, TV, Wi-Fi.

Syntagma

Syntagma Square is the center and heart of Athens. It's bustling, elegant and hectic with a wide selection of hotels from classic old-timers to trendy newcomers and everything in between.

Best For: People who want to stay in the center of things.

Drawbacks: It's not a spot for relaxing, as the area is busy night and day and sometimes (say, during protest demonstrations), it can be a little too "busy."

VERY EXPENSIVE

Grande Bretagne ★★★ The Grande Bretagne, one of Athens's most distinguished 19th-century buildings, is back after a renovation that preserved the Beaux Arts lobby while making dingy rooms grand once more, and adding indoor and outdoor swimming pools. From Winston Churchill to Sting, the guests who stay here expect the highest level of attention. The Grande Bretagne prides itself on its service; you are unlikely to be disappointed. Ask for a room with a balcony overlooking Syntagma Square, the Parliament building, and the Acropolis.

Syntagma Sq., 10564 Athens. www.grandebretagne.gr. © **210/333-0000.** Fax 210/333-0160. 328 units. 277€–285€ double. AE, DC, MC, V. Metro: Syntagma. **Amenities:** 2 restaurants; 2 bars; free airport pickup; concierge; health club and spa w/Jacuzzi; 2 pools (indoors and outdoors); room service; smoke-free rooms; 1 room for those w/limited mobility. *In room:* A/C, TV, hair dryer, Internet, minibar.

King George II ★★ Next door to the beautiful Grande Bretagne, the King George II is another of Athens's great historical hotels, opulent and classy. With only 102 rooms, it feels like a personalized boutique hotel rather than an Athenian landmark. Everything is immaculate from the antiques to the modern gym/health club. The rooms are individually designed with handmade furniture, silk and satin upholstery, and spacious, gray marbled bathrooms with sunken tubs and glass-encased showers. The **Tudor Bar** on the rooftop has excellent views of the city and its landmarks, while the power Greek-dining **Tudor Restaurant** is sublime. The infamous ninth-floor penthouse suite—whose occupants have included Aristotle Onassis, Maria Callas, Grace Kelly and Prince Rainier, Marilyn Monroe, and Frank Sinatra, among others—is said to be spectacular, as it should be for the small fortune it costs to stay there.

Vas Georgiou A2, Syntagma Sq., 10564 Athens. www.lux-hotels.com. © **210/322-2210** or 210/728-0350. Fax 210/325-0564 or 210/728-0351. 220€–260€ double. AE, DC, MC, V. Metro: Syntagma. **Amenities:** Rooftop bar/restaurant; bar; health club; indoor swimming pool; smoke-free rooms; spa; rooms for those with limited mobility. *In room:* A/C, TV, Internet.

EXPENSIVE

New Hotel ★ The "Yes" (Young Enthusiastic Seductive) hotel chain, responsible for some of the city's finest and trendiest hotels ("Semiramis," "Periscope," "21") has done it again and this time right in Syntagma Square and close to the Plaka, on the site of the former Olympic Palace Hotel. Designed by award-winning Brazilian architects and brothers Fernando and Humberto Campana, this supertrendy hotel—think jagged mirrors, nice-size rooms, contemporary furnishings from recycled materials, original art pieces throughout, and balconies with side street views—is a sophisticated newcomer. As with all the aforementioned hotels of the "Yes" chain, guests receive a 10% discount at the well-regarded Zouboulakis Art Gallery.

16 Fillelinon St., 10557 Athens. www.yeshotels.gr. © **210/628-4565.** Fax 210/628-4640. 79 units. 160€–200€ double. **Amenities:** Breakfast room; bar; restaurant; gym; Internet. *In room:* A/C, TV, hair dryer, minibar, Wi-Fi.

MODERATE

Athens Cypria ★★ 🏠   In a convenient location on a (usually) quiet street, the Cypria overlooks the Acropolis from unit nos. 603 to 607. With bright white halls and rooms, cheerful floral bedspreads and curtains, and freshly tiled bathrooms with new fixtures, the Cypria is a welcome addition to the city's moderately priced hotels. The breakfast buffet offers hot and cold dishes from 7 to 10am. The hotel can be infuriatingly slow in responding to faxed reservation requests.

5 Diomias, 10562 Athens. www.athenscypria.com. © **210/323-8034.** Fax 210/324-8792. 115 units. 117€ double; 143€ triple. Reductions possible off season. Rates include buffet breakfast. AE, MC, V. Take Karayioryi Servias out of Syntagma Sq.; Diomias is on the left, after Lekka. **Amenities:** Breakfast room; bar; snack bar; luggage storage. *In room:* A/C, TV, hair dryer, Internet, minibar.

Electra Hotel ★ 🍴   On pedestrian Ermou, the Electra boasts a location that is quiet and central—steps from Syntagma Square. Most of the guest rooms have comfortable armchairs, large windows, and modern bathrooms. Take a look at your room before you accept it: Although most are large, some are quite tiny. The front desk is sometimes understaffed but the service is generally acceptable, although it can be brusque when groups are checking in and out.

5 Ermou, 10563 Athens. www.electrahotels.gr. © **210/322-3223.** Fax 210/322-0310. 110 units. 140€ double; 260€ suite. Rates include buffet breakfast. AE, DC, MC, V. Metro: Syntagma. The Electra is about 2 blocks down on the left as you walk along Ermou with Syntagma Sq. behind you. **Amenities:** Restaurant; bar. *In room:* A/C, TV, hair dryer, minibar, Wi-Fi.

INEXPENSIVE

Hotel Carolina ★★   The friendly, family-owned and -operated Carolina, on the outskirts of the Plaka, is a brisk 5-minute walk from Syntagma and has always been popular with students. In the last few years, the Carolina has undertaken extensive remodeling and now attracts a wide range of frugal travelers. Double-glazed windows and air-conditioning make the guest rooms especially comfortable. Many rooms have large balconies, and several (such as no. 308) with four or five beds are popular with families and students. The congenial atmosphere may be a bit too noisy for some.

55 Kolokotroni, 10560 Athens. www.hotelcarolina.gr. © **210/324-3551.** Fax 210/324-3350. 31 units. 90€ double; 110€ triple; 130€ quad. Rates include breakfast buffet. MC, V. Take Stadiou out of Syntagma Sq. to Kolokotroni (on left). **Amenities:** Breakfast room; bar; Internet cafe. *In room:* A/C, TV, Wi-Fi.

Kolonaki

Kolonaki has always been the posh section of downtown. Galleries, upscale shops, cafes, boutique hotels, and eateries line the trendy streets, many of them pedestrianized.

Best For: Travelers who want to be in a more cosmopolitan section of the city, ideal for shopping marathons and discovering some of the city's most eclectic dining and nightlife options. Also for those seeking to experience the city as locals do and away from most other tourists.

Drawbacks: The lack of budget accommodations and it's a bit away from the sites.

EXPENSIVE

St. George Lycabettus Hotel ★★   As yet, the distinctive, classy St. George does not get many tour groups, which contributes to its tranquil, sophisticated tone. The rooftop pool is a real plus, as is the excellently redesigned rooftop restaurant, **Le Grand Balcon,** much favored by wealthy Greeks for private events. Floors have differing decorative motifs, from Baroque to modern Italian. Most rooms look toward pine-clad Mount Likavitos; some have views of the Acropolis. Others overlook a small park or have interior views. This impeccable boutique hotel is steps from chic restaurants, cafes, lounges, and shops. Check out the **Frame** lounge in the hotel lobby after dark; this ultrahip lounge/bar is one of the hottest Athenian destinations.

2 Kleomenous, 10675 Athens. www.sglycabettus.gr. ⓒ **210/729-0711.** Fax 210/721-0439. 154 units. 148€–170€ double; 280€ suite. Continental breakfast 20€. AE, DC, MC, V. Parking 14€ per day. From Kolonaki Sq., take Patriarchou Ioachim to Loukianou and follow Loukianou uphill to Kleomenous. Turn left on Kleomenous; the hotel overlooks Dexamini Park. **Amenities:** 2 restaurants; 2 bars; concierge; pool; room service; smoke-free rooms; rooms for those w/limited mobility. *In room:* A/C, TV, hair dryer, minibar, Wi-Fi.

MODERATE

Athens Lycabettus Hotel ★   This stylish boutique hotel is on Valeoritou, a pedestrian street filled with trendy cafes, bars, restaurants, and lounges for the fashion-conscious crowd. Apart from its ideal location, the hotel has made a name for itself for its outstanding service. Rooms, though on the small side, are pleasant and bright with contemporary furnishings and nice-size marble bathrooms. The hotel also has a popular **bar/cafe restaurant.**

6 Valeoritou and Voukourestiou St., 10671 Athens. www.athenslycabettus.gr. ⓒ **210/360-0600.** 25 units. 110€–130€ double; 160€–200€ suite. Metro: Syntagma. **Amenities:** Restaurant/bar; Wi-Fi. *In room:* A/C, TV, hair dryer, minibar.

Periscope ★   The Periscope is a concept hotel with an unusual concept: surveillance. The 22 guest rooms, spread over six floors, are all black and white with large beds, industrial-style bathrooms, and ceilings decorated with aerial pictures of Athens taken from a helicopter. The penthouse suite has exclusive use of the rooftop deck with its Jacuzzi and breathtaking views of the city, including the Acropolis and Mount Lycabettus all the way to Piraeus. The **lobby bar** broadcasts live images of the city on huge flatscreen monitors—the images are shot from the **rooftop bar,** by a camera which is controlled by loungers in the lobby area. This has led to a lively bar scene. The neighborhood is upscale, with many posh boutiques, stylish cafes and eateries nearby. The hotel's restaurant (π) is one of the most popular in the city.

22 Haritos, 10675 Athens. www.yeshotels.gr. ⓒ **210/623-6320.** Fax 210/729-7206. 22 units. 127€–136€ double; 204€ suite. AE, DC, MC, V. **Amenities:** Cafe/bar; restaurant, gym; smoke-free rooms. *In room:* A/C, TV, DVD player, minibar, Wi-Fi.

Embassy District (Museum Mile)

The **Embassy** district (or **Museum Mile**) near trendy Kolonaki, is home to some of the city's finest museums and galleries as well as the **Athens Music Hall.**

Best For: Travelers who want to be a bit out of the tourist frenzy but minutes away via Metro from the sites. It's also close to some of the city's finer smaller museums and the fashionable Kolonaki district.

Drawbacks: The lack of budget accommodations.

EXPENSIVE

Hilton Athens ★★★　The Hilton remains one of the best hotels in the city. Small shops, a salon, cafes, and restaurants surround the glitzy lobby. The guest rooms (looking toward either the hills outside Athens or the Acropolis) have large marble bathrooms and are decorated in the generic but comfortable international Hilton style, with some Greek touches. The Plaza Executive floor of rooms and suites offers a separate business center and a higher level of service. Facilities include a large outdoor pool, conference rooms, and a spa. Even if you're not staying here, you can dine at the superb **Milos** seafood restaurant and **Byzantinon** restaurant and have a drink around sunset at the **Galaxy** rooftop bar with its impressive city views. For 15€, visitors can use the pool for the day. Ask about special/promotional rates before booking.

46 Leoforos Vas. Sofias, 11528 Athens. www.hilton.com. ✆ **800/445-8667** in the U.S., or 210/728-1000. Fax 210/728-1111. 527 units. 179€–339€ double; 274€ triple. AE, DC, MC, V. Parking 27€ per day. Metro: Evangelismos. **Amenities:** 4 restaurants; 3 bars; free airport pickup; babysitting; concierge; health club and spa w/Jacuzzi; 2 pools (outdoor and indoor); room service; smoke-free rooms/floors; rooms for those w/limited mobility. *In room:* A/C, Internet TV, hair dryer, minibar, Wi-Fi.

Koukaki & Makrigianni (Near the Acropolis)

The **Makrigianni** district is home to the **Acropolis Museum** and a stone's throw away from the **Plaka** and the **Acropolis. Markigianni** and **Koukaki** have a wide variety of accommodations, are largely residential and centrally located to all the sites.

Best For: Travelers who want to be conveniently located to the sites, the **Plaka,** and the **Archaeologial Promenade** and still feel as if they're locals.

Drawbacks: The area is becoming very popular with tourists. This might be an advantage or a drawback for some.

MODERATE/EXPENSIVE

Athens Gate Hotel ★　This small boutique accommodation is stylish, elegant and close to the sights and the metro. The seven-floor hotel has 99 rooms; the front rooms on the busy Leof. Syngrou have Temple of Olympian Zeus views; you'll find a partial view of the Acropolis from the lower-floor back rooms (which are also quieter); the rooms on the seventh floor have spectacular Acropolis and city views. The rooms are comfortable and spacious with polished wood floors, modern furnishings, comfortable beds, and good-size bathrooms. The top floor **restaurant** with its spellbinding views is also a major plus.

10 Syngrou Ave., Makrigianni, 11742 Athens. www.athensgate.gr. ✆ **210/923-8302.** Fax 210/237-4993. 99 units. 130€–185€ double; 195€ triple. Rates include breakfast buffet. AE, DC, MC, V. Metro: Akropolis. **Amenities:** Restaurant; 2 bars/cafe; concierge; room service; smoke-free rooms. *In room:* A/C, TV, hair dryer, Internet, minibar.

Divani-Palace Acropolis ★★　Just 3 blocks south of the Acropolis, in a quiet residential neighborhood, this place does a brisk tour business but also welcomes independent travelers. The bland guest rooms are large and comfortable, and some of the large bathrooms even have two washbasins. The cavernous marble-and-glass lobby contains copies of classical sculpture; a section of Athens's 5th-century-B.C. defensive wall is preserved behind glass in the basement by the gift shop. The breakfast buffet is extensive, the hotel's two restaurants are quite good (particularly the summer-only rooftop **Acropolis Secret Roof Garden**) and the outdoor pool is a nice touch.

19–25 Parthenonos, Makrigianni, 11742 Athens. www.divaniacropolis.gr. ☎ **210/922-2945.** Fax 210/921-4993. 253 units. 110€–180€ double; 300€ suite. Rates include breakfast buffet. AE, DC, MC, V. Metro: Akropolis. **Amenities:** 2 restaurants; 2 bars; concierge; outdoor pool; room service; smoke-free rooms. *In room:* A/C, TV, hair dryer, Internet, minibar.

MODERATE

Acropolis Hill ★   This boutique hotel, near the Filopappos Hill (Hill of the Muses), is pretty, spacious, clean, and in a quiet location. Here you'll find nice rooms with modern furnishings and polished wood floors, marble bathrooms, and many of the rooms on the top floor have balconies commanding Acropolis views. There's also a nice **rooftop restaurant/bar** and a small outdoor pool. It's up a rather steep hill, if that makes a difference to you.

7 Mouson, Filopappou, 11742 Athens. www.acropolishill.gr. ☎ **210/923-5151.** Fax 210/924-7350. 36 units. 130€ double; 150€ triple. Rates include breakfast buffet. AE, DC, MC, V. Metro: Syngrou-Fix. From Syngrou-Fix station ascend Drakou St. for a few blocks to Mouson St. and turn left. **Amenities:** 2 restaurants; 2 bars; concierge; outdoor pool; room service; smoke-free rooms. *In room:* A/C, TV, hair dryer, minibar, Wi-Fi.

Hera Hotel ★ 🔰   The Hera has a stunning indoor courtyard behind its breakfast room and great views of the Acropolis from its rooftop garden where the elegant **Peacock Lounge** has become one of the most popular bar/restaurants in the city—especially a little after sunset for its breathtaking views. The units are comfortable and tastefully furnished; the ones on the fourth floor and the suites on the fifth floor have the best views and large verandas.

9 Falirou, Makrigianni, 11742 Athens. www.herahotel.gr. ☎ **210/923-6682.** Fax 210/923-8269. 38 units. 135€ double; 180€ junior suite. AE, DC, MC, V. Free parking. Metro: Akropolis. **Amenities:** 2 cafe/bar/restaurants (1 on the rooftop); shared Internet terminal; smoke-free rooms; rooms for those w/limited mobility. *In room:* A/C, TV, hair dryer, Internet.

INEXPENSIVE

Art Gallery Hotel   Once home to several artists, this small hotel in a 50-year-old house maintains an artistic flair (and an old-fashioned cage elevator). Rooms are small and plain but comfortable, many with polished hardwood floors and ceiling fans. A Victorian-style breakfast room on the fourth floor is furnished with marble-topped tables and velvet-covered chairs. The top-floor **bar/lounge** has beautiful views of Filopappou Hill and the Acropolis.

5 Erechthiou, Koukaki, 11742 Athens. www.artgalleryhotel.gr. ☎ **210/923-8376.** Fax 210/923-3025. 22 units. 70€–100€ double; 80€–100€ triple. 7€ buffet breakfast. AE, MC, V. Metro: Syngrou-Fix. *In room:* A/C, TV.

Athens Studios 📱   You wouldn't realize that Athens Studios is a hostel if I hadn't told you. Located on Veikou street, down the Makrigianni pedestrian block from the Acropolis Metro station between a laundromat and the fun and affordable Athens Sports Bar, the studio apartments come with either two or four beds (some with six), and are bright, modern, and spacious, each with a kitchenette and balcony. The higher floor apartments have larger balconies and better views but all in all, this is a wonderful place in a great location with a warm homey feel to it that won't break the bank.

3a Veikou, Makigianni, 11742 Athens. www.athensstudios.gr. ☎ **210/923-5811.** 15 units. 60€–65€ double. AE, MC, V. Metro: Akropolis. *In room:* A/C, TV, Internet.

Marble House Pension ★   Named for its marble facade, which is usually covered with bougainvillea, this small hotel, whose front rooms offer balconies overlooking quiet Zinni Street, is famous among budget travelers (including many teachers) for its friendly staff. Over the last several years, the pension has been remodeled and redecorated, gaining new bathrooms and guest-room furniture (including small fridges). Two units have kitchenettes. If you're spending more than a few days in Athens, this is a homey base.

35 A. Zinni, Koukaki, 11741 Athens. www.marblehouse.gr. ✆ **210/923-4058.** Fax 210/922-6461. 16 units, 12 with bathroom. 45€ double without bathroom; 49€ double with bathroom. 9€ supplement for A/C. Monthly rates available off season. No credit cards. Metro: Syngrou-Fix. **Amenities:** 2 rooms for those w/limited mobility. *In room:* A/C (9 units), TV, minibar.

Practical Hotel Information

THE BIG PICTURE

Athens hotel rooms come in basically the same size as most of their European counterparts and generally smaller than their U.S. ones. Athens has a large range of accommodations, from luxury historic hotels to designer boutiques and everything else in between, nearly all of them offer the same amenities, including at the very least an Internet corner if not Wi-Fi in the room, comfortable bathrooms (again on the small size), decent beds, a minibar, and a large number of the rooms have balconies.

On the whole Athens hotels are less expensive per average than the rest of Europe and bargains can be found even during peak season.

GETTING THE BEST DEAL

High season is considered from Easter to October with the height of the season between July and late September but deals can be found even then if you begin your search early enough. If you're making your plans last minute you can also find quite decent deals especially if you're willing to compromise and not stay in Makrigianni and the Plaka districts. At press time, the best deals were to be found in or near Omonoia Square, including some hotels recommend in previous editions, like the Melia Athens and the Art Hotel. All three are exceptional and offer very good deals but are in a part of town that can get unpleasant, if not dangerous, after dark which prompted their removal from the list. If Omonoia ever comes back to life again and the hotels manage to survive the area's downgrading, we will certainly include them again. Deals for all hotels, can be found online but its best to contact the hotel personally and negotiate the online deal you have found or have a reputable local travel agency do the work for you. **Off-peak season** visitors will discover a cooler (temperature wise) Athens with less tourists, far less crowded sites and great deals.

Reservation Services: To get the best deals in town, you will need a reputable local travel agency that will do the hard work for you. Thankfully Athens has many, but our three favorites are: **Fantasy Travel,** 19 Filelinon (✆ 210/331-0530; www.fantasy-travel.gr); **CHAT Tours,** 4 Stadiou (✆ 210/323-0827; www.chatours.gr); and **Key Tours,** 4 Kalliroïs (✆ 210/923-3166; www.keytours.gr).

Alternative Accommodations: Athens has many hotel options (including the hostels recommended), but you can also rent or swap apartments, if you're in town for a longer stay. In that case, popular websites to check out would be **www.expatriates.com**, **www.vacationrentals.com**, **www.craigslist.gr**, **www.homeaway.com**, and **www.worldhomeexchanges.com**. As always, proceed with care, and if a deal sounds too good to be true, it probably is.

WHERE TO EAT

Epicurian Athens is a foodie's delight, from the old-fashioned tavernas to the trendiest gourmet eateries; world cuisines are nicely represented as well. The plethora of

PRICE CATEGORIES

Very Expensive	100€ and up
Expensive	40€–100€
Moderate	20€–40€
Inexpensive	Under 20€

dining options is dizzying and the settings range from city sidewalks, quiet courtyards and gardens, verandas with breathtaking Acropolis and city views to dining on the beach. A meal in Athens, particularly dinner, is to be relished, never rushed and preferably enjoyed alfresco.

The Plaka

Some of the most charming old restaurants in Athens are in the Plaka—as are some of the worst tourist traps. Here are a few things to keep in mind when you head off for a meal in the Plaka.

Some restaurants station waiters outside who pursue you with an unrelenting sales pitch. The hard sell is almost always a giveaway that the place caters to tourists. (That said, remember that announcements of what's for sale are not invariably ploys reserved for tourists. If you visit the Central Market, you'll see and hear stall owners calling out the attractions of their meat, fish, and produce to passersby—even waving particularly tempting fish and fowl in front of potential customers.)

In general, it's a good idea to avoid places with floor shows; many charge outrageous amounts (and levy surcharges not always stated on menus) for drinks and food. If you get burned, stand your ground, phone the **tourist police** (𝄞 **171**), and pay nothing before they arrive. Often the mere threat of calling the tourist police has the effect of causing a bill to be lowered.

MODERATE

Daphne's ★★ CONTEMPORARY GREEK Frescoes adorn the walls of this neoclassical 1830s home, which includes a shady garden courtyard displaying bits of ancient marble found on-site. Diners from around the world sit at Daphne's tables. The courtyard makes it a real oasis in Athens, especially when summer nights are hot. The food here—recommended by the *New York Times, Travel + Leisure,* and just about everyone else—gives you all the old favorites with new distinction (try the zesty eggplant salad), and combines familiar ingredients in innovative ways (delicious hot pepper and feta cheese dip). We could cheerfully eat the hors d'oeuvres all night. We have also enjoyed the *stifado* (stew) of rabbit in *mavrodaphne* (sweet-wine) sauce and the tasty prawns with toasted almonds. Live music plays unobtrusively in the background on some nights. The staff is attentive, endearing, and beyond excellent.

4 Lysikratous. 𝄞/fax **210/322-7971.** www.daphnesrestaurant.gr. Reservations recommended. Main courses 30€–40€, with some fish priced by the kilo. AE, DC, MC, V. Daily 7pm–1am.

INEXPENSIVE

Damigos (The Bakaliarakia) ★★ GREEK/SEAFOOD This basement taverna, with enormous wine barrels in the back room and an ancient column supporting the roof in the front room, has been serving deep-fried codfish and eggplant, as well as chops and stews, since 1865. The wine comes from the family vineyards. There are few pleasures greater than sipping retsina (if you wish, you can buy a bottle to take away) while you watch the cook turn out meal after meal in his absurdly small kitchen. Don't miss the *skordalia* (garlic sauce), good with cod, eggplant, bread—well, you get the idea.

41 Kidathineon. ☏ **210/322-5084.** Main courses 6€–18€. No credit cards. Daily 7pm to anytime from 11pm–1am. Usually closed June–Sept. From Syntagma Sq., head south on Filellinon or Nikis to Kidathineon; Damigos is downstairs on the left just before Adrianou.

Giouvetsakia ★ TRADITIONAL GREEK   Run by the same family since 1950, this traditional taverna at a bustling junction is perfect for people-watching in a scenic environment while enjoying some delicious, traditional fare. Try the Giouvetsi (stewed lamb in orzo—still the house's specialty and its namesake) and be sure to leave room for the complimentary fruit dish topped with cinnamon.

144 Adrianou and Thespidos. ☏ **210/322-7033.** Main courses 6€–18€. MC, V. Daily 10am–2am.

Kouklis Ouzeri (To Yerani) ★ GREEK/MEZEDES   Besides Kouklis Ouzeri and To Yerani, Greeks call this old favorite with its winding staircase to the second floor the "Skolario" because of the nearby school. Sit down at one of the small tables and a waiter will present a large tray with about a dozen plates of *mezedes*—appetizer portions of fried fish, beans, grilled eggplant, *taramasalata* (fish roe dip), cucumber-and-tomato salad, olives, fried cheese, sausages, and other seasonal specialties.

14 Tripodon. ☏ **210/324-7605.** www.sholarhio.gr. Appetizers 5€–18€. No credit cards. Daily 11am–2am. From Syntagma Sq., head south on Filellinon or Nikis to Kidathineon; take Kidathineon across Adrianou to Thespidos and climb toward Acropolis; Tripodon is 1st street on right after Adrianou.

Paradosiako ★ TRADITIONAL GREEK   Off the fringes of Plaka, removed from the tourist traps, is this great little place offering traditional fare (its name translates to "traditional"). We recommend the inexpensive and quite delicious whole grilled calamari and the baked chickpeas, but everything on the menu is quite tasty.

44A Voulis. ☏ **210/321-4121.** Main courses 7€–15€. No credit cards. Mon–Sat 10am–2am; Sun 10am–9pm.

Platanos Taverna ★★ TRADITIONAL GREEK   In good weather, this taverna on a quiet pedestrian square puts its tables beneath a plane tree (*platanos* means plane tree). Inside, where locals usually congregate to escape the summer sun at midday and where tourists gather in the evening, you can enjoy the old paintings and photos on the walls. The Platanos has been serving good *spitiko fageto* (home cooking) since 1932, and has managed to keep its regulars happy while enchanting visitors. If artichokes or spinach with lamb are on the menu, you're in luck: They're delicious. The casseroles (either lamb or veal with spinach or eggplant) are especially tasty. The wine list includes a wide choice of bottled wines from many regions of Greece, although the house wine is tasty. Plan to come here and relax, not rush, through a meal.

A Note on Credit Cards (or Bring Cash)

Many Athenian restaurants still do not accept credit cards, especially tavernas and "lower brow" places.

4 Diogenous. ☏ **210/322-0666.** Fax 210/322-8624. Main courses 7€–15€. No credit cards. Mon–Sat noon–4:30pm and 8pm–midnight; also Sun in Mar–May and Sept–Oct noon–4:30pm. From Syntagma Sq., head south on Filellinon or Nikis to Kidathineon. Turn right on Adrianou, and take Mnissikleos up 1 block toward the Acropolis; turn right onto Diogenous.

Athens Restaurants

5

ATHENS   Where to Eat

122

Kouklis Ouzeri
(To Verani) **20**
Kuzina **30**
Mamakas **7**
Mani Mani **18**
Melliotos **54**
Meson El Mirador **3**
Milos **50**
Nikitas **34**
O Santorinios **15**
Oineas **33**
Papandreou **38**
Paradosiako **24**
Platanos Taverna **23**
Prosopa **9**
Rhodia **51**
Sardelles **8**
Spondi **52**
Strofi Taverna **17**

EXARCHEIA
NEAPOLIS
National Library
University of Athens
Athens Academy
LIKAVITOS HILL
Rack Railway (Funicular) **45**
KOLONAKI
Kolonaki Square
SYNTAGMA
Syntagma Square
Parliament
NATIONAL GARDEN
Zappeion
Presidential Palace
National Art Gallery
Temple of Olympian Zeus
Panathenian Stadium
GRAND PROMENADE (Vas. Olgas)

Metro:
PANEPISTIMIO
SYNTAGMA
EVANGELISMOS
ZAPPEION

Ta Kioupia **47**
Taverna Skalas **43**
Taverna Tou Psiri **36**
Taverna Xinos **53**
Telis **39**
Thanasis **28**
To Kafeneio **49**
To Kouti **29**
To Omorfo **60**
To Ouzadiko **58**
To Prytaneion **57**
To Stekitouilia **12**
Tou Psiara **22**
Tzitzikaskai Mermigas **55**
Varoulko **6**
Vlassis **46**

ⓘ Information
Metro:
Ⓜ — Line 1
Ⓜ — Line 2
Ⓜ — Line 3
Ⓛ — Light Rail

5

Taverna Xinos ★ TRADITIONAL GREEK   Hidden just off Plaka's main square, where it has been run for over 70 years by the same family, is this little gem, offering traditional, home-cooked meals specializing in lamb dishes. Try it fricasseed (with lemon sauce) or stewed with pasta (Giouvetsi) or grilled. According to family lore, this taverna is where my grandfather proposed to my grandmother as a strolling duo serenaded them with Greek love songs accompanied by the accordion. Though I am certain it isn't the same pair of musicians, a duo still serenades diners nightly with beautiful love songs of a long-gone but not quite forgotten era. In warm weather you can dine in the tree-lined courtyard; in winter, warm yourself by the coal-burning stove and admire the frescoes.

4 Geronta. ℂ **210/322-1065.** Main courses 6€–18€. No credit cards. Daily 8pm to anytime from 11pm–1am; sometimes closed Sun. Usually closed part of July and Aug. From Syntagma Sq., head south on Filellinon or Nikis to Kidathineon; turn right on Geronta and look for the XINOS sign in the cul-de-sac.

Tou Psara ★ GREEK/SEAFOOD   One of the few remaining places in the Plaka that remains a cut above its tourist-trap neighbors, this spot is tucked away in a quiet corner under blooming mulberry trees. This might just be the only seafood option in Plaka seriously worth considering. The marinated octopus is truly out of this world.

16 Erechtheos and 12 Erotokritou. ℂ **210/321-8733.** Main courses 7€–18€. No credit cards. Daily noon–2am.

Monastiraki

MODERATE

Abyssinia Cafe ★ TRADITIONAL GREEK   This small cafe in a ramshackle building sports a nicely restored interior featuring lots of gleaming dark wood and polished copper. It faces Abyssinia Square off Ifaistou, where furniture restorers ply their trade and antiques shops sell everything from gramophones to hubcaps. You can sit indoors or out with a coffee, but it's tempting to snack on Cheese Abyssinia (feta scrambled with spices and garlic), mussels and rice pilaf, the marinated anchovies, or wild boar *keftedes* (meatballs). Everything is reasonably priced, but it's easy to run up a tab, because everything is so good—especially the *mezedes* that are superior to the main courses. For a quieter experience, book a table on the mezzanine with its awesome views.

7 Kinetou, Plateia Abyssinia, Monastiraki. ℂ **210/321-7047.** Appetizers and main courses 10€–29€. MC, V. Tues–Sat 11am–midnight; Sun 11am–7pm. Closed mid-July to mid-Aug. Metro: Monastiraki. Abyssinia Sq. is just off Ifaistou (Hephaistos) across from Ancient Agora's entrance on Adrianou.

To Kouti ★ CONTEMPORARY GREEK   Located along Adrianou Street next to the Ancient Agora, this place is great for people-watching. To Kouti (the Box) looks like children decorated it with bright-colored crayons—even the menu is handwritten on brightly illustrated children's book covers. Beyond decor, To Kouti has an unusual but tasty menu: Try the beef in garlic and honey or the shrimp in carrots, or opt for some of its vegetarian dishes. The homemade bread is served in (of course) boxes.

23 Adrianou, Monastiraki. ℂ **210/321-3229.** Main courses 15€–30€. AE, MC, V. Daily 1pm–1am. Metro: Monastiraki.

INEXPENSIVE

Bliss ★ MEDITERRANEAN/ORGANIC   Three levels in this extremely popular all day multiuse space include a wonderful cafe/restaurant that serves delicious organic fare: teas, coffee, smoothies, sandwiches, salads, and Greek taverna main courses; beginning with their first-rate breakfast. There's also yoga and alternative therapy rooms, a New Age bookstore, and gift shop.

24A Romvis St., Monastiraki. ✆ **210/325-0360.** www.purebliss.gr. Appetizers and main courses 5€–15€. MC, V. Daily 7am–2am. Metro: Monastiraki/Thissio.

Dioskouri ★ GREEK MEZEDES   On busy Adrianou—ideal for its Acropolis, Agora, and Temple of Hephaestus views, not to mention the countless passers-by—Dioskouri has been serving tasty seafood and meat *mezedes* at affordable prices for many years, becoming a favorite for locals and tourists alike.

37 Adrianou, Monastiraki. ✆ **210/325-3333.** Appetizers 5€–15€. No credit cards. Daily 11am–1am. Metro: Monastiraki/Thissio.

Diporto GREEK   This little place, sandwiched between olive shops, serves salads, stews, and delicious *revithia* (chickpeas) and *gigantes* (butter beans), both popular Greek winter dishes among stall owners, shoppers, and Athenians who make their way to the market for cheap and delicious food.

Central Market, Athinas. No phone. Main courses 8€–18€. No credit cards. Mon–Sat 6am–6pm. Metro: Monastiraki.

James Joyce Pub IRISH/AMERICAN   Yes, it's an Irish pub in downtown Athens, with excellent American-style buffalo wings, burgers, and stuffed potato skins; Irish dishes such as Connaught lamb chops and grilled salmon; great salads—and, of course, lots of beer. The James Joyce also has an excellent Irish breakfast and it's one of the few places where one can watch NFL football games and U.S. baseball as well as European soccer matches.

12 Astiggos, Monastiraki. ✆ **210/323-5055.** www.jjoyceirishpubathens.com. Main courses 9€–19€. No credit cards. Daily 9am–2am. Metro: Monastiraki/Thissio.

Papandreou GREEK   The butcher, the baker, and the office worker duck past the sides of beef hanging in the Meat Hall and head to this hole in the wall for zesty tripe dishes. Don't like tripe? Don't worry: Their menu offers choices that don't involve it. Papandreou has a virtually all-male clientele during the daytime but it's infamous for its early morning after-club crowd.

Central Market, Athinas. ✆ **210/321-4970.** Main courses 8€–18€. Daily 24 hr. Metro: Monastiraki.

Thanasis ★ GREEK/SOUVLAKI   Thanasis serves terrific souvlaki and pita—and exceptionally good french fries—both to go and at its outdoor and indoor tables. As always, prices are higher if you sit down to eat. On weekends, it often takes the strength and determination of an Olympic athlete to get through the door and place an order here. It's worth the effort: This is both a great budget choice and a great place to take in the local scene, which often includes a fair sprinkling of Gypsies.

69 Mitropoleos (just off the northeast corner of Monastiraki Sq.). ✆ **210/324-4705.** Main courses 6€–15€. No credit cards. Daily 9am–2am.

Psirri

EXPENSIVE/MODERATE

Godzilla ★ JAPANESE   For those late nights where drinking has left you ravenous but you can't stomach another souvlaki, Godzilla is the perfect option. Decorated like a Tokyo subway station, Godzilla is a great sushi bar whose popularity skyrocketed recently, but it remains reasonably priced and as tasty as ever. Sundays are a great deal for the hungry, with an all-you-can-eat lunch buffet for 27€ per person.

5 Riga Palamidou, Psirri. ✆ **210/322-1086.** Main courses 30€–40€. MC, V. Daily 9pm–2:30am.

Kuzina ★★ CONTEMPORARY GREEK   With seating on busy, beautiful pedestrian Adriannou with its views of the Temple of Hephaestus, the Agora, and the Acropolis, this gem of contemporary Greek cuisine has exceptional dishes, impeccable service, and a roof garden terrace to die for. The impressive menu does no wrong—everything we tried was excellent. Steamed mussels, dumplings with feta cheese and pomegranate syrup, crab cakes, grilled pork chops, and the grilled salmon with fennel pie were all outstanding, but our favorite was the yellowfin tuna sashimi and the lobster tail over Greek noodles. The wine list is impressive and the views amazing. There also is an art gallery on the second floor.

9 Adriannou St, Psirri. ✆ **210/324-0133.** www.kuzina.gr. Main courses 15€–35€. DC, MC, V. Daily 1pm–1am. Metro: Thissio/Monastiraki.

INEXPENSIVE

Nikitas ★★ TRADITIONAL GREEK   Amid all the new and glitzy bars and bar/restaurants of this hip area, Nikitas stands alone as an old-time, traditional taverna featuring its delicious classic fare all throughout the day and late into the night. A must.

19 Agion Anargyron, Psirri. ✆ **210/325-2591.** Main courses 6€–18€. No credit cards. Daily 10am–7pm. Metro: Monastiraki/Thissio.

Oineas ★★ TRADITIONAL GREEK   Delightful and delicious, this taverna in Psirri is popular with tourists and locals alike—the stamp of approval from both camps is deserved. The unusual appetizers (fried feta in light honey) may conspire to make you forget to order any main dishes, but don't—you can't go wrong in any of your selections here.

9 Aisopou. Psirri. ✆ **210/321-5614.** Main courses 8€–18€. DC, MC, V. Mon–Fri 7pm–2am; Sat–Sun noon–2am. Metro: Monastiraki.

Taverna Tou Psiri ★★ TRADITIONAL GREEK   The oldest taverna in Psiri is still one of the best in the area. You'll find delicious traditional taverna fare (the lamb chops are particularly good), hearty salads, good house wine, live music, moderate prices, and a nice outdoor garden.

12 Eshylou, Psirri. ✆ **210/321-4923.** Main courses 8€–18€. DC, MC, V. Daily 10am–2am. Metro: Thissio/Monastiraki.

Tellis ★ TRADITIONAL GREEK   It lacks style and decor (to put it mildly), but the hordes of locals couldn't care less with such delicious fare in this extraordinary meaterie, which serves gigantic portions at budget prices. The grilled lamb chops with oven-roasted lemon potatoes are amazing. Salads are good, too.

86 Evripidou, Psirri. ✆ **210/324-2775.** Main courses 6€–15€. No credit cards. Mon–Sat 9am–1am. Metro: Monastiraki.

Gazi, Kerameikos, Thissio & Petralona
VERY EXPENSIVE

Varoulko ★★★ INTERNATIONAL/SEAFOOD   This is widely considered the Athens area's finest seafood restaurant. We had one of our most memorable meals here—smoked eel; artichokes with fish roe; crayfish with sun-dried tomatoes; monkfish livers with soy sauce, honey, and balsamic vinegar—and the best sea bass and monkfish we have eaten. Sweetbreads, goat stew, and tripe soup have joined seafood on the menu. In summer there's a rooftop terrace with a gorgeous view of the Acropolis.

80 Piraios, Athens. ✆ **210/522-8400.** www.varoulko.gr. Reservations necessary several days in advance. Dinner for 2 from about 120€; fish priced by the kilo. DC, MC, V. Mon–Sat about 8pm–midnight. Metro: Kerameikos.

EXPENSIVE

Funky Gourmet ★ CONTEMPORARY GREEK   Housed in a beautiful neoclassical building, Funky Gourmet was a hit upon arrival. The gorgeous restaurant also has fine cuisine and, as the name suggests, a playful menu. Highlights on a recent visit included the beef filet in tartar sauce with mashed potatoes, exceptional lobster with pasta, and duck with mushrooms and cashew nuts. The desserts were out of this world, particularly the Black Forest cake.

13 Paramythias and Salaminos, Kerameikos. ⓒ **210/524-2727.** www.funkygourmet.com. Reservations essential. Main courses 31€–39€. AE, DC, MC, V. Tues–Sat 8:30pm–midnight. Metro: Kerameikos.

MODERATE

Butcher Shop ★ GREEK GRILL   As the name suggests, this postmodern taverna/grill house, on the city's hippest street between Sardelles and Mamacas, is a haven for meat lovers: tender pork chops, steaks, *biftekia* (burgers), grilled and roasted (organic) chicken, a myriad of sausages (try the wild boar sausages), wonderful meat soups, and large salads—with a rich selection of cheeses from all over Greece (try the Kasseri from the island of Lesbos) and the freshest vegetables.

19 Persefonis, Gazi. ⓒ **210/341-3440.** Main courses 15€–30€. No credit cards. Daily noon–1am. Metro: Kerameikos.

Chez Lucien ★ FRENCH/BELGIAN   Off pedestrian Apostolou Pavlou and tucked away in one of Thissio's many charming side streets (leading to Ano Petralona), you will find this popular French bistro with a small but excellent menu and a symposium-like atmosphere. They don't take reservations, so be prepared to wait and even share a table—it's worth the wait. Menu highlights include the French onion soup and the crème brûlée.

32 Troon, Petralona. ⓒ **210/346-4236.** Main courses 15€–30€. No credit cards. Tues–Sat 8pm–2am. Metro: Petralona.

Dirty Ginger ★ CONTEMPORARY GREEK   In trendy Gazi, on an impossibly popular street lined with some of the city's hottest bars and restaurants, Dirty Ginger stood out from the get-go, thanks to its courtyard, the party mood that takes over after 10pm, and the sought-after seats on the tiny pavement in front where you can watch beautiful people come and go. The light Mediterranean fare is delicious, too. I had the most delicious chop suey I've ever eaten there. The Tinos french fries (served in a cone) are also first rate, as are the grilled eggplant with garlic and diced tomato, the grilled chicken with curry, the souvlaki (in a pita), and the mouthwatering veal and lamb chops. Eat, drink, and linger to watch and participate in the highly infectious nightly party. You won't want to or need to go anywhere else for the night.

46 Triptopolemou and Persefonis, Gazi. ⓒ **210/342-3809.** www.dirtyginger.gr. Main courses 15€–25€. V, MC. Daily 8pm–2am. Metro: Kerameikos.

Mamacas ★★ GREEK   If any restaurant can be credited for kick-starting the transformation of Gazi from gritty to urban chic, it's Mamacas. A famous restaurant on the island of Mykonos, the city version of Mamacas has been irresistible to Athenians since 1998. With its modern, delicious twist on old favorites, whitewashed walls, chic clientele, and impossibly good-looking staff, Mamacas is still one of the best the ancient city has to offer. Check out the trays of cooked dishes *(magirefta)* and a range of dependable and delicious grills and appetizers (the spicy meatballs or *keftedakia* are a must). After dinner, linger a little at the bar as it picks up heat after midnight, or watch the world go by outside in the hippest place in the city after dark.

41 Persophonous, Gazi. ✆ **210/346-4984.** www.mamacas.gr. Main courses 15€–35€. AE, MC, V. Daily 1:30pm–1:30am. Metro: Kerameikos.

Meson el Mirador ★ MEXICAN   After years of having pseudo-Mexican fare, I finally had a genuine Mexican meal in Athens in the middle of Kerameikos, right off the ancient cemetery in a beautifully restored mansion. Top-notch enchiladas, quesadillas, and pork chops with beans—plus a vegetarian menu, excellent sangria, and margaritas—blow the would-be competitors out of the water. With the surroundings, food, and music in this atmospheric part of town, you can't go wrong. In summer the beautiful roof terrace with Acropolis views is open.

88 Agisilaou at Salaminas, Kerameikos. ✆ **210/342-0007.** www.el-mirador.gr. Main courses 15€–30€. MC, V. Mon–Fri 7:30pm–2am; Sat noon–2am; Sun noon–6pm. Metro: Thissio.

Prosopa ★ MEDITERRANEAN   This little restaurant (translated as "Faces") beside the train tracks on the outskirts of Gazi has plenty of atmosphere going for it in this once-forgotten section of the city. Wonderful Mediterranean fare, including a wide array of pasta and risotto entrees and some exceptional beef, chicken, and seafood dishes, make "Faces" a wonderful little place to discover. Leave enough room for the "trio of death"—cheesecake, chocolate brownie, and banana-cream pie.

4 Konstantinoupoleos and 52 Megalou Vassiliou, Gazi. ✆ **210/341-3433.** www.prosopa.gr. Main courses 25€–30€. No credit cards. Daily 8:30pm–2:30am. Metro: Kerameikos, then walk down to Konstantinoupoleos by the train tracks.

Sardelles ★ GREEK/SEAFOOD   "Sardines" is a friendly and simple modern taverna specializing in delicious seafood *mezedes*. Try the fried shrimp, the grilled cuttlefish, and the grilled *sardeles* (sardines), plus the large, fresh salads.

15 Persefonis St., Gazi. ✆ **210/347-8050.** Main courses 15€–30€. No credit cards. Daily noon–1am. Metro: Kerameikos.

INEXPENSIVE

Filistron ★★ GREEK/MEZEDES   Right on the Archaeological Promenade in Thissio, Filistron has a rooftop terrace with such awesome views of the dramatically lit Parthenon against the starry night sky, you won't want to leave. The delicious offerings will give you even more reason to linger. The menu is (mostly) *mezedes,* which means you can have many different dishes and try as many specialties as you'd like. And it's reasonably priced to boot. Begin with a glass of wine at dusk and watch the sky turn dark as the lights on the Acropolis come to life. After that, begin sampling the restaurant's many *mezedes*—my favorites are Byzantine salad and the grilled potatoes with smoked cheese. If you like all things salty, order the salted sardines from Spain.

23 Apostolou Pavlou, Thissio. ✆ **210/346-7554.** www.filistron.com. Reservations suggested for the rooftop. Appetizers 7€–18€. DC, MC, V. Mon–Sat 8pm–1am; Sun 1:30–5pm. Metro: Thissio.

Gazohori ★ GREEK/MEZEDES   "Gazi Village" has delicious fare (*mezedes*) at affordable prices, so its pretty courtyard is almost always packed with students. Festive, friendly, and fun, it also has live music. Try the hearty salads, the grilled meatballs and sausages, lemon potatoes, and slow-cooked eggplant.

2 Dekeloen, Gazi. ✆ **210/342-4044.** Appetizers 7€–15€. V, MC. Daily noon–1am. Metro: Kerameikos.

O Santorianios (The Man from Santorini) ★★ GREEK/MEZEDES   Delicious fare from the island of Santorini is served at this little gem, open only in the evening. You'll get traditional cuisine from the island in an old Athenian home with a small garden, run by a family from Santorini. Try the impeccable fava dip, cherry

QUICK bites IN SYNTAGMA

In general, Syntagma Square is not known for good food, but the area has a number of places to get a snack. **Apollonion Bakery**, 10 Nikis, and **Elleniki Gonia**, 10 Karayiori Servias, make sandwiches to order and sell croissants, both stuffed and plain. **Ariston** is a small chain of *zaharoplastia* (confectioners) with a location at 10 Voulis (just off Syntagma Sq.); it sells snacks as well as pastries and delicious cheese pies. For some of the best chocolate drinks in the city, stop by **Chocolate 56,** 56 Ermou St.

For the quintessentially Greek *loukoumades* (round doughnut hole–like pastries that are deep-fried, then drenched with honey and topped with powdered sugar and cinnamon), try **Doris,** 30 Praxitelous, a continuation of Lekka, a few blocks from Syntagma Square. If you're still hungry, Doris serves hearty stews and pasta dishes for low prices Monday through Saturday until 3:30pm. If you're nearer Omonia Square when you feel the need for *loukoumades* or a soothing dish of rice pudding, try **Aigaion** ★, 46 Panepistimiou.

Everest is another local chain worth trying; there's one a block north of Kolonaki Square at Tsakalof and Iraklitou. Also in Kolonaki Square, **Kotopoula Valsamakis** serves succulent grilled chicken to take out or eat in. In the Plaka, **K. Kotsolis Pastry Shop,** 112 Adrianou, offers excellent coffee and sweets; it's an oasis of old-fashioned charm in the midst of souvenir shops. **Oraia Ellada (Beautiful Greece)** ★★, a cafe at the Center of Hellenic Tradition, opens onto both 36 Pandrossou and 59 Mitropoleos near the flea market and has a spectacular view of the Acropolis. You can revive yourself here with a coffee and pastries. For the best espresso, cappuccino, Italian pastries, and brioche sandwiches in town, venture to **Alfiere Café** ★ in Kolonaki, right behind the Italian Embassy at 5 Sekeri.

tomato salad with chloro cheese, grilled octopus and red snapper, and their famous *tomatokeftedes* (tomato rissoles) paired with a fine wine from the island. You'll wish you were back there or planning a visit, but until then, you can always return here.

8 Doreion, Petralona. ℂ **210//345-1629.** Reservations strongly recommended Fri–Sat. Appetizers 8€–18€. No credit cards. Daily 8pm–midnight. Metro: Petralona.

To Steki Tou Ilia ★ TRADITIONAL GREEK GRILLHOUSE   On a quiet pedestrian street away from the bustling cafes and bars of lively Thissio, you can find this popular grill house ("Ilias' hangout"). The house specialty is its irresistible *paidakia*, chargrilled lamb chops served the old-fashioned way, with grilled bread sprinkled with olive oil and oregano. There's a second location at 5 Eptachalkou St., Thissio (ℂ **210/ 345-8052**), that keeps the same hours.

7 Thessalonikis, Thissio. ℂ **210/342-2407.** Main courses 8€–20€. No credit cards. Mid-June to mid-Sept Tues–Sat 8pm–1am; Sun 1:30–5pm (closed 2 weeks in Aug). Metro: Thissio.

Syntagma
EXPENSIVE

Aegli/Cibus ★★ INTERNATIONAL   For years, the bistro in the Zappeion Gardens was a popular meeting spot; when it closed, it was sorely missed. Now it's back, along with a cinema, a hip and highly recommended outdoor bar/club, and a fine restaurant. Once more, chic Athenian families head here, to the cool of the Zappeion

Gardens, for the frequently changing menu. Some of the specialties include foie gras, oysters, tenderloin with ginger and coffee sauce, profiteroles, fresh sorbets, strawberry soup, and yogurt crème brûlée. Tables indoors or outdoors by the trees offer places to relax with coffee. In the evening, take in a movie at the open-air cinema before dinner, or have a drink and a snack at one of the nearby cafes. In short, this is a wonderful spot to while away an afternoon or evening—and a destination for a special occasion.

Zappeion Gardens (adjacent to the National Gardens fronting Vas. Amalias Blvd.). © **210/336-9363.** Reservations recommended. Main courses 35€–53€. AE, DC, MC, V. Daily 10am–midnight. Sometimes closed in Aug. Metro: Syntagma.

MODERATE

Furin Kazan ★ JAPANESE Furin Kazan is continuously swarming with a mostly Japanese clientele—a sure stamp of approval. It's an ideal spot for lunch. Try the noodle and rice dishes, but it's best known for the sushi and sashimi.

2 Appolonos, Synatgma. © **210/322-9170.** www.furin-kazan.com. Main courses 15€–35€. AE, DC, MC, V. Mon–Sat 11:30am–11pm; Sun 2-11pm. Metro: Syntagma.

Tzitzikas kai Mermigas ★★ GREEK The Greek translation of Aesop's fable of the "Cricket and the Ant" has come to the heart of Athens after being a suburban favorite for years. Try as many *mezedes* as you like; all are delicious—the cheese pies, shrimp with ouzo and cream, and spicy meatballs with mozzarella are just some of our favorites. The desserts and ice creams are also excellent.

12-14 Mitropoleos, Syntagma. © **210/324-7607.** www.tzitzikas-mermigas.gr. Main courses 15€–25€. MC, V. Mon–Sat 1pm–1am. Metro: Syntagma.

INEXPENSIVE

Melilotos ★★ MEDITERRANEAN/ORGANIC Inside the lobby of a commercial building by Syntagma Square, this isn't the kind of place you go to for ambience. What you will come here for, and I suspect more than once, is the delicious, meticulously prepared, and inexpensive meals cooked on the spot from the finest, freshest ingredients under the guidance of award-winning chef Konstantinos Siopidis. Everything here is excellent: greens pies, fish (halibut and salmon), meat (beef), poultry (roasted chicken with potatoes), delicious soups, and salads; just leave enough room for the pastries prepared by the chef's mother-in-law, a recurring guest chef on Greek daytime TV. Come in, pick up your meal, and then head over to the National Gardens across the street for a wonderful picnic.

15 Xenofontos, Syntagma. © **210/322-2458.** Main courses 5€–13€. MC, V. Mon–Thurs 11am–7pm. Fri 11am–6pm.

Pangrati

EXPENSIVE

Spondi ★★★ MEDITERRANEAN Athinorama, the weekly review of the Athenian scene, has chosen Spondi several years running (2001–2007, 2011) as the best place in town. The menu features light dishes—the fresh fish, especially the salmon, is superb—as well as dishes you will find delightful (roast pork with myzithra cheese and a fig-and-yogurt sauce; sea bass in rose-petal sauce; hare and truffle mille-feuille). The setting, a 19th-century town house with a stone courtyard covered with bougainvillea, is lovely; the wine list offers over 1,000 labels; the service is excellent; and the desserts, created with Paris-based patisserie Bristol, divine. You'll probably want to take a cab here, costing you (from Syntagma Sq.) around 6€. Spondi won its first Michelin star in 2002 and its second in 2008. It is considered by many to be the best restaurant in Greece.

5 Pyrronos, Pangrati. ℂ **210/752-0658.** www.spondi.gr. Reservations recommended. Main courses 45€–130€. AE, DC, MC, V. Daily 8pm–midnight. Closed Sun in Aug. Pyrronos runs btw. Empedokleous and Dikearchou, behind the Olympic Stadium.

Kolonaki, Ambelokipi
EXPENSIVE
48 the Restaurant ★★ MEDITERRANEAN   One of the most popular places in the city, with a clientele of the famous and infamous, this former art gallery has high ceilings and a big industrial space with fantastic design and lighting. The food is exceptional—inspired dishes using traditional Greek ingredients in new ways. The menu changes daily according to the find of the day from the local markets. The wine list offers more than 500 labels from the owner's private vault in Paris.

Armatolon and 48 Klefton, Ambelokipi. ℂ **210/641-1082.** Main courses 45€–85€. AE, DC, MC, V. Mon–Sat 9pm–1am. Metro: Ambelokipi.

Horizons ★★ MEDITERRANEAN   For a table with a view, you can't do better than this. It sits on the top of Lycabettus hill, with the entire city laid under your feet like a sparkling map, and the view is sublime. The Mediterranean menu is very good as well. We started with the lobster salad gradine with Gorgonzola cheese, grilled vegetables, and the fried salmon with wasabi—all exceptional. The grilled shrimp, pasta risotto, and smoked pork tenderloin and lamb shank that followed were all top-notch too, as was the baklava dessert, but it was the view that stole the show. Arrive for sunset and enjoy.

Lycabettus Hill. ℂ **210/722-7065.** Reservations recommended. Main courses 40€–60€. AE, MC, V. Daily 1pm–1am. Taxi or walk to the top of Lycabettus to Ploutarchou St. to take the funicular (6€ with return), or walk up from Dexamini Sq.

Ta Kioupia ★★ CONTEMPORARY/REGIONAL GREEK   After relocating from Kifissia to a neoclassical building in Kolonaki, this excellent restaurant has ambience in spades and a menu to match, ranging from modern to traditional Greek cuisine from the islands and other regions. I strongly suggest the tasting menu (25€–40€), which offers samplings from over 30 dishes. The *trahana* soup (with rooster and bulgur wheat), the warm eggplant and pine nut salad, and the lamb baked in vine leaves are delicious, as are the samplings slow cooked in clay pots (thus the name of the restaurant).

Dinokratous and 22 Anapiron Polemou. ℂ **210/740-0150.** www.takioupia.com. Main courses 25€–54€. MC, V. Daily 1pm–1am. Metro: Evangelismos.

MODERATE
Filipou ★ TRADITIONAL GREEK   This longtime Athenian favorite almost never disappoints. The traditional dishes such as stuffed cabbage, stuffed vine leaves, vegetable stews, and fresh salads are consistently good. In the heart of Kolonaki, near the St. George Lykabettus Hotel, this is a place to head when you want good *spitiko* (home cooking) in the company of the Greeks and resident expats who prize the food.

19 Xenokratous. ℂ **210/721-6390.** Reservations recommended. Main courses 12€–25€. No credit cards. Mon–Fri 8:30pm–midnight; Sat lunch 1–5pm. Metro: Evangelismos.

Jackson Hall ★ AMERICAN   On hip and popular Milioni Street in the heart of Kolonaki, Jackson Hall—with its grilled burgers, steaks, large salads, appetizers, and cocktails—packs them in all year-round. Hearty, generous-size dishes and delicious cocktails, especially the daiquiris, highlight the menu. The T-bone steak is top-notch, as is the Montana filet (pork filet with mushrooms sautéed with Madeira wine). Try the DI Siena risotto with chicken, and the surprisingly good cheesecake.

4 Milioni St. ℃ **210/361-6098.** www.jacksonhall.gr. Main courses 15€–30€. AE, MC, V. Daily 10am–2am. Metro: Syntagma.

To Kafeneio ★★ GREEK/INTERNATIONAL   This is hardly a typical *kafeneion* (coffee shop/cafe). If you relax, you can easily run up a tab of 50€ for lunch or dinner for two, but you can also eat more modestly, yet equally elegantly. If you have something light, like the artichokes *a la polita*, leeks in crème fraîche, or onion pie (one, not all three), accompanied by draft beer or the house wine, you can finish with profiteroles and not put too big a dent in your budget. I've always found this an especially congenial spot when I'm eating alone (perhaps because I love people-watching and profiteroles).

26 Loukianou. ℃ **210/722-9056.** Reservations recommended. Main courses 8€–25€. MC, V. Mon-Sat 11am–midnight or later. Closed most of Aug. Metro: Evangelismos.

To Ouzadiko ★★ GREEK/MEZEDES   This ouzo bar offers at least 40 kinds of ouzo and as many *mezedes*, including fluffy *keftedes* that make all others taste leaden. To Ouzadiko is popular with Athenians young and old who come to see and be seen while having a snack or a full meal, often after concerts and plays. A serious foodie friend of mine comes here for the wide variety of *horta* (greens), which she says are the best she's ever tasted. If you see someone at a nearby table eating something you want and aren't sure what it is, ask your waiter and it will appear for you—sometimes after a bit of a wait, as the staff here is often seriously overworked.

25-29 Karneadou (in the Lemos International Shopping Center). ℃ **210/729-5484.** Reservations recommended. Most *mezedes* and main courses 8€–25€. No credit cards. Tues-Sat 1pm-12:30am. Closed Aug. Metro: Syntagma. From Kolonaki Sq. take Kapsali across Irodotou into Karneadou. The Lemos Center is the miniskyscraper on your left.

Vlassis ★★★ TRADITIONAL GREEK   Greeks call this kind of food *paradisiako* (traditional), but paradisiacal is just as good a description. This reasonably priced food is fit for the gods: delicious fluffy vegetable croquettes, a unique eggplant salad, and hauntingly tender lamb in egg-lemon sauce.

15 Meandrou, Ilissia. ℃ **210/725-6635.** Reservations recommended. Main courses 15€–30€. MC, V. Mon-Sat 1pm-midnight; Sun noon-5pm. Closed much of June-Sept. Metro: Megaro Mousikis. Once you exit the Metro, cross the avenue and head down (adjacent the hospital) toward Michalacopoulou St. Meandrou is 1 block before. Across the street from the Crowne Plaza hotel.

INEXPENSIVE

To Omorfo (The Beautiful) ★ GREEK   And indeed it is beautiful! Tucked in a beautiful, tranquil section of Kolonaki on pretty Xenokratous Street, on the slopes of Lycabettus mountain, this quiet (lunch and early dinner) tavern has tons of old-world charm. The dishes (*mageirefta*: ready-cooked meals) change daily according to the freshest ingredients and catch of the day from the local markets.

50 Xenokratous, Kolonaki. ℃ **210/722-6830.** Main courses 7€–15€. No credit cards. Mon-Sat 12:30–8:30pm. Metro: Evanggelismos. From the Evanggelismos Metro station exit, cross the avenue and walk up Marasli St. until you hit Xenokratous, 5 blocks away.

Omonia Square, Metaxourgeio & University Area (Near Exarchia Square/Archaeological Museum)

EXPENSIVE

El Bandoneon ★ SOUTH AMERICAN   In a beautiful theatrical space, this fine Argentine restaurant, with its excellent meat selection, is dominated by a large central dance floor, where professional tango dancers spin to tango rhythms and offer the diners free lessons. Many well-known Argentine singers and dancers often perform here. It's lots of fun, with great food, and an exceptional bar.

7 Virginias Benaki, Metaxourgeio. ✆ **210/522-4346.** www.elbandoneon.com. Main courses 40€–60€. AE, DC, MC, V. Wed–Sat 8pm–1:30am; Sun 8pm–2am (operates only as a bar and offers tango lessons). Closed late May to early Sept. Metro: Metaxourgeio.

MODERATE

Archaion Gefsis (Ancient Flavors) ★★ ANCIENT GREEK CUISINE   It's a little on the kitschy side (columns, torches, and waitresses in togas), but a brilliant idea nonetheless. With recipes from ancient Greece (recorded by the poet Archestratos), this is your one chance to dine like the ancients did. Offerings include cuttlefish in ink with pine nuts, wild-boar cutlets, goat leg with mashed vegetables, and pork with prunes and thyme. Just remember: You may use a spoon and a knife, but no fork—ancient Greeks did not use them. It's equally adored by locals, foodies, and tourists alike, and evenings here make for a unique dining experience.

22 Kodratou, Plateia Karaiskaki, Metaxourgeio. ✆ **210/523-9661.** www.arxaion.gr. Main courses 20€–33€. MC, V. Mon–Sat 8pm–1am. Metro: Metaxourgeio.

Giantes CONTEMPORARY GREEK/ORGANIC   With a charming location in a quaint, pretty garden by the open-air summer movie theater, Giantes has ambience and also serves tasty regional cuisine made with organic products. Many vegetarian dishes are on the menu, but our favorite was the chicken with honey, raisins, and coriander.

44 Valtetsiou, Exarchia. ✆ **210/330-1369.** Main courses 12€–27€. AE, DC, MC, V. Metro: Omonoia.

Kalliste Gefsis ★★ CONTEMPORARY GREEK   In a beautifully restored 19th-century house with polished wood floors and ornamental plaster ceilings, Kalliste manages to be both cozy and elegant and under its new management, seems to be bolder in its choices, yet always on the money. The constantly changing menu usually includes traditional dishes with a distinctive flair, such as lentil soup with pomegranate, and chicken with hazelnuts and celery purée. Even that old standby, crème caramel, is enlivened by the addition of rose liqueur.

137 Asklepiou, off Akadimias above the University of Athens. ✆ **210/645-3179.** Reservations recommended. Main courses 24€–30€. MC, V. Mon–Sat noon–2pm and 8pm–midnight. Metro: Panepistimio.

Kostoyiannis ★★ TRADITIONAL GREEK   Kostoyiannis has been doing everything right since the 1950s, serving a wide range of fresh seafood, grills, sweetbreads, and their signature *stifados* (rabbit or veal stews). Arriving here is a joy, as you walk past a display of what can be cooked for you. Inside the bustling restaurant, contented diners dig in to their choices. This is one of the nicest places in town to spend a leisurely evening watching more and more people arrive as concerts and theater performances let out across Athens.

37 Zaimi, Pedion Areos, behind the National Archaeological Museum. ✆ **210/822-0624.** Reservations recommended. Main courses 15€–25€; fish and shellfish by the kilo. No credit cards. Mon–Sat 8pm–midnight. Closed late July to Aug. Metro: Victoria.

Dining in Athens (as in any other European capital) will rarely come cheap at the quality restaurants and reservations are highly recommended, particularly on weekends. If you wish to dine with the locals, remember that Athenians do not dine before 10pm, so plan accordingly. Your tip should be 10% to 15% of the bill (check to see if service is included). Menus can be found in both Greek and English (if not, the waiter will help you with suggestions.) The current E.U. nonsmoking law that went into effect in 2009 did not have a major effect on the city's countless warm season al fresco dining and drinking establishments.

INEXPENSIVE

Athinaikon ★★ GREEK/OUZERI   Not many tourists come to this favorite haunt of lawyers and businesspeople who work in the Omonia Square area. You can stick to appetizers (technically, this *is* an ouzeri) or have a full meal. Appetizers include delicious *loukanika* (sausages) and *keftedes;* pass up the more expensive grilled shrimp and the seafood paella. The adventurous can try *ameletita* (lamb's testicles). Whatever you have, you'll enjoy taking in the old photos on the walls, the handsome tiled floor, the marble-topped tables and bentwood chairs, and the regular customers, who combine serious eating with animated conversation.

2 Themistokleous. ✆ **210/383-8485.** Appetizers and main courses 8€–20€. No credit cards. Mon–Sat 11am–midnight. Closed Aug. Metro: Omonia. From Omonia Sq., take Panepistimou a block to Themistokleous; the Athinaikon is almost immediately on your right.

Taygetos ★ 🍴 GREEK/SOUVLAKI   This is a great place to stop for a quick meal on your way to or from the National Archaeological Museum. The service is swift and the souvlaki and fried potatoes are excellent, as are the chicken and the grilled lamb. The menu sometimes features delicious *kokoretsi* (grilled entrails).

4 Satovriandou. ✆ **210/523-5352.** Grilled lamb and chicken priced by the kilo. No credit cards. Mon–Sat 9am–1am. Metro: Omonia or Panepisitimio. From Omonia Sq., take Patision toward National Museum; Satovriandou is the 3rd major turn on your left.

Koukaki & Makrigianni (Near the Acropolis)

MODERATE

Mani Mani ★★ CONTEMPORARY/REGIONAL GREEK   Delicious and moderately priced, Mani Mani's menu is based on traditional dishes from Mani in the south of the Peloponnese. The rooster *bardouniotikos* (rooster stewed with feta) we had was exceptional as was the lamb shank, cod fish and their homemade pasta (*hilopites*). Tasty appetizers included the *siglino* (cured pork that is first salted, then smoked, and finally boiled) and grilled sausages. The salads are also recommendable, and the service is wonderful.

10 Falirou, Makrigianni. ✆ **210/921-8180.** www.manimani.com.gr. Main courses 9.50€–17€. DC, MC, V. Tues–Sat 8pm–1am; Sun 2–5pm. Metro: Akropolis.

Strofi Tavern ★ TRADITIONAL GREEK   The Strofi serves standard Greek taverna fare (the *mezedes* and lamb and goat dishes are especially good here), but the view of the Acropolis is so terrific that everything seems to taste particularly good. Keep this place in mind if you're staying south of the Acropolis, an area not packed with restaurants. Strofi is popular with the after-theater crowd that pours out of the nearby Herodes Atticus Theater during the Athens Festival.

25 Rovertou Galli, Makriyianni. ℂ **210/921-4130.** Reservations recommended. Main courses 8€–25€. DC, MC, V. Mon–Sat 8pm–2am. Metro: Akropolis. Located 2 blocks south of Acropolis.

EXPLORING ATHENS

It's likely that you'll arrive in Athens in the afternoon, groggy and disoriented after a long flight. The ride into town from the airport is unlikely to help your spirits. You'll whiz along an efficient but anonymous highway that could be anywhere, before being fed into Athens's ferocious traffic; or you'll be underground in the Metro, itching to get to your hotel. Somewhere, you know, not far away, must be the blue Aegean and the lofty Acropolis. But where?

When you get to your hotel, jump into the shower, take a nap, and then set off for an evening stroll through elegant **Syntagma (Constitution) Square** past the House of Parliament. Take a few minutes to explore Syntagma's handsome marble **Metro** station, with its display of finds from the excavations here. Sit on a bench or at one of the cafes and have a cup of coffee or a snack as you take in the city, its citizens, and your surroundings. (Syntagma Sq. has free Wi-Fi, so you have many reasons to return here and linger during your stay.)

If it's too warm out, escape into the shade of the **National Gardens**—an oasis of calm and cool in the heart of Athens. You'll discover shady benches; a small cafe; the excellent Aigli restaurant in the adjacent, wider, and more formal **Zappeion Gardens;** and lots of opportunities to watch Greek families out for a stroll. Keep an eye out for the shockingly well-preserved Roman Baths, have a seat and linger by the Zappeion's handsome fountain for a while, and then head into the **Plaka,** the old neighborhood on the slopes of the Acropolis that has more restaurants, cafes, and souvenir shops than private homes. If you get off the Plaka's main drags, Kidathineon and Adrianou, and follow one of the streets such as Thespidos that run up

> **Athens Info Online**
>
> The Ministry of Culture information site for archaeological sites, monuments, and museums is **www.culture.gr**. Four invaluable websites with a wealth of information and daily updates are **www. visitgreece.gr, www.cityofathens.gr, www.breathtakingathens.com,** and **www.athens24.com.**

the slope of the Acropolis, you'll find yourself in **Anafiotika.** This district, built in the 19th century by immigrants from the Cycladic island of Anafi, retains much of its old village character. As you stroll, look up: You're bound to see the Acropolis, perhaps floodlit—the best reminder of why you came.

After you have had your first Greek meal, head for the **Archaeological Promenade,** stop by **Thissio** at the cafe/bar/restaurant **Athinaion Politeia** or the beautiful **Chocolat Café** for a glass of wine, and slowly head back to your hotel and get a good night's rest so that you'll be ready for your first real day in Athens.

The Top Attractions

The Acropolis ★★★ ◎ The Acropolis is one of a handful of places in the world that is so well known, you may be anxious when you finally get here. Will it be as beautiful as its photographs? Will it be, ever so slightly, a disappointment? Rest assured: The Acropolis does not disappoint—but it *is* infuriatingly crowded. What

Athens Attractions

Acropolis Renovations

At press time, The **Temple of Nike** was scaffold-free and reassembled, having just completed an extensive 9-year renovation; the temple's **frieze,** however, is in the Acropolis Museum. Work continues on the Parthenon and a minor section of the Propylaia. The climb up to the Acropolis is steep; if you don't want to walk, an elevator has been installed and the sacred hill is now wheelchair accessible as well.

you want here is time—time to watch the Parthenon's columns appear first beige, then golden, then rose, then stark white in changing light; time to stand on the Belvedere and take in the view over Athens (and listen to the muted conversations floating up from the Plaka); time to think of all those who have been here before you. *Tip:* There is no reason to head to the Acropolis during the day in summer; it's too crowded and hot. The best time to visit during the summer is after 5pm—the brilliant light of the late-afternoon hours will only enhance your experience.

When you climb the Acropolis—the heights above the city—you're on your way to see Greece's most famous temple, the **Parthenon.** People lived here as early as 5,000 B.C. The Acropolis's sheer size made it a superb natural defense, just the place to avoid enemies and to be able to see invaders coming across the sea or the plains of Attica. There was a spring here then, to provide water.

In classical times, when Athens's population had grown to around 250,000, people moved down from the Acropolis, which had become the city's most important religious center. The city's **civic and business center**—the **Agora**—and its **cultural center,** with several theaters and concert halls, bracketed the Acropolis. When you peer over the sides of the Acropolis at the houses in the Plaka, and the remains of the Ancient Agora and the Theater of Dionysos, you'll see the layout of the ancient city. Syntagma square, the heart of today's Athens, was well out of the ancient city center.

Even the Acropolis's superb heights couldn't protect it from the Persian assault of 480 B.C., when invaders burned and destroyed most of its monuments. Look for the immense column drums built into the Acropolis's walls. They are from the destroyed Parthenon. When the Athenian statesman Pericles ordered the Acropolis rebuilt, he had these drums built into the walls so that they would remember that they had rebuilt what they had lost. Pericles's rebuilding program began about 448 B.C.; the new Parthenon was dedicated 10 years later, but work on other monuments continued for a century.

You'll enter the Acropolis through **Beulé Gate,** built by the Romans and named for the French archaeologist who discovered it in 1852. You'll then pass through the **Propylaia,** the monumental 5th-century-B.C. entrance. It's characteristic of the Roman mania for building that they found it necessary to build an entrance to an entrance.

Just above the Propylaia is the elegant little **Temple of Athena Nike (Athena of Victory);** this beautifully proportioned Ionic temple was built in 424 B.C. and heavily restored in the 1930s. To the left of the Parthenon is the **Erechtheion,** which the Athenians honored as the tomb of Erechtheus, a legendary king of Athens. A hole in the ceiling and floor of the northern porch indicates where Poseidon's trident struck to make a spring gush forth during his contest with Athena to have the city named in his or her honor. Athena countered with an olive tree; the olive tree planted beside the Erechtheion reminds visitors of her victory—as, of course, does Athens's name.

Give yourself time to enjoy the delicate carving on the Erechtheion, and be sure to see the original **Caryatids** in the Acropolis Museum. The Caryatids presently holding up the porch of the Erechtheion are the casts put there when the originals were moved to prevent further erosion by Athens's acid *nefos* (smog).

The **Parthenon** is dedicated to Athena Parthenos (Athena the Virgin, patron goddess of Athens) and is the most important religious shrine here. Visitors are not allowed inside, both to protect the monument and to allow restoration work to proceed safely. If you're disappointed, remember that in antiquity only priests and honored visitors were allowed in to see the monumental—about 11m tall (36 ft.)—statue of Athena designed by the great Phidias, who supervised Pericles' building program. Nothing of the huge gold-and-ivory statue remains, but there's a small Roman copy in the Acropolis Museum—and horrific renditions on souvenirs ranging from T-shirts to ouzo bottles. Admittedly, the gold-and-ivory statue was not understated; the 2nd-century-A.D. traveler Pausanias, one of the first guidebook writers, recorded that the statue stood "upright in an ankle-length tunic with a head of Medusa carved in ivory on her breast. She has a figure of Victory about 2.5m (8 ft.) high, and a spear in her hand and a shield at her feet, with a snake beside the shield, possibly representing Erechtheus."

Look over the edge of the Acropolis toward the **Temple of Hephaistos** (now called the **Theseion**) in the Ancient Agora, and then at the Parthenon, and notice how much lighter and more graceful the Parthenon appears. Scholars tell us that this is because Ictinus, the Parthenon's architect, was something of a magician with optical illusions. The columns and stairs—the very floor—of the Parthenon all appear straight, because all are minutely curved. Each exterior column is slightly thicker in the middle (a device known as *entasis*), which makes the entire column appear straight. That's why the Parthenon, with 17 columns on each side and 8 at each end (creating an exterior colonnade of 46 relatively slender columns), looks so graceful, while the Temple of Hephaistos, with only 6 columns at each end and 13 along each side, seems squat and stolid in comparison.

The other reason the Parthenon looks so airy is that it is, quite literally, open to the elements. In 1687, the Venetians, in an attempt to capture the Acropolis from the Turks, blew the Parthenon's entire roof (and much of its interior) to smithereens. A shell fired from nearby Mouseion Hill struck the Parthenon—where the Turks were storing gunpowder and munitions—and caused appalling damage to the building and its sculptures.

 The Archaeological Promenade ★★★

One of the great pleasures in Athens is strolling through what's been dubbed the **Archaeological Promenade,** Europe's longest and arguably prettiest pedestrian promenade. It takes visitors past the most important of the city's ancient monuments. In preparation for the 2004 Olympics, the city laid out walkways from Hadrian's Gate past the Acropolis on Dionissiou Areopagitou to the Ancient Agora, past the Acropolis Museum through Thissio to the temple of Hephaistus, and on to Kerameikos and Gazi to the west, veering north through Monastiraki to the Plaka. Athenians use the walkways for their evening *volta* (stroll); the promenade helped change central Athens from a traffic-ridden horror to a delight.

The Acropolis by August Moonlight

For the past few years, 55 ancient sites throughout Greece—including, of course, the Acropolis—were open to the public on the night of the August full moon. The Culture Ministry plans to do this every August—and to stage free concerts at some of the moonlit sites.

An Englishman, Lord Elgin, carted off most of the remaining sculptures to London—including one Caryatid—in the early 19th century, when Greece was part of the Ottoman Empire, to decorate his mansion. When he fell into bankruptcy, he sold what became known as the **Elgin Marbles** to the British government, which has had them on display in the British Museum since 1816, causing ongoing pain to generations of Greeks, who continue to press for their return. Things heated up again in the summer of 1988, when English historian William St. Clair's book *Lord Elgin and the Marbles* was published. According to St. Clair, the British Museum "overcleaned" the marbles in the 1930s, removing not only the outer patina, but many sculptural details. The museum countered that the damage wasn't that bad—and that the marbles would remain in London. The Acropolis Museum—with stark-white reproductions of the missing Marbles in contrast to the originals, honey colored by the Attica sunlight—is the country's most eloquent and aggressive plea to Britain as of yet.

The Parthenon originally had sculptures on both of its pediments, as well as a frieze running around the entire temple. The frieze was made of alternating **triglyphs** (panels with three incised grooves) and **metopes** (sculptured panels). The east pediment showed scenes from the birth of Athena, while the west pediment showed Athena and Poseidon's contest for possession of Athens. The long frieze showed the battle of the Athenians against the Amazons, scenes from the Trojan War, and struggles of the Olympian gods against giants and centaurs. The message of most of this sculpture was the triumph of knowledge and civilization—that is, Athens—over the forces of darkness and barbarians. An interior frieze showed scenes from the Panathenaic Festival held each August, when citizens paraded through the streets with a new tunic for the statue of Athena. Only a few fragments of these sculptures remain in place.

On a smog-free and sunny day, you can see the gold and cream tones of the Parthenon's Pentelic marble at their most subtle. It may come as something of a shock to realize that in antiquity, the Parthenon—like most other monuments here—was painted in bright colors that have since faded, revealing the natural marble. If the day is a clear one, you'll get a superb view of Athens from the Belvedere at the Acropolis's east end.

Almost all of what you see comes from Athens's heyday in the mid–5th century B.C., when Pericles rebuilt what the Persians destroyed. In the following centuries, every invader who came built monuments, most of which were destroyed by the next wave of invaders. If you had been here a century ago, you would have seen the remains of mosques and churches, plus a Frankish bell tower. The archaeologist Heinrich Schliemann, discoverer of Troy and excavator of Mycenae, was so offended by the bell tower that he paid to have it torn down.

If you find the Acropolis too crowded, you can usually get a peaceful view of its monuments from one of three nearby hills (all signposted from the Acropolis): the **Hill of the Pnyx,** where the Athenian Assembly met; **Hill of the Areopagus,** where the Athenian Upper House met; and **Hill of Filopappos** (also known as the Hill of the Muses), named after the 2nd-century-A.D. philhellene Filopappos, whose funeral monument tops the hill. A visit to the sacred rock in itself however won't give you the complete picture of the temple's lavish past. The **Acropolis Museum** displays over 4,000 statues and artifacts that once adorned the temple—most of these treasures are being admired again for the first time in 200 years.

Dionissiou Areopagitou. ✆ **210/321-0219.** Admission 12€ adults; free Sun. Ticket, valid for 1 week, includes admission to the Acropolis, Ancient Agora, Theater of Dionysos, Karameikos Cemetery, Roman Forum, Tower of the Winds, and Temple of Olympian Zeus. Individual tickets may be bought (6€) at the other sites. Daily 8am–7pm. Ticket booth, small post office, and snack bar are located slightly below Acropolis entrance. Metro: Acropolis. From Dionissiou Areopagitou, follow the marble path up to the Acropolis.

Ancient Agora ★★　The Agora was Athens's commercial and civic center. People used these buildings for a wide range of political, educational, philosophical, theatrical, and athletic purposes—which may be why it now seems such a jumble of ancient buildings, inscriptions, and fragments of sculpture. This is a pleasant place to wander, enjoy the views up toward the Acropolis, and take in the herb garden and flowers planted around the amazingly well-preserved 5th-century-B.C. Temple of Hephaistos and Athena (the Theseion).

Find a shady spot by the temple, sit awhile, and imagine the Agora teeming with merchants, legislators, and philosophers—but very few women. Women did not regularly go into public places. Athens's best-known philosopher, **Socrates,** often strolled here with his disciples, including **Plato,** in the shade of the Stoa of Zeus Eleutherios. In 399 B.C., Socrates, accused of "introducing strange gods and corrupting youth," was sentenced to death. He drank his cup of hemlock in a prison at the southwest corner of the Agora—where excavators centuries later found small clay cups, just the right size for a fatal drink. **St. Paul** also spoke in the Agora; he irritated many Athenians because he rebuked them as superstitious when he saw an inscription here to the "Unknown God."

The one monument you can't miss in the Ancient Agora is the 2nd-century-B.C. **Stoa of Attalos,** built by King Attalos of Pergamon in Asia Minor, and completely reconstructed by American archaeologists in the 1950s. (You may be grateful that they included an excellent modern restroom.) The museum on the stoa's ground floor contains finds from 5,000 years of Athenian history, including sculpture and pottery, a voting machine, and a child's potty seat, all labeled in English. The stoa is open Tuesday through Sunday from 8:30am to 2:45pm.

As you leave the stoa, take a moment to look at the charming little 11th-century Byzantine **Church of the Holy Apostles,** also restored by the Americans. The church is almost always closed, but its delicate proportions are a relief after the somewhat heartless—too new and too well restored—facade of the Stoa of Attalos.

Striking Out in Athens

Strikes can close museums and archaeological sites without warning. Decide what you most want to see, and go there as soon as possible after you arrive.

Below the Acropolis at the edge of Monastiraki (entrance is on Adrianou, near Ayiou Philippou Sq., east of Monastiraki Sq., and on Ayiou Apostoli, the road leading down into Plaka from the Acropolis). ✆ **210/321-0185.** Admission (includes museum) 4€, or free with purchase of 12€ Acropolis ticket. Summer daily 8am–7pm; winter daily 8:30am–6pm (sometimes as early as 2:30pm). Metro: Monastiraki.

Tourism Information in Athens

The **Greek National Tourism Organization (EOT,** also known as the Hellenic Tourism Organization) is at 26 Amalias (**ℰ 210/870-0000;** www.visitgreece.gr), across the street from the tram stop at Syntagma. The office is officially open Monday through Friday 9am to 3pm and is closed weekends.

Hadrian's Arch ★   The Roman emperor Hadrian built a number of monuments in Athens, including this enormous triumphal arch with its robust, highly ornamental Corinthian columns. Although Hadrian was a philhellene (lover of things Greek), he didn't hesitate to use his arch to let the Athenians know who was boss: An inscription facing the Acropolis side reads THIS IS ATHENS, THE ANCIENT CITY OF THESEUS. On the other side it states THIS IS THE CITY OF HADRIAN, NOT OF THESEUS. Ironically, much more of ancient Athens is visible today than of Hadrian's Athens, and much of Roman Athens lies unexcavated under modern Athens. Hadrian's Arch is still a symbolic entrance to Athens: A number of times when demonstrations blocked traffic from the airport into central Athens, taxi drivers told us that they could get us as far as Hadrian's Gate, from which we'd have to walk into town.

On Leoforos Amalias, near Temple of Olympian Zeus, easily seen from the street. Free admission. Summer daily 8am–7pm; winter daily 8:30am–6pm (sometimes as early as 2:30pm). Metro: Acropolis.

Kerameikos Cemetery ★   Ancient Athens's most famous cemetery, just outside the city walls, is a lovely spot. Many handsome monuments from the 4th century B.C. and later line the Street of the Tombs, which has relatively few visitors. You can sit quietly and imagine **Pericles** putting the final touches on his **Funeral Oration** for the Athenian soldiers killed during the first year of fighting in the Peloponnesian War. Athens, Pericles said, was the "school of Hellas" and a "pattern to others rather than an imitator of any." Offering comfort to the families of the fallen, he urged the widows to remember that the greatest glory belonged to the woman who was "least talked of among men either for good or for bad"—which must have caused a few snickers, since Pericles's mistress, Aspasia, was the subject of considerable gossip.

Ancient Greek words often hide in familiar English words, and that's true of Kerameikos. The name honors the hero Keramos, who was something of a patron saint of potters, giving his name both to the ceramics made here and to the district itself. The Kerameikos was a major crossroads in antiquity, rather like today's Omonia Square. You can see remains of the massive **Dipylon Gate,** where most roads converged, and the **Sacred Gate,** where marchers in the Panathenaic Festival gathered before heading through the Ancient Agora and climbing to the Parthenon. What you can't see are the remains of **Plato's Academy,** which was in this district but has thus far eluded archaeologists. The well-preserved statue of a *kouros,* found in the Kerameikos in 2000, is in the Kerameikos Museum, along with photos showing its discovery.

The **Oberlaender Museum,** with a collection of finds from the Kerameikos, including terra-cotta figurines, vases, and funerary sculptures, is usually open when the site is. Be sure to see the handsome classical statue of a youth known as the *Kerameikos Kouros,* and the lion and sphinx pieces. You may also want to visit Athens's enormous **First Cemetery,** near Athens Stadium; it has acres of monuments, many as elaborate as anything you'll see at the Kerameikos.

148 Ermou. © **210/346-3553.** Admission 2€, or free with purchase of 12€ Acropolis ticket. Summer Tues–Sun 8am–7pm; winter Tues–Sun 8:30am–6pm (sometimes as early as 2:30pm). Metro: Monastiraki or Thisio on line 1. Walk west from Monastiraki Sq. past Thisio Metro station on the Archaeological Promenade; cemetery is on the right.

Roman Agora (Forum) ★   One of the nicest things about the Roman Agora is that if you don't want to inspect it closely, you can take it in from one of the Plaka cafes and restaurants on its periphery. In addition to building a number of monuments on the Acropolis and in the Ancient Agora, Roman leaders, beginning with Julius Caesar, built their own agora, or forum, as an extension of the Greek agora. Archaeologists want to explore the area between the Greek and Roman agoras; Plaka merchants and fans of the district do not want more digging. At present, the Roman Agora is a pleasant mélange of monuments from different eras, including a mosque built here after the Byzantine Empire was conquered by Mehmet II in 1453.

The Roman Agora's most endearing monument is the octagonal **Tower of the Winds (Aerides),** with its relief sculptures of eight gods of the winds, including Boreas blowing on a shell. Like so many monuments in Athens—the Parthenon itself had a church inside it for centuries—the Tower of the Winds has had a varied history. Built by a 1st century-B.C. astronomer as a combination sundial and water-powered clock, it became a home for whirling dervishes in the 18th century. When Lord Byron visited Athens, he lodged near the tower, spending much of his time writing lovesick poetry to the beautiful "Maid of Athens."

You can usually find the remains of the Roman latrine near Tower of the Winds by following the sound of giggles to people taking pictures of each other in the seated position. The less-well-preserved remains of the enormous and once-famous **library of Emperor Hadrian** go largely unnoticed. Draw your own conclusions.

Enter from corner of Pelopida and Eolou. Admission 2€, or free with 12€ Acropolis ticket. Usually summer Tues–Sun 8am–7pm; winter Tues–Sun 8:30am–6pm (sometimes as early as 2:30pm). Metro: Monastiraki.

Temple of Olympian Zeus (Olympieion) ★★   Hadrian built this massive temple—or rather, finished the construction that began in the 6th century B.C. and continued on and off (more off than on) for 700 years. At 108m long and 43m wide (360×143 ft.), the **Olympieion,** also known as the **Kolonnes (Columns),** was one of the largest temples in the ancient world. The 17m-high (56-ft.) Pentelic marble columns that remain standing, as well as the one sprawled on the ground, give a good idea of how impressive this forest of columns must have been—although it may be more appealing as a ruin than it ever was as a contender for the title "mother of all temples." Inside, side by side, were once statues of Zeus and of Hadrian.

At Leoforos Vas. Olgas and Amalias, easily seen from the street. © **210/922-6330.** Admission 2€. Summer Tues–Sun 8am–7pm; winter Tues–Sun 8:30am–6pm (sometimes as early as 2:30pm). Metro: Acropolis.

Theater of Dionysos & Odeion (Odeum) of Herodes Atticus ★★   This theater of Dionysos was built in the 4th century B.C. to replace and enlarge the earlier theater in which the plays of the great Athenian dramatists were first performed. The new theater seated some 17,000 spectators in 64 rows of seats, 20 of which survive. Most spectators sat on limestone seats—and probably envied the 67 grandees who got to sit in the front row on thronelike seats of handsome Pentelic marble. The most elegant throne belonged to the priest of Dionysos (god of wine, revels, and theater); carved satyrs and bunches of grapes appropriately ornament the priest's throne.

Herodes Atticus, a wealthy 2nd-century-A.D. philhellene, built the Odeion—also known as the Odeum or Irodio (Music Hall). It is one of an astonishing number of monuments funded by him. If you think it looks well preserved, you're right: It was reconstructed in the 19th century. Although your 2€ entrance ticket for the Theater of Dionysos allows you entrance to the Odeion, this is misleading. The Odeion is open only for performances. The best ways to see the Odeion are by looking down from the Acropolis or, better yet, by attending one of the performances staged here during the Athens Festival each summer. If you do this, bring a cushion: Marble seats are as hard as you'd expect, and the cushions provided are lousy.

Dionissiou Areopagitou, on the south slope of the Acropolis. ✆ **210/322-4625.** Admission 2€ (for both monuments), or free with purchase of 12€ Acropolis ticket. Theater of Dionysos: summer Tues–Sun 8am–7pm; winter Tues–Sun 8:30am–6pm (sometimes as early as 2:30pm). Odeion: open during performances and sometimes on performance day. Metro: Acropolis.

The Top Museums

The Acropolis Museum ★★★ 📷 Designed by Bernard Tschumi (and Michalis Fotiadis), the 21,000-sq.-m (226,000-sq.-ft.) glass-and-concrete museum is stunning. The treasures it displays (most of them in storage for almost 200 years) are breathtaking. At once awe inspiring and humbling, the museum has over 4,000 treasures on display (10 times more than the previous Acropolis museum), making this *the* must-see museum for anyone visiting Athens for the first time (it doesn't hurt that the museum's **restaurant** is top notch as well).

Ramps take visitors to the ongoing excavations in the museum's lower levels, where you can peer through glass panels at an ancient Athenian neighborhood (where houses, baths, workshops, and roads have been uncovered) and an early Christian settlement.

The artifacts, statues, sculptures, and free-standing objects that used to adorn the sacred rock (plus some little-known treasures from the Temple of Artemis Braurona) are all displayed throughout the first two floors, preparing visitors for the final moment when they ascend to the top floor, the **Parthenon Gallery.** The glassy gallery is different than the other floors. Rotated 23 degrees off its axis to mirror the layout of the Parthenon—visible throughout the gallery—it handsomely displays what remains in Greece of the original Parthenon sculptures and frieze—36 of the 115 original panels, alongside stark white plaster casts of the originals (The "Elgin Marbles") in London. This is where one gets the full picture; the grandeur of the past, the importance of this incredible legacy and the ugly truth that this is a work of art that has been looted. Even though fragments of the Parthenon frieze were returned in early 2009 from Italy, Germany, and the Vatican, they are but fragments of the whole of a spectacular work. The missing marbles break apart a poem carved in stone as a unity that tells a single story. There are also missing body parts, turning the splendid into the grotesque—the goddess Iris has her head in Athens and her body in London; Poseidon's rear is in Athens while his torso is in London, and so on and so forth.

As magnificent as the museum is, in its design and in its treasures, one cannot walk away without an even deeper appreciation of a glorious era in human history. Yet one also leaves with a sense of sadness knowing that this tremendous work of art has been looted, vandalized, and ravaged far too many times. We want to believe it is only a matter of time until the British Museum undoes the most recent wrong.

15 Dionisiou Aeropagitou. ✆ **210/900-0901.** www.theacropolismuseum.gr. Admission 5€. Tues–Sun 8am–8pm; Fri 8am–10pm. Metro: Acropolis.

Benaki Museum ★★ Housed in an elegant neoclassical mansion, the Benaki Museum was founded by art collector Antoni Benaki in 1931. This stunning private collection of about 20,000 small and large works of art includes treasures from the Neolithic era to the 20th century. The folk art collection (including magnificent costumes and icons) is superb, as are the two rooms from 18th-century northern Greek mansions, ancient Greek bronzes, gold cups, Fayum portraits, and rare early Christian textiles. The museum shop is excellent. The **cafe** on the roof garden offers a spectacular view, as well as a 25€ buffet dinner on Thursdays. This is a pleasant place to spend several hours—as many Athenians do, as often as possible. After you visit the Benaki, take in its new branch, **Benaki Museum of Islamic Art** (below).

1 Koumbari (at Leoforos Vasilissis Sofias, Kolonaki, 5 blocks east of Syntagma Sq.). © **210/367-1000.** www.benaki.gr. Admission 6€; free Thurs. Mon, Wed, and Fri-Sat 9am-5pm; Thurs 9am-midnight; Sun 9am-3pm. Metro: Syntagma or Evangelismos.

Benaki Museum of Islamic Art ★★ The world-class collection, in a 19th-century neoclassical building complex, displays Islamic art (ceramics, carpets, woodcarvings, and other objects, plus two reconstructed living rooms from the Ottoman times and a 17th-century reception room from a Cairo mansion) that date from the 14th century to the present. Labels are in Greek and English.

22 Agion Asomaton and Dipylou, Psirri. © **210/367-1000.** www.benaki.gr. Admission 5€. Tues and Thurs-Sun 9am-3pm; Wed 9am-9pm. Metro: Thissio.

Byzantine and Christian Museum ★★ If you love icons (paintings, usually of saints and usually on wood) this is the place to go. This museum is devoted to the art and history of the Byzantine era (roughly 4th–15th c. A.D.). You'll find selections from Greece's most important collection of icons and religious art, along with sculptures, altars, mosaics, religious vestments, Bibles, and a small-scale reconstruction of an early Christian basilica. The museum originally occupied the 19th-century Florentine-style villa overlooking the new galleries now used for special exhibits. Allow at least an hour for your visit; 2 hours is better if a special exhibit is featured. The small museum shop sells books, CDs of Byzantine music, and icon reproductions.

22 Vasilissis Sofias Ave. © **210/723-1570.** www.byzantinemuseum.gr. Admission 4€. Tues-Sun 9am-3pm (Wed until 9pm). Metro: Evangelismos.

Greek Folk Art Museum ★★ This endearing museum showcases embroideries and costumes from all over the country. Seek out the small room with zany frescoes of gods and heroes done by the eccentric artist Theofilos Hadjimichael, who painted in the early part of the 20th century. We stop by every time we're in Athens, always finding something new—and always glad we weren't born Greek women 100 years ago, when we would have spent endless hours embroidering, crocheting, and weaving. Much of what is on display was made by young women for their *proikas* (dowries) in the days when a bride was supposed to arrive at the altar with enough embroidered linen, rugs, and blankets to last a lifetime. The museum shop is small but good.

17 Kidathineon, Plaka. © **210/322-9031.** www.culture.gr. Admission 2€. Tues-Sun 9am-2pm. Metro: Acropolis.

Ilias LALAoUNIS Jewelry Museum ★ 📱 The 3,000 pieces of jewelry on display are so spectacular that even those with no special interest in baubles will enjoy this glitzy museum, founded by one of Greece's most successful jewelry designers. The first floor contains a boutique and small workshop. The second and third floors display pieces honoring ancient, Byzantine, and Cycladic designs, as well as plants, animals, and insects. The shop carries copies of some of the displays, and jewelers in the museum's workshop take orders in case you want your own gold necklace inspired by insect anatomy.

12 Kalisperi (at Karyatidon). ✆ **210/922-1044.** Fax 210/923-7358. www.lalaounis-jewelrymuseum.gr. Admission 4€. Mon and Thurs–Sat 9am–4pm (free Sat 9–11am); Wed 9am–9pm (free 3–9pm); Sun 11am–4pm. Metro: Acropolis. Walk 1 block behind Acropolis Museum.

Museum of Popular Greek Musical Instruments ★★ Photographs show the musicians, while recordings let you listen to the tambourines, Cretan lyres, lutes, pottery drums, and clarinets on display. Not only that, but this museum is steps from the excellent **Platanos Taverna** (p. 121), so you can alternate the pleasures of food, drink, and music. When we were here, an elderly Greek gentleman listened to some music, transcribed it, stepped out into the courtyard, and played it on his own violin. The shop has a wide selection of CDs and cassettes and the courtyard hosts many musical performances throughout the summer.

1-3 Diogenous (around the corner from Tower of the Winds). ✆ **210/325-0198.** Free admission. Tues and Thurs-Sun 10am–2pm; Wed noon–6pm. Metro: Acropolis or Monastiraki.

National Archaeological Museum ★★★ Considered one of the top 10 museums in the world, its collection of ancient Greek antiquities is unrivaled and stunning even to those who have been here quite a few times. The Akrotiri frescoes are on display again (after being damaged in the 1999 earthquake) as are many "new" items, recently returned to Greece from Los Angeles, Italy, Belgium, Britain, and Germany. In order to appreciate the museum and its treasures, try to be at the door when it opens, so you can see the exhibits and not the backs of other visitors. Early arrival, except in high summer, should give you at least an hour before most tour groups arrive; alternatively, get here an hour before closing or at lunchtime, when the tour groups may not be as dense. If you can come more than once, your experience will be a pleasure rather than a marathon. *Tip:* Be sure to get the brochure on the collection when you buy your ticket; it has a handy, largely accurate description of the exhibits.

The **Mycenaean Collection** includes gold masks, cups, dishes, and jewelry unearthed from the site of Mycenae by Heinrich Schliemann in 1876. Many of these objects are small, delicate, and hard to see when the museum is crowded. Don't miss the stunning **burial mask** that Schliemann misnamed the "Mask of Agamemnon." Archaeologists are sure that the mask is not Agamemnon's, but belonged to an earlier, unknown monarch. Also not to be missed are the **Vaphio cups,** showing mighty bulls, unearthed in a tomb at a seemingly insignificant site in the Peloponnese.

The museum also has a stunning collection of **Cycladic figurines,** named after the island chain. Although these figurines are among the earliest known Greek sculptures (about 2000 B.C.), you'll be struck by how modern the idols' faces look, comparable to those wrought by Modigliani. One figure, a musician with a lyre, seems to be concentrating on his music, oblivious to his onlookers. If you like these, be sure to visit the superb collection at the N. P. Goulandris Foundation Museum of Cycladic Art (p. 147).

The **Stathatos Gallery** has stunning jewelry, vases, figurines and objects from the middle Bronze Age to the post-Byzantine era. The **Egyptian Art Collection,** is considered one of the world's finest. Spanning more than 3,000 years from the predynastic period to Roman times, this awe-inspiring collection's centerpiece is the

The Vases & Frescoes of Santorini

One of the museum's greatest treasures is its vast collection—not surprisingly, the finest in the world—of **Greek vases** and a wonderful group of **frescoes** from the Akrotiri site on the island of Santorini (Thira).

Around 1450 B.C., the volcanic island exploded, destroying not only most of the island but also, some say, the Minoan civilization on nearby Crete. Could Santorini's disappearance have created the myth of Atlantis? Perhaps. Fortunately, these beautiful frescoes survived and were brought to Athens for safekeeping and display.

Just as Athens wants the Elgin Marbles back, the present-day inhabitants of Santorini want their frescoes back, hoping that the crowds who come to see them in Athens will come instead to Santorini. There are as many theories on what these frescoes show as there are tourists in the museum on any given day. Who were the boxing boys? Were there monkeys on Santorini, or does the scene show another land? Are the ships sailing off to war, or returning home? No one knows, but it's impossible to see these lilting frescoes and not envy the people of Akrotiri who looked at such beauty every day.

bronze statue of princess-priestess **Takushit,** dating from around 670 B.C. She was found in Alexandria in 1880 and wears a crown covered in hieroglyphs.

The museum's staggeringly large sculpture collection invites you to wander, stopping when something catches your fancy. We stop for the **bronzes,** from the tiny jockey to the monumental figure variously identified as Zeus or Poseidon. Much ink has been spilled trying to prove that the god was holding either a thunderbolt (Zeus) or a trident (Poseidon). And who can resist the bronze figures of the handsome young men, perhaps athletes, seemingly about to step forward and sprint through the crowds?

44 Patission. ℂ **210/821-7724.** Fax 210/821-3573. www.namuseum.gr. Admission 6€, or 12€ with admission to the Acropolis. Mon 12:30–5pm; Tues–Fri 8am–5pm; Sat–Sun and holidays 8:30am–3pm. Metro: Panepistimio or Victoria. The museum is .5km (⅓ mile; 10 min. on foot) north of Omonia Sq. on the road named Leoforos 28 Octobriou, but usually called Patission.

National Gallery ★★ Greece's premier art gallery exhibits a stunning collection of more than 9,500 paintings, sculptures, and engravings as well as miniatures and furniture, showcasing modern Greek art and hosting major international exhibits. Currently, its prize exhibits are three El Greco masterpieces. The museum is currently being expanded—the new wing will more than double the size of the existing museum and will also include an amphitheater, educational facilities, a reception area, and a gift shop—and is expected to be completed in 2013.

50 Vasileos Konstantinou. ℂ **210/723-5857.** www.nationalgallery.gr. Admission 6.50€. Mon and Wed–Sat 9am–3pm and 6–9pm; Sun 10am–2pm. Metro: Evangelismos.

N. P. Goulandris Foundation Museum of Cycladic Art ★★ Come here to see the largest collection of Modigliani-like Cycladic art outside the National Archaeological Museum. This handsome museum—the collection of Nicolas and Aikaterini Goulandris—opened its doors in 1986 and displays more than 200 stone and pottery vessels and figurines from the 3rd millennium B.C. This museum is as satisfying as the National Museum is overwhelming. It helps that the Goulandris does not get the same huge crowds, and that the galleries here are small and well lit, with labels throughout in Greek and English. The collection of Greek vases is small and exquisite—the ideal place to find out if you prefer black or red figure vases. The museum's elegant little shop has a wide selection of books on ancient art, as well as reproductions of items from the collection, including a pert Cycladic pig. When you've seen all you want to (and have perhaps refreshed yourself at the basement snack bar or courtyard cafe), walk through the courtyard into the museum's newest acquisition, the elegant 19th-century **Stathatos Mansion.** The mansion, with some of its original furnishings, provides a glimpse of how wealthy Athenians lived 100 years ago.

4 Neophytou Douka. ✆ **210/722-8321.** www.cycladic.gr. Admission 5€. Mon and Wed–Fri 10am–4pm; Sat 10am–3pm. Metro: Evangelismos.

Ancient Monuments

One small, graceful monument you might easily miss is the 4th-century-B.C. **Choregic Monument of Lysikrates,** on Lysikratous in the Plaka, located a few steps from the excellent **Daphne's** restaurant (p. 120). This circular monument with Corinthian columns and a domed roof bears an inscription stating that Lysikrates erected it when he won the award in 334 B.C. for the best musical performance with a "chorus of boys." A frieze shows Dionysos busily trying to turn evil pirates into friendly dolphins.

Three hills near the Acropolis deserve a respectful glance: **Areopagus, Pnyx,** and **Filopappos. Areopagus** is the bald marble hill across from the entrance to the Acropolis; it is so slippery, despite its marble steps, that it is never an easy climb, and it is treacherous in the rain. This makes it hard to imagine the Athenians who served on the council and court making their way up here. Still harder to imagine is St. Paul on this slippery perch thundering out criticisms of the Athenians for their superstitions.

From the Areopagus and Acropolis, you can see two nearby wooded hills. The one with the monument visible on its summit is **Filopappos (Hill of the Muses).** The monument is the funeral stele of the Roman consul after whom the hill is named. You can take pleasant walks on the hill's wooded slopes; view a Byzantine church, **Ayios Demetrios;** and see the **Dora Stratou Theater,** where you can watch folk dances being performed (p. 153). If you climb to the summit (at night, don't try this alone or wander here or on Pnyx hill) and face the Acropolis, you can imagine the moment in 1687 when the Venetian commander Morosini shouted "Fire!"—and cannon shells struck the Parthenon.

Pnyx hill, crowned by the Athens Observatory, is where Athens's citizen assembly met. As much as any spot in Athens—which is to say, anyplace in the world—it is the "birthplace of democracy." Here, for the first time, every citizen could vote on every matter of common importance. True, citizens did not include women, and there were far more slaves than citizens in Athens—as was the case in most of the world for a very long time after this democracy was born.

Organized Tours

Some independent travelers eschew organized tours. Nonetheless, such a tour can be an efficient and easy way to get an overview of an unfamiliar city. We're impressed by the number of people we know who confess that they are glad they took a tour, which helped them get oriented and figure out which sights they wanted to see more thoroughly. Most tour guides must pass stiff tests to get their licenses.

The **CitySightseeing bus** (**www.city-sightseeing.com**; 18€ adults, 8€ children) is an open-top double-decker bus that begins and ends its journey at Syntagma Square. The ride through central Athens lasts 90 minutes, with stops at the Acropolis, Temple of Zeus, Plaka, the university, Omonia Square, Kerameikos, Monastiraki, Psirri, Thission, the Benaki Museum, the National Gallery, the Central Market, and the Panathenaiko Stadium. Prerecorded commentaries are available in English, Greek, Spanish, French, German, Italian, Russian, and Japanese. Tickets are valid for 24 hours and buses depart every half-hour from 7am to 6pm. Also, **Hop in Sightseeing** (✆ **210/428-5500**; www.hopin.com) allows you to get on and off the bus tour over 2 days and even does hotel pickups.

Fantasy Travel, 19 Filelinon (✆ **210/331-0530**; www.fantasytravel.gr), is one of our favorite travel agencies in the city as it has splendid deals and can come up with excellent suggestions and ideas on the spot. They offer half-day and full-day tours of the city, an Athens Segway tour (which is a great way to get around the city), an "Athens by Night" tour for 62€ including dinner at the Mikrolimano harbor and great packages for the islands. Our other favorites are **CHAT Tours,** 4 Stadiou (✆ **210/323-0827**; www.chatours.gr), and **Key Tours,** 4 Kalliroïs (✆ **210/923-3166**; www.keytours.gr). To take any of these tours, you must book and pay in advance. At that time, you will be told when you will be picked up, or where you should meet the tour. **Athens Walking Tours** (✆ **210/884-7269**; www.athenswalkingtours.gr) also has some nice packages, including a "shopping tour" and a very popular "food tour."

Each company also offers excursions from Athens. A visit to the popular **Temple of Poseidon at Sounion** costs about 60€ for a half-day trip, including swimming and a meal. A trip to **Delphi** usually costs about 110€ for a full day, and often includes stops at the Monastery of Osios Loukas and Arachova village. If you want to spend the night in Delphi (included are hotel, site, and museum admissions, as well as dinner, breakfast, and sometimes lunch), the price ranges from 50€ to 160€. Rates for excursions to the **Peloponnese,** taking in Corinth, Mycenae, and Epidaurus, are similar to those for Delphi. If your time in Greece is limited, you may find one of these day trips considerably less stressful than renting a car for the day and driving yourself.

If you want to hire a private guide, speak to the concierge at your hotel or contact the **Panhellenic Guides Federation,** 9a Apollonas (✆ **210/322-9705**). Expect to pay 90€ for a 4-hour tour. Through **Athenian Days** (✆ **210/864-0415**; www.athenian days.co.uk) you will have classicist Andrew Farrington lead you through tailor-made cultural and historical tours of the city for up to six people. **Rania Vassiliadou** (✆ **210/940-3932**; www.raniavassiliadou.virtualave.net) offers tours of Athens's archaeological sites and day trips for up to six people.

For the more adventurous, there are two ways of sightseeing that will offer you a unique perspective on the city—the first one is on the ground and the second above. *Pame Volta* (**Let's Go for a Ride**), 20 Hadjichristou, Acropolis (✆ **210/922-1578**; www.pamevolta.gr; Wed–Fri 9am–5pm, Sat–Sun 11am–7pm), offers bicycles for rent and **bicycle tours** around the city. It's a unique and fun way to explore the city.

Much more expensive (with prices ranging from 1,800€–3,380€ for groups of up to five), but also much more spectacular is the **Helicopter Sightseeing Tour** of Athens by **Hop In Zinon Tours,** 29 Zanni St., Piraeus (✆ **210/428-5500**; www. hopin.com). Seeing Athens from above, especially at night when all the monuments are lit, is an unforgettable (if pricey) experience.

SHOPPING

Your hotel room may have a copy of the monthly magazines *Athens Today* or *Now in Athens,* both of which have a shopping section.

You're in luck shopping in Athens, because much of what tourists want can be found in the central city, bounded by Omonia, Syntagma, and Monastiraki squares. You'll also find most of the shops frequented by Athenians, including a number of large **department stores** and malls.

Monastiraki has a **flea market,** which is especially lively on Sunday. Although there's a vast amount of tacky stuff, you can uncover real finds, including retro clothes and old copper. Many Athenians furnishing homes head here to pick up old treasures.

The **Plaka** has cornered the market on souvenir shops, with T-shirts, reproductions of antiquities (including antique imagery reproduced on obscene playing cards, drink coasters, bottle openers, and more), fishermen's sweaters (increasingly made in the Far East), and jewelry (often not real gold)—enough souvenirs to encircle the globe.

In the Plaka-Monastiraki area, shops worth seeking amid the endlessly repetitive souvenir shops include **Stavros Melissinos,** "the Poet-Sandalmaker of Athens," relocated after 50 years to his new location at 2 Agias Theklas (℡ 210/321-9247; www.melissinos-poet.com), where his son Pantelis has taken over; **Iphanta,** a weaving workshop, 6 Selleu (℡ 210/322-3628); the **Center of Hellenic Tradition,** 59 Mitropoleos and 36 Pandrossou (℡ 210/321-3023), which sells arts and crafts; and the **National Welfare Organization,** 6 Ipatias and Apollonos, Plaka (℡ 210/325-0524), where a portion of the proceeds from everything sold (including handsome woven and embroidered carpets) goes to the National Welfare Organization, which encourages traditional crafts. **Amorgos,** 3 Kodrou (℡ 210/324-3836; www.amorgos art.gr), has authentic Greek folk art, ceramics, embroideries, wood-carved furniture, and all sorts of collectibles; **Greece Is for Lovers,** 13a Kariatidon (℡ 210/924-5064; www.greeceisforlovers.com), as kitsch as it might sound, has some fun stuff and **Koukos,** 21 Navarhou Nikodimou (℡ 210/322-2740), has a great collection of antique ceramics, jewelry and all sorts of goodies. For more personalized gifts visit **www.kokicreations.gr**, an extremely successful online store that has taken Greece by storm. Even Oprah is a fan.

Kolonaki, on the slopes of Mount Likavitos, is boutique heaven. However, it's a better place to window-shop than to buy, since much of what you see here is imported and heavily taxed. During the January and August sales, you may discover bargains. If not, it's still fun to work your way up pedestrian Voukourestiou and along Tsakalof, Skoufa and Anagnostopoulou (with some of the most expensive boutiques in Athens) before you collapse at a cafe on one of the pedestrian streets in Kolonaki Square—perhaps fashionable Milioni. Then you can engage in the other serious business of Kolonaki: people-watching. Give yourself about 15 minutes to figure out the season's must-have accessory.

Pedestrianized **Ermou Street** is the prime shopping district in the city, with more stores than you will ever have the time to visit, and you could spend a pleasant day (and a lot of money) exploring it.

Markets & Groceries

The **Central Market** ★ on Athinas is open Monday through Saturday from about 8am to 6pm. You may not want to take advantage of all of the bargain prices (two sheep's heads for the price of one is our all-time favorite), but this is a great place to buy Greek spices, herbs, cheeses, and sweets—and to see how Athens is fed.

Insider Shopping

Serious shoppers should look for the "Best of Athens" issue of the English-language magazine *Odyssey*. Published in July or August and available at bookstores and kiosks, the issue is filled with shopping tips—and scoops on what's "in" in Athens.

Every Friday from about 8am until 2pm, **Xenokratous** in Kolonaki turns into a street market selling flowers, fruits, and vegetables. This is a very different scene from the rowdy turmoil of the Central Market, although it's lively enough. Kolonaki matrons come here with their Filipino servants, who lug their purchases home while the ladies head off for shopping and light lunches (perhaps at fashionable **To Kafenio,** ✆ **210/722-9056**). Every neighborhood has a weekly market; if you want to take in a number of them, ask at your hotel. **Green Farm** (✆ **210/361-4001**), also in Kolonaki, sells only organic produce.

In Plaka, **Mesogeia,** 52 Nikkis (✆ **210/322-9146**), with organic produce, is one of a number of small "boutique" groceries springing up in Athens.

Sweets/Ice Cream

You'll have no problem satisfying your sweet tooth in Athens. If anything, you'll come up gasping for air as you eat the seriously sweet sweets adored by most Greeks.

The long-established **Aristokratikon,** 9 Karayioryi Servias, just off Syntagma Square (✆ **210/322-0546;** www.aristokratikon.com), makes excellent chocolates, glazed pistachio nuts, and *loukoumia* (Turkish delight). Beware—even chocoholics may find the truffles coated with white chocolate too sweet. That said, **Chocolate 56,** 56 Ermou ✆ **210/322-9919**), serves some of the finest chocolate drinks in the city. **Karavan,** the hole in the wall at 11 Voukourestiou (no phone), has the best Levantine delights in town. Serving excellent coffee and sweets, **K. Kotsolis Pastry Shop,** 112 Adrianou, is an oasis of old-fashioned charm in the midst of the Plaka. **Sermpetia of Psiri,** 3 Aishilou (✆ **210/324-5862**), has some of the best desserts in the city, period.

Loukoumades are the Greek doughnuts with a difference—each is about the size of an American doughnut hole, drenched in honey, covered with cinnamon, and served hot. *Delicious!* If you're near Syntagma Square, try **Doris,** 30 Praxitelous (✆ **210/323-2671**). If you're nearer Omonia Square, try **Aigaion,** 46 Panepistimiou (✆ **210/381-4621**). Better yet, try both.

Looking for the best **gelato** in town? Venture into Psirri at **Gelatomania,** 21 Taki and Aisopou (✆ **210/323-0001**), for authentic homemade Italian ice cream.

ATHENS AFTER DARK

Greeks enjoy their nightlife so much that they take an afternoon nap to rest up for it. The evening often begins with a leisurely *volta* (stroll); you'll see this in most neighborhoods, including the main drags through the Plaka and Kolonaki Square. Most Greeks don't think of dinner until at least 9pm in winter, 10pm in summer. Around midnight, the party may move on to a club for music and dancing.

Check the *Athens News* (published Fri) or the daily *Kathimerini* insert in the *International Herald Tribune* for listings of current cultural and entertainment events,

THE festivals: ATHENS (HELLENIC), LYCABETTUS & EPIDAURUS

Tickets for the Athens, Lycabettus, and Epidaurus festivals are available at the **Hellenic Festival Box Office,** 39 Panepistimiou (in the arcade; ✆ **210/928-2900**). Hours are Monday through Friday 8:30am to 4pm, Saturday 9am to 2:30pm. (The name "Hellenic Festival" is an umbrella term for a number of summer festivals, including the Athens and Epidaurus festivals.) Advance booking for most events starts 3 weeks before each performance, 10 days before each event for the Lycabettus Festival. Ticket reservation and telephone booking are also possible by credit card, with the exact date and performance, number and category of tickets, and number and expiration date of the credit card. Tickets (if available) also go on sale at the **box offices** at each theater 2 hours before each performance. Events at the Odeion of Herodes Atticus on the slopes of the Acropolis are usually sold out by the day of the performance; for information, call ✆ **210/323-2771.**

Additional information is available at www.greekfestival.gr, www.athens24.com, and www.breathtakingathens.gr.

including films, lectures, theater, music, and dance. The weekly *Hellenic Times* and monthly *Now in Athens* list nightspots, restaurants, movies, theater, and much more.

The Performing Arts

The acoustically marvelous **Megaron Mousikis Concert Hall,** 89 Leoforos Vas. Sofias (✆ **210/729-0391** or 210/728-2333; www.megaron.gr; Metro: Megaro Mousikis), hosts a wide range of classical music programs that include operas symphonies, and recitals. On performance nights, the box office is open Monday through Friday from 10am to 6pm, Saturday from 10am to 2pm, and Sunday from 6 to 10:30pm. Tickets are also sold Monday through Friday from 10am to 5pm in the Megaron's convenient downtown kiosk in the Spiromillios Arcade, 4 Stadiou. Ticket prices run from 5€ to as much as 100€, depending on the performance. The Megaron has a limited summer season but is in full swing the rest of the year.

The **Greek National Opera** performs at **Olympia Theater,** 59 Akadimias St. (✆ **210/361-2461;** www.nationalopera.gr; Metro: Panepistimio). The indoor opera season runs from November to May. During the summer months the company plays at the **Odeon of Herodes Atticus** and occasionally tours the country and/or abroad.

Pallas Theater, 5 Voukourestiou (✆ **210/321-3100;** www.ticketshop.gr; Metro: Syntagma), hosts jazz and rock concerts, as well as some classical performances in a stunning space, restored to its former glory in the CityLink building. Prices vary from performance to performance, but you can get a cheap ticket from about 10€.

The **Hellenic American Union,** 22 Massalias between Kolonaki and Omonia squares (✆ **210/362-9886;** www.hau.gr; Metro: Panepistimio), often hosts performances of English-language theater and American-style music (tickets 10€ and up). If you arrive early, check out the art shows or photo exhibitions in the adjacent gallery.

The **Athens Center,** 48 Archimidous (✆ **210/701-8603;** www.athenscentre.gr), often stages free performances of ancient Greek and contemporary international plays in June and July. It is behind the Panethinaiko Stadium (old Olympic Stadium).

At the **National Theater,** 22–24 Agiou Konstantinou (☎ **210/522-3242;** www. n-t.gr; Metro: Omonia), you will find a variety of shows from classical theater to musicals in a beautiful neoclassical building. Tickets range from 15€ to 20€.

Since 1953, **Dora Stratou Folk Dance Theater** ★ has been giving performances of traditional Greek folk dances on Filopappos Hill. At present, performances take place May through September, Tuesday through Sunday at 9:30pm, with additional performances at 8:15pm on Wednesday and Sunday. You can buy tickets at the **box office,** 8 Scholio, Plaka, from 8am to 2pm (☎ **210/921-4650** after 5:30pm; www.grdance.org; Metro: Acropolis). Tickets are 15€. Tickets are also available at the theater before the performances. The program changes every 2 or 3 weeks.

The **Onassis Cultural Center,** 107-109 Syngrou Ave. (☎ **210/178-0000;** www. sgt.gr), hosts events, theater, visual art, and music performances.

The Club, Music & Bar Scene

Given the vicissitudes of Athens nightlife, your best bet is to have a local friend; failing that, you have this guide and you can always ask someone at your hotel for a recommendation. The listings in the weekly *Athinorama* (Greek) or in publications such as the English-language *Athens News,* the *Kathimerini* insert in the *Herald Tribune,* and hotel handouts such as *Best of Athens* and *Welcome to Athens,* can be very helpful. If you ask a taxi driver, he's likely to take you to either his cousin's joint or the place that gives him drinks for bringing you.

If you head to a large club, you're likely to face a cover charge of at least 10€ to 20€, which will likely include a drink. Thereafter, each drink will probably cost over 10€. It's best to go only to clubs with or recommended by someone *trustworthy* who knows the scene or that have come recommended from reliable sources (such as this guide). In large clubs, don't sit at a table unless you want to purchase a bottle of alcohol (100€), whether you want it or not.

TRADITIONAL MUSIC

Walk the streets of the Plaka on any night and you'll find plenty of tavernas offering pseudo-traditional live music. As noted, many are serious clip joints, where if you sit down and ask for a glass of water, you'll be charged 100€ for a bottle of scotch. At most of these places, there's a cover of 10€. We've had good reports on **Taverna Mostrou,** 22 Mnissikleos (☎ 210/324-2441), which is large, old, and best known for traditional Greek music and dancing. Shows begin around 11pm and can last until 2am. The cover of 30€ includes a fixed-menu supper. A la carte fare is available but expensive (as are drinks). Nearby, **Palia Taverna Kritikou,** 24 Mnissikleos (☎ 210/322-2809), is another lively open-air taverna with music and dancing.

Tavernas offering low-key music include **Daphne's,** 4 Lysikratous (☎ 210/322-7971); **Nefeli,** 24 Panos (☎ 210/321-2475); **Dioyenis,** 4 Sellei (☎ 210/324-7933); **Stamatopoulou,** 26 Lissiou (☎ 210/322-8722); and favorites **Klimataria,** 5 Klepsidrias (☎ 210/324-1809), and **Xinos,** 4 Agelou Geronta (☎ 210/322-1065).

BARS/CLUBS

Greek nightlife has a reputation for just getting started when the rest of Europe has already gone to bed. It's true. The nightlife in Athens is sophisticated and varied. From large clubs by the beach to trendy lounges in **Kolonaki, Neo Psihiko,** and **Panormou** street, to indie and intimate bars in **Karitsi Square** and **Psirri** to clubs and red-hot bars in **Gazi,** this is a city that never sleeps. Apart from a few waterfront choices, visitors will find most places located in the center. For those wishing to visit the beach clubs, keep in mind the tram runs on a 24-hour schedule during the weekends, making getting to and from the coast easy and inexpensive. Some of the best lounges/bars in the city these days are in hotels. Don't forget to have a drink at the top-floor **Galaxy** bar at the **Hilton** hotel for an amazing city view. For the best Acropolis view head to the **Hera Hotel's Peacock Lounge;** for the most happening scene visit the **Frame Bar-Lounge** at **St. George Lycabettus Hotel** and **Ochre & Brown** lounge.

Plaka/Makrigianni
(For Plaka Metro: Syntagma/Acropolis. For Makrigiannni Metro: Acropolis)

Athens Sports Bar, 3a Veikou, Makrigianni (✆ **210/923-5811;** www.athenssportsbar.com), is just that, with snacks, projection screens, karaoke, and theme nights; happy hour is nightly 7–8pm. **Brettos Bar,** 41 Kydathineon, Plaka (✆ **210/323-2110;** www.brettosplaka.com), with its backlit wall of bottles, has been an Athenian landmark for more than a century. **Chandelier,** 4 Benizelou, Plaka (✆ **210/631-6330**), is a cozy and laid-back lounge with a jazz soundtrack on the ground floor of a neoclassical building. **Duente Bar,** 2 Tzireon, Makrigianni (✆ **210/924-7069**), is an elegant old-world brasserie with a Rat Pack soundtrack, ideal for quiet evenings. **Melina Café,** 22 Lyssiou 22, Plaka (✆ **210/324-6501;** www.melinacafe.gr), is a charming cafe/bar that celebrates the life of Greek actress and politician Melina Mercouri and is popular with the French tourists. **Tiki Athens,** 15 Falirou, Makrigianni (✆ **210/923-6908;** www.tikiathens.com), as the name suggests, is a fun and funky place with '50s exotic decor, Asian-inspired cuisine, and infectious good times.

Monastiraki
(Metro: Monastiraki)

Dude, 14 Kalamiotou (✆ **210/322-7130;** www.thedudebar.com), is named after the cult-favorite character from *The Big Lebowski* and is a funky bar where the dude himself would abide. **Gallery Café** (cafe/bar), 33 Adrianou (✆ **210/324-9080**), on busy Adrianou, is a delightful and edgy cafe serving breakfast and snacks throughout the day. At night, the lights dim and it morphs into an equally charming bar. When electronica-loving hipsters bought **Inoteka,** 3 Plateia Avyssinias (✆ **210/324-6446**), they redid the space into a funky bar. During the summer, the candlelit tables spill out on the *plateia*—a great place to linger at all night long. **Keyser Soze,** 12 Avramiotou (✆ **210/323-4341**), is named for the enigmatic character from *The Usual Suspects* and has an inspired and intriguing film noir theme: old detective novels adorn the walls and there's even an outlined body on the floor as a rock soundtrack and weekly theme parties add to the fun. **Magaze,** 33 Eolou (✆ **210/324-3740;** www.magaze.gr), is an all-day cafe and laid-back evening bar with a mixed and friendly crowd on pedestrian Eolou. **TAF–The Art Foundation** includes an art bar at 5 Normanou (✆ **210/323-8757;** www.theartfoundation.gr). Off Ermou Street, in a seemingly abandoned alley, the blink-and-you-missed-it door leads into a restored neoclassical building complex from the 19th century that houses the Art Foundation, a series of galleries, music, and theater showings. In the middle of the complex is the lively courtyard bar.

Psirri
(Metro: Monastiraki)

Cantina Social, 6-8 Leokoreiou (✆ **210/325-1668**), is a bar directly across from the "Ochre & Brown" boutique hotel, inside an old arcade. This unconventional bar has flourished due to word of mouth, in a space (including a "courtyard") between abandoned buildings. Old movies play on tarnished walls, the crowd is alternative and friendly, the music fun and the drinks (5€–7€) a real find. **Cubanita** at 28 Karaiskaki (✆ **210/331-4605;** www.cubanita.gr) offers—hands down—one of the best nights to be had in the city, where Latin beats and excellent Cuban cuisine combine to make a great place to party until the early morning hours. On some nights there's live Cuban music. **El Pecado,** a bar/restaurant/club at 11 Tournavitou (✆ **210/324-4049;** www.elpecado.gr), came about from the unorthodox union of a medieval Spanish-style church and erotic murals inspired by Bible themes. Confused? Don't be. Follow the fun into this sinfully enjoyable venue (cover is 10€).

Thissio
(Metro: Thissio)

Athinaion Politeia (cafe/bar/restaurant), 30 Apostolou Pavlou and 1 Akamanthos (✆ **210/341-3794;** www.athinaionpoliteia.gr), is in a grand restored building (a grocery store in the 19th c.) right on the Promenade, with views of the Acropolis and passersby. **Dust,** 3 Irakleidon, (✆ **210/342-6794**), is a wonderful all-day cafe and cool bar at night with DJs, live performances, and weekly art events. **Loop,** 3 Plateia Agion Asomaton (✆ **210/324-7666**), features industrial decor, rotating DJs, and a fun crowd. **Stavlos** (multifunctional urban coolness), 10 Iraklidon (✆ **210/346-7206;** www.stavlos.gr), is off the Archaeological Promenade on pedestrian Iraklidon Street. It was the royal stables in the 1880s. Now it is a cafe during the day with an Italian restaurant and laid-back bar/club at night with outdoor seating in either the terrace, the tree-lined courtyard, or on the busy sidewalk.

Gazi
(Metro: Kerameikos)

And here we are: nightlife central. Trying to pick a place here is tricky because most of the bars and clubs in Gazi are good. For starters, take a stroll to scope out the scene. Walk down Persefonis Street and Triptopolemou in either direction: The Kerameikos Metro station is a landscaped *plateia* (Gazi Sq.) that covers an entire city block and is surrounded on either side by extremely popular bars, cafes and eateries. Once the bars reach full capacity, patrons head to the street and the *plateia,* drinks in hand.

There is always something cool going on at **Bios,** 84 Pireos (✆ **210/342-5335;** www.bios.gr), an art-space/cafe/bar/club, from avant-garde performances to exhibitions and foreign art film showings. A basement nightclub sways to a mostly rock soundtrack. An excellent place to begin the night is at **45 degrees,** 18 Iakhou, corner of Voutadhon (✆ **210/347-2729**). This rock bar/club has a rooftop terrace overlooking Gazi and the Acropolis. The oldest bar in Gazi **Gazaki,** 31 Triptopolemou (✆ **210/346-0901**), remains one of the best. The music is always excellent, as are the drinks. The no-pretense mixed crowd makes this a sure bet for any night of the week and the roof terrace is another plus.

Across from Gazaki, you will find **Dirty Ginger,** 46 Triptopolemou (✆ **210/342-3809;** www.dirtyginger.gr), a bar/restaurant with table seating on one of the most active streets in the city, a palm-tree-lined garden, and excellent Mediterranean cuisine and pumping soundtrack. **Eighth Sin,** 141 Megalou Alexandrou (✆ **210/347-7048**), is a beautiful space, smartly decorated, with a mixed crowd and excellent cocktails based on, you got it, the seven deadly sins, plus an eighth one: the delicious and potent namesake's signature cocktail. **Gazarte,** 32–34 Voutadon (✆ **210/346-0347;** www.gazarte.gr), is a three-level urban chic space with various weekly art exhibitions, a good restaurant, and a lovely bar on the roof terrace with sweeping views.

Hoxton, 42 Voutadon (☎ **210/341-3395**), is a hip bar with a seriously addictive rock/new wave soundtrack. At **Tapas Bar,** 44 Triptopolemou (☎ **210/347-1844**), the action begins with light snacks and a jazzy soundtrack that segues into Latin beats as patrons down the margaritas, mojitos, and rum-based drinks.

K44, 33 Leof. Konstantinoupoleos (☎ **210/342-6804;** www.k44.gr), is a multi-level warehouse that is a popular cafe/bar with live music performances on the ground floor and art exhibitions upstairs. **Nipiagogio (Kindergarten)** at Elasidon and 8 Kleanthous (☎ **210/345-8534**) is a former elementary school that has been turned into one of the hottest bar/clubs in the city. On Saturday nights the former classrooms and playground stay hot until 6am. **Villa Mercedes,** Andronikou and 11 Jafferi (☎ **210/342-3606;** www.mercedes-club.gr), is an impressive nightclub with many rooms and an internal courtyard (plus a restaurant) that's always hopping. (Cover is 10€–15€.) *Tip:* Any night you're in Gazi, stop by **Mamacas** bar/lounge (inside the popular modern tavern; p. 127) and have a drink at the bar to check out the scene. Something interesting is always going on here.

Zappeio/Syntagma
(Metro: Syntagma)

Banana Moon, 1 Adrittou (☎ **210/347-8716**), is an all-day cafe and evening bar/club in the middle of Adrittou avenue (formerly On the Road) across the street from the Old Olympic Stadium, with great music and decor and a wonderfully rowdy atmosphere. **Booze Coopertiva,** 57 Koloktroni (☎ **210/324-0944;** www.booze coopertiva.com), is an all-day hangout cafe with art exhibitions, screenings and performances, and lively bar at night. Inside the Aigli complex you will find the **Lallabai** lounge/club, 9 Zappeion (☎ **210/336-9340**). Tastefully decorated, this is a great place to soak up the serene garden surroundings or the boisterous scene as the lounge turns into a club. (Cover is 10€.) **Six D.O.G.S.,** 6-8 Avramiotou (☎ **210/321-0510;** www.sixdogs.gr), is an all-day cafe and gallery space, with live music performances and energetic bar in the evenings. **Kalua,** 6 Amerikis (☎ **210/360-8304**), a bar near Syntagma Square, packs partiers into one of the city's most outrageously fun spots. **Stin Priza (Plugged In),** 1 Christou Lada. (☎ **210/324-4101**), a popular bar on Karitsi Square (decorated in sockets—thus its name), is mellow during the day but picks up serious heat after 9pm and still manages to feel more like a friend's party than a bar. **The Gin Joint,** 1 Christou Lada. (☎ **210/321-8646**), is a bar that explores a U.S. Prohibition-era "speakeasy" style, showcasing its bottles behind fenced windows and sways to a jazz and swing soundtrack. **The Seven Jokers,** 7 Voulis (☎ **210/321-9225**), is a quiet cafe during the day, intimate bar in the early evening, and insanely busy after-hours bar with a serious crush on the Stones.

Exarheia
(Metro: Panepistimio)

Circus, 11 Navarinou (☎ **210/361-5255;** www.circusbar.gr), is a bar on the border of Kolonaki and Exarheia, where posh meets bohemian. **Decadence,** 87 Emmanouil Benaki, Exarcheia (☎ **210/381-3685;** www.decadence.gr), is a landmark Athenian rock club in a beautiful neoclassical mansion that used to belong to royalty. It's popular with all ages and touring bands that stop in after their shows. **Recital,** 64 Eressou (☎ **210/380-5556**), is a club in an ivy-covered mansion that hosts live performances by Greek and foreign rock bands; you can also hang out on the terrace. Catch a rock concert at **Gagarin 205,** 205 Liossion (☎ **210/854-7601;** www.gagarin205.gr), a large indoor space in Athens in the winter, or its other space on the coast in the summer.

Kolonaki/Ambelokipi

(Metro for Kolonaki: Syntagma or Evaggelismos; for Ambelokipi: Ambelokipi)

Balthazar, 27 Tsoha and Soutsou, Ambelokipi (© **210/644-1215;** www.balthazar. gr), has been a favorite Athenian destination since the '80s, and has a fine restaurant, but it is the bar in the mansion's lantern-lit courtyard that's the nightlife spot. Show up late (after midnight) for drinks in this romantic location with the pretty people. **Baraonda,** 43 Tsoha, Ambelokipi (© **210/644-4308;** www.baraonda.gr), features red velvet curtains, candles, stone and tiled walls, chandeliers, two bars, a VIP section, summer courtyard, a stylish clientele, and tasty Mediterranean cuisine. **Mike's Irish Bar,** 6 Sinopis, Ambelokipi (© **210/777-6797;** www.mikesirishbar.gr), is a popular pub that's packed with expatriates and locals alike. **Mai Tai,** 18 Ploutarhou, Kolonaki (© **210/725-83062;** www.mai-tai.gr), is an all-day hangout place, with a tasty menu, good drinks, and an attractive 30-plus crowd. **Mommy Open,** 4 Delfon, Kolonaki (© **210/361-9682**), offers an impressive space—with a smart decor, art exhibitions, an excellent Mediterranean menu, and great drinks. It gets pumping after midnight, and also has an excellent Sunday brunch. **Scala Vinoteca,** 50 Sina, Kolonaki (© **210/361-0041**), is a beautiful, stylish wine bar/restaurant tucked between the stairs ascending to Lycabettus mountain, a perfect spot to begin the evening.

Seaside Clubs

Akrotiri Club Restaurant, Leof Vas Georgiou B5, Agios Kosmas (© **210/985-9147;** www.akrotirilounge.gr; tram to Elliniko stop), is a massive (capacity 3,000), beautiful and stylish open-air club next to the beach, with an elegant tropical decor, a huge pool, dance floors, deck seating by the beach, sea views, excellent (but pricey) Med-fusion cuisine (50€–70€), which has been popular since the '80s and shows no signs of stopping. (Cover, including a drink, 11pm–5am Mon–Thurs and Sun is 10€, Fri–Sat 15€.) **B.E.D.,** 58 Leoforos Poseidonos (© **210/894-1620;** tram to Plateia Glyfadas then 5-min. walk), is inside the Asteras Glyfada complex, and you can party right by the waves and the pool. (Cover, including drink Wed–Fri and Sun 11pm–5am is 10€; Fri–Sat 15€.) **Sea and City,** 14 Karamanli, Voula (© **210/895-9645;** tram to Plateia Glyfadas, then bus no. A2 or a taxi), is in a beautiful seafront mansion with a terrace right above the waves. It's a trendy cafe during the day that slowly morphs into a lounge/restaurant until its final reincarnation as a pumping club. Romantic **Island ★**, Limanakia Vouliagmenis (© **210/965-3563;** www.islandclubrestaurant. gr; tram to Plateia Glyfadas and from there take a taxi or bus no. 114 and get off at Limanakia), is out of the way but worth the trip. Set on a cliff top with sea vistas, where you can enjoy excellent finger food, sushi, and Mediterranean dishes, this is the quintessential Athenian summer nightspot. Things get louder after 1am. Show up early or make dinner reservations—prices are moderate to expensive (20€–70€)—or you can enjoy tapas at the bar. The door policy is annoying—if you arrive on foot you won't get in unless it's very early (10pm) or you have dinner reservations. (No cover with dinner reservations, 15€ without.)

REMBETIKA & BOUZOUKIA

Visitors interested in authentic *rembetika* (music of the urban poor and dispossessed) and bouzoukia (traditional and pop music featuring the bouzouki, a kind of guitar, today almost always loudly amplified) should consult their hotel concierge or check the listings in *Athinorama,* the weekly *Hellenic Times,* or *Kathimerini* (the daily insert in the *International Herald Tribune*). Another good place to ask is at the shop of the Museum of Popular Greek Musical Instruments (p. 146). *Rembetika* performances usually don't start until nearly midnight, and though there's rarely a cover, drinks can cost as much as 20€. Many clubs close during the summer.

One of the more central places for *rembetika* is **Stoa Athanaton,** 19 Sofokleous, in the Central Meat Market (© **210/321-4362**), which has been serving good food and live music since 1930 from 3 to 7:30pm and after 11pm. **Taximi,** 29 Isavron, Exarchia (© **210/363-9919**), is consistently popular. Drinks cost 12€. It's closed Sunday and Monday and during July and August. The downscale, smoke-filled **Rembetiki Istoria,** in a neoclassical building at 181 Ippokratous (© **210/642-4967**), features old-style *rembetika,* played to a mixed crowd of older regulars and younger students and intellectuals. The music usually starts at 11pm, but arrive earlier to get a seat. The legendary Maryo I Thessaloniki (Maryo from Thessaloniki), described as the Bessie Smith of Greece, sometimes sings *rembetika* at **Perivoli t'Ouranou,** 19 Lysikratous (© **210/323-5517** or 210/322-2048), in Plaka. Expect to pay at least 10€ per drink in these places, most of which have a cover from 20€—except Rembetiki Istoria, which due to its student clientele is more affordable than most such places.

JAZZ

A number of clubs and cafes specialize in jazz, but also offer everything from Indian sitar music to rock to punk. The popular—and well thought of—**Half Note Jazz Club,** 17 Trivonianou, Mets (© **210/921-3310;** www.halfnote.gr), schedules performers who play everything from medieval music to jazz; set times vary from 8 to 11pm and later. (Cover is 30€ with one drink.) In Gazi, at the **Art House,** 46 Konstantinou-poleos (© **210/461-1535;** www.art-house-athens.gr), you can often hear jazz from 11pm. (Cover depends on event.) **Cabaret Voltaire,** 30 Marathonos, Metaxourgeio (© **210/522-7046;** Metro: Metaxourgeio), has live jazz every Sunday. **Jazz n' Jazz,** 4 Deinokratous (© **210/725-8362;** Tues–Sat 8pm–3am), a small, cozy and charming jazz museum/bar in Kolonaki, is a great place to take in the vibe and listen to their extensive jazz collection. If you're visiting in late May, check out the **European Jazz Festival** at **Technopolis,** 100 Pireos (© **210/346-0981;** www.technopolis.gr). Also check out what's happening at the **Pallas Theater,** 5 Voukourestiou (© **210/321-3100;** www.ticketshop.gr), which hosts frequent jazz concerts. Also, the beautiful **Athens Plaza Hotel** (www.njvathensplaza.gr) hosts weekly live jazz performances.

Gay & Lesbian Athens

There are lots of gay bars, cafes, and clubs in Athens, even though the gay male venues by far outnumber the lesbian ones. The scene used to be in Makrigianni and Kolonaki, and the legendary gay bars and clubs of the past remain and are still popular but Gazi has taken over, with the hippest gay or gay-friendly scene. The weekly publications *Athinorama* and *Time Out* often list gay bars, discos, and special events in the nightlife section. You can also look for the Greek publication ***Deon Magazine*** (© **210/953-6479;** www.deon.gr) or surf the Web at www.gaygreece.gr, www.greekgayguide.eu, www.gayathens.gr, or www.lesbian.gr. **Gay Travel Greece,** at 377 Syngrou Ave. in central Athens (© **210/948-4385;** www.gaytravelgreece.com), specializes, as its name proclaims, in travel for gay and lesbian visitors.

Gay and lesbian travelers will not encounter difficulties at any Athenian hotel, but one with a largely gay and lesbian clientele is 41-room **Hotel Rio Athens** (© **210/522-7075;** www.hotel-rio.gr), at 13 Odysseos off Karaiskaki Square in a restored neoclassical building. The popular Alexander Sauna has nice, clean apartments for rent above the bathhouse at affordable prices at **Alexander Apartments,** 134 Megalou Alexandrou and Iera Odos, Gazi (© **210/698-0282;**

www.alexander-apartments.gr). Below are some selections we have made of the city's more fun gay and lesbian bars/clubs. Also remember that **Athens Pride** (**www.athenspride.eu**) takes place in early June.

GAY & LESBIAN BARS/CLUBS

Alexander Sauna, 134 Megalou Alexandrou and Iera Odos, Gazi (✆ **210/698-0282;** www.alexandersauna.com; Sun–Thurs 7pm–3am, Fri–Sat 7pm–8am; admission 9€–15€), is a very popular bathhouse with sauna, gym, Jacuzzi, private rooms, bar, garden, and many events and theme parties. **Bear Code Club,** 8 Konstantinoupoleos, Gazi (✆ **694/888-3241;** www.bearcode.gr; Thurs–Sun 10pm–5am), is a bar/club with events and live performances for bears, cubs, and their admirers. **Blue Train,** 84 Konstantinoupoleos, Gazi (✆ **210/346-0677;** www.bluetrain.gr; daily 8pm–4am), is right by the railway tracks on the edge of Gazi. The friendly scene here is a great place to begin the evening, preferably at a sidewalk table, where you can watch the trains and the boys go by, except on Fridays when the night belongs to the girls.

Group Therapy, 11 Lepenioutou, Psirri (✆ **210/323-4977;** daily 10pm–4am), is an intimate, friendly, and sexy lesbian bar, popular with the beautiful, yet attitude-free girls and their friends. **Fou Club,** 8 Keleou, Gazi (✆ **210/346-6800;** www.fouclub.gr; daily 10pm–5am), is a fun place with theme nights, special events, and an attitude-free crowd. **Kazarma,** first floor, 84 Konstantinoupoleos, Gazi (✆ **210/346-0667;** Thurs–Sat midnight–5am), is above Blue Train, one of the best gay clubs in the city. During summer, the fun moves to the terrace (**El Cielo**). **Lamda Reloaded,** 15 Lembessi and 9 Syngrou, Makrigianni (✆ **210/922-4202;** www.lamdaclub.gr; Thurs–Sun 11pm–5am), has been popular for so long, it has become an Athenian institution. The energy on the ground floor is mostly laid back, while things in the basement get far rowdier. **Mayo,** 33 Persefonis, Gazi (✆ **210/342-3066;** daily 8pm–4am), is a quiet bar with a great inner courtyard and a rooftop terrace with a killer view. **Micraasia,** 70 Konstantinopoleos, Gazi (✆ **210/346-4851;** daily 7:30pm–4am), whose name means "Asia Minor," has a decor with something of the Middle Eastern vibe of the old Greek world in that region (now Turkey). Red lighting, colored tiles, chaises, and belly dancers all contribute to making this an atmospheric venue (mostly for girls). There is also seating on its "secret" rooftop.

My Bar, 6 Kakourgiodikiou, Monastiraki (✆ **210/486-2161;** www.mybar.gr; daily 11pm–4am), is a more intimate, less rowdy bar than its Gazi counterparts but just as energetic. The girls have made **Noiz,** 41 Evmolpidon and Konstantinoupoleos, Gazi (✆ **210/342-4771;** www.noizclub.gr; Mon–Fri 10:30pm–4am, Sat–Sun 10:30pm–6am), into the most popular lesbian bar/club in town. With its good music and dynamic scene, Noiz offers the ultimate lesbian party. **Sodade,** 10 Triptopolemou, Gazi (✆ **210/346-8657;** Mon–Fri 10:30pm–4am, Sat–Sun 10:30pm–6am), was the first gay bar to open in Gazi, and it's become an institution, unbearably packed on weekends but always irresistible. **S'Cape,** Iera Odos and 139 Meg. Alexandrou, Gazi (✆ **210/345-2751;** www.s-cape-club.blogspot.com; Mon–Fri 10:30pm–4am, Sat–Sun 10:30pm–6am), is a large club with army bunks, military-style motif, and a sexy crowd; it's fun and very cruisy, but never takes itself too seriously. Monday is karaoke night, Thursday is Greek night.

RESTAURANTS/CAFES

Del Soul, 44 Voutadon, Gazi (✆ **210/341-8169**), is an all-day cafe, snacks, and late-night bar, along with **Magaze,** 33 Eolou, Monastiraki (✆ **210/324-3740;** www.magaze.gr). **Myrovolos,** 12 Giatrakou, Metaxourgeio (✆ **210/522-8806**), is a popular restaurant in a large piazza that opens at 11am daily as a cafe. It then becomes a very good restaurant before morphing into a busy bar for girls who love other girls, and their friends. **Kanella,** 70 Leof. Konstantinoupoleos, Gazi (© **210/347-6320**), is a good, moderately priced modern taverna with a mixed clientele. Everybody loves the cafe **Wunderbar,** 80 Themistokleous, Exarchia (© **210/381-85577**), especially the girls. The popular restaurants **Mamacas** (p. 127) and **Prosopa** (p. 128) are both mainstream but very gay friendly.

PIRAEUS: ATHENS'S PORT

Piraeus has been the port of Athens since antiquity, and it is still where you catch most island boats and cruise ships. What's confusing is that Piraeus has **three harbors: Megas Limani (Main Harbor),** where you'll see everything from tankers to cruise ships; **Zea Limani (Zea Marina),** the port for most of the swift hydrofoils that dart to the islands; and **Mikrolimano (Little Harbor),** also called Turkolimano, or Turkish Harbor by the old-timers, one of the most charming and picturesque harbors in the Mediterranean, lined with a number of fish restaurants, cafes, and bars.

The absence of helpful signs at both the Main Harbor and Zea Limani, however, along with their constant bustle, means that this is not an easy place to navigate. To be on the safe side, even if you have your tickets, get there an hour before your ship is scheduled to sail—and don't be surprised if you curse this advice because your ship sails later than announced.

As in antiquity, today's Piraeus has the seamier side of a sailors' port of call as well as the color of an active harbor—both aspects, somewhat sanitized, were portrayed in the 1960 film *Never on Sunday* that made Melina Mercouri an international star. Piraeus also has a sprawling street market just off the Main Harbor, where you can buy produce that arrives each day on island boats, including bread baked that morning on distant islands. If you find yourself here with some time to spare, take a stroll along Mikrolimano, Zea Marina (otherwise known as Pasalimani, with countless cafes and shopping stores), and the pretty residential area of Kastella.

Essentials

These prices were accurate at press time and may have (and probably will have) gone up by the time you arrive here.

Preparing for Piraeus

From mid-July through the end of August, boats leaving Piraeus for the islands are heavily booked, and often overbooked. It is sometimes possible to get deck passage without a reservation, but even that can be difficult when as many as 100,000 passengers leave the ports on a summer weekend (as often happens in July–Aug). Most ships will not allow passengers to board without a ticket, so buy your tickets in advance.

Because schedules depend on the weather, and sailings are often delayed or canceled, it's not a good idea to plan to return to Athens by boat less than 24 hours before your flight home. Also, as with most ports, this is not a good place to wander around in the wee hours—unless you are looking for a walk on the wild side.

Piraeus

Megas Limani (Main Harbor)

Zea Limani (Zea's Harbor)

Mikrolimano (Little Harbor/Turkish Harbor)

Greece
Athens
Piraeus
Aegean Sea
Mediterranean Sea
CRETE

International Ferries	1
Istioploikos	9
Jimmy and the Fish	8
Pisina (The Swimming Pool)	3
Plous-Podilatou	7
Vosporos	5

Ammos	6
Cellier Zea	4
Dourambeis	10
Flying Dolphins	2

GETTING THERE **By Metro** The fastest and easiest way to Piraeus from central Athens is to take the Metro from Omonia Square, Monastiraki, or Thissio to the last stop (1.20€), then cross the footbridge to the domestic port.

By Bus From Syntagma Square, take the (very slow) Green Depot bus no. 40 from the corner of Filellinon; it will leave you a block from the international port, about a 10-minute walk along the water from the domestic port. From the airport, bus no. X96 goes to Piraeus; the fare is 5€.

By Taxi A taxi from Syntagma Square can cost up to 15€. The flat rate from Athens International Airport to the port is 35€ during the day and 50€ after midnight. For more info visit **www.athenstaxi.info**.

RETURNING TO ATHENS The easiest way is to take the Metro to central Athens, to either Monastiraki, Thissio, or Omonia stations. Most taxi drivers waiting at the dock will try to overcharge tourists disembarking from the boats. They often offer a flat rate that's two or three times the legal fare. The options are to pay up, get a policeman to help you, or walk to a nearby street, hail a cab, and hope for a fair rate.

VISITOR INFORMATION For boat schedules, transit information, and other tourist information 24 hours a day, dial ℂ **171** or 1441. The **Piraeus Port Authority**

can be reached at ☏ **210/451-1311** to -1317 (www.olp.gr). The *Athens News* and the *Kathimerini* insert in the *International Herald Tribune* print major ferry schedules. The **Greek National Tourism Organization (EOT)** office (☏ **210/452-2591**) is inconveniently located on the street above Zea Marina (the hydrofoil port), on the second floor of a shopping arcade stocked with yacht supplies. It's open Monday through Friday from 9am to 2:30pm, but its limited resources probably won't warrant the 20-minute walk from the ferry piers. The small **tourist office** (☏ **210/412-1181**) in the Piraeus Metro station on Akti Poseidonos is open daily from 8am to 8pm. The numbers for the **harbor police** are ☏ **210/412-2501** or 210/451-1311.

FAST FACTS　Several **banks** are along the waterfront. **National Bank,** on Ethniki Antistaseos, has extended hours in summer. A portable **post office** opposite the Aegina ferry pier offers currency exchange; it's open Monday through Saturday from 8am to 8pm and Sunday from 8am to 6pm. The **main post office** is on Tsamadoy; it's usually open daily from 8am to 4pm. There is also a substation in the Metro office on Akti Poseidonos. The **telephone office (OTE)** is a block away from the post office and is open 24 hours. There is another branch by the water, on Akti Miaouli at Merarchias, open daily from 7am to 9:30pm. You'll find secure **luggage storage** in the Metro station at the **Central Travel Agency** (☏ **210/411-5611**; www.athensferries.gr); hours are from 6am to 8pm. The website has all its info regarding departing and returning ferries to and from most major islands.

TICKETS TO THE ISLANDS　The quay of the Main Harbor is lined with **ticket agents,** many concentrated in Plateia Karaiskaki; some sell tickets for one or two lines or destinations only, some for more. A sign in the window should tell you what the agent sells. Almost every agent will tell you that you're getting a good deal; almost no agent will give you one.

FERRIES TO THE ISLANDS　You will be confused as to where to catch your boat; this is inevitable. Allow yourself plenty of time. Even the person you buy your ticket from may give you a bum steer. *Tip:* Information below may change at any moment. Sorry—but we thought you should know the truth.

　　Ferry tickets can be purchased at a ticket office up to 1 hour before departure; after that they can usually be bought on the boat. To book first-class cabins or buy advance-sale tickets, see one of the **harborside travel agents** (around Karaiskaki Sq. by the domestic ferries and along Akti Miaouli, opposite the Crete ferries). Most open at 6am, and some will hold your baggage for the day (but without security). The **Greek National Tourism Organization** publishes a list of weekly sailings. The **tourist police** (☏ **171**) or the **Port Authority** (☏ **210/451-1311** to -1317) can provide you with schedule information. Also check out the **Central Travel Agency** of Piraeus's website at **www.athensferries.gr** for schedules and info. As always it's the better and safer idea to book your tickets through a reputable local travel agency.

　　Boats for the eastern Cyclades (including Mykonos and Santorini) leave in the morning from Akti Tzelepi across from Plateia Karaiskaki. Aegina boats leave from Akti Poseidonos. Boats for Rhodes sail in the afternoon from Akti Miaouli. Boats for the western Cyclades (including Sifnos) sail in the early evening from Akti Kalimassioti near Plateia Karaiskaki. Boats for Crete sail in the early evening from Akti Kondyli. Many additional island boats leave from the quay opposite the Metro station. Boats heading out of Greece depart the quay on Akti Miaouli farthest away from the quays near the Metro and train stations. Boats for Aegina, Poros, Hydra, Spetses,

Peloponnesian ports, and Kithira depart from Zea Marina, which is across the Piraeus peninsula and opposite the Main Harbor; the walk there takes 30 minutes.

What to See & Do

If you're stuck between boats, you may want to walk inland from the harbor on Demosthenous or Vas. Georgiou to Plateia Korai, which leads to a cafe where you can sit with a book. If you want to be by the sea, stroll or take the no. 904 bus (.50€) from the Main Harbor to Akti Themistokleous, where you can also find cafes.

If you're in Piraeus in the summer, a more energetic suggestion is an **open-air theatrical performance** at the Kastella Theater, a few blocks inland from Mikrolimano. In 2000, the first **Poseidon Festival,** with a wide range of concerts, took place in Piraeus; it's becoming an annual event. Get details at **Piraeus Municipal Theater,** Ayiou Konstantinou (📞 **210/419-4550**).

In the winter, performances are staged indoors, at the **Public Theater** on the green at Leoforos King Constantine. The Sunday **flea market** on and around Alipedou and Skylitsi is an equally crowded variation on the Monastiraki flea market, with generally lower-quality goods. The daily **street market** just off the Main Harbor is a good place to get **picnic supplies** for your boat trip.

The **Maritime Museum** (*Akti Themistokleous*), near the pier for hydrofoils (📞 **210/451-6264**), has handsome models of ancient and modern ships. Don't miss the classical warship (*trireme*); scholars still don't know how all those oarsmen rowed in unison. The museum is open Tuesday through Saturday from 9am to 2pm; admission is 3€. If you have time, stop by the **Archaeological Museum ★**, 31 Harilaou Trikoupi (📞 **210/452-1598**), to see three superb monumental bronzes, one depicting a youth (some say Apollo) and two of goddesses (some say Athena and Artemis). Museum hours are Tuesday through Sunday from 8:30am to 3pm; admission is 3€.

Where to Stay

Because Athens is so accessible by Metro, we don't recommend an overnight stay in Piraeus. However, if it makes sense in your travel plans, try one of these decent, moderately priced choices (usually no more than 100€): The 74-unit **Hotel Mistral,** 105 Vas. Pavlou, Kastella (www.mistral.gr; 📞 **210/411-7150**), has a nice roof garden. The 31-unit **Ideal Hotel,** 142 Notara (www.ideal-hotel.gr; 📞 **210/429-4050**) is clean and convenient. For something a bit nicer, try 32-unit **Hotel Castella,** 75 Vas. Pavlou (📞 **210/411-4735**), or **Piraeus Theoxenia Hotel,** 23 Karaoli and Dimitriou (www.theoxeniapalace.gr; 📞 **210/411-2550**), a five-star hotel with 76 rooms in a pretty neoclassical building. Frugal traveling friends always stay at 56-unit **Hotel Triton,** 8 Tsamadou (📞 **210/4173-4578**), which they praise for its quiet location—and double-glazed windows that cut down what noise there is.

Where to Eat

While there are some good restaurants in Piraeus, most of the places to eat along the harbor are mediocre at best. You'll do better if you walk a few blocks along Demosthenous to Plateia Korai, where the small cafes and restaurants are actually patronized by Greeks. If you decide on one of the seafood restaurants in central Piraeus or Mikrolimano, make sure you know the price before ordering; some of these places prey on the unwary. If the final tab seems out of line, insist on a receipt, phone the tourist police, and sit tight. Despite that warning, however, it would be a shame if such a postcard-perfect spot such as Mikrolimano had nothing to offer but ambience. Ignore the aggressive restaurant staff that try to get you to dine in their establishments (far worse than their Plaka counterparts) and try one of the restaurants listed below.

Jimmy & the Fish ★★ SEAFOOD   In addition to its excellent location and great summer deck right by the marina, this restaurant offers excellent food and impeccable service. The lobster spaghetti is out of this world, as is the octopus in red wine and virtually everything on the menu.

46 Akti Koumoundourou, Mikrolimano. ✆ **210/412-4417.** www.jimmyandthefish.gr. Reservations recommended. Main courses 35€-40€. MC, V. Daily noon-1am.

Margaro ★ 🍴 SEAFOOD   This fish taverna near the Main Harbor offers good value (along with excellent cooking) by keeping the menu simple: fish (large or small), crayfish, and salads. Service is brisk, although this place gets very crowded.

126 Hatzikyriakou. ✆ **210/451-4226.** Fish prices (by the kilo) change frequently. No credit cards. Mon-Sat 11am-midnight; Sun lunch only.

Plous Podilatou ★★ SEAFOOD   You'll find elegant dining on picturesque Mikrolimano in this pricey but excellent restaurant. The seafood and crab salads left us begging for more; the squid stuffed with feta cheese and seafood spaghetti are excellent, as are the three risottos (with chicken, shrimp, or leeks).

42 Akti Koumoundourou, Mikrolimano. ✆ **210/413-7910.** www.plous-podilatou.gr. Reservations recommended. Main courses 39€-46€. MC, V. Daily noon-1am.

Vassilenas ★ SEAFOOD/GREEK   Vassilenas has been serving its flat-fee menu for decades. Come here hungry, and even then you likely won't be able to eat everything in the more than 15 courses set before you. There's plenty of seafood, plus good Greek dishes. This is a great place to bring friends, so you can compare notes on favorite dishes or share them. Since Vassilenas is a fair hike from the waterfront, you may want to take a taxi.

72 Etolikou, Ayia Sofia. ✆ **210/461-2457.** Reservations recommended Fri-Sat. Main courses 25€. No credit cards. Mon-Sat 8pm-midnight. Closed Aug.

Vosporos ★ GREEK   In the midst of the pretty marina and all the seafood restaurants, Vosporos specializes mostly in meat dishes, serving excellent souvlaki, gyros, burgers, and hearty salads in very generous portions at reasonable prices.

20 Akti Koumoundourou, Mikrolimano. ✆ **210/412-7324.** Main courses 18€-22€. No credit cards. Daily noon-1am.

Hanging Out in Piraeus

Cellier Zea   Cellier Zea is a good restaurant, but its claim to fame is its beautiful multilevel neoclassical building overlooking Zea Marina, with superb views from the roof terrace, and a fine wine store on the first floor. Enjoy dinner (wonderful Mediterranean fare) on the roof terrace or a glass or two of their many wines while taking in the romantic view.

51 Akti Themistokleous, Zea Marina. ✆ **210/418-1049.** www.cellier.gr. Main courses 18€-30€. AE, MC, V. Daily 8pm-2am.

Istioploikos   Surrounded by sailboats right on picturesque Mikrolimano, Istioploikos (named after the private Yacht Club of Greece) features delicious variations on classic Greek cuisine, but it is the cafe that steals the show with its incredible vistas. Later on in the night, the cafe turns into a bar.

Akti Mikrolomano. © **210/413-4084.** www.istioploikos.gr. Main courses 35€–40€. AE, DC, MC, V. Daily 10am–4am.

Pisina (The Swimming Pool)   Ultratrendy Pisina is centered around a large swimming pool (thus its name), offering amazing views of Zea Marina throughout the day and night. This is a great place to sit by the pool during the day, overlooking the yachts, and to dine and/or enjoy drinks by the candlelight at night.

Zea Marina. © **210/451-1324.** www.pisinacafe.gr. Main courses 22€–26€. AE, DC, MC, V. Daily 10am–4am.

THE SARONIC GULF ISLANDS

by Sherry Marker

The islands of the Saronic Gulf are so close to Athens that each summer Athenians flee there for some relief from the heat and the crowds. The summer of 2007 was the hottest in at least 90 years—until the summer of 2010. If these summer scorchers continue, more and more Athenians will try to escape the pulverizing heat of Athens and head for the Saronic Gulf islands on as many summer weekends as possible. In addition, these islands are popular destinations for European and American travelers with limited time, who are determined not to go home without seeing at least one Greek island. You can make a day trip to any of these islands, and some day cruises out of Piraeus rush you on and off three islands. Usually, that involves quick stops at Hydra, Poros, and Spetses before you're deposited back on the mainland. If you plan to spend the night on any of these islands in summer, book well in advance. The website www.windmills travel.com is a useful resource for all the islands. Also useful is www. greeka.com, where you can access a website for each of the Saronic Gulf islands by typing www.greeka.com/saronic into your browser, followed by the name of the island—for example, www.greeka.com/saronic/poros. For ferry schedules, check out www.openseas.gr or www.gtp.gr.

The easiest island to visit is **Aegina,** just 30km (17 nautical miles) from Piraeus. The main attractions—in addition to the ease of the journey—are the graceful Doric **Temple of Aphaia,** one of the best-preserved Greek temples; several good beaches; and verdant pine and pistachio groves. That's the good news. The bad news is that Aegina is so close to the metropolitan sprawl of Athens and Piraeus, that it's not easy here to get a clear idea of why the Greek islands are so beloved as refuges from urban life. Aegina has become a bedroom suburb for Athens, with many of its 10,000 inhabitants commuting to work by boat. That said, Aegina town still has its pleasures, and both the Temple of Aphaia and deserted medieval town of **Paleohora** are terrific. If you come here, try to avoid weekends and the month of August.

Poros is hardly an island at all; only a narrow (370m/1,214-ft.) inlet separates it from the Peloponnese. There are several decent beaches, and the landscape is wooded, gentle, and rolling, like the landscape of the adjacent mainland. Alas, Poros's pine groves were badly damaged by the summer fires that swept through Greece in 2007. Poros is popular with tour groups as well as young Athenians (in part because the Naval Cadets'

Lemon Groves of Limonodassos **5**
Monastery of Ayios Nektarios **1**
Monastery of the Prophet Elijah (Profitis Elias) **6**
Monastery of Zoodhochou Pigis **4**
Temple of Aphaia **2**
Temple of Poseidon **3**

With some of the hydrofoils and ferries that serve the Saronic Gulf islands, it is impossible to book a round-trip. If you cannot buy a round-trip ticket, head for the ticket office as soon as you arrive at your island destination, and book a return ticket. If you do not do this, you may end up spending longer than you planned—or wished—on one or more of the islands. At press time, both Minoan Flying Dolphins and Ceres Flying Dolphins had been absorbed by Hellenic Seaways (www.hellenic seaways.gr), the former Hellas Flying Dolphins, but there may be more ownership and name changes by the time you arrive.

Training School here means that there are lots of young men eager to party). On summer nights, the waterfront is either very lively or hideously crowded, depending on your point of view.

Hydra (Idra), with its bare hills, superb natural harbor, and elegant stone mansions, is the most strikingly beautiful of the Saronic Gulf islands. One of the first Greek islands to be "discovered" by artists, writers, and bon vivants in the '50s, Hydra, like Mykonos, is not the place to experience traditional village life. The island has been declared a national monument, from which cars have been banished. Its relative quiet is increasingly being infiltrated by motorcycles. A major drawback: Few of the beaches are very good for swimming, although you can swim from the rocks in and just out of Hydra town. **Spetses** has always been popular with wealthy Athenians, who built—and continue to build—handsome villas here. If you like wooded islands, you'll love Spetses, although summer forest fires over the last few years have destroyed some of Spetses's pine groves.

When to Go

If possible, avoid June through August, unless you have a hotel reservation and think that you'd enjoy the hustle and bustle of high season. Also, mid-July through August, boats leaving Piraeus for the islands are heavily booked—often seriously overbooked. It is sometimes possible to get a deck passage without a reservation, but even that can be difficult when as many as 100,000 Athenians leave Piraeus on a summer weekend. Most ships will not allow passengers to board without a ticket.

Something to consider: Some hydrofoils leave from the Piraeus Main Harbor while others leave from the Piraeus Marina Zea Harbor—and some leave from both harbors. It's a good idea to arrive early, in case your boat is leaving from a spot other than the one you expect.

If you go to one of these islands on a **day trip,** remember that, unlike the more sturdy ferryboats, hydrofoils cannot travel when the sea is rough. You may find yourself an unwilling overnight island visitor, grateful to be given the still-warm bed in a private home surrendered by a family member to make some money. I speak from experience. For more information, see "Getting There," below. *Greek Island Hopping,* published annually by Thomas Cook, is, by its own admission, out of date by the time it sees print. That said, it's a very useful volume for finding out where (if not when) you can travel among the Greek islands.

AEGINA

30km (17 nautical miles) SW of Piraeus

More travelers come to Aegina (Egina), the largest of the Saronic Gulf islands, than to any of the other Greek islands. Why? The answer, as so often, is location, location, location. Aegina is so close to Athens that it draws thousands of day-trippers. As the day-trippers arrive in the morning, many of the 10,000 who live on Aegina and commute daily to work in Athens depart. If you have only 1 day for one island, you may decide on Aegina, where you can see one famous temple (the Doric **Temple of Aphaia**), visit one romantic medieval hill town **(Paleochora),** have lunch at one of the harborside tavernas in Aegina town, and munch the island's famous pistachio nuts as you sail back to Athens.

Most ships arrive and depart from the main port and capital of **Aegina town** on the west coast, though a few stop at the resort town of **Souvala** on the north coast and at the port of **Ayia Marina** on the east coast. Ayia Marina is about as charmless as it's possible to be, but this port is your best choice, if your principal destination is the Temple of Aphaia.

Despite massive tourism and the rapid development devouring much farmland, the area still has its share of almond, olive, and especially **pistachio** orchards. In fact, Aegina has an endemic water problem simply because of the water necessary for the pistachio groves. Wherever you buy pistachios in Greece, the vendor may assure you that they are from Aegina to indicate their superior quality.

GETTING THERE   **Car ferries** and **excursion boats** to Aegina usually leave from Piraeus's Main Harbor; confusingly, **hydrofoils** leave both from the Main Harbor and from Marina Zea Harbor. Hydrofoil service is at least twice as fast as ferries and at least 40% more expensive (except to Aegina, for which the charge is only about 10% more). The sleek little hydrofoils are outfitted like broad aircraft with airline seats, toilets, and a minimum of luggage facilities. (The fore sections offer better views, but they're also bumpier.) The newer Super Cats are bigger, faster, and more comfortable, with food and beverage service. Reservations are usually vital on weekends. Often, in order to continue to another Saronic Gulf island by hydrofoil, you must return to Piraeus and change to another hydrofoil. Some ferries go from Aegina to the other Saronic Gulf islands. *Warning:* Schedules—and even carriers—can change, so double-check information you get—and then be prepared for last-minute schedule and carrier changes. For ferry schedules, check out **www.openseas.gr** or **www.gtp.gr**.

Daily hydrofoil and ferry service to the Saronic Gulf islands is offered by **Hellenic Seaways** (© **210/419-9200;** www.hellenicseaways.gr). **Saronikos Ferries**

Avoid the Crowds

If Aegina turns out to be too crowded for you, take the short ferry ride to little Angistri, where **Rosy's Little Village** (© **22970/91-610;** www.rosyslittle village.com) is as charming as its name, with 16 whitewashed rooms tucked in a pine grove. The restaurant serves organic food, there's swimming in a rocky cove, and many guests meditate and relax, either on their own or in one of a number of holistic workshops. Summer doubles start at 50€ and go to around 75€ in August.

Culture Calls

If you visit the islands of the Saronic Gulf in July and August, keep an eye out for posters announcing exhibitions at local museums and galleries. There are often exhibits at the **Citronne Gallery** (*✆* 22980-22-401; www.citronne.com), on Poros, and at the **Koundouriotis Mansion** (*✆* 22980/52-210), on Hydra. In addition, many Athenian galleries close for parts of July and August, and some have shows on the islands. The **Athens Centre,** 48 Archimidous (*✆* 210/701-2268; www.athenscentre.gr), sometimes stages plays on Spetses and Hydra. The center offers a modern-Greek-language summer program on Spetses in June and July.

(*✆* 210/417-1190) takes passengers and cars to Aegina, Poros, and Spetses; cars are not allowed to disembark on Hydra. **Euroseas** (*✆* 210/411-3108) has speedy catamaran service from Piraeus to Poros, Hydra, and Spetses. Boats often—but not always—leave from gates E8 and E9 in the main Piraeus harbor. You can usually visit any one of the Saronics for between 20€ and 65€ day return; the faster the ship, the higher the price. Several cruises offer day trips to Hydra, Poros, and Aegina; for details, see chapter 4, "Cruising the Greek Islands."

For information on schedules for most Argo-Saronic ferries, you can try one of the various numbers of the **Piraeus Port Authority** (*✆* 210/422-6000, 210/410-1480, or 210/410-1441), but phones are not always answered. On Aegina, try *✆* 22970/22-328.

VISITOR INFORMATION   Aegina Tourist Office (*✆* 22970/22-220) is in Aegina Town Hall, where you can pick up the handy free *Mini Guide,* published each year in English and Greek. There's a string of travel agencies at the harbor, including the usually efficient **Aegina Island Holidays,** 47 Demokratias (*✆* 22970/26-439; fax 22970/26-430). To learn a little about Aegina's history, look for Anne Yannoulis's *Aegina* (Lycabettus Press), usually on sale at **Kalezis Boatokshop** on the harbor (*✆* 22970/25-956), which stocks foreign newspapers. Check the websites **www.aeginagreece.com** and **www.greeka.com/saronic/aegina** for info in English.

GETTING AROUND   A left turn as you disembark takes you east to the **bus station** (*✆* 22970/22-787) on Plateia Ethneyersias. There's good service to most of the island, with trips every hour in summer to the Temple of Aphaia and Ayia Marina (3€); tickets must be purchased before boarding. Every Saturday and Wednesday in summer, **Panoramic Bus Tours** (*✆* 22970/22-254) offers a 3½-hour bus tour (6€) of the island, taking in the Temple of Aphaia, several beaches and villages, and the Wildlife Center and Hospital (*✆* 22970/28-267; www.ekpaz.gr) at Pachia Rachi. The tour has a commentary in Greek and English and is a great introduction to the island. **Taxis** are easy to find in Aegina town; if you want to take a taxi tour of the island, negotiate the fare before you set off. Your hotel can usually get you a decent price to rent either **bicycles** or **mopeds;** if you just show up at a rental place, the price is usually higher. An ordinary bike should cost about 12€ per day; mopeds, from 25€—except on summer weekends, when the sky is the limit. Motorcycle and moped agents are required to—but do not always—ask for proof that you are licensed to drive such vehicles and give you a helmet. Be sure to check the tires and brakes.

FAST FACTS The **National Bank of Greece** is one of four waterfront banks with currency-exchange service and ATMs; some travel agents, including **Island Holidays** (© **22970/23-333**), often exchange money both during and after normal bank hours, usually at less favorable rates. The island **clinic** (© **22970/22-251**) is on the northeast edge of town; for **first aid,** dial © **22970/22-222.** The **police** (© **22970/23-343**) and the **tourist police** (© **22970/27-777**) share a building on Leonardou Lada, about 200m (656 ft.) inland from the port. The **port authority** (© **22970/22-328**) is on the waterfront. The **post office** is in Plateia Ethatneyersias, around the corner from the hydrofoil pier. The **telephone office (OTE)** is 5 blocks inland from the port, on Aiakou. There are several Internet cafes, including **Prestige** and **Nesant,** on and just off the waterfront. *Tip:* Try to pick up the useful guides *Essential Aegina* and *Mini Guide,* often available from travel agents, hotels, and the tourist police.

What to See & Do
EXPLORING AEGINA TOWN

Aegina town's neoclassical buildings date from its brief stint as the first capital of newly independent Greece (1826–28). Most people's first impression of this harbor town, though, is of fishing boats and the small cargo vessels that ply back and forth to the mainland. Have a snack at one of the little restaurants in the **fish market** (follow your nose!) just off the harbor. This is where the men who catch your snacks of octopus and fried sprats come to eat their catches. The food is usually much better here than the food at the harborfront places catering to tourists.

If you take a horse-drawn carriage or wander the streets back from the port, you'll easily spot neoclassical buildings, including the **Markelos Tower,** home of the island cultural center, where there are sometimes exhibits. The Cathedral of **Ayios Demetrios,** with its square bell towers, is nearby. Carriage ride prices fluctuate wildly, but are usually between 15€ and 25€. In 1827, the first government of independent Greece held sessions both in the tower and at the cathedral. Fans of Nikos Kazantzakis may want to take a cab to **Livadi,** just north of town, to see the house where he lived when he wrote *Zorba the Greek.* North of the harbor, behind the town beach, and sometimes visible from boats entering the harbor, is the lone worn Doric column that marks the site of the **Temple of Apollo** (known locally as Kolona), open Tuesday through Sunday from 8:30am to 3pm. The view here is nice, the ruins very ruined. The small museum (© **22970/22-637**) has finds from the site, notably pottery; it's open Tuesday through Sunday 8:30am to 3pm; combined admission is 3€.

About 4.8km (3 miles) out of Aegina town, the ruins of **Paleohora,** capital of the island from the 9th to the 19th centuries, sprawl over a steep hillside. During the centuries when pirate raids threatened seaside towns, the people of Aegina sensibly chose to live inland. This is a wonderful spot to explore (be sure to wear sturdy shoes and a sun hat). You'll see ruined houses and a number of carefully preserved churches, and have fine views over the island. The bus to the busy beach resort of Ayia Marina makes a stop in Paleohora. If you come here, allow several hours for the excursion.

Lovers of wildlife will want to visit the **Wildlife Center and Hospital** (© **22970/28-267;** www.ekpaz.gr) in Pachia Rachi. The center is open daily from 9:30am to 7pm and cares for thousands of injured and abandoned birds and beasts each year. The Wildlife Center welcomes volunteers as well as visitors.

If you're on Aegina in August, you can enjoy some of the 20 or so concerts on tap during the **Aegina Music Festival** (© **698/131-9332**); offerings vary from classical

A Swim & a Snack

There's a small beach in the seaside, still charming, village of **Perdika** (served by bus from Aegina town). This is also a good place to have a meal by the sea; Antonis (☎ 22970/61-443) is the best-known and priciest place, but lots of other appealing (and much cheaper) places are nearby. If you visit Aegina with children, you may want to head to **Faros** (also served by bus from Aegina town) to the **Aegina Water Park** (☎ 22970/22-540). There are several pools, waterslides, snack bars, and lots of overexcited children; on hot days, this is a very popular destination for Athenian families.

to casual and take place by the Temple of Aphaia, in churches, and on beaches. If you show up in September, you can celebrate Aegina and Greece's most famous nut, the pistachio (*fistiki*), which has its own festival, the **Aegina Fistiki Fest** (www.aegina fistikifest.gr), usually held on a mid-September weekend.

SEEING THE TEMPLE OF APHAIA ★★

The 5th-century-B.C. **Temple of Aphaia**, set on a pine-covered hill 12km (7½ miles) east of Aegina town (☎ 22970/32-398), is one of the best-preserved and most handsome Greek temples. No one really knows who Aphaia was, although it seems that she was a very old, even prehistoric, goddess who eventually became associated with both the hunter-goddess Artemis and Athena, the goddess of wisdom. According to some legends, Aphaia lived on Crete, where King Minos, usually preoccupied with his labyrinth and Minotaur, fell in love with her. When she fled Crete, he pursued her, and she finally threw herself into the sea off Aegina to escape him. At some point in the late 6th or early 5th century B.C., this temple was built, on the site of earlier shrines, to honor Aphaia.

Thanks to the work of restorers, 25 of the original 32 Doric columns still stand. The pedimental sculpture, showing scenes from the Trojan War, was carted off in 1812 by King Ludwig of Bavaria. Whatever you think about the removal of art treasures from their original homes, Ludwig probably did us a favor by taking the sculptures to the Glyptothek in Munich: While he was doing this, locals were busily burning much of the temple to make lime and hacking up other bits to use in building their homes. Admission to the site is 4€; it's open Monday through Friday from 8:30am to 7pm, Saturday and Sunday from 8:30am to 3pm. Allow at least 4 hours for your visit, if you come here by the hourly bus from Aegina town; by taxi, you might do a visit in a couple of hours.

Where to Stay

In addition to the places mentioned below, you might consider two other very appealing hotels in Aegina town: the **Hotel Brown** (☎ 22970/22-271; www.hotelbrown. gr) overlooks a sandy beach and is a short walk from the center of town. The beach is just across a busy road, but friends who have stayed there have not been bothered by the traffic; ask for a room on one of the two upper floors. The stone building is a former sponge factory, converted into a hotel in 1959, and most recently updated in 2008. This stylish 28-room hotel has sea views from front rooms in the main building, its own restaurant, and a cluster of bungalow-like units in its garden; doubles from 75€. Well-traveled friends of mine joke that they go to Greece purely to stay here. That's what makes it so confusing to receive several recent reports of sloppy housekeeping; do let us know what you think. If you want a suite with a kitchenette, try the 11-unit **Rastoni** (✆ **22970/270-39;** www.rastoni.gr), a 5- to 10-minute hike from the harbor, which has a lovely garden and sea views; many rooms have balconies (from 80€). All these places often have special offers, especially off season and for long stays.

Eginitiko Archontiko ★★ This mansion near the cathedral, only a couple of hundred feet from the harbor, was built in the 1700s, expanded in the 1800s, and later renovations have preserved much original detail, including some walls and ceilings with paintings; the suite is especially charming. The small guest rooms are traditionally furnished, comfortable, and quiet (although here, as elsewhere in Greece, motorcycle noise can be intrusive). The pleasant downstairs lobby retains much 19th-century charm, and the glassed-in sunroom is a delight. The owners care about this handsome building and make guests comfortable. This is not the place to stay if you want lots of modern conveniences; it *is* the place to stay if you want to imagine life 100 years or so ago in an elegant island townhouse. I would love to stay here in the winter, when the motorcycles would be quiet, and soak up the atmosphere of this wonderful house.

Ag. Nikolaou and 1 Eakou, 18010 Aegina. www.lodgings.gr. ✆ **22970/24-968.** 12 units. 70€–90€ double; 120€ 2-room suite. AE, MC, V. **Amenities:** Breakfast room; communal kitchen; garden; sun room. *In room:* A/C.

Hotel Apollo ★ ☺ Large resort hotels are not my cup of tea and the resort of Ayia Marina leaves me pretty cold. That said, friends with small children who stayed at this beach hotel were pleased with the large bathrooms and simple bedrooms, most with balconies. In short, on my own on Aegina, I'd head for any of the places above; with the kids, I'd head here.

Ayia Marina, 18010 Aegina. www.apollohotel.gr. ✆ **22970/32-271.** 107 units. 100€–150€ double. Compulsory breakfast buffet 10€. Daily and weekly meal plans available. AE, DC, MC, V. Closed Nov–Mar. **Amenities:** Restaurant; bar; fresh- and saltwater pools; tennis; Wi-Fi. *In room:* A/C, TV, hair dryer, minifridge.

Where to Eat

Keep in mind that fish is priced by the kilogram at most restaurants. The price varies from catch to catch, so it's a good idea to ask before you order. One place where the fish is always fresh is **Antonis** (✆ **22970/61-443**), harborside in Perdika. In Ayia Marina, **Kyriakakis** (✆ **22970/32-165**) has been packing them in since the 1950s; the fish is fresh, the veggie dishes tasty, and the french fries are still homemade. If you don't mind being away from the fish and the sea, try **Vatsoula** (✆ **22970/22-711**) in Aegina town; any local can direct you there. Call ahead, as this place with the pleasant garden and tasty *spitiko* (home) cooking keeps idiosyncratic hours.

Maridaki ★ GREEK This lively portside spot offers a wide selection of fish, grilled octopus, and the usual taverna fare of souvlaki and moussaka. The *mezedes* here are usually very good, and you can make an entire meal of them if you wish. Come on a quiet evening, and you will have the sense of going back in time to an earlier Greece.

Demokratias. ✆ **22970/25-869.** Main courses 8€–20€; seafood priced by the kilo. DC, MC. Daily 8am–midnight.

Mezedopoleio To Steki ★★ *MEZEDES* Locals and Athenians head to this little place by the fish market for its delicious *mezedes,* including succulent grilled octopus. You can make a meal of them. If you eat as the Greeks do, wash it all down with ouzo. (If you're not used to ouzo, wash the ouzo down with lots of water.)

45 Pan Irioti. ✆ **22970/23-910.** *Mezedes* 6€–15€. No credit cards. Daily 8am–midnight.

Aegina After Dark

At sunset, the harbor scene gets livelier as everyone comes out for an evening *volta* (stroll). As always, this year's hot spot may be closed by the next season. As no one answers the phones at these places, we do not list phones. In Aegina town, **Avli** and **Perdikiotika,** in another one of Aegina's handsome 19th-century houses, are durable favorites. On summer weekends, **En Egina** and **Kyvrenio** have live music and occasional traditional *rembetika* music—often from around midnight 'til dawn. On summer weekends, **Armida,** a bar/restaurant in a converted caique moored at the harbor, is open from breakfast until, well, breakfast. There are also several outdoor cinemas in town, including the **Olympia** and the **Faneromeni.** Young bloods and yachties rub shoulders after dark at the **Muzik Bar Café** on the Perdika beach. If you decide you want some late-night ouzo and octopus back in Aegina town, try **Tsias** or **Pelaisos** by the fish market.

POROS

55km (31 nautical miles) SW of Piraeus

Poros shares the gentle, rolling landscape of the adjacent Peloponnesian coastline, and has several good beaches, some decent tavernas, and lively summer nightlife. If that sounds like lukewarm praise, it just may be. For me, Poros lacks the sense of being a world unto itself that makes most Greek islands so delicious to visit. And, in July and August, the island virtually sinks under the weight of day-trippers and tour groups.

As someone once said, "Geography is destiny." Poros (the word means "straits" or "ford") is separated from the Peloponnese by a narrow channel only 370m (1,214 ft.) wide. Poros is so easy to reach from the mainland that weekending Athenians and many tourists flock here each summer. In fact, a car ferry across the straits from Galatas to Poros town leaves almost every 20 minutes in summer, which means that there are a *lot* of cars here.

Technically, Poros is separated by a narrow canal into two islands: little **Sferia,** where Poros town is, and larger **Kalavria,** where everything else is. If you wish, you can use Poros as a base for visiting the nearby attractions on the mainland, including Epidaurus, ancient Troezen (modern Trizina), and the lemon groves of Limonodassos. In a long day trip, you can visit Nafplion (Nafplio) and Epidaurus; in a very long day trip, you could also see Mycenae and Tiryns.

Essentials

GETTING THERE   Daily hydrofoil and ferry service to Poros and other Saronic Gulf islands is offered by **Hellenic Seaways** (*☎* 210/419-9200; www.hellenicseaways. gr). **Saronikos Ferries** (*☎* 210/417/1190) takes passengers and cars to Aegina, Poros, and Spetses; cars are not allowed to disembark on Hydra. **Euroseas** (*☎* 210/ 411-3108) has speedy catamaran service from Piraeus to Poros, Hydra, and Spetses. For information on schedules for most Argo-Saronic ferries, you can try one of the various numbers of the **Piraeus Port Authority** (*☎* 210/422-6000, 210/410-1480, or 210/410-1441), but phones are not always answered. On Poros, try *☎* **22980/22-274.** For ferry schedules, check out **www.openseas.gr** or **www.gtp.gr**.

The other Saronic Gulf islands are all easy to reach from Poros. In addition, in summer **Marinos Tours** (*☎* **22980/22-297**) offers excursions to Saronic and Cycladic islands.

VISITOR INFORMATION The waterfront hotels are generally too noisy for all except heavy sleepers, so if you want to stay in town, we suggest you check with **Marinos Tours** (© 22980/22-297), which handles several hundred rooms and apartments, as well as many island hotels. We've had good reports of **Saronic Gulf Travel** (© 22980/24-555; www.saronicgulftravel.gr), which usually has an excellent free map of the island. To learn more about Poros, look for Niki Stavrolakes's enduring classic, *Poros* (Lycabettus Press), for sale on the island. The websites **www.poros.com.gr** and **www.greeka.com/saronic/poros** have information in Greek and English.

GETTING AROUND You can walk anywhere in Poros town. The island's **bus** can take you to the beaches or to the **Monastery of the Zoodhochou Pigis** and the remains of the **Temple of Poseidon;** the conductor will charge you according to your destination. The **taxi station** is near the hydrofoil dock, or you can call for one at © **22980/23-003;** the fare to or from the Askeli beach should cost about 14€. **Kostas Bikes** (© 22980/23-565), opposite the Galas ferry pier, rents bicycles for about 12€ per day, and mopeds from about 20€ per day—except on summer weekends, when the sky is the limit.

FAST FACTS The **National Bank of Greece** is one of a handful of waterfront banks with an ATM where you can also exchange money. The **police** (© 22980/22-256) and **tourist police** (© 22980/22-462) are on the *paralia* (harbor). The **port authority** (© 22980/22-274) is on the harborfront. For **first aid,** call © 22980/22-254. The **post office** and **telephone office (OTE)** are also on the waterfront; their hours are Monday through Friday from 8am to 2pm. In summer, in addition to normal weekday hours, the OTE is open Sunday 8am to 1pm and 5 to 10pm. **Dionysus Internet Café** and **Kentrou Typou** (also a newsagent with foreign newspapers) are both on the harborfront and offer Internet service for about 8€ per hour.

What to See & Do

ATTRACTIONS IN POROS TOWN

As you make the crossing to the island, you'll see the streets of the island's capital, Poros town, which sprawls up a hill topped with a clock tower. The church of Agios Yeoryios (St. George) is well worth having a look at: the frescoes were done by a famous 20th-century Greek painter, Constantine Parthenis. As you wander, you'll realize that what you've read is true: Poros town is itself an island, joined to the rest of Poros by a causeway. The narrow streets along the harbor are usually crowded with visitors inching their ways up and down past the restaurants, cafes, and shops. At night, the adjacent hills are, indeed, alive with the sound of music; the "Greek" music is often heavily amplified American rap.

Poros town has a **Naval Cadets' Training School**—which means that a lot of young men are looking for company here. Anyone wishing to avoid their attention should visit the small **Archaeological Museum** (© 22980/23-276), with finds from ancient Troezen. It's usually open daily from 9am to 3pm; admission is free. Lovers of seashells may want to visit the Public Library, where the Poros Shell Museum (© 22980/22-936; www.poroshellmuseum.gr) is housed. This free museum is open Monday through Friday 9am to 1pm and 5 to 8pm.

EXPLORING THE ISLAND

By car or moped, it's easy to make a circuit of the island in half a day. What remains of the 6th-century-B.C. **Temple of Poseidon** is scattered beneath pine trees on the low plateau of Palatia, east of Poros town. The site is usually open dawn to dusk;

As you take in Poros, when you look out to sea, you may well see some of the cadets from the **Naval Cadets' Training School** practicing rowing. The school has produced a number of world-class rowing teams, and you will often see cadets practicing close to shore.

admission is free. The ruins are scant, largely because the inhabitants of the nearby island of Hydra plundered the temple and hauled away most of the marble to build their harborside Monastery of the Virgin.

The Temple of Poseidon was the scene of a famous moment in Greek history in 322 B.C., when Demosthenes, the Athenian 4th-century orator and statesman, fled here for sanctuary from Athens's Macedonian enemies. When his enemies tracked him down, the great speechwriter asked for time to write a last letter—and then bit off his pen nib, which contained poison. Even in his death agonies, Demosthenes had the presence of mind to leave the temple, lest his death defile the sanctuary. It seems fitting that Demosthenes, who lived by his pen, died by the same instrument.

Those who enjoy monasteries can continue on the road that winds through the island's interior to the 18th-century **Monastery of the Zoodhochou Pigis (Monastery of the Life-Giving Spring),** south of Poros town. There are usually no monks in residence, but the caretaker should let you in from about 9am to 2pm and from 4 to 7pm. It's appropriate to leave a small donation in the offerings box. There's a little taverna nearby.

Poros's beaches are not enchanting. The beach easiest to visit after seeing the temple of Poseidon is Vagonia, one of the nicer ones. **Love Bay** and Monastiriou both have shade from pine trees and small restaurants. Both the sea and beach at **Megalo Neorio,** northwest of town, are sometimes polluted. Neorio has a string of places renting personal watercraft, water skis, and windsurfing equipment.

OFF THE ISLAND: A FESTIVAL, ANCIENT TROEZEN & LEMON GROVES

If you're in Poros in mid-June, you might want to catch the ferry across to Galatas and take in the annual **Flower Festival,** with its floral displays and parades of floats and marching bands. (Lots of posters in Poros town advertise the festival.)

From Galatas, you can catch a bus the 8km (5 miles) west to **Trizina** (ancient Troezen), birthplace of the great Athenian hero Theseus. It's also where his wife, Phaedra, tragically fell in love with her stepson, Hippolytus. When the dust settled, both she and Hippolytus were dead and Theseus was bereft. There are the remains of a temple to Asclepius here—but again, these ruins are very ruined.

About 4km (2½ miles) south of Galatas near the beach of Aliki, you'll find the olfactory wonder of **Limonodassos (Lemon Grove),** where more than 25,000 lemon trees fill the air with their fragrance each spring. Alas, many were harmed in a harsh storm in March 1998, and in yet another storm in 2002; very hot summers in recent years damaged more. Some trees have survived, and more have been planted. Several cafes nearby serve freshly squeezed lemonade. When the trees aren't in bloom, there's not much point in visiting here, as several readers have irately brought to our attention.

Where to Stay

There are a great many places to stay on Poros; we suggest two appealing choices in Poros town. If you are interested in a long stay, check out the **Villa Tryfon** (C **22980-25-854;** www.poros.com.gr/tryfon-villa), which has six simply furnished apartment-like units up the hill, away from the harbor (but with great views down to the harbor), just off Plateia Georgiou; open year-round, call for prices.

Hotel 7 Brothers ★★   This small hotel with the handsome neoclassical facade was built in 1901 and converted into a hotel some 20 years ago. The simple, cheerful, and comfortable rooms have balconies, the hospitality is old-fashioned, and the tips on what to see and do are up to date. An excellent choice, it was charming when I first stayed there a number of years ago and is still charming today. This is not a full-service hotel, but the owners take care of you very well indeed.

18020 Poros Island. www.7brothers.gr. C **22980/23-412.** 16 units. 80€ double. DC, V. **Amenities:** Breakfast. *In room:* A/C.

Sto Roloi ★★   Another small hotel with charm, Sto Roloi is a 2-century-old town house well out of the hustle and bustle of the harbor, near the island's famous *roloi* (clock tower). The owner rents the building as two suites: a garden apartment and a terrace apartment. A separate garden studio is also available. Many of the original details of the building (tiles, woodwork) have been preserved, and a serious attempt has been made to furnish Sto Roloi with appropriate island furniture (rather than the flashy modern furnishings often used in upmarket island hotels). This would be a very good place to spend a week; you can take advantage of the substantial price reduction for a week's stay, watch performances at Epidaurus, tour the eastern Peloponnese, or simply relax (several units have a Jacuzzi). The owners will arrange caique excursions for guests and will help watersports enthusiasts hook up with Passage Watersports. In addition to the original three units in Sto Roloi, they have the Anemone House (with pool), Little Tower, and Limeri House and Studio (with a shared pool).

13 Karra, 18020 Poros, Trizinias. www.storoloi-poros.gr. C **22980/25-808.** 7 units. Sto Roloi: 80€ studio, 150€ garden apt., 180€ terrace apt.; Anemone House and Limeri House 250€; Little Tower and Limeri Studio 110€. No credit cards. **Amenities:** Breakfast room; bar. *In room:* A/C, TV, hair dryer, mini-fridge, Wi-Fi.

Where to Eat

If you're willing to give up your view of the harbor, head into town, a bit uphill, and try one of the restaurants near the church of Ayios Yeorgios, such as **Platanos, Dimitris, Karavolos,** or **Kipos.** As is often the case, these places tend to draw a more Greek crowd than the harborside spots. Fish is priced by the kilogram at most restaurants; ask for prices before you order.

Caravella Restaurant GREEK   This portside taverna prides itself on serving organic homegrown vegetables and local (not frozen) fish. Specialties include traditional dishes such as snails, veal *stifado,* moussaka, souvlaki, and stuffed eggplant, as well as seafood and lobster.

Paralia, Poros town. C **22980/23-666.** Main courses 8€–18€. AE, MC, V. Daily 11am–1am.

Taverna Grill Oasis ★ GREEK   This taverna has been here since the mid-1960s. Its harborside location, with indoor and outdoor tables, excellent fresh fish, and a cheerful staff, make it live up to its name as a pleasant oasis for lunch or dinner. One not-so-traditional item on the menu: pasta with lobster.

Paralia, Poros town. © **22980/22-955.** Main courses 8€–19€; seafood priced by the kilo. No credit cards. Daily 11am–midnight.

POROS AFTER DARK

There's endless evening entertainment in Poros town, including serious people-watching strolls up and down the harbor, past the solid bar/disco/restaurant territory. As always, this year's hot spot may be closed by the next season. As no one answers the phones at these places, we do not list phones. In town, **Symbosio** often has live bouzouki (stringed music instrument, resembling a mandolin), and **Cine Diana Café** has elaborate cocktails, background music, and views over the harbor. If you want to dance, try **Lithos, Orion,** in town, and **Poseidon,** about 2km (1¼ miles) out of town; all are popular discos. **Petros** at Megalo Neorio beach often has live Greek music late at night—or early in the morning, depending on your point of view.

HYDRA (IDRA)

65km (35 nautical miles) S of Piraeus

Hydra is one of a handful of places in Greece that seemingly can't be spoiled. Along with Mykonos, this was one of the first Greek islands to be "discovered" by the beautiful people back in the '50s and '60s. Today, there are often more day-trippers here than "beautiful people," although when elegant Athenians flee their stuffy apartments for their Hydriote hideaway each summer, the harborfront turns into an impromptu fashion show. If you can, arrive here in the evening, when most of the day visitors have left, and spend a day or two avoiding the day-trippers and rejoicing in the cool of the evening. Whatever you do, be sure to be out on the deck of your ship as you arrive, so you can see Hydra's bleak and steep hills suddenly reveal its perfect horseshoe harbor overlooked by the 18th-century clock tower of the Church of the Dormition. This truly is a place where arrival is half the fun. But the best truly is yet to be, when you step ashore.

Let's start with the cars—or, more precisely, the absence of cars. With the exception of a handful of municipal vehicles, there are no cars on Hydra. You'll probably encounter at least one example of a popular form of local transportation: the donkey. When you see Hydra's splendid 18th- and 19th-century stone *archontika* (mansions) along the waterfront and on the steep streets above, you won't be surprised to learn that the entire island has been declared a national treasure by both the Greek government and the Council of Europe. You'll probably find Hydra town so charming that you'll forgive its one serious flaw: no top-notch beach. Do as the Hydriots do, and swim from the rocks at Spilia and Hydronetta, just beyond the main harbor, or hop on one of the caiques that ply from Hydra town to the relatively quiet island beaches.

Essentials

GETTING THERE Daily hydrofoil and ferry service to Hydra and other Saronic Gulf islands is offered by **Hellenic Seaways** (© **210/419-9200;** www.hellenic seaways.gr). **Saronikos Ferries** (© **210/417/1190**) takes passengers and cars to Aegina, Poros, and Spetses; cars are not allowed to disembark on Hydra. **Euroseas** (© **210/411-3108**) has speedy catamaran service from Piraeus to Poros, Hydra, and Spetses. For information on schedules for most Argo-Saronic ferries, you can try one of the various numbers of the **Piraeus Port Authority** (© **210/412-4585,** 210/422-6000, or 210/410-1480), but phones are not always answered. On Hydra, try

On a June weekend—often, but not always, the third weekend in June—Hydra celebrates the **Miaoulia,** which honors Hydriot Admiral Miaoulis, who set much of the Turkish fleet on fire in the Battle of Geronta in 1821. The plucky admiral rammed the Turkish fleet with explosives-filled fireboats; casualties on both sides were understandably considerable, with more Greek than Turkish ships left afloat. Celebrations include a reenactment of the sinking of a model warship; if you're not on Hydra for the festivities, you may see the fireworks light up the sky from other Saronic islands and the adjacent Peloponnesian mainland. In early July, Hydra has an annual **puppet festival** that, in recent years, has drawn puppeteers from countries as far away as Togo and Brazil. As these two festivals are not on set dates, check for schedules with the **Greek National Tourist Office** (© 210/870-0000; www.gnto.gr) or the **Hydra tourist police** (© 22980/52-205).

© **22980/52-279.** For ferry schedules, check out **www.openseas.gr** or **www.gtp. gr**. Reservations are a must on summer and on holiday weekends. *Tip:* Lots of porters, some with and some without mules, meet the boats. If you have enough luggage to require their services, agree on a price before you hand it over; be prepared to pay at least 14€.

VISITOR INFORMATION The free publications *Holidays in Hydra* and *This Summer in Hydra* are widely available and contain much useful information, including maps and lists of rooms to rent; shops and restaurants pay to appear in these publications. **Hydra View,** available in print and on line (www.hydraview.gr) is another useful resource. **Saitis Tours** (© 22980/52-184), in the middle of the harborfront, can exchange money, provide information on rooms and villas, book excursions, and help you make long-distance calls or send faxes. For those wanting to pursue Hydra's history, we recommend Catherine Vanderpool's *Hydra* (Lycabettus Press), on sale on the island. You may also want to check **www.greeka.com/saronic/hydra** or **www.hydradirect.com**.

GETTING AROUND Walking is the only means of getting around on the island itself, unless you bring or rent a donkey or a bicycle. **Caiques** provide water-taxi service to the island's beaches (Bilsi has extensive watersport facilities) and to the little offshore islands of Dokos, Kivotos, and Petasi, as well as to secluded restaurants in the evening; rates run from around 14€ to outrageously steep amounts, depending on destination, time of day, and whether or not business is slow.

FAST FACTS The **National Bank of Greece** and **Commercial Bank** are on the harbor; both have ATMs. Travel agents at the harbor will exchange money from about 9am to 8pm, usually at less favorable rates. The small **health clinic** is signposted at the harbor; cases requiring complicated treatment are taken by boat or helicopter to the mainland. The police and tourist **police** (© 22980/52-205) share quarters on the second floor at 9 Votsi (signposted at the harbor). The **port authority** (© 22980/53-150) is on the harborside. The **post office** is just off the harborfront on Ikonomou, the street between the two banks. The **telephone office (OTE),** across from the police station on Votsi, is open Monday through Saturday from 7:30am to 10pm, Sunday from 8am to 1pm and 5 to 10pm. For **Internet access,** try HydraNet (☎ **22980/54-150**), signposted by the OTE.

What to See & Do

ATTRACTIONS IN HYDRA TOWN

Why did all those "beautiful people" begin to come to Hydra in the '50s and '60s, and why is the island so popular today? As with the hill towns of Italy, the main attraction here is the architecture and setting of the town itself—and all the chic shops, restaurants, hotels, and bars that have taken up quarters in the handsome old stone buildings. In the 18th and 19th centuries, ships from Hydra transported cargo around the world and made this island very rich indeed. Like ship captains on the American island of Nantucket, Hydra's ship captains demonstrated their wealth by building the fanciest houses money could buy. The captains' lasting legacy: the handsome stone *archontika* (mansions) overlooking the harbor that give Hydra town its distinctive character. If you want to know more about Hydra's history, stop in at the harbor side **Historical Archives and Museum** (☎ **22980/52-355**; admission 4€; daily 9am–3pm and 7–8pm), which has old paintings, wonderful elaborately carved and painted ship figureheads, and costumes. There are sometimes temporary exhibits of work by local artists in a gallery here.

One *archontiko* that you can hardly miss is the **Tombazi mansion,** which dominates the hill that stands directly across the harbor from the main ferry quay. This is now a branch of the School of Fine Arts, with a hostel for students, and you can usually get a peek inside. Call the mansion (☎ **22980/52-291**) or **Athens Polytechnic** (☎ **210/619-2119**), for information about the program or exhibits.

The nearby **Ikonomou-Miriklis mansion** (also called the **Voulgaris**) is not open to the public, but the hilltop **Koundouriotis mansion,** built by an Albanian family that contributed generously to the cause of independence, is now a house museum. The mansion, with period furnishings and costumes, is usually open from April until October, Tuesday to Sunday 10am to 4pm; 4€. If you wander the side streets on this side of the harbor, you will see many more handsome houses, some of which are being restored so that they can once again be private homes, while others are being converted into still more boutique hotels.

Hydra's waterfront is a mixed bag, with a number of ho-hum shops selling little of distinction—and a handful of jewelry shops and elegant clothing boutiques—one bold (or honest) enough to call itself **Spoiled!** (☎ **22980/52-363**). Most of the elegant shops are either on side streets off the harbor, or in the area below the Tombazi mansion. Alas, the wobbly global economy has threatened a number of the nicest shops, and you may not find everything still there when you visit. **Elena Votsi** (www.elenavotsi.com) sells her original designs (including a graceful gravity-defying sterling silver clothes hanger for baby's first designer outfit) here and at her shop in Athens's Kolonaki district. **Hermes Art Shop** (☎ **22980/52-689**) has a wide array of jewelry, some good antique reproductions, and a few interesting textiles. **Domna Needlepoint** (☎ **22980/52-959**) has engaging needlepoint rugs and cushion covers, with Greek motifs of dolphins, birds, and flowers. **Vangelis Rafalias's Pharmacy** is a lovely place to stop in, even if you don't need anything, just to see the jars of remedies from the 19th century.

When you've finished with the waterfront, walk uphill on Iconomou (it's steep) to browse in more shops. **Meltemi** (☎ **22980/54-138**) sells original jewelry (including drop-dead-gorgeous earrings) and ceramics. Although the shop is small, just about everything here is borderline irresistible—especially the winsome blue ceramic fish. Across from Meltemi, **Emporium** (no phone) shows and sells works by Hydriot and other artists. If you want to take home a painting or a wood or ceramic model of an island boat, try here.

Like many islands, Hydra boasts that it has 365 churches, one for every day of the year. The most impressive, the mid-18th-century **Monastery of the Dormition of the Virgin Mary (E Kimisis tis Panagias)** is by the clock tower on the harborfront. This is the monastery built of the marble blocks hacked out of the (until then) well-preserved Temple of Poseidon on the nearby island of Poros. The buildings here no longer function as a monastery, and the cells are now municipal offices. The church itself has rather undistinguished 19th-century frescoes, but the elaborate 18th-century marble iconostasis (altar screen) is terrific. Like the marble from Poros, this altar screen was "borrowed" from another church and brought here. Seeing it is well worth the suggested donation.

EXPLORING THE ISLAND: A MONASTERY, A CONVENT & BEACHES

If you want to take a vigorous uphill walk (with no shade), head up Miaouli past Kala Pigadia (Good Wells), still the town's best local source of water. A walk of an hour or two, depending on your pace, will bring you to the **Convent of Ayia Efpraxia** and **Monastery of the Prophet Elijah (Profitis Elias).** Both have superb views, both are still active, and the nuns sell their hand-woven fabrics. (*Note:* Both nuns and monks observe the midday siesta from 1–5pm. Dress appropriately—no shorts or tank tops.)

Unfortunately, most of Hydra's best **beach,** at **Mandraki,** a 20-minute walk east of town, is the private preserve of the Miramare Hotel. If you're on Hydra briefly, your best bet is to swim off the rocks just west of Hydra town at **Spilia** or **Hydronetta,** or head out to sandier (and fashionable) **Kaminia.** Still farther west are the pretty pine-lined coves of **Molos, Palamida,** and **Bisti** (all three as sandy as it gets on Hydra), best reached by water taxi from the main harbor. The **Kallianos Dive Centre** (www.kallianosdivingcenter.com) offers PADI scuba lessons and excursions off Kapari island, near Hydra.

The island of **Dokos,** northwest off the tip of Hydra, an hour's boat ride from town, has a good beach and excellent diving conditions; it was here that Jacques Cousteau found a sunken ship with cargo still aboard, believed to be 3,000 years old. You may want to take a picnic with you, as the taverna here keeps unpredictable hours.

Where to Stay

Hydra has an impressive number of small, charming hotels in thoughtfully restored 19th-century buildings. In addition to the following choices, you might try the 19-unit **Hotel Greco,** Kouloura (© **22980/53-200;** fax 22980/53-511), in a former fishing-net factory in a quiet neighborhood; the 20-unit **Misral Hotel** (© **22980/52-509**), a restored island home off the harbor; or the 27-unit **Hotel Leto** (© **22980/53-385;** www.letohydra.gr), which is airy and bright, with large bedrooms, a large garden courtyard, and one wheelchair-accessible room. If you're traveling with friends, you might investigate the **Kiafa,** once a 19th-century sea captain's mansion, now a boutique hotel with a pool, in the Historic Hotels of Europe group, that rents to groups of up to nine people (© **210/364-0441;** www.yadeshotels.gr).

Hotel Angelica ★   The whitewashed Angelica complex, just off the main island road and just outside Hydra town, continues to expand its cluster of red-tile-roofed buildings, offering accommodations ranging from the very nice ("Standard" VIP doubles and an apartment) to the luxurious ("Superior" VIP rooms and a villa, which share a pool). Almost all the rooms have high ceilings and a balcony or terrace, with rooms in the pension annex more simply furnished than the VIP units. If you stay here, try to splurge on the VIP quarters so that you are not tormented by the sounds of other guests splashing in that pool, while you stand under your shower or sink into your Jacuzzi to cool down. The breakfast buffet is highly praised.

42 Miaouli, 18040 Hydra. www.angelica.gr. © **22980/53-264.** 21 units. 140€–200€ double; villa from 300€. MC, V. **Amenities:** Breakfast room; VIP pool; garden. *In room:* A/C, TV, fridge, Wi-Fi.

Hotel Bratsera ★ The Bratsera, in a restored 1860s sponge factory that's only a short stroll from the harbor, keeps turning up on everyone's list of the best hotels in Greece; unfortunately, this is a telling comment on the state of most Greek hotels. Throughout, there's lots of wood and stone, many distinctive Hydriot touches (paintings, engravings, ceramics), and many units with antique four-poster beds. The small pool, with wisteria-covered trellises, is very attractive; breakfast and meals are often served poolside in fair weather. We've had reports that room-service trays left in the hall after breakfast were still not collected by dinnertime, and I know from personal experience that messages left for guests aren't always delivered—nor does staff express any surprise or chagrin when this is brought to their attention. Still, many readers report having leaving here hoping they will be back soon. In short, for some the Bratsera produces memories of a relaxing stay in an architecturally charming hotel with a welcome pool and very central Hydra town location; for others, cavalier service is their most lasting memory.

Tombazi, 18040 Hydra. www.bratserahotel.com. © **22980/53-971.** Fax 22980/53-626. 253 units. 165€–220€ double; from 280€ suite. Rates include breakfast. AE, DC, MC, V. Closed mid-Jan to mid-Feb. **Amenities:** Restaurant; bar; pool. *In room:* A/C, hair dryer, minibar, Wi-Fi.

Hotel Hydra ★★ 🍴 This is one of the best bargains in town—if you don't mind the steep walk up to the beautifully restored two-story, gray-stone mansion on the western cliff, to the right as you get off the ferry. The guest rooms have high ceilings and are simply furnished; many have balconies overlooking the town and harbor.

8 Voulgari, 18040 Hydra. www.hydra-hotel.gr. © **22980/53-420.** Fax 22980/29-798. 12 units, 8 with bathroom. 130€ double without view, from 160€ double with view. MC, V. **Amenities:** Breakfast room. *In room:* A/C. TV, hair dryer, Wi-Fi.

Hotel Miranda ★★ Once, when we were trapped for the night on Hydra by bad weather that grounded the ferry boats, we were lucky enough to get the last guest room at the Miranda. The unit was small, with a tiny bathroom and no real view—so it's a tribute to this hotel that we have wonderful memories of that visit. Most of the guest rooms here are decent size, with nice views of the town and the Miranda's own lovely garden courtyard (where breakfast is often served). The handsome 1820 captain's mansion is decorated throughout with Oriental rugs, antique cabinets, worn wooden chests, marble tables, contemporary paintings, and period naval engravings. There's even a small art gallery—in short, this is a very classy place. We're distressed and, frankly, surprised, at a recent report of indifferent service; please let us know how you find things here.

Miaouli, 18040 Hydra. www.mirandahotel.gr. © **22980/52-230.** Fax 22980/53-510. 14 units. 150€–225€ double. AE, V. Closed Nov–Feb. **Amenities:** Breakfast room. *In room:* A/C, TV, hair dryer, minibar, Wi-Fi.

Hotel Orloff ★ This restored mansion, just a short walk from the port, on one of Hydra town's main squares, was built in the 18th century by the Russian admiral Count Orloff, who led a naval campaign against the Turks. Today it's a comfortable small hotel, distinctively decorated with antique furnishings, but with light and bright bedrooms, with white walls and blue accents in rugs and curtains. Some bedrooms and bathrooms are on the small side, and you may want to go for a superior or luxury double, with a sitting area. Still, the garden is lovely; the views are terrific; breakfast (served in the garden or breakfast room, which was redecorated in 2011) is excellent; and the in-house bar is pleasant.

9 Rafalia, 18040 Hydra. www.orloff.gr. © **22980/52-564.** Fax 22980/53-532. 10 units. 160€–200€ double. Rates include buffet breakfast. AE, MC, V. Closed Nov–Mar. **Amenities:** Dining room; bar, Internet. *In room:* A/C, TV, hair dryer.

Where to Eat

The harborside eateries are predictably expensive and mostly not very good, although the views are such that you may not care. The cost of fish, priced by the kilogram at most restaurants, varies from catch to catch, so it's a good idea to ask the price before you order. Two longtime favorites off the harbor are still going strong: **Manolis** (© **22890/29-631**) and **Kyria Sophia** (© **22980/53-097**), both with lots of vegetable dishes, as well as stews and grills. Kyria Sophia's is tiny, so it's vital to try to book a table. A number of cafes also lie along the waterfront, including **To Roloi (The Clock),** by the clock tower. **Omilos** (© **22980/53-800**), by Hydra town's rocky bathing spot, Hydronetta, has terrific salads, with a wide variety of hard-to-find greens and inventive dressings. Out on Kamini beach, **Castello** (© **22980/54-101;** www.castello hydra.gr) is open from early to late, serving up snacks and full meals to elegantly casual young Athenians who like the mushroom-stuffed hamburgers and foreigners who toy with *mezedes* and Greek salads; there's a resident DJ, a master bartender (apple and pear martinis, anyone?), and great views over the sea for sunset—or sunrise.

Marina's Taverna ★ GREEK   Several readers report that they have enjoyed both the food and the spectacular sunset at this seaside taverna, appropriately nicknamed Iliovasilema ("Sunset"). Perched on the rocks west of town, it's a 12€ water-taxi ride from town. The menu is basic, but the food is fresh and carefully prepared by Marina; her *kleftiko* (pork pie), an island specialty, is renowned.

Vlihos. © **22980/52-496.** Main courses 10€–15€. No credit cards. Daily noon–11pm.

To Steki ✇ GREEK   This small taverna, a few blocks up from the quay end of the harbor, has simple food and reasonable prices. The walls inside have framed murals showing an idealized traditional island life. The daily specials, such as moussaka and stuffed tomatoes, come with salad, vegetables, and dessert. The fish soup is memorable.

Miaouli. © **22980/53-517.** Main courses 7€–18€; daily specials 8€–15€; seafood priced by the kilo. No credit cards. Daily noon–3pm and 7–11pm.

Hydra After Dark

Hydra has a very energetic nightlife, with restaurants, bars, and discos all going full steam ahead in summer. In theory, bars close at 2am. As always, this year's hot spot may be closed by the next season. Portside, there are plenty of bars. As no one answers the phones at these places, we do not list phones. **The Pirate,** near the clock tower, is one of the longest living (since the 1970s) and loudest. **Veranda** (up from the west end of the harbor, near the Hotel Hydra) is a wonderful place to escape the full frenzy of the Hydra harbor scene, sip a glass of wine, and watch the sunset. **Hydronetta** tends to play more Western than Greek music—although the music at all these places is so loud that it's hard to be sure. Friends report enjoying drinks at the **Amalour,** just off the harbor, where they were surrounded by hip, black-clad 30-somethings and listened to jazz, rap, and vintage heavy metal. There are still a few local haunts left around the harbor; you'll be able to recognize them easily. You'll also easily spot the **Saronicos:** If you don't hear the music, just look for the fishing boat outside the front door.

SPETSES ★★

98km (53 nautical miles) SW of Piraeus; 3km (2 nautical miles) from Ermioni

First, here's one real plus—with quibbles—for visitors to Spetses: Cars are not allowed to circulate freely in Spetses town. Here's the quibble: This would make for admirable tranquillity if motorcycles were not increasingly endemic. Now, a closer look at the island.

Despite a recent series of dreadful forest fires, Spetses's pine groves still make this the greenest of the Saronic Gulf islands. Even in antiquity, this island was called Pityoussa (Pine-Tree Island). Over the centuries, many of Spetses's pine trees became the masts and hulls of the island's successive fleets of fishing, commercial, and military vessels. In time, Spetses was almost as deforested as its rocky neighbor Hydra is to this day.

In the early 20th century, the wealthy local philanthropist Sotiris Anargyros bought up more than half the island and replanted barren slopes with pine trees. Anargyros also built himself one of the island's most ostentatious mansions, flanked by palm trees, which you can see just off Spetses's main harbor, the Dapia. Amargyros also built the massive harborfront Hotel Poseidon to jump-start upper-class tourism. Then he built Anargyros College (modeled on England's famous Eton College) to give the island a first-class prep school; John Knowles taught here in the early 1950s and set his cult novel *The Magus* on Spetses.

Today, Spetses's pine groves and wonderful architecture are its greatest treasures: The island has an unusual number of handsome *archontika* built in the 19th and 20th centuries by wealthy residents, many of them shipping magnates, many now owned by their descendants or by well-heeled Athenians. Many Spetses homes have lush gardens and handsome pebble mosaic courtyards; if you're lucky, you'll catch a glimpse of some when garden gates are ajar. Like Andros, another island beloved of wealthy Athenians, Spetses communicates a sense that there's a world of private privilege that exists undisturbed by the rough and tumble of tourism, which—let's not mince words—means you and me.

Fortunately for attentive visitors, a number of Spetses's dignified villas have been converted into appealing small hotels where it's possible to escape the world of the package tour, mostly based at Ayia Marina.

Essentials

GETTING THERE   Daily hydrofoil and ferry service to Spetses and other Saronic Gulf islands is offered by **Hellenic Seaways** (✆ **210/419-9200;** www.hellenic seaways.gr). **Saronikos Ferries** (✆ **210/417-1190**) takes passengers and cars to Aegina, Poros, and Spetses; cars are not allowed to disembark on Hydra. **Euroseas** (✆ **210/411-3108**) has speedy catamaran service from Piraeus to Poros, Hydra, and Spetses. For information on schedules for most Argo-Saronic ferries, you can try one of the various numbers of the **Piraeus Port Authority** (✆ **210/412-4585,** 210/422-6000, or 210/410-1480), but phones are not always answered. On Spetses, try ✆ **22980/72-245.** For ferry schedules, check out **www.openseas.gr** or **www.gtp.gr.**

VISITOR INFORMATION The island's travel agencies include **Alasia Travel** (✆ **22980/74-098**) and **Spetses & Takis Travel** (✆ **22980/72-215**). Andrew Thomas's *Spetses* (Lycabettus Press), usually on sale on the island, is the book to get if you want to pursue Spetses's history. You can also check out **www.greeka.com/saronic/spetses** and the very helpful **www.spetsesdirect.com**.

GETTING AROUND The island's limited public transportation consists of several municipal **buses** and a handful of **taxis.** Motorcycle and moped agents are required to, but do not always, ask for proof that you are licensed to drive such vehicles and give you a helmet. Be sure to check the tires and brakes; mopeds start at 15€ a day, motorcycles start at 20€, except on summer weekends, when the sky is the limit. **Bikes** are also widely available, and the terrain along the road around the island makes them a good means of transportation; three-speed bikes cost about 12€ per day, while newer 21-speed models go for about 15€. **Horse-drawn carriages** can take you from the busy port into the quieter back streets, where most of the island's handsome old mansions are located. Take your time choosing a driver; some are friendly and informative, others are surly. Fares are highly negotiable.

The best way to get to the various beaches around the island is by **water taxi.** Locals call it a *venzina* (gasoline); each little boat holds about 8 to 10 people. Here, too, fares are negotiable. A tour around the island costs about 50€. Schedules are posted on the pier. You can also hire a water taxi to take you anywhere on the island, to another island, or to the mainland. Again, prices are highly negotiable.

FAST FACTS The **National Bank of Greece** is one of several banks on the harbor with an ATM. Most travel agencies (9am–8pm) will also exchange money, usually at less favorable rates than banks. The local health **clinic** (✆ **22980/72-201**) is inland from the east side of the port. The **police** (✆ **22980/73-100**) and **tourist police** (✆ **22980/73-744**) are to the left off the Dapia pier, where the hydrofoils dock, on Boattassi. The **port authority** (✆ **22980/72-245**) is on the harborfront. The **post office** is on Boattassi near the police station; it's open from 8am to 2pm Monday to Friday. The **telephone office (OTE),** open Monday to Friday from 7:30am to 3pm, is to the right off the Dapia pier, behind Hotel Soleil. **Internet access** is available at Delphina Net-Café on the harborfront for 5€ an hour.

What to See & Do

EXPLORING SPETSES TOWN (KASTELLI)

Spetses town (aka Kastelli) meanders along the harbor and inland in a lazy fashion, with most of its neoclassical mansions partly hidden from envious eyes by high walls and greenery. Much of the town's street life takes place on the main square, the **Dapia,** the name also given to the harbor where the ferries and hydrofoils now arrive. The massive bulk of the 19th-century Poseidon Hotel dominates the west end of the harbor. The Old Harbor, **Baltiza,** largely silted up, lies just east of town, before the popular swimming spots at **Ayia Marina.**

If you sit at a cafe on the Dapia, you'll eventually see pretty much everyone in town—who wants to be seen—passing by. The handsome black-and-white pebble mosaic commemorates the moment during the War of Independence when the first flag, with the motto "Freedom or Death," was raised. Thanks to its large fleet, Spetses played an important part in the War of Independence, routing the Turks in the Straits of Spetses on September 8, 1822. The victory is commemorated every year on the weekend closest to **September 8,** with celebrations, church services, and the burning of a ship that symbolizes the defeated Turkish fleet.

As you stroll along the waterfront, you'll notice the monumental bronze statue of a woman, her left arm shielding her eyes as she looks out to sea. The statue honors one of the greatest heroes of the War of Independence, **Laskarina Bouboulina,** the daughter of a naval captain from Hydra. Bouboulina financed the warship *Agamemnon*, oversaw its construction, served as its captain, and was responsible for several naval victories. She was said to be able to drink any man under the table, and strait-laced citizens sniped that she was so ugly, the only way she could keep a lover was with a gun. You can see where Bouboulina lived when she was ashore by visiting **Laskarina Bouboulina House** (© 22980/72-077; www.bouboulinamuseum spetses.gr), in Pefkakia, just off the port. It keeps flexible hours (posted on the house), but is usually open mornings and afternoons from Easter until October. An English-speaking guide often gives a half-hour tour. Admission is 5€. If the **Spetses Mexis Museum** (© 22980/72-994), in the handsome stone Mexis mansion (signposted on the waterfront), has reopened by the time you visit, you can even see Bouboulina's bones, along with archaeological finds and mementos of the War of Independence. Check when you arrive for the new hours and fee. If you head east away from the Dapia, you'll come to the picturesque **Paleo Limani** (aka the Baltiza or **Old Harbor**), where many wealthy yacht owners moor their boats and live nearby in villas hidden behind high walls. The **Cathedral of Ayios Nikolaos (St. Nicholas)** was built in the 17th century as the church of a monastery, now no longer functioning. The great moment here took place on April 3, 1821, when the flag of Spetses first flew from St. Nicolas's campanile as support for the War of Independence against the Turks. A bronze flag beside the church's war memorial commemorates this moment and a pebble mosaic commemorates the War of Independence (look for the figure of Bouboulina). While you're at the Old Harbor, have a look at the boatyards, where you can often see caiques being made with tools little different from those used when Bouboulina's mighty *Agamemnon* was built here.

Beaches

Ayia Marina, signposted and about a 30-minute walk east of Spetses town, is the best, and busiest, town beach. It has a number of tavernas, cafes, bars, including the locally famous **Paradise,** and discos. West of Spetses town, **Ayii Anaryiri** has one of the best sandy beaches anywhere in the Saronic Gulf, a perfect C-shaped cove lined with trees, and, increasingly, almost more bars and tavernas than trees. The best way to get here is by water taxi. **Paradise beach** is crowded, littered, and, for me at least, not very appealing. Now I hate to mention this, as all of us travel writers try to keep some secrets, but **Zageria** is as undeveloped a beach as you will find here. If you are interested, ask around for directions. Whichever beach you pick, go early, as beaches here get seriously crowded by midday.

Fans of *The Magus* may want to have a look at the beach at **Ayia Paraskevi,** which is bordered by pine trees. Located here are a cantina and **Villa Yasemia,** residence of the Magus himself. West over some rocks is the island's official nudist beach.

Where to Stay

Great news: The former **Hotel Posidonion** (© 22980/74-553; www.poseidonion. com), now justifiably called the **Poseidonion Grand Hotel,** situated on the harbor and impossible to miss, reopened in 2009 after renovations so extensive that they constituted rebirth. Not, repeat not, cheap, but what a great spurge to stay in this glorious 55-room grand hotel, now merging modern luxury and convenience with

Belle Epoque elegance—and, of course, there's a spa and a trendy Japanese restaurant. When I win the lottery, I am heading here, pronto. Summer doubles are around 300€; excellent off-season prices are often available.

Economou Mansion ★★   Small and elegant, this 19th-century sea captain's mansion has mosaics with sea motifs in the garden, and views far out to sea from most rooms. Unlike many boutique hotels, where you feel almost smothered in muslin curtains and embroidery, the Economou Mansion rooms are cozy and elegant, but never pretentious. The owners are attentive, but never intrusive. The breakfast buffet is extensive and delicious. Friends who had never been particularly enamored of Spetses stayed here in 2006, returned in 2010, and report that the hotel made them fall in love with the island itself.

Kounoupitsa, Spetses town. 18050 Spetses. www.economouspetses.gr. ✆ **22980/73-400.** 8 units. 200€ double; 220€ studio; 280€ deluxe suite. DC, MC, V. **Amenities:** Breakfast room; pool; Wi-Fi. *In room:* Fridge in rooms, kitchens in suites.

Hotel Faros ★ 🍴   Though there's no *faros* (lighthouse) nearby, this older hotel shares the busy central square with a Taverna Faros, a Faros Pizzeria, and other establishments whose tables and chairs curb the flow of vehicular traffic. Try for the top floor, where the simple, comfortable, twin-bedded rooms are relatively quiet (for the main square) and have balcony views of the island.

Plateia Kentriki (Central Sq.), 18050 Spetses. ✆ **22980/72-613.** Fax 22980/74-728. 50 units. 85€ double. No credit cards. **Amenities:** Breakfast room. *In room:* A/C, TV.

Hotel Nissia ★   If you're planning a lengthy stay, check out the Nissia, which is open all year. In an increasingly popular trend in Greece, the Nissia has restored a 1920s industrial building and made it the main building of a boutique hotel. Don't be dubious—it works. The Nissia has a wide range of accommodations, including double rooms, maisonettes, studios, and flats clustered around a pool to simulate traditional village residences. The hotel is a 10-minute walk from the center of Spetses town. When you get there, you can sink into the very welcome pool.

Kounoupitsa, 16675. 18050 Spetses. www.nissia.gr. ✆ **22980/75-000.** 77 units. From 220€ double. AE, MC, V. Amenities: Bar/lounge; pool; room service. In room: A/C, TV, minibar.

Orloff Resort ★★   This elegant little resort, about a 10-minute walk from the Old Harbor, was built in 1975, totally renovated in 2004, and won a place in *Odyssey* magazine's selection of the best hotels in Greece in 2007. The complex, with a swimming pool and sea and garden views, occupies the land and some of the buildings of the 1865 Orloff estate. Accommodations range from rooms, suites, and maisonettes (some with kitchenettes), to a self-contained house. The decor is simple, but not stark, with red accents perking up the pristine white and understated grays and beiges. If you play tennis and pull a muscle, not to worry: aromatherapy and massage are available.

Old Harbour, Spetses. www.orloffresort.com. ✆ **22980/75-444.** 22 units. 210€–250€ double; 400€ suite; 500€ maisonette for 4; 1,200€ house. Rates include breakfast. DC, MC, V. **Amenities:** Restaurant; bar; babysitting; pool; spa facilities; tennis. *In room:* A/C, TV, minibar.

Star Hotel 🍴   We are talking good value here. This blue-shuttered, five-story hotel—the best in its price range—is flanked by a pebble mosaic, making it off limits to vehicles. Almost all guest rooms have balconies, the front ones with views of the harbor. Each large bathroom has a tub, shower, and bidet. The rooms are very simple and could really use sprucing up. The staff is not terribly attentive. Breakfast is available, a la carte, in the lobby.

Plateia Dapia, 18050 Spetses. ☎ **22980/72-214** or 22980/72-728. Fax 22980/72-872. 37 units. From 75€ double. No credit cards. **Amenities:** Breakfast room. *In room:* A/C, TV.

Where to Eat

Spetses's restaurants can be packed with Athenians on weekend evenings, so you may want to eat unfashionably early (about 9pm) to avoid the crush. Count on spending at least 25€ at any of these places—unless you are very careful. If the price of your fish is not on the menu, ask for it; fish is usually expensive and priced by the kilogram. **Liotrivi** (☎ **22980/72-269**), in the Old Harbor, is a great place for simple grilled fish or *makaronada tou psara* (fish, tomato sauce, and pasta) or *mayiatiko a la Spetsiate* (fish stewed with tomatoes and herbs).

For standard Greek taverna food, including a number of vegetable dishes, try the rooftop taverna **Lirakis,** Dapia, over the Lirakis supermarket (☎ **22980/72-188**), with a nice view of the harbor. **To Kafeneio,** a long-established coffeehouse and ouzo joint, on the harborfront, is a good place in which to sit and watch the passing scene, as is **To Byzantino.** Or try **Orloff,** on the road to the Old Harbor, which has a wide variety of *mezedes.* The island's popularity with tour groups seems to have led to a decline in the quality of restaurant fare.

Spetses has some of the best **bakeries** in the Saronic Gulf; all serve a Greek specialty especially beloved on the islands: *amygdalota,* small, usually crescent-shaped almond cakes, flavored with rosewater and covered with powdered sugar. You'll see why this is usually served with a tall glass of cold water when you bite into all that powdered sugar.

The Bakery Restaurant GREEK/CONTINENTAL   This restaurant is on the deck above one of the island's more popular patisseries. There are a few ready-made dishes, but most of your choices are prepared when you order them. The chef obviously understands foreign palates and offers smoked trout salad, grilled steak, and roasted lamb with peas, in addition to the usual Greek dishes.

Dapia. No phone. Main courses 8€–20€. No credit cards. Daily 6:30pm–midnight.

Exedra Taverna ★ GREEK/SEAFOOD   This traditional taverna on the Old Harbor, where yachts from all over Europe moor, is also known by locals as Sioras or Giorgos. This is a good place to try fish Spetsiota (a broiled fish-and-tomato casserole). The freshly cooked zucchini, eggplant, and other seasonal vegetables are also excellent. If you can't find a table for supper, try the nearby **Taverna Liotrivi,** also known for good seafood.

Paleo Limani. ☎ **22980/73-497.** Main courses 8€–20€; fish priced by the kilo. MC, V; cash preferred. Daily noon–3pm and 7pm–midnight. Closed Feb–Nov.

Lazaros Taverna ★ GREEK   Another traditional place, Lazaros caters less to the yachties than Exedra does and more to locals. Lazaros is decorated with potted ivy, family photos, and big kegs of homemade retsina lining the walls. It's popular with locals (always a good sign), who come here for the good, fresh, reasonably priced food. The small menu features grilled meats and daily specials, such as goat in lemon sauce.

Dapia. No phone. Main courses 7€–14€. MC, V; cash preferred. Daily 6:30pm–midnight. Closed mid-Nov to mid-Mar. Inland and uphill about 400m (1,312 ft.) from the water.

Spetses After Dark

Spetses has plenty of bars, discos, and bouzouki clubs from the Dapia to the Old Harbor to Ayia Marina, and even to the more remote beaches. As always, this year's hot spot may be closed by the next season. For bars, try golden oldies **Bratsera** or

Stavento, in the heart of Dapia. For discos, there's **Figaro,** with a seaside patio and international funk until midnight; afterward, the music switches to Greek, and the dancing follows suit, often until dawn. The **1800 Bar & Internet Café,** in Kounoupitsa, Spetses town, is the place to go if you want to listen to music, keep an eye on a TV, check your e-mail, and take in the narghile lounge, where you can smoke a water pipe, with some flavored tobacco, for 2 hours (10€). **Fox** often has live Greek music and dancing; obvious tourists are encouraged to join the dancing.

CRETE

by John S. Bowman

The birthplace of Zeus, the cradle of Minoan civilization, the site of Zorba's feats—Crete is steeped in at least 5,000 years of myth, history, and culture. Greece's largest island sometimes feels more like a country: You can go from the tropical palm grove of Vai to the snowy heights of the White Mountains in a day. The great Minoan palaces, the splendor of Venetian Rethymnon, the precipitous Samaria Gorge, the luxury beach resorts—if ever an island could claim it has something for everyone without sounding like a boastful cliché, it is surely Crete.

BEACHES   There are so many beaches around Crete's coastline that it is hard to decide which to single out: the sugar-fine sand and water the color of a tropical lagoon at **Elafonisi** and **Vai; Matala**'s crescent beach, embraced by promontories into which legendary chambers have been carved; **Kommos Bay,** which attracts both nesting loggerhead turtles and nudists; or even major resort centers such as **Mallia** and **Hersonissos.** A drive along almost any stretch of coast reveals beaches that can offer anything from complete solitude to a full menu of amenities.

THINGS TO DO   Slip back to the seafaring Minoan world by wandering through the labyrinthine **Palace of Knossos,** legendary home of the Minotaur, or viewing the treasures of Minoan palaces in Iraklion's **Archaeological Museum.** Later Greek remains surprise visitors at **Gortyna;** frescoed **Byzantine chapels** dot the land; **El Greco**'s birthplace village, Fodhele, and contemporary paintings in Iraklion are unanticipated encounters; and elegant **Venetian structures** in several cities are equally unexpected. Then there are the **minarets** and **mosques** that remain from the 250 years of Ottoman Turkish rule.

EATING & DRINKING   Crete's distinctive natural cuisine is the prototype of the much-touted **"Mediterranean diet."** Although some main city restaurants now cater to more "cosmopolitan" tastes, you can find traditional Cretan fare such as sautéed goat, snails, and *marathopita* (fennel pie) in mountain villages. Eat fresh seafood along **Rethymnon's Venetian harbor** or overlooking **Ayios Nikolaos's lagoon.** Try a *bougatsa* (sugar-sprinkled cheese turnover) in Iraklion's Fountain Square. But above all, indulge in the fresh vegetables and fruits, the cheeses, and yogurt.

NATURE   A great pleasure of traveling on Crete is the awareness of the mountains that form its ever-present spine. Enjoy them simply as spectacular views or as providing trails for modest hikes and peaks for more ambitious climbs. **Mt. Idha,** for one, tops out at 2,456m (8,058 ft.). At

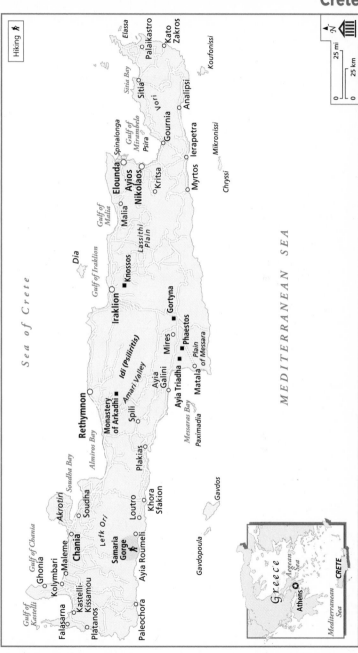

Hiking 🏃

Sea of Crete

MEDITERRANEAN SEA

Elassa
Palaikastro
Kato Zakros
Koufonissi
Sitia Bay
Sitia
Vori
Analipsi
Gournia
Gulf of Mirambelo
Psira
Spinalonga
Ierapetra
Mikronissi
Elounda
Ayios Nikolaos
Kritsa
Myrtos
Chryssi
Gulf of Malia
Malia
Lassithi Plain
Dia
Gulf of Iraklion
Knossos
Iraklion
Gortyna
Idi (Psiliritis)
Amari Valley
Phaestos
Mires
Plain of Messara
Rethymnon
Monastery of Arkadhi
Spili
Ayia Galini
Ayia Triadha
Matala
Messaras Bay
Paximadia
Almiros Bay
Soudha Bay
Plakias
Akrotiri
Lefk Ori
Soudha
Loutro
Khora Sfakion
Gavdos
Gulf of Chania
Ghonia
Kolymbari
Maleme
Chania
Samaria Gorge
Ayia Roumeli
Gavdopoula
Gulf of Kastelli
Falasarna
Kastelli-Kissamou
Platanos
Paleochora

Greece
Aegean Sea
Athens
CRETE
Mediterranean Sea

191

Crete's Wildflowers

Among the glories of Crete are its wild-flowers: A walk in almost any locale outside the center of cities provides a glimpse of their diversity and loveliness. There are said to be at least 1,500 individual species, of which some 200 are endemic or indigenous to Crete. One need not be a botanist or even especially knowledgeable about flowers to appreciate them, although there are several available guides to be found in bookstores and stalls around the island. But there is a hitch: The greatest profusion is in the spring, which comes early on Crete—early March to early April is prime time. However, those who cannot be there for the spring showing will be treated throughout much of the summer to the miles and miles of blooming oleanders that line the national highway from Chania to Ayios Nikolaos.

the other extreme, the **Samaria Gorge** hosts an excursion that thousands of people now make annually. Bird lovers will see many species, familiar and unfamiliar, and everyone can enjoy the wild flowers and flowering bushes that bedeck the landscape.

Strategies for Seeing the Island

Per square mile, Crete must be one of the most "loaded" places in the world—loaded, that is, in the diversity of its history, archaeological sites, natural attractions, tourist amenities, and just plain surprises. In a world where more and more travelers have "been there, done that," Crete is an endlessly fascinating and satisfying destination.

If possible, go in June or September, even late May or early October, unless your goal is simply a sun-drenched beach: Crete has become an island on overload in July and August—and it's very hot. The overnight ferry from Piraeus is still the purist's way to go, but the 50-minute flight by plane from the Athens airport gives you more time for activities. The island offers enough to do to fill up a week, if not a lifetime of visits. By flying, you could actually see several major sites in 2 packed days. To make full use of your time, you can fly into Iraklion and out of Chania, or vice versa.

I recommend the following destinations, if you have 5 to 7 days. This mix of activities even allows you time to collapse on a beach at the end of the day. Iraklion is a must, with its archaeological museum and nearby Knossos. An excursion to Phaestos, its associated sites, and the caves at Matala can easily occupy most of day 2. If you don't need to see that second Minoan palace, I recommend you move on at the end of the first day to overnight in Chania or Rethymnon—each or both can fill another day of strolling. Choose your route: The old road from Iraklion that winds through the mountains and villages has its charms, while the coastal expressway offers impressive vistas and a "tunnel" of flowering oleanders. If you set off in the morning, you could stay on the coastal highway and just before Rethymnon take the side trip through the Amari Valley (p. 225). Once in Chania, the walk through the famed Samaria Gorge requires 1 long day for the total excursion (p. 217). Those seeking less strenuous activity might prefer a trip east from Iraklion to Ayios Nikolaos and its nearby attractions—especially the many fine beaches along the way. Another alternative is a visit to the Lasithi Plain and the Dhiktaion Cave: This can be taken from either Iraklion or Ayios Nikolaos (p. 206). Various other side trips are described in the appropriate places. Although public transportation or tour groups are possibilities, you should really rent a car (although not for use in the cities or towns) so you

If you visit Crete during the summer, check to see when major sites and museums are open. According to the tourist office, they should be open from	8am to 7:30pm, but some may close earlier in the day and all are usually closed 1 day a week.

can leave the overdeveloped tourist trail and explore countless villages, spectacular scenery, beaches at the ends of the roads, and lesser known archaeological, historical, and cultural sites.

IRAKLION (HERAKLION)

Iraklion is the gateway to Knossos, the most impressive of the Minoan palace sites, while the museum here is home to the world's only comprehensive collection of Minoan artifacts. Beyond that, the town has magnificent fortified walls and several other testimonies to the Venetians' time of power. Iraklion is also big enough (Greece's fifth-largest city) and confident enough to have its own identity as a busy modern city. It often gets bad press because it bustles with traffic and commerce and construction—the very things most travelers want to escape. At any rate, give Iraklion a chance. Follow the advice below, and you just may come to like it.

Essentials

GETTING THERE   By Plane   Aside from the many who now fly from European cities directly to Crete on charter/package tour flights, most visitors will take the 50-minute flight from Athens to Iraklion or Chania on **Olympic Air** (✆ 210/926-9111; www.olympicair.com) or **Aegean Airlines** (✆ 801/112-0000; www.aegeanair. com). Fares vary greatly depending on time of year and time of day, and so can run from 130€ to 260€ round-trip. Olympic also offers at least one direct flight a week between Iraklion and Rhodes; and, in high season, the airline offers service between Athens and Sitia (in eastern Crete). Otherwise, flights between Crete and other points in Greece (such as Santorini, Mykonos, or Thessaloniki) go through Athens. Reservations are a necessity in high season.

Iraklion's airport is about 5km (3 miles) east of the city, along the coast. Major car-rental companies have desks at the airport. A taxi to Iraklion costs about 25€; the public bus, 4€. To get back to the airport, you have the same two choices—taxi or public bus no. 1. You can take either from Plateia Eleftheria (Liberty Sq.) or from other points along the way. Inquire in advance at your hotel about the closest stop.

By Boat   Throughout the year, there is at least one ship per day (and as many as two or three in high season) from Piraeus to Iraklion, and other ships to Chania and Rethymnon. Most trips take about 10 hours, but as of 2007 there is a "high-speed" service from Piraeus to Chania that is supposed to cut the trip down to under 5 hours. Check online at **www.ferries.gr**. In the summer season, **ANEK Lines** (www.anek. gr) operates traditional ferries about twice a week to and from Crete and Rhodes (and Karpathos, Kassos, and Khalki, the islands between the two) and Santorini and some of the other Cycladic islands en route to or from Piraeus. Occasional ferries also link Crete to Thessaloniki and various Greek ports en route. In high season, occasional ships from Italy, Cyprus, and Israel put into Iraklion. And catamarans operated by **Hellenic Seaways** link Iraklion with several Cycladic islands (Santorini, Ios, Paros, Naxos, and Mykonos). These run daily in high season, four times weekly other times; check online (www.greekislands.gr), or contact their Athens office (☏ 210/419-9000). For information on all ships, inquire at a travel agency, search online (www.gtp.gr), or contact **Paleologos Agency** (www.ferries.gr).

If you have arrived at Iraklion's harbor by ship, you'll most likely want to take a taxi up into the town, as it's a steep climb. Depending on where you want to go, the fare ranges from 8€ to 15€. Or you can take a bus from the depot.

By Bus   Visitors also come to Iraklion by public bus from other cities on the island. Where you arrive depends on where you've come from. Those arriving from points to the west, east, or southeast—Chania or Rethymnon, for instance, or Ayios Nikolaos or Sitia to the east—end up along the harbor. To get into the center of town, you must walk, take a taxi, or hop a public bus. The bus starts its route at the terminal where buses from the east and southeast stop; directly across the boulevard is the station for the Rethymnon-Chania buses. Visitors arriving from the south—Phaestos, Matala, and other towns—will end up at Chania Gate, on the southwest edge of town; walking may not appeal to most people, but you can take a public bus or taxi.

VISITOR INFORMATION   The **National Tourist Office** (☏ 2810/228-225; fax 2810/226-020) is at 1 Xanthoudidou, opposite the Archaeological Museum. Its hours are Monday through Friday 9am to 5pm. Maps and pamphlets are provided free, but the information is often a bit "general." For specifics you might do better to contact one of the more reliable travel agencies in Iraklion: **Creta Travel Bureau,** 49B Dikeossinis (☏ 2810/300-610; fax 2810/223-749), or **Arabatzoglou Travel,** 30 25th Avgusto (☏ 2810/301-398; fax 2810/301-399). For those interested in renting an apartment or villa on Crete, see the agencies listed in "Tips on Accommodations," in chapter 13.

GETTING AROUND   By Bus   You can see much of Crete by using the public bus system. The buses are cheap, relatively frequent, and connect to all but the most isolated locales. The downside: Remote destinations often have schedules that cater to locals, not tourists. The long-distance bus system is operated by **KTEL,** which serves all of Greece. Ask your travel agent, or call ☏ 2810/221-765 to find out more about KTEL buses to Rethymnon-Chania and points west. For buses to Ayios Nikolaos, Sitia, Ierapetra, and points east, call ☏ 2810/245-019. For buses to Phaestos and other points south, call ☏ 2810/255-965.

By Car & Moped   A car gives you maximum flexibility in seeing the island. All the familiar car-rental agencies are available at the main centers of Crete, including the airports, and most travelers have their preferences. In Iraklion, aside from these, I recommend the locally owned **Motor Club,** 18 Plateia Agglon, at the bottom of 25th Avgusto, overlooking the harbor (☏ 2810/222-408; www.motorclub.gr). **Europrent,** with its home office in Chania, can also provide cars in Iraklion (☏ 28210/27-810; www.europrent.gr). If a moped or motorcycle looks tempting, be *very* sure you can control such a vehicle in chaotic urban traffic and on dangerous mountain roads (with few shoulders but lots of potholes and gravel). Try the Motor Club for rentals.

By Taxi   Taxis are reasonable if two or three people share a trip to a site; no place on Crete is more than a day's round-trip from Iraklion. Ask a travel agent to find you a driver who speaks at least rudimentary English; he can then serve as your guide as

Iraklion

HOTELS ■

Aquila Atlantis Hotel **6**
Atrion Hotel **1**
Galaxy Hotel **10**
Lato Boutique Hotel **4**
Megaron Hotel **5**

RESTAURANTS ◆

Brillant Gourmet Restaurant **4**
Ippocampus **2**
Kyriakos **9**
Loukoulos **7**
O Vrakos **3**
Pantheon **8**

7

CRETE | Iraklion (Heraklion)

📎 **Biking on Crete**

In general, I am reluctant to encourage the casual visitor to Greece to rent and ride a bicycle—either to get around cities and towns or to set off for the countryside. In the former case, Greek drivers are not accustomed to bicycle riders, and their driving habits make it extremely dangerous; in the latter case, the terrain is usually quite mountainous, roads are often not that well maintained, and there is little shoulder to ride on. That having been said, Crete has become a major attraction for serious bikers. Various specialized tour operators run bicycle tours on Crete—extending over several days, doing a segment each day, with accommodations at each stop over; you could bring your own, but these firms also rent them. Some tours are described as requiring truly top-level conditioning, while others are less demanding, but all involve a lot of hills. (And in summer, any activity can be quite draining.) If you want to pursue this, try **Trekking Plan** (www.cycling.gr) to learn about their offerings. If you are intent on renting on your own for some limited excursion, major tourist centers usually have some outfit that will rent a bike (usually a mountain bike); in Iraklion, for example, try **Blue Aegean Holidays** (www.blueaegean.com) or **MotoExress** (www.motoexpress.gr). Note that many online sites that advertise bikes for rent are referring to motorbikes.

well. It might cost 100€ to tour the city and get out to Knossos, but for a party of three or four it is well worth it.

By Boat Several excursion boats take day trips to offshore islands or to isolated beaches—occasionally even to Santorini; inquire at a travel agency.

FAST FACTS The official **American Express** agency is Adamis Travel Bureau, 23 25th Avgusto (📞 **2810/346-202;** fax 2810/224-717). There are numerous **banks** and **ATMs** (as well as several currency-exchange machines) throughout the center of Iraklion, with many along 25th Avgusto. The **British Consul** (📞 **2810/224-012**) is at 16 Papa Alexandrou, opposite the Archaeological Museum; there is no American consulate in Iraklion. **Venizelou Hospital** (📞 **2810/237-502**) is on Knossos Road. For general **first-aid** information, call 📞 **2810/222-222.** For Internet access, try the InSpot Cafe, at 6 Korai, or the Cyberpoint Cafe, 117 Paraskiyopoulou. Both open midmorning and close at midnight. The access fee at both is now about 4€ per hour.

The most convenient place to do **laundry** is at 25 Merebellou (behind the Archaeological Museum); its hours are Monday through Saturday from 9am to 9pm. You can leave **luggage** at the airport for 5€ per piece per day; most hotels will hold luggage for brief periods. The **tourist police** are at 10 Dikeossenis, on the main street linking 25th Avgusto to Plateia Eleftheria (📞 **2810/283-190**); they are open daily from 7am to 11pm. The main **post office** (📞 **2810/289-995**) is on Plateia Daskaloyiannis and is open daily from 7:30am to 8pm. The **telephone office (OTE),** 10 Minotaurou (far side of El Greco Park), is open daily from 6am to 11pm.

What to See & Do

ATTRACTIONS

The Archaeological Museum ★★★ This—the world's premier collection of art and artifacts from the Minoan civilization—surprises most visitors, who are amazed by the variety of objects, styles, and techniques of the treasures inside. Many of the most spectacular objects are from Knossos; the rest, from other sites on the island. Among the most prized objects are **snake goddesses** from Knossos, the **Phaestos Disc** (with its still-undeciphered inscription), the **bee pendant** from Mallia, **carved vases** from Ayia Triadha and Kato Zakros, and objects depicting young men leaping over the horns of charging bulls. Upstairs you'll find the **original frescoes from Knossos** and other sites, their restored sections clearly visible (the frescoes now at Knossos are copies of these). Most displays have decent labels in English, but you may want to invest in one of the guidebooks for sale in the lobby. You will need at least 1 hour for even a quick walk-through. To avoid the tour groups in high season, plan to visit very early, late in the day, or on Sunday.

1 Xanthoudidou. ℂ **2810/226-092.** Admission 6€ adults, 3€ students with official ID and E.U. citizens 65 and over; free Sun Nov–Mar, and some Sun in summer. Combination ticket for museum and Palace of Knossos 10€. Apr to mid-Oct Tues–Sun 8am–8pm, Mon 12:30–8pm; mid-Oct to Mar Tues–Sun 8am–5pm, Mon 12:30–5pm. Far corner of Plateia Eleftheria. Parking in immediate area impossible—best to park below, along commercial harbor road.

Cretaquarium ☺   Hardly a world-class aquarium, but there's more than enough here to occupy your kids on a day when you need a break from the beach. Located on the edge of the former U.S. Air Force station, its several tanks house over 2,500 specimens from hundreds of Mediterranean and tropical species of fish and invertebrates—from hunter sharks to tiny sea horses to jellyfish. Various underwater terrains have also been replicated—it is definitely a professional operation. The whole complex, known as Thalassocosmos (Sea World), belongs to the Hellenic Center for Marine Research. A restaurant and souvenir shop are also on the premises.

At Gournes, 16km (10 miles) east of Iraklion. ℂ **2810/337-788.** www.cretaquarium.gr. Admission 8€ adults; 6€ students, children 5–17, and seniors over 65. June–Sept daily 9am–9pm; Oct–May daily 10am–5:30pm. Bus from station at Iraklion port.

Harbor Fort (the Koules) ☺   You may feel as if you're walking through a Hollywood set—but this is the real thing. The harbor fort, built on the site of a series of earlier forts, went up between 1523 and 1540, and although greatly restored, it is essentially the Venetian original. Both its exterior and interior are impressive in their dimensions, workmanship, and details: thick walls, spacious chambers, great ramparts, cannonballs, and Lion of St. Mark plaques. It's well worth an hour's visit.

At breakwater on old harbor. ℂ **2810/288-484.** Admission 4€. Daily 9am–1pm and 4–7pm.

 Museum's Temporary Display

When this edition went to press, Iraklion's Archaeological Museum was still closed for major renovations and additions, although it was claimed it would be open by the spring of 2012. However, they have installed a wonderful selection of all the major holdings in a new building at the rear of the museum. Its hours have been Tuesday through Sunday 8:30am to 5pm, and Monday noon to 5pm. Admission is 4€; 2€ for students and E.U. seniors. To be frank, this greatly reduced selection is probably enough for most visitors—all the notable pieces are on display. One drawback is that the floor space is limited even more than usual, so try to visit there during off hours—very early in the morning or late in the day.

Historical Museum of Crete ★ This museum picks up where the Archaeological Museum leaves off, displaying artifacts and art from the early Christian era up to the present. You get some sense of the role the Cretans' long struggle for independence still plays in their identity. On display are traditional Cretan **folk arts;** the re-created study of **Nikos Kazantzakis,** Crete's great modern writer; and two paintings by **El Greco,** another of the island's admired sons. Even if you take only an hour for this museum, it will reward you with surprising insights about the island.

7 Lysimakos Kalokorinou (facing coast road, 450m/1,500 ft. west of harbor). ☏ **2810/283-219.** www.historical-museum.gr. Admission 5€ adults, 3€ students. Mar–Oct Mon–Sat 9am–5pm. Closed Sun and holidays.

The Palace of Knossos ★★★ ☺ This is undeniably one of the great archaeological sites of the world, yet until Arthur Evans began excavating here in 1900, little was known about the ancient people who inhabited it. Using every possible clue and remnant, Evans rebuilt large parts of the palace—walls, floors, stairs, windows, and columns. Visitors must now stay on a walkway, but you still get a good sense of the structure's labyrinthine nature. You are looking at the remains of two major palaces, plus several restorations made up to about 1250 B.C. This was not a palace in the modern sense of a royal residence, but a combination of that and the Minoans' chief religious/ceremonial center, as well as their administrative headquarters and royal workshops. Take the time for a guided tour here; it's worth the expense (your hotel or a travel agency can arrange it). On your own, you'll need at least 2 hours for a cursory walk-through. The latter part of the day and Sunday tend to be less crowded. And if time is an issue, splurge on a taxi, usually 12€ one way.

Knossos Rd., 5km (3 miles) south of Iraklion. ☏ **2810/231-940.** Admission 6€, 3€ students with official ID and E.U. citizens 65 or over; free Sun Nov–Mar and some Sun in summer. Combination ticket for the Palace of Knossos and Archaeological Museum (above) 10€. Apr to mid-Oct daily 8am–8pm; mid-Oct to Mar Mon–Fri 8am–5pm, Sat–Sun 8:30am–3pm. Frequent buses from center of Iraklion. Free parking down slope on left, 90m (300 ft.) before main entrance.

Venetian Walls & Tomb of Nikos Kazantzakis ★ ☺ These great walls and bastions were part of the fortress-city the Venetians called Candia. Two of the great city gates have survived fairly well: the Pantocrator or Panigra Gate, better known now as the Chania Gate (dating from about 1570), at the western edge; and the Gate of Gesu, or Kainouryia Gate (about 1587), at the southern edge. Walk around the outer perimeter of the walls to get a feel for their sheer massiveness. They were built by the forced labor of Cretans. On the Martinengo Bastion at the southwestern corner of the great walls is the grave of Nikos Kazantzakis (1883–1947), a native of Iraklion and author of *Zorba the Greek* and *The Last Temptation of Christ.* Here, too, is one of the best views to the south. Mount Iouktas appears in profile as the head of a man— some say the head of the buried god Zeus. A dedicated visit requires a solid hour from the city center, especially if you want to examine the nearby Kainouryia Gate and a segment of the wall.

Tomb is on Martinengo Bastion, at southwestern corner of the walls, along Plastira. Free admission. Daily sunrise–sunset.

A STROLL AROUND IRAKLION

Start your stroll at **Fountain Square** (also known as Lions Sq., officially Plateia Venizelou), after trying a plate of *bougatsa* at one of the two cafes here serving this local pastry: Armenian Greeks introduced this cheese- or cream-filled delicacy to Crete. This square, long one big traffic jam, is now for pedestrians only. Francesco

Morosini, Crete's Venetian governor, installed the **fountain ★** here in 1628. Note the now fading but still elegant relief carvings around the basin. Across from the fountain is the **Basilica of St. Mark,** restored to its original 14th-century Italian style and used for exhibitions and concerts.

Proceeding south 50m (164 ft.) to the crossroads, you'll see the **market street** (officially from 1866); alas, it is increasingly taken over by tourist shops but is still a must-see, with its purveyors of fresh fruits and vegetables, meats, and wines.

At the far end of the market street, look for **Kornarou Square,** with its lovely Turkish fountain; beside it is the **Venetian Bembo Fountain** (1588). The modern statue at the far side of the square commemorates the hero and heroine of Vincenzo Kornarou's Renaissance epic poem *Erotokritos,* a Cretan-Greek classic.

Turning right onto Vikela, proceed (always bearing right) until you come to the imposing, if not artistically notable, 19th-century **Cathedral of Ayios Menas,** dedicated to the patron saint of Iraklion. Below and to the left, the medieval **Church of Ayios Menas** boasts old woodcarvings and icons.

At the far corner of the cathedral (to the northeast) is the 15th-century **Church of St. Katherine ★.** During the 16th and 17th centuries, this church hosted the Mount Sinai Monastery School, where it is alleged that Domenico Theotokopoulou studied before moving on to Venice and Spain; there he became known as **El Greco.** The church houses a small museum of icons, frescoes, and woodcarvings. It's open Monday through Saturday from 10am to 1pm, and Tuesday, Thursday, and Friday from 4 to 6pm. Admission is 5€.

Take Ayii Dheka, the narrow street that leads directly away from the facade of St. Katherine's, and you'll arrive at **Leoforos Kalokerinou,** the main shopping street for locals. Turn right onto it and proceed up to the crossroads of the market street and 25th Avgusto—now set aside for pedestrians. Turn left to go back down past Fountain Square and, on the right, you'll see the totally reconstructed **Venetian Loggia,** originally dating from the early 1600s. Prominent Venetians once met here to conduct business affairs; it now houses city government offices.

A little farther down 25th Avgusto, also on the right, is the **Church of Ayios Titos,** dedicated to the patron saint of Crete (Titus of the Bible), who introduced Christianity to Crete. Head down to the **harbor,** with a side visit to **the Koules (Harbor Fort)** if you have time (see above), then pass on the right the two sets of great **Venetian arsenali**—where ships were built and repaired. (The sea at that time came in this far.) Climbing the stairs just past the arsenali, turn left onto Bofort and curve up beneath the **Archaeological Museum** to **Plateia Eleftheria (Liberty Sq.),** where you can pride yourself on having seen the main attractions of Irakion and reward yourself with a refreshing drink at one of the many cafes on the far side.

SHOPPING

Costas Papadopoulos, the proprietor of **Daedalou Galerie,** 11 Daedalou, between Fountain Square and Plateia Eleftheria (© **2810/346-353**), has been offering his tasteful selection of traditional Cretan-Greek arts and crafts for several decades—icons, jewelry, porcelain, silverware, pistols, and more. Some of it is truly old, and he'll tell you when it isn't.

Eleni Kastrinoyanni-Cretan Folk Art, 3 Ikarou, opposite the Archaeological Museum (© **2810/226-186**), is the premier store in Iraklion for some of the finest in embroidery, weavings, ceramics, and jewelry. The work is new but reflects traditional Cretan folk methods and motifs. Get out your credit card, and go for something you'll enjoy for years to come. It's closed October through February.

Stores that sell local agricultural products have sprung up all over Iraklion (as well as most of Crete). Crete's olive oil—among the finest in the world—stands side by side with honey, wines and spirits, raisins, olives, herbs, and spices. One store is as good as the other.

Where to Stay

In recent years, mass tourism on Crete has led to a demand for beach hotels outside of the cities, but Iraklion still offers a range of hotels. Reservations are a must in high season.

INSIDE THE CITY

Our search for a good hotel here tries hard to feature the criterion of quiet. Iraklion lies under the flight patterns of many commercial planes and the occasional Greek Air Force jet fighter. The noise factor probably adds up to less than 40 minutes every 24 hours, so the sounds of scooters and motorcycles outside your hotel at night will probably be more annoying. Closed windows and air-conditioning promise the best defenses.

Very Expensive

Megaron Hotel ★★★ The "grand hotel" of Iraklion was formerly an old and abandoned commercial/apartment building on the site of a bastion of the old Venetian walls and high above the harbor. Opening in 2003, the owners installed a hotel that is elegant in its decor, facilities, and service. All rooms have an exterior view, leaving the core of the structure as a great atrium. All the public areas bespeak understated luxury, and rooms are more generous than in many Greek hotels, as well as far more stylish. The various amenities and the service are of the highest standard. Special elements include a small library/reading area, plasma TV, free wireless in public areas, private dining options, rooms for those with disabilities. The Megaron is convenient for walking to any place in the core of the city.

9 Beaufort, 71202 Iraklion (on street below Archaeological Museum). www.gdmmegaron.gr. ✆ **2810/305-300.** 58 units. 164€–354€ double. Rates include full breakfast. AE, DC, MC, V. Private parking arranged. **Amenities:** Restaurant; 2 cafes (1 by pool); bar; airport pickup by arrangement; babysitting; health club and gym w/Jacuzzi massage room, sauna, and steam bath; rooftop pool; room service; smoke-free rooms; Wi-Fi. *In room:* A/C, TV, fridge, hair dryer, Internet, minibar.

Expensive

Aquila Atlantis Hotel ★★ Although Iraklion boasts a more luxurious hotel, the Atlantis is probably more than adequate for most travelers' tastes. This Class A hotel is in the heart of Iraklion, yet removed from city noise (especially if you use the air-conditioning). The staff is friendly and helpful, and although the Atlantis is popular with conference groups—it has major conference facilities—individuals get personal attention. Guest rooms (insist on smoke-free if that matters), although neither plush nor especially large, are comfortable, and you can swim in the rooftop pool.

2 Iyias, 71202 Iraklion (behind the Archaeological Museum). www.aquilaatlantis-crete.com. ✆ **2810/229-103.** 162 units. High season 155€ double; low season 140€ double. Rates include breakfast. Reduction possible for longer stays. Special rates for business travelers; half board available. AE, DC, MC, V. Private parking arranged. **Amenities:** Restaurant; 2 bars; airport pickup by arrangement; babysitting; children's playground (across street); Jacuzzi; small indoor pool; room service; smoke-free rooms; tennis court across street. *In room:* A/C, TV, fridge, hair dryer, minibar, Wi-Fi.

Galaxy Hotel ★ With a reputation as one of the finer hotels in Iraklion, the Galaxy is classy once you get past its rather forbidding gray exterior. The interior was completely renovated in 2008. The public areas are striking if airport modern, and the

Galaxy boasts (for now, at least) the largest indoor swimming pool in Iraklion. Guest rooms are stylish—international modern—but don't expect American-style size. Ask for an interior unit, as you lose nothing in a view and gain in quiet. The hotel also offers several expensive suites, as well as rooms especially designed for those with limited mobility. Although a reader once reported a less-than-gracious tone from desk staff, I have always found them courteous, if brisk. All in all, the Galaxy appeals most to travelers who prefer a familiar, international ambience to folksiness.

67 Leoforos Demokratias, 71306 Iraklion (about 1km/½ mile out main road to Knossos). www.ellada.net/galaxy. ☎ **2810/238-812.** 127 units, some with shower, some with tub. High season 110€ double; low season 100€ double. Rates include buffet breakfast. AE, DC, MC, V. Parking on adjacent streets. Frequent bus to town center within yards of entrance. **Amenities:** 2 restaurants; bar; pastry shop; babysitting; health club; indoor pool; room service; sauna; smoke-free rooms; Wi-Fi. *In room:* A/C, TV, hair dryer, Internet, minibar.

Moderate

Atrion Hotel   Nothing spectacular here, but I have liked this hotel for many years, if only for its location. It's in a quiet, seemingly remote corner that is in fact only a 10-minute walk to the center of town, and an even shorter walk to the coast road and the harbor. True, the adjacent streets are not that attractive, but they are perfectly safe; once inside the hotel, you can enjoy your oasis of comfort and peace. Thoroughly renovated in 2004, this hotel has well-appointed public areas—a lounge, a refreshing patio garden—and pleasant, good-size guest rooms. Guests often rave about the breakfast.

9 Chronaki (behind the Historical Museum), 71202 Iraklion. www.atrion.gr. ☎ **2810/229-225.** 60 units, some with shower, some with tub. High season 85€ double; low season 75€ double. Rates include buffet breakfast. Reductions for children. AE, MC, V. Parking on adjacent streets. Public bus within 200m (656 ft.). **Amenities:** Restaurant; bar; babysitting; room service; smoke-free rooms. *In room:* A/C, TV, hair dryer, Internet, minibar.

Lato Boutique Hotel ★ 🍴   Long one of my favorites in Greece, the Lato provides value, a stylish environment, and warm hospitality. Renovations scheduled for completion by 2012 will refurbish the public areas, transform the rooms' decor and furnishings, and add new state-of-the art bathrooms. A few rooms are a bit small for more than one, five are handsome suites, but all are perfectly adequate. The buffet breakfast is especially satisfying. A major plus: its location, convenient to the town's center while offering rooms with harbor views (just ask for one). A rooftop restaurant is also one of the attractions of this hotel, combining alfresco dining with a spectacular view. The hotel has its own luxury restaurant next door and in 2011 it opened a completely renovated former hotel across the street as an annex. The staff is always ready to help you make the most of your stay in Iraklion.

15 Epimenidou, 71202 Iraklion. www.lato.gr. ☎ **2810/228-103.** 58 units, some with shower only. High season 115€–125€ double; low season 100€–115€ double. Rates include buffet breakfast. 10% discount for Internet reservations; 50% discount for children 6–12. AE, DC, MC, V. Valet parking by desk staff. **Amenities:** 2 restaurants (see Brillant Gourmet below); breakfast room; bar; Jacuzzi; minigym; room service; smoke-free rooms; steam room. *In room:* A/C, TV, hair dryer, Internet, minibar.

Inexpensive

Poseidon 🍴   This is by no means for everyone, but in a contest among longtime Frommer's loyalists for a favorite hotel in Iraklion, the Poseidon would probably win. And it's not just because of good value for the money. Owner/host John Polychronides established a homey atmosphere, a tone maintained by the desk staff (fluent in English). The street is not especially attractive—but that's true at most of Iraklion's hotels, and few can match the fresh breezes and an unobstructed view over the port.

Rooms are on the small side and showers are basic, but everything is clean and functional. The sound-insulated windows keep out most exterior noise, but overhead air traffic can be annoying at times. Frequent buses and cheap taxi fares let you come and go into Iraklion center, a 20-minute walk.

54 Poseidonos, Poros, 71202 Iraklion. www.hotelposeidon.gr. © **2810/222-545.** 26 units, all with shower only. High season 75€ double; low season 65€ double. Rates include continental breakfast. For e-mail reservations and cash payments, a 10% discount for 1–2 nights, 1%–5% discount for stays over 2 nights. AE, MC, V. Parking all around hotel. Frequent public buses, 180m (590 ft.) at top of street. About 2.5km (1½ miles) from Plateia Eleftheria, off the main road to the east. *In room:* A/C (8€ daily surcharge), TV, fridge.

OUTSIDE THE CITY

Assuming you want to be fairly close to Iraklion, stay on the coast, if you want to avoid city noise. If you just want to stay near a remote beach on Crete, such accommodations are described later in this chapter. Although the hotels below can be reached by public bus, a car or taxi will save you valuable time.

Expensive

Candia Maris Resort and Spa ★ ☺   After a couple of years under Swiss management, this hotel has returned to Greek ownership. Located on the western edge of Iraklion—you have to pass through a rather dreary edge of Iraklion to get here—it's close enough to town to allow for easy excursions. Its beach makes it especially attractive to families with children, and it offers just about everything, from special Cretan Nights, with traditional music and dancing; to a squash court; to the newest fad, thalassotherapy (seawater treatment). The exterior and layout are a bit severe, but the rooms are good-size and cheerful, the bathrooms up-to-date. Besides, you won't spend much time looking at the building's exterior, so don't let it deter you from trying this resort hotel. Guests tend to praise the food and friendly staff. It was also one of the first hotels in Greece to offer accessibility for those with limited mobility.

Amoudara, Gazi, 71303 Iraklion. www.candiamaris.gr. © **2810/377-000.** 285 units. 165€ double in hotel; 210€ bungalow. Closed Nov–Mar. Rates include buffet breakfast. Varied fees for extra person in room and for children; half-board plan available. AE, DC, MC, V. Parking on grounds. Public bus every half-hour to Iraklion. On beach about 6km (4 miles) west of Iraklion center. **Amenities:** 4 restaurants; 4 bars; babysitting; basketball; bikes; billiards; bowling; children's programs; health club; minigolf; 7 pools (2 outdoor, 4 indoor, 1 children's); room service; spa; tennis and squash courts; thalassotherapy; volleyball; watersports; Wi-Fi in public areas for fee; rooms for those w/limited mobility. *In room:* A/C, TV, fridge, hair dryer, Internet (for fee), minibar.

Where to Eat

Avoid eating a meal at either Fountain Square or Liberty Square (Plateia Eleftheria), unless you want the experience of being at the center of activity—the food at those areas' establishments is, to put it mildly, nothing special. Save these spots for a coffee or beer break.

EXPENSIVE

Brillant Gourmet Restaurant ★★ INTERNATIONAL   Since opening in 2007, this restaurant has emerged as offering the finest dining experience in Iraklion. The decor is quite striking but this would mean nothing if it were not matched by the menu and service, which are of the highest quality. The ingredients are basically Greek—even local Cretan—but prepared in combinations that make for some unexpected treats: Appetizers might include a tomato-brie puff pie and goat cheese with prosciutto, while entrees include tender filets of beef or pork, as well as chicken and fish dishes. The basic menu changes at least twice a year and specials are offered most nights. The wine list is equally special—trust the waiter to suggest a wine appropriate for your entree and you may be surprised at how good, say, one of the better Cretan wines can be.

15 Epimenidou (adjacent to the Lato Boutique Hotel). ☎ **2810/334-959.** www.brillantrestaurant.gr. Reservations recommended for dinner in high season. Main courses 18€–25€ (lobster dishes extra). AE, DC, MC, V. Daily 7:30pm–12:30am. Lato Hotel can help with parking, but best just to walk here.

MODERATE

Kyriakos ★ GREEK   In recent years, this restaurant has gained the reputation of offering some of the finest cooking in Iraklion. The menu is essentially traditional Greek, but its specialties include artichokes with potatoes and lettuce, lamb fricassee, and eggplant stuffed with feta. Snails are another delicacy, and if that doesn't tempt you, come back at Christmas for the turkey. The wine choices are appropriately fine and expensive. Two people should expect to drop between 50€ and 75€ for the full works here, but think what you'd pay at home for such a meal. Its location might disappoint some; it's on a busy boulevard on the edge of town and lacks Cretan "atmosphere." It's a bit stodgy, but if you're serious about what's on your plate, coming here is an occasion.

53 Leoforos Demokratias (about 1km/½ mile from center on the road to Knossos). ☎ **2810/224-649.** Reservations recommended for dinner in high season. Appetizers 4€–8€; main courses 6€–28€. AE, DC, MC, V. Daily noon–5pm and 7pm–1am. Closed Sun June 2–July 10.

Loukoulos ★ ITALIAN/GREEK   Here's another restaurant that has gained a stylish reputation. It's in the very heart of the city on a back street, crammed into a tiny patio with fanciful umbrellas shading the tables. The chairs are comfortable, the table settings lovely, and the selection of *mezedes* (appetizers) varied. The creative Italian menu features lots of pasta dishes, such as a delicious rigatoni with a broccoli-and-Roquefort cream sauce. Treat yourself at least once to Iraklion's "in" place.

5 Korai (one street behind Daedalou). ☎ **2810/224-435.** Reservations recommended for dinner in high season. Main courses 6€–20€; fixed-price lunch 18€. AE, DC, V. Mon–Sat noon–1am; Sun 6:30pm–midnight. Street closed to vehicles.

O Vrakos ★ GREEK   A once modest taverna that has gained an enthusiastic following from both Greeks and foreigners, it has the added advantage of providing its diners a view over the old Venetian harbor and its imposing fortress. Seafood is a specialty, but if you aren't looking to spend at the high end, stick with the basic taverna fare. You could make a meal from their tasty *mezedes*—the fried zucchini, the lamb meatballs, and a tasty Greek salad. The staff is especially hospitable and if you've spent for a full meal, you are apt to be served a complimentary dessert (and raki) after you've asked for the check.

1 Marinelli (at foot of street at the traffic circle at the harbor). ☎ **2810/243-243.** Main courses 6€–18€. No credit cards. Mon–Sat 11:30am–midnight; Sun 5:30pm–midnight. Parking on adjacent side streets.

INEXPENSIVE

Ippocampus MEZEDES   This is an institution among locals, who line up for a typical Cretan meal solely of appetizers. The zucchini slices, dipped in batter and deep fried, are fabulous. A plate of tomatoes and cukes, another of sliced fried potatoes, small fish, perhaps fried squid—that's it. A couple could assemble a meal for as little as 20€—but go early. Ippocampus is down along the coast road. You can sit indoors or on the sidewalk, a bargain either way.

3 Mitsotaki (along the waterfront, to left of traffic circle as you come down 25th Avgusto). ℂ **2810/282-081.** Appetizers 2.50€–8€. No credit cards. Mon–Fri 1–3:30pm and 7pm–midnight. Parking on adjacent side streets.

Pantheon 📷 GREEK Anyone who spends more than a few days in Iraklion should take at least one meal in Dirty Alley, where this restaurant is a longtime favorite. Although it lost its rough-hewn atmosphere long ago, Dirty Alley still seems an indigenous locale. The menu at Pantheon (much the same as the menus at the other Dirty Alley places) offers taverna standards—meat stews; chunks of meat, chicken, or fish in tasty sauces; and vegetables such as okra, zucchini, or stuffed tomatoes. These places are not especially cheap—the proprietors know to charge for the atmosphere—but the food's tasty. And if you sit in the Pantheon, on the corner of the market street, you'll get a choice view of the scene outside.

2 Theodosaki (Dirty Alley, connecting the market street and Evans). ℂ **2810/241-652.** Main courses 6€–16€. No credit cards. Mon–Sat 11am–11pm.

Iraklion After Dark

To spend an evening the way most Iraklians do, stroll and then sit in a cafe and watch others stroll by. The prime locations for the latter have been Plateia Eleftheria (Liberty Sq.) or Fountain Square, but the crowded atmosphere of these places—and some overly aggressive waiters—has considerably reduced their charm.

For a more relaxed atmosphere, go to **Marina Cafe,** at the old harbor (directly across from the restored Venetian arsenali). For as little as 2€ for a coffee or as much as 9€ for an alcoholic drink, you can enjoy the breeze as you contemplate the illuminated Venetian fort, which looks much like a stage set. Another possibility if you're looking to have a late meal and hang out with a younger crowd is to try the small cafe/restaurant right on the 1866 Street (the Market street), **Peninda-Peninda.**

There is no end to the number of **bars** and **discos,** featuring everything from international rock 'n' roll to Greek pop music, although they come and go from year to year to reflect the latest fads. **Disco Athina,** 9 Ikarou, just outside the wall on the way to the airport, is an old favorite with the young; or try any of the clubs along Epimenidou—the **Villa Lokka** or **Privilege**—or **Vogue** or **Envy** along the seafront.

Most Class A hotels now host a **Cretan Night,** when performers dance and play **traditional music.** For more of the same, take a taxi to either **Aposperides,** out on the road toward Knossos, or **Sordina,** about 5km (3 miles) to the southwest of town.

During the summer, Iraklion's **arts festival** (though hardly competitive with the major festivals of Europe) brings in world-class performers (ballet companies, pianists, and others), but mostly featured are ancient and medieval-Renaissance Greek dramas, Greek-themed dance, or traditional and modern Greek music. Many performances take place outdoors in one of three venues: on the roof of **the Koules** (the Venetian fort in the harbor), **Kazantzakis Garden Theater,** or **Hadzidaksis Theater.** Ticket prices vary from year to year, but are well below what you'd pay at such cultural events elsewhere. Maybe you didn't come to Crete expecting to hear Vivaldi, but why not enjoy it while you're here? The festival begins in late June and ends in mid-September.

Side Trips from Iraklion

Travel agencies arrange excursions setting out from Iraklion to virtually every point of interest on Crete, such as **Samaria Gorge** in the far southwest (p. 217). In that sense, Iraklion can be used as the home base for all your touring on Crete. If you have only 1 extra day on Crete, I recommend the following trip.

GORTYNA, PHAESTOS, AYIA TRIADHA & MATALA ★★

If you have an interest in history and archaeology, and you've already seen Knossos and Iraklion's museum, this is the trip to make. The distance isn't that great—a round-trip of about 165km (100 miles)—but you'd want a full day to take it all in. A taxi or guided tour is advisable, if you haven't rented a car. Bus schedules won't allow you to fit in all the stops. (You can stay, of course, at one of the hotels on the south coast, but they're usually booked long in advance of high season.)

The road south takes you up and across the **mountainous spine** of central Crete. At about 40km (25 miles), you'll leave behind the **Sea of Crete** (to the north) and see the **Libyan Sea** to the south. You then descend onto the **Messara,** the largest plain on Crete (about 32km/20 miles × 5km/3 miles) and a major agricultural center. At about 45km (28 miles), you'll see on your right the **remains of Gortyna;** many more remnants lie scattered in the fields off to the left. Gortyna (or Gortyn or Gortys) first emerged as a center of the Dorian Greeks who moved to Crete after the end of the Minoan civilization. By 500 B.C., they had advanced enough to inscribe a code of law into stone. The stones were found in the late 19th century and reassembled here, where you can see this unique—and to scholars, invaluable—document testifying to the legal and social arrangements of this society.

After the Romans took over Crete (67 B.C.), Gortyna enjoyed another period of glory when it served as the capital of Roman Crete and Cyrenaica (Libya). Roman structures—temples, a stadium, and more—litter the fields to the left. On the right, along with the **Code of Gortyna ★**, you'll see a small **Hellenistic Odeon,** or theater, and the remains of the **Basilica of Ayios Titos** (admission 5€; daily 8am–7pm high season, reduced hours off-season). Paul commissioned Titos (Titus) to lead the first Christians on Crete. The church, begun in the 6th century, was later greatly enlarged.

Proceed down the road another 15km (10 miles), turn left at the sign for Phaestos, and ascend to the ridge where the **palace of Phaestos ★★** sits in all its splendor (admission 6€; daily 8am–7pm high season, reduced hours off-season). Scholars consider this the second most powerful Minoan center; many visitors appreciate its attractive setting on a prow of land that seems to float between the plain and the sky. Italians began to excavate Phaestos soon after Evans began at Knossos, but they decided to leave the remains much as they found them. The **ceremonial staircase** is as awesome as it must have been to the ancients, while the **great court** remains one of the most resonant public spaces anywhere. And you can have a meal at the restaurant on the terrace overlooking the site.

Leaving Phaestos, continue down the main road 4km (2½ miles) and turn left onto a side road. Park here and make your way to pay your respects to a Minoan minipalace complex known as **Ayia Triadha.** To this day, scholars aren't certain exactly what it was—something between a satellite of Phaestos and a semi-independent palace. Several of the most impressive artifacts in the Iraklion Museum, including the painted sarcophagus (on the second floor), were found here.

Back on the road, follow the signs to **Kamilari** and then **Pitsidia.** Now you've earned your rest and swim, and at no ordinary place: the nearby **beach at Matala ★**. It's a small cove enclosed by bluffs of age-old packed earth. Explorers found **chambers,** some complete with "bunk beds" that probably date back to the Romans (most likely no earlier than A.D. 100). Cretans long used them as summer homes, the German soldiers used them as storerooms during World War II, and hippies took them over in the 1960s. You can visit them during the day; otherwise, they are off limits. Matala has become one more overcrowded beach in peak season, so after a dip and some refreshment, make your way back to Iraklion (straight up, via **Mires,** so you avoid the turnoff back to Ayia Triadha and Phaestos).

LASITHI PLAIN ★

Here's an excursion that combines some spectacular scenery, a major mythological site, and an extraordinary view on a windy day. Long promoted as "the plain of 10,000 windmills," alas, the Lasithi Plain can no longer really boast of this: The many hundreds, if not thousands, of white-sailcloth-vaned windmills have largely been replaced by gasoline-powered generator windmills (and wooden or metal vanes), but it is still an impressive sight as you come over the ridge to see these windmills turning. What they are doing is pumping water to irrigate the crops that fill the entire plain: No buildings are allowed on this large plateau (some 40 sq. km/15 sq. miles) because its rich alluvial soil (washed down from the surrounding mountains) is ideal for cultivating potatoes and other crops.

Having come this far—the plain is some 56km (35 miles) from Iraklion—you must go the next 16km (10 miles) to visit one of the major mythological sites of all Greece: the Dhiktaion Cave, regarded since ancient times as the birthplace of Zeus and the cave where he was hidden so that his father, Cronus, could not devour him. Driving around the outer edge of the plain (via Tzermiadhes, Drasi, Ayios Constantinos, and Ayios Georgiios), you come to the village of Psykhro on the slopes on the southern edge of the plain. Psykhro and the cave are geared for tourists who come from all over the world (admission 4€). After you reach the tourist pavilion, you still face a relatively steep climb to the cave; you are advised to take on one of the guides because the descent into the cave can be slippery and tricky (it's best to wear rubber-soled, sturdy footwear), and you will not know what you are looking at. Although long known as the cave associated with Zeus—it appears in numerous ancient myths and texts—it was not excavated until 1900, and successive "digs" in the decades since have turned up countless artifacts, confirming that it was visited as a sacred shrine for many centuries. It should be admitted that other caves on Crete and elsewhere claim the honor of Zeus's birthplace, but the Dhiktaion Cave seems to have won out, and having visited it, you can claim to have been at one of the more storied sites of the ancient world.

Lasithi Platin can also be visited as a side trip from Ayios Nikolaos (see later in this chapter). You head back westward on the old road to Iraklion and, at about 8km (5 miles), turn left (signed DRASI); then climb another 25km (15 miles) up to the plain.

CHANIA (HANIA/XANIA/ CANEA) ★★

150km (93 miles) W of Iraklion

Until the 1980s, Chania was one of the best-kept secrets of the Mediterranean: a delightful provincial town nestled between mountains and sea, a labyrinth of atmospheric streets and structures from its Venetian-Turkish era. Since then, tourists have flocked here, and there's hardly a square inch of the old town that's not dedicated to satisfying them. Chania was heavily bombed during World War II; ironically, some of its unique atmosphere is due to still-unreconstructed buildings that are now used as shops and restaurants.

What's amazing is how much of Chania's charm has persisted since the Venetians and Turks effectively stamped the old town in their own images, between 1210 and

Korai

Akti Miaouli

Minoos

SPLANTZIA

Plateia 1821

Kalergon

Karon

Ikaron

Sifaka

Vourdouba

A. Melidoni

Nikiforou Episkopou

Daskaloyiannis

Niklos Foka

El. Venizelou

Konstantinou

Tzanakaki

Akti Enoseos

Arholeon

Tsouderon

Municipal Market

Skindlof

Karaoli - Dimitriou

Skindlof

Hadzimikhali Giannari

Kriari

Plateia 1866

Apokoronou

Peridou

Sfakianaki K.

Zimivrakidon

Grigoriou E.

Zambeliou

Kondilaki

Halidon

Bus Terminal

Skalidi

Theotokopouli

Atki Koumounioutou

Pireos

NEA HORA

Manousogianakidon

Kidonias

Konstantinopoleos

Apostolidou

Akti Kanari

Patriarhou Nikiou

Patriarhou Gerasimou

Metaxaki

Marigoniou

Xepapa G.

Sea of Crete

Sea of Crete

100 m
100 y

Greece

Aegean Sea

Athens

Mediterranean Sea

Chania CRETE

1898. Try to visit any time except July and August; whenever you come, dare to strike out on your own and see the old Chania.

Essentials

GETTING THERE By Plane Olympic Air offers at least three flights daily to and from Athens in high season. (Flight time is about 50 min.) Flights to Chania from other points in Greece go through Athens. **Aegean Airlines** also offers several flights daily to and from Athens. See "Getting There," in the section on Iraklion, earlier in this chapter, for contact information. The airport is located 15km (10 miles) out of town on the Akrotiri. Public buses meet all flights except the last one at night, but almost everyone takes a taxi (about 20€).

By Boat One ship makes the 10-hour trip daily between Piraeus and Chania, usually leaving early in the evening (www.ferries.gr). But as of 2007, during the tourist season **Hellenic Seaways** runs a once-daily high-speed catamaran between Piraeus and Chania that cuts the trip down to about 5 hours (www.greekislands.gr). All ships arrive at and depart from Soudha, a 20-minute bus ride from the stop outside the municipal market. Many travel agents around town sell tickets. In high season, if you're traveling with a car, make reservations in advance, or check with the **Paleologos Agency** (www.ferries.gr).

By Bus Buses run almost hourly from early in the morning until about 10:30pm, depending on the season, connecting Chania to Rethymnon and Iraklion. (Round-trip fare to Iraklion for example, is 25€.) There are less frequent, and often inconveniently timed, buses between destinations in western Crete. The main **bus station** to points all over Crete is at 25 Kidonias (© **28210/93-306**). Get there plenty early—it can be a madhouse in high season.

By Car All the usual agencies can be found in the center of town, but I've always had reasonable and reliable service with **Europrent,** at 87 Halidon (© **28210/27-810;** www.europrent.gr).

By Taxi It should be noted that in July 2009, the taxi drivers of Chania agreed to observe the posting of standard fares to some of the most frequented destinations in and around the city's center (such as the airport or points on the Akrotiri, or from one edge of the city to the other). These postings are supposed to be visible at major taxi pickup points, and although the actual charge cannot always be held to the exact penny (due, say, to traffic conditions that cause long waits), these posted costs should be useful in an appeal to the Tourist Police if you feel you have been grossly overcharged. Having said that, don't forget that taxi drivers are allowed a number of surcharges—late at night, extra luggage, and so on.

VISITOR INFORMATION The official Tourist Information office is at 40 Kriari, off 1866 Square (© **28210/92-943**), but it keeps unreliable hours. You're better off turning to private travel agencies. On the scene, I recommend **Lissos Travel,** Plateia 1866 (© **28210/93-917;** fax 28210/95-930), or **Diktynna Travel,** 6 Archontaki (© **28210/43-930;** www.diktynna-travel.gr); from your home abroad, try **Crete Travel,** in the nearby village of Monoho (© **28250/32-690;** www.cretetravel.com). A useful source of insider's information is **The Bazaar,** 46 Daskaloyiannis, on the main street down to the new harbor (to the right of the Municipal Market). This shop sells used foreign-language books and assorted "stuff." Owned and often staffed by non-Greeks, it maintains a listing of all kinds of helpful services.

A Taxi Tip

To get a taxi driver who is accustomed to dealing with English-speakers, call **Nikos,** at his mobile phone (② **69774/ 45-585**). With Nikos, you get an informative guide as well as a driver.

GETTING AROUND You can walk to most tourist destinations in Chania. Public buses go to nearby points and to all the major destinations in western Crete. But if you want to explore the countryside or more remote parts of western Crete, I recommend that you rent a car to make the best use of your time.

FAST FACTS **Banks** in the new city have ATMs. For the **tourist police,** dial ② **171.** The **hospital** (② **28210/27-231**) is on Venizelou in the Halepa quarter. There are now several **Internet** cafes: I like the Vranas Studios Cafe, behind the cathedral and at the corner of Aghion Deka, or Cafe Santé (on the second floor at the far west corner of the old harbor). There are also several **Laundromats** in the old town, including the ones at 38 Karoli and Dimitriou, or 38 Kanevero. In the new town, Speedy Laundry, at 17 Kordiki, is on the corner of Koroneou, a block west of Plateia 1866. If you prefer to leave your laundry off, you can't beat **Oscar,** at 1 Kanevero, at the corner of the harbor square. For **luggage storage,** try the KTEL bus station on Kidonias, although your hotel may also offer this service. The **post office** is at 6 Peridou (an extension of Plastira that leads directly away for the municipal market); hours are Monday through Friday from 8am to 8pm, Saturday from 8am to noon. The **telephone office** (OTE) is on Tzanakaki (leading diagonally away from the municipal market); it is open daily from 7:30am to 11:30pm. **Foreign-language publications** are available at 8 Skalidi (main street heading west, at top of Halidon).

What to See & Do

In summer, several small **excursion ships** offer 1- to 5-hour trips to the waters and islets off Chania. These trips depart from the old and new harbors and include stops for swimming at one or another of the islets; some provide free snorkeling gear. On the glass-bottomed *Evangelos* and *Aphrodite,* you can see underwater life. The cost ranges from 10€ to 25€ adults; free for children 11 and under. Those more curious about the terrestrial environment might want to take an informative **walk through Old Chania** with Dr. Alexandra Ariotti, a local archaeologist; she can be contacted via e-mail at alex@ chania-oldtown-walks.gr. The cost starts at 25€, but can be lower, depending on the number who go along. **Diktynna Travel Agency** (② **28210/41-458;** www.diktynna-travel.gr) sponsors a **day at a farm** outside Chania where you get lessons in cooking Cretan specialties; participate in cheese, wine, and olive tastings; and cap the day with a meal. There is also what is said to be the highest **bungee-jumping** site from a bridge in Europe at the Aradaina Bridge, near the south coast, just west of Khora Sfakion.

Archaeological Museum ★ Even short-term visitors should stop here, if only for a half-hour's walk-through. The museum, housed in the 16th-century Venetian Catholic Church of St. Francis, was carefully restored in the early 1980s and gives a fascinating glimpse of the different cultures that have played out on Crete, from the Neolithic through the Minoan and on to the Roman and early Christian. You'll come away with a sense of how typical people of these periods lived, as opposed to the elite classes featured in so many museums.

30 Halidon. ② **28210/90-334.** Admission 2€, 1€ 65 and over. Tues–Sun 8:30am–3pm (but always subject to change). No parking.

Two fairly new possibilities on Crete should appeal to eco-tourists. One is **Milia** (⏍ **28210/46-774**; www.milia.gr), a long-abandoned village in the mountains of western Crete that has been converted into a retreat for those willing to stay in old stone houses, do without modern hotel facilities (although there is electricity), and eat a limited but delicious natural diet. It is operated by native Cretans, and you are left pretty much on your own to enjoy the wild natural setting. I want to avoid guidebook superlatives, but I feel confident in predicting that if you are looking for a truly natural stay in Greece, no place beats this. The second is the **Dalabelos Estates** (⏍ **28340/22-155**; www.dalabelos.gr), 10 houses (new and with all amenities) located in the countryside outside Rethymnon. Here you are on a working farm and, depending on the season, can participate in such activities as grape- or olive-picking or even sheep-shearing.

Both places realistically require a vehicle to reach, even though the proprietors would pick you up at a nearby bus station. Milia is a solid 2-hour drive from Chania and requires a willingness to travel the last miles up a rather hairy dirt road; once there, you would probably want to take all your meals at the simple dining room. Dalabelos Estates is only about a half-hour's drive from Rethymnon but not served by public transportation; in any case you would want a car to have the freedom to move about the island. For those wavering about which to take on, note that at Milia you have no view but you step out of your cabin into a wooded area bursting with wildlife. The Dalabelos Estates is a bit more like a resort in that it offers both handsome accommodations and a selection of diversions.

The Minoan Ship ★   Here's something unique that in recent years has become a major attraction: a full-size replica (or at least an attempt at one) of a Minoan ship. It was constructed during 2 years leading up to the Athens Olympic Summer Games of 2004, allegedly using materials and tools only available to the ancient Minoans (although one photo shows them using a modern pulley). Launched in December 2003, 22 oarsmen rowed it by stages to Piraeus where it was on display during the Olympics. Now part of the Maritime Museum annex in the Venetian arsenal at the far end of the new harbor, it is placed in the harbor once or twice a year just to keep it seaworthy. There are many supporting displays including a video, but make sure you view the display board showing the ancient depictions (frescoes, vase paintings, and so on) that were used as sources for the reconstruction.

Akti Kountourioti. ⏍ **28210/91-875.** www.mar-mus-crete.gr. Admission 2€, 1€ 65 and over. High season Mon–Sun 10am–2pm and 5–9pm; call for low-season reduced hours. Parking behind arsenal.

A WALK AROUND OLD CHANIA

Start at **Plateia Venizelou,** the large clearing at the far curve of the old harbor—now distinguished by its marble fountain. Head along the east side to see the prominent domed **Mosque of Djamissis** (or of Hassan Pasha), erected soon after the Turks conquered Chania in 1645. Proceeding around the **waterfront** toward the **new harbor,** you'll come to what remains of the great **arsenali,** where the Venetians made and repaired ships; exhibitions are sometimes held inside. Go to the far end of this inner harbor and you can visit the Minoan ship (see above) In any case, you can walk out along the breakwater to the 19th-century lighthouse (thoroughly restored in

2006). Go back to the far corner of the long set of arsenali and Arnoleon, where you turn inland, and then proceed up Daskaloyiannis; on the left, you'll come to **Plateia 1821** and the **Orthodox Church of St. Nicholas.** Begun as a Venetian Catholic monastery, it was converted by the Turks into a mosque—thus its campanile and minaret. The square is a pleasant place to sit and have a cool drink. Go next to Tsouderon, where you turn right and, passing another minaret, arrive at the back steps of the great **municipal market** (ca. 1911)—worth wandering through, although and alas, it has been largely taken over by touristic shops.

If you exit at the opposite end of your entrance, you'll emerge at the edge of the **new town.** Turn right and proceed along Hadzimikhali Giannari until you come to the top of **Halidon,** the main tourist-shopping street. The stylish **Municipal Art Gallery,** at no. 98, sits at the top right side (hours posted). As you continue to make your way down Halidon, you'll pass on the right the famous **Skridlof,** with its leather workers; the **Orthodox Cathedral** or the Church of the Three Martyrs, from the 1860s; and on the left the **Archaeological Museum** (see above).

As you come back to the edge of Plateia Venizelou, turn left one street before the harbor, onto **Zambeliou.** Proceed along this street; you can then turn left onto any of the side streets and explore the **old quarter** (now, alas, also overwhelmed by modern tourist enterprises). If you turn up at Kondilaki, follow the signs and turn right at the alley that leads to the **Etz Hayyim Synagogue;** built in the 17th century (on site of still earlier synagogues) and destroyed in World War II, it has now been beautifully restored and is well worth a visit. (Hours have been Mon–Fri 10am–5pm. Check www.etz-hayyim-hania.org to learn about the history and activities of the synagogue.) Back to Zambeliou, continue along, taking a slight detour to Moskhou to view **Renieri Gate,** from 1608. On Zambeliou again, you'll ascend a bit until you come to **Theotokopouli;** turn right here and take in the architecture and shops of this Venetian-style street as you make your way down to the sea.

At the end of the street, on the right, the recently restored **Church of San Salvatore** was converted into a fine little museum of Byzantine and post-Byzantine art (www.culture.gr; irregular hours; admission 2€). After the museum, you'll be just outside the harbor; turn right and pass below the walls of the **Firkas,** the name given to the fort that was a focal point in Crete's struggle for independence at the turn of the 20th century. If you're into naval history, the **Naval Museum** (© 28210/26-437) has some interesting displays and artifacts (daily 10am–4pm; admission 5€); or you can take a seat for welcome refreshment at one of the cafes near the museum entrance.

SHOPPING

Jewelers, leather-goods shops, and souvenir stores are everywhere—but it's hard to find that very special item that's both tasteful and distinctively Cretan. To single out one, there's **Kaparakis** at 32 Portou (the street running below the Venetian wall, approached from the top of Kondolaki; © 28210/99-205). **Carmela,** at 7 Anghelou (the narrow street across from the Naval Museum's entrance; © 28210/90-487), has some elegant ceramics and jewelry—all original, but inspired by ancient works of art and even employing some of the old techniques.

Below, I highlight some things you will not find anywhere else. And unless otherwise noted, these shops are open daily.

XPOMA (Chroma) at 42 Daskoloyiannis (no phone) has a truly fine (and not cheap) selection of old prints and maps. The new **Notos Bookstore** at 10 Kondolaki (© 28210/86-771) has a surprisingly sophisticated (for its location) selection of books in several foreign languages. Call ahead if you have a special title in mind.

Step into **Cretan Rugs and Blankets,** 3 Angheliou (© **28210/98-571**), to experience a realm not found anywhere else on Crete. It's an old Venetian structure filled with gorgeously colored rugs, blankets, and kilims. Prices range from 100€ to 2,000€. Or visit **Roka Carpets,** 61 Zambeliou (© **28210/74-736**), where you can watch a traditional weaver at his trade. The carpets come in patterns, colors, and sizes to suit every taste; prices start at 20€. These are not artsy textiles, but traditional Cretan weaving.

There is no end of shops selling ceramics, trinkets, and souvenirs of all kinds, for a more sophisticated selection of Greek handicrafts, try **Mitos** at 44 Halidon, opposite the Orthodox Cathedral (© **28210/88-862**). **Castello Vecchio,** at 61 Episkopi Chrysanthos (© **28210/46-463**), has an unusual selection of ceramics and wood ware. For a varied selection by amateur Cretan artisans, visit the **Local Artistic Handicrafts Association** (© **28210/41-885**), located just where the new harbor turns the corner into the old harbor.

Where to Stay

EXPENSIVE

Casa Delfino ★★   When did you last have the chance to stay in a 17th-century Venetian mansion, with fresh orange juice for breakfast? Its quiet neighborhood (also dating from the 1600s) is conveniently located a block from the harbor. The owners transformed the stately house into stylish independent suites and studios, whose tastefully decorated rooms are among the most elegant you will find on Crete. All have modern bathrooms (nine with Jacuzzi), and three have kitchenettes. ***But be warned:*** Several rooms have beds on a second level—little more than sleeping lofts—forcing you to go up and down stairs to get to the bathroom. (You should request other rooms unless the price differential deters you.) Especially attractive is the rooftop terrace, where lights meals can be had. The reception desk may be informal, but the friendly staff will provide a wide range of services, from airport transport to tour arrangements.

8 Theofanous, 73100 Chania, Crete. www.casadelfino.com. © **28210/87-400.** 24 units. High season 200€–330€ double, 265€–335€ suite; low season 150€–220€ double, 210€–320€ suite. Rates include buffet breakfast. AE, MC, V. Free parking nearby. **Amenities:** Courtyard breakfast area; rooftop terrace cafe; bar; babysitting; Internet access; Jacuzzi; room service. *In room:* A/C, TV, hair dryer, minibar, Wi-Fi.

MODERATE

Doma ★★   Long regarded as one of the most distinctive hotels on Crete, the neoclassical, turn-of-the-20th-century Doma was once a fine mansion, former home of the Austrian consulate. Authentic Cretan heirlooms and historical pictures decorate its public areas. Bedrooms and bathrooms are not especially large but are perfectly adequate. The four suites are roomier. All the rooms are plainly decorated—even a bit severe, with muted wall colors and rather old-fashioned furniture. Front rooms have great views of the sea, but also the sounds of passing traffic. The third-story dining room offers fresh breezes and a superb view of old Chania; breakfast here includes several homemade delights. An elevator provides access for those who can't take stairs. Among the hotel's special features is a museum-quality display of headdresses from all over the world. The Doma is not for those seeking luxury, but it appeals to travelers who appreciate a discreet old-world atmosphere.

124 Venizelou, 73100 Chania, Crete. www.hotel-doma.gr. © **28210/51-772.** 25 units (22 with shower only). 140€ double; 190€–280€ suite. Rates include buffet breakfast. Special rates for more than 2 persons in suite; reduced rates for longer stays. AE, MC, V. Free parking on adjacent streets. Closed Nov–Mar. Bus to Chania center; can be reached on foot. 3km (2 miles) from the town center along the

lower coastal road. **Amenities:** Restaurant; bar; smoke-free rooms. *In room:* A/C in suites, ceiling fan in rooms, TV, hair dryer, minibar.

Hotel Porto Veneziano ★ Thanks to the owner/manager "on the scene," this hotel combines the best of old-fashioned Greek hospitality with good, modern service. As a member of the Best Western chain, it has to maintain certain standards. The tasteful bedrooms (standard international style) are relatively large; the bathrooms are modern but small. Many rooms have a fine view of the harbor. (Be warned; that can also mean harbor noise early in the morning.) Six suites offer even more space. Located at the far end of the old harbor (follow the quay from the main harbor all the way around to the east, or right). There are many restaurants within a few yards of the hotel. Refreshments from the hotel's own Cafe Veneto may be enjoyed in the garden or at the front overlooking the harbor. The desk personnel are genuinely hospitable and will make tour arrangements.

Akti Enosseos, 73100 Chania, Crete. www.portoveneziano.gr. ✆ **28210/27-100.** 57 units (48 with shower only). High season 120€–145€ double; low season 110€–130€ double. Rates include buffet breakfast. AE, DC, MC, V. Free parking nearby. **Amenities:** Breakfast room; cafe/bar; babysitting; Internet; room service. *In room:* A/C, TV, hair dryer, minibar.

Mistral Hotel ★ This is an unusual hotel—one designed expressly for mature singles. But *not* a hotel for "swinging singles"; if you are looking for all-night carousing, go over to Mallia or Chersonnisos. The Mistral is for the independent single traveler who has come to Crete to enjoy its special features. Thus, the many excursions that are offered: bicycles for rent, early breakfast, and packed lunches for those setting out on their own. The hotel offers all manner of in-house facilities and activities—tai chi, and classes in watercolor, dance, cooking, and photography. The beach is about a 3-minute walk away; frequent buses take you to Chania. You can relax in the garden where much of their organic produce is grown to be used in their meals.

Maleme, 73100 (16km/10 miles west of Chania, left turn off coastal road). www.singlesincrete.com. ✆ **28210/62-062.** 33 units. High season 90€–100€ per person; low season 88€–97€. Rates include half board. AE, DC, MC, V. Free parking on grounds. **Amenities:** Breakfast room; bar; Internet; Jacuzzi; 2 pools; spa; Wi-Fi. *In room:* A/C (5€ per day), hair dryer.

INEXPENSIVE

Eria Resort Hotel ★ 👬 Here is a truly distinctive establishment—probably unique in all of Greece: A resort hotel designed, built, and operated expressly for those with physical disabilities. The project of a Cretan pharmacist who has done well with a chain of medical supply stores, all of its public areas and rooms are accessible to travelers who use wheelchairs. Specialist doctors can be seen by appointment and mechanized wheelchairs, bed hoists, and all kinds of specialized equipment may be rented at reasonable rates. Its swimming pool has a sloping ramp (and it provides waterproof chairs to allow entry into the water); it also offers special life jackets, a spa, physiotherapy, and special water games—some with extra fees. The hotel has its own handicapped accessible van to transport clients on excursions. Some clients have complained about the rough surfaces adjacent to the hotel grounds, making it hard to leave the premises, but above all, the staff is sensitive to and prepared to serve those with physical disabilities.

Maleme, 73104 (on coastal road some 21km/13 miles from Chania). www.eria-resort.gr. ✆ **28210/62-790.** 13 units, including 2 suites accommodating up to 4 adults (all with specially equipped bathrooms for those with limited mobility). High season 75€ double; low season 65€ double. Rates include buffet breakfast. Half board 23€, full board 38€. MC, V. Parking on premises. **Amenities:** Restaurant; bar; gym w/modified equipment; physiotherapy; pool; spa; watersports equipment/rentals; boccie field; basketball; volleyball, Wi-Fi free in lobby. *In room:* A/C, TV, beds w/hoist bars, hair dryer, minibar.

Hotel Palazzo   This Venetian-style town house, now a handsome little hotel, delivers the feeling of old Crete without skimping on amenities. A fridge in every room, a TV in the bar, and a roof garden with a spectacular view of the mountains and sea make this a comfortable hotel. Nothing fancy about the rooms (furnishings are traditional Cretan rustic, knotty-pine style), but they are good size. Those at the front have balconies, so you are exposed to street and restaurant noise—perhaps a small price to pay for staying on Theotokopouli, the closest you may come to living on a Venetian canal. The owners speak English and will graciously help you with all your needs, including laundry service, car rentals, and tours. You can drive up the street to unload and load but must park at a nearby square.

54 Theotokopouli, 73100 Chania, Crete. www.palazzohotel.gr. ℰ **28210/93-227.** 11 units, some with shower, some with tub. High season 90€ double; low season 65€ double. Rates include breakfast. MC, V. Free parking 50m (164 ft.) away. Closed Nov–Mar (but will open for special groups). Within easy walking distance of all of Chania, around the corner from the west arm of harbor. **Amenities:** Breakfast room; bar; roof garden. *In room:* A/C, TV, fridge.

Pandora Suites   Centrally located, with views over the harbor, this hotel may seem a bit unpromising from its street-side entrance but inside is a quietly elegant hostelry, a completely renovated 17th-century Italian town house. All eight doubles and three suites (for four persons) have kitchenettes, but it should be said that the suites' beds are on an interior "second level" (see the website to get a clear sense of this). Two of the doubles have private balconies, and everyone is free to enjoy the rooftop terrace to take breakfast or an evening drink with a fabulous view of Chania's celebrated harbor. This is just the place for those who like a bit of old-world funkiness.

29 Lithinon, 73132 Chania, Crete. www.pandora-hotel.com. ℰ **28210/43-588.** 11 units. High season 110€–115€ double; 155€ suite. Rates include breakfast. MC, V. Parking on street or nearby streets. Closed Nov–Mar (but will open for special groups). Within easy walking distance of all of Chania, around the corner from the west arm of harbor. **Amenities:** Breakfast room; roof terraces; Wi-Fi. *In room:* A/C, kitchenette.

Botanical Park of Crete

It's rare to come up with something brand new, different, and engaging after years of seeking out places of interest on Crete, but here is just such a place. Three Cretan brothers, having lost their olive grove to a great forest fire in 2003, chose to convert their mountain slopes into a **botanical garden ★**, with hundreds of species of trees, bushes, herbs, and flowers from all over the world. One walks along groomed paths up and down the slopes with most of the plants identified (in Greek and English) and their distinctive characteristics and uses (many are medicinal) described. There's a small collection of animals at the base, including Crete's famous wild goat. At a leisurely pace, you can spend 2 to 2½ hours here; with shortcuts, it can be done in half that time. The final ascent can be a bit demanding, but at the end you get to eat a meal prepared from virtually 100% local products while sitting on the restaurant terrace and enjoying the spectacular panoramic view. The garden is located about 19km (12 miles) southwest of Chania, just beyond the town of Fournes. It's open daily April to October, 8am to 8:30pm. Admission is 4€ and includes a bottle of water and the use of a walking stick if desired; children 12 and under free. See www.botanical-park.gr for more details.

Where to Eat

Chania offers a wide variety of dining experiences. At one extreme are places catering mainly to foreigners, such as the **Tamam,** at 49 Zambeliou (the main street behind and parallel to the old harbor); widely publicized, it's popular for its vaguely "fusion" cuisine and reasonable prices. If you want a place more favored by Chania's own, seek out **Karnayio,** located in an open square abutting the *arsenali* on the new harbor. I'd pass up most of the restaurants on the old harbor, but almost any of the restaurants at the far end of the new harbor—the **Antigone** for one—can be counted on for good meals and decent prices. But don't be afraid to take a chance here and there.

EXPENSIVE

Nykterida ★★ GREEK   Location is a major part of this dining experience. It's on a high point with spectacular nighttime views of Chania and Soudha Bay—but be sure to insist on a table with that view—so save it for when you can eat outdoors on a summer evening. An institution in Chania since 1933, its founder claims to have taught Anthony Quinn the steps he danced in *Zorba*. The cuisine is traditional Cretan-Greek, but many of the dishes have an extra something. For an appetizer, try the *kalazounia* (cheese pie speckled with spinach) or the special *dolmades* (squash blossoms stuffed with spiced rice and served with yogurt). Any of the main courses will be well done, from the basic steak filet to the chicken with okra. Complimentary *tsoukoudia* (a potent Cretan liquor) is served at the end of the meal. Traditional Cretan music is played on Monday, Thursday, and Friday evenings until the end of October.

Korakies, Crete. ℂ **28210/64-215.** www.nykterida.gr. Reservations recommended for parties of 7 or more. Main courses 6€–22€. MC, V. Mon–Sat 6pm–1am. Parking on-site. Taxi or car required. About 6.4km (4 miles) from town on road to airport; left turn opposite NAMFI Officers Club.

MODERATE

Amphora Restaurant GREEK   At some point, almost everyone who spends any time in Chania will want to eat a meal right on the old harbor. Frankly, most of the restaurants there are undistinguished at best, but this old favorite still offers a decent meal at a reasonable price. As with any Greek restaurant, if you order fish or steak, you'll pay a hefty price, but you can assemble a good meal here at modest prices. To start, try the eggplant croquettes and the specialty of the house, a lemony fish soup. The restaurant belongs to the adjacent Amphora Hotel, and this is probably what has maintained its food and friendly service.

49 Akti Koundouriotou (near the far right, western curve of the harbor). ℂ **28210/71-976.** Main courses 6€–20€. AE, MC, V. Daily 11:30am–midnight. Closed Oct–Apr.

The Well of the Turk ★★ MIDDLE EASTERN/MEDITERRANEAN   Here's a restaurant that rises above others in Chania because of its unexpected menu, tasty cooking, and unusual setting. At the heart of the old Turkish quarter (Splanzia), in a historic building that contains a well, there is a quiet outside court where diners may sit in the summer. The chef's imaginative touches make the cuisine more than standard Middle Eastern. In addition to tasty kabobs, specialties include meatballs mixed with eggplant, and *laxma bi azeen* (a pita-style bread with a spicy topping). Middle Eastern musicians sometimes play here, and you can settle for a quiet drink at the bar.

1-3 Kalinikou Sarpaki (on small street off Daskaloyiannis). ℂ **28210/54-547.** Reservations recommended for parties of 7 or more. Main courses 7€–20€. No credit cards. Wed–Mon 7pm–midnight.

INEXPENSIVE

Enomayirio SEAFOOD   Here's a special treat for diners who can handle eating in a cramped, unstylish restaurant smack in the center of Chania's public market. The fish and other seafood come from stalls barely 3m (10 ft.) away. All the other ingredients also come straight from the nearby stands. Food doesn't get any fresher than this. Sit here and watch the world go by.

In the public market, at the "arm" with the fish vendors. No phone. Main courses 5€–18€; gigantic platter of mixed fish for 2 is 26€. No credit cards. Mon–Sat 9am–3:30pm.

Portes ★ GREEK/MEDITERRANEAN   Here's an unpretentious restaurant that offers a different menu, congenial service, and a setting off the beaten track. Perhaps it's because of the "hybrid" Irish and Greek proprietors, but since discovering Portes (and eating there several times), I've come to think of it as worth seeking out. Along with some traditional Greek fare, dishes such as roasted vegetable salad or spicy chicken livers make dining here a special experience. And although you're not on the harbor, a candlelit table against the Venetian wall on a summer evening has its own cachet. And during the winter season, there is live music on the weekends.

48 Portou (the street against the Venetian wall, btw. the tops of Kondolaki and Douka). ℭ **28210/76-261.** Main courses 6.50€–9€. MC, V. Mon–Sat noon–1am; Sun 5pm–1am.

Psitopoleio (The Grill) GREEK   Known to the foreign community of Chania as the Meatery, this is not for the fainthearted (or vegetarians). Its clientele is almost 100% Cretan. To call its decor "basic" is a major understatement: It is a long, bare space, with the butcher's block at the rear and the grill at the front. Your meat course is butchered at the former and cooked at the latter. The specialties are lamb chops, pork chops, kidneys, spareribs, and sausages; excellent french fries; salads, both the standard Greek and a cabbage version; soup; and *tzatziki*. House wine, beer, and soft drinks help you wash down the tasty and unforgettable food.

48 Apokorono. ℭ **28210/91-354.** Main courses 5€–14€. No credit cards. Daily noon–3pm and 7:30pm–1am. With your back to the municipal market, walk along the main street leading diagonally away, off to the right.

Remezzo Cafe INTERNATIONAL   Sooner or later, we all say, "Enough Greek salads!" and want to indulge in a club sandwich or tuna salad. Remezzo, at Venizelou Square on the old harbor, is a great choice for breakfasts and light meals (omelets, salads, and so on). It also offers a full range of coffee, alcoholic drinks, and ice cream desserts. Sitting in one of the heavily cushioned chairs as you sip your drink and observe the lively scene, you'll feel like you have the best seat in the house.

16A Venizelou (on corner of main square at old harbor). ℭ **28210/52-001.** Main courses 5€–14€. No credit cards. Daily 7am–2am.

Chania After Dark

At night, instead of seeking out a packed club/bar/disco or walking around the harbor and old town, wander into Chania's back alleys to see the old Venetian and Turkish remains. Sit in a quayside cafe and enjoy a coffee or a drink, or treat yourself to a ride in a horse-drawn carriage at the harbor. At the other extreme, stroll through the new town; you might be surprised by the modernity and diversity (and prices) of the stores patronized by typical Chaniots.

   Clubs come and go from year to year. Some popular spots include **El Mondo** and the **Happy Go Lucky,** both on Kondilaki (the street leading away from the center of the old harbor); **Idaeon Andron,** 26 Halidon; and **Ariadne,** on Akti Enoseos (around the corner, where the old harbor becomes the new). On Anghelou (up from the Naval Museum) is **Fagotta,** a bar that sometimes offers jazz.

Cafes are everywhere, but two stand out because of their special locations. At **Pallas Roof Garden Cafe-Bar,** on Akti Tobazi (right at the corner where the new harbor meets the old harbor), you can sit high above the harbor, watch the blinking lights, listen to the murmur of the crowds below, and nurse a refreshing drink or ice cream. However, you must climb 44 stairs to get here; as the sign says, IT'S WORTH IT. If you'd prefer to hear traditional Cretan songs, try **Cafe Lyriaka,** 22 Kalergon (behind the arsenali along the harbor).

The gay community in Chania does not seem to have any single gathering place, but the **DioLuxe** cafe, at 8 Sarpidonas (behind the Porto Veneziano hotel, on the new harbor), is reported to be gay-friendly.

A **summer cultural festival** sometimes features dramas, symphonic music, jazz, dance, and traditional music. These performances take place from July to September at several venues: **Firka** fortress at the far left of the harbor; the **Venetian arsenali** along the old harbor; **East Moat Theater** along Nikiforou Phokas; or **Peace and Friendship Park Theater** on Demokratias, just beyond the public gardens. For details, inquire at one of the tourist information offices when you arrive in town.

A Side Trip from Chania: Samaria Gorge ★★

Everyone with an extra day on Crete—and steady legs and solid walking shoes—should consider hiking through the Samaria Gorge. The endeavor involves first getting to the top of the gorge, a trip of about 42km (26 miles) from Chania. Second comes the actual descent and hike through the gorge itself, some 18km (11 miles). Third, a boat takes you from the village of Ayia Roumeli, at the end of the gorge, to Khora Sfakion; from there, it's a bus ride of about 75km (46 miles) back to Chania. (Some boats go westward to Paleochora, approximately the same distance by road from Chania.)

Most visitors do it all in a long day, but you can put up for the night at one of the modest hotels and rooms at Ayia Roumeli, Paleochora (to its west), Souya (to its east), Khora Sfakion (main port to meet buses), and elsewhere along the south coast. But for most people, I strongly advise signing up with one of the many travel agencies in Chania that get people to and from the gorge. This way, you are guaranteed seats on the bus (there and back) and on the boat. One agency I recommend is **Diktynna Travel,** 6 Archontaki St. (© **28210/41-458;** www.diktynna-travel.gr); it offers a day excursion—including all transportation to and from the Samaria George—for 65€ per person. In recent years, Samaria Gorge has been so successfully promoted as one of the great natural splendors of Europe that on the most crowded days, you can find yourself walking single file with several thousand other people. Starting very early is one way to beat the worst of the crowd; alternatively, start on in the afternoon and plan to spend the night in Ayia Roumeli. The gorge is open from about mid-April through mid-October (depending on weather conditions); the best chance for a bit of solitude means hiking near the beginning or end of the season. The hike is relatively taxing; and here and there, you will scramble over boulders. Bring water and snacks, and wear sturdy, comfortable shoes. Admission is 5€.

The gorge offers enough opportunities to break away from the crowds. You'll be treated to the fun of crisscrossing the water, not to mention the sights of wildflowers (but don't pick them!) and dramatic geological formations, the sheer height of the gorge's sides, and several unexpected chapels—it will all add up to a worthwhile experience, one that many regard as the highlight of their visit to Crete.

RETHYMNON (RETHIMNO)

72km (45 miles) E of Chania; 78km (50 miles) W of Iraklion

Whether visited on a day trip from Chania or Iraklion or used as a base for a stay in western Crete, Rethymnon can be a most pleasant town—provided you pick the right Rethymnon.

The town's defining centuries came under the Venetians in the late Middle Ages and the Renaissance, then under the Turks from the late 17th century to the late 19th century. Its maze of streets and alleys is now lined with shops, its old beachfront is home to restaurants and bars, and its new beach-resort facilities (to the east of the old town) offer a prime (some might say appalling) example of how a small town's modest seacoast can be exploited. Assuming you have not come to see these "developments," we'll help you focus your attention on the old town—the side of Rethymnon that can still work its charm on even the casual stroller.

Essentials

GETTING THERE   Rethymnon lacks an airport but is only about 1 hour from the Chania airport and 1½ hours from the Iraklion airport.

By Boat   Rethymnon does have its own ship line, which offers direct daily trips to and from Piraeus (about 10 hr.).

By Car   Many people visit Rethymnon by car, taking the highway from either Iraklion (about 78km/50 miles) or Chania (72km/45 miles). The public parking lot at Plateia Plastira, at the far western edge, just outside the old harbor, is best approached via the main east-west road along the south edge of the town. But unless you plan to take some side trips en route to Rethymnon, taking the bus there might be the best way to go from either of those other cities.

By Bus   If you don't have your own vehicle, the bus offers frequent service to and from Iraklion and Chania—virtually every half-hour from early in the morning until midevening. In high season, buses depart Rethymnon as late as 10pm. The fare is about 15€ round-trip. The **KTEL** bus line (✆ **28310/22-212**) that provides service to and from Chania and Iraklion is located at Akti Kefaloyianithon, at the city's western edge (so allow an extra 10 min. to get there).

VISITOR INFORMATION   The **National Tourism Office** (✆ **28310/29-148**) is on Venizelou, the main avenue that runs along the town beach. In high season, it's open Monday through Friday from 8am to 2:30pm; off-season, its hours are unpredictable. But there are numerous private travel agencies in town that can

---

 For Wine Lovers

Rethymnon's annual wine festival takes place for about 10 days starting near the end of July. It's centered on the public gardens, with music and dancing to accompany the samplings of local wines. The modest affair is a welcome change from larger, more staged festivals elsewhere.

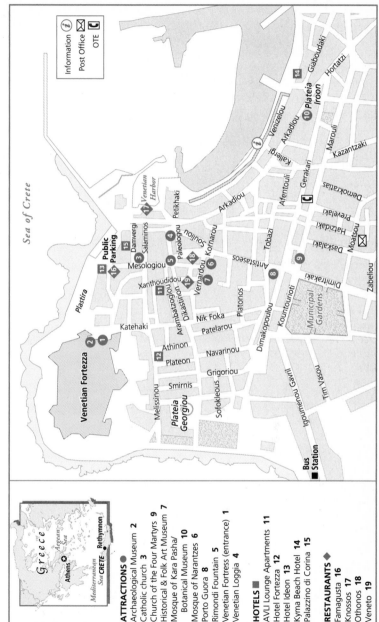

Information *i*
Post Office ⊠
OTE ☎

Sea of Crete

Venetian Harbor

Venetian Fortezza

Public Parking

Bus Station

Plateia Georgiou

Municipal Gardens

Plateia Iroon

Greece

Aegean Sea

Athens

Mediterranean Sea **CRETE** • Rethymnon

ATTRACTIONS ●
Archaeological Museum **2**
Catholic church **3**
Church of the Four Martyrs **9**
Historical & Folk Art Museum **7**
Mosque of Kara Pasha/
  Botanical Museum **10**
Mosque of Narantzes **6**
Porto Guora **8**
Rimondi Fountain **5**
Venetian Fortress (entrance) **1**
Venetian Loggia **4**

HOTELS ■
AVLI Lounge Apartments **11**
Hotel Fortezza **12**
Hotel Ideon **13**
Kyma Beach Hotel **14**
Palazzino di Corina **15**

RESTAURANTS ◆
Famagusta **16**
Knossos **17**
Othonos **18**
Veneto **19**

arrange trips to virtually anywhere on the island. I recommend **Ellotia Tours** at 155 Arkadhiou (www.rethymnoatcrete.com).

GETTING AROUND   Rethymnon is a walker's town. Bringing a car into the maze of streets and alleys is more trouble than it's worth—in fact, it's virtually impossible. The sights to see are never more than a 20-minute walk from wherever you are.

To see the countryside of this part of Crete, unless you have unlimited time to use the buses, you'll need to rent a car. Among the many agencies with offices in Rethymnon are **Motor Club** (✆ **28310/54-253**), **Budget** (✆ **28310/56-910**), **Europeo** (✆ **28310/51-940**), and **Hertz** (✆ **28310/26-286**).

FAST FACTS   Several **banks** in both the old town and the new city have ATMs and currency-exchange machines. The **hospital** is at 7–9 Trantallidou in the new town (✆ **28310/27-491**). For **Internet access,** try Caribbean Bar Cafe (behind Rimondi Fountain) or Alana Taverna (on Salaminas near Hotel Fortezza). The most convenient place to do **laundry** is next to the Youth Hostel, 45 Tombazi; its hours are Monday through Saturday from 8am to 8pm. The **tourist police** (✆ **28310/28-156**) share the same building with the tourist office along the beach. The **post office** is east of the public gardens at 37 Moatsu (✆ **28310/22-571**); its hours are Monday through Friday from 8am to 8pm, Saturday from 8am to noon. The **telephone office (OTE)** is at 40 Kountourioti; it's open daily from 7:30am to midnight.

What to See & Do

ATTRACTIONS

Historical and Folk Art Museum ★   Housed in a centuries-old and architecturally significant Venetian mansion, this small museum displays ceramics, textiles, jewelry, artifacts, implements, clothing, and other vivid reminders of the traditional way of life of most Cretans across the centuries. Well worth a brief visit.

30 Vernardou. ✆ **28310/23-398.** Admission 3€ adults, 1€ students, free for children. Mon–Fri 10am–2pm.

The Venetian Fortezza ★   Dominating the headland at the western edge of town, this massive fortress is the one site everyone should give at least an hour to visit. Built under the Venetians (but *by* Cretans) from about 1573 to 1580, its huge walls, about 1,130m (3,700 ft.) in perimeter, were designed to deflect the worst cannon fire of its day. In the end, of course, the Turks simply went around it and took the town by avoiding the fort. There's a partially restored mosque inside as well as a Greek Orthodox chapel. It's in this vast area that most of the performances of the annual **Rethymnon Renaissance Festival** take place (see below).

A STROLL THROUGH THE OLD TOWN

Rethymnon's attractions are best appreciated by walking through the old town. Start by getting a free map from the tourist office down along the beachfront, or follow the numbers on our Town Plan.

If you have limited time, first visit the **Venetian Fortress** (1) (see the Rethymnon map, above). If you have the time or inclination, look into the **Archaeological Museum** (2). Then make your way down to Melissinou and turn left and proceed to the **Catholic Church** (3) at the corner of Mesologiou. Proceed down Salaminos to Arkadiou; make a left here to the western edge of the **old harbor.** Curving right down to the harbor is an unexpected sight: the wall of restaurants and bars that effectively obliterates the quaint harbor that drew them here in the first place. Making your way through this obstacle course, you'll emerge at the southeast corner of

Rethymnon's cultural festival offers mostly musical and theatrical events from July to early September. Productions range from ancient Greek dramas to more contemporary artistic endeavors (and now include folk and rock concerts). Most performers are Greek; some are foreigners. The majority of performances are staged in the Fortezza itself; there's nothing quite like listening to 17th-century music or seeing a Renaissance drama in this setting. For details, inquire at the tourist information office.

this curved harbor and come to a square that faces the town's long beach, its broad boulevard lined with even more restaurants and cafes. Turn right up Petikhaki, and at the first crossroads, you'll see the **Venetian Loggia** (ca. 1600) (4)—for many years the town's museum and now a Ministry of Culture gallery that sells officially approved reproductions of ancient Greek works of art. Continue up past it on Paleologou to the next crossroads. On the right is **Rimondi Fountain** (ca. 1623) (5).

Leaving the fountain, head onto Antistaseos toward the 17th-century **Mosque of Nerantzes** (6) (originally a Christian church) near the corner of Vernardou; you can climb the minaret Monday to Friday 11am to 7:30pm, Saturday 11am to 3pm (closed Aug). Again, if you have the time, proceed up Vernardou to the **Historical and Folk Art Museum** (7). If you follow Antistaseos to its end, you'll come to **Porta Guora** (8), the only remnant of the Venetian city walls.

Emerging at that point onto the main east-west road, opposite and to the right are the **municipal gardens.** On your left is the **Orthodox Church of the Four Martyrs** (9), worth a peek as you walk east along Gerakari. You then come to **Platei Iroon,** the large circle that serves as the junction between the old town and the new beachfront development.

Turning back into the old town on Arkadiou, you'll see on your left the restored **Mosque of Kara Pasha** (10), now a botanical museum (daily 9am–6pm). Continue along Arkadiou, and in addition to the modern shops, note the surviving remains of the Venetian era—particularly the **facade of no. 154.** From here, you're on your own to explore the narrow streets, go shopping, or head for the waterfront for a cool drink.

OUTDOOR PURSUITS

If you're interested in horseback riding, try the **Riding Center,** southeast of town at Platanias, 39 N. Fokas (✆ **28310/28-907**), or **Zoraida's Horse Riding** at Georgioupolis, about midway between Chania and Rethymnon (✆ **28250/61-745**). Among the newer diversions offered in Rethymnon are daily **excursion boats** that take people on day trips for **swimming** on the beach either at **Bali** (to the east) or **Marathi** (on the Akrotiri to the west). The price, which is about 40€ for adults, includes a midday meal at a local taverna as well as all the wine you care to drink. You can sign on at the far end of the harbor. **Manias Tours,** 5 Arkadiou (✆ **28310/56-400**), offers an **evening cruise** that provides a view of Rethymnon glittering in the night.

SHOPPING

Here, as in Chania and Iraklion, you may be overwhelmed by the sheer number of gift shops offering mostly souvenirs. Looking for something different? Try Nikolaos Papalasakis's **Palaiopoleiou,** 40 Souliou, which is crammed with some genuine antiques, old textiles, jewelry, and curiosities such as the stringed instruments made by the proprietor. At **Olive Tree Wood,** 35 Arabatzoglou, the name says it all—the store carries bowls, containers, and implements carved from olive wood. **Evangeline,** 36 Paleologlou, has a good selection of textiles, while **Haroula Spridaki,** 36 Souliou, has a nice selection of Cretan embroidery. **Talisman,** 32 Arabatzoglou, sells an interesting selection of blown glass, ceramics, plaques, paintings, and other hand-made articles. And the AVLI Hotel's **Raki Baraki,** at 22 Xanthoudidou, has a large and varied selection of natural products from all over Greece.

Where to Stay

There is no shortage of accommodations in and around Rethymnon—but it has become hard to find a place in town that offers location, authentic atmosphere, and a quiet night's sleep. Our choices try to satisfy the last-mentioned criterion first. Note that many places in Rethymnon shut down in winter.

EXPENSIVE

AVLI Lounge Apartments ★   This boutique hotel is a restored mansion dating from 1530, now loaded with elements from various centuries and cultures and with every possible modern convenience. The rooms are suites in the sense that they are large enough to assign areas to different functions—sleeping, working, relaxing—two even have working fireplaces. Clients are warned that some rooms are in a separate building across a narrow (pedestrian-only) street and there are no elevators in either this or the main building. Rooms along the street are not well soundproofed and should be avoided by light sleepers. Also, because there are only seven units, you have little chance of switching. Insist on your room's location when making a reservation. Final word: You are paying a high price for more luxuries than you may need on Crete.

1622 Xanthoudidou, 74100 Rethymnon. www.avli.gr. ✆ **28310/58-250.** 7 units. High season 190€–500€ double; low season 165€–210€ double. Rates include buffet breakfast. Surcharge for 3rd person sharing room; babies stay free. AE, DC, MC, V. Parking on public lot, 10-min. walk away. **Amenities:** Restaurant; bar; babysitting; pool; room service; yoga and massage. *In room:* A/C, TV, hair dryer, Internet, Jacuzzi, minibar.

Palazzino di Corina ★   Setting a new benchmark for stylish accommodations in Rethymnon, this boutique hotel is in a centuries-old Venetian mansion restored with taste and restraint. Each of the 21 rooms is named after one of the Greek gods or goddesses, and each has some distinctive configuration and appearance; size varies considerably but all have comfortable beds and private bathrooms. A courtyard offers a delightful place to retreat from your city walks or wider excursions—plus a small pool in which to cool off. Its location offers closeness to the old town's center while providing a quiet night, but there is one drawback for some: There is no elevator and some rooms are on what Americans call a third floor; however, there is a room for those limited in their mobility. Definitely for those who appreciate subdued luxury and are willing to spend a bit for such an environment.

7-9 Damvergi and A. Diakou, 74100 Rethymnon. www.corina.gr. ✆ **28310/21-205.** 21 units. High season 130€–230€ double; low season 115€–180€ double. Rates include buffet breakfast. Surcharge for 3rd person sharing room; babies stay free. MC, V. Parking on public lot, 10-min. walk away. **Amenities:** Restaurant; bar; babysitting; pool; room service. *In room:* A/C, TV, hair dryer, hydromassage, Internet, minibar.

MODERATE

Hotel Fortezza ★   Fortezza has long been one of the more popular hotels in Rethymnon, mainly because of its location and moderate prices, and since its total renovation in 2010–11, it now offers more pleasant accommodations and ambience. You're only a few blocks from the inner old town and then another couple of blocks to the town beach and the Venetian Harbor. It's convenient, too, for driving and parking a car. The Venetian Fortezza rises just across the street. Guest rooms are decent size with modern bathrooms (some with shower, some with tub); most have balconies. It is essential, however, to ask for one of its inside rooms, which overlook the small but welcome pool—streetside rooms can be noisy. This hotel has become so popular that you must make reservations for the high season.

16 Melissinou, 74100 Rethymnon. www.fortezza.gr *C* **28310/55-551.** 53 units. High season 85€–92€ double; low season 64€–76€ double. Family room for 4, high season 135€; low season 95€. Rates include buffet breakfast. Surcharge for 3rd person sharing room; babies stay free. AE, DC, MC, V. Free parking nearby. On the western edge of town, just below the Venetian Fortezza, which is approached by Melissinou. **Amenities:** Restaurant; bar; babysitting; pool; Wi-Fi. *In room:* A/C, TV, hair dryer, Internet.

Mare Monte Beach Hotel ★ ☺   If you stay at the Mare Monte, some 24km (15 miles) west of Rethymnon, you'll feel like you're living in a remote hideaway, with the sea before you and the mountains behind. This first-class resort hotel gets its highest ratings for its beautiful beach. Guest rooms are of moderate size with basic Greek hotel furnishings, but fully modern bathrooms. Some rooms are wheelchair accessible. Activities include minigolf, archery, and horseback riding by arrangement. Although it lacks the luxury of the grand resorts to the east of Rethymnon, the Mare Monte is a good alternative for those who want to focus their Cretan stay on Rethymnon, Chania, and western Crete, yet prefer to be based well away from a noisy town. The village of Georgioupolis is close enough for an evening stroll.

73007 Georgioupolis, Crete. www.mare-monte-beach.com. *C* **28250/61-390.** 200 units. High season 115€; low season 85€ double. Rates include only breakfast, but most guests take half board. DC, MC, V. Parking on-site. Closed Nov–Mar. 25 min. west of Rethymnon, on the main road to Chania. **Amenities:** 2 restaurants; 2 bars; babysitting; children's playground; gym; 2 pools (adult and children's); room service; 2 night-lit tennis courts; extensive watersports equipment/rentals; Wi-Fi. *In room:* A/C, TV, hair dryer.

INEXPENSIVE

Hotel Ideon   This longtime favorite is a solid choice for its location and price. It also boasts a pool with a sunbathing area. The friendly desk staff will arrange for everything from laundry service to car rentals. The guest rooms are the standard modern of Greek hotels—but insist on one away from the street, as an adjacent area is a popular gathering spot in summer. I like this place because it offers an increasingly rare combination in a Rethymnon hotel: It's near the active part of the old town and near the water (although it is several hundred meters to a swimming beach).

10 Plateia Plastira, 74100 Rethymnon. www.hotelideon.gr. *C* **28310/28-667.** 86 units, some with shower, some with tub. High season 85€ double; low season 60€ double. Rates include buffet breakfast. Reduced rates for 3rd person in room or for child in parent's room. AE, DC, MC, V. Parking on nearby lot. Closed Nov to mid-Mar. On coast road just west of the Venetian Harbor. **Amenities:** Restaurant; terrace cafe; 2 bars; babysitting; pool. *In room:* A/C, TV (in suites), fridge, kitchenette.

Kyma Beach Hotel   This is a modern, city hotel—not a resort hotel—designed for people who want to take in Rethymnon and then retire to a stylish but no-nonsense hotel. It's close to the attractions of old town and to the beach. The somewhat austere gray exterior might put off some people, but in fact the hotel is well designed and has been totally renovated by 2011. Although rooms are hardly spacious, they are neatly furnished. Some have sleeping lofts, so if this doesn't appeal to you, speak up. Bathrooms are up to date. All rooms have balconies: ask for one with a sea view and insist on a higher floor to escape street noise. The outdoor cafe is a popular watering hole for locals; you won't feel as if you're in a foreigners' compound.

Agnostou Stratioti Sq. 74111 Rethymnon. www.kyma-beach.com. ℂ **28310/55-503.** 35 units, some with shower, some with tub. High season 85€ double; low season 65€ double. Rates include continental breakfast. AE, MC, V. Parking on adjacent streets. Public buses nearby. At eastern edge of old town and its beach. **Amenities:** 2 restaurants; 2 bars; babysitting. *In room:* A/C, TV, minibar, Wi-Fi.

Where to Eat

Rethymnon may not have the choice of restaurants of Iraklion or Chania, but there is a choice for a range of budgets. For truly elegant dining and wining, try the **AVLI Lounge**'s restaurant (see above); it boasts of its wine selection and also provides private dinners, special celebration dinners, wine-tasting evenings, and even cooking lessons. Or try the **Veneto,** a 600-year-old Venetian mansion at 4 Epimenidou (a small street halfway between Nerantzes Mosque and the Folk Museum). Either offers truly special cuisine but may be more expensive than most travelers are budgeting for.

EXPENSIVE

Knossos ★ GREEK/SEAFOOD   Visitors who appreciate dining in a 600-year-old taverna head for this small, charming family-owned restaurant along the old Venetian harbor. It specializes in fish as fresh as the day's catch, and all meals are lovingly prepared by Maria Stavroulaki and her mother. You can't go wrong with the grilled whole fish with fresh vegetables, or baked lobster with pasta. Happiness is snagging the single table on the open second-floor balcony overlooking the blinking harbor lights.

40 Nearchou (the old port). ℂ **28310/25-582.** Reservations recommended. Main fish courses 20€–40€. MC, V. Daily 11am–midnight. Closed Nov–Mar.

MODERATE

Famagusta GREEK/INTERNATIONAL   This well-tested seaside restaurant is far from the hustle of the harbor yet convenient to the center's attractions. The menu offers Cretan specialties such as breaded, deep-fried zucchini with lightly flavored garlic yogurt or *halumi,* a grilled cheese. Grilled fish and filets are the core of the main courses, but the adventurous chef includes Chinese-style Mandarin beef and that old basic, chili con carne. Eating here makes you feel like you're at an old-fashioned seaside restaurant, not some touristic confection.

6 Plastira Sq., Rethymnon. ℂ **28310/23-881.** Main courses 6€–18€. AE, DC, MC, V. Daily 10am–midnight. Closed Christmas through New Year's. Parking lot nearby. Near Ideon Hotel, on coast road just to west of Venetian Harbor.

Othonos GREEK   Just as Americans claim to trust a diner where the truckers are parked, you can trust a Greek restaurant where the locals gather, and the Othonos is such a place. It offers tasty taverna food and a front-row seat for the passing scene. Minor variations—such as a Roquefort dressing on a salad, cheese and ham pies, artichokes with the lamb dish—liven up the traditional fare such as rabbit *stifado* (stew). Just right for dropping in when you are on a walking tour of the town.

27 Pethihaki Sq., Rethymnon. ℂ **28310/55-500.** Main courses 6€–20€. MC, V. Daily 10am–midnight. In center of old town, so park on edge of old town.

A Side Trip from Rethymnon: Monastery of Arkadhi

The events that took place here can help put modern Cretan history in perspective. The **Monastery of Arkadhi** sits some 23km (14 miles) southeast of Rethymnon and can be reached by public bus. A taxi might be in order if you don't have a car. If you ask the driver to wait an hour, the fare should total about 80€. What you'll see is a surprisingly Italianate-looking church facade, for although it belongs to the Orthodox priesthood, it was built under Venetian influence in 1587.

Like many monasteries on Crete, Arkadhi provided support for the rebels against Turkish rule. During a major uprising on November 9, 1866, many Cretan insurgents—men, women, and children—took refuge here. Realizing they were doomed to fall to the far larger besieging Turkish force, the abbot, it is claimed, gave the command to blow up the powder storeroom. Whether it was an accident or not is debatable, but hundreds of Cretans and Turks died in the explosion. The event became known throughout the Western world, inspiring writers, revolutionaries, and statesmen of several nations to protest, at least with words. To Cretans it became and remains the archetypal incident of their long struggle for "freedom or death." (An ossuary outside the monastery contains the skulls of many who died in the explosion.) Even if you never thought about Cretan history, a brief visit to Arkadhi should go a long way in explaining the Cretans you deal with.

An Excursion from Rethymnon: The Amari Valley

Everyone who has more than a few days to spend on Crete should try to make at least one excursion into the interior to experience three of the elements that have traditionally characterized the island: eons-old rugged mountains, age-old village life, and centuries-old chapels and monasteries. The Amari Valley, south of Rethymnon, offers just such an opportunity. It's not much more than a 161km (100-mile) round-trip, but given the mountainous roads and allowing for at least some stops to see a few villages and chapels, a full day should be budgeted. Your own vehicle or a hired taxi is a must (unless, of course, you get a travel agency to arrange a tour); if you go on your own, a good map of Crete is also a necessity. Heading east out of Rethymon, some 5km (3 miles) along at Platanias, you take the road south to Prassies and Apostoli, always climbing and zigzagging. At Apostoli, a turnoff to the left leads to Thronos and its Church of the Panayia, built on the mosaic floor of an early Christian church. Back on the main road, you proceed toward Monasteraki but take the turnoff to the left to visit the Monastery of Asomatos. Founded in the 10th century, its present building dates from the Venetian period; it served as a center of resistance and Greek culture under the Turks. Proceed on down to Fourfouras (a starting point for the ascent to Crete's highest peak, Psiloritis). Continue south to Nithavris and Ayios Ioannis, then head north via Ano Meros, Gerakari, Patsos, and Pantanassa until you rejoin the road where a left starts you back north and down to the coast. Along the way you will have passed through many other villages and be directed to other chapels, but best of all you will have spent an unforgettable day in the Cretan mountains.

AYIOS NIKOLAOS

69km (43 miles) E of Iraklion

Ayios Nikolaos tends to inspire strong reactions, depending on what you're looking for. Until the 1970s, it was a lazy little coastal settlement with no archaeological or historical structures of any interest. Then, the town got "discovered," and the rest is the history of organized tourism in our time.

For about 5 months of the year, Ayios Nikolaos becomes one gigantic resort town, taken over by the package-tour groups who stay in beach hotels along the adjacent coast and come into town to eat, shop, and stroll. During the day, Ayios Nikolaos vibrates with people. At night, it vibrates with music—the center down by the water is one communal nightclub.

Somehow, the town remains a pleasant place to visit, and it serves as a fine base for excursions to the east of Crete. And if you're willing to stay outside the very center, you can take in only as much of Ayios Nikolaos as you want, and then retreat to your beach or take off to explore the east end of the island. And anyone who's come as far as Ayios Nikolaos should get over to Elounda at least once: It's some 12km (8 miles), but in addition to taxis there are buses every hour back and forth. It's slower paced and less fashionable than Ayios Nikolaos, but all the more pleasant for being so.

Essentials

GETTING THERE **By Plane** Ayios Nikolaos does not have its own airport but can be reached in about 1 hour by taxi or bus (1½ hr.) from the Iraklion airport. During the high season, **Olympic Airways** offers a few flights weekly to Sitia, the town to the east of Ayios Nikolaos, but the drive from there to Ayios Nikolaos is also a solid 1½ hours, so you'd do just as well to fly into Iraklion.

By Boat At least during the summer season, several ships a week each way link Ayios Nikolaos and Piraeus (about 11 hr.).; these ships usually run from Ayios Nikolaos to Sitia (just east along the coast) and on to Rhodes via the islands of Kassos, Karpathos, and Khalki. In summer, ships may link Ayios Nikolaos to Santorini (4 hr.), and then to Piraeus via several other Cycladic islands. Schedules and even ship lines vary so much from year to year that you should wait until you get to Greece to make specific plans, but you can try checking www.gtp.gr in advance.

By Bus Bus service almost every half-hour of the day each way (in high season) links Ayios Nikolaos to Iraklion; almost as many buses go to and from Sitia. The **KTEL** bus line (© **28410/22-234**) has its terminal in the Lagos neighborhood (behind the city hospital, which is up past the Archaeological Museum).

VISITOR INFORMATION The **Municipal Information Office** (© **28410/22-357**; gr_tour_ag_nik@acn.gr) is one of the most helpful in all of Greece, perhaps because it's staffed by eager young seasonal employees (mid-Apr to Oct daily 8am–10pm). In addition to providing maps and brochures, it can help arrange accommodations and excursions. (To the left, just around the corner, is a small Folklore Museum, open usually 10am–6pm; admission 3€.) Of several travel agencies in town, I recommend **Nostos Tours,** 30 R. Koundourou, along the right arm of the harbor (© **28410/26-383**).

GETTING AROUND The town is so small that you can walk to all points, although taxis are available. The KTEL buses (see above) serve towns, hotels, and other points in eastern Crete. If you want to explore this end of the island on your own, it seems as if car and moped/motorcycle rentals are at every other doorway. I found some of the best rates at **Alfa Rent a Car,** 3 Kap. Nik. Fafouti, the small street between the lake and the harbor road (© **28410/24-312**; fax 28410/25-639). I should point out that parking is such a problem in the center of town that you might like to know of a small **private parking lot** at the corner of Kyprou and Koziri, just off the square (signed) at the top of Koundourou, the main street leading up from the harbor.

FAST FACTS Several **ATMs** and currency-exchange machines line the streets leading away from the harbor. The **hospital** (© **28410/22-369**) is on the west edge of town, at the junction of Lasithiou and Paleologou. For **Internet access,** try either

Ayios Nikolaos

To Elounda

Sea of Crete

0   100 m
0   100 y

Archaeological Museum

To Bus Terminal

Miatou

Koritsas

Prigipos Georgiou

Koraka

Paleologou

Ethnikis Antistaseos

Theotokouloud

Kobnarouv

D. Solomos

Titou

Plastira

Akti Koundourou

Kantanoleorntos

Katehaki

Kondilaki

Lake Voulismeni

Quay

Koundourou

Lasthenous

Pasifias

Ariadnis

Miiou

Ebans

M. Sfakianaki

Alexomanoli

Omirou

28 Octobriou

Koundourou

25 Martiou

K. Sfakianaki

Manousogianakis

Kitroplatia Beach

Filellinon

Plateia Venizelou

El. Venizelou

Polytechniou

Bus Station

Tavla

Koziri

Akti Atlantidos

Information (i)
Post Office ✉
OTE C

Greece

Athens

Aegean Sea

Mediterranean Sea   CRETE   Ayios Nikolaos

HOTELS ■

Iberostar Hermes **2**

Minos Beach Art Hotel **1**

RESTAURANTS ◆

Hollands Restaurant—
  De Molen (The Mill) **4**

Itanos **6**

La Casa **5**

Pelagos **3**

the bookstore/cafe **Polychromos,** at 28 October, or the **Atlantis Café,** 15 Akti Atlantidos; they tend to be open daily in high season from 9am to 11pm. (2€ an hour). The most convenient place to do **laundry** is Xionati Laundromat, 10 Chortatson (a small street leading up from the beach on Akti Nearchou); it's open Monday through Friday from 8am to 2pm and 5 to 8pm, Saturday from 8am to 4pm. **Luggage storage** is available at the main bus station. The **tourist police** (✆ 28410/26-900) are at 34 Koundoyianni. The **post office** is at 9 28th Octobriou (✆ 28410/22-276). In summer, it's open Monday through Saturday from 7:30am to 8pm; in winter, Monday through Saturday from 7:30am to 2pm. The **telephone office (OTE),** 10 Sfakinaki, at the corner of 25th Martiou, is open Monday through Saturday from 7am to midnight, Sunday from 7am to 10pm.

What to See & Do

The focal point in town is the small pool, formally called **Lake Voulismeni,** just inside the harbor. You can sit at its edge while enjoying a meal or a drink. Inevitably, it has given rise to all sorts of tales—that it's bottomless (it's known to be about 65m/213 ft. deep); that it's connected to Santorini, the island about 104km (65 miles) to the north; and that it was the "bath of Athena." Originally it was a freshwater pool, probably fed by a subterranean river that drained water from the mountains inland. A 20th-century channel now mixes the fresh water with sea water.

Archaeological Museum ★   This is a fine example of one of the relatively new provincial museums that have opened up all over Greece—in an effort both to decentralize the country's rich holdings and to allow local communities to profit from the finds in their regions. It contains a growing collection of Minoan artifacts and art being excavated in eastern Crete. Its prize piece, the eerily modern ceramic **Goddess of Myrtos,** shows a woman clutching a jug; it was found at a Minoan site of this name down on the southeastern coast. The museum is well worth at least a brief visit.

74 Paleologou. ✆ **28410/24-943.** Admission 4€. Tues–Sun 8:30am–3pm. Closed all holidays (reduced hours possible in low season, so call ahead).

SHOPPING

Definitely make time to visit **Ceramica,** 28 Paleologou (✆ **28410/24-075**). You will see many reproductions of ancient Greek vases and frescoes for sale throughout Greece, but seldom will you have a chance to visit the workshop of one of the masters of this art, Nikolaos Gabriel. His authentic and vivid vases range from 25€ to 300€. He also carries a line of fine jewelry, made by others to his designs. Across the street, at no. 1A, **Xeiropoito** sells handmade rugs. **Pegasus,** 5 Sfakianakis, on the corner of Koundourou, the main street up from the harbor (✆ **28410/24-347**), offers a selection of jewelry, knives, icons, and trinkets—some old, some not. You'll have to trust the owner to tell you which is which. For something a bit different in women's clothing, step into **Vendemma,** 11 Koundourou.

For something truly Greek, what could be better than an icon—a religious or historic painting on a wooden plaque? The tradition is kept alive in Elounda at the studio/store **Petrakis Workshop for Icons,** 22 A. Papendreou, on the left as you come down the incline from Ayios Nikolaos, just before the town square (✆ **28410/41-669**). Georgia and Ioannis Petrakis work seriously at maintaining this art. Orthodox churches in North America as well as in Greece buy icons from them. Stop by and watch the artists at their painstaking work—you don't have to be Orthodox to admire or own one. The store also carries local artisans' jewelry, blown glass, and ceramics.

Where to Stay

IN TOWN

Iberostar Hermes   Taken over by the Spanish international Iberostar hotel chain in 2011, the former Hotel Hermes remains the best choice if you want to stay close to the center of town. Yet the Hermes is just far away enough—around the corner from the inner harbor—to escape the nightly din. One drawback is that it requires at least half board (breakfast and dinner), but this makes its rates relatively moderate—leaving you free to try local eateries now and then. Above all, it's a compromise between the deluxe beach resorts and the cheaper in-town hotels. Guest rooms are done in the standard style, and most enjoy views over the sea. There's a private terrace (not a beach) on the shore, just across the boulevard. The roof has a pool, with plenty of space to sunbathe. Probably not the town's best fit for adults with children.

If the Hermes is booked, you might try **Hotel Coral,** next door (✆ **28410/28-253**). It's almost as classy, and slightly cheaper.

Akti Koundourou, Ayios Nikolaos, 72100 Crete. www.iberostar.com. ✆ **28410/28-253.** 206 units. High season 125€ double; low season 85€ double. Rates include buffet breakfast; special rate for longer stays. AE, DC, MC, V. Parking on opposite seawall (but beware of spray). Closed Nov–Mar. On the shore road around from the inner harbor. **Amenities:** 2 restaurants; 2 bars; conference facilities; fitness center; pool; sauna. *In room:* A/C, TV, fridge on request, hair dryer.

Minos Beach Art Hotel ★★   I have to admit that I recommend this place out of loyalty to the first of the luxury beach-bungalow resorts in all of Greece. It remains a favorite among many returnees, but I must also admit that the common areas are not as well maintained as those at newer resorts, and its grounds now look a bit over-grown. But the individual accommodations are just fine, although as with almost all Greek hotels, the rooms and bathrooms are small (given the price). The hotel does have a civilized air, which is enhanced by the original, modern works of sculptors (several world famous) scattered around the grounds. It's a great place to enjoy complete peace and quiet not too far from Ayios Nikolaos. It will appeal to those who like a touch of the Old World when they go abroad and aren't looking for a lot of glitz.

Amoudi, Ayios Nikolaos, 72100 Crete. www.minos-beach-art-hotel.com. ✆ **28410/22-345.** 132 units. High season 285€–900€ double/bungalow; low season 175€–765€ double/bungalow. Rates include buffet breakfast. Special rates for children. AE, DC, MC, V. Parking on-site or nearby. Closed late Nov to late Mar. A 10-min. walk from center of Ayios Nikolaos. Frequent public buses to Ayios Nikolaos or Elounda. **Amenities:** 5 restaurants; 2 bars; airport transport arranged; babysitting; bike rentals; concierge; conference center; health club; Internet; saltwater pool; room service; sauna; table tennis; night-lit tennis court; TV room; watersports equipment/rentals. *In room:* A/C, TV, hair dryer, Jacuzzi (in some bungalows), minibar.

OUT OF TOWN

Istron Bay ★★   This beautiful and quiet beach resort, nestled against the slope on its own bay—has the atmosphere of a tropical paradise atmosphere that makes it a special place. Family owned, it maintains traditional Cretan hospitality; for example, newcomers are invited to a cocktail party to meet others. The comfortable guest rooms have modern bathrooms and spectacular views. If you can tear yourself away from here, you're well situated to take in all the sights of eastern Crete. The main dining room has a fabulous view to go with its award-winning cuisine; it takes special pride in offering choices based on the "Cretan diet," internationally recognized as especially healthy. The resort offers activities such as scuba diving at an authorized school, nature walks in the spring and autumn, wine tastings, fishing trips, and Greek lessons.

72100 Istro, Crete (12km/7 miles east of Ayios Nikolaos). www.istronbay.gr. ✆ **28410/61-347.** 145 units, including 27 bungalows. High season 145€–225€ double, 185€–310€ suite or bungalow; low season

105€–145€ double, 155€–210€ suite or bungalow. Rates include half board with buffet breakfast. Special rates for extra beds in room, for children, for June, and for breakfast only. AE, DC, MC, V. Parking on premises. Closed Nov–Mar. Public buses every hour to Ayios Nikolaos or Sitia. **Amenities:** 3 restaurants; 2 bars; airport transport arranged; babysitting; children's program; concierge; conference facilities; seawater pool and children's pool; room service; night-lit tennis court; watersports equipment/rentals. *In room:* A/C, satellite TV, hair dryer, minibar.

Where to Eat

Ayios Nikolaos and nearby Elounda have so many restaurants that it's hard to know where to start or stop. When deciding, consider location and atmosphere; those factors have governed our recommendations below. But if you're looking for just a basic taverna with traditional but tasty food, try the **Trata,** on the Akti Pangalou overlooking the town's Kitroplatia Beach. Standing at the port and facing the open sea, walk around the harbor to the right and then take a right onto Milou Street; follow that to the beach front and you will see the Trata on the right.

EXPENSIVE

Pelagos ★ GREEK/SEAFOOD   Looking for a change from the usual touristy seafront restaurant—something a bit more cosmopolitan? Try Pelagos, in a handsome old house a block up from the hustle and bustle of the harbor. As its name suggests, it specializes in seafood and this is what makes it a bit more expensive. From squid to lobster (not really recommended in Greece), it's all done with flair. You can sit indoors in a subdued atmosphere or out in the secluded garden; either way you'll be served with style. This restaurant lets you get away from the crowd for a more intimate meal.

10 Ketahaki (at corner of Koraka, a block up from the waterfront). ☎ **28410/25-737.** doxan45@hot mail.com. Reservations recommended in high season. Main courses 6€–20€; some fish by the kilo. MC, V. Daily noon–1am. Closed Nov–Feb. Parking on adjacent streets impossible in high season.

MODERATE

Hollands Restaurant—De Molen (The Mill) DUTCH/INDONESIAN   Looking for a change from the basic Greek menu? Aside from offering a (possibly) new experience for your palate, this place commands the most dramatic nighttime view of Ayios Nikolaos. Specialties include pork filet in a cream sauce. Vegetarian? Try the crepe with eggplant, mushrooms, carrots, and cabbage, tied up with leeks. I sampled the popular Indonesian dish *nasi goreng*—a plate heaped with rice, vegetables, and pork in a satay (peanut) sauce. Perhaps it's the setting, but everything here is especially good.

10 Dionysos Solomos. ☎/fax **28410/25-582.** Main courses 6€–18€; combination plates offered. V. Daily 10am–11:30pm. Closed Nov–Mar. A taxi is your only choice if you can't make it up the hill. It's the road at the highest point above the lake.

La Casa GREEK/INTERNATIONAL   With its lakeside location, tasty menu, and friendly Greek-American proprietress, this might be many travelers' first choice in Ayios Nikolaos. You'll enjoy the fine meals Marie Daskaloyiannis cooks up, including fried rice with shrimp, lamb with artichokes, and rabbit *stifado.* Or try the "Greek sampling" plate—moussaka, dolmades, stuffed tomato, meatballs, and whatever other goodies Marie heaps on. There's always a slightly special twist to the food here.

31 28th Octobriou. ☎ **28410/26-362.** Main courses 6€–14€. AE, DC, DISC, MC, V. Daily 9am–midnight.

Vritomartes GREEK/SEAFOOD   The 12km (8-mile) trip to get to this Elounda taverna takes a bit of effort, but a seat by the water makes it worthwhile. You can't beat dining at this old favorite—there's been at least a lowly taverna here long before the beautiful people and tour groups discovered the area. (In high season, come early or make a reservation.) The specialty, no surprise, is seafood. (You may find the proprietor literally "out to sea," catching that night's fish dinners.) If you settle for the red mullet and a bottle of Cretan white Xerolithia, you can't go wrong. The dining area itself is plain, but this is one place you won't forget.

On the breakwater, Elounda. ☏ **28410/41-325.** Reservations recommended for dinner in high season. Main courses 6€–32€; 2-person fish-platter special 58€. MC, V. Daily 10am–11pm. Closed Nov–Mar.

INEXPENSIVE

Itanos GREEK   A now familiar story on Crete: A simple local taverna where you go to experience "authenticity" becomes overrun by tourists, changing the scene. But the fact is, the food and prices haven't changed *that* much. Standard taverna oven dishes are still served—grilled meats; no-nonsense chicken, lamb, or beef in tasty sauces; and hearty helpings of vegetables. The house wine comes from barrels. Low seasons and during the day, you sit indoors, where you'll experience no-nonsense decor and service. But at night during the hot months, tables appear on the sidewalk, a roof garden opens up on the building across the narrow street, and fellow travelers take over. Come here if you need a break from the harbor scene and want to feel you're in a place that still exists when all the tourists go home.

1 Kyprou. ☏ **28410/25-340.** Reservations not accepted, so come early in high season. Main courses 6€–12€. No credit cards. Daily 10am–midnight. Just off Plateia Venizelos, at top of Koundourou.

Side Trips from Ayios Nikolaos

Almost everyone who spends any time in Ayios Nikolaos makes the two short excursions to Spinalonga and Kritsa. Each can easily be visited in a half day.

SPINALONGA

Spinalonga is the **fortified islet** in the bay off Elounda. The Venetians built one of their many fortresses here in 1579, and it enjoyed the distinction of being their final outpost on Crete, not taken over by the Turks until 1715. When the Cretans took possession in 1903, it was turned into a leper colony, but this ended after World War II. Now Spinalonga is a major tourist attraction. In fact, there's not much to do here except walk around and soak in the atmosphere and ghosts of the past. Boats depart regularly from both Ayios Nikolaos harbor and Elounda as well as from certain hotels. It's not especially romantic, more like an abandoned site, so visitors are left to populate it with their own imaginations.

KRITSA ★

Although a walk through Spinalonga can resonate as a historical byway, if you have time to make only one of these short excursions, I advise taking the 12km (8-mile) trip into the hills behind Ayios Nikolaos to the village of Kritsa and its 14th-century **Church of Panagia Kera ★**. The church is architecturally interesting, and scholars regard its **frescoes,** dating from the 14th and 15th centuries, as among the jewels of Cretan-Byzantine art. They have been restored, but their impact still emanates from the original work. Scenes depict the life of Jesus, the life of Mary, and the Second Coming. Guides can be arranged at any travel agency or at the Municipal Information Office in Ayios Nikolaos. After seeing the church, visit the village of Kritsa itself and enjoy the view and the many fine handcrafted goods for sale.

THE CYCLADES

by Sherry Marker

When most people think of the isles of Greece, they're usually thinking of the Cyclades. This rugged, often barren chain of islands in the Aegean Sea has villages with dazzling white houses that, from a distance, look like so many sugar cubes. The Cyclades got their name from the ancient Greek word meaning "to circle or surround," because the islands encircle Delos, the birthplace of the god Apollo. Today, especially in the summer, it's the visitors who circle these islands, taking advantage of the swift boats and hydrofoils that link them. The visitors come to see the white villages, the blue-domed chapels, and the fiery sunsets over the cobalt blue sea. They also come to relax in chic boutique hotels, eat in varied and inventive restaurants, and to enjoy an ouzo—or a chocolate martini—in some of the best bars and cafes in Greece.

When you visit the Cyclades, chances are that one island will turn out to be your favorite. Here are some of our favorites, for you to shortlist when you set out to explore the islands that lie in what Homer called the "wine dark sea." We'll start in the north Aegean and make our way south, before circling back north.

Unlike many of the Cyclades, where you can easily hear more English, French, and German spoken in summer than Greek, almost everyone who comes to **Tinos** is Greek. The island is often nicknamed the "Lourdes of Greece" because its famous church of the Panagia Evangelistria is Greece's most important pilgrimage destination. Don't even think of coming here on the Feast of the Assumption of the Virgin (Aug 15) without a reservation unless you enjoy sleeping alfresco—with lots of company. Tinos is also famous for its villages ornamented with the ornate marble doors and window fanlights carved here. Tinos also has intricate dovecotes that, from afar, can be mistaken for miniature villages perched on hills and hidden in valleys.

The "beautiful people" discovered **Mykonos** back in the 1950s and 1960s, drawn by its perfect Cycladic architecture—and, in those days, cheap, cheap prices. Today, despite seriously high prices here, travelers still come to see the famous windmills and sugar-cube houses. Now, they also come for the boutique hotels, the all-night cafe life, and some serious shopping. In short, Mykonos—along with Santorini—is still one of the Cyclades that just about everyone wants to see. If you come here in August, you'll think that just about everyone has arrived with you, and finding a hotel, or even a place at one of the chic, nouvelle-Greek-cuisine restaurants, will not be easy.

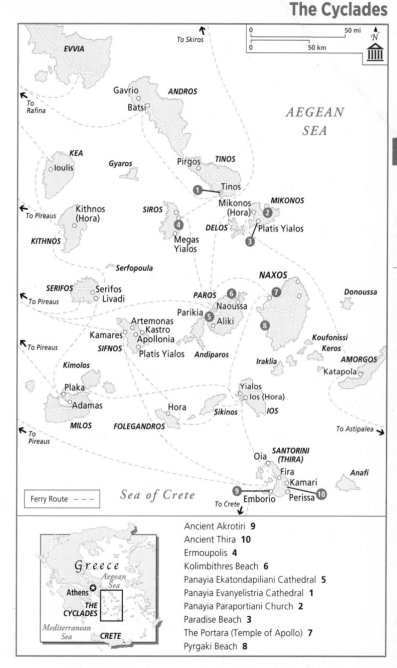

Ancient Akrotiri **9**
Ancient Thira **10**
Ermoupolis **4**
Kolimbithres Beach **6**
Panayia Ekatondapiliani Cathedral **5**
Panayia Evanyelistria Cathedral **1**
Panayia Paraportiani Church **2**
Paradise Beach **3**
The Portara (Temple of Apollo) **7**
Pyrgaki Beach **8**

That's one reason some travelers prefer **Paros,** which has something of a reputation as the poor man's Mykonos, with excellent windsurfing and a profusion of restaurants and nightspots less pricey and crowded than those on its famous neighbor, Mykonos. Paros also has one preposterously picturesque seaside village—Naoussa—and one very scenic inland village—Lefkes.

The largest and most fertile of the Cyclades, **Naxos** somehow has yet to attract hordes of summer visitors. You know what that means: Go there soon! The hills—sometimes green well into June—are dotted both with dovecotes and a profusion of endearing Byzantine chapels. The main town is crowned by a splendid kastro (castle) and a number of stately houses that the Venetians built between the 12th and 16th centuries; some of the houses are still lived in by the descendants of those very Venetians. Furthermore, although Naxos is a rich enough island that it does not have to woo tourists, there are some good small hotels and restaurants here.

Santorini (Thira) is famous from a thousand travel posters, showing its black-lava pebble-and-sand beaches and sheer blood-red cliffs. Only a crescent-shaped sliver remains of the once-sizeable island that was blown apart in antiquity by the volcano that still steams and hisses today. The first serious tourist invasion here began in the 1970s, as word got out about Santorini's deep harbor, framed by its sheer cliffs and its odd villages, cut out of the lava. The first travelers here were willing to put up with the most modest of accommodations in local homes. (On my first visit here I was installed in a bed from which the owner's grandmother had just been ejected.) Today, Santorini gives Mykonos a serious run for the money as Boutique Hotel Central, with some of the best food in all Greece. Santorini also has one of the most impressive ancient sites in all Greece: ancient Akrotiri, where you can walk down streets some 3,500 years old. It is so well-preserved that it is often compared to Pompeii.

Folegandros is the perfect counterbalance to Santorini. As yet, this little island is not overwhelmed with visitors, but the helipad suggests that this generation's beautiful people have discovered this still-tranquil spot. Folegandros's capital—many say it's the most beautiful in all the Cyclades—is largely built into the walls of a medieval kastro. Just outside the kastro is another reason to come here: the elegant cliffside Anemomilos Apartments Hotel.

Sifnos, long popular with Athenians, increasingly draws summer visitors to its handsome whitewashed villages, which many consider to have the finest architecture in all the Cyclades. In the spring, this is one of the greenest and most fertile of the islands. In summer, it's a place for the young at heart: In the capital Apollonia, it's easier to count the buildings that have not (yet) been converted into shops, restaurants, and discos than those that have been.

Siros, on the other hand, is as "undiscovered" as a large Cycladic island can be. Its distinguished capital, Ermoupolis, has a startling number of handsome neoclassical 19th-century buildings, including the Cyclades's only opera house, modeled on Milan's La Scala. Ano Siros, the district on the heights above the port, has sugar-cube Cycladic houses and both Catholic and Orthodox monasteries. Like Tinos and Naxos, Siros welcomes, but does not depend on, foreign tourists.

If you wanted to describe the Cyclades in their entirety, you could do worse than to string together well-deserved superlatives: Wonderful! Magical! Spectacular! The sea and sky really are bluer here than elsewhere, the islands on the horizon always tantalizing. In short, the Cyclades are very "more-ish"—once you've visited one, you'll want to see another, and then another, and then, yes, yet another.

Strategies for Seeing the Islands

A few practicalities: As you might expect, the Cyclades are crowded and expensive during high season—roughly mid-June to early September—and high season seems to get longer every year. If summer crowds and prices don't appeal to you, visit during the off-season; the best times are mid-September through October or from mid-April to early June. Keep in mind that April can still be cold in the islands and winter winds can be unremittingly harsh. Should you visit in winter or spring, keep in mind that many island hotels have minimal heating; find out if your hotel has genuine heat *before* you check in. And, keep in mind that island boat service is much less frequent off-season, and that many hotels, restaurants, and shops close for the winter (usually Nov–Mar). Whenever you visit, you'll discover that most hotels charge a **supplementary fee of 10%** for a stay of fewer than 3 nights. Finally, it's useful to remember that on most of these islands, the capital town has the name of the island itself. In addition, "Hora," or "Chora," meaning "the place," is commonly used for the capital. The capital of Paros, Parikia, for example, is also called Hora, as is Apollonia, the capital of Sifnos. Just to keep you on your toes, Apollonia/Hora is also called Stavri. When you're in island capitals, try to pick up the handy Sky Map, available at many travel agencies; there's a map for almost every Cycladic island. Although the businesses on these maps pay to be included, the maps are quite useful.

Although the Cyclades are bound by unmistakable family resemblance, each island is rigorously independent and unique, making this archipelago an island-hopper's paradise. Frequent ferry service makes travel easier—although changes in schedules can keep travelers on their toes (often on their toes as they pace harborside for ships to appear at unpredictable hours). Hydrofoils, in particular, are notoriously irregular, and even summer service is often canceled at the whim of the *meltemi* (blasting winds). Still, the growing fleet of catamarans is greatly facilitating travel between the ports of Piraeus and Rafina and the Cycladic islands.

Tip: If you haven't travelled here before, or for a while, here's some good news: You can now buy interisland tickets on almost any island. In the past, often you could only buy a ticket from, for example, Tinos to Paros; then, on Paros, you could buy a ticket to Naxos; on Naxos, you could buy a ticket to Sifnos; and so forth. Ticket purchase is much more streamlined now and you can also get many tickets online.

> ### Foodie Alert!
>
> Miles Lambert's *Greek Salad: A Dionysian Travelogue* (The Wine Appreciation Guild, 2004) is a great guide to finding the tastiest local delicacies—here in the Cyclades and elsewhere in Greece.

SANTORINI (THIRA) ★★★

233km (126 nautical miles) SE of Piraeus

Santorini is the travel poster Greek island destination that just about everyone wants to experience. Don't fly here; come by boat, for the view that never palls: blindingly white sugar-cube houses perched atop the high cliff tops of the island's deep caldera (crater). Add in the cobalt-blue Aegean and a light so pure and bright it makes you blink and you've arrived at Santorini. The volcano that created the caldera some 3,500 years ago is still smoldering, just part of the unique beauty of an island that gave birth to the lost-city-of-Atlantis myth. This is the Greece of ancient myths and photogenic sunsets, of blue-domed churches and donkey rides—and more boutique hotels, shops, and restaurants than there are churches.

BEACHES   Santorini's coastline is pure drama, from the steep cliffs that frame the caldera to the gentle slopes of pebble beaches whose pebbles come from the lava of the long-ago explosion that rent the island in half. **Red Beach, White Beach,** and **Black Beach,** named for their distinctly colored pebbles, lie in the southwest. The lively southeast trio of **Perissa, Agios Georgios,** and **Perivolos** are best for nightlife and watersports. Rock formations create a striking backdrop in family-friendly **Monolithos.** For more seclusion, descend the cliffs or hitch a donkey ride to one of **Oia**'s postage-stamp beaches, with deep and startlingly blue water.

THINGS TO DO   **Akrotiri** is an archaeological wonder: a Minoan town decimated by that huge volcanic eruption some 3,500 years ago, and preserved under lava until excavations began in 1967. Some of Akrotiri's treasures, including frescoes and pottery, are displayed at the **Museum of Pre-Historic Thira** in Fira. If Akrotiri is closed, don't despair: A vertiginous hike or ride brings you to the Greek, Roman, and Byzantine ruins at **Ancient Thira,** straddling a high promontory. The beautiful, bustling, whitewashed capital **Fira** is rivaled only by **Oia**'s equally dramatic clifftop mosaic of white houses and blue church domes. For sheer beauty, and greater tranquillity, little **Imerovigli,** with its offshore islet crowned by a medieval kastro, bests its more famous neighbors.

EATING & DRINKING   In Fira, you can get both acclaimed and inventive food (tiramisu with smoked eggplant mousse, anyone?) and a fantastic crater view at **Koukoumavlos.** At **Katina's** in Oia, postsunset relaxation goes well with the grilled fish and crisp white Assyrtiko wine from Santorini's volcanic vines. Over in the charming village of Pyrgos, you can snack at the bistro or dine at the restaurant at **Selene,** one of the best restaurants in all Greece, where the drop-dead gorgeous and delicious food uses the freshest of local ingredients. Order the sea bass with stuffed zucchini flowers and you'll suspect that the fish almost swam to your table, gathering the fresh zucchini flowers as it swam.

NATURE   One of the biggest volcanic eruptions in history shook Santorini some 3,500 years ago and created its unique **caldera.** The best way to appreciate the views from its vertiginous cliffs is by **hiking** along the rim from Fira to Oia. Take a boat trip to see the **volcano** in all its steaming glory, stopping for a therapeutic dip in **sulphur** hot springs. The vineyards of **Megalohori** and **Pyrgos** produce volcanic wines such as dry white Assyrtiko and sweet, amber-hued Vinsanto.

Essentials

GETTING THERE   **By Plane**   **Olympic Air** (✆ **810/114-4444** or 210/966-6666 [though they're almost never answered]; www.olympicair.com) offers daily flights between Athens and the Santorini airport **Monolithos** (✆ **22860/31-525**), which also receives European charters. There are frequent connections with Mykonos and Rhodes, and service two or three times per week to and from Iraklion, Crete. **Aegean Airlines** (✆ **810/112-0000**; www.aegeanair.com) also has several flights daily between Athens and Santorini. A bus to Fira (4€) meets most flights; the schedule is posted at the bus stop, beside the airport entrance. A taxi to Fira costs about 13€. *Tip:* The website of Athens International Airport (www.aia.gr) is a useful resource for domestic airline schedules.

By Boat Ferry service runs to and from Piraeus at least twice daily; the trip takes 9 to 10 hours by car ferry on the Piraeus-Paros-Naxos-Ios-Santorini route, or 4 hours by catamaran, if you go via Piraeus-Paros-Santorini. Boats are notoriously late and/or early; your travel or ticket agent will give you an *estimate* of times involved in the following journeys. *Remember:* That's estimate, as in guesstimate. In July and August, ferries connect several times a day with **Ios, Naxos, Paros,** and **Mykonos;** almost daily with **Anafi** and **Siros;** five times a week with **Sikinos** and **Folegandros;** and twice weekly with **Sifnos.** Service to **Thessaloniki** (17–24 hr.) is offered four to five times per week. There is an almost daily connection by excursion boat with **Iraklion** in Crete, but because this is an open sea route, the trip can be an ordeal in bad weather and is subject to frequent cancellation. For ferry schedules, check out **www.openseas.gr** or **www.gtp.gr**. Confirm ferry schedules with the Athens **GNTO** (© **210/870-0000;** www.gnto.gr), the **Piraeus Port Authority** (© **210/451-1311,** 210/451-1440, or -1441; phone not always answered), or the **Santorini Port Authority** (© **22860/22-239**).

Almost all ferries dock at **Athinios,** where buses meet each boat and then return directly to Fira (one-way to Fira costs 3€); from the Fira dock, buses depart for many other island destinations. Taxis are also available from Athinios, at nearly five times the bus fare. Athinios is charmless; when you come here to catch a ferry, it's a good idea to bring munchies, water, and a good book.

The exposed port at **Skala,** directly below Fira, is unsafe for the larger ferries but is often used by small cruise ships, yachts, and excursion vessels. If your boat docks here, head to town either by cable car (5€), mule, or donkey (5€); or you can do the 45-minute uphill walk. Be prepared to share the narrow path with the mules. We recommend a mule up and the cable car down. If you suffer from acrophobia, try taking the cable car both ways with your eyes firmly shut.

VISITOR INFORMATION   Nomikos Travel (☎ 22860/23-660; www.nomikos villas.gr), **Bellonias Tours** (☎ 22860/22-469), **Pelican Travel** (☎ 22860/22-220; www.pelican.gr), and **Kamari Tours** (☎ 22860/31-390) are well established. Bellonias, Nomikos, and Pelican offer bus tours of the island, boat excursions around the caldera, and submarine tours beneath the caldera. Expect to pay about 40€ for a bus tour to Akrotiri or ancient Thira, about the same for a day-trip boat excursion to the caldera islands, and about twice that for the submarine excursion.

GETTING AROUND   **By Bus**   The **central bus station** is just south of the main square in Fira. Schedules are posted here: Most routes are served every hour or half-hour from 7am to 11pm in high season. A conductor on board will collect fares, which range from 2€ to 5€. Destinations include Akrotiri, Athinios (the ferry pier), Oia, Kamari, Monolithos (the airport), Perissa, Perivolas Beach, Vlihada, and Vourvoulos. Excursion buses go to major attractions; ask a travel agent for details.

By Car   The travel agents listed above can help you rent a car. Be sure to take full insurance. Of the better-known agencies, try **Budget Rent-A-Car,** at the airport (☎ 22860/33-290), or in Fira, a block below the small square that the bus station is on (☎ 22860/22-900); a small car in high season should cost about 60€ a day, with unlimited mileage. If you reserve in advance through Budget in the U.S. (☎ 800/527-0700), you should be able to beat that price.

Warning: If you park in town or in a no-parking area, the police will remove your license plates, and you, not the car-rental office, will have to find the police station and pay a steep fine to get them back. There's free parking—often full—on the port's north side.

By Moped   The travel agents listed above can help you rent a moped. Many roads on the island are narrow and winding; add local drivers who take the roads at high speed, and visiting drivers who aren't sure where they're going, and you'll understand the island's high accident rate. If you're determined to use two-wheeled transportation, expect to pay about 25€ per day, less during off-season. Greek law now requires wearing a helmet; not all agents supply the helmet.

 Safety First

Use caution when walking around Santorini, especially at night. Keep in mind that many drivers are newcomers to the island and may not know every twist and turn. Those who do know every twist and turn tend to take them at full throttle.

By Taxi   The taxi station is just south of the main square. In high season, book ahead by phone (☎ 22860/22-555 or 22860/23-951), if you want a taxi for an excursion; be sure that you agree on the price before you set out. For most point-to-point trips (Fira to Oia, for example), the prices are fixed. If you call for a taxi outside Fira, you'll be charged a pickup fee of at least 2€; you're also required to pay the driver's fare from Fira to your pickup point. Bus service shuts down at midnight, so book a taxi in advance if you'll need it late at night.

FAST FACTS   The **National Bank** (Mon–Fri 8am–2pm), with an ATM, is a block south of the main square, on the right, near the taxi station. The **health clinic** (✆ **22860/22-237**) is on the southeast edge of town, on Ayiou Athanassiou, immediately below the bus station and the new archaeological museum. There are a number of **Internet** cafes on the main square, including **PC World** (✆ **22860/25-551**). There are several do-it-yourself launderettes in Fira; if you want your wash done for you, **Penguin Laundry** (✆ **22860/22-168**) is at the edge of Fira on the road to Oia, 200m (656 ft.) north of the main square. The **police** (✆ **22860/22-649**) are several blocks south of the main square, near the post office. For the **port police,** call ✆ **22860/22-239.** The **post office,** open Monday through Friday from 8am to 1pm, is south of the bus station. The **telephone office (OTE)** is off Ipapantis, up from the post office; hours are Monday through Friday from 8am to 3pm.

The Top Attractions

The top attraction here is the island itself; this is one of the most spectacular islands in the world. Many Greeks joke, somewhat begrudgingly, that there are foreigners who know where Santorini is—but are confused about where Greece is. Especially if you arrive by sea, you won't confuse Santorini with any of the other Cyclades. What will confuse you is that the island is also known as Thira. While large ships to Santorini (pop. 12,000) dock at the port of Athinios, many small ships arrive in Skala, a spectacular harbor that's part of the enormous caldera (crater) formed when a volcano blew out the island's center sometime between 1600 and 1500 B.C. One thing that just about everyone agrees on: The sunsets over the caldera are spectacular. The best views are from the ramparts of the kastro and from the footpath between Fira and Oia.

   The real wonder is that Santorini exceeds all glossy picture-postcard expectations. Like an enormous crescent moon, Santorini encloses the pure blue waters of its caldera, the core of an ancient volcano. Its two principal towns, **Fira** and **Oia** (also transliterated as **Ia**), perch at the summit of the caldera; as you approach by ship, bending back as far as possible to look as far up the cliffs as possible, whitewashed houses look like a dusting of new snow on the mountaintop. Up close, you'll find that both towns' main streets have more shops (*lots* of jewelry shops), restaurants, and discos than private homes. If you visit off-season—say in early May—you'll still find Fira's streets, shops, and restaurants crowded. In August, you'll experience gridlock.

   Akrotiri is Santorini's principal archaeological wonder: a town destroyed by the volcano eruption here, but miraculously preserved under layers of lava. As soon as you reach Santorini, check to see if Akrotiri is open; the site's protective roof collapsed in 2005, and the site has been closed partially or totally since then. If Akrotiri is closed, don't despair: If it weren't that Akrotiri steals its thunder, the site of **ancient Thira** would be the island's must-see destination. Spectacularly situated atop a high promontory, overlooking a black lava beach, the remains of this Greek, Roman, and Byzantine city sprawl over acres of rugged terrain. Ancient Thira is reached after a vertiginous hike or drive up (and up) to the acropolis itself.

   Don't feel compelled to race from attraction to attraction. It's far better to make haste slowly, linger on the black beach at Kamares, and stroll Thira in the early morning when the town belongs to its inhabitants, who are buying loaves sprinkled with sesame seeds at the bakery, and sweeping and washing the pavement outside all those jewelry stores. Most importantly, wherever you are, enjoy the view. There's nowhere else in the world, let alone in the Cyclades, with that caldera view. A great way to see the caldera is to take one of the **sunset cruises** offered by replica 18th-century sailing ships the Thallasa and the Bella Aurora (*©* **22860/24-024**). Some cruises include a light dinner. Most travel agents sell tickets from around 45€, or check out www.santorini.com/sailing and www.santoriniyachting.com.

Tip: If you plan to visit the ancient sites and their associated museums, get the economical 10€ ticket that's good for the Archaeological Museum, ancient Akrotiri (if open), prehistoric Thira, and ancient Thira. Even if the ticket price goes up, as it almost certainly will, and even if Akrotiri is closed, as it may be, this is a good buy.

Ancient Akrotiri ★★★ As noted, Akrotiri has been open only intermittently since the protective roof over the site collapsed in 2005. If even part of Akrotiri is open, go. If the entire site is closed when you want to visit, there's no point in coming here in the hopes of catching a glimpse of the remains: Unlike many sites, Akrotiri is *not* visible from the road.

Since excavations began in 1967, this site has presented the world with a fascinating look at life in the Minoan period. Akrotiri—sometimes nicknamed the "Minoan Pompeii"—was frozen in time sometime between 1600 and 1500 B.C. by a cataclysmic eruption of the island's volcano. Many scholars think that this powerful explosion destroyed the prosperous Minoan civilization on Crete. Pots and tools still lie where their owners left them before abandoning the town; the absence of human remains indicates that the residents had ample warning of the town's destruction.

Akrotiri Trivia

In 1860, Santorini workers quarrying blocks of volcanic ash—for use in building the Suez Canal—discovered ancient remains here. The quarry was relocated and, some 100 years later, the excavation of Akrotiri began. Who knows what unnoticed treasures may have been walled into the canal if the workers had not been alert.

You enter the Akrotiri site along the ancient town's main street, on either side of which are the stores or warehouses of the ancient commercial city. *Pithoi* (large earthen jars) found here contained traces of olive oil, fish, and onion. To get the best sense of the scale and urban nature of this town, go to the triangular plaza, near the exit, where you'll see two-story buildings and a spacious gathering place. Imagine yourself 3,000 years ago leaning over a balcony and spying on the passersby. As you walk along the path through town, look for the descriptive plaques in four languages. A few poor reproductions of the magnificent wall paintings are here; the best frescoes were taken off to the National Archaeological Museum in Athens, although Santorini continues to agitate for their return. For now, you can see some originals in the Museum of Prehistoric Thira and a splendid recreation in the Thira Foundation. As you leave the site, you may notice a cluster of flowers beside one of the ancient walls. This marks the burial spot of Akrotiri's excavator, Professor S. Marinatos, who died in a fall at Akrotiri. Allow at least an hour here.

Akrotiri. *©* **22860/81-366.** Admission 6€. Tues–Sun 8:30am–3pm.

Ancient Thira ★★ A high rocky headland (Mesa Vouna) separates two popular beaches (Kamari and Perissa), and at its top stand the ruins of ancient Thira. It's an incredible site, where cliffs drop precipitously to the sea on three sides and there are dramatic views of Santorini and neighboring islands. This extensive group of ruins is

Winery Tours

For information on a number of winery tours on Santorini, check out www. santonet.gr/wineries. **Boutari** (☎ 22860/ 81-011; www.boutari.gr) is the island's largest winery, and Greece's best-known wine exporter. A variety of tours are offered at their winery in Megalochiri on the road to Akrotiri, from a simple tasting of three wines (6€) to the "Libation to Santorini," with four wines, serious nibblies, and a multimedia show. This is a pleasant way to spend an hour or so (but never on Sun, when the winery, like most on Santorini, is closed). If you want to sample other local wines, stop by the underground **Volcan Wine Museum** (☎ 22860/31-322; www.volcanwines.gr), just outside Fira, on the mail road to Kamari. The museum, which occupies subterranean caves and tunnels, has an audio tour and reconstructions of the winemaking process (6€). Volcan's once-a-week Greek Night, featuring dinner and belly dancers, is popular with large tour groups. Check the website of individual wineries for their varied hours.

not easy to take in because of the many different periods on view—Roman baths jostle for space beside the remains of Byzantine walls and Hellenistic shops. One main street runs the length of the site, passing first through two agoras. The arc of the theater embraces the town of Kamari, Fira beyond, and the open Aegean.

Greeks lived here as early as the 9th century B.C., though most buildings are much later and date from the Hellenistic era (4th c. B.C.). You may not decipher everything, but do take in the view from the large Terrace of the Festivals. This is where naked lads danced to honor Apollo (inadvertently titillating, some of the graffiti suggests, a number of the spectators).

You can reach the site by bus, car, or taxi or, if you wish, on foot, passing on the way a cave that holds the island's only spring (see "Walking," under "Outdoor Pursuits," below). Excursion buses for the site of Thira leave from Fira and from the beach at Kamari. Allow yourself at least 5 hours to view the site, if you walk up there and walk back down; if you come and go by transport, allow at least an hour at the site.

Kamari. ☎ **22860/31-366.** Admission 4€. Tues–Sun 8am–2:30pm; site sometimes open later in summer. On a hilltop 3km (2 miles) south of Kamari by road.

Museum of Prehistoric Thira ★ Come here to see frescoes and other finds from ancient Akrotiri, along with objects imported from ancient Crete and the Northeastern Aegean Islands. Some pottery—cups, jugs, and *pithoi*—is delicately painted with motifs similar to those of the wall paintings (see Thira Foundation, below). If possible, visit both the museum and archaeological site at ancient Akrotiri on the same day. Allow an hour here.

Across the street from the bus stop in Fira; entrance is behind the Orthodox Cathedral. ☎ **22860/22-217.** Admission 5€. Tues–Sun 8:30am–3pm.

Thira Foundation: The Wall Paintings of Thira ★★ This exhibition created copies of the Akrotiri wall paintings, using a sophisticated technique of three-dimensional photographic reproduction that closely approximates the originals. The displays present some of the paintings in a re-creation of their original architectural context. The terrace in front of the foundation offers an astonishing view toward Fira and Imerovigli. Allow an hour here. The center hosts Thira's Music Festival each August and September.

Petros Nomikos Conference Center, Fira. © **22860/23-016.** www.therafoundation.org. Admission 4€. Recorded tour 3€. On the caldera, 5 min. past the cable car, on the way to Firostephani.

Exploring the Island

FIRA

Location, location, location: To put it mildly, Fira has a spectacular location on the edge of the caldera. Just when you think you've grown accustomed to the view down and out to sea and the offshore islands, you'll catch a glimpse of the caldera from a slightly different angle—and be awed yet again. If you're staying overnight on Santorini, take advantage of the fact that almost all the day-trippers from cruise ships leave in the late afternoon. Try to explore Santorini's capital, Fira, in the early evening, between the departure of the day-trippers and the onslaught of the evening revelers. As you stroll, you may be surprised to discover that, in addition to the predictable Greek Orthodox cathedral, Fira has a Roman Catholic cathedral and convent, legacies from the days when the Venetians controlled much of the Aegean. The name Santorini is, in fact, a Latinate corruption of the Greek for St. Irene. **Megaron Gyzi Museum** (© **22860/22-244**), in a stately old house by the cathedral, has church and local memorabilia, an icon workshop, and before-and-after photographs of the island at the time of the devastating earthquake of 1956. It is open Monday to Saturday 10:30am to 1pm and 5 to 8pm, and Sunday 10:30am to 4:30pm. Admission is 4€.

Not surprisingly, Fira is Santorini's busiest and most commercial town. The abundance of **jewelry stores** is matched in the Cyclades only by Mykonos—as are the crowds in July and August. At the north end of Ipapantis (also known as "Gold Street," for all those jewelry stores), you'll find the **cable-car station.** The Austrian-built system, the gift of wealthy ship owner Evangelos Nomikos, can zip you down to the port of Skala in 2 minutes. The cable car makes the trip every 15 minutes from 7:30am to 9pm for 5€, and it's worth every euro, especially on the way up.

Up and to the right of the cable-car station is the small **Archaeological Museum** (© **22860/22-217**), which contains early Cycladic figurines, finds from ancient Thira, and erotic (or obscene, depending on the eye of the beholder) Dionysiac figures. It's open Tuesday through Sunday from 8:30am to 3pm. Admission is 4€. You can easily spend a day or more enjoying Fira, but don't count on getting much sleep: Fira has a wild all-night-every-night bar scene, with every bar seemingly competing for the award for attaining the highest decibel level with amplified music.

OIA ★

Oia gets most visitors' votes as the most beautiful village on the island. The village made an amazing comeback from the 1956 earthquake, which left it a virtual ghost town for decades. Several fine **19th-century mansions** survived the earthquake and have been restored, including the elegant **Restaurant-Bar 1800** and the **Naval Museum** (see below). Much of the reconstruction continues the ancient Santorini tradition of excavating dwellings from the cliff's face, and the island's most beautiful cliff dwellings can be found here. The village has basically two streets: one with traffic, and the much more pleasant inland pedestrian lane, paved with marble and lined with an increasing number of jewelry shops, tavernas, and bars.

The **Naval Museum ★** (© **22860/71-156**) is a great introduction to this town where, until the advent of tourism, most young men found themselves working at sea and sending money home to their families. The museum, housed in a restored neoclassical mansion, was almost completely destroyed during the 1956 earthquake. Workers meticulously rebuilt the mansion using photographs of the original structure.

The museum's collection includes ship models, figureheads, naval equipment, and fascinating old photographs. Its official hours are Wednesday through Monday from 12:30 to 4pm and 5 to 8:30pm, although this varies considerably. Admission is 3€.

The battlements of the ruined **kastro** (fortress), at the western end of town, are the best place to catch the famous Oia sunset. Keep in mind that many cruise ships disgorge busloads of passengers who come here just to catch the sunset; unless you are here on a rainy February day, you may prefer to find a more secluded spot, where the click of camera shutters is less deafening (see "Imerovigli," later). Below the castle, a long flight of steps leads down to the pebble beach at **Ammoudi,** which is okay for swimming and sunning, and has some excellent fish tavernas (see "Where to Eat," later in this chapter). To the west is the more spacious and sandy **Koloumbos Beach.** To the southeast, below Oia is the fishing port of **Armeni,** where ferries sometimes dock and you can catch an excursion boat around the caldera.

OUT ON THE ISLAND: SOME VILLAGES

It's easy to spend all your time in Fira and Oia, with excursions to the ancient sites and beaches, and to neglect other villages. Easy, but a shame, as there are some very charming villages on the island. As you travel, keep an eye out for the troglodytic **cave houses** hollowed into solidified volcanic ash. Another thing to look for: In many fields, you'll see what look like large brown circles of intertwined sticks neatly placed on the ground. What you're looking at is a vineyard. Santorinians twist the grape vines into wreaths that encircle the grapes and protect them from the island's fierce winds.

At the south end of the island, on the road to Perissa, is the handsome old village of **Emborio.** The town was fortified in the 17th century, and you can see its towers, a graceful marble statue of the muse Polyhymnia in the cemetery, and modern-day homes built into the ruins of the citadel.

Pyrgos, a village on a steep hill just above the island's port at Athinios, is a maze of narrow pathways, steps, chapels, and squares. Until the mid–19th century, this quiet hamlet hidden away behind the port was the island's capital. Near the summit of the village is the crumbling Venetian kastro, with sweeping views over the island. There is less tourism in Pyrgos than in many island villages, and the central square, just off the main road, has just about all the shops and cafes. Try the **Café Kastelli,** with tasty snacks, *glyka tou koutalou* (spoon sweets of preserved fruits), and fine views. If you want a sweet-and-sour treat, try the preserved *nerangi* (bitter orange).

In the hamlet of **Gonias Episkopi ★**, the Church of the Panagia is an astonishingly well-preserved 11th- to 12th-century Byzantine church. As is often the case, the builders pillaged classical buildings. You will see the many fragments they appropriated incorporated into the walls—and two ancient marble altars supporting columns. Among the frescoes, keep an eye out for the figure of a dancing Salome.

THE CALDERA ISLETS ★

These tantalizing **islands** in the caldera are part of the glory of Santorini's seascape, reminders of the larger island that existed before the volcano left today's crescent in the sea. Fortunately, you can visit the islands and get a view of Santorini from there.

Thirassia is a small, inhabited island west across the caldera from Santorini; a clifftop village of the same name faces the caldera, and is a relatively quiet retreat from Santorini's summer crowds. You can reach the village from the caldera side only by a long flight of steep steps. (Travelers once had to get to Fira and Oia the same way.) Full-day **boat excursions** departing daily from the port of Fira (accessible by cable car, donkey, or on foot) make brief stops at Thirassia, just long enough for you to have a quick lunch in the village; the cost of the excursion—which includes Nea Kameni, Palea Kameni, and Ia—is about 50€ per person; check out www.santorini. com/sailing and www.santoriniyachting.com. Another option is local **caiques,** which make the trip in summer from Armeni, the port of Oia; ask for information at your hotel or at one of the Fira travel agents (see "Visitor Information," earlier in this chapter).

The two smoldering dark islands in the middle of the caldera are **Palea Kameni (Old Burnt),** the smaller and more distant one, which appeared in A.D. 157; and **Nea Kameni (New Burnt),** which began to appear sometime in the early 18th century. The day excursion to Thirassia (a far more enjoyable destination) often includes these two (unfortunately often litter-strewn) volcanic isles.

Outdoor Pursuits

BEACHES   Santorini's beaches may not be the best in the Cyclades, but the volcanic black and red sand here is unique in these isles—and gets very hot, very fast. **Kamari,** a little over halfway down the east coast, has the largest beach on the island. It's also the most developed, lined by hotels, restaurants, shops, and clubs. In fact, Kamari is now so overrun with tour groups that I no longer recommend the string of hotels there. The natural setting is excellent, at the foot of cliffs rising precipitously toward ancient Thira, but the black-pebbled beach becomes unpleasantly crowded in July and August. **Volcano Diving Center** (✆ 22860/33-177; www.scubagreece. com) at Kamari, offers guided snorkel swims for around 25€ and scuba lessons from around 60€. **Perissa,** to the south, is another increasingly crowded beach resort, albeit one with beautiful black sand. The **Santorini Dive Center,** at Perissa, also has scuba and snorkel facilities and instruction (✆ 22860/83-190; www.divecenter. gr). **Red Beach (Paralia Kokkini),** at the end of the road to ancient Akrotiri, gets its name from its small red volcanic pebbles; it is—but for how long?—usually less crowded than Kamari and Perissa. All three beaches have umbrellas and chairs to rent, cafes, and tavernas.

BICYCLING   Santorini's roads are in fairly good condition; it's the drivers you need to worry about. Local drivers know the roads with their eyes shut (and sometimes seem to drive that way), and visitors study maps as they drive. That said, you can rent high-quality suspension mountain bikes from 15€ per day from **Moto Chris** (✆ 22860/ 23-431), in Fira, and **Moto Piazza** (✆ 22860/71-055), in Oia. It's always a good idea to check the brakes and steering before you set off.

WALKING   If it's not too hot when you are here, there are a great many walks you can enjoy. Here are a few.

o **Fira to Oia ★★**   The path from **Fira** to **Oia** (10km/6 miles) follows the edge of the caldera, passes several churches, and climbs two substantial hills along the way. Beginning at Fira, take the pedestrian path on the caldera rim, climbing past the Catholic Cathedral to the villages of Firostephani and Imerovigli. In Imerovigli, signs on the path point the way to Oia; you'll be okay so long as you continue north, eventually reaching a dirt path along the caldera rim that parallels the vehicular road. The trail leaves the vicinity of the road with each of the next two ascents, returning to the road in the valleys. The descent into Oia eventually leads to the main pedestrian street in town. Allow yourself at least 2 hours. If you end up at Oia around sunset, you'll feel that every minute of the walk was worth it.

- **Imerovigli & Skaros ★★**   In **Imerovigli,** a rocky promontory jutting into the sea is known locally as **Skaros.** From medieval times until the early 1800s, this absurdly small spot was home to the island's administrative offices. There is little to be seen of the Skaros castle now; it probably collapsed during a 19th-century earthquake. Skaros's fantastic view of the caldera is especially nice at sunset. Getting out on the promontory takes just enough effort that it is usually a tranquil haven from the crowds and bustle of the adjacent towns. The trail (signposted) descends steeply to the isthmus connecting Skaros with the mainland. The path wraps around the promontory after 1.6km (1 mile), reaching a small chapel with a panoramic view of the caldera. On the way, note the cliffs of glassy black volcanic rock, beautifully reflecting the brilliant sunlight. People used this rock to decorate many of the older buildings in Santorini.
- **Kamari to Ancient Thira ★**   The trail from Kamari to the site of **ancient Thira** is steep but doable. It passes the beautiful site of Santorini's only freshwater spring, which you will wish to drink dry. To reach the trail head from Kamari, take the road (in the direction of ancient Thira) past the Kamari beach parking, and turn right into the driveway of the hotel opposite Hotel Annetta, to the right of a minimarket. The trail begins behind the hotel. Climbing quickly by means of sharp switchbacks, the trail soon reaches a small chapel with a terrace and olive trees at the mouth of a cave. You can walk into the cave, which echoes with purling water, a surprising and miraculous sound in this arid place. Continuing upward, the trail rejoins the car road after a few more switchbacks, about 300m (984 ft.) from ancient Thira. The full ascent from Kamari takes a good hour.

Shopping

If you're interested in fine **jewelry,** keep in mind that many prices in Fira are higher than in Athens, but the selection here is fantastic. Santorini's best-known jeweler, with lovely reproductions of ancient baubles, is probably **Kostas Antoniou** (✆ 22860/22-633), on Ayiou Ioannou, north of the cable-car station. **Porphyra** (✆ 22860/22-981), in the Fabrica Shopping Center, near the cathedral, also has impressive work. As signaled by its name, the **Bead Shop** (✆ 22860/25-176), by the Archaeological Museum, sells beads. What makes them special is that most are carved from island lava. And there are plenty of shops between the two. Generally, the farther north you go, the higher the prices and the less certain the quality. In Firostephani, **Cava Sigalas Argiris** (✆ 22860/22-802) stocks all the local **wines,** including their own. Also for sale are locally grown and **prepared foods,** often served as *mezedes: fava,* a spread made with chickpeas; *tomatahia,* small pickled tomatoes; and *kapari* (capers). The main street in Oia, facing the caldera, has many interesting stores, several with prints showing local scenes, in addition to the inevitable souvenir shops. **Replica** (✆ 22860/71-916) is a source of contemporary statuary and pottery as well as museum replicas; it will ship purchases to your home at post office rates. Farther south on the main street is **Nakis** (✆ 22860/71-813), which specializes in amber jewelry and, not surprisingly, has a collection of insects in amber.

Where to Stay

The best advice we can offer is to avoid visiting during the months of July and August. Santorini experiences an even greater transformation during the peak season than other Cycladic isles. With visitors far in excess of the island's capacity, trash collects in the squares, and crowds make strolling the streets of Fira and Oia next to impossible. *Tip:* Some accommodations rates can be marked down by as much as 50% if you come off-season. Virtually all accommodations are marked up by at least as much for desperate arrivals without reservations in July and August.

The summer of 2011 was not a good one for tourism in the Cyclades. Consequently, many hotels did not raise their prices. The minute that things improve, prices will go up, so be especially sure to double-check prices when you make your trip.

As noted, Santorini is stuffed to the gills with visitors in July and August; try to make a reservation with a deposit at least 2 months in advance. We also hear tales of hotels more than doubling the price on remaining rooms. Except in July and August, don't accept lodging offered at the port unless you're exhausted and don't care how meager the room is and how remote your lodging is from what you want to see when you wake up the next morning. That said, in July and August, be grateful for whatever you get if you show up without a reservation.

The island's unusual **cave houses** have inspired many hotel designers. Barrel-vaulted ceilings and perhaps even a bathroom carved into the rock distinguish a typical **cave house.** Built for earthquake resistance and economy, some of the spaces may at first strike you as cramped; like most newcomers, you'll soon see them as part of the island's special charm. The best of them are designed with high ceilings, airy rooms, and good cross-ventilation, and because they are carved into the cliff face, they remain relatively cool throughout the summer.

Many apartments and villas have efficiency kitchens, but the facilities may be minimal. If you plan to do much cooking, check first to see what's in the drawers and cupboards, or you may find yourself frustrated if you try to prepare anything more elaborate than a cup of coffee.

If you are after the best of the best in hotels, look at www.santoriniluxuryhotels. com; keep in mind that it is usual for hotels to pay a fee to be listed in these services.

FIRA

In addition to the choices below, we continue to get good reports on the long-popular and usually quiet 25-room **Hotel Atlantis** (© **22860/22-232;** www.atlantishotel. gr), where guests can spend the sunset hours with a bottle of wine on the balcony overlooking the caldera. The tony eight-unit **Enigma Apartments** (www.enigma hotel.com) appeared in *Odyssey* magazine's "Best Hotels of 2009." Furnishings are elegantly simple; the views of the caldera and sunsets are spectacular. The Enigma is the sister hotel of another long-time entry in *Odyssey*'s best hotels list:

A perfect Santorini vacation would be divided between these two hotels: Enigma, in the island capital, and **ASTRA Suites,** in Imerovigli, one of Santorini's most perfect villages. For a (much) more modest place, consider **Loizos Apartments** (www. loizos.gr); no caldera view, but a quiet Fira location and helpful owners.

Note: Due to the noise throughout Fira, you may want to consider staying in one of the villages out on the island, unless you stay in one of the quieter hotels we suggest.

Aigialos ★★   In a quiet caldera location, occupying 16 restored 18th- and 19th-century town houses, the Aigialos proclaims its intention to be a "Luxury Traditional Settlement." The oxymoron aside—rather few traditional settlements here or elsewhere have had Jacuzzis, swimming pools, and counter-swim exercise pools—this is a nifty place. The units have all the modern conveniences and all the creature comforts. As the price goes up, you get more space (two bathrooms, not just one) and more privacy. Some units have their own garden and/or balcony, veranda, or terrace, while others share a garden, a veranda, or a terrace. There's an extensive breakfast buffet and an in-house, guests-only restaurant.

Fira, 84700 Santorini. www.aigialos.gr. ☏ **2860/25-191.** 16 units. 400€–550€ double; 800€–1,300€ honeymoon suite. Rates include breakfast. AE, DC, MC, V. Closed Nov–Mar. **Amenities:** Pool bar; pool; room service. *In room:* A/C, TV, fridge, hair dryer, Wi-Fi.

Hotel Aressana ★★   This hotel (popular with Greek and foreign honeymooners) compensates for its lack of a caldera view with a large swimming pool and excellent location—tucked away behind the Orthodox Cathedral, in a relatively quiet setting. Most rooms have balconies or terraces; many have the high barrel-vaulted ceilings typical of this island. Unusual in Greece are the nonsmoking rooms. The breakfast room opens onto the pool terrace, as do most of the guest rooms; the elaborate buffet breakfast includes numerous Santorinian specialties. The Aressana also maintains seven nearby apartments facing the caldera, starting at 250€, which includes use of the hotel pool.

Fira, 84700 Santorini. www.aressana.gr. ☏ **2860/23-900.** Fax 22860/23-902. 50 units, 1 with shower. 275€–350€ double; 350€–405€ suite. Rates include full breakfast. AE, DC, MC, V. Closed mid-Nov to Feb. **Amenities:** Snack bar; bar; freshwater pool; room service. *In room:* A/C, TV, hair dryer, minibar.

Hotel Keti ★★ ⬧   This simple little hotel offers one of the best bargains on the caldera. All of the (smallish) rooms have traditional vaulted ceilings, white walls, and beds with coverlets, and open onto a shared terrace overlooking the caldera. The bathrooms, at the back of the rooms, are carved into the cliff face. Clearly, the Keti is doing something right: Not many places this modest make it into Alastair Sawday's *Special Places*. One drawback, if you have trouble walking: It's a steep 5- to 10-minute walk from the Keti's quiet cliffside location to Fira itself.

Fira, 84700 Santorini. www.hotelketi.gr. ☏ **2860/22-324.** 7 units. 100€–150€ double. No credit cards. Closed Nov to mid-Mar. **Amenities:** Breakfast room; bar. *In room:* A/C, TV, fridge.

FIROSTEPHANI

This quieter and often less expensive neighborhood is just a 10-minute walk from Fira. The views of the caldera are just as good, if not better.

Tsitouras Collection ★   This is one of those places where, if you have to ask what a room costs, you probably can't afford to stay there. This top-of-the-line luxury hotel will either dazzle or dismay you. Understatement is conspicuous by its absence here, where antiques and reproductions jostle for space in five themed villas (including "House of Portraits" and "House of Porcelain"). The villa you stay in (decorated with art from the private collection of artist and mogul Demitris Tsitouras) is all yours, which ensures blissful privacy. Some spa services are available. Guests are encouraged to meet with the chef to discuss "constructing" a meal; a very expansive breakfast (and free copy of the *International Herald Tribune*) is included in the room price. We've had almost as many thumbs down for the indifferent service as we have had raves for the serious luxury and quiet location.

Firostefani, 84700 Santorini. www.tsitouras.gr. ☏ **2860/23-747.** Fax 22860/23-918. 5 villas (for 4 or more). 1-bedroom villa 500€–850€; 6-person villa 3,500€. MC, V. **Amenities:** Restaurant; cafe. *In room:* A/C, TV/CD/DVD, wet bar, hair dryer, kitchenette, Wi-Fi.

IMEROVIGLI

The next village north along the caldera rim is so named because it is the first place on the island from which you can see the rising sun. The name translates as "day vigil." By virtue of its height, Imerovigli also has the best views on this part of the caldera.

While everyone else is jostling for a place to see the sunset at Oia, head to Imerovigli and take the path over to the promontory of Skaros, with the picturesque remains of its medieval kastro. Amazingly, this deserted and isolated spot was the island's medieval capital. It's a blissful place to watch the sunset.

Imerovigli and Oia have a considerable number of attractive and comfortable places to stay. In addition to the places listed below, you might want to consider **La Maltese** (✆ **22860/24-701;** www.lamaltese.com), a member of Relais & Châteaux, in a restored sea captain's neoclassical mansion, now fitted out with indoor and outdoor pools, *hamam* and sauna, restaurant and piano bar, and, of course, that caldera view.

ASTRA Suites ★★★   The 27-suite ASTRA is very special; although it looked perfect to me, ASTRA was completely renovated in 2010–11. Perched on a cliff, with spectacular views, this is one of the nicest places to stay in all of Greece. There are other places nearby that also have spectacular pools with spectacular views, but manager George Karayiannis is a large part of what makes ASTRA so special: He is always at the ready to arrange car rentals, recommend a wonderful beach or restaurant—or even help you plan your wedding and honeymoon here. The ASTRA Suites look like a tiny, whitewashed village (with elegant pools) set in the village of Imerovigli, which is still much less crowded than Fira or Oia. Nothing is flashy here; everything is just right. The vibrant blue of the bed coverlets is echoed in the blue paint on the cupboards. Although each unit has its own kitchenette, breakfast can be served on your private terrace or balcony, and you can order delicious salads and sandwiches from the bar day and night. There are spa services (massage, sauna, and Jacuzzi) and a Greek-Mediterranean full-service restaurant that emphasizes local cuisine.

Imerovigli, 84700 Santorini. www.astrasuites.com. ✆ **22860/23-641.** Fax 22860/24-765. 27 suites, 1 villa. 280€–800€ suite; villa from 1,500€. MC, V. **Amenities:** Bar; restaurant; pool; spa services. *In room:* A/C, TV/CD/DVD, hair dryer, kitchenette, radio, Wi-Fi.

Chromata ★★   Along with Katikies (see below), this is one of a small group of luxury hotels (www.katikies.com) on Santorini. Here you'll get a wonderful view out over the island, an inviting pool, and excellent service. The lovely rooms sport comfortable, stylish chairs and hand-loomed rugs. If it weren't that George Karayiannis makes its neighbor, ASTRA, so special, Chromata would be the place to stay. If ASTRA is full, you'll be happy here. Some of the suites have small, private plunge pools.

Imerovigli, 84700 Santorini. www.chromata-santorini.com. ✆ **22860/24-850.** 17 units. 200€–300€ double; 500€–800€ suite. AE, MC, V. **Amenities:** Bar; restaurant; Internet; pool. *In room:* A/C, TV, hair dryer, minibar.

KARTERADOS

About 2km (1¼ miles) southeast of Fira, this small village knows the tourist ropes, and has many new hotels and rooms to let. Buses stop at the top of Karterados's main street on their ways to Kamari, Perissa, and Akrotiri. Nevertheless, the location is somewhat inconvenient, not especially close to Fira or to the beach. Karterados beach is a 3km (2-mile) walk from the center of town. Get to Monolithos, a longer beach, by continuing south along the water's edge an additional half-mile.

Pension George ★ 🍴   With a small pool, simple wood furnishings, attractive and reasonably priced rooms, and helpful owners, the pension offers good value if you're on a budget. To save even more money, opt for a room without a balcony. If you want more space, ask about their five new apartments at Karterados beach. George Halaris and his English wife, Helen, will help you arrange car and boat rentals.

P.O. Box 324, Karterados, 84700 Santorini. www.pensiongeorge.com. ⓒ **22860/22-351.** 25 units. 60€–90€ double. No credit cards. **Amenities:** Breakfast on request; free transportation to airport or harbor. *In room:* A/C, TV (in some), fridge.

OIA

Oia's chic shops (check out **the Art Gallery** and **Art Gallery Oia** on Oia's meandering main drag), boutique hotels, and gorgeous sunsets make it an increasingly popular place to stay or to visit—especially for travelers who find Fira too frenetic.

If you're running low on reading material by the time you get to Santorini, head to **Atlantis Books** (ⓒ **22860/72-346;** www.atlantisbooks.org) in Oia, run by a group of expat Brits and Americans as well as several Greeks. You'll find everything from guidebooks and detective novels for the beach to poetry and philosophy.

Chelidonia ★ Chelidonia (the Greek name for the swallows that you'll see here) is a carefully restored and reconstructed slice of Oia that was destroyed in the 1956 earthquake. Most units are former homes, each with its unique layout—another unit was a bakery, yet another a stable. Rooms are large, the bathrooms luxuriously large, and the interiors simple, but elegant. Skylights illuminate many rooms from above. Most have truly private terraces, many with small gardens of flowering plants and herbs. All units enjoy the famous Oia view across the caldera toward Imerovigli, Fira, and the southern end of the island. If you want room service, this is not the place for you, but there is daily maid service. There's usually a 3-night minimum for stays.

Ia, 84702 Santorini. www.chelidonia.com. ⓒ **22860/71-287.** Fax 22860/71-649. 10 units. 185€ studio; 260 suite; 290€ villa. No credit cards. *In room:* A/C, TV, kitchenette.

Finikia Place 🍴 This small, appealing hotel has a number of rooms with the domed ceilings traditional to Santorini architecture. Some rooms boast local weavings and artifacts. Most units have semiprivate balconies or terraces with views toward the sea—the hotel is on the east slope of the island, so the view is gentle rather than spectacular. The pool is good size and the restaurant/bar is open almost all day. Irene and Theodoris Andreadis are helpful and friendly hosts. They have adjacent apartments for rent as well.

Finikia, 84702 Santorini. www.finikiaplace.com. ⓒ **22860/71-373** or 210/654-7944 in winter. Fax 22860/71-118. 15 units. From 100€ double. Rates include breakfast. MC, V. Closed Nov–Mar. **Amenities:** Restaurant; bar; pool; Wi-Fi. *In room:* A/C, minibar.

Katikies ★★ Along with Chromata (see above), this is one of a small group of luxury hotels in Oia (www.katikies.com). If you find a more spectacular pool anywhere on the island, let us know. The main pool—one of four here—runs almost to the side of the caldera. You'll enjoy a world-class view. Katikies began as a small hotel, then added suites (some with their own plunge pools), and now has a seven-unit villa (with, of course, its own pool). The hotel's island-style architecture incorporates twists and turns, secluded patios, beamed ceilings, and antiques. If the people in the next room like to sing in the shower, you might hear them, but most people who stay here treasure the tranquillity. After all, this is a member of the Small Luxury Hotels of the World. The top-of-the-line honeymoon suite has its own Jacuzzi, just in case you can't be bothered going to either outdoor pool. The new White Cave restaurant has only a handful of tables, so be sure to book ahead. Or head to one of Katikies' three other restaurants. A masseur is on call at the small spa on-site.

Oia, 84702 Santorini. www.katikies.com. ⓒ **22860/71-401.** Fax 22860/71-129. 22 units. 540€ double; 610€–1,650€ suite. Rates include breakfast. MC, V. **Amenities:** 4 restaurants; bar; concierge; currency exchange; health club and spa; library; 4 pools; Wi-Fi. *In room:* A/C, TV, hair dryer, minibar, Wi-Fi.

Perivolas Traditional Settlement ★★ You could be forgiven for thinking that this is a pool with a nice little hotel (with seriously splashy bathrooms) attached: The *Condé Nast Traveler* cover photo of Perivolas's pool meeting the edge of the sky and the lip of the caldera put this place on the jet-setters' map. The 17 houses that make up the hotel offer studios and junior and superior suites. Price differences reflect the sizes of the three categories; each unit has a kitchenette and a terrace. The superior suites have a separate bedroom, whereas the other units are open plan. The architecture—wall niches, skylights, stonework—and some of the furnishings of these greatly enhanced cave dwellings are traditional. Everything is elegant—including the in-house library. The only downside: Few units have terraces with significant degrees of privacy, but that is true of almost every Santorini hotel—and certainly true of genuine traditional village settlements.

Ia, 84702 Santorini. www.perivolas.gr. © **22860/71-308.** Fax 22860/71-309. 19 units. 520€ studio; 620€–950€ suite; 1,500€–2,000€ villa. Rates include buffet breakfast. No credit cards. Closed mid-Oct to mid-Apr. **Amenities:** Cafe; bar; pool. *In room:* A/C, TV, hair dryer, kitchen.

MEGALOHORI

Villa Vedema Hotel ★★ The sleepy village of Megalohori is not where you'd expect to find a luxury hotel, but Santorini is full of surprises. The hotel is a self-contained world, surrounded by a wall like a fortified town. A member of the Small Luxury Hotels of the World group, the Vedema is justly proud of its attentive but unobtrusive service. The residences are set around several irregular courtyards, much like those found in a village. Each apartment is comfortable, with sink-into-them chairs and at least one huge marble bathroom. The restaurant is excellent, and the candlelit wine bar is located in a 300-year-old wine cellar. The principal disadvantage of a stay here is the location: Megalohori is not a particularly convenient base for exploring the island. But with this amount of luxury, you may not want to budge.

Megalohori, 84700 Santorini. www.vedema.gr. © **22860/81-796** or 22860/81-797. 45 units. 500€–750€ double/suite; from 1,000€–3,600€ villa. Minimum 3-night stay. AE, DC, MC, V. Closed mid-Oct to mid-Apr. **Amenities:** Restaurant; bar; concierge; pool; room service. *In room:* A/C, TV/CD/DVD, hair dryer, minibar, Wi-Fi.

PYRGOS

Zannos Melathron ★★ The relatively uncrowded village of Pyrgos sits inland between Megalohori and Kamari. This 12-room boutique hotel, on one of the highest points on the island, occupies two adjacent former private mansions, one dating from the 18th century and one built in the early 19th century. Both are handsome and handsomely restored. The rooms mix antiques with modern pieces, the island views are lovely, the pool is welcoming, and some rooms have Jacuzzis. If you want nightlife, this is not the place for you; if you want a peaceful retreat and near-perfect service in—not outside—a village, this may be just the spot. If you want a cigar bar, look no further. Something to consider: In 2011, most rooms here were available only for stays of 3 nights or more. One big plus of staying here: the island's best restaurant, Selene (see below), moved to Pyrgos in 2011.

Pyrgos, 84700 Santorini. www.zannos.gr. © **22860/28-220.** 12 units. 250€–550€ double; 550€–1,000€ suite. MC, V required to make reservation; payment is cash only. **Amenities:** Restaurant; bar; airport pickup; concierge; Jacuzzi; pool; room service. *In room:* A/C, TV, hair dryer, minibar, Wi-Fi.

Where to Eat

FIRA

First, if you are coming here to eat at the island's best restaurant, Selene, you should know that in 2010, Selene moved to the village of Pyrgos (see below). Second, as you might expect, restaurants in Fira range from blah to beatific. The bad ones stint on quality and service because they know that most tourists are here today and gone tomorrow. The good places cater to the discriminating tourist and to Greek and foreign visitors who come back again and again.

If all you want is breakfast or a fast cheap meal, try **Corner Crepes,** just off the main square (no phone). The popular taverna **Camille Stefani** (✆ 22860/28-938), long in Kamari, is now in Fira, at the Fabrica shopping center. With a caldera view, **Lithos** (✆ 22860/23-203; www.lithossantorini.com) turns out good *spitiko* (home-style) cooking at moderate prices.

Note: Many of the restaurants on the caldera and near the cable car fall into the forgettable category. In addition, some of these restaurants have been known to present menus without prices, and then charge exorbitantly for food and wine. If you are given a menu, make sure prices are listed.

Koukoumavlos ★★ GREEK The terrace at Koukoumavlos enjoys the famous caldera view, but unlike most caldera restaurants where a spectacular view compensates for mediocre food, here the view is a distraction from the inventive, even idiosyncratic, menu. Two examples: the grilled foie gras with raisin paste and ouzo jelly, and the lobster and monkfish terrine with anchovy-caviar sour cream in a forest-fruit tea sauce. In short, you are likely to be either titillated or terrified by the combination of ingredients in most dishes. You'll definitely remember the food, and probably find the prices equally memorable (salads start at around 20€). Despite the lofty character of the cuisine, the staff is usually both helpful and attentive.

Below the Hotel Atlantis, facing the caldera. (✆ **22860/23-807.** www.koukoumavlos.eu. Reservations recommended for dinner. Main courses 25€ and up. AE, MC, V. Daily noon–3pm and 7:30pm–midnight.

Taverna Nikolas ★ 🍴 GREEK This is another one of the few restaurants in Fira where locals and tourists both turn up regularly—high praise, for a place that has been here forever. There aren't any surprises; you'll get traditional Greek dishes prepared very well. The lamb with greens in egg-lemon sauce is particularly tasty. The dining room is always busy, so arrive early or plan to wait.

Just up from the main square in Fira. No phone. Main courses 12€–15€. No credit cards. Daily noon–midnight.

OIA

If you want to be by the sea, head down to **Ammoudi,** Oia's port, hundreds of feet below the village, huddled between the cliffs and the sea. We recommend **Katina's** fish taverna there (see below). If you don't want to trek all the way down to the beach, stop along the way at **Kastro** (✆ 22860/71-045), where you'll still have a fine view and can enjoy Greek dishes, pasta, or fresh fish. To get there, follow the stepped path down from the vicinity of Lontza Castle, hire a donkey (5€), or call a taxi. We recommend the walk down (to build an appetite) and a taxi or donkey up.

8

Katina's ★★ SEAFOOD   Fresh fish, grilled by the sea—what more could one ask for? Well, for one thing, a taxi back up the hill when it's time to leave. Just ask your waiter and a taxi will appear.

Ammoudi. ✆ **22860/71-280.** Fish priced by the kilo. No credit cards. Daily 10am–midnight (usually).

Restaurant-Bar 1800 ★★ MEDITERRANEAN   For many years recognized as the best place in Oia for a formal dinner, the 1800 has a devoted following among visitors and locals. Many items are Greek dishes with a difference, such as the tender lamb chops with green applesauce, and the cheese pie, filled not just with feta, but with five cheeses. The restaurant, housed in a splendidly restored 19th-century neo-classical captain's mansion, has undeniable romantic charm whether you eat indoors or on the amazing rooftop terrace. After you eat, you can decide whether the owner (an architect and chef) deserves more praise for his skill with the decor or with the cuisine. "Each plate resembles a canvas," this restaurant proclaims.

Odos Nikolaos Nomikos. ✆ **22860/71-485.** www.oia-1800.com. Main courses 18€–35€. AE, DC, MC, V. Daily 8pm–midnight.

Skala ★ 🍴 GREEK   Skala has perfectly fine taverna food, at prices that are less steep than those at many other places here. All the staples of traditional Greek (if not local Santorini) food are reliably good; the management is helpful and friendly. Veggies are not overcooked, as so often happens in Greece, and the grills and stews are tasty. If you've never tried rabbit stew *(stifado kouneli),* but are curious, this is a good place to see whether you agree that rabbit tastes a lot like, well, chicken.

Odos Nikolaos Nomikos. ✆ **22860/71-362.** Main courses 9€–20€. MC. Daily 1pm–midnight.

PYRGOS

Selene ★★★ GREEK   If you eat only one meal on Santorini, eat it here. This is the best restaurant on Santorini—and one of the best in Greece. Selene was in Fira from 1986 to 1910, when it moved to Pyrgos to continue to delight guests with what owner George Haziyannakis calls the "creative nature of Greek cuisine." The appetizers, often including a delicious sea urchin salad on artichokes and fluffy fava balls with caper sauce, are deservedly famous. Entrees include *brodero* (seafood stew). The baked mackerel with caper leaves and tomato wrapped in a crepe of fava beans will convert even the most dedicated meat eaters. The local lamb, quail, rabbit, and beef are all excellent. In short, everything—beautiful surroundings, perfect ambience, and service—comes together to form the best imaginable setting for the delicious, inventive, but never coy food. And, if you want something a little more casual and less expensive, you can have an equally great meal at Selene's bistro-cafe-patisserie-wine bar.

Pyrgos. ✆ **22860/22-249.** Fax 22860/24-395. www.selene.gr. Reservations recommended. Main courses at restaurant 17€–30€. Snacks/drinks at the bistro from 6€; main courses from 12€. MC, V. Restaurant open daily 7–11:30pm, early Apr to late Oct; bistro open daily noon–11pm, early Mar to late Oct.

Santorini After Dark

The height of the tourist season is also the height of the music season in Santorini. If you are here in July, you may want to take in the annual Santorini Jazz Festival (www.jazzfestival.gr), which has been bringing international jazz bands and artists here every summer since 1997. Many performances are on Kamari beach. In August and September, the 2-week **Santorini International Music Festival** (✆ **22860/23-166**), with international singers and musicians, gives performances of classical music at the Nomikos Centre, in Fira. Admission to most events starts at 15€.

If you want to kick off your evening with a drink on the caldera as you watch the spectacular sunset, **Franco's** and **Tropical** (both on Marinatou St.) are still the most famous spots for this magic hour; be prepared to pay 15€ and up (and up) for a drink. **Kira Thira** and **Koo** (two of the wall-to-wall places on Stavrou St.) pack people in later in the day (and through the night). If you are willing to forego the caldera view, you'll find almost too many spots to sample along the main drag and around the main square, including the inevitable Irish pub, **Murphy's. Kirathira Bar** plays jazz at a level that permits conversation, and the nearby **Art Café** offers muted music. And don't forget that the island's best restaurant, **Selene,** now in Pyrgos, has its own cafe bar for a quiet drink and snack.

Discos come and go, and you need only follow your ears to find them. **Koo** (see above), with at least five different bars, is the biggest; **Tithora** is popular with a young, heavy-drinking crowd. There's usually no cover, but the cheapest drinks at most places are at least 10€.

Out on the island, in Oia, **Zorba's** is a popular cliffside pub. The fine **Restaurant-Bar 1800** (see above) is a quiet and sophisticated place to stop in for a drink—and certainly for a meal.

Kamari Beach has lots of disco bars, including **Disco Dom, Mango's, Yellow Donkey,** and **Valentino's,** all popular with the youngish tour groupers who grope about here.

FOLEGANDROS ★★

181km (98 nautical miles) SE of Piraeus

Tell people that you're off to Folegandros and you're likely to get one of two reactions: quizzical expressions from those who have not been here and envious glances from those who know the island. Folegandros has one of the most perfect capitals in the islands: More village than town, Hora huddles at the edge of cliffs some 250m (820 ft.) above the sea. As with so many Cycladic towns, this one was built far inland, to make it almost invisible to marauding pirates. The town has a series of interlocked plateias (squares), whose streets are made of green and blue paving slates outlined in brilliant white. As you prowl the streets, you'll gradually realize that much of Hora is built into the walls of the kastro, a medieval castle. Small houses with steep front staircases and overhanging wooden balconies weighed with pots of geraniums line the narrow lanes.

As for the main port, **Karavostasi:** If you didn't know about Hora and the island's beguiling interior landscape, you could be forgiven for continuing to the next port of call and not getting off here. Karavostasi means "ferry stop," and the name really just about sums up all there is to say about this desultory little port; although, in recent years, a sprinkling of cafes and jewelry shops began to offer visitors a chance to shop and have an espresso. Still, Karovostasi has little of architectural interest and few of the energetic charms of most Cycladic ports.

If you want to explore Folegandros, you can do a good deal by local bus, but if you like to walk, this is a great place for it. Even if you rent a car, you'll have to leave it from time to time—no cars are allowed in Hora and several other villages—and continue on foot. The island's paved roads are still fairly minimal and there is still an elaborate—and, as yet, unasphalted for cars—network of foot and donkey paths over beautiful terraced hillsides. Look closely and you'll see that some of these paths are paved with ancient marble blocks; others are hacked from the natural bedrock. Hills are crisscrossed with the stone walls that enclose the terraced fields that allow local farmers to grow barley on the island's steep slopes. Rocky coves shelter some appealing pebble beaches (best reached by caique). Try to allow at least a day and a night on Folegandros—and don't be surprised if you decide to stay a lot longer. *Tip:* There's no bank here, and the ATM in Hora is not always reliable, so you may want to bring some extra cash. That said, hotels and the travel agencies will change money for you.

Essentials

GETTING THERE By Boat   Three ferries a week stop at Folegandros on the Santorini-Folegandros-Sikinos-Ios-Naxos-Paros-Piraeus route; it's about 10 hours from Piraeus to Folegandros. Information is available at the **Piraeus Port Authority** (© **210/451-1311,** or 210/451-1440 or -1441), which seldom answers the phone. Boats are notoriously late and/or early; your travel or ticket agent will give you an *estimate* of times involved in the following journeys. Several ferries per week stop on the Folegandros-Milos-Sifnos-Paros-Mykonos-Tinos-Siros hydrofoil run. During the off-season, infrequent service and bad weather can easily keep you here longer than you intend. **Folegandros Port Police** are at © **22860/41-530.** For ferry schedules, check out **www.openseas.gr** or **www.gtp.gr**.

VISITOR INFORMATION   Maraki Travel Agency (© **22860/41-273;** maraki@syr.forthnet.gr) and **Sottovento Travel** (© **22860/41-444;** www.sottovento. eu) exchange money, help with travel arrangements, sell maps of the island, and offer Internet facilities. Sottovento also serves as the local Italian consulate and its owner Flavio Facciolo runs the tasty Café del Viaggiatori in Hora, with Italian-style snacks and great espresso.

GETTING AROUND By Bus   The bus (© **22860/41-425**) to Hora meets all ferries in peak season and most ferries during the rest of the year; it also makes eight or nine trips a day on the road running along the island's spine between Hora and Ano Meria at the island's northern end. The fare is 2€.

By Moped Jimmy's Motorcycle (© **22860/41-448**), in Karavostassi, and **Moto Rent** (© **22860/41-316**), in Hora, near Sottovento Travel, both rent mopeds. As always, check the brakes before you head off.

By Boat   Mid-June through August, boat taxis or caiques provide transport to the island's southern beaches. From Karavostassi, boats depart for Katergo and Angali (10€ round-trip); another boat departs from Angali for Ayios Nikolaos, Livadaki, and Ambeli (10€ round-trip). There is also a 7-hour tour of the island's beaches that departs from Karavostassi at least three times weekly in summer, and makes stops at five beaches; the cost is 30€ per person, including lunch. Reservations can be made at Diaplous or Sottovento Travel (see above); note that tickets must be purchased a day in advance.

By Taxi   If you don't find a taxi at the port or in Hora, dial © **22890/22-400** or 22860/41-048.

FAST FACTS   Folegandros has neither bank nor ATM, but you can exchange money at travel agents and hotels. Commissions on money exchange can be steep, because you are something of a captive audience here. It may be wise to arrive with enough cash for your visit. The **post office** and **telephone office (OTE)** are right off the central square in Hora, open Monday through Friday from 8am to 3pm. The **police station** (© **22860/41-222**) is behind the post office and OTE.

What to See & Do

Unless you are determined to be by the sea, you probably won't want to linger in **Karavostassi,** perhaps the least enticing port in the Cyclades. Best to hop on a local bus and chug the 4km (2½ miles) up to Hora.

Cliffside **Hora ★★** is centered on five closely connected squares, connected by meandering streets, lined with houses, restaurants, and shops. Even from the bus-stop square, the sheer drop of the cliff offers an awesome sight. On the right in the next square, you'll find **the Kastro:** two narrow pedestrian streets connected by tunnel-like walkways, squeezed between the town and the sea cliffs, within the remaining walls of the Hora's medieval castle. One majestic church, **Kimisis The-otokou,** dominates the skyline of Hora. It's particularly beautiful at night, when it's illuminated. Built at the highest point in town—and with fine views over the island—the church stands on the foundations of the ancient Greek town. If you walk up here even once, your admiration for the ancient Folegandrians who lived here and did the walk up and down to their fields daily will soar. Today, townspeople parade through the village with the church's icon of the Virgin, with great ceremony, each Easter Sunday. The other church to see here is the deserted **Monastery of the Panagia,** north of town, also with lovely views.

OUT ON THE ISLAND

As you rush from island to island, checking in and out of hotels, it's not always easy to feel the rhythm of island life. One great way to do that is to visit Folegandros's small **Folk Museum,** in Ano Meria. If you want to see some countryside, head west from Hora to the village of **Ano Meria.** This tiny hamlet of scattered farms is the island's second-largest village. Some of the tools and household items on view in the museum have been used for generations, and you can see some still in use today. The museum (no phone; free admission, but donation appreciated) is open 5 to 8pm weeknights in July and August, and the local bus can drop you a pleasant stroll away. If the museum is closed, console yourself that this, too, is an insight into the rhythms of island life.

BEACHES

You can swim at the port of Karavostasi, or get a caique (10€ round-trip) from there to the island's best beach, **Katergo ★**, which is protected from the sometimes fierce winds here by rocky headlands. You can also get by caique to **Angali,** the largest and most crowded fine-sand beach on the island. There are a few tavernas on the beach and rooms to let.

WALKING

The footpaths through the northern part of the island, for the most part, are well used and easy to follow. Numerous paths branch off to the southwest from the paved road through Ano Meria; the hills traversed by these trails, between the road and the sea, are particularly beautiful. Here's one walk you may enjoy; if you want to try more walks, check with someone at the Sottovento Travel agency for tips. There may even be a walker's map by the time you visit.

Ayios Andreas to Ayios Yeoryios. An easy path leads you from **Ayios Andreas** to the bay at **Ayios Yeoryios.** Take the bus to the next-to-last stop, at the northern end of Ano Meria; it will let you off by the church of Ayios Andreas. At the stop, the sign AG. GEORGIOS 1.5, points to the right. Follow the sign, and continue along a road that quickly becomes a path and descends steeply toward the bay. Follow the main path at each of several intersections; you'll be able to see the bay for the last 20 minutes of the walk. You'll find a small pebble beach at the bay of Ayios Yeoryios, but no fresh water, so be sure to bring plenty. Allow 2 hours for the round-trip.

Where to Stay

For some time there have been two special places to stay here: **Anemomilos Apartments** and the **Castro Hotel.** The Castro was closed for renovations during the 2011 season, but promises to be back better than ever in 2012. Since 2006, the 32-room **Chora Resort** (📞 **22860/415-90;** www.choraresort.com), with spa facilities, a 500-sq.-m. (5,382 sq. ft.) pool, and its own restaurant, has offered sybaritic pleasures and attractive package deals. If you want simpler accommodations, the 11-room **Meltemi Hotel** (📞 **22860/41-425;** www.greekhotel.com), across from Anemomilos, is a good buy, with decent rooms, but no view or pool. The island's limited facilities are always fully booked in July and August, when advance reservations are essential; other times, reservations are recommended here. If you want to stay by the sea, the **Aeolos Beach Hotel** (📞 **22860/41-205**), just outside Karavostassi, is across the road from the beach and has simple but perfectly acceptable studios (minifridge) from 85€ to 120€ double in high season.

Anemomilos Apartments ★★   This congenial place began to turn up on lists of the "best island retreats" soon after it opened in 1998—and made *Odyssey* magazine's best-of-the-year list again in 2007. Spectacularly situated at the edge of a cliff overlooking the sea, all but two of the units here have terraces; all units have either a full or partial sea view. A well-stocked kitchenette means you can actually cook here. If you don't want to make your own breakfast, Cornelia Patelis, who manages the hotel with her husband, Dimitris, makes a delicious sweet breakfast pie with local cheese. The hotel also serves breakfast and snacks throughout the day on the pool terrace. One apartment is accessible for travelers with disabilities. Transport to and from the port, arranged by the hotel, costs about 5€ per person one-way.

Hora, 84011 Folegandros. www.anemomilosapartments.com. 📞 **22860/41-309.** 22 units. 160€–240€ double. Breakfast 15€. V. Closed mid-Oct to Easter. Near the central bus stop. **Amenities:** Breakfast room/bar; pool. *In room:* A/C, TV, hair dryer, kitchenette, Wi-Fi.

Castro Hotel ★   The Castro was closed for renovations at press time, so I cannot speak to what precisely you will find when this charming small hotel reopens in 2012. It will certainly still have its wonderful location, in a Venetian castle dating from 1212; it's the oldest part of Hora, wedged against the cliffs and facing the Aegean 250m (820 ft.) below. I assume that the guest rooms will still be small, but even more comfortable than before. Seven rooms have phenomenal views. Even if you do not get a room with a balcony and view, you can enjoy the view from the shared rooftop terrace. The charming Mrs. Danassi, whose family has owned this house for five generations, will make you feel at home. And her homemade fig jam gets high praise.

Hora, 84011 Folegandros. www.hotel-castro.com. 📞 **22860/41-230** or 210/778-1658 in Athens. Fax 22860/41-230 or 210/778-1658 in Athens. 12 units. Rates for 2012 not available at press time; call for post-renovation rates. AE, V. Closed Nov–Apr.

Where to Eat

Main courses for all the restaurants listed run about 8€ to 20€; hours are generally from 9am to 3pm and 6pm to midnight.

The local specialty, *matsata,* is made with fresh pasta and rabbit or chicken. The best place to sample it is **Mimi's,** in Ano Meria (*✆* **22860/41-377**), where the pasta is made on the premises. Look for two other restaurants in Ano Meria: **Sinandisi** (*✆* **22860/41-208**), also known as Maria's, which has good *matsata* and swordfish (take the bus to the Ayios Andreas stop); and **Barbakosta** (*✆* **22860/41-436**), a tiny room that serves triple duty as bar, taverna, and minimarket (the bus stop has no name, so ask the driver to alert you).

Hora has a number of tavernas, whose tables spill onto and partially fill the central squares. At the bus-stop square, **Pounda** (*✆* **22860/41-063**) serves a delicious breakfast of crepes, omelets, yogurt, or coffeecake; lunch and dinner, including veg-etarian dishes, are also available. **Silk** (*✆* **22860/41-515**), on the *piatsa* (third) square, offers delicious variations on taverna fare, including numerous vegetarian options. **Piatsa** (*✆* **22860/41-274**), also on the third square, is a simple taverna with tasty food. **O Kritikos** (*✆* **22860/41-219**) is another local favorite, known for its grilled chicken. After dinner, if you want some nightlife, you'll find some bars and discos sprouting on the outskirts of the Kastro; **Greco Café Bar, Kolpo, Aquarius,** and **Ba-Raki** were popular in recent years.

SIFNOS ★★

172km (93 nautical miles) SE of Piraeus

Just about everyone thinks that Sifnos is the most beautiful of the western Cyclades. This island has long been a favorite of Greeks, especially Athenians; but now, in sum-mer, it is an all-too-popular destination for European tourists. August here can be more than hectic, with rooms hard to find, cars impossible to rent, and the village buses sardine-can full.

The mountains that frame Sifnos's deep harbor, Kamares, are barren, but once you've left the port, you will see elegantly ornamented dovecotes above cool green hollows, old (no one really knows just how old) fortified monasteries, and watchtowers that stand astride the summits of arid hills. The beautiful slate and marble paths across the island are miracles of care, although an increasing number are now covered over with concrete and asphalt to accommodate motorcycles and cars. Nonetheless, Sifnos is a hiker's—even a stroller's—delight and astonishingly green, not only in spring but well into the summer. In addition, beaches along the southern coast offer long stretches of fine amber sand; several smaller rocky coves are also excellent for swimming.

Sifnos is small enough that any town can be used as a base for touring; the most beautiful are the **seven settlements** spread across the central hills—notably Apol-lonia (sometimes called Stavri) and Artemonas—and Kastro, a small medieval forti-fied town atop a rocky pinnacle on the eastern shore. Buses now run from Cheronissos in the north to Vathi in the south, and the bus, combined with some walking, will take you to the island's top attractions: the ancient acropolis at **Ayios Andreas,** the town of **Kastro** and its tiny but excellent **archaeological museum,** the southern **beaches,** the once-isolated beaches at **Vathi** and **Cheronisso,** and, for the ambitious, the walled **Monastery of Profitis Elias** on the summit of the island's highest mountain. Brown and gold signs in Greek and English now mark most places of archaeological and historical interest.

In Greece, Sifnos has long been famous for its ceramics, although fewer and fewer locals work as potters and fewer still use local clay. Some of the island's best potters are in Kamares and Platis Yialos. Sifnos is also famous for its olive oil and sophisticated cooking; in fact, "Tselementes," a slang term for a cookbook, is a tribute to the famous 20th-century Siphmian chef and cookbook writer Nikos Tselementes.

Essentials

GETTING THERE   By Boat   Weather permitting, there are at least four boats daily from Piraeus, including car ferries and HighSpeeds and SeaJets, some of which do and some of which do not take cars. Check ferry schedules with a travel agency, or with the **Piraeus Port Authority** (℗ **210/451-1311,** -1440, or -1441; phone not always answered) or **Sifnos Port Authority** (℗ **22840/33-617**). Ferries travel on ever-changing schedules to other islands, including **Serifos, Kimolos Milos, Tinos, Paros,** and **Kithnos.** Boats are notoriously late and/or early; your travel or ticket agent will give you an estimate of times involved in above journeys. For ferry schedules, check out **www.openseas.gr** or **www.gtp.gr**.

Tip: If you have time to kill waiting for your boat, have a seat by the **Poseidonas** cafe, where an ouzo and *mezedes* were a stunningly reasonable 2€ in 2011.

VISITOR INFORMATION   The best place on the island for information and help getting a hotel room, boat tickets, car, or motorbike (and arranging hiking excursions) is **Aegean Thesaurus Travel and Tourism ★★**, with offices at the port (℗ **22840/ 32-152;** www.thesaurus.gr) and on the main square in Apollonia (℗ **22840/33-152**). Aegean Thesaurus handles tickets for all hydrofoils and ferries. Check at either office to get the helpful information packet on Sifnos for 2€. Just off the main square in Apollonia, **Xidis Travel** (℗ **22840/32-373;** www.xidis.com.gr) is another good travel agent.

GETTING AROUND   By Bus   Apollonia's central square, **Plateia Iroon** (which locals simply call the **Plateia** or **Stavri**), is the main bus stop for the island. Buses run regularly to and from the port at Kamares, north to Artemonas and Cheronisso, east to Kastro, and south to Faros, Platis Yialos, and Vathi. Pick up a schedule at Aegean Thesaurus Travel (see "Visitor Information," above).

By Car & Moped   Many visitors come to Sifnos for the wonderful hiking and mountain trails, but still want the convenience of a car or motorcycle. Reliable agencies include **Aegean Thesaurus** (℗ **22840/33-151**), in Apollonia and **Proto Moto Car** (℗ **22840/33-792;** www.protomotocar.gr), with a quay-side office in Kamares and offices in Apollonia and Plati Yialos. In high season, you should reserve ahead. As always, exercise caution if you decide to rent a car or moped; many drivers, like you, will be unfamiliar with the island roads. The daily rate for an economy car with full insurance is from 30€; a moped rents from 20€.

By Taxi   Apollonia's main square is the island's primary taxi stand. There are about 10 taxis on the island, each privately owned, so you'll have to get their **mobile phone numbers** available at travel agents. Most hotels, restaurants, and shops will call a taxi for you; offer to pay for the call.

FAST FACTS   Visitor services are centered in or just off the main square in Apollonia. This is where you will find the **National Bank** (℗ **22840/31-317**), with an ATM; the **post office** (℗ **22840/31-329**); the **telephone office (OTE);** and the **police** (℗ **22840/31-210**), For **medical emergencies,** call ℗ **22840/31-315.** The municipal website **www.sifnos.gr** is useful.

What to See & Do

In antiquity, Sifnos was a very wealthy island, thanks to its gold deposits. If you've been to Delphi, you'll have seen the sculpture from the impressive Treasury the Siphnians build there. When the island was an important center of shipping, pottery, and trade in the 19th century, wealthy Sifnians built the handsome houses you'll see across the island. After World War II, when shipping dried up, the island had some very lean years. Now, Sifnos's fortunes follow the fortunes of Greek tourism, although the island seems to have enough year-round Greek visitors to ward off more seriously lean years.

The capital town of the island, **Apollonia ★** (also called Hora and Stavri) is the name given jointly to the **seven settlements** on these lovely interior hills. It's 5km (3 miles) inland from Kamares; a local bus makes the trip hourly (from about 6am–midnight) every day in summer. The town's central square is the transportation hub of the island. All vehicle roads converge here, and this is where you'll find the bus stop and taxi stand. The small **Popular and Folk Art Museum** (great old photographs) cunningly does not post its hours, but is often open July 1 to September 15 from 10am to 1pm and 6 to 10pm (admission is 2€). From the square, pedestrian paths of flagstone and marble—lined with boutiques, restaurants, and cafes—wind upward through the beautiful town. If you stumble upon the Church of the Panagia, keep an eye out for the carving of St. George besting the dragon, over the door, and the ancient marble column in the courtyard. The column was probably looted from a temple dedicated to Apollo, after whom Apollonia was named. As you go up and up the stepped-stone streets, once you get past the enormous Cathedral, you'll find yourself in residential neighborhoods, with small courtyards, some with enormous caper and rose bushes. This is a great place to wander, admire the perfect whitewashed sugar-cube houses, get a bit lost, and hope you end up at the wonderful **Gerontopoulos** pastry shop for a restorative espresso and some sweet, dense chocolate pudding.

Tip: If you rent a car and have trouble finding a parking place in Apollonia—and you almost certainly will—head down the hill toward Kamares and turn right into the large municipal parking lot just out of Apollonia. From the parking lot, avoid walking up the main road by taking the side street that runs back up hill into the Main Square.

Kastro ★★ is one of the best-preserved medieval towns in the Cyclades, built on the dramatic site of an ancient acropolis. Until several decades ago, Kastro was almost entirely deserted; as tourists began to infiltrate the island, Kastro sprouted cafes, restaurants, and shops. The 2km (1¼-mile) walk from Apollonia is easy, except under the midday sun. Start out on the footpath that passes under the main road in front of Hotel Anthoussa, and continue through the tiny village of Kato Petali, finishing the walk into Kastro on a paved road, or the marked footpath. Whitewashed houses, some well preserved and others eroding, adjoin one another in a defensive ring abutting a sheer cliff. Venetian coats of arms are still visible above doorways of older houses. Within the maze of streets are a few tavernas and some beautiful rooms to let. The little **Archaeological Museum** (© **22840/31-022**) here has a good collection of pottery and sculpture found on the island; it's often open Tuesday through Saturday from 9am to 2pm, Sunday and holidays from 10am to 2pm. Admission is free.

Artemonas ★, about 2km (1¼ miles) north of Apollonia, is a small village with streets lined with very handsome 19th-century mansions built by wealthy Siphnian ship owners. The walk here from Apollonia in not-too-hot weather is lovely; if you drive, there is a good-sized parking lot just as you come into town. When you get to

Artemonas, you can have some homemade almond sweets (amygdalia) at any of the excellent local sweet shops.

About 2km (1¼ miles) south of Apollonia, on the road to Vathi, is a trail leading to the hilltop church of **Ayios Andreas.** Until recently, this was an excursion to make simply for the amazing, almost 360-degree view of Sifnos and neighboring islands. Since 2011, there has been another reason to visit here: the excavations of an **ancient acropolis,** and its excellent small site museum. Broad stone steps begin a long climb to the summit; count on at least 20 vigorous minutes to make the ascent. Having done this excursion previously on foot and on donkey back, I am happy to say that when I visited in 2011, I drove on the new road right up to the summit. People have lived on this spot from perhaps the 13th century B.C. until at least the 4th century B.C. The site was protected by massive defense walls that once stood some 6m (20 ft.) high and still reach more than 3.5m (12 ft.) in height. The walls encircled the settlement, with its sanctuary of Artemis, and small houses. Standing on the summit on a lovely early summer day it is hard to imagine how miserable life must have been here when winter winds whipped across the site and people huddled in their tiny, dark, cold dwellings. From the site, you can see the remains of some of Sifnos's more than 80 ancient stone towers that were used for defense and for communication: Bonfires could flash messages quickly across the island from tower to tower. All this and more is explained in the excellent museum, where everything is labeled both in Greek and English. The site and museum are usually open Tuesday through Sunday 8:30am to 3pm; entrance was free in 2011, but a fee is to be expected soon.

The pottery on display in the museum is a reminder that pottery-making flourished on Sifnos well into the 1980s. Now only a handful of potteries remain. The distinctive brown-and-blue glazed Sifnian pottery still being made has become something of a collector's item. If you fall for a piece, buy it—with more potteries closing down, you can't be sure you'll find this distinctive ware again. (See "Shopping," below.)

BEACHES

Sifnos has several really good beaches. You can reach many of them by caique shuttle services from Kamares; Aegean Thesarus Travel in Apollonia or Kamares can let you know the schedules. Not surprisingly, **Plati Yialos,** the island's longest sand beach, is easy to reach by taxi or public transportation. There are plenty of tavernas and cafes along the crescent sand beach where you can have a bite. (You can also hike from Platis Yialos to the Panagia tou Vounou monastery; see "Walking," below.) Not surprisingly, Plati Yialos—which boasts that it is the longest beach in the Cyclades—can be crowded in summer. If you have time, you may want to explore some of the island's other beaches. Here are some suggestions.

From Platis Yialos, it's a half-hour walk east through the olive groves and intoxicating oregano and thyme patches over the hill to **Panagia Chrissopiyi,** a double-vaulted whitewashed church on a tiny island. There's good swimming at **Apokofto,** a cove with a long sand beach and several shade trees just beyond the monastery, where rocky headlands protect swimmers from rough water. **Pharos** and **Fasolou,** two other east-coast beaches (reachable from Platis Yialos on foot by the resolute), are easier to get to by taking the bus from Apollonia. The excellent **Dimitris taverna** (© 22840/71-493) is by the sea at Fasolou.

Until 1997, the beach at **Vathi**—one of the best on the island—was accessible only on foot or by boat, but there's now a road and regular bus service. Sifnos's first posh resort, **Elies,** opened here in 2005. The beach does not have the dense development of the port of Kamares and Platis Yialos, but there's every sign that it may yet. Of the several tavernas here, my friends with houses on Sifnos praise **To Livada** (© 22840/ 71-123). I couldn't agree more: great salads, grills, stews, and a pleasantly cool spot to sit, just off the beach, surrounded by trees. The beach at **Cheronisso,** at the island's northern end, is a spectacular spot to watch the sun go down.

WALKING

More and more asphalt roads are appearing on Sifnos to accommodate wheeled vehicles, but you'll still be able to do lots of your walking on the island's distinctive flagstone and marble paths. You'll probably see village women whitewashing the edges of the paving stones, transforming the monochrome paths into elaborate abstract patterns. Throughout the island, you'll find dovecotes, windmills, and small white chapels in amazingly remote spots.

One wonderful walk on the island leads west from **Apollonia to Profitis Elias,** passing through a valley of extraordinary beauty to the summit of the island's highest mountain (wraparound amazing views). A short detour lets you also take in the church and ruined monastery at Skafis. Pick up a walking map at one of the local travel agencies. The 12th-century walled monastery of Profitis Elias is a formidable citadel, its interior courtyard lined with the monks' cells. The lovely chapel has a fine marble iconostasis. Continue straight where the summit path branches right and walk through the next intersection. You'll soon reach the church of Skafis, situated within the ruins of an old monastery and overlooking a small valley shaded by olive trees. Look for the remains of paintings on the walls of the ruined monastery, in what must have been a tiny chapel. Allow about 4 hours for the round-trip to Profitis Elias, with an additional half-hour for the detour to Skafis.

From Plati Yialos (see "Beaches," above), you can hike to the **Panagia tou Vounou** by following a paved road that leads off the main road to Plati Yialos; although the monastery (which has fine views over the island) is signposted, it is best to have a good island map. The church is usually unlocked in the morning, locked in the afternoons.

SHOPPING

Famed in antiquity first for its riches, then for its ceramics, Sifnos still produces some wonderful brown glaze pottery with minimalist white decorative swirls. As you criss-cross the island, you'll see signs advertising pottery workshops, although the clusters of potters in Plati Yialos are, alas, gone. **Simos and John Apostolidis** (© 22840/71-258) are among the few potters who still have a ceramics workshop in Plati Yialos. In Kamares, **Antonis Kalogerou** (© 22840/31-651) sells folk paintings of island life and the typical pottery of Sifnos, which is manufactured in his showroom from the deep gray or red clay mined in the inland hill region. In Apollonia, Kastro, and Artemona a number of shops sell pottery, much of which is from neighboring Paros, not Sifnos. You can spot the Parian pottery by its bright colors, shiny glazes, and scenes of fruit, flowers, and island life. For those in search of distinctive jewelry rather than ceramics, Spyros Koralis's **Ble** (© 22840/33-055), in Apollonia, does innovative work in silver and gold. I counted 20 jewelry shops in one short stroll recently in Apollonia, so you should find something you like here.

Where to Stay

If you feel like a little serious indulgence, check out the top-of-the-line **Elies Resort** (© 22840/34-000; www.eliesresorts.com), which opened in 2005 on a hillside stretching down to the beach in Vathi. Elies immediately won and has kept a place in *Odyssey* magazine's annual feature on the 50 best hotels in Greece. The glistening white (inside and out) resort, shaded by olive trees (*elies* is Greek for olive trees), is designed to look like a traditional Cycladic village—albeit a village with tennis courts, villas with private pools, and a spa offering aromatherapy and massage. Doubles begin at 340€, suites at 550€, and villas at 950€. You may also want to check out the **Verina Complex** (www.verina.gr), whose holdings, in addition to the Hotel Petali (see below), include the Verina Suites, at Plati Yialos; the Verina Astra Suites, in the village of Poulati; and a villa at Vathy. Keep in mind that many Sifnian hotels insist on a stay of more than one night in high season.

APOLLONIA

Apollonia is the most central place to use as a base on Sifnos. Buses depart from the central square to most island towns, and stone-paved paths lead to neighboring villages. Keep in mind that many Athenians vacation on Sifnos, particularly on summer weekends, when it can be virtually impossible to find a room, car, or, unless you start early, even a meal. If you plan to be here during the high season, be sure to make reservations by May. If you're here during off season, many hotels are closed.

With advance notice, the efficient **Aegean Thesaurus Travel** (see "Visitor Information," above) can usually place you in a rented room with your own bathroom, in a studio with kitchenette, or in other, more stylish accommodations. A simple double in a place with no view can cost 100€ in high season.

Hotel Anthoussa   This hotel is above the excellent and popular Yerontopoulos cafe and patisserie (free Internet service), on the main road around Apollonia, less than a 5-minute walk from the main square. That sounds convenient, and is, but although streetside rooms offer wonderful views over the hills, they overlook both a main road and the late-night sweet-tooth crowd in the cafe/patisserie. In truth, it is usually very noisy here at night. Back rooms are somewhat quieter and overlook a beautiful bower of bougainvillea. In short, the location is the problem for an otherwise appealing place.

Apollonia, 84003 Sifnos. ℂ **22840/31-431.** 13 units. 90€ double. MC, V. **Amenities:** Breakfast room. *In room:* A/C, TV.

Hotel Petali ★★   Here's a quiet hotel with great views not far—but all uphill—from Apollonia's main square. The Petali is on a largely pedestrianized side street, with lovely distant views of the sea beyond the town's many houses. After a day's sightseeing, it's especially nice to enjoy those views from the Petali's pool or poolside terrace. Each guest room has a large terrace, handsome and comfortable chairs, good beds, and modern bathrooms. A small restaurant serves delicious Sifnian specialties. Although the Hotel Petali does not accept credit cards, its managing office, **Aegean Thesaurus Travel Agency** (ℂ **22840/32-152;** www.thesaurus.gr), accepts MasterCard and Visa. Like many island hotels, the Petali insists on a stay of at least 4 nights in high season.

Apollonia, 84003 Sifnos. www.hotelpetali.gr. ℂ/fax **22840/33-024.** 11 units. 200€ double. No credit cards (see listing for details). **Amenities:** Restaurant; bar; Internet; Jacuzzi; pool; sauna. *In room:* A/C, TV, hair dryer.

Hotel Sifnos ★★   The hospitable owners here have tried hard to make their hotel reflect island taste, using local pottery and weavings in the smallish but cheerful rooms. The hotel restaurant (see "Where to Eat," below) offers good basic meals beneath a broad arbor; it's just as popular with locals as it is with travelers and hotel guests. The excellent restaurant makes this a good place to stay if you don't want to search out a place for dinner; like almost everything in town, traffic and pedestrian noise can be a problem here.

Apollonia, 84003 Sifnos. ✆ **22840/31-624.** 9 units. 90€ double. AE, MC, V. **Amenities:** Restaurant; bar. *In room:* A/C, TV.

ARTEMONA

There are several small hotels and rooms to rent in Artemona. Although the 25-room **Hotel Artemon** (✆ **22840/31-303;** www.hotel-artemon.com) is just outside the village on the main road from Apollonia to Artemona, the road is usually not horribly noisy at night. The rooms (simple, but just fine) at the back overlook a garden, all rooms have balconies, there's a very good restaurant, and the owners get high praise from the many guests who come back year after year. The Artemon is open year-round; doubles start at 80€; and the fixed-price dinner is 17€.

KASTRO

Aris Rafeletos Apartments   These traditional rooms and apartments are distributed throughout the medieval town of Kastro. Most have exposed ceiling beams, stone ceilings and floors, and the long narrow rooms typical of this fortified village. The two smallest units are somewhat dark and can be musty, but the three apartments are spacious and charming. All apartments have kitchenettes and terraces; three have splendid sea views. The largest apartment is on two levels and can comfortably sleep four. If the antiquity and charm of this hilltop medieval village appeals to you, and you don't want hotel service but a chance to experience village life, then these accommodations may be the perfect base for your exploration of the island.

Kastro. ✆/fax **22840/31-161.** 6 units. 85€–180€ apts. No credit cards. The rental office is at the village's north end, about 50m (164 ft.) past the Archaeological Museum. **Amenities:** Breakfast room/bar. *In room:* Kitchenette in some units.

KAMARES

The port of Kamares has the greatest concentration of hotels and pensions on the island, but unfortunately, it has little of the beauty of Sifnos's traditional villages. You can swim here, but the water is not as clean as at the island's less commercial beaches. Two moderately priced hotels are the 14-unit harborside **Hotel Stavros** (doubles from 80€) and the 18-unit **Hotel Kamari** (doubles from 60€), a 10-minute walk from the beach and harbor. Information is available on both, from Stavros and Sarah Kalogirou (✆ **22840/33-383;** www.sifnostravel.com). This helpful couple (Sarah is English) also has a car-rental agency and the very attractive **Elonas** apartments to rent in Apollonia (units sleeping up to five, from 125€). They also run the YaMas Internet Cafe Bar, in Kamares.

Hotel Boulis   This hotel, capably managed by two more members of the Kalogirou family, Lyn and Antonis, is right on the port's beach—you'll see it from the ferry as you approach Kamares. The large, carpeted rooms have balconies or patios, most with beach views; all have fridges and ceiling fans. The hotel has a spacious, cool, marble-floored reception area and a sunny breakfast room.

Kamares, 84003 Sifnos. www.hotelboulis.gr. ✆ **22840/32-122.** 45 units. 100€–130€ double. Rates include breakfast. AE. Closed Oct–Apr. Follow the main street 300m (984 ft.) from the ferry pier, turning left opposite the Boulis Taverna (operated by the same family). The hotel is on your left. **Amenities:** Breakfast room/bar. *In room:* Fridge.

PLATIS YIALOS

A busy beach resort on the island's south coast, Plati Yialos serves as a convenient base, especially if you are traveling with children. (I speak from happy experience at the Hotel Platis Yialos.) The town exists for tourism during high season. If Hotel Platis Yialos is full, there are lots of other choices, including the attractive beachside 20-room **Hotel Efrosini** (𝄐 **22840/71-353;** www.hotel-efrosini.gr), popular with Greek families, or the stylish **Verina** (𝄐 **22840/71-525;** www.verina.gr), across from the beach, but with a lovely garden and big pool.

Akti Hotel Platis Yialos ★★ ☺   The island's oldest and most family-friendly beach hotel—completely renovated in 2010–11—overlooks the beach on the west side of the cove, set apart from the rest of the town's densely populated beach strip. The hotel's location, on an excellent sand beach that slopes gently into the sea, is an ideal location if you are traveling with young children—or, for that matter, on your own. Originally a government-owned Xenia hotel, its design follows the usual Xenia rectangle motel-like format, but the public rooms are now very bright and attractive, as are the guest rooms. The ground-floor guest rooms, with patios facing the garden and water, are especially desirable if you are traveling with children; rooms on the upper stories have balconies and better sea views. There are also two suites, one with its own Jacuzzi. Works of art by local artists are displayed throughout the hotel. The Platis Yialos's flagstone sun deck extends from the beach to a dive platform at the end of the cove. A bar and restaurant share the same Aegean views.

Platis Yialos, 84003 Sifnos. www.platys-gialos.gr. 𝄐 **22840/71-324** or 28310/22-626 in winter. 23 units. 100€–180€ double; from 270€ small suite, from 320€ large suite. Rates include breakfast. No credit cards. Closed Oct–Mar. **Amenities:** Restaurant; bar. *In room:* A/C, hair dryer, Wi-Fi.

Where to Eat

APOLLONIA

If you want a sweet, head for the wonderful **Gerontopoulos Pastry Shop** (𝄐 **22840/32-220**) in the Hotel Anthousa. I can vouch for their cookies, cakes, ice creams, and preserved fruits. Oh, yes, and the chocolate pudding is divine. For a snack, try **Veranda** or **Sifnos Café-Restaurant** (no phones). Both serve breakfasts and sweets all day—and, along with many other places, have the island specialty of *revithia* (chickpeas) most Sundays. **Okyalos** (𝄐 **22840/32-650**), on Apollonia's main drag, succeeds in its aim of serving "Mediterranean gourmet cuisine." The food is beautifully displayed on the plate and very tasty, with lots of local touches (local cheese on the salad, fresh herbs galore).

Sunset (To Troullaki) ★ GREEK   This is a good place to go at sunset or any other time. About 8km (5 miles) out of Apollonia in a peaceful setting by the road to Cheronisso, this family-run taverna serves delicious island food. The sunsets here are spectacular. Much of the meat and vegetables is organic. The *Mastello,* melt-in-the-mouth lamb on vine leaves, is slowly baked in an earthenware pot (local, of course).

Apollonia. 𝄐 **22840/31-970.** Main courses 7€–15€. No credit cards. Lunch and dinner most days.

ARTEMONAS & ENVIRONS

There are a number of sweet shops and cafes in Artemonas. On the main plateia, **Margarita's** (𝄐 **22840-32-058**) is open virtually all day and has snacks, salads, and light meals. The Hotel Artemon's restaurant **Lambessis** (𝄐 **22830/31-303**), just outside Artenonas on the road to Apollonia, gets high praise from locals and visitors.

A Baker's Dozen & Then Some

As you travel around Sifnos, you'll notice a lot of bakeries (a bakery is called a *furno* in Greece) and sweet shops. According to local lore, long ago a baker named Benios (pronounced Venios) had a baker's dozen of children—and almost all the children and their children's children and successive generations of the Benios family became bakers. That's why many bakeries in Sifnos to this day are owned by one or another member of the Benios family. Many families and some restaurants send their *revithia* (chickpeas) in a Siphnian clay pot to a Benios bakery to be slow-cooked overnight for the traditional Sunday dinner.

Chrysso ★★ GREEK   Once you get to Artemonas, follow the small white signs with the blue arrow pointing on to "Chrysso." You'll pass neoclassical mansions and be sure you're lost in the lanes at least once until you come to the wide terrace with the wonderful view. Better yet, the food is delicious: tender *paidakia* (lamb chops) grilled on charcoal, hearty stews, luscious salads. Maria the owner and cook does a wonderful job and most of my friends with homes on Sifnos say that this is their favorite place, both for the ambience and view, and for the food.

Apollonia. ✆ **22840/31-322.** Main courses 8€–12€. No credit cards. Lunch and dinner most days. Sometimes closed in winter.

To Liotrivi (Manganas) ★ GREEK   We're still mentioning To Liotrivi because it has been an island favorite for a long time. Unfortunately, recent reports from readers and friends suggest that this place is resting far too heavily on its laurels. It was one of the first restaurants on the island to have a varied and inventive menu.

Artemona. ✆ **22840/31-246.** Main courses 8€–10€. No credit cards. Daily noon–midnight. From Apollonia, follow the pedestrian street north from the main plateia, past Mama Mia and Hotel Petali; the walk takes a pleasant 10–15 min.

KAMARES

Boulis Taverna ★ GREEK   With an unexceptional location at the top of the town's busy main street, this isn't the place to go for a romantic evening, but it does offer some very good food. The taverna is operated by Andonis Kalogirou, of Hotel Boulis, who uses vegetables, cheeses, and meats raised on the family's organic farm. The walls of the vast interior room are lined with wooden wine casks. Outside, lamb, chicken, and steak cook on the grill.

At the top of the main street through town. ✆ **22840/31-648.** Main courses 7€–15€. No credit cards. Daily 11am–1am.

Kapitain Andreas ★ SEAFOOD   This place, with its sometimes gruff host, Andreas, who is both proprietor and fisherman, serves good food and grills.

On the town beach. ✆ **22840/32-356.** Main courses 8€–15€; fish priced by the kilo. No credit cards. Daily 1–5pm and 7:30pm–12:30am.

Poseidonas (Sophia's) ★★ GREEK   The first restaurant you pass after disembarking the ferry is easily the best place to eat in Kamares: Sophia Patriarke and her daughters are hospitable to strangers and serve tasty grills, truly fresh salads, and fabulous *rivithokeftedes rena* (chickpea croquettes).

✆ **22840/32-362.** Fish priced by the kilo. No credit cards. Daily 1–5pm and 7pm–midnight.

8

THE CYCLADES

Sifnos

265

A Special Feast

Prophet Elijah's feast day (July 20–22) is one of the most important religious holidays on Sifnos, which has had a monastery dedicated to this saint for at least 800 years. The celebration begins with a mass outing to the monastery of Profitis Elias on the summit of the island's highest mountain, and continues through the night with dancing and feasting.

KASTRO

To Astro ★ GREEK   Simple food on a lovely shaded terrace with long views over the island on the outskirts of one of Sifnos's most charming villages.

© **22840/31-476.** Main courses 6€–10€. Most days from 10am–midnight.

PLATIS YIALOS

Sofia's (To Steki) ★★ GREEK   Platis Yialos's best restaurant for traditional Siphnian home cooking taverna fare is popular for its outdoor terrace with tamarik trees.

At the beach's east end. *©* **22840/71-202.** Main courses 8€–18€. No credit cards. Daily 8pm–1am.

Sifnos After Dark

The main street of Apollonia vibrates to the sound of music from virtually wall-to-wall bars all summer. Of these, the **Argo Bar** has been around for years; it plays European and American pop music with some Greek tunes thrown in.

In Kamares, there's another longtime survivor of the bar wars: the picturesque **Old Captain's Bar.** For classical music, the **Cultural Society of Sifnos** sometimes schedules summer concerts in Artemonas.

PAROS ★★

168km (91 nautical miles) SE of Piraeus

Paros is accurately (but hardly enticingly) known as the "transportation hub" of the Cyclades: Almost all island boats stop here en route to someplace else. As a result, Paros has suffered from the reputation of the place on the way to the place where you're going. At present, Paros is still cheaper than either Mykonos or Santorini—in fact, some call it the "poor man's Mykonos"—although rising prices are rapidly making that nickname anachronistic. Comparisons aside, Paros's good beaches and nightlife have made it a very popular destination in its own right. Because of the absence of any single five-star attraction—there's no antiquity here to rival Santorini's ancient Akrotiri and nothing to rival the beauty of Mykonos's perfect Cycladic architecture—a lot of visitors come here simply to have a good time, windsurfing, sunbathing, and partying.

Still others—not necessarily opposed to having a good time—are drawn back over and over again to Paros because of its other attractions. Admittedly, if you come by ship, your first impression after docking at the main port and capital **Parikia** will be of the kitsched-up windmill on the quay, travel agents, cafes, and the not terribly enticing fast-food joints lining the harborfront. Where, you'll wonder, is the town described as "charming"? Take a few steps inland, and you'll find it. **Parikia** has an energetic marketplace and the Ekatondapiliani, the 100-doored church designed in the 6th century by the famous architect Isodore of Miletus. Winding streets, the paving stones meticulously marked off with whitewash, lead off from the main square. One street meanders up and up, passing marble fountains and modest houses with elaborate door frames, to the remains of a medieval castle, largely built with chunks pillaged from various local ancient temples.

Somehow, Parikia manages to be both cozy and cosmopolitan. The town has a lively cultural life: The Archilochos Cultural Society stages a winter film festival and hosts a summer music festival (www.archilochos.gr). This is also the home of the Aegean Center for the Fine Arts, which has exhibitions and lectures, and offers several 3-month-long sessions in painting and literature each year (www.aegeancenter.org). Not surprisingly, there are lots of shops and galleries exhibiting and selling work by artists who spend all or part of the year here.

Out on the island, there's a scattering of appealing villages and two must-see spots: the hillside village of Lefkes, deep in the interior, and the picture-postcard seaside hamlet of Naoussa. Paros also has enough good beaches to keep almost any visitor happy.

Paros is large enough that even if you're just here for a day, renting a car makes sense. If you're here in May or June, you can make an around-the-island tour that includes a morning visit to **Petaloudes (Valley of the Butterflies),** a visit to Lefkes, a stop for a good lunch in Naoussa, a swim at your beach of choice, and a night back in Parikia, where you visit the wonderful Byzantine Ekatondapiliana Cathedral and then n shop and stroll the evening away. Other months, when the butterflies are not on Paros, you may want to spend more time visiting the cathedral, and taking in the nearby archaeological museum, combined with a boat trip from Parikia or Pounta to the little island of Andiparos.

Essentials

GETTING THERE **By Plane** **Olympic Air** offers daily flights between Athens and Paros, which also receives European charters. **Aegean Airlines** also has several flights daily between Athens and Paros. (For contact information for both, see "Essentials" under "Santorini," earlier in this chapter.) In Parikia, you can call ✆ **22840/21-900** for flight information, but you'll do much better to use a local travel agent. *Tip:* The website of Athens International Airport (www.aia.gr) is a useful resource for domestic airline schedules.

By Boat Paros has more connections with more ports than any other island in the Cyclades. The main port, Parikia, has connections at least once daily with Piraeus by ferry (5–6 hr.) and high-speed ferry (3–4 hr.). Confirm schedules with the Athens **GNTO** (✆ **210/327-1300** or 210/331-0562) or **Piraeus Port Authority**

Check Your Calendar

The Feast of the Dormition of the Virgin (Aug 15) is one of the most important religious holidays in Greece—and the most important, after Easter, in Paros. Pilgrims come here from throughout the Cyclades to attend services at the Panagia Ekatondapiliani, which is dedicated to the Virgin. If you come here then, make reservations well in advance, or you will probably find yourself sleeping rough. And, on the subject of dates: If you want to visit Paros to see its famous **butterflies,** remember that they come here in May and June.

(☎ **210/926-9111**). Boats are notoriously late and/or early; your travel or ticket agent will give you an *estimate* of times involved in the following journeys. Daily ferry and hydrofoil service links Parikia with Ios, Mykonos, Santorini, and Tinos. Several times a week, boats depart for Folegandros, Sifnos, and Siros. There are daily excursion tours from Parikia or Naoussa (the north-coast port) to Mykonos. The high-speed services usually take half as long and cost twice as much as the slower ferries. There's also overnight service to Ikaria and Samos several times a week. (From Samos you can often arrange a next-day excursion to Ephesus, Turkey.) In high season, there's hourly caique service to Andiparos from Parikia and Pounda, a small port 6km (4 miles) south of Parikia, with regular connection by bus. The east-coast port of Piso Livadi is the point of departure for travelers heading to the "Little Cyclades." Ferries depart four times weekly for Heraklia, Schinoussa, Koufonissi, and Katapola. For ferry schedules, check out **www.openseas.gr** or **www.gtp.gr**.

For general ferry and other travel information, try **Santorineos Travel** (☎ **22840/24-245**) or **Polos Tours** (☎ **22840/22-092**), both on the harbor in Parikia. The **port authority** can be reached at (☎ **22840/21-240**). Many agents around Mavroyenous Square and along the port sell ferry tickets; schedules are posted along the sidewalk.

VISITOR INFORMATION There is a **visitor information office** on Mavroyenous Square, just behind and to the right of the windmill at the end of the pier. This office is often closed, but there are numerous travel agencies on the seafront, including **Santorineos Travel** and **Polos Tours** (see above). The municipality information office in the Parikia town hall can be reached at ☎ **22840/22-078.** The island has a number of helpful websites, including **www.parosweb.com** and **www.paroslife. com**. The quarterly English-language magazine *Paros Life and Naxos Life* (2€), is very useful and has a good calendar of upcoming events.

GETTING AROUND **By Bus** The cunningly unmarked **bus office and main station** (☎ **22840/21-395**) in Parikia is on the waterfront, to the left as you face the windmill. There is often hourly service between Parikia and Naoussa, from 8am to midnight in high season. The other buses from Parikia run frequently, from 8am to 9pm, in two general directions: south to Aliki or Pounda, and southeast to the beaches at Piso Livadi, Chrissi Akti, and Drios, passing the Marathi Quarries and the town of Lefkes along the way. Schedules (not always up to date) are usually available at the Parikia bus office.

Warning: Buses on Paros usually have no visible indication of their destination; the place where you are let off in Naoussa, for example, is seldom the place you should be waiting to be picked up for the return trip. Try to get this useful information on which bus is yours and where you should be for your return trip from the bus office staff or bus driver. Be persistent.

By Car & Moped Paros is large enough that renting a car makes sense. There are many agencies along the waterfront, and except in July and August, you should be able to bargain. **Iria Cars and Bikes** (☎ **22840/21-232**), **Santorineos Travel** (☎ **22840/24-245**), and **Stefanos** (☎ **22840/21-521**) get praise from travelers. Expect to pay from 30€ per day for a car and from 15€ per day for a moped. Be sure to get full insurance and check the brakes.

By Taxi Taxis can be booked (☎ **22840/21-500**) or hailed at the windmill taxi stand. Taxi fare to Naoussa with luggage should run about 15€. Be sure to agree on a fare before you set out.

American Students Here?

The Aegean Center for the Fine Arts (www.aegeancenter.org) offers courses in painting, photography, music, creative writing, and other artistic endeavors, including two 3-month sessions. You'll see the mostly teen and 20-something students all over Parikia and out on the island.

FAST FACTS   There are several **banks** with ATMs in Parikia on Mavroyenous, the main Square, and one on the square in Naoussa; their hours are Monday through Thursday from 8am to 2pm, and Friday from 8am to 1:30pm. The private **Medical Center of Paros** (✆ 22840/24-410) is to the north of the pier, across from the post office; the public **Parikia Health Clinic** (✆ 22840/22-500) is on the central square, down the road from the Ekatondapiliani Cathedral. Much of Paros now has **Wi-Fi,** but **Internet access** is available on the Wired Network (www.parosweb.com) at eight locations around the island; you can buy a "smart card" that stores your personal settings and provides access at any of these locations for about 6€ per hour. The main wired network location—often noisy and crowded—is in Parikia, on Market Street (✆ 22840/22-003). **Cyber Cookies** (✆ 22840/21-610), the cafe just past the square with the ficus tree and Distrato Café, on the nameless street that runs from the cathedral into Market Street, is much nicer, with very helpful multilingual staff.

The **Laundry House** is on the *paralia* (shore road), near the post office (✆ 22840/24-898). For the Paraikia **police,** call ✆ 22840/23-333; in Naoussa, call ✆ 22840/51-202. The **post office** in Parikia (✆ 22840/21-236) is left of the windmill on the waterfront road, open Monday through Friday from 7:30am to 2pm, with extended hours in July and August. Parikia's **telephone office** (**OTE;** ✆ 22840/22-135) is just to the right of the windmill; it's usually open daily in summer from 7:30am to 2pm. (If the front door is closed, go around to the back, as wind direction determines which door is open.) A branch in Naoussa has similar hours. If you don't have your own phone, it is usually much easier to forget about the OTE office and make a phone call with a phone card, on sale at almost all kiosks.

What to See & Do

THE TOP ATTRACTIONS IN PARIKIA

Archaeological Museum   The museum's most valued holding is a fragment of the famous Parian Chronicle, an ancient chronology. The Ashmolean Museum at Oxford University has a larger portion of the chronicle, which is carved on Parian marble tablets. Why is this document so important? Because it lists dates for actual and mythical events from the time of Cecrops until about 260 B.C. Cecrops was the legendary first king of Athens, whose dates—indeed, existence—cannot be proven. Just to confuse and irritate historians, the chronicle gives information about artists, poets, and playwrights—but doesn't bother to mention many important political leaders or battles. The museum also contains a number of sculptural fragments as well as a splendid running Gorgon (with a delicate incised border on its skirt) and a Winged Victory from the 5th century B.C. There's also part of a marble monument with a frieze of Archilochus, the important 7th-century-B.C. lyric poet, known as the inventor of iambic meter and for his ironic detachment. ("What breaks me, young friend,

The Ancient Cemetery

If you face Parikia's harborside windmill and then turn and walk to your right, in about 15 minutes you will come to the ancient cemetery. If you want to go there from the Archaeological Museum, walk downhill to the sea, turn right, and you'll soon be there. Excavations at the cemetery since the 1980s have revealed much about the island's history between 11th century B.C. and the Roman period. Many of the graves contained the bones and weapons of warriors, often buried in handsome ceramic jars and marble urns, some of which are on view at the Archaeological Museum. The cemetery, which still has a number of marble tombs, is sometimes illuminated at night. If you want to have a drink or meal and contemplate mortality, try the excellent harborside Porphyra Seafood Restaurant (☏ **22840/23-410**), which overlooks the cemetery.

is tasteless desire, lifeless verse, boring dinners.") The courtyard has lots of marble monuments (and excellent toilet facilities).

Parikia. ☏ **22840/21-231**. Admission 3€. Tues–Sun 8:30am–3pm. Behind the cathedral, opposite the playing fields of the local school.

Panagia Ekatondapiliani Cathedral ★★ This is a magical spot. According to tradition, the Byzantine cathedral of Panagia Ekatondapiliani (Our Lady of a Hundred Doors) was founded by St. Helen, the mother of Constantine the Great, the emperor whose conversion to Christianity led to its establishment as the official religion of the Roman Empire. St. Helen is said to have stopped on Paros en route to the Holy Land, where the faithful believe that she found the True Cross. Fragments of the Cross are revered relics in many a church. Helen's son fulfilled her vow to found a church here, and successive emperors and rulers expanded it—which may in part explain the church's confusing layout, an inevitable result of centuries of renovations and expansions, which include the six side chapels. The work has not stopped: The cathedral was extensively restored in the 1960s, and the large square in front was expanded in 1996 for the church's 1,700th birthday.

The cathedral is hidden behind its high, thick wall, built to protect the shrine from pirates and other marauders. Cut into the wall are rows of monks' cells, some of which now house offices and a shop and ecclesiastical museum. After you step through the outer gate, the noise of the town vanishes, and you enter a garden with lemon trees and flowering shrubs. Ahead is the cathedral, its elegant arched facade a memento both of the Venetian period and of classical times (several of the columns were brought here from ancient temples).

Inside, the cathedral is surprisingly spacious. Almost every visitor instinctively looks up to the massive dome, supported on vaults ornamented with painted six-winged seraphim. Take time to find the handsome icons, including several set in the iconostasis (altar screen), side chapels, and an elegant little 4th-century baptistery, with a baptismal font in the shape of a cross. In the arcade, the museum contains a small but superb collection of 15th- to 19th-century icons, religious vestments, and beautiful objects used in Orthodox Church ceremonies. Everything is labeled in Greek and in English.

The small shop, also in the arcade, features religious books and memorabilia, as well as books on Paros. Panayotis Patellis's *Guide Through Ekatontapiliani* (4€) is both useful and charming. When you leave the cathedral precincts, turn left slightly uphill toward the Archaeological Museum for a fine view of the entire cathedral complex with its red-tile roofs.

Parikia. No admission fee for cathedral, although it is customary to leave a small offering. Daily 8am–8pm, but usually closed 2–5pm in winter. Museum ✆ **22840/21-243.** Admission 2€. Daily 10am–2pm and 6–9pm. On Parikia's central square, opposite and north of the ferry pier.

THE TOP ATTRACTIONS OUT ON THE ISLAND

Marathi Marble Quarries   The inland road to Lefkes and Marpissa will take you up the side of a mountain to the marble quarries at Marathi, source of the famous Parian marble. Ancient sculptors prized Parian marble for its translucency and fine, soft texture, and they used it for much of their best work, including the *Hermes* of Praxiteles and the *Venus de Milo.* The turnoff to the quarries is signposted, and an odd, rather foolishly monumental, marble-paved path leads up the valley toward (but not to) a group of deserted buildings and the ancient quarries. The buildings, to the right of the path, once belonged to a French mining company, which, in 1844, quarried the marble for Napoleon's tomb; the company was the last to operate here. The quarry entrances are about 46m (150 ft.) beyond the marble path's end, on the left. The second, very wide quarry on the left has a 3rd-century-B.C. relief of the gods at its entrance, encased in a protective cage. In Roman times, as many as 150,000 slaves labored here, working day and night to the flickering lights of thousands of oil lamps. There isn't much to see today inside the quarries unless you're a spelunker at heart, in which case you'll find it irresistible to explore the deep caverns opened by the miners high above the valley. Bring a flashlight, wear appropriate clothing, and don't explore alone.

Marathi. Open site.

The Valley of Petaloudes & Convent of Christou stou Dhassous ★   Another name for this oasis of plum, pear, fig, and pomegranate trees is Psychopiani (Soul Softs). The butterflies, actually tiger moths (*Panaxia quadripunctaria poda*), look like black-and-white-striped arrowheads, until they fly up to reveal their bright red underwings. They have been coming here for at least 300 years because of the freshwater spring, flowering trees, dense foliage, and cool shade; they're usually most numerous in early mornings or evenings in June. Donkey or mule rides from Parikia to the site

---

Murder in the Cathedral

As you visit the Panagia Ekatondapiliani Cathedral, watch for the two squat sculptured figures that support the columns of the monumental gate by the chapel of St. Theodosia, to the left of the main cathedral entrance. According to popular legend, the two figures are Isidore of Miletus, the best-known architect here, and his pupil Ignatius. As the story has it, Isodore was so envious of Ignatius's talent that he pushed him off scaffolding high inside the church's dome. As he fell, Ignatius grabbed onto Isidore and they both tumbled to their deaths. The sculptor has shown Isidore pulling on his beard (evidently a sign of apology) and Ignatius rubbing his head—perhaps in pain, perhaps as he cogitates on revenge. It's a nice story, but, in fact, archaeologists think that the two figures come from a temple of Dionysos that stood here and represent two satyrs—yet another example of how often successive generations reused building materials and re-created appropriate legends.

along a back road cost about 12€. You can take the Pounda and Aliki bus, which drops you off at the turnoff to the nunnery; you'll have to walk the remaining 2.5km (1½ miles) in to Petaloudes. Be sure to scowl at any visitors who clap and shout to alarm the butterflies and make them fly, often causing the fragile insects to collapse. A small snack bar serves refreshments; men can wait here, while women visit the nearby Convent of Christou sto Daso, which does not customarily welcome male visitors. (Cooling their heels in the courtyard, the men can console themselves by thinking of visiting Mount Athos, which is forbidden to female visitors.)

Petaloudes. Admission 3€. Mid-May to mid-Sept daily 9am–1pm and 4–8pm. Head 4km (2½ miles) south of Parikia on the coast road, turn left at the sign for the nunnery of Christou stou Dhassous, and continue another 2.5km (1½ miles).

BEACHES

Paros has some fine-sand beaches. If you're really pressed for time, you can walk in less than 15 minutes from where the ferry docks past where the fishing boats and small pleasure boats are moored to sandy Livadia beach, which has cafes and umbrellas If you can visit a couple of out-on-the-island beaches, here are some suggestions. All have chairs and umbrellas to rent and lots of tavernas and cafes. **Chrissi Akti (Golden Beach)** ★, on the island's southeast coast, is a kilometer (half-mile) of fine golden sand (with umbrellas and chairs to rent, tavernas, and cafes), is generally considered the best beach on the island. It's also the windiest, although the wind is usually offshore. As a result, this has become the island's primary windsurfing center and has hosted the World Cup championship every year since 1993. **Aegean Diving College** (✆ 22840/43-347; www.aegeandivingcollege.com) and the **Aegean Diving School** (22840/92-071; www.eurodivers.gr) offer scuba instruction and guided dives. There's frequent bus service here from both Parikia and Naoussa. If you're interested in kiteboarding, try (crowded, built-up) **Pounda** (see "Windsurfing & Scuba," below).

One of the island's best and most famous, picturesque **Kolimbithres** ★ is also served by bus from Parikia and Naoussa. It has smooth giant rocks that divide the gold-sand beach into several tiny coves—and appear on lots of island postcards. As at Golden Beach, there are umbrellas and chairs to rent and lots of places to have a bite.

There's bus and caique service from Naoussa to **Santa Maria beach** ★, one of the most beautiful on the island. It has particularly clear water and shallow dunes (rare in Greece) of fine sand along the irregular coastline. It also offers some of the best windsurfing on Paros. The **Santa Maria Surf Club** (✆ 22840/52-490) provides windsurfing gear and a brief lesson for about 20€ per hour.

TOWNS & VILLAGES: NAOUSSA & LEFKES

If your time on Paros is limited, do try to see Naoussa and Lefkes. If you have more time, you'll enjoy rambling about the island discovering other villages. One to keep in mind is **Marpissa** and the nearby monastery of **Agios Antonios,** from which there are fine views over the island.

Until recently, the fishing village of **Naoussa** remained relatively undisturbed, with simple white houses in a labyrinth of narrow streets, but it's now a growing resort center with increasingly fancy restaurants, trendy bars, boutiques, and galleries. Most of the new building here is concentrated along the nearby beaches, but a multiplicity of boutiques and restaurants has infiltrated deep into Naoussa. Some shops are just great, with drop-dead gorgeous summer togs, but if you want a sense of the village itself, walk inland and uphill until you get lost in the winding streets. Then wander

THE cave OF ANDIPAROS

There was a time not so long ago when people went to Andiparos, the islet about a nautical mile off Paros, for two reasons: to see the famous cave and to get away from all the crowds on Paros. The cave is still a good reason to come here, but Andiparos has been put firmly on the tourist map. Tom Cruise cruised by here, other stars followed in their yachts, Madonna dropped in by helicopter, and the wannabes began to come by ferryboat. There's been a lot of charmless building here to accommodate holiday makers, and it's hard to think of a reason to linger after you see the cave. In short, Parikia and Naoussa knock the socks off AndiParos for people watching, window shopping, and good food.

The cave (4€) is open in summer from 11am to 3pm; excursion caiques run hourly from 9am from Parikia and Pounda to Andiparos (3€ one-way). A shuttle barge, for vehicles as well as passengers, crosses the channel between Paros's southern port of Pounda and Andiparos continuously from 9am; the fare is 2€ or 10€ with a car; you can take along a bicycle for free. Buses (1.50€) run back and forth from the port to the cave. Something to keep in mind: Greeks have a soft spot for caves, and the Andiparos cave is often as crowded as an Athens bus.

Tourists once entered the cave by rope, but today's concrete staircase offers more convenient—if less adventurous—access. The cave is about 90m (300 ft.) deep, but the farthest reaches are closed to visitors. Through the centuries, visitors have broken off parts of the massive stalactites as souvenirs and left graffiti to commemorate their visits, but the cool, mysterious cavern is still worth exploring. As usual, Lord Byron, who carved his name into a temple column at Sounion, left his signature here. The Marquis de Nointel celebrated Christmas mass here in 1673 with 500 attendants; a large stalagmite served as the altar and the service was concluded with fireworks and explosions at the stroke of midnight.

back to the harbor after seeing some of the charming houses and little tourist-shop-free squares that Naoussa still has. In short, Naoussa retains its charm—but for how long? Colorful local fishing boats jostle for space beside visiting yachts, and fishermen calmly go about their work on the docks, all in the shadow of a half-submerged ruined Venetian minifortress—and, increasingly, tour buses. A narrow causeway links the Venetian fortress with the quay; the little kastro is absurdly picturesque when illuminated at night. The best night to see the fortress is during the **festival** held on or about **August 23,** when the battle against the pirate Barbarossa is reenacted by torch-lit boats converging on the harbor. Much feasting and dancing follows. On July 2, the Festival of Fish and Wine is celebrated here and elsewhere on Paros.

There's frequent bus service from Parikia to Naoussa in summer. Signs along Naoussa's harbor advertise caique service to nearby beaches. Daily excursion tours from Naoussa to Mykonos are usually offered in summer; inquire at any of the travel agencies in Parikia, or here at any local travel agency, such as **Nissiotissa Tours** (© **22840/51-480;** fax 22840/51-189).

Hilltop **Lefkes** ★ is the medieval capital of the island. Its whitewashed houses with red-tile roofs form a maze around the central square, with its little *kafeneion* (coffeehouse) with its unexpectedly grand neoclassical facade. The *kafeneion;* a barbershop; a shop selling crafts; and a plateia, paved with stone slabs accented with fresh whitewash—this is surely the most perfect little plateia in the Cyclades, unless the plateia in Pyrgos on Tinos has a slight edge because of its fountain house. Like so many Cycladic hamlets, Lefkes was purposely built in an inaccessible location and with an intentionally confusing pattern of streets to thwart pirates. Test your own powers of navigation by finding **Ayia Triada (Holy Trinity) Church,** whose carved marble towers are visible above the town. The Lefkes Village Hotel is one of the nicest places on the island to stay, although it's not easy to get a room there on summer weekends, when it is very popular with Greek families for wedding receptions.

OUTDOOR PURSUITS

WALKING Paros has numerous old stone-paved roads connecting the interior towns, many of which are in good condition and perfect for walking. One of the best-known trails is the **Byzantine Road,** between Lefkes and Prodromos, a narrow path paved along much of its 4km (2.5-mile) length with marble slabs. Begin in Lefkes, as from here the way is mostly downhill. There isn't an easy way to find the beginning of the Byzantine Road among the labyrinthine streets of Lefkes; we suggest starting at the church square, from which point you can see the flagstone-paved road in a valley at the edge of the town, to the west. Having fixed your bearings, plunge into the maze of streets and spiral your way down and to the right. After a 2-minute descent, you emerge into a ravine, with open fields beyond, and a sign indicates the beginning of the Byzantine Road. It's easy going through terraced fields, a leisurely hour's walk to the Marpissa Road, from which point you can catch the bus back to Parikia. Check the schedule and exact pickup point beforehand.

WINDSURFING & SCUBA ★★ The continuous winds on Paros's east coast have made it a favorite destination for windsurfers. Golden Beach has hosted the **Windsurfing World Cup** for the past 17 years. The best months are July and August, but serious windsurfers may want to visit earlier or later in the season to avoid the crowds. The free *Paros Windsurfing Guide* is available at most tourist offices in Parikia or Naoussa; www.diving-greece.net is also a good resource. On Golden Beach, the **F2 Windsurfing Center** (✆ 22840/41-878) has lessons and sponsors the **Windsurfing World Cup.** The **Aegean Diving College** (✆ 22840/43-347; www.aegean divingcollege.com) offers scuba instruction; director and marine archaeologist Peter Nikolaides is also connected with the Aegean Center in Parikia. At the port town of **Pounda,** the **Paros Kite Pro Center** (✆ 22840/92-071; www.paroskite-procenter. com) gives kiteboarding and windsurfing lessons (from 25€ for 1 hr.).

SHOPPING

Market Street in Parikia is the shopping hub of the island, with lots and lots of tempting jewelry, leather, pottery, and—as always in Greece—shoe shops. This may not be a nation of foot fetishists, but it certainly is a nation of shoe lovers. The **Jewelry Workshop** (✆ 22840/24-359) is precisely that, with the work of several local designers. You may not be looking for things to decorate your home, but if you are, check out **Yria Interiors** (✆ 22840/24-359; www.yriaparos.com) and Yvonne von der Decken's shop **Palaio Poleio ★** (✆ 22840/21-909), both on Market Street, both with pottery, home furnishings, and some old pieces from Greece and Europe. **Audiophile** (✆ 22840/22-357) has an extensive collection of CDs of Greek and international music, at prices a bit higher than you might pay in Athens. On the harbor, **InterNews** (✆ 22840/22-513) sells international newspapers, guidebooks, maps, and some novels.

Studio Detour

En route to or from Marathi, consider a detour to the nearby **Studio Yria** (*©* **22840/29-007;** www.yriaparos. com), signposted by the village of Kostos. A number of artists, including sculptors, painters, and potters, have set up shop here, and their wares are impressive. Many works draw on traditional Byzantine and island designs, whereas others are modern.

Several shops that sell local produce, including cheeses, honey, and wine, all merit your attention. **Pariana Proionta (Parian Produce)** ★ (*©* **22840/22-181**), run by the Agricultural Collective, is on Manto Mavroyennis Square; **Topika Proionta (Local Produce)** ★ (*©* **22840/24-940**) is on Market Street; and **Paktia** (*©* **22840/ 21-029**) is just off Market Street, just around the corner from the tempting Dodona ice cream parlor. Farther along the unsignposted street that leads from Market Street to the cathedral, the congenial **Distrato Café** ★ (*©* **22840/24-789**) has its own shop with organic produce from Paros and elsewhere in the Cyclades.

Across the island, in the old part of Naoussa, **Metaxas Gallery** (*©* **22840/52-667**) holds exhibitions of paintings by local artists, which are sometimes for sale; you can also find locally crafted jewelry here. **Hera,** just down the lane from the **Naoussa Sweet Shop** (*©* **22840/53-566**), sells local pottery, jewelry, carpets from Greece and Turkey, and fine-arts books of local interest. Owner Hera Papamihail is a talented photographer whose prints are available for purchase. The **kiosk** on the main plateia has some international newspapers. **Paria Lexis Bookstore** (*©* **22840/ 51-121**) offers a selection of travel guides, maps, and novels.

In Lefkes, **Anemi** (*©* **22840/41-182**), by the *kafeneion* on the plateia, has hand-loomed and embroidered fabrics. In addition, nuns in several of the island's convents often sell crafts.

Where to Stay
PARIKIA

The port town has three basic hotel zones: **agora** (the market area), **harbor,** and **beach;** alas, all can be very noisy at night. As always in Greece, bring earplugs, in case people walking the streets talk louder than you'd wish after you've gone to bed.

Here are some suggestions for potentially quiet places to stay. In addition to the places listed below, the **Pandrossos** (*©* **22840/22-903;** www.pandrossoshotel.gr), on a hill overlooking Parikia and the harbor, has a pool and a quiet location and was completely renovated in 2008. Here's the problem: About half the people who tell me about their stay there were very happy. The others found the location fine, the facilities fine, but the service dreadful. Most hotels here offer significant off-season discounts.

Captain Manolis Hotel ★ A tempting flower-covered entrance on Market Street, by the National Bank, leads into a passageway to this small hotel, which renovated its rooms in 2011. Rooms have balconies or terraces, the small lobby is comfy, and friends who have stayed here praise the staff and say that they were astonished at the tranquillity of this hotel in the heart of Market Street. As with all hotels with balconies and terraces opening on a shared courtyard, noise can be a problem if a large party takes over a number of rooms. I should also mention that there have been some recent reports of lax housekeeping.

Market St., Parikia, 84400 Paros. www.paroswelcome.com. (© **22840/21-244.** Fax 22840/25-264. 14 units. From 70€ double. No credit cards. **Amenities:** Breakfast room. *In room:* A/C, TV, fridge, hair dryer, Wi-Fi.

Hotel Dina ★★ 🍴   This is a charming place run by a charming couple. You reach the Dina through a narrow, plant-filled courtyard at the quiet end of Market Street. This is definitely a place to take time to smell the flowers, especially the gardenias in the courtyard. More pension than hotel, half the rooms and bathrooms were completely redone in 2010 (great new showers, reading lights, and some elegant brass bedsteads), and the rest were scheduled to be done in 2011. Three spacious rooms overlook Market Street; no. 2, with a balcony and brass bed calls out for a honeymoon couple. The balcony in room no. 8 (my favorite) looks onto a quintessentially Greek blue-domed church across a narrow lane; the other rooms face the garden courtyard. Dina Patellis has been the courteous and friendly proprietor for nearly 3 decades, and her personal touch keeps guests coming back year after year. Her husband wrote the excellent *Guide Through Ekatontapiliani*, available in local bookshops.

Market St., Parikia, 84400 Paros. www.hoteldina.com. (© **22840/21-325** or 22840/21-345. Fax 22840/23-525. 8 units. 50€–65€ double. No credit cards. Just off Market St., next to the Apollon Restaurant and across from the Pirate Bar. *In room:* A/C, TV, hair dryer, minifridge, Wi-Fi.

SOUTH OF PARIKIA

Yria Resort Hotel ★★ ☺   This resort complex is the place if you are traveling with young children and want a great pool and beach for them and a nifty spa for you. The beach is about 150m (492 ft.) away from the resort, whose architecture imitates the cluster of whitewashed Cycladic village houses. While not all rooms (most done in soft pastels, some with bright blue and white motifs) have a sea view, the grounds are so nicely landscaped that you won't feel deprived if your room faces inward. If you find the restaurant and bar too crowded, you can let it be known that you would like to be served in a private dining pavilion. The staff has been praised as helpful.

Parasporos, 84400 Paros. www.yriahotel.gr. (© **22840/24-154.** Fax 22840/21-167. 60 units. From 300€ double; from 370€ suite; from 550€ maisonette. Rates include full buffet breakfast. AE, DC, MC, V. Closed mid-Nov to Apr. Located 2.5km (1½ miles) south of the port. **Amenities:** Restaurant; bar; concierge; fitness center; freshwater pool; tennis. *In room:* A/C, TV, hair dryer, minibar, Wi-Fi.

NAOUSSA

In addition to the places listed below, you might consider the coyly named **Heaven Naoussa** (© **22840/51-549;** www.heaven-naoussa.com), with four doubles, five suites, and two maisonettes (with shared pool). Doubles run from 120€, suites from 200€, and maisonettes from 1,600€ per week. Rates for rooms and suites, but not villas, include an extensive breakfast buffet. The architecture is, appropriately, Cycladic, the decor is eclectic and stylishly casual, and restaurants and the harbor are steps away. If you're unable to find a room in Naoussa, try **Nissiotissa Tours** (© **22840/51-480**), just off the east (left) side of the main square.

Astir of Paros ★   The most luxurious hotel on the island is built like a self-contained Cycladic village within a luxurious garden, with a private beach, 3-hole golf course, good pool, tennis court, gym, and a small art gallery. What the Astir does not have is something to make it really memorable. Double rooms are unexceptional, with simple beds, tables, and chairs. The spacious suites have a bit more personality, with armchairs, desks, and attempts at fancy window drapes. Four units are equipped for travelers with disabilities. Produce for the two hotel restaurants is grown on a nearby farm; the breakfast buffet (not included in the room rates) features more than 70 items. Some people come here and don't budge; if you want to see something of the island, Astir can arrange a car rental.

Kolimbithres Beach, 84401 Paros. www.astirofparos.gr. ℂ **22840/51-976** or 22840/51-707. Fax 22840/51-985. 61 units. 200€–240€ double; 210€–450€ suite. Rates include continental breakfast. AE, DC, MC, V. Closed Oct 20–Easter. West of Naoussa, off the south end of the beach. **Amenities:** Restaurant; bar; concierge; 3-hole golf course; health club; freshwater pool; tennis; 4 rooms for those w/limited mobility. *In room:* A/C, TV/DVD, hair dryer, minibar, Wi-Fi.

Hotel Petres ★★   Clea and Sotiris Hatzinikolakis combine warm hospitality with helpful efficiency to meet the needs of their guests. The large, comfortable rooms, with private terraces or balconies, cluster around the big pool. Throughout, antiques and paintings, many done by Clea herself, give the Petres the charm and comfort so sadly lacking in most Greek hotels. The extensive, inventive, and delectable buffet breakfast/brunch, served from 9 to 11:30am, may well be the highlight of your stay on Paros. Dinner is usually available on request; and most Saturdays in summer, there's a barbecue at the poolside grill. The view is of farm fields, with the sea in the distance; if you want to get into Naoussa, the hotel offers a frequent, free minibus shuttle. In short, the only drawback to the Petres is that the temptation to relax by the pool may entice you to put off sightseeing until *aurio* (tomorrow).

Naoussa, 84401 Paros. www.petres.gr. ℂ **22840/52-467.** Fax 22840/52-759. 16 units. From 125€ double. Rates vary depending on location and length of stay and include extensive buffet breakfast. DC, MC, V. Closed Nov–Mar. 3km (5 miles) from town. **Amenities:** Breakfast room/bar; airport/port pickup; Jacuzzi; freshwater pool; sauna; tennis; Wi-Fi. *In room:* A/C, TV, hair dryer, minibar.

LEFKES

The Lefkes Village Hotel is quite special, but if it is full when you visit, or if you want to spend less, the simple 14-unit **Pantheon** (ℂ **22840/41-646**) is perfectly decent and a lot cheaper (doubles from 65€).

Lefkes Village Hotel ★★★   This handsome hotel, some 10km (6 miles) from Parikia, is designed to look like a small island village. It helps that Lefkes is probably the most charming inland village on the island. The spectacular views reach across the countryside to the sea. The pool is so nice that you may not mind not being on the sea. Guest rooms are light and bright, with good bathrooms; some have balconies with wonderful views. In addition to all the things you'd expect in a tasteful hotel, there's a small Museum of Popular Aegean Culture and a winery. This is a popular place for wedding receptions; some summer weekends, wedding parties take over the entire hotel, which means that you may listen to music, dancing, and toasts, until dawn.

P.O. Box 71, Lefkes Village, 84400 Paros. www.lefkesvillage.gr. ℂ **22840/41-827** or 210/251-6497. Fax 2284/41-0827. 25 units. 200€–210€ double. Rates include buffet breakfast. MC, V. **Amenities:** Restaurant; bar; Jacuzzi; freshwater pool. *In room:* A/C, TV, hair dryer, minibar, Wi-Fi.

Where to Eat

A favorite standby on the harbor, below the Kastro and especially nice at sunset time, **To Spitiko** (ℂ **22840/24-956**) promises to serve "tasty answers to hungry questions"—just what you'd expect from a place whose name means home cooking; 20€ will let you eat lots here.

On Market Street, as it bends toward the Ekatondapiliani Cathedral at the Dodona Café, you'll find **Daphne** (ℂ **22840/22-575**); **Tamarisko** (ℂ **22840/24-689**) is just off Market Street. Both have very nice gardens and both have excellent food. Daphne has elegant Mediterranean cuisine, while Tamarisko has a lighter touch (more salads and rice dishes). On the continuation of Market Street into town (as opposed to where it bends toward the Ekatondapiliani), **Franca Scala** (ⓒ **22840/24-407**) has a great rooftop terrace, possibly the best place in town for people-watching. If I were sitting there with a glass of white wine, I might toy with an order of smoked salmon rolls with eggplant mousse. Dinner at Daphne, Tamarisko, or Franca Scala could run as little as 20€ or easily twice that, depending on your choices.

PARIKIA

Apollon Garden ★ GREEK   THE PLACE TO GO, THE PLACE TO BE SEEN says the business card, and while that may be true, this is also a place with a lovely garden with flowers and palm trees and excellent food. You will find all the Greek standards here—stuffed vegetables in season, grills, stews—and the quality is consistently good.

Market St., Parikia. ⓒ **22840/21-875.** Main courses 8€–20€. No credit cards. Daily 7pm–midnight. On Market St., just past the HOTEL DINA sign. Sometimes closed in winter.

Dionysos ★★ GREEK   The first thing you notice is the palm tree that goes up and up and is draped with the fiery orange flowers of a trumpet vine. There's a nice garden and terrific food that is both elegant and hearty: pork filet stuffed with sun-dried tomatoes, fresh basil, and asparagus, and duck breast with mango sauce are often on the menu, as well as a house favorite, spaghetti with lobster. If possible, save room for dessert, and try to decide between the chocolate fondant and the chocolate tiramisu.

Market St., Parikia. ⓒ **22840/25-194.** Main courses 15€–40€. No credit cards. Daily in season 11am–3pm and 6pm–1am. Usually closed in winter.

Distrato Café ★★ GREEK/INTERNATIONAL   On the street that runs from the cathedral to Market Street, beneath the spreading branches of a ficus tree, this is as nice a place as any to spend an hour or two; some habitués seem to start the day with a coffee and croissant here and end it with wine and one of the tasty spaghettis. Distrato serves crepes, sandwiches, ice creams, pasta dishes, and inventive salads. If you're still hungry, the shop stocks nicely packaged organic Greek produce. If there are no tables at Distrato, try **Symposio,** a few steps away, with tasty snacks (great mozzarella and tomato baguette sandwich), but no shady tree.

Paralia. ⓒ **22840/22-311.** Snacks and main courses 8€–15€. No credit cards. Daily 10am–midnight. Look for the big ficus tree as you walk from the cathedral to Market St.

Levantis ★★ GREEK/INTERNATIONAL   This place gets high praise for its offbeat dishes that combine local produce with international ingredients. Where else on the island will you find Thai dishes alongside stuffed eggplant? Owner-chef George Mavridis likes to cook and likes to talk food, so you can enjoy what you eat while learning about the kitchen. His daily specials are an indication of how much he enjoys experimenting and trying out new dishes. The desserts are well worth saving room for, especially if you're a chocoholic. If you're too full for dessert, you can relax and enjoy the pleasant garden.

Paralia, on Market St. ⓒ **22840/23-613.** Main courses 8€–22€. AE, V. Daily 7pm–midnight. Closed Nov–Easter.

Porphyra ★★ GREEK/FISH   Locals say Porphyra (overlooking the ancient Roman cemetery and the harbor) serves the best fish in town. It's small, and the nondescript, utilitarian service and decor are typical of your average taverna. The difference here is that the owner cultivates the shellfish himself, resulting in exceptional mussels *saganaki* (mussels cooked with tomato, feta, and wine) and a great fish soup.

The *tzatziki* (cucumber-yogurt dip) and other traditional cold appetizers are also very good. The fish is predictably fresh, and offerings vary with the season. The same owners operate the nearby **Art Café;** drinks and snacks are served at the small gallery and cafe, which sometimes features live music.

Paralia. ✆ **22840/22-693.** Main courses 8€–20€; fish priced by the kilo. AE, MC, V. Daily 6:30pm–midnight. Closed Jan–Feb. Past the cathedral, btw. the pier and the post office, just back from the waterfront, about a 10-min. walk from Market St.

NAOUSSA

Naoussa's restaurants are either harborside, or tucked away in town. Your best way to find the in-town restaurants is to ask. Streets are winding and street signs are virtually nonexistent. Don't worry: You'll get lost, but you'll find what you're looking for, often with the help of gaggles of giggling schoolchildren.

Barbarossa Ouzeri ★ GREEK/*MEZEDES*   This longtime local ouzeri is right on the port. Wind-burned fishermen and scores of chic Athenians sit for hours nursing their milky ouzo in water and their miniportions of grilled octopus and olives. If you want more of a meal, this is a fine fish restaurant. If you wonder what language the staff here is speaking, it's often Arabic or Russian—more evidence that the world is indeed becoming a global village.

Naoussa waterfront. ✆ **22840/51-391.** *Mezedes* 6€–15€. Fish priced by the kilo. No credit cards. Daily 1pm–1am.

Le Sud ★ GREEK/INTERNATIONAL   I happened to be on Paros when this small place opened in 2003. I must admit, I wondered if a new restaurant with serious French-influenced cuisine could lure diners away from the popular harborside tavernas. I needn't have worried. Le Sud, with its charming garden, has been a great success. There's often terrine of vegetables, bream with ginger, lamb with lemon and cardamom confit, and blinis. In short, although all the ingredients are fresh and almost all are local, the cuisine is somewhat eclectic. Try to reserve one of the handful of tables in the small garden; it's a good idea to call in advance in summer.

Off the harbor. ✆ **22840/51-547.** Main courses 15€–25€. No credit cards. Daily 7pm–midnight. About 200m (656 ft.) back from the port.

Mitsi's ★★ GREEK/SEAFOOD   This is the sort of seafood taverna you dream about finding and will always remember. We stopped at this little place on the beach beyond the harbor one evening just to have an ouzo and watch the sun set—and left 4 hours later after a number of ouzos and a leisurely dinner of fresh greens, fresh fish, and something tasty that the *patron* called "grandmother's stew." When we sat down, we were the only customers; by the time we left, every table was taken, about half by locals, half by visitors to the island. The retsina wine, which the engaging owner (Mitsi himself) makes, is terrific.

 Beware the *Bomba*

Several places on the strip in Parikia offer very cheap drinks or "buy one, get one free." What you'll get, most likely, is locally brewed alcohol that the locals call *bomba.* This speak-easy brew is made privately and often illegally. It's a quick way to get drunk—and to feel awful after you get sober.

Harborside. ✆ **22840/51-302.** Main courses 8€–15€; fish priced by the kilo. No credit cards. Daily 7pm–midnight.

Papadakis ★ INNOVATIVE GREEK   Fresh fish is one of the specialties here, but be sure not to rush to the main course—the appetizers are admirable: The *tzatziki* with dill is delicious and refreshingly different; the traditionally prepared *melitzanosalata* (a cold eggplant salad, usually made with lots of garlic) is redolent of wood-smoked eggplant. The desserts are worth sampling, especially *kataifi ekmek*, a confection conjured from honey, walnuts, cinnamon, custard, and cream.

Naoussa waterfront. ✆ **22840/51-047.** Reservations recommended. Main courses 10€–30€. AE, V. Daily 7:30pm–midnight.

Pervolaria ★ GREEK/CONTINENTAL   There's something for everyone here. The restaurant is set in a garden, lush with geraniums and grapevines, behind a white stucco house decorated with local ceramics. There's pasta and pizza, and *schnitzel a la chef* (veal in cream sauce with tomatoes and basil). If you want to eat Greek, order the souvlaki and varied appetizers' special.

Off the harbor. ✆ **22840/51-598.** Main courses 7€–15€. MC, V. Daily 7pm–midnight. About 100m (328 ft.) back from the port.

Paros After Dark

Keep an eye out for posters announcing concerts and art exhibits and check out the listings in the current issue of the quarterly *Paros Life and Naxos Life* (2€). If you're on Paros in July and like jazz, check to see if the Greek International Jazz Summer School (www.innovaros.com) is meeting and giving performances. **Music-Dance Naoussa Paros** (✆ **22840/52-284;** www.parosweb.com) often performs Greek dances; the group wears costumes and is quite good.

Just behind the windmill in Parikia is a local landmark, **Port Cafe,** a basic *kafenion* lit by bare incandescent bulbs and filled day and night with tourists waiting for a ferry, bus, taxi, or fellow traveler. The cafe serves coffee, pastry, and drinks; it's a good place for casual conversation.

Pebbles Bar ★ often has classical music and good jazz; as does the **Pirate Bar** ★, a few doors from Hotel Dina in the agora. Both are very congenial places, as popular with Greeks as with foreign visitors. **Alexandros,** in a restored windmill by the harbor, is awfully attractive and a perfect spot to enjoy being on an island, by the harbor, watching the passing scene. In Naoussa, check out **Agosta** or **Café del Mar** by the harbor or for an after-dinner drink. If you want to watch the sun rise after you see it set, head along the harbor to where the fishing boats are moored, and **Lindardo's** often goes all night. You'll find the serious discos on the outskirts of town and by the bus station; **Vareladikos,** by the bus station, often goes all night.

NAXOS ★★

191km (103 nautical miles) SE of Piraeus

Unlike many of its neighbors, whose prosperity depends on the summer tourist season, green, fertile Naxos is largely self-sufficient. This is the largest of the Cyclades, with wonderful groves of olives and fruit trees, wheat fields, and good grazing land for the cows, sheep, and goats whose milk goes into a wide variety of Naxian cheeses. Visitors here will find lots of blessings to count: for starters, there are rolling green hills and valleys with clusters of Byzantine churches, medieval towers, and villages with handsome neoclassical houses. There are long sand beaches, and a capital that has grown up in and around its own massive Venetian castle in the island's capital, Hora. The Venetians ruled Naxos from 1207 until the island fell to the Turks in 1566. The influence of **Venetian architecture** is obvious in Hora's kastro, some handsome mansions here and there in Hora, and many of the *piryi* (fortified towers) that punctuate the hillsides. The presence on the island of descendants of the Venetians means that Naxos has both Catholic and Orthodox churches—sometimes side by side and even sharing a central wall, as at the Bellonia Tower (p. 285). Having said that, the glory of Naxos's church architecture is the remarkable abundance of small **Byzantine chapels,** many of which contain exceptional frescoes dating from the 9th to the 13th centuries. These chapels escaped destruction by Naxos's various overlords and remain to charm visitors—if, that is, you can find them. Many are poorly signposted and elusive, which means that you will feel triumphant when you track them down. Paul Hetherington's *Greek Islands* is an invaluable guide to the medieval and Byzantine monuments.

The island's mountain villages, on the lower slopes of Mount Zas, the highest mountain in the Cyclades, preserve the rhythms of agrarian life. The lush—for Greece—area known as the **Tragea** has plains of olive trees, upland valleys, and a cluster of villages, Venetian towers, and Hellenistic watchtowers. Just about everybody's favorite village is **Apiranthos,** with some marble-paved streets, a particularly handsome Venetian tower, and small shaded plateias.

The airport, good interisland ferry service, and speedy high-speed ferries make Naxos easy to visit. New hotels have appeared in the port, and more hotels cluster on island beaches—which are among the best in the Cyclades. In short, tourism has arrived—but, as yet, in a way that makes visiting here easy and pleasurable. As always, it is handy to have a car, although the local bus service is good, if leisurely. If you just want to see Naxos town, a day will do you, but longer will let the charms of the little streets in the old fortress sink in. And, as you would expect of the largest of the Cyclades, there's lots to see out on the island. Unfortunately, some of what you see may still show signs of damage from several severe summer forest fires in 2009.

Essentials

GETTING THERE   By Plane   Olympic Air offers daily flights between Athens and the Santorini airport Monolithos (✆ **22860/31-525**), which also receives European charters. **Aegean Airlines** also has several flights daily between Athens and Naxos. (For contact information for both, see "Essentials" under "Santorini," earlier in this chapter.) A bus meets most flights and takes passengers into Naxos town (2€).

By Boat   From Piraeus, there is at least one daily ferry (6 hr.) and one daily high-speed ferry (4 hr.). Check schedules at the Athens **GNTO** (**210/870-0000;** www.gnto.gr), the **Piraeus Port Authority** (✆ **210/451-1311,** -1440, or -1441), or **Naxos Port Authority** (✆ **22850/22-300**). Boats are notoriously late and/or early; your travel or ticket agent will give you an *estimate* of times involved in the following journeys. There is at least a once-daily ferry connection with Ios, Mykonos, Paros, and Santorini. There is ferry connection several times weekly by high-speed ferry or hydrofoil with Siros, Tinos, and Samos, and somewhat less frequently with Sifnos and with Folegandros. For ferry tickets, try **Zas Travel** (✆ **22850/23-330**), on the *paralia* opposite the ferry pier. For ferry schedules, check out **www.openseas.gr** or **www.gtp.gr**.

VISITOR INFORMATION   The privately operated **Naxos Tourist Information Center** (✆ **22850/22-993;** fax 22850/25-200), across the plaza from the ferry pier, is the most reliable source of information and help. (Don't confuse it with the small office on the pier itself, which is often closed.) The center, run by the owner of the Chateau Zevgoli (p. 290), provides ferry information; books charter flights between various European airports and Athens, accommodations, cars, and mopeds; arranges excursions; sells maps; exchanges money; holds luggage; assists with phone calls; and provides 2-hour laundry service. Naxos has a helpful website, **www.naxosnow.com**, with maps and a photo tour of the island.

If you enjoy map reading, get a good map as soon as possible, as Hora (Naxos town) is old, large, and complex, with a permanent population of more than 3,000. The free *Summer Naxos* magazine has the best map of the city. That said, map or no map, prepare to get lost at least once in the little streets in and around the Kastro. The *Harms-Verlag Naxos* is the best map of the island, but it's pricey at 7€. John Freely's *Naxos* (1976) remains delightful and helpful.

GETTING AROUND   By Bus   The bus station is on the harbor; bus schedules are often posted at the station, and free schedules are sometimes available. Regular bus service is offered throughout most of the island two or three times a day, more frequently to major destinations. In summer, there's service every 30 minutes to the nearby south-coast beaches at Ayios Prokopios and Ayia Anna. A popular day trip is to Apollonas, near the northern tip. In summer, the competition for seats on this route can be fierce, so get to the station well ahead of time.

In addition to the public buses, **Zas Travel** (✆ **22850/23-300**) offers day excursions around the island in season, usually from 25€.

By Bicycle & Moped   Moto Naxos (✆ **22850/23-420**), on Protodikiou Square, south of the *paralia,* has the best mountain bikes as well as mopeds for rent. A basic bike is about 15€ per day. For a moped, expect to pay from 30€ per day. Naxos has some major inclines that require a strong motor and good brakes, so a large bike (80cc or greater) is recommended (as is checking the brakes before you set off).

By Car   It's a good idea to inquire first about car rental at the Naxos Tourist Information Center (see "Visitor Information," above), which usually has the best deals. Car is the ideal mode of transport on this large island, and most travel agencies in Naxos town rent them, including the oddly named **Naxos Vision** (✆ **22850/26-2000; www.naxosvision.com), AutoTour** (✆ **22850/25-480), Auto Naxos** (✆ **22850/ 23-420), and Palladium** (✆ **22850/26-200**).

By Taxi   The taxi station (✆ **22850/22-444**) is at the port. Taxi fares are slated to go up in 2012, but in 2011, a taxi trip within Naxos town cost around 4€. The fare to Ayia Anna Beach was about 8€; to the handsome inland village of Apiranthos, 20€.

FAST FACTS   Commercial Bank, on the *paralia,* has an ATM. It and other banks are open Monday through Thursday from 8am to 2pm, Friday from 8am to 1:30pm. Naxos has a good 24-hour **health center** (✆ **22850/23-333**) just outside Hora on the left off Papavasiliou, the main street off the port. **Holiday Laundry,** on Periferiakos Road, Grotta area (✆ **22850/23-988**), offers drop-off service. The **police** (✆ **22850/22-100**) are beyond Protodikiou Square, by the Galaxy Hotel. The **telephone office (OTE)** is at the port's south end; summer hours are daily from 7:30am to 2pm. The **post office** is south of the OTE by the basketball court; it's opposite the court on the left, on the second floor (Mon–Fri 8am–2pm).

What to See & Do
THE TOP ATTRACTIONS IN HORA ★★

Kastro is the name both for the 13th-century Venetian kastro (castle), which is Hora's greatest treasure, and for the neighborhood around it, where the Venetian nobility lived from the 13th to the 16th century. You should allow yourself at least several hours to explore the Kastro area of Hora—preferably by meandering, getting a bit lost, and then being pleasantly surprised at the architectural treasures (and nice little cafes) that you happen upon. If you take in Kastro's two museums, it's nice to have at least half a day here. To get to Kastro, you have to climb up from the **harbor,** through **Bourgo,** Hora's lower town. This route goes from harborside, through Bourgo, to Kastro. This is a pleasant way to spend a day—or, if pressed, several hours.

The Portara and Myrditiotissa ★★   If you come here by sea, you'll see two of Naxos's most famous monuments as you sail into the harbor: the little whitewashed **Myrditiotissa** chapel, on an islet off the quay, and the **Portara (Great Door),** connected to the quayside by a causeway. The Myrditiotissa was built around 1207 by the Venetian Marco Sanudo, ruler of the Venetian Duchy of the Archipelago and a nephew of the doge of Venice. Sanudo also built much of the Kastro (see below). The massive Portara entrance door is all that remains of an obviously enormous Temple of Apollo. A 6th-century tyrant, Lygdamis, began the temple; when he died, construction stopped and demolition began. Over the centuries, most of the temple was carted away to build other monuments and buildings, including parts of both the Catholic and Orthodox cathedrals and much of the kastro. Fortunately, the massive posts and lintel of the Portara were too heavy for the Venetians to handle. Each of the four surviving blocks in the gates weighs about 20 tons.

Some scholars have thought that this temple was dedicated to the god Dionysos, who spent some time in his youth on Naxos dallying with local nymphs. Many locals believed that this was the palace of Ariadne, the Cretan princess who taught Theseus the mysteries of the labyrinth and helped him to slay the Minotaur. Her reward was to be abandoned here by Theseus as he sailed back to Athens, an event commemorated by Strauss in his opera *Ariadne auf Naxos.* Dionysos took pity on the discarded princess and married her, which gave rise to the nice legend that this great door was the entrance to the bridal palace. Now, most scholars think that the temple was dedicated to Apollo, in part because of a brief reference in the Delian Hymns and in part because it directly faces Delos, Apollo's birthplace.

One of the nicest ways to see the Portara is at sunset, from one of the harborside cafes. If you feel like a swim, join the locals swimming off the rocks below the temple door.

Panagia Zoodochos Pigi Cathedral (Mitropolis) and Mitropolis Site Museum ★   As is so often the case in Greece, the modern town sits atop successive ancient settlements. Excavations undertaken around the Panagia Zoodochos Pigi Cathedral from 1982 to 1985 revealed a layered history of continuous occupation here from Mycenaean times to the present, with significant remains of the classical agora and the later Roman city. The cathedral is often locked; frustratingly, when I have seen a priest unlock a side door and go in, he has assured me that the cathedral is shut—and slammed the door in my face. The Mitropolis museum, located in the square facing the cathedral, preserves the open space of the square while providing

What's in a Name?

There are many churches in Greece called Panagia Zoodochos Pigi (Virgin of the Life-Giving Spring). Here, the name is especially appropriate: The church was built near the ancient Nymphaeum (fountain house). Much of the handsome marble in the cathedral was pillaged from ancient buildings both on Naxos and from neighboring islands, including Delos. Since Venetian times, this neighborhood has been known as Fontana, because of the spring that still flows here.

access to a segment of the excavated archaeological site below. You'll probably want to spend at least half an hour here.

Hora. ⓒ **22850/24-151.** Free admission. Tues–Sun 8am–2:30pm. Turn in from the *paralia* at Zas Travel and continue about 100m (328 ft.) until you see the Mitropolis Cathedral Sq. on your right.

Bourgo/Kastro/Archaeological Museum/Venetian Museum ★★★   In Venetian times, the grandees lived at the top of the hill, in Kastro, and the Greeks lived down the hill, in Bourgo. To get to the kastro, wend your way up through Bourgo, along one of the streets that snakes uphill. There's also a signposted lane leading up from the harborside, but almost any street going uphill will get you there, although perhaps not directly to one of the entrances through the kastro's thick walls.

The kastro had three main entryways, of which the most impressive today is the north entry, known as the **Trani Porta (Strong Gate),** signposted on Apollon Street. This narrow marble arched threshold marks the transition from the commercial bustle of Bourgo to the Kastro's medieval world. Look for the incision on the right column of the arch, which marks the length of a Venetian yard, and was used to measure the cloth brought here for aristocratic Venetian ladies to consider purchasing. Exploring the Kastro's byways, it's hard not to wish to be able to levitate up over the lofty walls and look inside one of these Venetian mansions, with their walled gardens and coats of arms carved over doorways. Fortunately, one typical aristocratic Venetian house, the 800-year-old Della Roca family home, located just inside the Trani Porta, is open to the public. The 40-minute tour, offered in English and Greek, of the **Domus Venetian Museum** (ⓒ **22850/22-387;** www.naxosfestival.com) is a wonderful chance to get an inside look at one of the surviving great Venetian homes; you'll see and learn about the reception rooms, chapel, and vaults, and end in a small shop with local produce and handicrafts. A wide variety of concerts and Greek dance performances take place in the garden here during each summer's **Domus Naxos Festival** (ⓒ **22850/22-387;** www.naxosfestival.com). Tours are not given when there is an evening concert.

Tip: Performances here are very popular and often sold out Naxos is now getting enough tour groups that all the tickets for a performance can be gobbled up well before a concert. If you want a ticket, try to book in advance.

At the center of the kastro is the perhaps too heavily restored 13th-century **Catholic cathedral,** with its brilliant marble facade. To the right, behind the cathedral, is the French School of Commerce and the former **Ursuline Convent and School,** where young ladies of the Venetian aristocracy were educated. The nearby French School has housed schools run by several religious orders, and among its more famous students was the (famous irreligious) Cretan writer Nikos Kazantzakis, who studied here in 1896. The school now houses the **Archaeological Museum ★**. One of the highlights here is the astonishingly large group of the rare white marble Cycladic figurines. These are the often violin-shaped marble figurines (dating from as long ago as 3000 B.C.) whose stark outlines some have compared to figures painted by Modigliani. The museum also has an extensive collection of late-Mycenaean-period (1400 B.C.–1100 B.C.) pottery found near Grotta, a district in the northern part of Hora, including vessels with the octopus motif that still appears in local art. The museum has lousy lighting in many galleries, but a great view from its terrace and balconies to the hills of Naxos.

Hora. Archaeological Museum: ℭ **22850/22-725.** Admission 3€. Tues–Sun 8am–3pm; sometimes open evenings in summer. Venetian Museum: ℭ **22850/22-387.** Admission and tour 6€. Daily 10am–3pm and 6–9pm.

THE TOP ATTRACTIONS OUT ON THE ISLAND

People who know Greece well often think that Naxos is both the most beautiful of the Cyclades and the nicest to visit—and revisit. The island has a magical landscape, with somewhat mysterious valleys, fertile fields, and even the highest mountain in the Cyclades. That's Mount Zas, associated in antiquity with Zeus, who felt at home on lofty eminences. If you climb Mount Zas, you'll find out just how lofty it is. Naxos also has wonderful old chapels, some of the best infuriatingly hard to find tucked away in those valleys, absurdly picturesque villages, and—let's not mince words—often crowded beaches. You could spend a lifetime exploring this island.

Ancient & Medieval Monuments

In addition to the Temple of Demeter, Naxos has two unfinished kouroi (monumental statues of men) that are well worth seeing, in villages that are themselves worth seeing. See "The Villages," below, for the kouros of Apollonas and the kouros of Flerio.

Sangri and the Temple of Demeter ★   The village of Sangri is an agglomeration of several villages in a valley below Mount Profitias Elias. There's a deserted 16th-century monastery, Timios Stavros, on the mountain's lower slopes and the remains of a 13th-century Venetian kastro on its summit. The temple of Demeter is signposted (5km/3 miles) out of Stavri. Until about 10 years ago, the temple, built in the 6th century B.C., was in a state of complete ruin; it had been partially dismantled in the 6th century A.D. to build a chapel on the site, and what was left was plundered repeatedly over the years. Then it was discovered that virtually all the pieces of the original temple were on the site, either buried or integrated into the chapel. A long process of reconstruction began. Most of the work has been completed, and it's possible to see the basic form of the temple—one of the few known square-plan temples. There's also a small site museum, often irritatingly closed.

Temple of Demeter at Ano Sangri. Free admission. Depart from Hora on the road to Filoti, and after about 10km (6 miles), turn onto the signposted road to Ano Sangri and the Temple of Demeter. From here it's another 3.5km (2 miles) to the temple, primarily on dirt roads (major turns are signposted).

The Bellonia, Frangopoulos, Angelopoulos & Himarros Towers ★

The Naxian countryside is dotted with the towers (some defensive, some dwellings) that the Venetians built here. If you visit island villages, you'll inevitably see some of the towers, such as the 17th-century Frangopoulos tower in the hamlet of Chalki, some 17km (10 miles) south of Hora. The easiest to see from Hora is the Bellonia, just 5km (3 miles) south of town, outside the village of Galando. The tower, once the residence of the Catholic archbishop of Naxos, is privately owned, but you can get a good look at the exterior without making the owners feel that they are under attack. The chapel beside the tower is really two chapels: one Catholic, one Orthodox; the arch between the chapels rests on an ancient column capital. About 10km (6 miles) north of Chora, a track road leads to the Monastery of Our Lady Upsilotera (Angelopoulos's Castle). This impressive 17th-century fortified building has a small sign giving its open hours and is usually closed. There are sometimes impressive turkeys wandering the grounds.

Lovers of Hellenistic fortifications and of hiking may wish to see the 20m-tall (45-ft.) Hellenistic Himaros tower, outside the hamlet of Filoti; the tower is signposted in Filoti as Pirgos Himarou, but ask for supplementary directions locally and allow at least 3 hours to hike there and back from Filoti.

Byzantine Churches ★★

You can easily spend a week seeing the Byzantine churches of Naxos, or you can see the handful mentioned below in a day. Getting to each one involves at least some walking and some luck: In order to see the interiors, you'll have to have the luck to find the caretaker. The churches are kept locked, due to increasing theft, although the caretaker often makes an early-morning or early-evening visit.

The remarkable numbers of small Byzantine chapels on Naxos mostly date from the 9th to the 15th centuries, many in or near some of the island's loveliest villages (see below). The prosperity of Naxos, during this period of Byzantine and Venetian rule, meant that wealthy patrons funded elaborate frescoes, many of which can still be seen on the interior walls of the chapels. Restoration has revealed multiple layers of frescoes and, whenever possible, the more recent ones have been removed intact during the process of revealing the initial paintings. Several frescoes removed in this way from the churches of Naxos can be seen at the Byzantine Museum in Athens.

Just south of Moni (23km/14 miles east of Hora), near the middle of the island, is the important 7th-century monastery of **Panagia Drossiani (Our Lady of Refreshment) ★**, which contains some of the finest—and oldest, dating from the 7th century—frescoes on Naxos (St. George and his dragon are easy to spot). Locals believe the icon of the Virgin ended a severe drought on the island shortly after the frescoes were painted. The church, with its huddled arched apses and domes, is all that survives of what we are told was an extensive monastery; what an appealing place for a contemplative life! Visits are allowed at all hours during the day; when the door is locked, ring the church bell to summon the caretaker (remember to dress appropriately). To get here, drive about 1km (½ mile) south from Moni and look for the low, gray, rounded form of the church on your left.

About 8km (5 miles) from Hora along the road to Sangri, you'll see a sign on the left for the 8th-century Byzantine cathedral of **Ayios Mamas,** which fell into disrepair during the Venetian occupation but has recently been partly restored. The **view** from this charming church alone: *vaut le voyage!* Sangri (the Greek contraction of Sainte Croix) today is made up of three villages, and includes the ruins of a medieval castle. The church of Ayios Nikolaos, which dates to the 13th century, has well-preserved frescoes, with a lovely figure of the personified River Jordan. To view them, ask around to find out which villager has the keys.

The Villages ★★

Many of the nicest villages and churches are in the lush **Tragaea Valley ★** at the center of the island. Each village is tempting, and you can easily spend several days, or several years, exploring them. The bus between Hora and Apollonas makes stops at each of the villages mentioned below, but you'll have considerably more freedom if you rent a car. You'll find cafes at all the villages, and restaurants in most.

SOME TRAGAEA VALLEY VILLAGES   The Tragaea is sometimes called a "little Mistra," which I find misleading. First, the Tragea is spread out across a good deal of central Naxos, unlike Byzantine Mistra in the Peloponnese, which is built on one steep hill. Secondly, Mistra's churches are the magnificent products of a wealthy center of empire, all within walking distance of the ruler's palace. The Byzantine chapels of the Tragaea are largely appealing because they were built by locals in small, scattered villages between the 7th and 15th centuries. In any event, the Tragaea is green, fertile, and charming, with particularly appealing town squares in Halki and Filoti. **Halki,** 16km (10 miles) from Hora, has a lovely central square shaded by a magnificent plane tree. Side streets have some rather grand 19th-century neoclassical homes. The fine 11th-century white church with the red-tiled roof, **Panagia Protothronos (Our Lady Before the Throne),** has well-preserved frescoes and is sometimes open in the morning. Turn right to reach the **Frankopoulos (Grazia) Tower.** The name is Frankish, but it was originally Byzantine; a marble crest on the tower indicates 1742, when it was renovated by the Venetians. Climb the steps for an excellent view of Halki and across to Filoti, one of the island's largest inland villages.

The brilliant white houses of **Filoti,** 2km (1¼ miles) up the road from Halki, elegantly drape the lower slopes of **Mount Zas,** the highest peak in the Cyclades. This is the largest town in the Tragaea, and the center of town life is the main square, shaded like Halki's square by a massive plane tree. There's a *kafenion* at the center of the square and two tavernas within 50m (164 ft.). In the town's center, the church of **Kimisis tis Theotokou (Assumption of the Mother of God)** has a lovely marble iconostasis and a Venetian tower. In the hamlet of Chalki, which has some wonderful neoclassical mansions and a shady plateia, the **Panagia Protothrone,** signposted down a pleasantly winding country path, has 13th-century frescoes and is usually open mornings.

Apiranthos ★, 10km (6 miles) beyond Filoti, the most enchanting of the mountain villages, is remarkable in that many of its buildings, streets, and even domestic walls are built of the brilliant white Naxos marble, others of a golden hued local stone. Many of the narrow lanes are covered with arches that join houses. The people of Apiranthos were originally from Crete; they fled their homes during a time of Turkish oppression. Be sure to visit **Taverna Lefteris,** the excellent cafe/restaurant just off the main square (see below); day tours of the island often stop here, so you may want to eat early or late. If you have time, have a look in the small folk museum signposted on the main square; it keeps irregular hours, but has some great old photos, farm implements, costumes, and a sweet wooden cradle. There's also a small archaeological museum that's sometimes open.

THE VILLAGES WITH THE KOUROI (MONUMENTAL ANCIENT MARBLE STATUES) ★   **Apollon,** at the northern tip of the island (54km/33 miles from Hora), is a small fishing village on the verge of becoming a wannabe resort. It has a sand cove, a pebbled beach, plenty of places to eat (tour groups come here to see the kouroi), rooms to let, and a few hotels. From the town, you can drive or take the path that leads about 1km (½ mile) south to the famous **kouros** (a monumental statue of a nude young man). The kouros, about 10m tall (33 ft.), was begun in the 7th century B.C. and abandoned, probably because the stone cracked during carving. Some archaeologists believe the statue was meant for the nearby temple of Apollo, but the kouros's

If you're going to spend some time on the island and want to explore on foot, pick up a copy of Christian Ucke's excellent guide, *Walking Tours on Naxos.* You can take an island bus to reach most of the start and finish points for the walks. It's available for 15€ at **Naxos Tourist Information Center** on the *paralia.* As with all off-the-beaten-track walks, be equipped with water, a hat, good shoes, sun block, a map, a compass—and a good sense of direction.

beard suggests that it may be Dionysos. Naxos's other kouros is in the village of **Flerio** (also known as Melanes), about 7km (4 miles) east of Naxos town. The 8m (26-ft.), probably 6th-century-B.C. kouros lies abandoned as though asleep in a lovely garden. Both kouroi sites are open to the public and free; in Flerio you can sip refreshments (including the local *kitron,* a lemon liqueur) served at the cafe run by the family that owns the garden and cares for the kouros. When you visit the National Museum in Athens, you can view a number of successfully completed kouroi statues.

BEACHES ★★

Naxos has the longest and some of the best beaches in the Cyclades, although you wouldn't know it from crowded **Ayios Yeoryios** beach just south of Hora. Windsurfing equipment and lessons are available at Ayios Yeoryios from Naxos Surf Club (✆ **22850/29-170**). **Ayios Prokopios,** just beyond Ayios Yeorgios, is another sand beach, some of which is now dominated by the new Lagos Mare Hotel (see "Where to Stay," below). You can rent windsurfing gear at **Plaka Beach,** south of Ayios Prokopios, from **Plaka Watersports** (✆ **22850/41-264**). Continuing south, **Kastraki Beach** is 7km (4½ miles) long and has won awards for its clean waters.

SHOPPING

Hora is a fine place for shopping, for both value and variety. **Zoom** (✆ **22850/23-675**), on the waterfront, is the place to head for books and magazines. To the right and up from the entrance to the Old Market is **Techni ★** (✆ **22850/24-767**), which has two shops within 20m (66 ft.) of each other. The first shop contains a good array of silver jewelry at fair prices; farther along the street, the second and more interesting of the two features textiles, many hand-woven (including some antiques) by island women. Nearby, **Loom** (✆ **22850/25-531**), as its name suggests, has hand-woven fabrics and garments.

On the *paralia,* next to Grotta Tours, is tiny **Galini** (✆ **22850/24-785**), with a collection of local ceramics. Also on the *paralia,* the venerable **Promponas Wines** (✆ **22850/22-258**) has been here since 1915; the local *kitron* liqueur is a house specialty, along with a wide variety of Naxian wines. If you want something to eat with your wine, head along the *paralia* to the OTE, turn left on the main inland street, Papavasiliou, and proceed up the left side of the street until your nose leads you into **Tirokomika Proïonda Naxou ★** (✆ **22850/22-230**). This delightful old store is filled with excellent local cheeses (*kephalotiri,* a superb sharp cheese, and milder *graviera*), barrels of olives, local wines, honey and spices.

There are a lot of shops on the streets leading up to Kastro, and because the streets are winding and cross each other, and seldom have visible street signs, I'm just going to suggest that you wander and keep an eye out for these. As always in the Cyclades, there are a great many jewelry shops, many selling cheap trinkets imported from China, but some with local work. You'll see the difference. Near the main entrance to the Kastro, **Paraporti** (☎ 22850/25-795) has an appealing selection of local and off-island crafts. The **Byzantium Gallery** (☎ 22850/22-478) has reproduction and original icons as well as a wide range of church art and gifts. **Techni** (☎ 22850/24-767) has side-by-side shops selling traditional weaving and embroidery (understandably, because all is handmade, is not cheap, but is lovely) done by Naxian women. In the kastro itself, **Antico Veneziano** ★ (☎ 22850/26-206) has just that—antiques from the island's Venetian period—as well as glassware, woodcarvings, and old weavings from throughout Greece. This is a lovely place to browse; it's in a handsome Venetian-period house. *Tip:* As you wander, keep an eye out for **Elia** (☎ 22950/24-884), a delightful cafe/restaurant on the old market street up to the kastro. This is a lovely spot for a coffee and a snack. If you want to stop at the accurately described "highest elevated restaurant in town," head to **Oniro** (☎ 22850/23-846; www.oniro-naxos.info). Oniro is perched outside the main entrance to kastro, and unless they only serve sawdust, I want to eat there soon. (They happened to be closed when I was last on Naxos.)

Where to Stay

Hora's harbor is too busy for quiet accommodations; the following hotels in Kastro and Bourgo are within a 10-minute walk of the port; hotels in Grotta are a bit farther away, and places in Ayios Yeoryios are just outside of Hora. Insect repellent is advised wherever you stay. In addition to the following, you might consider the 19-unit **Hotel Anixis** (☎ 22850/22-112; www.hotel-anixis.gr), near the Kastro's Venetian tower. Rooms are small, but about half have balconies, and the Kastro location is appealing; as always with a Kastro, the walk there is steep. If you want to be on a beach, consider Anixis's sister hotel, the seven-unit **Anixis Resort** (☎ 22850/26-475; www.hotel anixis.gr), a 10-minute walk from town, 30m (98 ft.) from Ayios Yiorgos Beach. The family management at both is highly praised; prices start at 70€. If you want to be in a quiet location, but near a number of Hora's night spots, including the disco **Soul,** as well as a supermarket, bus stop, and beach, check out **Margo Studios** (☎ 22850/27-644; www.naxosmargo.com), which has nine rooms, seven studios, two apartments, a nice garden terrace, and very helpful English-speaking owners; doubles from 50€, studios from 60€, apartments sleeping up to five for 90€.

KASTRO

Castro ★ Not quite a B&B, not quite self-sufficiency apartments, the two units here are rather fey studio apartments just inside the Kastro, with a shared terrace and a view across town to the Portara and the sea—and that's quite a view! This is the sort of place that makes you have pleasant fantasies of holing up and writing a novel (or at least a novella) and spending enough time exploring the Kastro neighborhood that you would get lost only once a day. Try to get the top-floor unit with its own balcony so that you can watch the passing scene. Both units have wrought-iron beds and plenty of shelf space, with some interesting knickknacks; you can add to the collections of seashells if you wish. The Castro also rents several nearby apartments (usually by the week). The Castro, Apollon, and Chateau Zevgoli Hotels are associated.

Kastro, Hora, 84300 Naxos. www.naxostownhotels.com. ☎ **22850/25-201.** 2 units. 80€–100€ studio; 110€–130€ apt. No credit cards. Closed Nov–Apr. *In room:* Kitchenette.

BOURGO

Apollon ★   What more appropriate spot to stay, on an island famous for its marble, than in a former marble workshop—although, I have to confess that if I had not been told this, I never would have guessed it. The Apollon has both a quiet and very convenient location a block from the waterfront shops and restaurants and steps from the Greek Cathedral. Rooms have verandas or balconies (always a big plus) and are simply furnished (twin beds, table, chair). Although there is no garden to speak of, there are plants everywhere. The breakfast room is pleasant and the staff attentive. Try to get one of the corner sea-view rooms, which are especially nice.

Fontana, Hora, 84300 Naxos. www.apollonhotel-naxos.gr. ℂ **22850/22-468.** 13 units. 100€–150€ double. Rates include breakfast. DC, MC. **Amenities:** Breakfast room/bar; Internet. *In room:* A/C, TV, hair dryer, minifridge.

Chateau Zevgoli ★★   This small hotel, easily the most attractive in Naxos, lies at the foot of the 13th-century kastro walls. The Chateau is often fully booked months in advance; plan well ahead if you want to stay here. The energetic and helpful owner, Despina Kitini, decorated the lobby and dining area with antiques and family heirlooms. All guest rooms open onto a central atrium with a lush garden; there's also a roof terrace. The units are small but distinctively furnished with dark wood and drapes. Room no. 8, for example, features a canopy bed and a private terrace. Several rooms have views of the harbor. Ms. Kitini also rents four apartments in her house, also within the kastro walls, and only 100m (328 ft.) from the hotel. These share a large, central sitting room; throughout are handsome stone walls and floors. The honeymoon suite has a balcony overlooking the town and the sea. Kitini also sometimes has studios for rent in town, often at excellent long-term rates.

Bourgo, Hora, 84300 Naxos. www.naxostownhotels.com. ℂ **22850/25-201** or 22850/22-993. Fax 22850/25-200. 14 units, including 4 apts. 90€–120€ double; call for apt. rates. Hotel rates include breakfast. AE, MC, V. Closed Nov–Mar. **Amenities:** Breakfast room/bar; Internet. *In room:* A/C, TV, hair dryer, minifridge.

OUT ON THE ISLAND

Hora has plenty of charm and makes a pleasant base, but if you want to be near a pool or the sea, Ayios Prokopios Beach, 5km (2 miles) out of Hora, has two good choices. The 42-unit **Lianos Village Hotel** (ℂ **22850/26-362;** www.lianosvillage. com) has a pool, snack bar, Internet cafe, and good views out toward the sea, and is a 15-minute walk from the beach (from 130€ double). The fancier 30-unit **Lagos Mare** (ℂ **22850/42-844;** www.lagosmare.gr) opened in 2006 with two restaurants, two pools, spa facilities, Internet, children's playground, snorkeling lessons, and a beachside position (225€–275€ double).

Where to Eat

HORA

The Bakery, on the *paralia* (ℂ **22850/22-613**), sells baked goods at fair prices. Farther north, across from the bus station, **Bikini** (ℂ **22850/24-701**) is a good place for breakfast and crepes. **Meltemi** (ℂ **22850/22-654**) and **Apolafsis** (ℂ **22850/ 22-178**), on the waterfront, both offer all the Greek staples; Apolafsis's has a great view of the passing scene, great mussels in garlic sauce, and live music many summer nights.

The Old Inn ★★   GERMAN/INTERNATIONAL   Yearning for some homemade pâté or sausages? Dieter Ranizewski makes them at the Old Inn. The Germanic menu (this is one of relatively few places in the Cyclades where you can get jellied or smoked pork) offers a distinctive alternative to standard taverna fare. The food is hearty, abundant, and delicious, with lots of local touches. As for the decor, the courtyard offers a green haven from the noise and crowds of the *paralia*. The restaurant, once a small monastery, inhabits several buildings surrounding a courtyard. The wine cellar is situated in a former chapel. Another vaulted room houses an eclectic collection of old objects from the island and from Dieter's native Berlin. The chef often doubles as waiter so things can be leisurely here, especially if there is a German team playing soccer; on those occasions, a TV usually appears in the garden.

100m (328 ft.) in from the port off the street leading to the Apollon Hotel; it's well signposted. ✆ **22850/26-093.** Main courses 8€–20€. No credit cards. Daily 6pm–2am. Sometimes closed in winter.

Popi's Grill ★ GREEK　As the business card proclaims, this is the "oldest family tavern in Naxos," serving grills and stews since 1948. You sit under an awning to avoid sun or rain, watch Naxians belting down ouzo with their meal, and relax, perhaps over your own ouzo. The food is well-prepared typical Greek restaurant fare, the service is smooth, and the customers are mainly locals. If you like Popi's, you'll also like nearby **Nicos** (✆ **22850/23-153**), especially for fresh fish.

Paralia. ✆ **22850/22-389.** Main courses 7€–12€; fish priced by the kilo. No credit cards. Daily 11am–midnight or later.

Taverna To Kastro ★ GREEK　Just outside the kastro's south gate, you'll find small Braduna Square, which is packed with tables on summer evenings. There's an excellent view toward the bay and St. George's beach; at dusk, a pacifying calm pervades the place. The specialty here is rabbit stewed in red wine with onions, spiced with pepper and a suggestion of cinnamon. The local wines are light and delicious.

Braduna Sq. ✆ **22850/22-005.** Main courses 7€–15€. No credit cards. Daily 7pm–2am.

APIRANTHOS

Taverna Lefteris ★★ GREEK　One of the island's best restaurants is in Apiranthos, perhaps Naxos's most beautiful town. The menu features the staples of Greek cooking, prepared in a way that shows you how good this food can be. The dishes highlight the freshest of vegetables and meats, prepared with admirable subtlety; the hearty homemade bread is delicious. A cozy marble-floored room faces the street, and in back is a flagstone terrace shaded by two massive trees. The homemade sweets are an exception to the rule that you should avoid dessert in tavernas.

Apiranthos. ✆ **22850/61-333.** Main courses 7€–12€. No credit cards. Daily 11am–11pm.

Naxos After Dark

Naxos doesn't compete with Mykonos and Paros for wild nightlife, but it has a lively and varied scene. For several years, a disco called **Soul,** has been packed. Ask for directions; it's a bit tricky to find, but only a 10-minute walk from the main dock. **Portara,** by its namesake at the far end of the harbor, is an excellent place to enjoy the sunset. Next, you can join the evening *volta* (stroll) along the *paralia.* **Fragile,** through the arch in the entrance to the Old Town, is one of the older bars in town and worth a stop. **Lakridi,** off the *paralia* and not easy to find (ask for directions), often has jazz, classical, and other mellow selections. On the *paralia,* **Ocean Dance** and **Super Island** are lively and usually go all night in summer. Ask for directions to the part of town called **Pigadakia,** and then follow the sounds of music to two neighboring bar/discos, **Jam** and **On the Rocks.**

MYKONOS (MIKONOS)

By Peter Kerasiotis

177km (96 nautical miles) SE of Piraeus

What is it about Mykonos that has captured the world's imagination for over 40 years and refuses to let go? Though it is an undeniably beautiful island, it isn't the prettiest Greek island, or even of the Cyclades for that matter. Santorini is far more striking, and Folegandros and Naxos have prettier towns and beaches than Mykonos does, and are green and lush compared to Mykonos's barren land. It used to be it was the island's cosmopolitan lifestyle, luxury hotels, and nightlife, but today many of the more popular islands claim to be able to compete with that. It used to be its title as the party capital of all Mediterranean islands that set it apart, yet today Spain's Ibiza shares that title. So what is it then?

It all began with the picture-perfect town of labyrinthine roads leading you in circles around the beautiful cubist Cycladic architecture that attracted the likes of Jackie Kennedy and Aristotle Onassis in the '60s. With their stamp of approval, Mykonos became *the* place to be for anybody who was anybody. Soon, in the hedonistic '70s, it became the island version of Studio 54, making world headlines on celebrity pages and magazines. The sheer contrast of a traditional Greek fishing village and the type of tourists it attracted—gay partiers, international jet-setters, celebrities, and models—made the island a unique place to visit, and it captured the world's imagination.

If this is your first visit, you'll find lots to enjoy—especially if you avoid mid-July and August, when it seems that every one of the island's million annual visitors is here. Then again, what is Mykonos if you can't experience some of its legendary nighttime vibe for yourself? I suggest (for first timers) an early July visit. It's busy enough so you can understand what all the fuss is about, but not choked with visitors like late July and August, when even finding a table at a restaurant can be difficult. Keep in mind that **it's very important to arrive here with reservations in the high season,** unless you enjoy sleeping outdoors and don't mind being moved from your sleeping spot by the police, who are not always charmed to find foreigners alfresco.

If you come in mid-September or October, you'll find a quieter Mykonos, with a pleasant buzz of activity, and streets and restaurants that are less clogged. Unlike many of the islands, Mykonos remains active year-round. In winter, it hosts numerous cultural events, including a small film festival. Many who are scared off by the summer crowds find a different, tranquil Mykonos during this off-season, demonstrating Hora's deserved reputation as one of the most beautiful towns in the Cyclades.

Essentials

GETTING THERE By Plane Olympic Air has several flights daily (once daily in off-season) between Mykonos and Athens/Thessaloniki. Book flights in advance and reconfirm with Olympic in Athens or on Mykonos (✆ **22890/22-490** or 22890/22-237). The Mykonos office is near the south bus station; it's open Monday through Friday from 8am to 3:30pm. Travel agencies on the port sell Olympic tickets as well. **Aegean Airlines** has daily service to Mykonos in summer. (For contact information for both airlines, see "Essentials" under "Santorini," earlier in this chapter.)

By Boat Mykonos now has two ports: the old port in Mykonos town, and the new port, north of Mykonos town, at Tourlos. Check before you travel to find out schedules and which port your boat will use (www.greekferries.gr). From Piraeus, the **Blue Star Ithaki** has departures once daily at 7:30am. The **Pegasus** has two afternoon departures during summer at 7:30pm (Mon and Sat). The **High Speed** has two departures daily, one at 7:15am and 4:45pm; and the **Marina** has three departures weekly, at 11:50pm on Tuesdays, 5pm Thursday and Saturday. From Rafina, **the Super Ferry** has one departure daily at 8am; the **Super Jet 2** has two departures daily at 7:40am and 4pm. The **Aqua Jewel** has one departure daily at 5pm while the **Penelope** leaves at 7:35pm daily. **High Speed** boats line **2** and **3** have daily afternoon departures at 7:30pm and 4:30pm respectively. Schedules can be checked with the **port police** (✆ 22890/22-218). There are daily ferry connections between Mykonos and Andros, Paros, Siros, and Tinos; five to seven trips a week to Ios; four a week to Iraklio, Crete; several a week to Kos and Rhodes; and two a week to Ikaria, Samos, Skiathos, Skyros, and Thessaloniki. **Hellenic Seaways** offers Flying Dolphin hydrofoil service from **Piraeus** (✆ 210/419-9100 or -9000; www.hellenicseaways.gr) in summer. From the port of Lavrio, the **Fly Cat 3** has an 11:15am departure daily to Mykonos.

On Mykonos, your best bet for getting up-to-date lists of sailings is to check at individual agencies. Or you can check with the **port authority,** by National Bank (✆ 22890/22-218); **tourist police,** at the north end of the harbor (✆ 22890/22-482); or **tourist office,** also on the harbor (✆ 22890/23-990; fax 22890/22-229).

Hydrofoil service to Crete, Ios, Paros, and Santorini is often irregular. For information, check at **Piraeus Port Authority** (✆ 210/451-1311 or 210/422-6000; phone seldom answered), **Piraeus Port Police** (✆ 210/451-1310), **Rafina Port Police** (✆ 22940/23-300), or **Mykonos Port Police** (✆ 22890/22-218).

Warning: Check each travel agency's current schedule, because most ferry tickets are not interchangeable. Reputable agencies on the main square in Mykonos (Hora) town include **Sunspots Travel** (✆ 22890/24-196; fax 22890/23-790); **Delia Travel** (✆ 22890/22-490; fax 22890/24-440); **Sea & Sky Travel** (✆ 22890/22-853; fax 22890/24-753); and **Veronis Agency** (✆ 22890/22-687; fax 22890/23-763).

Visitor Information **Mykonos Accommodations Center,** at the corner of Enoplon Dhinameon and Malamatenias (✆ 22890/23-160; www.mykonos-accommodation.com), helps visitors find accommodations. It also functions as a tourist information center. **Windmills Travel ★** (✆ 22890/23-877; www.windmillstravel.com) has an office at Fabrica Square, where you can get general information, book accommodations, arrange excursions, and rent a car or moped. Look for the free *Mykonos Summertime* magazine, available in cafes, shops, and hotels throughout the island.

 Finding an Address

Although some shops hand out maps of Mykonos town, you'll probably do better finding restaurants, hotels, and attractions by asking people to point you in the right direction—and saying *efcharisto* (thank you) when they do. Don't panic at how to pronounce *efcharisto;* think of it as a name and say "F. Harry Stowe." Most streets do not have their names posted. Also, maps do not always show lots of small, twisting, streets—and Mykonos has almost nothing but small, twisting, streets. The map published by **Stamatis Bozinakis,** sold at most kiosks for 2€, is quite decent. The useful **Mykonos Sky Map** is free at some hotels and shops.

Getting Around   One of the best things to happen to Mykonos was the government decree that made Hora an architectural landmark and prohibited motorized traffic from its streets. You will see a few small delivery vehicles, but the only ways to get around town are to walk—or to ride a bike or donkey. Many of the town's large hotels ring the busy peripheral road, and a good transportation system serves much of the island.

By Bus   Mykonos has one of the best bus systems in the Greek islands; the buses run frequently and on schedule. Depending on your destination, a ticket costs about 1.60€ to 6€. There are two bus stations in Hora: one near the Archaeological Museum and one near the Olympic Airways office (follow the helpful blue signs). At the tourist office, find out which station the bus you want to take leaves from, or look for schedules in hotels. Bus information in English is sometimes available from **KTEL** office (✆ **22890/23-360**).

By Boat   Caiques to Super Paradise, Agrari, and Elia depart from Platis Yialos every morning, weather permitting; there is also service from Ornos in high season (July–Aug) only. Caique service is highly seasonal, with almost continuous service in high season and no caiques October through May. Excursion boats to Delos depart Tuesday through Sunday between 8:30am and 1pm, from the west side of the harbor near the tourist office. (For more information, see a travel agent; guided tours are available.)

By Car & Moped   Rental cars are available from about 50€ per day, including insurance, in high season; most agencies are near one of the two bus stops in town. **Windmills Travel** (see "Visitor Information" above) can arrange a car rental for you and get good prices. The largest concentration of moped shops is just beyond the south bus station. Expect to pay about 15€ to 30€ per day, depending on the moped's engine size. Take great care when driving: Island roads can be treacherous.

Warning: If you park in town or in a no-parking area, the police will remove your license plates. You—not the rental office—will have to find the police station and pay a steep fine to get them back.

By Taxi   There are two types of taxis in Mykonos: standard **car taxis,** for destinations outside town, and tiny, cart-towing **scooters** that buzz through the narrow streets of Hora. The latter are seen primarily at the port, where they wait to bring new arrivals to their lodgings in town—a good idea, as most in-town hotels are a challenge to find. Getting a car taxi in Hora is easy: Walk to Taxi (Mavro) Square, near the statue, and join the line. A notice board gives rates for various destinations. You can also call **Mykonos Radio Taxi** (✆ **22890/22-400**).

Fast Facts   **Commercial Bank** and **National Bank of Greece** are on the harbor a couple blocks west of Taxi Square; both are open Monday through Friday from 8am to 2pm. ATMs are available throughout town. **Mykonos Health Center** (✆ **22890/ 22-274** or 22890/22-398) handles routine medical complaints; serious cases are usually airlifted to the mainland. The **tourist police** (✆ **22890/22-482**) are on the west side of the port near the ferries to Delos; the local **police** (✆ **22890/22-716**) are behind the grammar school, near Plateia Laka. The **post office** (✆ **22890/22-238**) is next to the police station; it's open Monday through Friday from 7:30am to 2pm. The **telephone office** (**OTE;** ✆ **22890/22-499**) is on the north side of the harbor, beyond the Hotel Leto, and is open Monday through Friday 7:30am to 3pm. For **Internet** access, keep in mind that most hotels on the island have at least an Internet corner, and most cafes have free Wi-Fi.

What to See & Do
BEACHES

The beaches on the island's **south shore** have the best sand, views, and wind protection. However, these days they are so popular that you'll have to navigate through a forest of beach umbrellas to find your square yard of sand. A few (**Paradise, Super Paradise**) are known as party beaches, and guarantee throbbing music and loud revelry until late at night. Others (**Platis Yialos** and **Ornos**) are quieter and more popular with families. **Psarrou** has gone from being a family beach to being perhaps the trendiest beach of them all (for visiting Athenians mostly). With all the south-coast beaches, keep in mind that most people begin to arrive in the early afternoon, and you can avoid the worst of the crowds by going in the morning. The **north-coast beaches** are less developed but just as beautiful. Because the buses and caiques don't yet make the trip, you'll have to rent a car or scooter; you'll be more than compensated for the trouble by the quiet and the lack of commercial development.

For those who can't wait to hit the beach, the closest to Mykonos town is **Megali Ammos (Big Sand),** about a 10-minute walk south—it's very crowded and not particularly scenic. To the north, the beach nearest town is 2km (1¼ miles) away at **Tourlos;** however, because this is now where many ships dock at the new harbor, it's not a place for a relaxing swim. **Ornos** is popular with families; it's about 2.5km (1½ miles) south of town and has a fine-sand beach in a sheltered bay, with extensive hotel development along the shore. Buses to Ornos run hourly from the south station between 8am and 11pm.

With back-to-back hotels and tavernas along its long sandy beach, **Platis Yialos** is extremely easy to get to from the town and has pristine aqua-blue waters and a variety of watersports. Due to its proximity to town however, it is always crowded and lacks character. It's ideal for a swim if you're too hung over to make it to farther beaches. Here you can catch a caique to the more distant beaches of Paradise, Super Paradise, Agrari, and Elia as well as a small boat to Delos. The bus runs every 15 minutes from 8am to 8pm, then every 30 minutes until midnight. Nearby **Psarou** is the first stop on the bus from town to Platis Yialos and it is a much more highbrow version of its neighbor. It is actually a beautiful stretch of beach, with white sand and greenery, overlooked by the terraces of tavernas and hotels. The excellent **N'Ammos** restaurant is right here, as is the sublime hotel **Mykonos Blu,** of the Grecotel chain. A rowdy beach bar here has patrons dancing on whatever free inch of space they can find. During high season, and especially during the weekends when the trendy Athenians flock to this beach, even chaise longues require reservations. Psarou is also popular when the *meltemi* winds strike the island, as it offers protection in its bay to many yachts, boats, and swimmers. Its watersports facilities include **Diving Center Psarou,** water-skiing, and windsurfing. **Paranga,** farther east, is small and picturesque and can be reached easily on foot via an inland path from Platis Yialos; this small cove is popular for nude sunbathing and doesn't get too crowded, but is never too quiet either as the loud music from the neighboring beaches can be heard. From here you can take a hill path that will lead you to another beach, **Agia Anna (St. Anne).** Agia Anna is a pebbles beach with a beautiful landscape and sweeping views from the top of the hill.

Reach **Paradise ★**, the island's most famous beach, on foot from Platis Yialos (about 2km/1¼ miles), by bus, or by caique. The more adventurous arrive by moped on roads that are incredibly narrow and steep. Seeing how very few leave this beach sober, it is in your best interest (even if you have rented a moped) to get back to town

Beach Notes

Activity on the beaches is highly seasonal, and all the information offered here pertains only to the months of June through September. The prevailing winds on Mykonos (and throughout the Cyclades) blow from the north, which is why the southern beaches are the most protected and calm. The exception to this rule is a southern wind that occurs periodically during the summer, making the northern beaches more desirable for sunning and swimming. In Mykonos town, this southern wind is heralded by particularly hot temperatures and perfect calm in the harbor. On such days, those in the know will avoid Paradise, Super Paradise, and Elia, heading instead to the northern beaches of Ayios Sostis and Panormos—or simply choose another activity for the day.

by bus. This is the island's original nude beach, and it still attracts many nudists. A stand of small trees provides some shade, and the beach is well protected from the predominant north winds. Lined with bars, tavernas, and clubs, Paradise is never a quiet experience—it is the premier party beach of the island and shows no signs of stopping. The **Tropicana Beach Bar** and the **Sunrise Bar** are both havens for the party crowd that goes all day, long after the sun has set. On top of the hill, the popular and internationally known **Cavo Paradiso Club** is a large, open-air nightclub with rotating international DJs and doors that do not open until after 2am. In fact the "cool crowd" begins to arrive only after 5am. On the beach, Paradise Club is the club destination from 6pm to midnight, reopening from 2am to 6am. One beach party on Paradise you shouldn't miss is the **Full Moon Party,** once a month. The only other party that compares to it is the **Closing Party** every September that has become an island institution. As in most of the island, the water here is breathtakingly beautiful, but hardly anybody comes to Paradise for the sea.

Super Paradise (Plindri) is in a rocky cove just around the headland from Paradise; it's somewhat less developed than its neighbor, but no less crowded. You can get to the beach on foot, by bus, or by caique; if you go by car or moped, be very careful on the extremely steep and narrow access road. The left side of the beach is a nonstop party in summer, with loud music and dancing, while the right side is mostly nude and gay, with the exclusive **Coco Club** providing a relaxed ambience for its chic clientele until after 5pm, when things get rowdy and loud. On the right side, there are similar party bars for the straight crowd. The waters here are beautiful but very deep, so it isn't the best swimming option for families with small children. Farther east across the little peninsula is **Agrari,** a lovely cove sheltered by lush foliage, with a good little taverna and a beach that welcomes bathers in all modes of dress and undress.

Elia, a 45-minute caique ride from Platis Yialos and the last regular stop (also accessible by bus from the town), is a sand-and-pebble beach with crowds nearly as overwhelming as at Paradise and little shade and bamboo windbreaks. Nevertheless, this beautiful beach is one of the longest on the island. The beach is surrounded by a circle of steep hills, has an attractive restaurant/cafe/bar, and offers umbrellas, sun beds, and watersports. There is a gay section to this beach that is clothing optional. Despite its popularity, there is no loud bar/club here, so the atmosphere is more sedate than the Paradise beaches. The next major beach is **Kalo Livadi (Good Pasture).** Located in a farming valley, this long, beautiful beach is about as quiet as a beach on

Mykonos's southern coast gets. There's bus service from Mykonos town's north station. Adjacent to the beach are a taverna and a few villas and hotels on the hills.

The last resort area on the southern coast accessible by bus from the north station is **Kalafatis ★**. This fishing village was once the port of the ancient citadel of Mykonos, which dominated the little peninsula to the west. A line of trees separates the beach from the rows of buildings that have grown up along the road. This is one of the longest beaches on Mykonos, and its days of being uncrowded are, alas, over. The waters are pristine, however, and the hotels offer water-skiing, surfing, and windsurfing lessons. Here you will also find a good beach restaurant and bar and many boats throughout the day to take you to **Dragonisi,** an islet that has many caves ideal for swimming and exploring. You might also catch a glimpse of rare monk seals at the islet; its caves are reportedly a breeding ground for them. Adjacent to Kalafatis in a tiny cove is lovely **Ayia Anna** (not to be confused with the other beach of the same name, by Paranga beach), a short stretch of sand with a score of umbrellas. Several kilometers farther east, accessible by a fairly good road from Kalafatis, is **Lia,** which has fine sand, clear water, bamboo windbreaks, and a small, exceptional, and shockingly low-priced taverna.

Most of the north-coast beaches are too windy to be of interest to anyone other than windsurfers and surfers. Though windsurfing has always been extremely popular in Greece, surfing is a relatively new sport here and Greece is a newly discovered destination for many surfers. All over the country, from Athens to beach towns and villages that line both coasts and many islands, surfers are suddenly realizing Greece with its many coasts has more to offer than clear waters that aren't shark infested. Though Mykonos doesn't appear in the top 10 list of favorite places to surf in Greece, it should; already many of the island's wind-battered north-coast beaches attract many European surfers in the know. When the north winds hit the island relentlessly, waves can swell up to impressive sizes and the lack of competition provides an uninterrupted haven for surfers and windsurfers alike. In order to enjoy this scene, however, you have to have either a car or a moped, as public transportation, regrettably or not, hasn't made it here yet. **Fokos** is a superb sandy beach that has only recently begun to get noticed by tourists. The scenery is raw, wild, and beautiful, and there is a small taverna here that is quite good. Fokos was the first beach to get noticed by the surfers. The huge Panormos Bay has three main beaches. The one closest to town is **Ftelia,** and it is a long fine-sand beach, easily one of the best on the island, but for the force of the north wind, which has made it popular with surfers and windsurfers. There are, however, two well-sheltered northern beaches, and because you can only reach them by car or moped, they're much less crowded than the southern beaches. Head east from Mykonos town on the road to Ano Mera, turning left after 1.5km (1¼ miles) on the road to Ayios Sostis and Panormos. At **Panormos,** you'll find a cove with 100m (328 ft.) of fine sand backed by low dunes. Another 1km (½ mile) down the road is **Ayios Sostis ★**, a lovely small beach that sits just below a village. There isn't any parking, so it's best to leave your vehicle along the main road and walk 200m (656 ft.) down through the village. An excellent small taverna just up from the beach operates without electricity, so it's open only during daylight hours. Panormos and Ayios Sostis have few amenities—no beach umbrellas, bars, or snack shops—but they do offer a break from the crowds. Ayios Sostis is wild, windswept, and beautiful, as are all north-coast beaches, offering a completely different landscape than their far more popular southern counterparts. When the *meltemi* winds are at their strongest, during July and August into September, the waves can be awesome and unrelenting and the water is filled with surfers. Ayios Sostis, however, is becoming the new "in" beach during the high season, when the visiting Athenians escape here when the winds aren't too strong.

Beaches to avoid on Mykonos because of pollution, noise, and crowds include **Tourlos** and **Korfos Bay.**

With so many sun worshipers on Mykonos, local merchants have figured out that they can charge pretty steep prices for suntan lotions and sunscreens. You probably want to bring some with you. If you want to try a Greek brand, the oddly named Carrot Milk is excellent.

DIVING

Mykonos is known throughout the Aegean as one of *the* places for diving. Scuba diving on many islands is prohibited to protect undersea archaeological treasures from plunder. The best month is September, when the water temperature is typically 75°F (24°C) and visibility is 30m (98 ft.). Certified divers can rent equipment and participate in guided dives; first-time divers can rent snorkeling gear or take an introductory beach dive. The best established dive center is **Mykonos Diving Center,** at Paradise beach (©/fax **22890/24-808;** www.dive.gr), which offers 5-day PADI certification courses in English from about 500€, including equipment. **Psarou Diving Center** in Mykonos town (© **22890/24-808**) has also been around for a long time. As always, before you sign up for lessons, be sure that all instructors are PADI certified. The **Union of Diving Centers in Athens** (© **210/411-8909**) usually has up-to-date information. In general, certified divers can join guided dives from 50€ per dive; beginners can take a 2-hour class and beach dive from 60€. There's a nearby wreck at a depth of 20 to 35m (65–114 ft.); wreck dives run from 60€.

ATTRACTIONS

Ask anybody who has visited the Greek islands and they will tell you that apart from the beaches, nothing compares to the early-evening stroll in the islands' towns. The light of the late hour, the pleasant buzz, the narrow streets filled with locals and tourists alike, and the romantic ambience in the air as you stroll along streets can lead you to anything from a modern restaurant, a pleasant taverna, a fortress, or an ancient, unassuming site.

Despite its intense commercialism and seething crowds in high season, Hora is still the quintessential Cycladic town and is worth a visit to the island in itself. The best way to see the town is to venture inland from the port and wander. Browse the window displays, go inside an art gallery, a store, or an old church that may be open but empty inside. Keep in mind that the town is bounded on two sides by the bay, and on the other two by the busy vehicular District Road, and that all paths funnel eventually into one of the main squares: **Plateia Mantos Mavroyenous,** on the port (called **Taxi Square** because it's the main taxi stand); **Plateia Tria Pigadia;** and **Plateia Laka,** near the south bus station.

Hora also has the remains of a small **Venetian kastro** and the island's most famous church, **Panagia Paraportiani (Our Lady of the Postern Gate),** a thickly whitewashed asymmetrical edifice made up of four small chapels. Beyond the Panagia Paraportiani is the **Alefkandra** quarter, better known as **Little Venice ★★**, for its cluster of homes built overhanging the sea. Many buildings here have been converted into fashionable bars prized for their sunset views; you can sip a margarita and listen to Mozart most nights at the **Montparnasse** or **Kastro Bar,** or check out the sunset and stay all night at **Caprice.** (See "Mykonos After Dark," later in this chapter.)

Another nearby watering spot is the famous **Tria Pigadia (Three Wells)** ★★. Local legend says that if a virgin drinks from all three, she is sure to find a husband, but it's probably not a good idea to test this hypothesis by drinking the brackish well water. After your visit, you may want to take in the famous **windmills of Kato Myli** and enjoy the views back toward Little Venice.

Save time to visit the island's clutch of pleasant small museums. **The Archaeological Museum** (☎ **22890/22-325**), near the harbor, displays finds from Delos; it's open Wednesday to Monday 9am to 3:30pm. Admission is 3€ (free Sun). **Nautical Museum of the Aegean** (☎ **22890/22-700**), across from the park on Enoplon Dinameon Street, has just what you'd expect, including handsome ship models. It's open Tuesday to Sunday 10:30am to 1pm and 6 to 9pm; admission is 3€. Also on Enoplon Dinameon Street, **Lena's House** (☎ **22890/22-591**) re-creates the home of a middle-class 19th-century Mykonos family. It's usually open daily Easter through October; admission is free. **Museum of Folklore** (☎ **22890/25-591**), in a 19th-century sea captain's mansion near the quay, displays examples of local crafts and furnishings. On show is a 19th-century island kitchen. It's open Monday to Saturday 4 to 8pm, Sunday 5 to 8pm; admission is free.

When you've spent some time in Hora, you may want to visit **Ano Mera,** 7km (4 miles) east of Hora near the center of the island, a quick bus ride from the north station. Ano Mera is the island's only other real town, and we especially recommend this trip for those interested in religious sites—the **Monastery of Panagia Tourliani** southeast of town dates from the 18th century and has a marble bell tower with intricate folk carvings. Inside the church are a huge Italian baroque iconostasis (altar screen) with icons of the Cretan school; an 18th-century marble baptismal font; and a small museum containing liturgical vestments, needlework, and woodcarvings. One kilometer (½ mile) southeast is the 12th-century **Monastery of Paleokastro,** in one of the island's greenest spots. Ano Mera also has the island's most traditional atmosphere; a fresh-produce market on the main square sells excellent local cheeses. This is the island's place of choice for Sunday brunch.

SHOPPING

Mykonos has a lot of shops, many selling overpriced souvenirs, clothing, and jewelry to cruise-ship day-trippers. Having said that, there are also a number of serious shops here, selling serious wares—at serious prices. **Soho-Soho,** 81 Matoyanni (☎ **22890/26-760**), is by far the most well known clothing store on the island; pictures of its famous clientele (Tom Hanks, Sarah Jessica Parker, and so forth) carrying the store's bags have been in gossip publications around the world. Maria will help the female clientele find the perfect outfit while just across the street, at the men's store, Bill will recommend the latest men's arrivals. Luxury fashion boutique **Scoop NYC** (☎ **22890/25-122;** www.scoopnyc.com) opened its first European location in the Belvedere Hotel. Its exquisite jewelry line by native Mykonian designer Ileana Makri sets this store apart from its New York counterpart. The finest jewelry shop on the island remains **LALAoUNIS** ★, 14 Polykandrioti (☎ **22890/22-444**), associated with the famous LALAoUNIS museum and shops in Athens. It has superb reproductions of ancient and Byzantine jewelry as well as original designs. When you leave LALAoUNIS, have a look at **Yiannis Galantis** (☎ **22890/22-255**), which sells clothing designed by the owner. If you can't afford LALAoUNIS, you might check out one of the island's oldest jewelry shops, the **Gold Store,** right on the waterfront (☎ **22890/22-397**). **Delos Dolphins,** Matoyanni at Enoplon Dimameon (☎ **22890/22-765**), specializes in copies of museum pieces; **Vildiridis,** 12 Matoyianni (✆ **22890/23-245**), also has jewelry based on ancient designs. Also be sure to check out **Karkalis,** 17 Matoyanni (✆ **22890/24-022;** www.gold.gr), the newest arrival to hit the town, with striking original and contemporary designs. **Actipis Sea Pebble Jewelry,** Ayion Spiridon and Ayias Annas (✆ **22890/25-747;** www.actipis.com), has beautiful and unique hand-made pieces. Mykonos is also well-known for its house-designed sandals in many colors and styles; perhaps no better selection can be found in the entire island than at **Eccentric by Design,** 11 Fiorou Zouganelis St. (✆ **22890/28-499**), where you can even find sandals encrusted with Swarovski crystals. For more traditional sandals, check out **Kostas Rabias,** on Matoyianni Street (✆ **22890/22-010**).

Mykonos has lots of art galleries, including some based in Athens that move here for the summer season. **Scala Gallery ★**, 48 Matoyianni (✆ **22890/23-407;** fax 22890/26-993; www.scalagallery.gr), is one of the best galleries in town. All the artists represented are from Greece, many of them quite well known. There is a selection of jewelry, plus an interesting collection of recent works by Yorgos Kypris, an Athenian sculptor and ceramic artist. Nearby on Panahrandou is **Scala II Gallery** (✆ **22890/26-993**), where the overflow from the Scala Gallery is sold at reduced prices. In addition, manager **Dimitris Roussounelos,** (✆/fax **22890/26-993;** scala@ otenet.gr) of Scala Gallery, manages a number of studios and apartments in Hora, so you might find lodgings as well as art at Scala.

There was a time when Mykonos was world famous for its vegetable-dyed hand-loomed weavings, especially those of the legendary Kuria Vienoula. Today, **Nikoletta** (✆ **22890/27-503**) is one of the few shops where you can still see the island's traditional loomed goods. Eleni Kontiza's tiny shop **Hand Made** (✆ **22890/27-512**), on a lane between Plateia Tria Pigadia and Plateia Laka, has a good selection of hand-woven scarves, rugs, and tablecloths from around Greece.

The best bookstore on Mykonos is **To Vivlio ★** (✆ **22890/27-737**), on Zougan-eli, one street over from Matoyianni. It carries a good selection of books in English, including many works of Greek writers in translation, plus some art and architecture books and a few travel guides.

Works of culinary art can be found at **Skaropoulos** (✆ **22890/24-983**), 1.5km (1 mile) out of Hora on the road to Ano Mera, featuring the Mykonian specialties of Nikos and Frantzeska Koukas. Nikos's grandfather started making confections here in 1921, winning prizes and earning a personal commendation from Winston Churchill. Try their famed *amygdalota* (an almond sweet) or the almond biscuits (Churchill's favorite). You can also find Skaropoulos sweets at **Pantopoleion,** 24 Kaloyerou (✆ **22890/22-078**), along with Greek organic foods and natural cosmetics; the shop is in a beautifully restored 300-year-old Mykonian house.

When you finish your shopping, treat yourself to another almond biscuit (or two or three) from **Efthemios,** 4 Florou Zouganeli (✆ **22890/22-281**), just off the harbor-front, where biscuits have been made since the 1950s.

Where to Stay

In summer, reserve a room 1 to 3 months in advance (or more), if possible. Ferry arrivals are often met by a throng of people hawking rooms, some in small hotels, others in private homes. If you don't have a hotel reservation, one of these rooms may be very welcome. Otherwise, book as early as you can. Many hotels are fully booked all summer by tour groups or regular patrons. Keep in mind that Mykonos is an easier, more pleasant place to visit in the late spring or early fall. Off-season hotel rates are sometimes half the quoted high-season rate. Also note that many small hotels, restaurants, and shops close in winter, especially if business is slow.

Mykonos Accommodations Center (MAC), 10 Enoplon Dinameon (✆ **22890/ 23-160** or 22890/23-408; fax 22890/24-137; www.mykonos-accommodation.com), is a very helpful service, especially if you are looking for hard-to-find inexpensive lodgings. The service is free when you book a hotel stay of 3 nights or longer. If you plan a shorter stay, ask about the fee, which is sometimes a percentage of the tab and sometimes a flat fee.

IN HORA

Andronikos Hotel ★★ Beautiful, elegant, and right in town, this impeccably designed hotel offers spacious verandas or terraces with incredible vistas of the sea and the town, a very good on-site restaurant, an edgy gallery, and a spa, at affordable (for Mykonos) prices.

Hora 86400, Mykonos. www.andronikoshotel.com. ✆ **22890/24-231.** Fax 22890/24-691. 53 units. 180€–230€ double; 240€–290€ double with Jacuzzi; 310€–380€ suite. AE, DC, MC, V. **Amenities:** Restaurant; bar; gallery; gym; pool; spa. *In room:* A/C, TV/DVD, hair dryer, Jacuzzi (in some rooms), minibar, Wi-Fi.

Apanema Resort Hotel ★★ This intimate and pretty boutique hotel is also ideally located only a 10-minute walk from town. The young owner has decorated her hotel in impeccable taste, with personal touches throughout, such as handcrafted pottery and rugs, which create a homey feeling even amid the elegance. Another big plus (apart from the stunning view from the pool) is the hotel's ample and delicious American buffet breakfast, served from 7am to 2pm, for those that cannot get out of bed before 1pm. The on-site Mediterranean fusion restaurant, **Apanema,** is another excuse to stay.

Hora, Tagoo 84600 Mykonos. www.apanemaresort.com. ✆ **22890/28-590.** Fax 22890/79-250. 17 units. 179€–300€ double; 510€ suite. Rates include American buffet breakfast. Considerable off-season reductions. AE, MC, V. Free parking. **Amenities:** Restaurant; bar; pool; tennis court. *In room:* A/C, TV, hair dryer, Internet, minibar.

Belvedere Hotel ★★ The all-white oasis of the Belvedere, in part occupying a handsomely restored 1850s town house on the main road into town, has stunning views over the town and harbor, a few minutes' walk away. Rooms are nicely, if not distinctively, furnished. Stay here if you want many of the creature comforts of Mykonos's beach resorts but prefer to be within walking distance of Hora. The ultrachic poolside scene buzzes all night and day, in part due to Nobu Matsuhisa's only open-air restaurant, the impeccable **Matsuhisa Mykonos.** Also on-site are the excellent Greek restaurant **Club Belvedere** and the wonderful **CBar Lounge**—ideal for its sweeping sunset views. In season, the hotel often offers massage, salon, and barber service. Off-season, look for excellent specials; after a 4-night stay, this might mean a free Jeep for a day or a fifth night free. This is the Delano of Mykonos; stylish, always popular, and in a class of its own.

Hora, 84600 Mykonos. www.belvederehotel.com. ✆ **22890/25-122.** Fax 22890/25-126. 48 units. 230€–460€ double; 650€ suite. Rates include American buffet breakfast. Considerable off-season reductions. AE, DC, MC, V. **Amenities:** 2 restaurants; bar/lounge; fitness center; Jacuzzi; pool; sauna. *In room:* A/C, TV, hair dryer, Internet, minibar.

Cavo Tagoo ★★ This exceptional hotel, set into a cliff, with spectacular views over Mykonos town, is hard to resist—and consistently makes it onto *Odyssey* magazine's list of 10 best Greek hotels. Cavo Tagoo's island-style architecture has won awards, and its gleaming marble floors, nicely crafted wooden furniture, queen- and king-size beds, and local-style weavings are a genuine pleasure. An impressive redesign has left it better than ever before. Elegantly minimalist with marble, spacious bathrooms and large balconies with stunning sea vistas, Cavo Tagoo features suites with private pools, a spa center, stunning lounge, and pool areas. Hora's harbor is only a 15-minute walk away, although you may find it hard to budge: A saltwater pool and a good restaurant are located at the hotel.

Hora, 84600 Mykonos. www.cavotagoo.gr. ☏ **22890/23-692** to -695. Fax 22890/24-923. 69 units. 225€–420€ double. Rates include buffet breakfast. AE, DC, MC, V. Closed Nov–Mar. **Amenities:** Restaurant; bar; gym; saltwater pool; sauna. *In room:* A/C, TV, hair dryer, Internet, minibar.

Elysium ★★   The smartest gay hotel on the island is located on a steep hillside right in the old town; a walk down the steep hill will have you back in town in 3 minutes. Gardens, a pool, great views, a gym, a sauna, and a very relaxed atmosphere keep guests coming again and again.

Mykonos Old Town, 84600 Mykonos. www.elysiumhotel.com. ☏ **22890/23-952.** Fax 22890/23-747. 42 units. 180 € double; 246€ suite; 800€–1,126€ royal suite. AE, DC, MC, V. **Amenities:** Bar/cafe; gym; hydromassage; pool; sauna; spa. *In room:* A/C, TV, hair dryer, Internet.

Hermes Mykonos ★   Atop a hill with stunning vistas of the town, the port, the windmills, and the sea, Hermes Hotel has clean and comfortable rooms, a breakfast area, and a lovely pool with breathtaking views. The 10-minute walk down the hill to town is effortless but the same walk on your way back up can easily run you longer and can be exhausting—the only drawback to this charming hotel. However, the magnificent views and good value compensate for the extra calories burned.

Drosopezoula, Hora, 84600 Mykonos. www.mykonoshermes.gr. ☏ **22890/24-242.** Fax 22890/25-640. 24 units. 130€–190€ double. Rates include buffet breakfast. AE, MC, V. **Amenities:** Cafe/bar; pool. *In room:* A/C, TV.

Mykonos Theoxenia ★★   When the Mykonos Theoxenia reopened its doors in 2004 after an extensive makeover, it quickly became the talk of the town once again as it was in the '60s. With its stone-clad walls and orange and turquoise fabrics, the mood is already set before you venture beyond the reception. In the 52 rooms and suites, funky '60s-inspired furniture and loud colors dominate the decor with spacious bathrooms (stuffed with luxuries) enclosed in glass walls. The location, right by the windmills and impossibly romantic Little Venice, could not be any more ideal. A wonderful pool and restaurant are the perfect finishing touches. When you arrive at the hotel you will be treated to a welcoming drink, a fruit basket, and bottle of wine.

Kato Mili, Hora, 84600 Mykonos. www.mykonostheoxenia.com. ☏ **22890/22-230.** 52 units. 282€–420€ double, depending on balcony and view; 625€ junior suite; 830€ 2-bedroom suite. AE, DC, MC, V. Free parking. **Amenities:** Restaurant; bar; pool. *In room:* A/C, TV, hair dryer, Internet.

Mykonos View ★   With a view that you'll be hard-pressed to beat, the Mykonos View is ideally situated: On a hill above the town is a complex of apartments (independent studios, apartments, and maisonettes) all connected via cobblestone paths, giving you the sense of having your own island apartment, which is infinitely more alluring for some than feeling they are in a hotel. The swimming pool hangs over the Aegean and the town. The hotel's awesome **Oneiro Bar (Dream Bar)** has become an island-must sunset destination.

Hora, 84600 Mykonos. www.mykonosview.gr. ☏ **22890/24-045.** Fax 22890/26445. 30 units. 130€–160€ studio; 160€–220€ superior studio; 180€–250€ apt.; 200€–280€ maisonette. AE, DC, MC, V. **Amenities:** Restaurant; bar; pool. *In room:* A/C, TV, hair dryer, Internet.

Ostraco Suites ★ This mod-meets-island decor is ideal for young, hip couples or a group of young friends who are looking for something stylish (but not outrageously pricey or chic) and a 5-minute walk to town. It consists of five white villas, and manages to be affordable and trendy at the same time. Two of the suites were renovated by the late, renowned Greek interior designer Angelos Angelopoulos.

Drafaki, 84600 Mykonos. www.ostraco.gr. ℂ **22890/23-396.** Fax 22890/27-123. 21 units. 185€–230€ double; 305€–380€ suite. Rates include buffet breakfast. AE, DC, MC, V. **Amenities:** Restaurant; bar; cafe; pool; spa; sun deck. *In room:* A/C, LCD TV/DVD, hair dryer, minibar.

Philippi Hotel Each room in this homey little hotel in the heart of Mykonos town is different, so you might want to look at several before choosing yours. The owner tends a lush garden that often provides flowers for her son's restaurant, the elegant **Philippi** (p. 308), which can be reached through the garden.

25 Kaloyera, Hora, 84600 Mykonos. www.philippihotel.com. ℂ **22890/22-294.** Fax 22890/24-680. 13 units. 90€ double. No credit cards. **Amenities:** Restaurant; breakfast room. *In room:* A/C, TV, fridge, hair dryer, Wi-Fi.

Semeli Hotel ★ Named after the mother of Dionysos, the god of wine, Semeli has an enviable location in the middle of town and charm in spades. Once a handsome stately home, the Semeli was turned into a four-star hotel without losing any of its distinctly Cycladic personality. The house's original furniture decorates the lobby and all the rooms abound with modern amenities. Rooms are bright and comfortable, with lovely verandas and good-size marble bathrooms. The Semeli's restaurant is very good.

Lekka St, Hora, 84600 Mykonos. www.semelihotel.gr. ℂ **22890/27-466.** 45 units. 310€ double. AE, DC, MC, V. **Amenities:** Restaurant; bar; cafe; gym; pool; spa. *In room:* A/C, TV, Internet.

Tagoo Hotel ★★ With a stunning view from every corner imaginable, it's still hard to beat the one from the wonderful rooftop pool. The rooms are light, cheerful, and spacious; the premises sparkle; and the staff is beyond helpful and endearing. For its price, it's certainly one of a kind.

Tagoo, Hora, 84600 Mykonos. www.hoteltagoo.gr. ℂ **22890/22-611.** Fax 22890/27-106. 20 units. 83€–180€ double. Rates include buffet breakfast. AE, MC, V. **Amenities:** Cafe/bar; pool. *In room:* A/C, TV.

Tharraoe of Mykonos ★★ Built on top of a hill, this small boutique hotel has spacious rooms with stunning sea and town vistas from the balconies; clean-lined wooden furniture; colorful bathrooms with funky, spacious tubs; and a wonderful pool area overlooking the sea and town. The top-notch **Barbarossa** restaurant, the in-house salon, and the Ayurvedic Spa complete the picture.

Hora, 84600 Mykonos. www.tharroeofmykonos.gr. ℂ **22890/27-370,** ext. 4. Fax 22890/27-375. 24 units. 150€–200€ double with island view; 226€ double with sea view; 380€–460€ suite. AE, DC, MC, V. Free parking. **Amenities:** Restaurant; bar; cafe; gym; pool; spa. *In room:* A/C, TV, hair dryer, Internet, minibar.

Villa Konstantin ★ Clean, spacious, and comfortable studios, apartments, and rooms highlight this location. Most units have their own balconies overlooking the Aegean Sea and the Old Port. A wonderful rooftop swimming pool also has awesome views.

Hora, 84600 Mykonos. www.villakonstantin.com. ℂ **22890/26-204.** Fax 22890/26-205. 9 units. 110€–150€ double. MC, V. Free parking. **Amenities:** Breakfast room; bar; cafe; Jacuzzi; pool; Wi-Fi. *In room:* A/C, TV, hair dryer, minibar.

OUT ON THE ISLAND

Although most visitors prefer to stay in Hora and commute to the beaches, there are some truly spectacular hotels on or near many of the more popular island beaches and many more affordable ones.

The beaches at Paradise and Super Paradise have private studios and simple pensions, but rooms are almost impossible to get, and prices more than double in July and August. Contact **Mykonos Accommodations Center** (☎ **22890/23-160**) or, for Super Paradise, **GATS Travel** (☎ **22890/22-404**), for information on the properties they represent. The tavernas at each beach may also have suggestions.

AT KALAFATI The sprawling **Aphrodite Hotel** (☎ **22890/71-367**; www. aphrodite-mykonos.com) has a large pool, two restaurants, and 150 rooms. It's a good value in May, June, and October, when a double costs about 100€. The hotel is popular with tour groups and Greek families.

AT ORNOS BAY Elegant **Kivotos Club Hotel ★★**, Ornos Bay, 84600 Mykonos (☎ **22890/25-795**; fax 22890/22-844; www.kivotosclubhotel.gr), is a small, superb luxury hotel about 3km (2 miles) outside Mykonos town. Most of the 45 individually decorated units overlook the Bay of Ormos, but if you don't want to walk that far for a swim, head for the saltwater or freshwater pool, the Jacuzzi and sauna, or the pool with an underwater sound system piping in music. Kivotos Clubhouse is small enough to be intimate and tranquil; the service (including frozen towels for poolside guests on hot days) gets raves from guests. If you're ever tempted to leave (and you may not be), the hotel minibus will whisk you into town. You can easily dine at the several restaurants on-site. Doubles cost 290€ to 390€; suites are priced from 650€ to 1,000€. The enormous **Santa Marina ★**, also at Ornos Bay (☎ **22890/23-200**; fax 22890/23-412; www.santa-marina.gr), has 90 suites and villas on 8 landscaped hectares (20 acres) overlooking the bay. If you don't want to swim in the sea, two pools and spa facilities are available at the hotel, which has its own restaurant as well. Suites with private pools are available from 1,500€. Doubles cost from 395€ to 600€, suites and villas from 625€ to 2,400€. The more modest 25-unit **Dionysos Mykonos Hotel** (☎ **22890/23-313**; www.dionysoshotel.gr) is steps from the beach and has a pool, restaurant, bar, and air-conditioned rooms with fridges and TV; doubles cost from 190€. The 42-unit **Hotel Yiannaki ★** (☎ **22890/23-393**; www. yiannaki.gr) is about 200m (656 ft.) away from the beach and has its own pool and restaurant; doubles begin at 125€. The nicest units have sea views and balconies.

Families traveling with children will find staying at one of the Ornos Bay hotels especially appealing. The beach is excellent and slopes into shallow, calm water. Furthermore, this is not one of Mykonos's all-night party beaches. If your hotel does not have watersports facilities, several of the local tavernas have surfboards and pedal boats to rent, as well as umbrellas. One minus: The beach is close to the airport, so you will hear planes come and go.

AT PLATI YIALOS The large and comfortable rooms of the 82-unit **Petasos Beach Resort ★**, Plati Yialos, 84600 Mykonos (☎ **22890/23-437**; fax 22890/24-101; www.petasos.gr), all have air-conditioning and minibars. Doubles go for about 150€. Each has a balcony overlooking the relatively secluded beach, which is less than 36m (118 ft.) away. The hotel has a good-size pool, sun deck, Jacuzzi, gym, and sauna. It offers free round-trip transportation to and from the harbor or airport, safety-deposit boxes, and laundry service. The seaside restaurant has a great view and serves a big buffet breakfast (a smaller continental breakfast is included in the room rate).

AT AYIOS IOANNIS **Mykonos Grand ★★** is a 100-room luxury resort a few kilometers out of Hora in Ayios Ioannis, 84600 Mykonos (✆ **22890/25-555;** www. mykonosgrand.gr). With its own beach and many amenities—pools, tennis, squash, Jacuzzis, a spa—this is a very sybaritic place. Doubles start at 225€. The **St. John Hotel ★★**, Ayios Ioannis, 84600 Mykonos (✆ **22890/28-752;** fax 22890/28-751; www.saintjohn.gr), has doubles from 310€ and suites from 590€. It's a breathtaking hotel, on a hillside over the Aegean, with spectacular sea vistas and a stunning infinity pool that has views over the cliff and into the sea. The St. John resembles a traditional blue-and-white village, complete with its own chapel. With 148 guest rooms and 9 opulent suites, the rooms are huge, stylishly decorated in warm hues of deep peach, with simple and elegant furniture, large marble bathrooms overflowing with products and their own Jacuzzi, and grand balconies with sea vistas as far as the eye can see. With a superb restaurant and fitness spa, three pools, and its own private beach, this is an experience in itself.

AT AYIOS STEPHANOS This popular resort, about 4km (2½ miles) north of Hora, has a number of hotels. Most close from November to March. The 38-unit **Princess of Mykonos ★**, Ayios Stephanos beach, 84600 Mykonos (✆ **22890/23-806;** fax 22890/23-031; www.princessofmykonos.gr), is lovely. The Princess has bungalows, a gym, a pool, and an excellent beach; doubles cost from 180€. **Hotel Artemis,** Ayios Stephanos, 84600 Mykonos (✆ **22890/22-345;** www.artemishotel. net), near the beach and bus stop, offers 23 units from 105€, breakfast included. Small **Hotel Mina,** Ayios Stephanos, 84600 Mykonos (✆ **22890/23-024**), uphill behind the Artemis, has 15 doubles that go for 80€. **Mykonos Grace ★★**, Ayios Stefanos, 84600 Mykonos (✆ **22890/26-690;** www.mykonosgrace.com), is an intimate yet undeniably stunning boutique hotel. Some of the hotel's 39 rooms might be on the small side, but the glass that separates the bathroom from the bedroom adds depth and the illusion of extra space, and huge balconies with stunning views more than compensate. Rooms range from standard to VIP suites, all with minimalistic design (230€–330€ double; 320€–420€ junior suite). Guests can swim in the sea off Ayios Stephanos beach, or in one of several hotel pools, or soak in the spa Jacuzzis or their suite's hot tub. Decor, food, and privacy all get high marks—as do the prices, which are less extravagant than at some of Mykonos's other boutique hotels. It's only a 5-minute walk to town to boot.

AT PSARROU BEACH **Grecotel Mykonos Blu ★★**, Psarrou Beach, 84600 Mykonos (✆ **22890/27-900;** fax 22890/27-783; www.grecotel.gr), is another of the island's serious luxury hotels with award-winning Cyclades-inspired architecture. Like Cavo Tagoo and Kivotos, this place is popular with wealthy Greeks, honeymooners, and jet-setters. The private beach, large pool, and in-house Poets of the Aegean restaurant allow guests to be as lazy as they wish (although there is a fitness club and spa for the energetic). Doubles run from 250€ to 450€.

Where to Eat

IN HORA

Camares Cafe (✆ **22890/28-570**), on Mavroyenous (Taxi) Square, has light meals and a fine view of the harbor from its terrace. It's open 24 hours and, for Mykonos, is very reasonably priced. Try the *striftopita* or crispy fried *xinotiro* (bitter cheese) and the thyme-scented grilled lamb chops (9am–2am; no credit cards). As is usual on the islands, most of the harborside tavernas are expensive and mediocre, although

Kounelas ★, on the harbor (no phone; no credit cards), is still a good value for fresh fish—as attested to by the presence of locals dining here.

Antonini's GREEK   Antonini's is one of the oldest of Mykonos's restaurants. It serves consistently decent stews, chops, and *mezedes*. Locals eat here, although in summer they tend to leave the place to tourists.

Plateia Manto. ℗ **22890/22-319.** Main courses 15€–20€. No credit cards. Summer daily noon–3pm and 7pm–1am. Usually closed Nov–Mar.

Avra Restaurant (the Breeze) ★ GREEK/MEDITERRANEAN   You can dine in this wonderful restaurant on either its busy terrace, in its more intimate interior, or in its lovely private garden. Try the octopus in white sauce, the stuffed chicken (with cheese, vegetables, and apricots), the stuffed lamb (with cheese, vegetables, and mustard), or the salmon risotto—all are excellent choices but the seafood pasta stole our hearts.

27 Kaloyera St. (behind Alpha Bank, on Matoyanni St.). ℗ **22890/22-298.** www.avra-mykonos.com. Main courses 15€–30€. DC, V. Daily 7pm–2am. Closed Nov–Mar.

Bakalo ★ GREEK TRADITIONAL/CONTEMPORARY   Housed inside a handsome house with a beautiful courtyard, Bakalo serves delicious traditional fare with a twist. Wonderful eggplant salad and fish roe dip began our evening and paved the way for deep fried codfish, shrimp saganaki, and grilled squid with spinach rice. Even classic traditional Greek dishes such as moussaka and chicken souvlaki were exceptional, as was their homemade pasta *(hilopites)*. Wonderful and with a very attentive and friendly staff—worth many repeat visits.

Lakka. ℗ **22890/78-121.** www.bakalo.gr. Main courses 15€–25€. AE, DC, MC, V. Daily 7pm–1:30am.

Chez Catrine ★★ GREEK/FRENCH   This is a pleasant place to spend the evening, enjoy a seafood soufflé or a seafood pasta, or try the chateaubriand. The candlelit dining room is so elegant that you won't mind being indoors. In addition to a wide variety of entrees, there is a range of excellent desserts. The feisty 70-year-old owner still makes her rounds night after night.

Agios Gerasimos Dilou. ℗ **22890/22-169.** Reservations recommended July–Aug. Main courses 22€–50€. AE, DC, MC, V. Daily 7pm–1am.

Chez Marinas ★ GREEK   Formerly known as Maria's Garden, this is another longtime favorite, with a lovely, lantern- and candlelit garden full of bougainvilleas and cacti, often animated by live music and fits of dancing. The vegetable dishes are always fresh and tasty, the lamb succulent, and the seafood enticing. In short, this is a place where ambience and cuisine come together to make a very successful restaurant. There's often a good-value set menu for around 25€.

30 Kaloyera. ℗ **22890/27-565.** Reservations recommended July–Aug. Main courses 22€–50€. DC, V. Daily 7pm–1am.

Club Belvedere ★★ GREEK   Inside the ultratrendy Belvedere Hotel, across the lantern-lit pool from where Matsuhisa Mykonos is housed, this restaurant offers Greek cuisine with a twist, by Greek-Australian chef George Calombaris. The *kerasma* menu (treat menu, 80€) is a great way to sample some of the restaurant's finest offerings, including mussels, spinach pie, and *saganaki*. The bread is made daily and is served with locally made olive oil as well as black sea salt from Cyprus's volcanic salt beaches (something you must experience to appreciate). Grilled fish, vegetable and/or meat skewers, and the hearty and fresh salads are also top notch. Add to this impeccable service and sublime setting, and you have an ideal dining experience.

At the Belvedere Hotel. © **22890/25-122.** www.belvederehotel.com. Reservations essential July–Sept. Main courses 35€–60€. AE, DC, MC, V. Daily 8pm–1am.

Danielle's Restaurant ★★ GREEK/MEDITERRANEAN   On the road from town to Ano Mera, this wonderful restaurant has excellent fare, combining traditional Greek island dishes with Mediterranean cuisine to stunning results. The salads are fresh and delicious, the pasta dishes are all excellent, and the wine is exceptional. Hands down one of the best restaurants in Mykonos.

On the road to Ano Mera. © **22890/71-513.** Main courses 25€–40€. MC, V. Daily 7pm–1am. Closed Nov–Feb.

El Greco ★ GREEK/CONTINENTAL   Put aside your suspicions of a place called El Greco and be prepared to enjoy traditional recipes collected from various regions of Greece. The eclectic menu includes traditional dishes; from Kerkira, for example, *bourdeto* is a monkfish-and-shellfish stew in tomato-and-wine sauce. Many concoctions feature local produce, such as mushrooms with Mykonian cheese.

Plateia Tria Pigadia. © **22890/22-074.** Main courses 25€–50€; fish priced by the kilo. AE, DC, MC, V. Daily 7pm–1am.

Fato a Mano ★★ GREEK/ITALIAN   Intimate like a friend's dinner party that gets rowdier and flirtier as the night goes on, this is an excellent choice for a wonderful dining experience. The shrimp spaghetti and the fettuccine with smoked salmon we had were just as excellent as we remembered; the pork filet, the grilled octopus, and the seafood pasta were all top-notch once again; and the complimentary fruit salad couldn't have been fresher. A great place to return again and again as we and many of the other diners have—mostly Italians whom we have gotten to know over the summers. The friendly staff and delicious wine don't hurt either.

Meletopoulos Sq. © **22890/26-256.** www.fatoamano.gr. Main courses 15€–30€. AE, DC, MC, V. Daily noon–2am.

Lotus ★ GREEK/TRADITIONAL   Made famous 30 years ago by the late Greek actress/politician Melina Mercouri, Lotus continues to cast its spell over the island. Tucked away off the busiest street in the entire island, the restaurant couldn't be more quiet and romantic. The traditional offerings are delicious—roast leg of lamb, moussaka, hearty salads—and the courtyard covered by bougainvillea is a wonderful touch. In winter there's seating around the fireplace.

47 Matogianni St. © **22890/22-881.** Main courses 15€–25€. No credit cards. Daily 7pm–1am.

Matsuhisa Mykonos ★★ JAPANESE   Nobu Matsuhisa has extended his sushi empire to the most happening hotel in town, the Belvedere. Right by the hotel's pool, with views of the sea and town, try the exceptional Japanese cuisine with Latin influences that will have you yearning for more, despite the high prices. Top-quality ingredients and sushi are flown in daily from Japan. Begin with a sakepirnha, the famous Brazilian cocktail made with sake instead of cachaça, and then continue to pick your way through the chef's choice tasting menu.

At the Belvedere Hotel. © **22890/25-122.** www.matsuhisamykonos.com. Reservations essential July–Sept. Main courses 60€–100€. AE, DC, MC, V. Daily 8pm–1am.

NiSa ★ GREEK/CONTEMPORARY   In the space once occupied by the very good Avra Restaurant (which has moved to a bigger space on the same street; see above), you will find this wonderful little restaurant. NiSa (named after owners Nikos and Sarah) is romantic, intimate, and lovely all around from its courtyard seating to its rooftop and the food is just as good. The beef burger with mushrooms in wine sauce was melt-in-your-mouth good as was the fresh salmon, but equally impressive were the mussels and shrimp spaghetti, the pork fillet stuffed with feta cheese and garlic, and the namesake chicken (stuffed with feta and rigotto cheese). Make sure to leave room for the desserts, including a very good chocolate soufflé.

10 Kaloyera St. ℂ **22890/78-550.** www.avra-mykonos.com/nisa.php. Main courses 15€–30€. AE, MC, V. Daily 7pm–1am.

Philippi ★ GREEK/CONTINENTAL One of the island's most romantic dining experiences, Philippi is in a quiet garden. Old Greek favorites share space on the menu with French dishes and a more than usually impressive wine list. What this restaurant provides in abundance is *atmosphere*, and that's what has made it a perennial favorite.

Just off Matoyianni and Kaloyera, behind the eponymous hotel. ℂ **22890/22-295.** Reservations recommended July–Aug. Main courses 20€–45€. AE, MC, V. Daily 7pm–1am.

Sea Satin Market ★ GREEK/SEAFOOD Below the windmills, beyond the small beach adjacent to Little Venice, the *paralia* ends in a rocky headland facing the open sea. This is the remarkable location of one of Hora's most charming restaurants. Set apart from the clamor of the town, it's one of the quietest spots in the area despite the fact that the closing scene of *The Bourne Identity* was filmed here. On a still summer night, just after sunset, the atmosphere is all you could hope for on a Greek island. At the front of the restaurant, the kitchen activity is on view, along with the day's catch sizzling on the grill. You can make a modest meal on *mezedes* here, or let it rip with grilled bon filet.

Near the Mitropolis Cathedral. ℂ **22890/24-676.** Main courses 30€–60€. AE, DC, MC, V. Fish priced by kilo. Daily 6:30pm–12:30am.

To Maireio (The Cookhouse) ★ GREEK TRADITIONAL With traditional island cuisine and home-cooked meals at affordable prices, this wonderful find is a treat and delight. Try Mama Arsenis' delicious village-style meatballs and hearty salads (with all produce from her own garden), and then order freely from the ready-cooked meals. Be sure to try the veal and pork in red peppers, in the "secret" island sauce; chicken in mushroom sauce; and tenderloin in vinaigrette reduction—all superb.

16 Kaloyera. ℂ **22890/28-825.** Main courses 15€–20€. MC, V. Daily 7pm–1:30am.

Uno con Carme ARGENTINE Set in the stunningly beautiful Art Deco space of a former open-air cinema, this fine restaurant also has an excellent bar and lounge for those wishing to take in the ambience with a drink. This steakhouse, apart from its excellent selection of meats (the T-bones are amazing) also has generously proportioned fresh salads and an excellent wine selection.

Panachra. ℂ **22890/24-020.** Main courses 28€–50€. AE, DC, MC, V. Daily 8pm–1am.

OUT-OF-TOWN DELIGHTS
Psarou

N'Ammos ★★ GREEK On hip and happening Psarou beach, N'Ammos, with its casual elegance and beachfront setting, is one of the island's finest restaurants. Wealthy Athenians stop by Mykonos just to have lunch here and taste the incredible lobster-pumpkin risotto. Other highlights are the spicy Mykonian meatballs, the marinated anchovies, fresh fish, and T-bone steaks.

Psarou Beach. ℂ **22890/22-440.** Main courses 25€–60€. AE, DC, MC, V. Daily 1pm–1am.

Ayios Sostis

Kiki's Taverna GREEK   A small, delightful, unspoiled taverna (with no sign, telephone number, or electricity), Kiki's is open only until sundown. Adjacent to the secluded Ayios Sostis beach, it serves island food the way it should taste. Meat and fish are grilled on a charcoal barbecue and served in the restaurant's shady courtyard. Be sure to try the tasty salads, too.

Ayios Sostis beach. No phone. Main courses 12€–20€. No credit cards. Daily 11am–6pm.

Fokos Beach

Fokos GREEK   On a secluded beach adored by surfers, Fokos serves up excellent traditional Greek cuisine that's unpretentious and delicious. Fresh local meat, fish of the day, and vegetables flown in daily from the owners' garden on the island of Crete make the unpretentious meals here some of Mykonos's best.

Fokos Beach. ℭ **22890/23-205.** Main courses 12€–20€. No credit cards. Daily 10am–7pm.

Mykonos After Dark

Once you arrive on Mykonos you will realize that the day has just as many party options as the night. As such, we've organized this section to give you party options for both day life and nightlife. Drinks in Mykonos are expensive; rarely will they cost less than 9€, but the good news is, if you are planning to head out at night, there are many supermarkets where you can buy a decent bottle of wine for no more than 6€ and begin your own party in your room or on your balcony before hitting the town.

DAY

Beach parties dominate the scene during the day. The most famous parties happen at Psarrou beach, where a hopping bar/club keeps the (mostly) Athenian crowd joyful. On Paradise beach, the **Tropicana Bar** and the **Sunrise Bar** cater to a more mixed crowd, and at Super Paradise, two loud bar/clubs on opposite sides of the beach cater to gay and mixed crowds, respectively. All three beaches have sunset parties, starting around 6pm, but it is Paradise Beach's **Paradise Club,** with its gigantic swimming pool in the middle of the club, that steals the show with its nightly fireworks and a wild party that lasts until midnight.

SUNSET

Back in town, things are less wild and more sophisticated around sunset. For over a quarter of a century, **Caprice** has been the island's sunset institution, with chairs lined along its narrow porch overlooking Little Venice, the windmills, and the sea. It is extremely popular with the Athenians (but it has caught on with the rest of the tourists as well). It isn't rare to come straight from the beach for the sunset and spend the entire night. The indoor area (set like a series of caves, with candlelit corners and a window opening up directly to the sea) is intimate and romantic. Another must-visit sunset destination is the **Oneiro Bar** perched on a beautiful deck overlooking the sea. Coming here will also give you a chance to check out the bar scene at the Mykonos View hotel. The **CBar Lounge,** set in the Belvedere Hotel, offers breathtaking sunset vistas with menu, drinks, and decor by renowned wedding designer Colin Cowie. Back in Little Venice—or "Sunset Central," as it's sometimes called—**Kastro,** near the Paraportiani Church, is famous for its classical music and frozen daiquiris. This is a great spot to watch or join handsome young men flirting with each other. **Montparnasse** is cozier, with classical music and Toulouse-Lautrec posters. At night this becomes a very popular (mostly with a gay crowd) piano bar. **Veranda,** in an old mansion overlooking the water with a good view of the windmills, is as laid back as its name might imply. **Galeraki** has a wide variety of exotic cocktails (and customers); the in-house art gallery gives this popular spot its name, "Little Gallery." After dark, it turns into a loud and fun bar/club. Next door, **Scarpa** and **Semelli** round up the top sunset destinations of the island and they too become rowdier once the sun has set.

With sunset out of the way, most head back to their rooms for a quick shower and change of wardrobe before heading out to dinner and then for after-dark fun.

AFTER DINNER

Chances are you'll find yourself more than once on the island's busiest strip, **Matoyanni street,** after dinner, strolling along with the majority of the island's population. Follow the crowd to **Astra,** the legendary bar and elegant lounge, with groovy modernist rooms and wonderful indoor and outdoor seating; its the perfect place to begin the night—or stay all night, as it morphs from a casual lounge to a pumping dance club when some of Athens's top DJs take over and **Egli,** another legendary Mykonian hot spot that is popular day and night as it morphs from quiet cafe to buzzing lounge and finally pumping club. As you continue up and down the strip, you will come across **Queen** (an extremely popular lounge-bar), **Diesel** (hip and trendy lounge bar), **Cosi** (casual and more relaxed), funky and decadent **Lola,** the almost tucked away (if not for its live jazz) **Alley,** popular day and night spot **Aroma,** popular newcomer **Rock n' Roll** and legendary gay bar **Pierro's.**

Athenian hot spot **Remezzo-W** is one of the island's most popular clubs -nights here don't begin before 2am and rarely end before 5am. By the church of Paraportiani, you will find **Jackie O',** the most popular gay bar on the island with wild party nights and nightly drag shows but also with great outdoor seating over the sea, ideal for sunsets and the more quiet and intimate early evening hours until the party begins. Next door, the equally popular **Babylon** has nice sea vistas, theme nights, drag shows, and many after-hours parties. Nearby, old-timer **Porta** remains a popular gay cruising spot, busy from 9pm onward.

The **Anchor** plays blues, jazz, and classic rock for its 30-something clients, as do **Argo, Stavros Irish Bar, Celebrities Bar,** and **Scandinavian Bar-Disco.** They draw customers from Ireland, Scandinavia, and quite possibly as far away as Antarctica. If you'd like to sample Greek music and dancing, try **Thalami,** a small club underneath the town hall. For a more intense Greek night out, head to **Guzel**—at Gialos, by the waterfront and near Taxi Square—the place to experience a super-trendy hangout, populated mostly by hip Athenians, with Greek and international hits that drive the crowd into a frenzy, with people dancing on the tables and on the bars. It's the sort of place that by the end of the night, you feel like you have partied with a group of close friends. Don't be intimidated if you aren't Greek. Go and have a blast! If you're looking for a club before 4am, try **Space Club,** by Lekka Square. It's extremely popular with the under-30 crowd, with a large dance floor and theme nights. The 10€ to 20€ entrance fee includes a drink.

If having a quiet evening and catching a movie is more your speed, head for **Cine Manto** (© **22890/27-190**), in the Municipal Garden of Meletopoulou, a small oasis of green on this arid island. Films show nightly around 9pm. Many films are American; most Greek films have English subtitles.

AFTER HOURS

To continue late into the night, head for Paradise beach (take the bus from town), to either **Cavo Paradiso** (www.cavoparadiso.gr), on the hill (cover 25€–50€ depending on DJ and event; nightly 2am–10am), or to **Paradise Club,** a large club by the beach (cover 15€–20€; nightly 2am–6am). Both clubs are extremely popular, with rotating international DJs, theme nights, huge pools, and great views. If you last until they close, you can just go for a swim and begin the day all over again. After all, sunset is only a few hours away.

For those who want to continue their partying after 4am but don't want to go all the way to Paradise beach to do so, there is **Yacht Club,** which is really the cafe by the old port that, for some reason, turns to a very popular mixed bar/club after hours. Wild flirting, drinking, and dancing ensue—this is the perfect place to end the night and to finally get together with the object of your affection. Being a mixed place, there is something for everybody here.

If you're visiting between July and September, find out what's happening at **Anemo Theatre** (📞 22890/23-944), an outdoor venue for the performing arts, in a garden in Rohari, just above town. A wide variety of concerts, performances, and talks are usually planned.

DELOS ★★★

There is as much to see at **Delos** as at Olympia and Delphi, and there is absolutely no shade on this blindingly white marble island covered with shining marble monuments. Just 3km (2 miles) from Mykonos, little Delos was considered by the ancient Greeks to be one of the holiest of sanctuaries, the fixed point around which the other Cycladic islands circled. It was Poseidon who anchored Delos to make a sanctuary for Leto, impregnated (as so many other maidens) by Zeus and pursued (as so many other maidens) by Zeus's aggrieved wife, Hera. Here, on Delos, Leto gave birth to Apollo and his sister, Artemis; thereafter, Delos was sacred to both gods, although Apollo's sanctuary was the more important. For much of antiquity, people were not allowed to die or give birth on this sacred island, but were bundled off to the nearby islet of Rinia.

Delos was not exclusively a religious sanctuary: For much of its history, the island was a thriving commercial port, especially under the Romans in the 3rd and 2nd centuries B.C. As many as 10,000 slaves a day were sold here on some days; the island's prosperity went into a steep decline after Mithridates of Pontus, an Asia Minor monarch at war with Rome, attacked Delos in 88 B.C., slaughtered its 20,000 inhabitants, and sailed home with as much booty as he could muster.

The easiest way to get to Delos is by caique from Mykonos; in summer, there are sometimes excursion boats here from Tinos and Paros. Try not to have a late night before you come here, and catch the first boat of the day (usually around 8:30am). As the day goes on, the heat and crowds here can be overwhelming. On summer afternoons, when cruise ships disgorge their passengers, Delos can make the Acropolis look shady and deserted. Sturdy shoes are a good idea here; a hat, water, munchies, and sunscreen are a necessity. *Tip:* Bring water and a snack; the snack bar on Delos, minimal at best, is often closed. Toilet facilities are rare here.

 Carpe Diem

Heavy seas can suddenly prevent boats docking at Delos. Follow the advice of the Roman poet Horace and *carpe diem* (seize the day). If you want to visit Delos, come here as soon as possible; if you decide to save your visit here for your last day in the area, rough seas may leave you stranded ashore.

Essentials

GETTING THERE From Mykonos, organized guided and unguided excursions leave starting about 8:30am about four times a day Tuesday through Sunday at the harbor's west end. Every travel agency in town advertises its Delos excursions (some with guides). Individual caique owners also have signs stating their prices and schedules. The trip takes about 30 minutes and costs about 10€ round-trip; as long as you return with the boat that brought you, you can (space available) decide which return trip you want to take when you've had enough. The last boat for Mykonos usually leaves by 4pm. The site is **closed** on Mondays.

Warning: If you're heading to Delos just to see the Avenue of the Lions, double-check to see if the lions are in place. Recent restoration activity and staff cutbacks have caused some of the noble beasts to have to endure the indignity of being put into storage. Some replicas have been substituted on the site.

Exploring the Site

Entrance to the site and museum costs 6€, unless this was included in the price of your excursion. At the ticket kiosk, you'll see a number of site plans and picture guides for sale; *Delos & Mykonos: A Guide to the History and Archaeology,* by Konstantinos Tsakos (Hesperos Editions), is a reliable guide to the site and the museum. Signs throughout the site are in Greek and French (the French have excavated here since the late 19th c.).

To the left (north) of the jetty where your boat will dock is the **Sacred Harbor,** now too silted for use, where pilgrims, merchants, and sailors from throughout the Mediterranean used to land. The commercial importance of the island in ancient times was due to its harbor, which made Delos an excellent stopping-off point between mainland Greece and its colonies and trading partners in Asia Minor.

The remains at Delos are not easy to decipher, but when you come ashore, you can head right, toward the theater and residential area, or left, to the more public area of ancient Delos, the famous avenue of the lions, and the museum. Let's head left, toward the **Agora of the Competialists,** built in the 2nd century B.C., when the island was a bustling free port under Rome. The agora's name comes from the *lares competales,* who were minor "crossroad" deities associated with the Greek god Hermes, patron of travelers and commerce. This made them popular deities with the Roman citizens here, mostly former slaves engaged in commerce. The agora dates from the period when Delos's importance as a port had superseded its importance as a religious sanctuary. To reach the earlier religious sanctuary, take the **Sacred Way**—once lined with statues and votive monuments—north from the agora toward the Sanctuary of Apollo. Although the entire island was sacred to Apollo, during Greek antiquity this was where his sanctuary and temples were. By retracing the steps of ancient pilgrims along it, you will pass the scant remains of several temples (most of the stone from the site was taken away for buildings on neighboring islands, including Naxos, Mykonos, and Tinos). At the far end of the Sacred Way was the **Propylaea,** a monumental marble gateway that led into the sanctuary. As at Delphi and Olympia, the sanctuary here on Delos would have been chockablock with temples, altars, statues, and votive offerings. You can see some of what remains in the **museum,** which has finds from the various excavations on the island. Admission to the museum is included in the site's entrance fee. Beside the museum, the remains of the Sanctuary of Dionysos are usually identifiable by the crowd snapping shots of the display of marble phalluses, many on tall plinths.

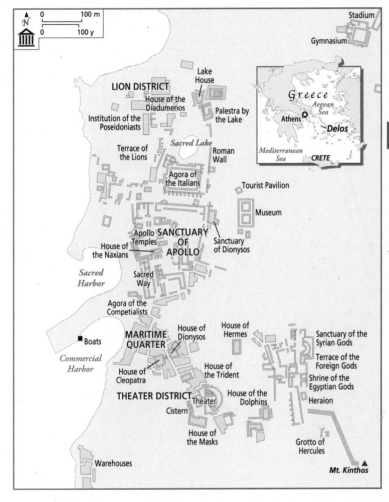

North of the museum and the adjacent tourist pavilion is the **Sacred Lake,** where swans credited with powers of uttering oracles once swam. The lake is now little more than a dusty indentation most of the year, surrounded by a low wall. Beyond it is the famous **Avenue of the Lions ★**, made of Naxian marble and erected in the 7th century B.C. There were originally at least nine lions. One was taken away to Venice in the 17th century and now stands before the arsenali there. The whereabouts of the others lost in antiquity remains a mystery; five were carted off to the museum for restoration some years ago and replaced by replicas. Beyond the lake to the northeast is the large square courtyard of the gymnasium and the long narrow stadium, where the athletic competitions of the Delian Games were held.

If you stroll back along the Sacred Way to the harbor, you can head next to the **Maritime quarter,** a residential area with the remains of houses from the Hellenistic and Roman eras, when the island reached its peak in wealth and prestige. Several houses contain brilliant **mosaics ★**, and in most houses the cistern and sewer systems can be seen. Among the numerous small dwellings are several magnificent villas, built around a central court and connected to the street by a narrow passage. The mosaics in the palace courtyards are particularly dazzling, and include such famous images as Dionysos riding a panther in the **House of the Masks,** and a similar depiction in the **House of Dionysos.** Farther to the south is the massive **Theater,** which seated 5,500 people and was the site of choral competitions during the Delian Festivals, an event held every 4 years that included athletic competitions in addition to musical contests. You may see donation boxes here: the Diazoma Organization, fearing that the Greek government has neither the funds nor the will to restore the theater, is attempting to finance the restoration privately. Behind the theater is a fine arched **cistern,** which was the water supply for the city. If you visit here in spring, the wildflowers are especially beautiful, and the chorus of frogs that live in and around the cisterns will be at its peak.

If you're not on a tour and have the energy, consider wrapping up your visit by getting an overview of the site—and of the Cyclades—from **Mount Kinthos ★**, the highest point on the island. On many days, nearby Mykonos, as well as Siros to the west, Tinos to the north, and Naxos and Paros to the south are easy to spot. On your way down, keep an eye out for the **Grotto of Hercules,** a small temple built into a natural crevice in the mountainside—the roof is formed of massive granite slabs held up by their own enormous weight.

TINOS ★★

161km (87 nautical miles) SE of Piraeus

Tinos has some very good restaurants, some fine beaches, exquisite dovecotes, and handsome villages with houses decorated with locally carved marble doorways and window fanlights. But that's not why most people come here. Each year, thousands of pilgrims come here to pray before the icon of the Virgin Mary in the church of the **Panagia Evangelistria (Our Lady of Good Tidings)**—sometimes called the "Lourdes of Greece." Thousands of others come here to baptize their babies at Greece's holiest shrine. Although Tinos is the most important destination in all of Greece for religious pilgrims, it remains one of the least commercialized islands of the Cyclades—and a joy to visit for that reason. Don't let your first sight of Tinos's undistinguished harbor alarm you: Behind the seaside sprawl of architecturally bland restaurants and cafes are lovely meandering lanes just waiting for you to get lost in them and discover their little courtyards and chapels.

From well out to sea, **Panagia Evangelistria**—illuminated at night—is visible atop a hill overlooking Tinos town. Almost any day of the year you can see people, particularly elderly women, crawling from the port on hands and knees up Megalocharis, the long, steep street that leads to the red-carpeted steps that are the final approach to the cathedral. Adjacent pedestrian-only Evangelistria is a market street, as well as a pilgrimage route for those who choose to walk it. The street is lined with stalls selling vials of holy water, incense, candles (up to 2m/7 ft. long), and mass-produced icons. There are also several jewelry and handicrafts shops, one or two cafes, groceries, old-fashioned dry-goods stores—and a surprising number of shops selling both incense and battery-powered kittens that roll over and meow.

Don't even think about arriving on Tinos without a reservation around **August 15** (Feast of the Assumption of the Virgin), when thousands of pilgrims travel here to

Looking for Dove . . .

Tinos is famous for its **dovecotes,** stout stone towers elaborately ornamented with slabs of the local shale, with ornamental perches and passageways for the doves. Venetians built the first dovecotes here. They brought with them the dovecote's distinctive miniature tower architecture. They used the doves' droppings as fertilizer, and the birds soon became an important part of the local diet. Locals still sometimes cook them, often in tomato sauce, as a winter dish. Some of the most elaborate of these birdhouses grace the towns of **Tarambados** and **Smardakito;** keep your eyes open. It is said that the island is home to 2,000 of them. Look for signs announcing detours to TRADITIONAL DOVE-COTES as you explore the island.

celebrate the occasion. **March 25** (Feast of the Annunciation) is the second-most important feast day here, but it draws fewer pilgrims because it is less easy to travel by sea in March. Pilgrims also come here on **July 23** (the anniversary of St. Pelagia's vision of the icon) and on **January 30** (the anniversary of the finding of the icon). Remember that Tinos is a *pilgrimage place:* It is considered very disrespectful to wear shorts, short skirts, halters, or sleeveless shirts in the precincts of the Evangelistria (or any other church, for that matter). Photographing the pilgrims, especially those approaching the shrine on hands and knees, is not appropriate. On the other hand, photographing the joyful baptismal parties approaching or leaving the church is fine.

Like Naxos, Tinos was ruled by Venice for several centuries and, like Naxos, Tinos still has a sizable Catholic population. You'll see signs of Tinos's Venetian heritage in the number of fine old Venetian mansions (locally known as *pallada,* the word also used for the harborfront), located on the streets off the harbor. Tinos town has a clutch of Catholic churches, including the harborfront churches of St. Anthony and St. Nicolas; out on the island, the **Church of the Virgin Mary Vrisiotissa,** near the village of Ag. Romanos, on the main Hora-Pirgos road, is an important Catholic pilgrimage shrine. The village of **Loutra** (see "Exploring the Island," below) has a folk-art museum in a Jesuit monastery, staffed by monks who come here from around the world.

The villages of Tinos are some of the most beautiful in the Cyclades. Many of the most picturesque are nestled into the slopes of **Exobourgo,** the rocky pinnacle crowned by a Venetian castle that is visible from the port. Many villages are connected by a network of walking paths that make this island a hiker's paradise. In these villages and dotting the countryside, you'll see the ornately decorated medieval *peristerion-ades* **(dovecotes)** for which the island is famous, as well as elaborately carved marble lintels, door jambs, and fan windows on village houses. According to one tradition (popular on virtually every one of the Cyclades), there are 365 churches scattered across the island, one for every day of the year; others boast that the island has 1,000 churches. The island's beaches aren't worthy of superlatives, but they are plentiful and uncrowded throughout the summer. All this may change if an airport is built here—all the more reason to visit Tinos now. If you want to do as the Greeks do, you'll spend a day or two here; do that once, and you may keep coming back to this *very* Greek island.

Essentials

GETTING THERE   Several ferries travel to Tinos daily from Piraeus (5 hr.). Catamaran (1½ hr.) and ferry services (4 hr.) are available daily in summer from Rafina.

Check schedules at the Athens **GNTO** (✆ **210/331-0562**); **Piraeus Port Author-ity** (✆ **210/459-3223** or 210/422-6000; phone seldom answered); or **Rafina Port Authority** (✆ **22940/22-300**). Several times a day, boats connect Tinos with nearby Mykonos (20–35 min.); there's daily service to Paros (and thence to many islands) in summer, and to and from Siros every day. Tinos has more winter connec-tions than most Cycladic isles due to its religious tourism, which continues through-out the year.

There are three ports in Tinos harbor. Be sure to find out from which pier your ship will depart—and be prepared for last-minute changes. The small catamarans (Seajet, Flying Cat, and Jet One) dock at the old pier in the town center; the large and high-speed ferries use the new pier to the north, on the side of town in the direction of Kionia. **Tinos Port Authority** (not guaranteed to be helpful) can be reached at ✆ **22830/22-348.**

VISITOR INFORMATION For information on accommodations, car rentals, island tours, and Tinos in general, contact Sharon Turner (sharon@thn.forthnet.gr) at **Windmills Travel ★★** (✆ **22830/23-398**; fax 22830/23-327; www.windmills travel.com). Sharon Turner is the friendly, amazingly helpful, and efficient Windmills Tinos representative, with unparalleled knowledge of Tinos and its neighboring islands. She sees clients at her office by appointment, but can solve almost any problem and supply amazing information on Tinos, the Cyclades, and beyond by phone and e-mail.

GETTING AROUND **By Bus** The **bus station** (✆ **22830/22-440**) is beside the Catholic church on the harbor, above the pier where the large island boats dock. Schedules are usually posted or available here. There are frequent daily buses to most island villages. The local bus company also offers a tour of the island, which usually departs from the Tinos town station daily from late June to late September at 10am; it returns to Tinos town around 5pm, after stopping at a number of villages and for lunch and a swim at Panormos. The 15€ charge does not include lunch. It is an excel-lent way to get an initial sense of the island. If you speak Greek, or feel adventurous, do this tour simply by hopping onto a variety of local buses.

By Car & Moped Vidalis Car Hire on the harbor at 2 Trion Hierarchon, where taxis congregate (✆ **22830/15-670**; www.vidalis-rentacar.gr), has a wide range of vehicles. Expect to pay from 40€ per day for a car, half that for a moped; prices lower off-season.

By Taxi Taxis hang out on Trion Hierarchon, which runs uphill from the harbor just before Palamaris supermarket and Hotel Tinion.

FAST FACTS There are several **banks** on the harbor, open Monday through Thursday from 8am to 2pm and Friday from 8am to 1:30pm; all have ATMs. The **first-aid center** can be reached at ✆ **22830/22-210.** There's a drop-off **laundry** service (✆ **22830/32-765**) behind the Lito Hotel—but be forewarned that it can be slow, up to 3 days in peak season. For **luggage storage,** try Windmills Travel (✆ **22830/23-398**). The **police** (✆ **22830/22-348**) are located just past the new pier, past Lito Hotel and Windmills Travel. The **post office** (✆ **22830/22-247**), open Monday through Friday from 7:30am to 2pm, is at the harbor's south end, next to Tinion Hotel. The **telephone office (OTE),** open Monday through Friday from 7:30am to 12:30pm, is on the main street leading to the church of Panagia Evange-listria, about halfway up on the right (✆ **22830/22-399**). The harborside **Tinos Cultural Foundation** (✆ **22830/29-070**) has a small permanent collection and temporary exhibitions; admission is sometimes charged for special exhibits. It's usually open Monday, Wednesday, and Friday 10am to 2pm and 7 to 9pm; weekend hours are 10:30am to 2pm and 7 to 9pm. It also has the cheapest Internet service in town, with a nearby cafe.

What to See & Do

Panagia Evangelistria Cathedral and Museums ★★★ Each year, the **Church of Panagia Evangelistria (Our Lady of Good Tidings)** draws thousands of pilgrims seeking the aid of the church's miraculous icon. According to local lore, in 1882 a nun named Pelagia repeatedly dreamed that the Virgin appeared to her and told her where to find a miraculous icon. A modest woman, Pelagia could not believe the Virgin would appear to her, but when the dreams did not stop, Pelagia finally sought out the bishop of Tinos, whom she hesitantly informed of her dreams. The bishop, convinced of her piety, ordered excavations to begin. Before long, the remains, first of a Byzantine church and then of the icon itself, were unearthed. As is the case with many of the most holy icons, this one is believed to be the work of St. Luke. The icon was initially housed where it was found, in the chapel of the Zoodohos Pigi, under the present cathedral. Astonishingly on such a small and poor island, the Parians built the massive church of the Panagia in just 2 years. The church is made of gleaming marble from Paros and Tinos, with a tall slender bell tower and handsome black-and-white pebble mosaics in the exterior courtyard.

At the end of Evangelistria Street, a broad flight of marble stairs leads you up to the church. Inside, hundreds of gold and silver hanging lamps illuminate the icon of the Virgin, to the left of the entrance. The icon is almost entirely hidden by votive offerings of gold, silver, diamonds, and precious gems dedicated by the faithful. Even those who do not make a lavish gift customarily make a small offering and light a candle. Keep an eye out for the silver ship with a fish hanging beneath it. According to tradition, a fierce storm threatened to sink a ship, which was taking in water through a breach in its hull. When the captain and crew called out to the Virgin for help, the storm abated and the ship reached harbor safely. When it was taken ashore for repairs, an enormous fish was discovered plugging the hole in the hull.

Beneath the church is the crypt with the chapel where the icon was found, surrounded by smaller chapels. The crypt is often crowded with Greek parents waiting to have their (usually howling) toddlers baptized here. Others come to fill vials with holy water from the spring.

Keep in mind that to enter the cathedral, men must wear long pants and shirts with sleeves, and women must wear dresses or skirts and blouses with sleeves. If there is a church service while you are here, you will hear the beautiful, resonant chanting that typifies a Greek Orthodox service—but remember that it's not appropriate to explore the church during a service. Services are usually held just after the church opens, just before it closes, and at other times during the day. A schedule of services is usually posted outside the main entrance.

Within the high walls that surround the church are various museums and galleries, each of which is worth a quick visit: a gallery of 14th- to 19th-century religious art, a gallery of more modern Tinian artists, and a sculpture museum. Admission is sometimes charged at these places.

Hora, Tinos. Free admission. Cathedral daily 8am–7pm (off-season hours vary); galleries Sat–Sun (some weekdays during July–Aug) 8am–8pm (off-season usually noon–6pm).

📎 **Trying Your Hand at Marble Carving**

Tinos has a long tradition of marble carving. If you want to try your hand, the **Dellatos Marble Sculpture School** (℃ **22830/23-664**; www.tinosmarble. com), just outside Tinos town, in Spitalia, offers 1- and 2-week workshops, from May through October, for would-be marble workers.

Exploring the Island

If it's a clear day, one of your first sights of Tinos from the ferry will be the odd mountain with a bare summit that looks bizarrely like a twisted fist. This is **Exobourgo ★★**, a mountain eminence crowned by the remains of a Venetian kastro (castle) about 15km (9 miles) outside of Hora. Sheer rock walls surround the fortress on three sides; the only path to the summit starts behind a Catholic church at the base of the rock, on the road between Mesi and Koumaros. As you make the 15-minute ascent, you'll pass several lines of fortification—the entire hill is riddled with walls and hollowed with chambers. As you might expect, the view over the Cyclades is superb from the summit (565m/1,854 ft.). The fortress itself has long been in ruins—and was never as imposing as, for example, the massive Venetian fortress at Nafplion in the Peloponnese. The Turks defeated the Venetians here in 1714 and drove them from the island.

The village of **Kambos ★** is not far from Exobourgo, and with a car, nothing in Tinos is very far from anything else. In 2011, the **Costas Tsoclis Museum** (℃ **22830/51-009;** tinos@tsoclismuseum.gr) opened here. The museum—more gallery than museum—showcases the work of the 20th-century Greek artist who was born in Athens, but had a home on Tinos. The museum occupies the former village school house, which had been abandoned when the village's population plummeted. Just outside the museum you'll see Tsoclis's metal sculpture showing the long, writhing scaly tail of the dragon slain by St. George. Inside, some 45 of Tsoclis's works are on display; the most memorable is perhaps the fiery display *Prometheus Imprudent,* which typifies Tsoclis use of what he called "living painting," the combination of painting and video projection that he helped to popularize. It's open Monday through Sunday, 9am to 1pm (sometimes also open 6–9pm; check for hours). Admission is free at present, but that may change.

A bus runs from Hora several times a day to the nearby **Convent of Kechrovouniou** (also known as the Monastery of Kurias Angellon/Our Lady of the Angels) **★★**, one of the largest in Greece—almost a town in its own right. It dates from the 10th century and was the home of Pelagia, the nun whose vision revealed the location of the island's famed icon; you can visit her cell and see a small museum of 18th- and 19th-century icons. The convent is usually closed from 1 to 4pm; if you arrive when the convent is closed, you can stroll outside the convent walls and visit the small deer park and the nearby chapel, with its impressive display of the skulls of deceased nuns and monks. If you have more time to spend, take in the hamlets of **Dio Horia, Arnados,** and **Triandaros,** all on the slopes topped by the convent. Arnados has a number of *stegasti,* tunnel-like streets formed by the overhanging second-floor rooms of village houses; Dio Hora has a wonderful village fountain; and Triandaros has several restaurants and nice side streets. Don't be surprised if you hear German spoken here; many Germans have bought homes in this area.

Loutra ★ is another especially attractive village with many *stegasti*. An imposing 17th-century Jesuit monastery contains a small museum of village life; implements for making olive oil and wine are on display alongside old manuscripts and maps. It's usually open mid-June to mid-September from about 10:30am to 3:30pm (no phone). If the door is locked, ring the cow bell at the entrance and hope for the door to open. From mid-July until the beginning of September, the Ursuline School is open for a fabulous tour that depicts the students' lives and studies, until the school closed in the 1950s. Admission is free at the museum and for the convent tour. Both places are usually closed during siesta time (3–5pm).

The **Museum of Traditional Pottery ★** (no phone) opened in 2009 in **Aetofolia,** one of the smallest and most charming Tinian villages. There are labels throughout in Greek and English, and museum guide Lila Tsigkriki speaks excellent English. The museum showcases pottery made—or found—not only on Tinos but also on the neighboring island of Sifnos, as well as other Cycladic islands. The displays are delightful as is the traditional 19th-century island house that is now the museum, with its kitchen filled with locally made pottery. Don't miss the little pottery barbecue, called a "foufou" from the sound made when cooks blow on the coals. Admission is 2€; it's open April through September, 10am to 4pm.

After touring the museum's well-stocked kitchen, you may be thinking of food, so head for the village of **Volax ★★**, where tall trees shade the excellent family-run **Taverna Volax** (*☎ 22830/41-021*), one of the very best places on Tinos to eat, relax, and enjoy the passing scene. Don't miss the local *loukanika* (sausages), best washed down with some Tinian wine. Volax is in a valley known for a bizarre lunar landscape of rotund granite boulders. On the theory of "if you have lemons, make lemonade," the villagers constructed a substantial stone amphitheater for theatrical productions; a schedule of summer performances is usually posted both in Volas and in Hora. Volax is also known for its local basket weavers, whose baskets are remarkably durable and attractive; you'll see signs pointing to their workshops. Be sure to visit the town spring, down a short flight of steps at the bottom of the village. Channels direct the water to the fields, and the basket weavers' reeds soak in multiple stone basins. From Volas, you may want to head on to **Koumaros,** a beautiful village on the road between Volax and Mesi, both of which have many of the arched *stegasti* passageways.

Pirgos ★★★, at the western end of the island, is one of Tinos's most beautiful villages, with an enchanting small plateia with enormous plane trees, a marble fountain, several cafes, and two tavernas, usually open for lunch and dinner in summer, less regularly off-season. Pirgos gets *lots* of visitors and, alas, the prices in the cafes and restaurants are high, the quality is mixed, at best, and the service is slow and often grumpy. Renowned for its school of fine arts, Pirgos is a center for marble sculpting, and many of the finest sculptors of Greece have trained here. In 2008, the superb **Museum of Marble Crafts** opened just outside Pirgos. On a terrace leading to the museum, huge marble blocks and quarry equipment recreate a Tinian marble quarry. Inside, the museum takes visitors into the lives of the sculptors and artisans of Tinos, with the help of photos and videos. Displays include examples of the more than 100 kinds of Greek marble, glorious fanlight windows, doorway ornaments, and grave monuments done by Tinian artists—and a good selection of the tools used to make them. The museum has a cafe (great coffee, great fresh orange juice, and, if you're not driving, fiery *tsiporo* liqueur and tasty *mezedes*) and an excellent small shop, with the cheapest, most endearing and portable souvenir I have ever seen: a small white eraser, decorated with a traditional Tinian carved braid pattern (1€). The museum is open Wednesday to Monday 10am to 6pm in summer, 10am to 5pm off-season (admission 3€).

In Pirgos itself, the **Museum of Yiannoulis Chalepas** and **Museum of Panormian Artists** occupy adjacent houses, and give visitors a chance not only to see sculpture by local artists, but to step into an island house. After you see the small rooms on the ground floor, you'll be surprised at how large the cool, flag-stoned lower story with the kitchen is. The museums are located near the bus station, on the main lane leading toward the village. Both are open Tuesday through Sunday from 11am to 1:30pm and 5:30 to 6:30pm; admission is 2€.

Although you may be tempted by the sculptures you see on sale in local workshops, even a small marble relief is not easy to slip into a suitcase. In the hardware shop across from Pirgos's two museums, **Nikolaos Panorios ★★★** makes and sells whimsical tin funnels, boxes, spoon holders, and dustpans, as well as dovecotes, windmills, and sailing ships. Each item is made of tin salvaged from olive oil and other containers, and every one is unique (some with scenes of Pallas Athena, others with friezes of sunflowers, olive gatherers, fruits, or vegetables). All these are delightful folk art; they cost from 15€. Nikolaos Panorios is usually in the shop mornings (© **22830/32-263**), from about 9am to 1pm.

BEACHES

The easiest place to take a dip from Tinos town is at **Kionia,** across from the site of the Temple of Poseidon, 3km (2 miles) west of Tinos town (see "A Swim, a Snack, an Ancient Site" box, below). Another beach close to town lies 2km (1¼ miles) east of town, at busy **Ayios Fokas.** West of Tinos town, a series of hairpin-turn paved and unpaved roads lead down—and when we say "down," we mean "way down"—to beaches at Ayiou Petrou, Kalivia, and Giannaki. From Tinos, there's bus service on the south beach road (usually eight times a day) to the resort of **Porto,** 8km (5 miles) to the east. Porto offers several long stretches of uncrowded sand, a few hotel complexes, and numerous tavernas, several at or near the beach. The beach at Ayios Ioannis, facing the town of Porto, is okay, but you'd be better off walking west across the small headland to a longer, less popular beach, extending from this headland to the church or Ayios Sostis at its western extremity; you can also get here by driving or taking the bus to Ayios Sostis. There are two beaches at **Kolimbithres,** on the north side of the island, which are easily accessed by car, although protection from the *meltemi* winds can be a problem. The smaller has more wind protection, beach umbrellas, a changing hut, and two tavernas. Just beyond Pirgos, the beach at **Panormos** is on the verge of turning into a holiday resort, but has a decent (usually windy) beach and several good fish tavernas, notably **Agoni Grammi ★** (© **22830/31-689**). If you eat here, be prepared for cars and buses to come very close to your seaside table.

WALKING

Tinos is a walker's paradise, with a good network of paths and remote interior regions waiting to be explored. Some of the best walks are in the vicinity of **Exobourgo**—paths connect the cluster of villages circling this craggy fortress, offering great views and many places to stop for refreshment along the way. There isn't a current English-language guide to walks in Tinos, but most decent maps of the islands indicate the paths, many of which are the former donkey and foot roads that connected villages.

A Swim, a Snack, an Ancient Site

If you're staying in Tinos town, the easiest place to take a dip is the beach at Kionia, about 3km (2 miles) west of Hora. Just across from the pebble-and-sand strand where you'll swim are the island's only excavated antiquities, the modest remains of the Temple of Poseidon and one of his many conquests, Amphitrite, a semidivine sea nymph (Tues–Sun 8:30am–3pm; admission 3€). When sheep or the custodians have trimmed the vegetation at the site, you can clearly make out the foundations of the 4th-century-B.C. temple, and a large altar and long stoa, both built in the 1st century B.C. As is inevitable with a site where Romans lived, there are the remains of a bath. Finds from the site are on display at the Tinos town Archaeological Museum (Tues–Sun 8:30am–3pm; admission 3€). When you head back to town, have a drink and a snack at either the Mistral or Tsambia taverna, both on the main road near the site. Closer to town, also on the main road, you can check your e-mail at the Para Pende cafe. Depending on your mood, you can do this excursion on foot, by public bus, or taxi. If on foot, keep to the side of the road and don't expect the trucks and motorcycles to cut you much slack.

SHOPPING

In Hora, Megaloharis is the main street from the harbor up to the cathedral. My two favorite shops in town are on Megalocharis: **Enosis,** a few steps up from the harbor, is the shop of the local **agricultural cooperative,** where pungent capers, creamy cheeses, olive oil, and the fiery local *tsiporo* liqueur are on sale (© 22830/21-184). If you like capers, stock up on a vacuum pack or two; I got mine safely back to Massachusetts and enjoyed them for months. Continue to 34 Megalocharis and you'll find **Nostos** © 22830/22-208). Everything here—ceramics, woodwork, jewelry, weavings—is handmade and just about everything will make you start plotting how you can fit it into your suitcase. The owner Litsa Malliari Toufekli, is a painter and many of her haunting scenes of Tinos, done on old wood panels, are on view.

Pedestrianized Evangelistria Street parallels Megalocharis Street. Shops and stalls lining Evangelistria sell icons, incense, candles, medallions, *tamata* (tin, silver, and gold votives), and various stuffed animals that nod, roll over, mew and squeal. You'll also find local embroidery, weavings, and a delicious local nougat, as well as *loukoumia* (Turkish delight) from Siros.

Two fine jewelry shops stand side-by-side on Evangelistria: **Artemis,** 18 Evangelistria (© 22830/23-781), and **Harris Prassas Ostria-Tinos,** 20 Evangelistria (© 22830/23-893;** fax 22830/24-568). Both have jewelry in contemporary, Byzantine, and classical styles; silverwork; and religious objects, including reproductions of the miraculous icon. Near the top of the street, on the left, in a neoclassical building, the small **Evangelismos Biotechni Shop,** the outlet of a local weaving school (© 22830/22-894), sells reasonably priced table and bed linens, embroidered aprons, and rugs.

Weekdays, a **Marko's fish market** and a **farmers' market** set up in the square by the docks. Keep an eye out for the rather pink-plumed pelican (Marko himself) that lives at the fish market and usually takes a morning stroll from there through the farmers' market to St. Anthony's Catholic church and back. Once back, he often takes a dip in his pool outside the fish market. There's a Palamidis supermarket, on the harbor, and an even larger one is just outside Tinos town, on the road to Pirgos.

You can get English language newspapers in the narrow street that parallels (to the extent that anything in Tinos runs straight enough to be said to parallel anything else) restaurant row, with the Metaxi Mas, Palaia Pallada, and Aithrio restaurants.

Where to Stay

Unless you have reservations, avoid Tinos during important religious holidays, especially **March 25** (Feast of the Annunciation) and **August 15** (Feast of the Assumption). It is also not a good idea to come here without an advance reservation on summer weekends, when Greeks travel here by the thousands for baptisms and pilgrimages. Most high-season weekend rates start at 80€ a night; rates off-season, especially during the week, are considerably lower. Several hotels and apartment complexes have Wi-Fi, but check on this before booking. There are also cafes in town with Wi-Fi available, such as **Sympsion** on Evangelistra (don't bother to phone; phone never answered); ask the price before you boot up. In addition to the following hotels, check out the good value **Asteria** (✆ 22830/22-830; asteriahotel@otenet. gr), perched above the harbor where the big boats dock. The Asteria was remodeled in 2010 and its lobby, breakfast room, and, most important, guest rooms and bathrooms are now very comfortable. As with many Tinos hotels, the Asteria does a brisk business in Greek tour groups. Doubles from 65€. If you are coming here for more than a night or two, consider the very appealing **Tiniotissa Studios** (✆ 22830/22-430; www.tiniotissa.gr), on a very quiet street off Megalocharis, between the Archaeology Museum and Grade School.

Oceanis Hotel ★   The Oceanis has a good quiet location, away from the main harbor hubbub, near where some of the fishing boats moor. Another plus: The Oceanis, formerly bland, down-at-the-heels, and charmless, has spruced itself up. The lobby is positively cheerful and the rooms have been repainted; only the exterior, a somber gray, could use some livening up. Be sure to ask for a front room: the balconies give a great view of the ships coming and going in Tinos's harbor, with views of Siros in the distance. The hotel is often taken over by Greek groups visiting the island's religious shrines. Don't bother with the restaurant, except for the breakfast buffet. The Oceanis stays open all year and has reliable heat in the winter.

Akti G. Drossou, Hora, 84200 Tinos. ✆ **22830/22-452.** Fax 22830/25-402. 47 units. From 70€ double. Rates include breakfast buffet. No credit cards. From the old harbor, walk south (right) along the *paralia* until you come to the Oceanis, whose large sign is clearly visible from the harbor. **Amenities:** Restaurant; bar. *In room:* A/C, TV, hair dryer, minifridge.

Porto Tango ★ ♨   I am only listing this place because it was once thought to be the breakthrough fancy place on the island, destined to leave the Tinos Beach Hotel in the dust. Porto Tango does have all the frills—restaurant, sauna, spa, health club, pool, and so forth. But the management seriously overbooks rooms, and then puts many arrivals elsewhere and tries to charge full price if guests use the hotel facilities. Did I mention that the beach is a 10-minute walk away, across a road? Or that the tennis court in June 2011 had weeds growing out of it? On the positive side, many rooms have balconies or terraces with sea views; some have both. In short, this is a place that has not got its act together, either in decor or in service. The Tinos Beach Hotel, below, is a much better choice.

Porto, 84200 Tinos. www.portotango.gr. ✆ **22830/24-411.** Fax 22830/24-416. 61 units. 150€ double; 450€ suite. Rates include breakfast buffet. AE, MC, V. **Amenities:** 2 restaurants; bar; health club; pool; spa. *In room:* A/C, TV, hair dryer, Internet, minibar.

Special Moments in Tinos Town

If you're lucky, while you're trying to decide what to have for lunch or dinner at a restaurant in Tinos town, you'll become aware of family celebrations taking place at other tables. Why, you may wonder, is that young couple dancing on one of the tables and passing their screaming toddler from guest to guest? Why is everyone kissing him and pinching his cheeks? Families come from all over Greece to baptize their children at the Panagia Evangelistria Cathedral. After the ceremony, it's time to celebrate (which means lots of food, wine, and dancing). If you're lucky, you may get to kiss the baby and toast the occasion. Be sure to say "Na sas zeesoun" ("May he live for you") to the proud parents.

Tinos Beach Hotel ★★ ☺ Despite a somewhat impersonal character, this is the best choice in a beachfront hotel. The decent-size rooms all have balconies, most with views of the sea and pool. The newly renovated superior doubles all face the sea and the suites are especially pleasant—large sitting rooms open onto poolside balconies. The pool is the longest on the island, and there's a separate children's pool as well. No one seems to praise either the ambience or the service here, but if you want to be near Tinos town, yet also on the beach, this is the place to be.

Kionia, 84200 Tinos. www.tinosbeach.gr. ✆ **22830/22-626** or 22830/22-627. Fax 22830/23-153. 180 units. 80€–100€ double. Rates include breakfast. Children 7 and under stay free in parent's room. AE, DC, MC, V. Closed Nov–Mar. 4km (2½ miles) west of Tinos town, on the coast road. **Amenities:** Restaurant; bar; children's pool; saltwater pool; tennis courts; watersports equipment rentals; Wi-Fi. *In room:* A/C, TV, hair dryer, minifridge.

Where to Eat

As usual, it's a good idea to avoid most harborfront joints, where food is generally inferior and service can be rushed—although, if you are catching a ferry and want a quick bite, the service can seem interminable. Be sure you know which quay your ferry is leaving from to avoid any last minute dashes through crowds of embarking and disembarking passengers. One special place to try that opened in 2010: **Etan Ena Mikro Karavi** ("There Was a Little Boat"; ✆ **22830/22-818;** www.mikrokaravi.gr) in a narrow alleyway off Trion Hierarchon. This place is gorgeous, with a lovely garden, elegant (but not fussy or pretentious) indoor dining room, and seriously inventive and delicious food (risotto with mushrooms, lamb with couscous, fresh fish, and a chocolate tart with homemade vanilla ice cream and caramel sauce). To my considerable distress, this place had not yet opened for the season when I was last on Tinos, and I had to make do with reading the menu and hearing from friends how very good everything is (dinner for two from around 50€). If, on the other hand, you just want a pizza (10€ and up), head to **Mesklies** (✆ **22830/22-151**) on the harbor. Mesklies also has some of the best pastry in town, at shops on the harbor and on Evangelista Street. For the best coffee—and a full pot of it for only 2€—try **Le Caffe** (no viable phone), also on the harbor. Le Caffe also has the best *loukoumades* (like donut holes, but drenched in honey, sprinkled with cinnamon, and, if you wish, topped with ice cream).

Metaxi Mas ★ GREEK   The zest that made the cooking at this longtime distinctive *mezedopoleio* (hors d'oeuvres place) so wonderful for so many years is flagging again. In short, Metaxi Mas is having its ups and downs. The varied *mezedes* are still very good, especially the vegetable croquettes, fried sun-dried tomatoes, piquant fried cheeses, and succulent octopus. But they aren't quite as good as they were a few years ago, when it was clear that the food here was better than its nearby competition. There's a cozy interior dining room with a fireplace, for when it's chilly, and tables outside in the pedestrianized lane, for good weather.

Kontoyioryi, Paralia, Hora. ⓒ **22830/24-857.** Main courses 8€–20€. No credit cards. Daily noon–midnight. Off the harbor, in a lane btw. the old and new harbors. Look for the sign over the door. Sometimes a METAXI MAS banner is strung across the lane.

Palaia Pallada ★★ GREEK   Palaia Pallada, next to Metaxi Mas, is a bit more down home than Metaxi Mas, a bit less inventive, but more consistently good. There are fewer ruffles and flourishes here, but the food (grills, stews, salads) in this family-run place is excellent, as is the local wine. You can eat indoors or outside in the lane. If you like Palaia Pallada, you're sure to like **Aithrio** (ⓒ **22830/22-033**), the third restaurant on this restaurant row.

Kontoyioryi, *Paralia*, Hora. ⓒ **22830/23-516.** Main courses 7€–15€. No credit cards. Daily noon–midnight. Off the harbor, in a lane btw. the old and new harbors. Look for the sign over the door, and the sign that overhangs the lane.

To Koutouki tis Eleni ★ GREEK   There's usually no menu at this excellent small taverna, known in town simply as To Koutouki. Basic ingredients are cooked into simple meals that remind you how delightful Greek food can be. Local cheese and wine, fresh fish and meats, delicious vegetables—these are the staples that come together so well in this taverna.

Paralia, Hora. ⓒ **22830/24-857.** Main courses 7€–15€. No credit cards. Daily noon–midnight. From the harbor, turn onto Evangelistria, the market street; take the 1st right up a narrow lane with 3 tavernas. Koutouki is the 1st on the left.

Tinos After Dark

Two sweets shops, **Epilekto** and **Meskiles** (fantastic *loukoumades* with ice cream), both on the waterfront, stay open late. In the streets beside restaurant row, where Palaia Pallada, Metaxi Mas, and Aithrio are located, there is a clutch of bars, with music, TV, and sometimes dancing, including **Koursaros, Kaktos, Volto,** and **Syvilla,** and, on the road toward Kiona, **Paradise.** If you want a late-night (or early-morning) coffee, try **Le Caffe,** on the harborfront; instead of a cup, this place brings you a delicious full pot of French filtered coffee. If you want to check your e-mail while you drink your coffee, try **Symposio,** which bills itself as a cafe/bar/restaurant. If you walk on the main road at night, watch out for the kamikaze motorcyclists.

SIROS (SYROS) ★★

144km (78 nautical miles) SE of Piraeus

Siros is very different from the other Cycladic islands. The capital, **Ermoupolis,** is not a twee Cycladic sugar-cube miniature town, nor a ramshackle port town, but the administrative capital of the Cyclades, with a large shipyard. If you live anywhere in the Cyclades and need a building permit, or a license, or a lawyer, you'll end up making at least one trip here. Consequently, Ermoupolis has a year-round businesslike bustle totally unlike any other town in the Cyclades. Ermoupolis has been the most important town in the Cyclades almost since it was founded in the 1820s by a flood of refugees from Asia Minor and the eastern Aegean islands. The settlers named the town after Hermes, the god of merchants. The name seems to have been an excellent

Siros has two impressive summer festivals, the **Ermoupoleia** (www.syros-live.gr) and the **Festival of the Aegean** (www.festivaloftheaegean.com). The Ermoupoleia runs almost all summer and has indoor and open-air concerts, plays, and performances. The Festival of the Aegean, usually held in mid-July, stages many of its performances—including several operas—at the glorious Apollon Theater. And Ano Siro, the community clustered on a peak above Ermoupolis, has its own festival in July and August (www.syros-live.gr).

choice: Soon, this was the busiest port in Greece—far busier than Piraeus—and a center of shipbuilding. You'll see several shipyards and dry docks along the harbor. Just inland are neighborhoods with handsome neoclassical mansions built by shipping magnates. When you walk into Plateia Miaoulis, the main square in town, you may find it hard to believe you're still in the Cyclades: The square is lined with truly grandiose public buildings, including a town hall that could hold its own beside any government building in Athens. Just off the Plateia is the Apollon Theater, a miniature of Milan's La Scala Opera House, with a summer music festival. Climb uphill from the Plateia Miaoulis and you'll find yourself in the oldest part of town, Ano Syros, which just happens to be a perfect little sugar-cube Cycladic neighborhood, albeit one with both a Capuchin and a Jesuit monastery. Although Ermoupolis saw a considerable period of decline in the 20th century, recent restoration efforts have brought back much of the city's glory; the entire town is now a UNESCO World Heritage Site.

I have to confess that Siros is one island where the capital town's pleasures are so considerable that I don't mind neglecting the island itself. However, the north end of Siros is a starkly beautiful region of widely dispersed farms, multilayered terraced fields, and village-to-village donkey and foot paths. Some of the island's best beaches are here, many accessible only on foot or by boat. The south is gentler, with a number of villages with the 19th-century country villas of the wealthy shipping magnates who had both a town house and a summer retreat; the villages of Manna, Ano Manna, and Dellagrazia have especially impressive villas. Throughout the island, the San Mihali and *kopanisti* cheeses are made, and delicious thyme honey is produced.

The best months to visit Siros are May, June, and September; the worst month is August. That's when vacationing Greek families—many bringing with them at least two cars—pour into their villas here, with the overflow taking up virtually every hotel room on the island. If you want to tour the island, having a car is the best way to get around, although bus service to the more settled, southern part of the island is good.

Essentials

GETTING THERE   By Plane   Olympic Air offers daily flights between Athens and Siros, which also gets European charters. **Aegean Airlines** also plans to start service between Athens and Siros. (For contact information for both, see "Essentials" under "Santorini," earlier in this chapter.) Buses from the airport to nearby Ermoupolis run frequently (4€); a taxi costs about 10€. A bus from the airport meets most flights; the schedule is posted at the bus stop, beside the airport entrance. A taxi to Fira costs about 13€.

By Boat   Ferries connect Siros at least once daily with Piraeus, Naxos, Mykonos, Paros, Tinos, and Santorini. The ferries connect once or twice weekly with Folegandros,

Sifnos, Iraklion, Samos, and Thessaloniki (12–15 hr.). There is service in summer from Rafina. Boats are notoriously late and/or early; your travel or ticket agent will give you an *estimate* of times involved in the following journeys. Remember: You'll find numerous ferry-ticket offices on the harborfront: **Alpha Syros** (✆ **22810/81-185**), opposite the ferry pier, and its sister company, **Teamwork Holidays** (✆ **22810/83-400;** www. teamwork.gr), sell tickets for all the ferries (and also handle plane tickets and hotel reservations). Ferry information can be verified with the Ermoupolis **port authority** (✆ **22810/88-888** or 22810/82-690). For ferry schedules, check out **www.openseas. gr** or **www.gtp.gr**.

VISITOR INFORMATION   The **Hoteliers Association of Siros** operates an information booth at the pier in summer; it's open daily from 9am to 10pm. There is a phone, but it is never answered; you'll have to go there. Note that the list of hotels they offer includes only hotels registered with their service. The website www.syros. com.gr is also very useful.

GETTING AROUND   By Bus   The **bus stop** in Ermoupolis is at the pier, where the schedule is posted. Buses circle the southern half of Siros hourly in summer (but never on Sun) between 8am and midnight. There is minimal bus service to the northern part of the island. **Teamwork Holidays** (✆ **22810/83-400;** www.teamwork.gr) offers an excellent value **bus tour** of the island during high season (Tues, Thurs, and Sat at 9am) for 20€, touring Ermoupoli and then heading out on the island for a visit to some southern villages, lunch (a la carte), and a swim before returning to town around 4:30pm. Teamwork also can arrange a day tour of Ermoupolis for 10€, and they rent cars (insurance included) from 35€.

By Car & Moped   In addition to **Teamwork Holidays** (see above), **Siros Rent A Car** (✆ **22810/80-409**), next to the GNTO office on Dodekanisou, a side street just to the left of the pier, is reliable. A small car will cost from 35€ per day, including insurance. A 50cc scooter rents from 15€ per day.

By Taxi   The taxi stand is on the main square, Plateia Miaoulis (✆ **2810/86-222**).

FAST FACTS   Several **banks** on the harbor have ATMs. The Ermoupolis hospital (✆ **22810/86-666**) is the largest in the Cyclades; it's just outside town to the west near Plateia Iroon. For free **luggage storage,** ask at Teamwork Holidays (✆ **22810/ 83-400**). The **police** (✆ **22810/82-610**) are on the south side of Miaoulis Square. The **port authority** (✆ **22810/88-888** or 22810/82-690) is on the long pier at the far end of the harbor, beyond Hotel Hermes. The **post office** (✆ **22810/82-596**) is between Miaoulis Square and the harbor, on Protopapadaki; it's open Monday through Friday from 7:30am to 2pm. The **telephone office (OTE)** is on the east side of Miaoulis Square (✆ **22810/87-399**); it's open Monday through Friday from 7:30am to 3pm. You can get online in the main square, Plateia Miaoulis, at the Internet facility, on the ground floor of the Town Hall, or at **Bizanas,** a nearby Internet cafe on Plateia Miaoulis; **Multirama,** at 54 Ethnikis Antistasis, the main drag along the harbor, also has Internet facilities.

What to See & Do
MUSEUMS

Archaeological Museum ★   The highlight of this museum's small collection is a room containing finds, including pottery and several fine Cycladic figurines, from Halandriani and Kastri, prehistoric sites in the northern hills of Siros. There are also finds from the Greek and Roman city here, which lies under modern Ermoupolis.

Because Ermoupolis is the capital of the Cyclades, the archaeological museum has holdings from many of the smaller Cycladic islands. Allow half an hour for your visit.

On the west side of the town hall, below the clock tower, Ermoupolis. ℂ **22810/86-900.** Admission 3€. Tues–Sun 8:30am–3pm.

Ermoupolis Industrial Museum ★★ Behind the cranes and warehouses of the Neorion Shipyard, at the southern end of the port, you'll find the Industrial Museum of Ermoupolis, which opened in a restored paint-works factory in 2000. There's an extensive collection of artifacts from the town's industrial past: weaving machines, metalworking tools, and, of course, items related to the town's famed shipyards (compasses, anchors, ships models). Also check out the fine collection of original drawings by the architects of Ermoupolis's neoclassical heyday, the wonderful old photographs and engravings depicting various aspects of island life, and the old maps of Siros and the Cyclades. The museum is a 20-minute walk or a short bus ride from the harbor. Allow an hour for your visit.

Ermoupolis. Just off Plateia Iroon and opposite the hospital. ℂ **22810/86-900.** Admission 3€; free on Wed. Tues–Sun 10am–2pm and 6–9pm.

EXPLORING ERMOUPOLIS ★★

If you arrive on Siros by boat, you'll immediately be aware of the two steep hills that tower over Ermoupolis. Originally, the term **Ano Siros** (which means "the area above Siros") was used to describe the peaks of both hills. Today, the term Ano Siros describes the taller hill seen to the left as you enter the harbor. This was, and still is, the Catholic quarter of the town, settled by the Venetians in the 13th century. Much of the intricate maze of narrow streets from that period remains today; cars can drive up Ano Siros and park outside the gates (as residents here do), and then continue on foot, but cars are not allowed inside. There's a **Jesuit monastery** and a **Capuchin monastery,** as well as the elaborately decorated **Church of Ayios Yeoryios** (mass Sun at 11am), at the crest of the hill. The real joy of visiting Ano Siros comes from wandering along its narrow lanes, peeking surreptitiously into courtyards, and stumbling across a tiny shop or cafe. Needless to say, there are great views over Ermoupolis and the island. Omirou, one of the streets that run uphill, is your best bet for an assault on foot on Ano Siros.

Ermoupolis's other hill, **Vrondado,** is crowned by the massive 19th-century blue-domed Greek Orthodox **Church of the Resurrection (Anastasi).** There's a fine view of Ermoupolis and the neighboring islands from the church's terrace. This area was built up as the town grew when Greeks from other islands, especially Chios, moved here at the time of the Greek War of Independence, in the 1820s. Narrow streets, marble-paved squares, and dignified pedimented mansions with elegant balconies make this neighborhood a quiet refuge from the bustling inner city.

Ermoupolis's central square, **Plateia Miaoulis,** and the elaborately elegant neoclassical **town hall** (designed by Ernst Ziller, who designed the Grande Bretagne Hotel in Athens) are conspicuous reminders of Ermoupolis's heyday. Ringed by high palm trees and facing the town hall, you really can't miss Plateia Miaoulis; if you do, go back to the harbor and head inland on Venizelou. This is the heart of Ermoupolis; this is where the island's most vigorous *volta* (promenade) takes place even if it takes place under umbrellas. Any of the cafes here is a nice place to sit, preferably with an elaborate ice-cream sundae, and watch the promenade.

A couple of blocks northeast of the town hall is the recently restored 19th-century **Apollon Theater ★**, a smaller version of Milan's La Scala, hence nicknamed "la piccola Scala." The theater is home to the **Festival of the Aegean** (www.festival oftheaegean.com), with its summer opera, classical, and pop music performances.

Even if you can't go to a performance here, step inside to see the elaborate painted ceilings and crystal chandeliers (entrance fee 2€). To the northeast is the imposing Greek Orthodox church of **Ayios Nikolaos.** The green marble iconostasis and the touching monument to the Unknown Soldier, in the park across from the church, were both done by Vitalis, a famed 19th-century marble carver from Tinos. A short stroll beyond the church will bring you to the neighborhood called **Vaporia,** appropriately named after the steamships that brought it great prosperity. Many of the town houses are built on the edge of the rocks that plunge into the sea. One other church on nearby Omirou Street is especially worth seeing: the Cathedral Church of the Transfiguration (Metamorphosi), with its glistening marble floors and precinct with wonderful pebble mosaics. This church, with its imposing arcade, is a grand tribute to the 19th-century prosperity of the Ermoupolis. One more church to visit: the Church of the Koimisis (Dormition), just off the harbor, a block or so from the casino. This 19th-century church, with a very cheerful blue and gold pulpit, houses (among much else) an icon of the Virgin, painted by Domenico Theotokopoulos, better known as El Greco. Exploring Ermoupolis is a very nice way to spend a day, or parts of any number of days.

BEACHES

Beaches are not the island's strongest suit, but there are a number of good places to swim and sun. **Mega Yialo,** as its name states, is the largest beach on the island and, not surprisingly, the most developed. Hotels there include the **Alexandra** (℃ 22810/ 42-540). **Kini Beach,** on the west coast is rapidly turning into a beach resort, with more and more rooms for rent and small hotels joining the restaurants and cafes.

On the west coast, **Galissas** (with its still charming village) has one of the best beaches on the island, a crescent of sand bordered by tamarisks. It also has a large campsite (for info, contact www.twohearts-camping.com) and a number of small hotels. Also on the west coast, **Finikas** has a slender beach and a cluster of hotels and restaurants. A few kilometers to the south, **Poseidonia** and **Agathopes** have sand beaches and less competition for a place in the sun. A bonus if you go to Poseidonia and Agathopes is that you can take in the charming village of Dellagrazia-Poseidonia, with its cluster of 19th-century villas.

Where to Stay

As you come off the ferry in Ermoupolis, you'll see the kiosk of the **Hoteliers Association of Siros,** which provides a list of island hotels. Note that hotels pay to become members of this association, so not all of the island's best lodgings are represented. In August, when vacationing Greeks pack the island, don't even think of arriving without a reservation. In addition to the following, you may want to consider the 16-unit **Syrou Melathron** (℃ 22810/85-963; syroumel@otenet.gr), in a handsome 19th-century town house. Only reports of indifferent service keep us from recommending this stylish little hotel wholeheartedly; doubles from 130€.

Hotel Apollonos ★   This small hotel on the water in Vaporia is one of Ermoupolis's restored mansion hotels. Those looking for a fully authentic restoration might be disappointed—the furnishings and lighting are partly contemporary in style—but the overall effect works. The best guest rooms are the two facing the water at the back of the house: Both are quite spacious, and one has a loft sleeping area with sitting room below. Bathrooms are large, with tile and wood floors. A large common sitting room faces the bay, while a breakfast room faces the street. If you want 24-hour service, this is not the place for you.

8 Apollonos, Ermoupolis, 84100 Siros. www.xenonapollonos.gr. ℂ **22810/81-387** or 22810/80-842. 3 units. 165€–200€ double. Rates include breakfast. No credit cards. **Amenities:** Breakfast room/bar. *In room:* A/C.

Hotel Ethrion ★ 🦟 This small, family-run hotel, with a quiet location in the heart of town, has rooms and studios (one with kitchenette) with terraces or balconies; five units have sea views from the balconies. The rooms are comfortably and pleasantly furnished (the ones on the top floors have fancier decor), the owners are very helpful (as is the website map), and the price is right. The more expensive rooms have a balcony and sea view. This is the sort of homey place that can tempt you to relax into getting to know Ermoupolis *siga, siga* (slowly, slowly).

24 J. Kosma, Ermoupolis 84100, Siros. www.ethrion.gr. ℂ **22819/89-006.** 8 doubles, 4 studios (1 with kitchenette). 70€–85€ double. MC, V. **Amenities:** Internet. *In room:* A/C.

Hotel Hermes ★ 🦟 The Hermes presents a bright, cheerful facade to busy Plateia Kanari at the harbor's east end. What you can't see from the street is that many of the better rooms directly face a quiet stretch of rocky coast at the back of the building. The functional, dull standard rooms have shower-only bathrooms and views of the street or a back garden. The rooms in the new wing are worth the extra money for their size, furnishings, and balconies that allow early risers to see the sunrise. If you get a room here on a summer weekend, be prepared to be the only guest not in a wedding party—and to see the sunrise from your balcony as the wedding reception winds down.

Plateia Kanari, Ermoupolis, 84100 Siros. ℂ **22810/83-011** or 22810/83-012. Fax 22810/87-412. 51 units. 100€ double. AE, DC, MC, V. **Amenities:** Restaurant; bar. *In room:* A/C, TV, hair dryer.

Hotel Omiros ★ The Omiros is in a nicely restored neoclassical house, with very comfortable and stylish public rooms, and much more simple guest rooms. The climb up to the hotel is steep and there is no elevator in the hotel itself. But the location is very quiet and the owners are very helpful. If you are coming to Siros for a long stay, this quiet spot might feel like home. If you are here for a short stay, the walk up and down to the Omiros might be wearing.

43 Omirou, Ermoupolis, 84100 Siros. ℂ **22810/84-910** or 22810/88-756. Fax 22810/86-266. 13 units. From 90€ double. Continental breakfast 10€. MC, V. **Amenities:** Breakfast room, lounge. *In room:* A/C, TV.

Hotel Vourlis ★★ On a hill overlooking the fashionable Vaporia district, the elegant Hotel Vourlis occupies one of the finest of the city's mansions. Built in 1888, the house has retained its grandeur and charm. The fine details that have sadly been lost in many other restored mansions are here in all their glory. The plaster ceilings in the front rooms are especially resplendent. Most furniture also dates from the 19th century, creating a period setting that incorporates all the comforts you expect from a fine hotel. Bathrooms are spacious and come with tubs. The two front rooms on the second floor have great sea views. Winter guests will be glad to know that the house is centrally heated. The adjacent five-unit **Ipatia Guesthouse** (ℂ **22810/83-575**) is in a nicely restored town house.

5 Mavrokordatou, Ermoupolis, 84100 Siros. ℂ/fax **22810/88-440** or 22810/81-682. 8 units. 135€–200€ double. Continental breakfast 9€. MC, V. **Amenities:** Breakfast room/bar. *In room:* A/C, TV.

Where to Eat

There are lots of excellent tavernas in and around Ermoupolis, but if you're only going to have one dinner here, head to **Thalami** (ℂ **22810/85-331**), in a 19th-century mansion with sea views and delicious food, especially seafood (great stuffed squid).

Main courses run 8€ to 15€ and much more, of course, if you have the fresh fish. Up in Ano Siros, try one of these places with great views: **Frangosiriani** (✆ 22810/84-888), down the street from the **Taverna Lilis,** or the nearby **Alithini** (✆ 22810/88-253), which specializes in rooster in wine sauce and *stifado,* a hearty stew with onions and veal or rabbit.

Taverna Lilis ★★ GREEK/SEAFOOD   The view is to die for and the food is good. Lilis is one of the best of the tavernas in Ano Siros, the quarter cresting the high conical hill behind Ermoupolis. From the terrace, there's a panoramic view of Ermoupolis, the bay, distant Tinos and, even farther out, the shores of Mykonos. The food is better-than-average taverna fare—meats and fish are grilled on a wood fire, and the ingredients are reliably fresh. There's sometimes *rembetika* music here (see "Siros After Dark," below).

Ano Siros. ✆ **22810/88-087.** Reservations recommended in July–Aug. Main courses 8€–20€. No credit cards. Daily 7pm–midnight. Follow Omirou from the center of Ermoupolis, past the Hotel Omiros, and continue straight up the long flight of steps that leads to Taverna Lilis's brightly lit terrace. You can also call a taxi.

To Arhontariki ★ GREEK   This small place fills the narrow street with tables that are precariously perched on cobblestones, and it is probably the best of the tavernas in Ermoupolis center. It's easy to find—just plunge into the maze of streets at the corner of Miaoulis Square, between Pyramid Pizzeria and Loukas Restaurant, and weave your way left—it's 2 blocks or so in, between Miaoulis and the harbor. Remember: if you get lost, you can ask for directions, and any local knows this place. The menu is largely composed of specials (several vegetarian) that change daily.

Ermoupolis. ✆ **22810/81-744.** Main courses 8€–18€. No credit cards. Daily noon–midnight.

To Koutouki Tou Liberis ★ GREEK   If you feel adventurous, take a taxi to this out-of-the-way place that is definitely worthwhile. There is no menu—the night's offerings are brought out to you on a massive tray, and each dish is explained in turn. The food is often innovative, making slight but significant departures from traditional recipes. The spicing is subtle, and good use is made of the season's best ingredients. The owner is renowned locally for his bouzouki playing—late at night, after the last diners have finished their meals, impromptu traditional music sessions sometimes take place.

Kaminia. ✆ **22810/85-580.** Reservations recommended several days in advance in high season. Main courses 8€–18€. No credit cards. Fri–Sat 9pm–1am. 2km (1¼ miles) from Ermoupolis center.

Siros After Dark

Siros was among the most fertile grounds for *rembetika,* the haunting songs of the dispossessed, marginally criminal underclasses that probably began in Asia Minor in the early 20th century. Markos Vambakaris, the Bob Dylan, as it were, of *rembetika,* was born on Siros, which still prizes his music. You can hear *rembetika* at **Xanthomalis** and at **Taverna Lilis,** in Ano Siros, which sometimes have late-night performances on the weekends; reservations are a must.

   Liquid Bar gets rave reviews from a taxi driver I talked to who likes his music very loud. You can also join in the evening *volta* **(stroll)** around Plateia Miaoulis, take a seat to watch it, or drop in at **Piramatiko, Agora,** or **Bizanas,** longtime music joints.

THE DODECANESE

By John S. Bowman

T he Dodecanese—the very name suggests someplace exotic, though it is merely Greek for "twelve islands"— if not exotic, have been providing visitors for many centuries a range of extraordinary attractions and experiences. Part of their special appeal comes from the fact that the Dodecanese mostly hug the coast of Asia Minor, far from the Greek mainland. As frontier or borderline territories, their struggles to remain free and Greek have been intense and prolonged. Although they have been recognizably Greek for millennia, only in 1948 were the Dodecanese formally reunited with the Greek nation.

By the way, "the twelve islands" are in fact an archipelago of 32 islands: 14 inhabited and 18 uninhabited. But they have been known collectively as the Dodecanese since 1908, when 12 of them joined forces to resist the revocation of the special status they had long enjoyed under the Ottomans.

The four islands selected for this chapter are certainly the most engaging of the Dodecanese. From south to north, they are **Rhodes, Simi, Kos,** and **Patmos.** Patmos and Simi are relatively arid in summer, while the interiors of Rhodes and Kos remain fertile and forested. Spectacular historical sights, such as ancient ruins and medieval fortresses, are concentrated on Patmos, Kos, and Rhodes; so are the tourists. Simi is the once-but-no-longer-secret getaway you will not soon forget.

Long accustomed to watching the seas for invaders, these islands now spend their time awaiting the tourists, who show up each spring and stay until October. The beginning of the tourist season sets into motion a pattern of activity largely contrived to attract and entertain outsiders. Such is the reality of island life today. As in the past, however, the islanders proudly retain their own character, even as they accommodate an onslaught of visitors.

Strategies for Seeing the Islands

In planning a visit, remember that Rhodes has the longest tourist season. So if you're rushing into the season in April, begin in Rhodes; if you're stretching the season into October, end up in Rhodes. In any case, if you can, avoid the Dodecanese July through August, when they are so crowded with tourists that they nearly sink.

In high season, at least, you can travel easily from one to the other of the three principal islands described here—**Rhodes, Kos,** and **Patmos** (although the excursion to Patmos really requires a minimum of 2 days). From the mainland, all are best reached by air. Rhodes and Kos have airports; Patmos is a short jaunt by hydrofoil from Samos, which also has an airport. From Kos and Rhodes, you can get just about anywhere in the eastern Aegean, including nearby **Turkey,** which is worth at least a day's excursion. **Simi** can be reached by ferry from Piraeus, but most people will approach it by boat as an excursion from Rhodes.

RHODES (RODOS) ★★

250km (135 nautical miles) E of Piraeus

Selecting a divine patron was serious business for an ancient city. Most Greek cities played it safe and chose a mainstream god or goddess, a ranking Olympian—someone such as Athena or Apollo or Artemis, or Zeus himself. It's revealing that the people of Rhodes chose **Helios,** the sun, as their signature god. Indeed, millennia later, the cult of the sun is alive and well on Rhodes, and no wonder: The island receives, on average, more than 300 days of sunshine a year. No wonder Rhodes has long been a destination for sun worshipers hailing from colder, darker, wetter lands around the globe.

But Rhodes gives visitors more than a mere tan. A location at the intersection of the East and West propelled the island into the thick of both commerce and conflicts. The scars left by its rich and turbulent history have become its treasures. Hellenistic Greeks, Romans, Crusader Knights, Turks, Italians—all invaders who brought some destruction but who also left behind fascinating artifacts.

Through it all, Rhodes has remained beautiful. Its beaches are among the cleanest in the Aegean, and its interior is still home to unspoiled mountain villages, rich fertile plains—and beautiful butterflies. Several days in Rhodes will allow you to appreciate its marvels, relax in the sun, and perhaps add a day trip to the idyllic island of Simi or to the coast of Turkey. If Rhodes is your last port of call in Greece, it will make a grand finale; if it is your point of departure, you can launch forth happily from here to just about anywhere in the Aegean or Mediterranean.

Essentials

GETTING THERE By Plane In addition to its year-round service between Rhodes and Athens and Thessaloniki, **Olympic Airways** offers summer service between Rhodes and the following Greek locales: Iraklion (Crete), Karpathos, and Santorini. The local Olympic office is at 9 Ierou Lohou (✆ **22410/24-571**). Flights fill quickly, so reserve in advance. **Aegean Airlines** (✆ **801/112-0000** in Greece; www.aegeanair.com), in addition to flights to Rhodes, offers at least high-season flights between Rhodes and Thessaloniki and Iraklion, Crete. Tickets for any flight in or out of Rhodes can be purchased directly from **Triton Holidays,** near Mandraki Harbor, 9 Plastira, Rhodes city (✆ **22410/21-690;** www.tritondmc.gr). Triton will either send your tickets to you or have them waiting for you at the airport.

The Rhodes **Paradissi Airport** (✆ **22410/83-214**) is 13km (8 miles) southwest of the city and is served from 6am to 10:30pm by bus. The bus to the city center (Plateia Rimini) is 6€. A taxi costs 22€. Some taxi drivers resist taking passengers to hotels in the Old Town (because of the slow going in the streets)—they will even claim they can't enter; note their number and threaten to report them, and they usually relent. Otherwise, make arrangements with your hotel to be met at one of the main gates.

The Dodecanese

Ancient Lindos **6**
Asklepion **2**
Monastery of St. John
  and the Cave of the Apocalypse **1**
Monolithos Castle **5**
Panormitis Monastery **3**
Petaloudes (Valley of the Butterflies) **4**

Greece

Aegean Sea

Athens

The Dodecanese

Mediterranean Sea

CRETE

PATMOS
Arki
Marathos
Kampos
Skala
Lipsi
Agathonisi
Megalo Horio
Farmakonisi
Partheni
LEROS
Lakki
Ksirokampos
Levitha
Emborios
Arginonta
Telendos
Massouri
Mirties
Kalimnos
KALIMNOS
Psarimos
Lambi
Mastihari
Tigaki
Kos
Ayios Fokas
Asfendiou
Kefalos
Kardamena
KOS
Nimos
Vathys
Yiali
Loutra
Simi
Pedi
SIMI
Analipsi
Mandraki
Emborios
Avlaki
Nisyros
Astypalea
Astypalea
Megalo Horio
Livadia
Tilos
Sirna
Rhodes
Ialisos
Maritsa
Soroni
Kalithea
Fanes
Faliraki
Alimia
Mandriko
RHODES
Afandou
Halki
Embonas
Archangelos
Monolithos
Laerma
Lindos
Apolakia
Messanagros
Gennadio
Kattavia
Plimiri
Tria Nissia
Sea of Crete
Saria
Diafani
Olymbos
KARPATHOS
Spoa
Piles
Karpathos
Arkassa
Armathia
Fri
Kassos
MEDITERRANEAN SEA
←**To Crete**

Ferry Routes

0   25 mi
0   25 km

N

By Boat   Rhodes is a major port with sea links not only to Athens, Crete, and the islands of the Aegean, but also to Cyprus, Turkey, and Israel. Service and schedules are always changing; check with the tourist office or a travel agency for the latest.

In late spring and throughout the summer, there are daily sailings—some with high-speed hydrofoils or catamarans—from and to Rhodes and many of the Dodecanense and other islands in the eastern Aegean: Kos, Kalimnos, Kastellorizo, Leros, Nissiros, Patmos, Samos, Simi, and Tilos. The advantage of hydrofoils and catamarans is that they make the voyage in half the time, but when the wind blows, the sailings are canceled. Air quality is also poor, especially compared to that on larger open-deck excursion boats or ferries. For more detailed information about the most active ship line, **Dodekanisos Seaways,** see www.12ne.gr.

Wherever you want to go, whether by ferry, hydrofoil, catamaran, or excursion boat, schedules and tickets are available from **Triton Holidays** (see above). Although several agents throughout Rhodes city and island can issue air and sea tickets, Triton has had a "special relationship" with Frommer's from the original "$5 a Day" guide.

VISITOR INFORMATION   During the high season only, you'll find a helpful **Rhodes Municipal Tourist Office** at Plateia Rimini, facing the port taxi stand (© 22410/35-945). It dispenses information on local excursions, buses, ferries, and accommodations, and offers currency exchange as well. Its hours are Monday through Saturday from about 9am to 9pm, Sunday from 9am to 2pm. The above-recommended **Triton Holidays** (see above) is also willing to answer any traveler's question, free of obligation, and is sometimes open when the tourist offices are closed.

GETTING AROUND   Rhodes is not an island you can see on foot. You need wheels of some sort: public bus, group-shared taxi, rental car, or organized bus tour for around-the-island excursions. Rhodes city is a different story. Walking is the only and most pleasurable mode of transport; you'll need a taxi only if you're going to treat yourself to a meal at one of the farther-flung restaurants. The fact is that even taxis are not allowed within the walls unless you have luggage and are arriving or leaving.

By Bus   Public buses provide good service throughout the island; the tourist office should be able to help with a schedule of routes and times. Buses to points **east** (except for the eastern coastal road as far as Falilraki) leave from the East Side Bus Station on Plateia Rimini, whereas buses to points **west,** including the airport, leave from the nearby West Side Bus Station on Averof. Buses for the eastern coastal road as far as Falilraki also leave from the West Side Bus Station. Island fares range from 1€ within the city to 20€ for the most remote destinations. The city bus system also offers six different tours; details are available from the tourist office.

By Bicycle, Moped & Motorcycle   Even where there are strips set aside for bicyclists, it can be risky cycling on Greek highways. You must have a proper license to rent anything motorized. We can recommend several outfits that rent motorbikes and bicycles: **Bicycle Center,** 39 Griva (© 22410/28-315); **Mike's Motor Club,** 23 Kazouli (© 22410/37-420); and **Moto Pilot,** 12 Kritis (© 22410/32-285). Starting prices per day are roughly 15€ for a mountain bike, from 25€ for a moped, and 40€ to 70€ for a motorcycle.

By Taxi   In Rhodes city, the largest of many taxi stands is in front of Old Town, on the harborfront in Plateia Rimini (© 22410/27-666). There, posted for all to see, are the set fares for one-way trips throughout the island. (A sample fare to Lindos is 40€ one way; add at least another 20€ if the taxi waits for you.) Since many of the cabdrivers speak sightseer English, a few friends can be chauffeured and lectured at

Rhodes Attractions

Rhodes

RHODES

0 — 330 m
0 — 330 y

Greece

Athens ✪   Aegean Sea

Mediterranean Sea   Rhodes

Aquarium

100 PALMS

Vas. Konstantinou

Othonos
Kritis
Ioannou Kazouli
Dragoumi
Amalias
Atti Miaouli
28 Octobriou
Amerikis
Vas. Marias
Martiou
Alexandrou
Vas. Amerkis Sofias
Ioannou
Metaxa
Diakou
Papalouka
NEW TOWN
Plateia Rimini
Palace of the Knights
Riga Fereou
Kennedy
Them. Sofouli
Pindou
Enoplon Dynameon
President
Chimairas
Pavlou Mela
Ioannou
Demokratias
City Walls
Diagondon
Ayiou
Komninon
Mount Smith 8
Ippoton
Sokratous
Fanouriou
Ippodamou
Omirou
OLD TOWN
Filellinon
Pythagora
Periklous
Vyronon
City Walls

Government Buildings

Fort St. Nicholas Lighthouse

Mandraki Harbor

Windmills   Akandia Harbor

Market
Eleftheria (Liberty) Gate
Mill Tower

Commercial Harbor
Customs House

9

THE DODECANESE | Rhodes (Rodos)

Acropolis of Rhodes **8**
Archaeological Museum
  of Rhodes **2**
Church of Our Lady
  of the Castle/
  Byzantine Museum **4**
Clock Tower **5**
Hospice of St. Catherine **9**
Mosque of Suleiman **6**
Municipal Art Gallery **3**
Municipal Baths **7**
Square of the Jewish
  Martyrs **10**
Street of the Knights **1**

Lighthouse

a reasonable cost. Taxis are metered, but fares should not exceed the minimum on short round-the-city jaunts. For longer trips, negotiate directly with the drivers. (I found Semis Limo Service to be reliable and friendly: semispa@yahoo.gr.) Better yet, **Triton Holidays** (see above), at no extra charge, will arrange for a private full- or half-day taxi with a driver who not only speaks fluent English, but will also respect your wishes regarding smoking or nonsmoking en route. For **radio taxis,** call ✆ **22410/ 69-800.** There is a slight additional pickup charge when you call for a taxi.

By Car   Once more, **Triton Holidays** agency can arrange for car rentals, both at the airport or in town. Apart from the array of international companies—among them **Alamo/National** (✆ **22410/73-570**), **Avis** (✆ **22410/82-896**), **Europcar** (✆ **22410/21-958**), and **Hertz** (✆ **22410/21-819**)—there are large numbers of local companies. The latter may offer the lowest rates but have only a handful of cars, so they may be unable to back you up, in the event of an accident. Be certain that you are fully covered, for all minor scrapes as well as major accidents, before signing anything. An established Greek company, with some 300 cars—reputedly the newest fleet on Rhodes—is DRIVE Rent-a-Car, now part of the **Budget** chain (✆ **22410/21- 690;** www.driverentacar.gr). It has an excellent reputation for personal service, as

The **Dodecanese Association for People with Special Needs** (✆ 22410/73-109 or 6940/463810 cellphone) provides free minibus door-to-door service from the port, airport, and hotels—or even if you want to go out for coffee or a swim.

well as low prices from about 40€ per day, depending on the season and demand. Some of the more remote roads on Rhodes require all-terrain vehicles, and rental-car companies usually stipulate that their standard vehicles be driven only on fully paved roads.

By Organized Tour & Excursion Boats   Several operators feature nature, archaeology, shopping, and beach tours. In Rhodes city, **Triton Holidays,** as one of the largest and most reliable agencies, specializes in trips designed for independent travelers. Triton offers day and evening cruises, hiking tours, and excursions in Rhodes, as well as in the other Dodecanese islands and in Mamaris in Turkey. We recommend the full-day guided tours, either the one to Lindos (50€) or the "Island Tour" (60€), which takes you to small villages, churches, and monasteries, and includes lunch in the village of **Embonas,** known for its local wines and fresh-grilled meat. There is also a fascinating half-day guided tour to Filerimos Monastery, Valley of the Butterflies, and the ancient city of Kamiros for 50€. Along Mandraki Harbor, you can find excursion boats that leave for **Lindos** at 9am and return around 6pm, costing about 50€, as well as daily excursions to **Simi** for 64€ round-trip. For an in-depth island experience, Triton Holidays also offers a combination package of car-rental and hotel accommodations in four small villages around the island (Kalavarda, Monolithos, Prasonisi, and Asklepion), ranging from 4 to 10 nights.

CITY LAYOUT   Rhodes is not the worst offender in Greece, but it does share the country's widespread aversion to street signs and numbers. You need a map marked with every lane, so that you can count your way from one place to another. My favorite is the map of Rhodes Town (Old and New) drawn by Mario Camerini; no longer widely available, I found it most recently at a gift shop at 65 Socratous.

Rhodes city (pop. 50,000) is divided into two sections: the Old Town, dating from medieval days, and the New Town. Overlooking the harbor, the **Old Town ★★** is surrounded by massive walls—4km (2½ miles) around and, in certain places, nearly 12m (40 ft.) thick—built by the Knights of St. John. The **New Town** embraces the old one and extends south to meet the **Rhodian Riviera,** a strip of luxury resort hotels. At its northern tip is the city beach, in the area called 100 Palms, and famed **Mandraki Harbor,** now used as a mooring for private yachts and tour boats.

FAST FACTS   Numerous **banks** in the New Town will exchange currencies as will commercial **exchange offices,** but most everyone now relies on the **ATMs** to be found not only on the banks' exteriors but at other locations frequented by tourists. For emergency care, call the **hospital** (✆ 22410/80-000) or, if necessary, an **ambulance** (✆ 166).

Internet cafes are now to be found everywhere throughout Rhodes Town and there is no sense in singling out one over another: select the place that is both most convenient and appealing at the time you need one—and of course you must purchase at least some beverage. **Express Laundry,** 5 Kosti Palama, behind Plateia

Rimini (☎ **22410/22-514**), is open daily from 8am to 11pm. **Wash-O-Matic,** on 33 Platonos (leading off Sokratous), keeps the same hours. **International Pharmacy,** 22 A. Kiakou in the New Town (☎ **22410/75-331**), is now but one of many pharmacies throughout the Old and New Towns. There are **public toilets** at 2 Papagou and across from 10 Papagou (the street leading up from Plateia Rimini); there is also one just outside the wall at the Marine Gate, by the Old Harbor. The **police** (☎ **22410/23-849**) in the Old Town can handle any complaints from 10am to midnight. The **tourist police** (☎ **22410/27-423**), on the edge of the Old Town, near the port, address tourists' queries, concerns, and grievances. The main **post office,** on Mandraki Harbor, is open Monday through Friday from 7am to 8pm.

What to See & Do in Rhodes City

Rhodes is blessed with first-rate sights and entertainment. As an international playground and a museum of both antiquity and the medieval era, Rhodes has no serious competitors in the Dodecanese and few peers in the eastern Mediterranean. Consequently, in singling out its highlights, we necessarily pass over sights and events that, on lesser islands, would be main attractions. Thus in late May to early June there is now a Medieval Festival with music, performances, and pageantry. Or in July there has been an International Ecofilm Festival with films based on environmental themes.

EXPLORING THE OLD TOWN

Best to know one thing from the start about Old Town: It's not laid out on a grid—not even close. There are roughly 200 streets or lanes that simply have no name. Getting lost here, however, is an opportunity to explore. When you feel the need to find your bearings, you can ask for **Sokratous,** which is the closest to a main street in Old Town.

Before setting out to visit Rhodes Old Town, there is at least one basic bit of history you should know: The great walls and most impressive of the medieval buildings you will be seeing are the result of the occupation of the island by the Knights of St. John (aka Hospitallers), who were forced by the Muslims to abandon the Holy Land in 1309. These men—known more generally as crusaders—were a mixed lot of Western Europeans who established a combination of an occupation army and charity foundation wherever they settled. In 1522, after a 6-month siege, the Muslims forced the knights to surrender and retreat to Malta. But we should realize that the magnificent structures we now see were built by the forced labor of native Rhodians.

When you approach the walls of Old Town, you are about to enter arguably the most impressive continuously inhabited medieval town in Europe. It's a thrill to behold. Although there are many gates, we suggest that you first enter through **Eleftheria (Liberty) Gate,** where you'll come to **Plateia Simi,** containing ruins of the **Temple of Venus,** identified by the votive offerings found here, which may date from the 3rd century B.C. The remains of the temple are next to a parking lot (driving is restricted in the Old Town), which rather diminishes the impact of the few stones and columns still standing. Nevertheless, the ruins are a reminder that a great Hellenistic city once stood here and encompassed the entire area now occupied by the city, including the Old and New towns. The population of the Hellenistic city of Rhodes is thought to have equaled the current population of the whole island (roughly 100,000).

Plateia Simi is also home to the **Municipal Art Gallery of Rhodes,** above the Museum Reproduction Shop (generally Mon–Sat 8am–2pm); admission is 4€. Its impressive collection comprises mostly works by eminent Modern Greek artists. The gallery now has a second beautifully restored venue in the Old Town (across from the

Of all the inns on the Street of the Knights, only the **Inn of France** is open to the public (Mon–Fri 8am–noon). The ground floor houses the Institut Français, but you can see its garden as well as an occasional art show in the second-floor gallery. The other inns are now offices or private residences and are closed to the public.

Mosque of Suleiman) to house its collection of antique and rare maps and engravings (Mon–Fri 8am–2pm). One block farther is the **Museum of Decorative Arts,** which contains finely made objects and crafts from Rhodes and other islands, most notably Simi (Tues–Sun 8:30am–3pm). Admission is 2€. Continue through the gate until you reach Ippoton, also known as the Street of the Knights. *Note:* If you are ready for serious sightseeing, purchase a ticket for 12€ that includes admissions to the Museum of Decorative Arts, Archaeological Museum, Church of our Lady of the Castle, and Palace of the Knights. It's available at all of the museums.

Street of the Knights ★★ (Ippoton is its name on maps) is one of the best-preserved and most delightful medieval relics in the world. The 600m-long (1,968-ft.) cobble-paved street was constructed over an ancient pathway that led in a straight line from the Acropolis of Rhodes to the port. By the early 16th century, it became the address for most of the inns of each nation (and known as "tongues," because of the languages they spoke), which housed Knights who belonged to the Order of St. John. The inns were used as eating clubs and temporary residences for visiting dignitaries, and their facades reflect the architectural details of their respective countries.

Begin at the lowest point on the hill, at **Spanish House,** now used by a bank. Next door is **Inn of the Order of the Tongue of Italy,** built in 1519 (as can be seen on the shield of the order above the door). Then comes the **Palace of the Villiers of the Isle of Adam,** built in 1521, housing the Archaeological Service of the Dodecanese. The **Inn of France,** constructed in 1492, now hosts the French Language Institute. It's one of the most ornate inns, with the shield of three lilies (fleur-de-lis), royal crown, and the crown of the Magister d'Aubusson (the cardinal's hat above four crosses), which is off center, over the middle door. Typical of the late Gothic period, the architectural and decorative elements are somewhat asymmetrical, lending grace to the squat building.

Opposite these inns is one side of the **Hospital of the Knights,** now the **Archaeological Museum,** whose entrance is on Museum Square. The grand and fascinating structure is well worth a visit. (As with so many public buildings in Rhodes, its hours are subject to change, but summer hours are generally Tues–Fri 8am–7pm and Sat–Sun 8:30am–3pm.) Admission is 3€. Across from the Archaeological Museum is the **Byzantine Museum,** housed in the **Church of Our Lady of the Castle** ★ (the Roman Catholic Cathedral of the Knights); it often hosts rotating exhibits of Christian art. Its hours vary but are generally Tuesday through Sunday from 8am to 7pm or later; admission is 3€.

The church farther on the right is **Ayia Triada** (open when it's open), next to the Italian consulate. Above its door are three coats of arms: those of France, England, and the pope. Past the arch that spans the street, still on the right, is the **Inn of the Tongue of Provence,** which was partially destroyed in 1856 and is now shorter than it once was. Opposite it on the left is the traditionally Gothic **Inn of the Tongue of Spain,** with vertical columns elongating its facade and a lovely garden in the back.

The culmination of this impressive procession should be **Palace of the Knights ★★★** (also known as Palace of the Grand Masters), but it was destroyed in a catastrophic accidental explosion in 1856. What you see before you now is a grandiose palace built in the 1930s to accommodate Mussolini's visits and fantasies. Its scale and grandeur are more reflective of a future that failed to materialize than of a vanished past. Today it houses mosaics stolen from Kos by the Italian military as well as a collection of antique furniture. Hours vary, but, in summer, are Monday from 12:30 to 7pm, Tuesday through Sunday from 8am to 7pm. Admission is 6€.

The **Mosque of Suleiman** and the public baths are two reminders of the Turkish presence in old Rhodes. Follow Sokratous west, away from the harbor, or walk a couple of blocks south, from the Palace of the Knights; you can't miss the mosque, with its slender, though incomplete, minaret and pink-striped Venetian exterior.

The **Municipal Baths** (what the Greeks call the "Turkish baths") are housed in a 7th-century Byzantine structure and have been considerably upgraded since 2000. They merit a visit by anyone interested in vestiges of Turkish culture that remain in the Old Town, and cost less than the showers in most pensions. The *hamam* (most locals use this Turkish word for "bath") is in Plateia Arionos, between a large old mosque and the Folk Dance Theater. Throughout the day, men and women go in via their separate entrances and disrobe in private shuttered cubicles. A walk across cool marble floors leads you to the bath area—many domed, round chambers sunlit by tiny glass panes in the roof. Through the steam, you'll see people seated around large marble basins, chatting, while ladling bowls of water over their heads. The baths are open Tuesday through Saturday from 10:30am to 4pm. Their use costs 5€. Note that on Saturday, the baths are extremely crowded with locals.

The Old Town was also home to the Jewish community, whose origins date to the days of the ancient Greeks. Little survives in the northeast or Jewish Quarter of the Old Town other than a few homes with Hebrew inscriptions, the Jewish cemetery, and the **Square of the Jewish Martyrs** (**Plateia ton Martiron Evreon,** also known as Sea Horse Sq., because of the sea horse fountain). The square is dedicated to the 1,604 Jews who were rounded up here and sent to their deaths at Auschwitz. On Dosiadou, leading off just below the square (signed), is a lovely synagogue, where services are held on Friday night; it is usually open daily from 10am to 3pm. A surprisingly elegant and informative museum is attached to it (Apr–Oct Sun–Fri 10am–3pm; free admission); those wishing to know more about this can e-mail **jcrhodes@otenet.gr**.

While at the Square of the Jewish Martyrs, be sure to visit the **Hospice of St. Catherine ★** (Mon–Fri 8am–2pm; free admission). Built in the late 14th century by the Order of the Knights of St. John (Knights Hospitaller) to house and entertain esteemed guests, it apparently lived up to its mission; one such guest, Niccole de Martoni, described it in the 1390s as "beautiful and splendid, with many handsome rooms, containing many and good beds." The description still fits, though only one "good bed" can be seen today. The restored hospice has exceptionally beautiful sea-pebble and mosaic floors, carved and intricately painted wooden ceilings, a grand hall and lavish bedchamber, and engaging exhibits.

After touring the sites of the Old Town, you might want to walk around the **walls.** The fortification has a series of magnificent gates and towers, and is a remarkable example of a fully intact medieval structure. Much of the structure can be viewed by walking around the outside, but to walk along the top of the walls requires an admission fee of 4€ for adults, 2€ for students. The museum operates a 1-hour tour for 6€ Tuesday and Saturday at 3pm, beginning at the Palace of the Knights.

Another possibility is the so-called **Land Train,** a familiar attraction in many tourist towns, which takes people on a 50-minute ride through the main streets for 5€; you join it at the main market in the New Town.

EXPLORING THE NEW TOWN

The New Town is best explored after dark, as it houses most of the bars, discos, and nightclubs, as well as innumerable tavernas. In the heat of the day, its beaches—**Elli beach** and the **municipal beach**—are also popular. What few people make a point of seeking out but also can't miss are **Mandraki Harbor** and the "neoimperial" architecture (culminating in the Nomarhia or Prefecture) along the harbor, all of which date from the Italian occupation (1912–44). Other draws are the lovely park and ancient burial site at **Rodini** (2km/1¼ miles south of the city), and the impressive ancient **Acropolis of Rhodes,** on Mount Smith. There's also a fairly decent aquarium by the harbor.

The remains of the ancient Rhodian Acropolis stand high atop the north end of the island, above the modern city, with the sea visible on two sides. This is a pleasant site to explore leisurely with a picnic; there's plenty of shade. The restored stadium and small theater are particularly impressive, as are the remains of the Temple of Pythian Apollo. Just a few pillars and a portion of the architrave remain, but they are provocative and pleasing, giving fodder to the imagination (no admission fee).

SHOPPING

In Rhodes city, the Old Town is most interesting to shoppers. *Note:* Most shops close at the end of November and don't reopen until March. You'll find classic and contemporary **gold and silver jewelry** almost everywhere. The top-of-the-line Greek designer **Ilias Lalaounis** has a boutique on Plateia Alexandrou. **Chrisochos Jewelry,** at 13 Sokratous, offers a more modestly priced selection. For a good selection of authentic and reproduction antique jewelry, as well as ceramics, silver, glass, and anything you'd expect in a bazaar, drop in at **Royal Silver,** 15 Apellou (off Sokratous).

For imported **leather goods** and **furs** (the former often from nearby Turkey, and the latter from northern Greece), stroll the length of Sokratous. Antiquity buffs should drop by the **Ministry of Culture Museum Reproduction Shop,** on Plateia Simi, which sells excellent reproductions of ancient sculptures, friezes, and tiles. True **antiques**—furniture, carpets, porcelain, and paintings—can be found at **Kalogirou Art,** 30 Panetiou, in a wonderful old building with a pebble-mosaic floor and an exotic banana-tree garden opposite the entrance to the Knights Palace.

Although most of what you find on Rhodes can be found throughout Greece, several products bear a special Rhodian mark. **Rhodian wine** has a fine reputation, and, on weekdays, you can visit two distinguished island wineries: **Cair,** at its winery 2km (1¼ miles) outside of Rhodes city, on the way to Lindo (www.cair.gr); and **Emery,** in the village of Embonas (www.emery.gr). Another distinctive product of Rhodes is a rare form of **honey,** made by bees committed to *thimati* (like oregano). To get this you may have to drive to the villages of Siana or Vati and ask if anyone has some to sell. It's mostly sold out of private homes, and locals are in no hurry to give it up. **Olive oil** is another local art, and again the best is sold out of private homes, meaning that you have to make discreet inquiries to discover the current sources.

Rhodes is also famed for handmade **carpets** and **kilims,** an enduring legacy from centuries of Ottoman occupation. Some 40 women around the island currently make carpets in their homes; some monasteries are also in on the act. There's a local carpet factory, known as **Kleopatra,** at Ayios Anthonias, on the main road to Lindos, near Afandou. In the Old Town, these and other Rhodian handmade carpets and kilims are sold at **Royal Carpet,** at 46 Aristotelos. Finally, there is "Rhodian" **lace** and **embroidery,** much of which, alas, now comes from Hong Kong. Insist on knowing the difference between what's local and what's imported.

SPORTS & OUTDOOR PURSUITS

Most outdoor activities on Rhodes are beach- and sea-related. For everything from **parasailing** to **jet skis** to **canoes,** you'll find what you need at **Faliraki beach** (see "Sights & Beaches Elsewhere on the Island," later in this chapter), if you can tolerate the crowds. If you've always wanted to try scuba diving, both **Waterhoppers Diving Schools** (☎/fax **22410/38-146;** www.waterhoppers.com) and **Dive Med** (☎ **22410/ 61-115;** www.divemedcollege.com) offer 1-day introductory dives for beginners, diving expeditions for experienced divers, and 4- to 5-day courses leading to various certifications. For wind- and kite-surfing, **Prasonisi beach** at the far southern end of Rhodes provides what has been described as a "surfer's heaven."

For a hike around the lesser-traveled parts of Rhodes, contact **Walking Rhodes** for guided excursions (☎ **69451/66-5850;** www.walking-rhodes.com).

No license is required for **fishing;** the best areas are reputed to be off Kamiros Skala, Kalithea, and Lindos. Try hitching a ride with the fishing boats that moor opposite Ayia Katerina's Gate. For sailing and yachting information, call the **Yacht Agency Rhodes** (☎ **22410/22-927;** fax 22410/23-393), the center for all yachting needs.

Other sports are available at **Rhodes Tennis Club** (☎ **22410/25-705**) in the resort of Elli, or at **Rhodes-Afandu Golf Club** (☎ **22410/51-225**), 19km (12 miles) south of the port. **Fitness Factory,** 17 Akti Kanari (☎ **22410/37-667;** www. rodosnet.gr/fitnessfactory), is a centrally located, fully equipped fitness center.

If you want to get some culture as you get in shape, information on traditional **Greek folk-dance lessons** was long obtainable at the **Old Town Theater** (☎ **22410/ 29-085**), but when the world-famous Nelly Dimoglou troupe was forced to suspend its performances after 2010, this service is no longer guaranteed. Instead, contact the **Traditional Dance Center,** 87 Dekelias, Athens (☎ **210/251-1080**); they usually offer weekly summer classes to teach dances from different regions of Greece.

Where to Stay in Rhodes City

IN THE OLD TOWN

Accommodations in the Old Town have an atmosphere of ages past, but character does not always equal charm. There are few really attractive options here, and they are in considerable demand, with all of the attending complications. One is that some hosts will hold you to the letter of your intent—so if you need or wish to cancel a day or more of your stay, they will do their best to extract every last pence. And there is some hedging, which means that the exact room agreed upon may be "unavailable" at the end of the day. Be explicit and keep a paper trail. And if any of this unsettles you, try booking a hotel through an agency such as Triton Holidays, which will go to bat for you in case of any problems.

Moderate

Marco Polo Mansion ★ Come here if you want a history lesson as well as a room with a touch of the exotic, but don't expect modern luxuries. What you will find, however, are extremely friendly and helpful proprietors and a comfortable environment. Featured in glossy fashion and travel magazines, the Marco Polo Mansion has captured attention with its stylish decor, its colors as if squeezed from tubes of ancient pigments and weathered in the bleaching sun. Each guest room is steeped in a history of its own and furnished with antiques and folk art. One was a harem, another a *hamam*. The Imperial Room has six windows, whereas the Antika 2 room, lined with kilims, has a view of minarets. The smaller garden rooms, nestled in fragrant greenery, reflect the house's Italian period.

42 A. Fanouriou, 85100 Rhodes. www.marcopolomansion.gr. ✆/fax **22410/25-562.** 7 units. 90€–160€ double. Rates include breakfast. AE, M, V. Free public parking with 10-min. walk. Closed Nov–Mar. **Amenities:** Restaurant, Wi-Fi. *In room:* A/C.

S. Nikolis Hotel and Apartments ★★   If you are the type who appreciates staying in a centuries-old building in a medieval town—which you really should do if you've come to experience Rhodes—this is the place. Proprietor and host Sotiris Nikolis has restored several medieval structures using the original stones, remaining as faithful as possible to the original style. The result is immensely pleasing. Many of the furnishings are true antiques. Some rooms have sleeping lofts; some suites and studios have Jacuzzis; some studios have basic kitchenettes; a special business suite comes with two bedrooms, two bathrooms, and a small office area with fax and computer (contact for rates). Breakfast and light meals are served in the rooftop garden. The S. Nikolis also has some less expensive, but equally pleasant, units—some including complete kitchens—in nearby annexes.

In the hotel's enclosed garden are a small fitness center and a computer nook with Internet access. There is also a cafe at the far end and an adjacent **Ancient Agora Bar and Restaurant** where, in 1990, a 10-ton marble pediment dating from the 2nd century was found beneath the medieval foundations. Note that smoking is not permitted in any of these areas.

61 Ippodamou, 85100 Rhodes. www.s-nikolis.gr. ✆ **22410/34-561.** 16 units. 60€–120€ double; 110€–180€ suite. Complete breakfast 15€ per person. AE, MC, V. Parking on nearby streets. Call ahead Nov–Mar to see if hotel is open. **Amenities:** Restaurant (rooftop); bar; kitchenette in suites; Wi-Fi. *In room:* A/C, TV, fridge, hair dryer, Jacuzzi in some suites.

Inexpensive

Hotel Andreas   This exceptionally well-run hotel (actually under Belgian ownership) offers relief from the cardboard walls and linoleum floors that haunt many of the town's budget choices. Housed in a restored 400-year-old Turkish sultan's house, it offers attractive rooms, some with panoramic views of the town. Others have wooden lofts, which can comfortably sleep a family of four. The bedrooms (with commendably firm beds) were once occupied by the sultan's harem, while the sultan held forth in room no. 11, a spacious corner unit with three windows and extra privacy. Breakfast is served on a shaded terrace that boasts gorgeous vistas of the town and the harbor—some of the best views in Old Town. The full bar has a wide-screen TV, and laundry service is provided. Room nos. 10 and 11 have the best views; room nos. 8 and 9 have private terraces.

28D Omirou (located btw. Omirou 23 and 20, *not* just before 29), 85100 Rhodes. www.hotelandreas.com. ✆ **22410/34-156.** 12 units, 6 with private bathroom. 55€–75€ double with private bathroom on corridor; 75€–110€ double with private bathroom in room. Breakfast 8€ per person extra. No credit cards. Public parking within 10-min. walk. Closed Nov–Feb. **Amenities:** Wi-Fi. *In room:* A/C (in some rooms).

Spot Hotel   Spotless would be a more suitable name for this small hotel. By Old Town standards, this building is an infant, barely 60 years old, but the proprietors have gradually added architectural enhancements that provide the hotel an island and medieval atmosphere more in keeping with its location. The garden and terrace sitting

Rhodes Accommodations & Dining

HOTELS ■
Esperia **3**
Hotel Andreas **17**
Hotel Mediterranean **2**
Ibiscus **1**
Marco Polo Mansion **12**
Rodos Palace **4**
Rodos Park **6**
S. Nikolis Hotel **14**
Spot Hotel **18**

RESTAURANTS ◆
Alexis Taverna **9**
Goniako Palati **5**
Hatzikelis **19**
Iannis Taverna **13**
Kafenio Turkiko **8**
Mama Sofia's **7**
Manolis Dinoris Fish Taverna **10**
Palia Historia **16**
Romeo **13**
Ta Kioupia **15**

areas have also been enlarged. The rooms are simple and tasteful, if not especially bright. Guests enjoy a large communal fridge; access to a phone, for free local calls; free limited use of a PC for e-mail; and free luggage storage. Spot is near the harbor, right off Plateia Martiron Hevreon, with convenient cafes.

21 Perikleous, 85100 Rhodes. www.spothotelrhodes.gr ☎ **22410/34-737.** 11 units. 70€–90€ double. Rates include continental breakfast. No credit cards. Parking on adjacent streets. **Amenities:** Wi-Fi. *In room:* A/C in some units, fridge, hair dryer.

IN THE NEW TOWN & ENVIRONS

Unlike the Old Town, the New Town doesn't prohibit new construction. You'll find a wild array of options, from boardinghouses to package-tour hotels to luxury resorts. Some are dazzling—take a look at the **Rodos Palace,** on the west-coast road running out of town, if your taste runs that way—but many are dull and so indistinguishable that you may forget which one you're in. I've tried to make a selection of those in different price ranges that stand out.

Very Expensive

Rodos Park Suites & Spa Hotel ★   This superb luxury hotel, with gleaming marble and polished wood interiors, enjoys a uniquely convenient yet secluded location. Guests are within a short stroll of the city's attractions—only a few minutes from the Old Town and Mandraki Harbor, yet conveniently close to the New Town shopping and dining areas. Some might regard the rooms as overdecorated, but they are certainly comfortable, with all the amenities you'd expect to find in a first-class hotel. This is not a beach resort—it's a fine city hotel open year-round. If you want a Jacuzzi in your room, opt for a suite, preferably one with a superb view of the Old Town walls. If you want to work off surplus calories from the in-house gourmet restaurant, head down to the fitness center or spa. A dip in the pool will offer the perfect finish to your regime.

12 Riga Fereou, 85100 Rhodes. www.rodospark.gr. ☎ **22410/89-700.** 59 units. High season 180€–260€ double; 310€–425€ suite; low season 150€–190€ double; 260€–305€ suite. Rates include breakfast. AE, MC, V. Parking on adjacent streets. **Amenities:** 3 restaurants; 2 bars; babysitting; health club; pool; room service; spa. *In room:* A/C, TV, hair dryer, Internet, Jacuzzi (in suites), minibar.

Moderate

Hotel Mediterranean ★ ☺   Directly across from Kos beach and close to the aquarium, this is a great spot for kids. The year-round hotel's interior, from the common to the private rooms, is stylish and sophisticated. Doubles have adjoining twin beds, pullout sofas, and spacious tiled bathrooms. Rates vary according to the view; of the three exposures, the spectacular sea view far outshines the garden (pool and veranda) or side (city) view. All suites have sea views, sitting areas, and king-size beds. All units have balconies. Rooms for travelers with limited mobility are available.

35 Kos beach, 85100 Rhodes. www.mediterranean.gr. ☎ **22410/24-661.** 241 units. 135€–145€ double. Rates include breakfast. AE, DC, MC, V. Free parking arranged. Frequent public buses. **Amenities:** 2 restaurants; bar; babysitting; outdoor freshwater pool; room service; night-lit tennis court nearby; watersports equipment/rentals. *In room:* A/C, TV, hair dryer, Internet, minibar.

Ibiscus ★   The Ibiscus is a well-situated and striking beachfront hotel. The spacious marble entrance hall opens into a stylish cafe/bar; you can take your drinks out front to the beach or back onto the poolside garden veranda. (The pool is small, but most everyone goes to the beach across the road.) The large, tasteful, fully carpeted double rooms have king-size orthopedic beds, large wardrobes, ample desk areas, and tile and marble bathrooms. The suites are especially appealing, with their two bedrooms (one with a king-size bed and one with twin beds). Every unit has a balcony, many of which face the sea.

Kos beach, 85100 Rhodes. www.rodos.com/ibiscus. ☎ **22410/24-421.** 205 units. 110€–150€ double. Rates include breakfast. AE, DC, MC, V. Free parking. Closed Nov–Mar. Frequent public buses. **Amenities:** Restaurant; bar; dipping pool. *In room:* A/C, TV, fridge, hair dryer.

Inexpensive

Esperia   This hotel, open year-round, will appeal most to budget-conscious travelers. The guest rooms are nothing special but are tasteful and clean, most with a large balcony with pleasant views. New double-glazed sliding balcony doors effectively seal the rooms from most of the town's noise. TVs are available on request, at a small additional cost. The bar, lounge, and breakfast room are inviting, and the walled outdoor pool and poolside bar are well above average for a modest hotel. The hotel is located near the restaurant district and only a short walk from the beach.

7 Griva, 85100 Rhodes. ☎ **22410/23-941.** 187 units. 60€–80€ double. Rates include breakfast. AE, DC, MC, V. Parking within 10-min. walk. **Amenities:** Breakfast room; bar; babysitting; pool. *In room:* A/C, fridge, hair dryer.

Where to Eat in Rhodes City

IN THE OLD TOWN

The Old Town is thick with tavernas, restaurants, and fast-food nooks, all doing their best to lure you into places that might be where you would want to be. If not, the more brazen their overtures, the more adamant you must be in holding to your course. Don't imagine, however, that all Old Town restaurants are tourist traps. Many Rhodians come to this area for what they consider the island's best food, particularly fish. Don't even think of driving to these places; walk through an entrance to the Old Town.

Very Expensive

Alexis Taverna ★ GREEK/SEAFOOD   For some 70 years, this restaurant has been the one to beat in Old Town, but you do have to be prepared to abandon restraint (and your budget). The proprietors preserve the traditions established by their grandfather to devise a seafood feast for you, accompanied by the perfect wine from the cellar (which represents vineyards all over Greece). The fish is selected daily down at the harbor and the proprietors have their own greenhouse on the outskirts of town to cultivate organic vegetables. Start with a bounteous seafood platter of delicately flavored sea urchins, fresh clams, and tender octopus carpaccio. Try the sargos, a sea-bream-type fish, chargrilled to perfection. In season, try the oysters. (At times they even have sushi.) The creamy Greek yogurt, with homemade green-walnut jam, is a perfect ending for a superb culinary experience. Every meal here begins with a chef's consultation and should end with applause.

18 Sokratous. ✆ **22410/29-347.** Reservations recommended. Individually prepared dinners without wine average 70€. AE, V. Mon–Sat 10am–4pm and 7pm–1am.

Manolis Dinoris Fish Taverna ★ GREEK/SEAFOOD   This restaurant, housed in the former stables of the 13th-century Knights of St. John's Inn, provides a unique setting to enjoy delicious and fresh seafood delights. You can order either a la carte or from the set menu of coquille St. Jacques, Greek salad, grilled prawns, swordfish, baklava, coffee, and brandy. In warm weather, the quiet side garden is delightful; in winter, a fire roars in the old stone hearth indoors.

14A Museum Sq. ✆ **22410/25-824.** Main courses 30€–65€; set menu 75€. AE, MC, V. Daily noon–midnight.

Expensive

Goniako Palati (Corner Palace) GREEK   The new Goniako Palati may not be a palace, but it is on the corner—a busy corner you overlook once the food arrives. Great canvas awnings cover the seating area, raised above street level. The extensive taverna menu is basic Greek, fresh and skillfully prepared in a slightly upscale environment at reasonable prices. This is one place local New Towners go for reliable taverna fare. The grilled swordfish souvlaki, served with a medley of steamed vegetables, is quite tasty. The *saganaki* (grilled cheese) here is a performance art, and delicious to boot.

110 Griva (corner of Griva and 28 Oktobriou). ✆ **22410/33-167.** Main courses 10€–28€. AE, MC, V. Daily 9am–midnight.

Ta Kioupia ★★ GREEK   Once rated by the *London Guardian* as one of the world's 10 best restaurants, this unique place offers a true gourmet experience. Much-lauded Greek chef Michael Koumbiadis founded it in 1972, and he has preserved the true harmonies of traditional Greek cuisine, using the best local ingredients and village recipes. The meal might begin with a choice of soups, followed by an amazing array of appetizers and accompanied by home-baked breads. Main dishes are equally superb—broiled veal stuffed with cheese and sprinkled with pistachio nuts in yogurt sauce; or delectable pork souvlaki, with yogurt and paprika sauce on the side. For dessert, try the light crepes filled with sour cherries and covered with chocolate sauce and vanilla crème. Many foods are prepared in clay pots in a traditional wood-burning oven. *Warning:* The grand fixed-price meal requires fasting, devotion, and time (about 3 hr.).

22 Menekleos (off Sokratous; follow signs to Hammam Bath). ℂ **22410/91-824.** Reservations required. Main courses 25€–30€; fixed-price meals 40€–75€ per person, wine extra. MC, V. Mon-Sat 8pm–midnight; Sun noon–3pm.

Moderate

Hatzikelis ★ GREEK/SEAFOOD   This delightful fish taverna enjoys a peaceful and pleasant setting in the midst of a small neighborhood park just behind the Church of Our Lady of the Burgh in the Square of the Jewish Martyrs. Although there is an extensive a la carte menu, the special dinners for two are probably the most appealing for many. The Fisherman's Plate consists of lobster, shrimp, mussels, octopus, squid, and a liter of wine, while the plates of traditional Rhodian dishes include specialties such as zucchini balls and shrimp *saganaki*. The portions are challenging, but the quality of the cuisine and the fact that you have until 2am to do your duty increase the odds in your favor. And top your meal off with some of their own pastries.

9 Alhadeff. ℂ **22410/27-215.** www.hatzikelis.gr. Main courses 9€–22€. No credit cards. Daily 11am–2am.

Mama Sofia's ★ GREEK/SEAFOOD/PIZZA   Don't let the name fool you—although it is in fact very much a family institution—this is Greek taverna food and atmosphere at its best. From pizza to fresh seafood, mezes to steaks, everything comes to the table prepared to perfection. You could make a meal out of nothing but their fabulous appetizers—scallops on the half shell, *tyrokafteri* (feta lightly spiced with chili), marinated octopus. Seafood is in fact their specialty and as always in Greece this can be a bit costly, depending on the variety chosen. The wine list offers some exceptional choices, from moderate to expensive. All this while you sit and watch the world go by at this choice location (including a roof garden).

Orfeos St. (behind the clock tower at top of Socratous). ℂ **22410/24-469.** www.mamasofia.gr. Main courses 8€–25€. AE, MC, V. Daily 8am–midnight. Closed mid-Nov to late Mar.

Romeo ★ GREEK/SEAFOOD/PIZZA   Though under siege by tourists, many locals gladly frequent the Romeo, as there is a good deal that's authentic within its walls (themselves some 500 years old). Beside the predictable taverna fare are the many local dishes on offer—including vegetarian options. Two house specialties are the mixed fish grill and the stuffed souvlaki. For the grill, you select your own fish from a generous array of fresh deep-sea options—the tender grilled octopus is especially good. The finely cut grilled souvlaki stuffed with melted cheese and tomatoes is a regional dish from the north end of the island. Their pizza is the thin-crust variety and quite tasty. The reasonably priced house wines go nicely with each entree. Set back in a quiet enclave, just off and out of the crush of Sokratous, Romeo offers courtyard and roof-garden seating, and tasteful, live traditional Greek music and song.

7-9 Menekleous (off Sokratous). ℂ **22410/25-186.** www.romeo-restaurant.com. Main courses 8€–26€. AE, MC, V. Daily noon–12:30am.

Inexpensive

Iannis Taverna ★ GREEK   For a budget Greek meal, visit Chef Iannis's small place on a quiet back lane. The moussaka, stuffed vegetables, and meat dishes are flavorful and well prepared by a man who spent 14 years as a chef in the Greek diners of New York. His Greek plate is one of the best to be found in Rhodes, with an unbelievably large variety of tasty foods. The breakfast omelets are a great deal. Portions are hearty and cheap, and the service friendly and informal.

41 Platonos. ☎ **22410/36-535.** Main courses 6€–18€. No credit cards. Daily 9am–midnight.

Kafenio Turkiko GREEK/SNACKS Located in a medieval structure, this is the only authentic place left on touristy Sokratous, otherwise replete with Swatch, Body Shop, Van Cleef, and a multitude of souvenir shops. Each rickety wooden table comes with a backgammon board for idling away the hours while you sip a Greek coffee or suck on a hookah pipe. The old pictures, mirrors, and bric-a-brac on the walls will enhance your feeling of bygone times.

76 Sokratous. No phone. Drinks/snacks 2€–9€. No credit cards. Daily 11am–midnight.

IN THE NEW TOWN & ENVIRONS
Moderate
Palia Historia (The Old Story) ★ GREEK If you're maxed out on run-of-the-mill Greek taverna fare, this is a good place to come—well worth a taxi ride from wherever you're staying. Most of the clientele is Greek, drawn by the subtle cuisine and lack of tourists. The marinated salmon and capers are worthy of the finest Dublin restaurant, and the broccoli with oil, mustard, and roasted almonds is inspired. As a main course, the shrimp *saganaki* leaves nothing to the imagination. With fish, the dry, white Spiropoulos, from Mantinia, is perfect. For a great finish, go for the banana flambé.

108 Mitropoleos (south in New Town, below modern stadium). ☎ **22410/32-421.** Reservations recommended. Main courses 12€–28€. AE, MC, V. Daily 7pm–midnight.

Rhodes City After Dark

During the high season, Rhodes claims one of the most active nighttime scenes in Greece outside of Athens. Granted, some of that energy is grounded in the resort complexes north of the city, but there is enough to go around.

Your own common sense is as good a guide as any in this ever-changing scene. In a city as compact as Rhodes, it's best to follow the lights and noise, and get a little lost. When you decide to call it quits, shout down a taxi (if you're outside the Old Town) to bring you back—just remember where you're staying.

As a rule of thumb, the younger foreign set will find the **New Town** livelier than the Old Town. **Cafe scenes** are located on the harbor, behind Academy Square, or on Galias near New Market. The **bar scene** tends to line up along Diakonou. In the Old Town, most of the clubs and bars are found along Miltiadhou—these tend to be more frequented by the local youth. There must be at least 100 **nightclubs** on Rhodes, so you're sure to find one to your liking.

Gambling is a popular nighttime activity in Greece. Rhodes, for many years, housed one of Greece's six legal casinos, a government-operated roulette and blackjack house adjoining the Grand Hotel. Now in private hands and known as the **Casino Rodos,** it is located in the **Grande Albergo delle Rose,** in the New Town; admission costs 15€, and patrons must be at least 23 years old.

Exploring the Island

Sun, sand . . . and the rest is history. Nowhere is that more true than on Rhodes, where ruins and beaches lure visitors out of Rhodes city. For the best **beaches,** head to the island's east coast. Visitors also flock to archaeological sites identical to the three original Dorian city-states, all nearly 3,000 years old: **Lindos, Kamiros,** and **Ialisos.** Of these, Lindos was and is preeminent; it is by far the top tourist destination outside of Old Town. So we begin here with Lindos, and then go back to Rhodes town to explore the island counterclockwise.

LINDOS

Lindos is the most picturesque town on the island of Rhodes. Because Lindos has been designated a historic settlement, the Archaeological Society controls development in the village, and the traditional white-stucco homes, shops, and restaurants form the most unified, classically Greek expression in the Dodecanese. Be warned, however, that Lindos is often deluged with tourists, and your first visit may be unforgettable for the wrong reasons. Avoid the crush of mid-July to August, if at all possible.

Frequent public buses leave Plateia Rimini for a fare of 8€; a taxi will cost 40€ one-way. There are two entrances to the town. The first and northernmost leads down a steep hill to the bus stop and taxi stand, and then veers downhill again to the beach. (However, if you're driving, park in the lot above the town.) At this square, from April through October daily from 9am to 10pm, you'll find the **Tourist Information Kiosk** (✆ **22440/31-900;** fax 22410/31-288). Here, too, is the commercial heart of the village, with the acropolis looming above. The rural **medical clinic** (✆ **22410/31-224**), **post office,** and **telephone office (OTE)** are nearby. The second road into town leads beyond it and into the upper village, blessedly removed from the hordes. This is the better route for people more aesthetically minded. Follow signs to the acropolis. You'll pass a stand where, for 8€, you can ride a donkey (also known as a "Lindian taxi") all the way to the top. If you walk, the sides of the walkway are strewn with embroidery and lace for sale, which may or may not be the handiwork of local women. Embroidery from Rhodes was highly coveted in the ancient world. In fact, it is claimed that Alexander the Great wore a grand Rhodian robe into battle at Gaugemila; and, in Renaissance Europe, French ladies used to yearn for a bit of Lindos lace. Much of what is for sale in Lindos today, however, is from Asia.

Before you start the final ascent to the acropolis, be sure to inspect the famous **relief carving of a trireme** ★, or three-banked ship, dating from the 2nd century B.C. At the top, from the fortress ramparts, are glorious views of medieval Lindos below, where most homes date from the 15th century. To the south you can see the lovely beach at St. Paul's Bay—legend claims St. Paul put ashore here—along with Rhodes's less developed eastern coastline. Across to the southwest rises Mount Krana, where caves, dug out to serve as ancient tombs, are thought to have sheltered cults to Athena well into the Christian period.

The **acropolis** ★ (✆ **22410/27-674**) is open Tuesday through Sunday from 8am to 7pm, Monday from 12:30 to 7pm. Admission is 6€ for adults and 3€ for students and children. This is one of three original Dorian acropolises in Rhodes. Within the much-later medieval walls stand the impressive remains of the **Sanctuary of Athena Lindos,** with its large Doric portico from the 4th century B.C. St. John's Knights refortified the acropolis with monumental turreted walls and built a small church to St. John inside. Today, stones and columns are strewn everywhere as the site undergoes extensive restoration.

On your descent, as you explore the labyrinthine lanes of medieval Lindos, you will come to the exquisite late-14th- or early-15th-century **Byzantine Church of the Panagia** ★. Still the local parish church (admission 2€), its more than 200 iconic frescoes cover every inch of the walls and arched ceilings. Dating from the 18th century, all of the frescoes have been painstakingly restored at considerable expense and with stunning results. Be sure to spend some time here; many of these icons are sequentially narrative, depicting the Creation, the Nativity, the Christian Passover, and the Last Judgment. And, after you've given yourself a stiff neck from looking up, look down at the extraordinary floor, made of sea pebbles.

Adjoining the Church of the Panagia is the **Church Museum** (✆ **22440/32-020**), open April through October daily from 9am to 3pm; admission is 2€. The historical and architectural exhibits and collected ecclesiastical items, including frescoes, icons, texts, chalices, and liturgical embroidery, comprise a collection. Frankly, most people prefer to spend their time looking elsewhere around the village.

Then, of course, there's the inviting **beach** below, lined with cafes and tavernas.

Where to Stay in Lindos & Environs

In high season, Lindos marks the spot where up to 10,000 day-trippers from Rhodes city converge with 4,000 resident tourists. As hotel construction is no longer permitted, almost all of the old homes have been converted into pensions (called "villas," in the brochures), by English charter companies. **Triton Holidays** (✆ **22410/21-690;** www.tritondmc.gr) books six-person villas, including kitchen facilities (reservations are often made a year in advance). In peak season, the local **Tourist Information Kiosk** (✆ **22440/31-900;** fax 22440/31-288) has a list of homes that rent rooms. Plan to pay at least 60€ for a double and 90€ to 125€ for a studio apartment.

Atrium Palace Thalassos Spa Resort ★ ☺ Just over 6.4km (4 miles) out of Lindos, on the long beach of crystal-clear Kalathos Bay, this luxurious resort hotel features an eclectic architectural design—a neo-Greek, Roman, crusader, and Italian pastel extravaganza. The rooms are colorful and comfortable; the inner atrium is an exotic, tropical garden of pools and waterfalls. The beautifully landscaped outdoor pool complex is an alternative to the nearby beach, and the indoor pool, sauna, and fitness club will keep you busy and now, as the name suggests, there is a spa that offers sea water treatment. To fully entertain the whole family on the rainy days that seldom occur, there are game rooms, a miniclub for young children, and an arcade of shops. The atmosphere here is relaxed, unpretentious, and friendly.

Kalathos beach, 85107 Rhodes. www.atrium.gr. ✆ **22440/31-601.** 316 units. 120€–155€ double. Rates include breakfast. AE, DC, MC, V. Parking on premises. Closed Nov–Mar. Pets allowed. **Amenities:** Restaurant; bars; babysitting; children's center; fitness club; Internet; Jacuzzi; pools; room service; sauna; spa. *In room:* A/C, TV, minibar.

Lindos Mare ★ This relatively small and classy cliff-side resort hotel is a prime site at which to drop anchor on the east shore. The rooms are a notch above comparable luxury hotels on the coast, and views of the bay below are glorious. A tram descends from the upper lobby, restaurant, and pool area to the lower levels of attractive Aegean-style bungalows, and continues onward down to the beach area (linked by a cable car), where you'll find umbrellas and watersports. The hotel is a 2km (1¼-mile) walk or ride into Lindos, although you might want to stay put in the evenings to enjoy in-house social activities, such as barbecues, folklore evenings, or dancing.

Lindos Bay, 85107 Rhodes. www.lindosmare.gr. ✆ **22440/31-130.** 141 units. 210€–240€ double; 250€–420€ suite. Rates include breakfast. With half-board plan (breakfast and dinner) 260€–290€ double. AE, DC, MC, V. Parking on premises. Closed Nov–Mar. **Amenities:** 2 restaurants; 2 bars; children's playground; 2 pools; room service; watersports equipment/rentals. *In room:* A/C, TV, fridge, hair dryer, Internet.

Melenos Lindos Exclusive Studios ★ This boutique hotel, admittedly, will appeal only to those able to afford a pricey luxury retreat, but, as such, it's a once-in-a-lifetime experience. It's in an authentically Lindian-style villa, with hand-painted tiles, local antiques, handcrafted lamps, fine linens—in short, traditional splendor combined with contemporary comforts and convenience. The terraces, landscaping, and views over the sea can make you forget that you are in the crowded Lindos, while you gaze up at the acropolis and muse about all the history that surrounds you.

Lindos Town, 85107 Rhodes. www.melenoslindos.com. ✆ **22440/32-222.** 12 units. 210€–310€ double; 230€–650€ suite. Rates include breakfast. AE, MC, V. Free parking nearby. **Amenities:** Restaurant; bar; room service. *In room:* A/C, TV, hair dryer, Internet, minibar.

Where to Eat in Lindos & Environs

You'll have a paralyzing array of restaurants and tavernas to choose from in tiny Lindos. On the beach, the expansive—but not expensive—**Triton Restaurant** gets a nod because you can easily change into your swimsuit in the bathroom, essential for nonresidents who want to splash in the gorgeous water across the way.

Argo Fish Taverna ★ GREEK/SEAFOOD   Haraki Bay is a quiet fishing hamlet with a gorgeous, crescent-shaped pebbly beach—and this excellent seafood taverna. Consider stopping here for a swim and lunch on a day trip to Lindos. You'll appreciate the freshness of the food, as well as a creative variation on a Greek salad that added mint, dandelion leaves, and other fresh herbs, served with whole-wheat bread. The lightly battered, fried calamari is tasty and a welcome relief from the standard over-battered fare. Mussels, baked with fresh tomatoes and feta cheese, are also something special.

Haraki beach (10km/6 miles north of Lindos). ✆ **22440/51-410.** Reservations recommended. Main courses 13€–55€. AE, MC, V. Easter–Oct daily noon–1am.

Mavrikos ★ GREEK/FRENCH   There's no denying that this is the most celebrated restaurant in Lindos—arguably in all of Rhodes—as attested to by the various rich and famous who have dined here in recent decades. It has its detractors, but most diners find that it lives up to its reputation, combining elegant food with the rustic charm of the tree-shaded terrace. Brothers Michalis and Dimitri Mavrikos continue a now-70-year-old family tradition of fine Greek and French cuisine, such as oven-baked lamb and nicely done beef filets, or the perfectly grilled and seasoned fresh red snapper. The food is especially distinguished by the subtle flavors provided by seasonings—butter beans in a sauce with carob, beef in a casserole with bergamot, and tuna with fenugreek. Vegetarians will also find much on the menu to satisfy their palates. The brothers Mavrikos also run an ice-cream parlor, **Geloblu,** serving homemade frozen concoctions and cakes. It's within the labyrinth of the Old Town, near the church.

Main Sq., Lindos. ✆ **22440/31-232.** Reservations recommended. Main courses 10€–30€. V. Daily noon–midnight.

SIGHTS & BEACHES ELSEWHERE ON THE ISLAND

A tour around the island provides you with a chance to view the wonderful variations of Rhodes's scenery. The sights described below, with the exception of Ialisos and Kamiros, are not of significant historical or cultural importance, but if you're tired of lying on the beach, they provide a pleasant diversion. The route outlined below traces the island counterclockwise from Rhodes city, with a number of suggested sorties to the interior. Even a cursory glance at a map of Rhodes will explain the many zigs and zags in this itinerary. Remember that not all roads are equal; all-terrain vehicles are required for some of the detours suggested below.

Ialisos (Ialyssos) was the staging ground for the four major powers that were to control the island. The ancient ruins and monastery on Mount Filerimos reflect the presence of two of these groups. The Dorians ousted the Phoenicians from Rhodes in the 10th century B.C. (An oracle had predicted that white ravens and fish swimming in wine would be the final signs before the Phoenicians were annihilated. The Dorians, quick to spot opportunity, painted enough birds and threw enough fish into wine jugs that the Phoenicians left without raising their arms.) Most of the Dorians left Ialisos for other parts of the island; many settled in the new city of Rhodes. During the 3rd to 2nd centuries B.C., the Dorians constructed a temple to Athena and Zeus Polios, whose ruins are still visible, below the monastery. Walking south of the site will lead you to a well-preserved 4th-century-B.C. fountain.

When the Knights of St. John invaded the island, they, too, started from Ialisos, a minor town in Byzantine times. They built a small, subterranean chapel decorated with frescoes of Jesus and heroic knights. Their little whitewashed church is built right into the hillside above the Doric temple. Over it, the medieval Italians constructed the **Monastery of Filerimos,** a lovely spot to visit (and with a most impressive cross at the top). Finally, Suleiman the Magnificent moved into Ialisos (1522) with his army of 100,000 and used it as a base for his eventual takeover of the island.

In summer, the site of Ialisos is open Monday through Saturday from 8am to 7pm; hours are irregular the rest of the year. Proper dress is required. Admission is 3€. Ancient Ialisos is 6km (3½ miles) inland from Trianda, on the island's northwest coast; buses leave from Rhodes frequently for the 14km (8½-mile) ride.

Petaloudes is a popular attraction because of the millions of black-and-white-striped **"butterflies"** (actually a species of moth) that overtake this verdant valley in July and August. When resting quietly on plants or leaves, the moths are well camouflaged. Only the wailing of infants and the Greek rock blaring from portable radios disturbs them. Then the sky is filled with a flurry of red, the moths' underbellies exposed as they try to hide from the summer crush. The setting, with its many ponds, bamboo bridges, and rock displays, is admittedly a bit too precious; and, the fact is, you cannot always be guaranteed of seeing the moths in flight. But it's worth at least a try. Petaloudes is 25km (16 miles) south of Rhodes and inland; it can be reached by bus but is most easily seen on a guided tour. It's open daily from 8:30am to 6:30pm; admission is 5€ from mid-June to late September, and 3€ the rest of the year.

The ruins at **Kamiros** are much more extensive than those at Ialisos, perhaps because this city remained an important outpost after the new Rhodes was completed in 408 B.C. The site is divided into two segments: the upper porch and the lower valley. The porch served as a place of religious practice and provided the height needed for the city's water supply. Climb to the top to see two aqueducts, which assured the Dorians of a year-round supply of water. The small valley contains ruins of homes and streets, as well as the foundations of a large temple. The site is well enough preserved to visualize what life in this ancient Doric city was like more than 2,000 years ago. Think about wearing a swimsuit under your clothes: Across from the site is a good stretch of **beach,** where there are some rooms to let, a few tavernas, and the bus stop. The site is open Tuesday through Sunday from 8:30am to 3pm. Admission is 4€. Kamiros is 34km (21 miles) southwest of Rhodes city, with regular bus service.

Driving south along the western coast from Kamiros for about a mile, you'll come to the late-15th-century knights castle of **Kastellos (Kritinias Castle),** dominating the sea below. From here, heading south and then cutting up to the northeast, make your way inland to **Embonas,** the wine capital of the island and home to several tavernas famed for their fresh meat barbecues. This village is on the tour-group circuit, and numerous tavernas offer feasts accompanied by live music and folklore performances. If you then circle the island's highest mountain, **Attaviros**

> ### 🎁 An Unexpected Delight
>
> One of the pleasures of traveling is to come across a place that you never expected to find. Just such a place is the **Kallithea Springs** north of Faliraki (and about 10km/6 miles from Rhodes city). The thermal waters of Kallithea had been praised for their therapeutic qualities by Hippocrates and had attracted visitors through the Middle Ages. But by the 20th century, the place had been forgotten and abandoned until in the 1920s the Italians restored the site as a classic curative spa, erecting an exotic complex of buildings in what is best described in an Arabic/art deco style. After World War II the place was once again abandoned until in the late 1990s work began on a complete and professional restoration of the site and its structures. This is what one sees today and possibly by the time this guide is in use people will even be able to at least drink the water. Meanwhile, there is a small bay here where people come to swim and snorkel or just sit in the cafe and contemplate the history of such an unexpected place. Not a major destination but well worth an afternoon's excursion—easily reached by frequent public buses.

(1,196m/3,923 ft.), you come to the village of **Ayios Issidoros,** where devoted trekkers can ask directions to the summit. (It's a 5-hr., round-trip hike from Ayios Issidoros to the top of Mount Attaviros.) Otherwise, proceed to the picturesque village of **Siana,** nestled on the mountainside. From here, head to **Monolithos,** with its spectacularly sited crusader castle perched on the pinnacle of a coastal mountain.

If you now decide to head for the eastern coast, you retrace your path back through Siana and Ayios Issidoros and then proceed on to **Laerma,** where you might consider taking a 5km (3-mile) seasonal road to **Tharri Monastery,** the oldest functioning monastery on the island, with beautiful though weather-damaged frescoes. From Laerma, it's another 10km (6 miles) to Lardos and the eastern coastal road, where you can either head straight to **Lindos** (see earlier) or take another detour to **Asklipio,** with its ruined castle and impressive Byzantine church. The church has a mosaic-pebbled floor and gorgeous cartoon-style frescoes, which depict the 7 days of Creation (check out the octopus) and the life of Jesus.

The **beaches** south of Lindos, from Lardos Bay to Plimmiri (26km/16 miles), are among the best on Rhodes, especially the short stretch between Lahania and Plimmiri. At the southernmost tip of the island, for those who seek off-the-beaten-track places, is **Prasonisi (Green Island),** connected to the main island by a narrow sandy isthmus, with waves and world-class windsurfing on one side, calm waters on the other.

Heading north from Lindos to Faliraki, there are a number of sandy, sheltered beaches with relatively little development. **Faliraki beach** is the island's most developed beach resort, offering every possible vacation distraction imaginable—from bungee jumping to laser clay shooting. For families with kids in tow, there is a **Water Park** and a sort of Disneyland-type amusement park, the **Magic Castle.** The southern end of the beach is less crowded and frequented by nude bathers. But for those who want to avoid the gigantic beach resort hotels, I can recommend the following.

Ladiko Bungalows Hotel   Anthony Quinn obtained permission to build a retirement home for actors on this pretty little bay on the road to Lindos, 3km (2 miles) south of the swinging beach resort of Faliraki, but never realized his plans. But you can see why the location attracted him—it is both quiet and convenient. This friendly family-operated lodge has activities for nature lovers (swimming, fishing, and hiking to nearby ruins and less frequented beaches), but is just a 20-minute walk to noisy, bustling Faliraki. The terrace bar and dining area with a splendid view of Ladiko Bay provide lovely tranquil spots for a drink or a meal. The guest rooms are not exceptional, but they are quite comfortable. Fourteen rooms come with fridges.

Faliraki, P.O. Box 236, 85100 Rhodes. ✆ **22410/85-560.** Fax 22410/80-241. 42 units. 65€–105€ double. Rates include breakfast. MC, V. Parking on premises. Closed Nov–Mar. **Amenities:** Coffee shop; fitness center. *In room:* A/C, some w/fridge, hair dryer.

SIMI (SYMI)

11km (7 miles) N of Rhodes

Tiny, rugged Simi is often called "the jewel of the Dodecanese." Arrival by boat affords you a view of pastel-colored neoclassical mansions climbing the steep hills above the broad, horseshoe-shaped harbor. Yialos is Simi's port, and Horio its old capital. The welcome absence of nontraditional buildings is due to an archaeological decree that severely regulates the style and methods of construction and restoration of all old and new buildings. Simi's long and prosperous tradition of shipbuilding, trading, and sponge diving is evident in its gracious mansions and richly ornamented churches. Islanders proudly boast that there are so many churches and monasteries that you can worship in a different sanctuary every day of the year.

During the first half of the 20th century, Simi's economy gradually deteriorated as the shipbuilding industry declined, the maritime business soured, and somebody went and invented a synthetic sponge. Simiots left their homes to find work on nearby Rhodes or in North America and Australia (a startling 70% eventually returned). Today, the island's picture-perfect traditional-style houses have become a magnet for moneyed Athenians and Italians in search of vacation homes. Simi is a highly touted off-the-beaten-path resort for European tour groups trying to avoid other tour groups. The onslaught of tourists generally arrives about 10:30am and departs by about 5pm.

In recent years, the **Simi Festival,** which goes on intermittently from July to September, has put Simi on the cultural map as an attractive seasonal contender, offering an eclectic menu of international music, theater, and cinema. Some of the performers have major international reputations.

Simi has no natural source of water—all water has to be transported by boat from nearby islands. Day visitors are scarcely aware of this, but everyone is asked to be careful to conserve water. Simi also has the reputation of being one of the hottest locales in Greece during the summer, so come prepared with a hat to sunscreen.

Essentials

GETTING THERE   Many (if not most) visitors to Simi arrive by boat from Rhodes. Several **excursion boats** arrive daily from Rhodes; schedules and itineraries for the boats vary, but all leave in the morning from Mandraki Harbor and stop at the main port of Simi, Yialos—some with an additional stop at Panormitis Monastery or the beach at Pedi—before returning to Rhodes later in the day. Currently, there are daily **car ferries** from Piraeus, and two **local ferries** weekly via Tilos, Nissiros, Kos, and Kalimnos. From late spring to summer, **hydrofoils** and a **catamaran** skim the waters daily from Rhodes to Simi, usually making both morning and afternoon runs. Round-trip fares run from 40€ to 64€, depending on the type (and speed) of the ship. Most travel agencies could make arrangements; in Rhodes town, use **Triton Holidays** (© **22410/21-690;** www.tritondmc.gr).

VISITOR INFORMATION   Check out the wonderfully helpful website operated by Simi's delightful and informative independent monthly, the *Symi Visitor* (© **22460/ 71-785;** www.symivisitor.com). Through the site's e-mail option, you can request information on accommodations, buses, weather, and more. Don't ask them, however, to recommend one hotel over another; explain exactly what you're looking for and they'll provide suggestions. Once you're on Simi, you'll find free copies of the latest *Symi Visitor* at tourist spots.

The long-established **Kalodoukas Holidays** (© **22410/71-077;** www.kalodou kas.gr) can help with everything from booking accommodations (often at reduced rates) to chartering a boat. Once you've arrived on Simi, drop by the office at the base of the stairway to Horio (where there is another office; Mon–Sat 9am–1pm and 5–9pm). In summer, this agency plans a special outing for every day of the week, from cruises to explorations of the island. Most involve a swim and a healthy meal.

A **tourist information kiosk** on the harbor keeps hours that remain a mystery. Information and a free pamphlet may also be obtained at the **town hall,** located on the town square behind the bridge.

GETTING AROUND   Ferries and excursion boats dock first at hilly **Yialos** on the barren, rocky, northern half of the island. Yialos is the liveliest village on the island and the venue for most overnighters. The clock tower, on the right as you enter the port, is used as a landmark when negotiating the maze of car-free lanes and stairs. Another landmark used in giving directions is the bridge in the center of the harbor's inlet.

Simi's main road leads to **Pedi,** a developing beach resort one cove east of Yialos, and a new road rises to **Horio,** the old capital, which is now overshadowed by Yialos. The island's 4,000 daily visitors often take an excursion boat that stops at Panormitis Monastery or at Pedi beach. **Buses** leave every hour from 8am until 11pm for Pedi via Horio (1€). Taxis at the center of the harbor charge a set fee of 8€ to Horio and 10€ to Pedi. **Mopeds** are also available, but due to the limited network of roads, you'll do better relying on public transportation and your own two feet. **Caiques** (converted fishing boats) shuttle people to various beaches: Nimborios, Ayia Marina, Ayios Niko-laos, and Nanou; prices range from 15€ to 25€, depending on distance. You can rent sun beds at these beaches.

FAST FACTS   For a **doctor,** call © **22410/71-316;** for a dentist, call © **22410/ 71-272;** for the **police,** © **22410/71-11.** The **post office** (© **22410/71-315**) and **telephone office** (OTE; © **22410/71-212**) are located about 50m (170 ft.) behind the clock tower on the waterfront; both open Monday to Friday from 7:30am to 3pm. Numerous cafes around the harbor now offer either **Internet access** or some with **Wi-Fi.**

What to See & Do

Simi's southwestern portion is hilly and green. Located here is the medieval **Panor-mitis Monastery,** dedicated to St. Michael, the patron saint of seafaring Greeks. The monastery is popular with Greeks as a place of pilgrimage and of refuge from modern life; young Athenian businessmen speak lovingly of the monks' cells and small apartments that can be rented for rest and renewal. There is also an almshouse that provides shelter for the elderly. Call the **guest office** (© **22410/72-414**) to

LOCAL industries

One skill still practiced on Simi is **ship-building.** If you walk along the water toward Nos beach, you may see boats under construction or repair. It's a treat to watch the men fashion planed boards into graceful boats. Simi was a boat-building center in the days of the Peloponnesian War, when spirited sea battles were waged off its shores.

Sponge fishing is almost a dead industry in Greece. Only a generation ago, 2,000 divers worked waters around the island; today only a handful undertake this dangerous work, and most do so in the waters around Italy and Africa. In the old days divers often went without any apparatus. Working at depths of 50 to 60m (164–197 ft.), many divers were crippled or killed by the turbulent sea and too-rapid depressurization. The few sponges that are still harvested around Simi—and many more imported from Asia or Florida—are sold at shops along the port. Even if they're not from Simi's waters, they make inexpensive and lightweight gifts.

book accommodations, ranging from 40€ to 75€ for an apartment or house. All units are self-contained, with their own stove and fridge. The least expensive units have shared outdoor toilets. Most sleep at least four people.

The whitewashed compound has a verdant, shaded setting and a 16th-century gem of a church inside. **Taxiarchis Mishail of Panormitis** boasts icons of St. Michael and St. Gabriel adorned in silver and jewels, and a superb iconostasis. The combined folk and ecclesiastical museums are well worth the 2€ entrance fee, which goes to support the almshouse mentioned above.

The town of **Panormitis Mihailis** is at its most lively and interesting during the annual November 8 Feast of Archangel Mihaili, but it can be explored year-round via local boats or bus tours from Yialos. The hardy can hike here—it's 10km (6 miles), about 3 hours from town—and then enjoy a refreshing dip in the sheltered harbor and a meal in the taverna.

In Yialos, if you are sure you are up to it, you can climb the 375 or so stone steps, known as the **Kali Strata** (the **Good Steps**), that take you to **Horio**—but this is not recommended for everyone in the heat of midsummer. This wide stairway ascends to a picturesque community that reflects a Greece that is in many ways long departed. Old women sweep the whitewashed stone paths outside their homes, and occasionally a young boy or an elderly man can be seen retouching the neon-blue trim over doorways and shutters. Nestled among the immaculately kept homes, which date back to the 18th century, are renovated villas now rented to an increasing number of tourists. And where tourists roam, tavernas, souvenir shops, and bouzouki bars soon follow but commercialization has yet to transform Horio.

Horio has a small **Archaeological and Folklore Museum** that houses archaeological and folklore artifacts that the islanders consider important enough for public exhibition. You can't miss the blue arrows that point the way. It's open Tuesday through Saturday from 9am to 2pm. Admission is 2€. Also, if you walk through the town you will pass on your right an iron-gated building that retains an intact old pharmacy; if not open, you can peer through the windows and see the jars with their curatives. The **Maritime Museum** in the port also costs 2€ and is open daily from 11am to 2:30pm.

Crowning Horio is the **Church of the Panagia.** The church is surrounded by a fortified wall and is therefore called the kastro (castle). It's adorned with the most glorious frescoes on the island, which can be viewed only when services are held (Mon–Fri 7–8am; all morning Sun).

Simi is blessed with many beaches, though they are not wide or sandy. Close to Yialos are two: **Nos,** a 15m-long (50-ft.) rocky stretch, and **Nimborios,** a pebble beach.

A bus to **Pedi,** followed by a short walk, takes you to **St. Nikolaos beach,** with shady trees and a good taverna, or to **St. Marina,** a small beach with little shade but stunning turquoise waters, as well as views of the St. Marina islet and its cute church.

The summertime cornucopia of outings provided by Kalodoukas Holidays has already been mentioned in "Visitor Information," above; but if you want to set out on your own, be sure to pick up a copy of *Walking on Symi: A Pocket Guide* or *Walks on Symi,* each available at Kalodoukas Holidays for about 7€. They describe numerous walks to help you discover and enjoy Simi's historic sites, interior forests, and mountain vistas.

Where to Stay

Many travelers bypass hotels for private apartments or houses. Between April and October, rooms for two, with shower and kitchen access, go for 45€ to 80€. More luxurious villa-style houses with daily maid service rent for 90€ to 150€. To explore this alternative, contact Kalodoukas Holidays or the Simi website (see "Visitor Information," above).

Dorian Studios   In a beautiful part of town, only 10m (33 ft.) from the sea, this rustically furnished hotel offers comfortable lodging (orthopedic beds) and a kitchenette in every room. Some studios have vaulted beamed ceilings and balconies or terraces overlooking the harbor, where you can enjoy your coffee or ouzo.

Yialos, 85600 Simi. www.symigreece.com/dorian.htm. ℂ **22460/71-307.** 9 units. 55€–80€ double. MC, V. Parking on adjacent streets. Closed Nov to mid-Apr. Just up from the Akti Gennimata, at the Aliki Hotel. *In room:* A/C (in 5 units), kitchenette.

Hotel Aliki ★   This grand Italianate sea captain's mansion, dating from 1895, is one of the more elegant tourist hostelries on Simi. It has the atmosphere of a boutique guesthouse, intimate and charming, and offers tastefully styled accommodations furnished with Italian antiques. Four rooms and two separate large apartments (for four to six persons) have balconies. Several units enjoy dramatic waterfront views, and the roof garden provides a spectacular 360-degree vista of the sea, town, and mountains. It is right on the waterfront, yet not in the built-up section. Because the Aliki has become a chic overnight getaway from bustling Rhodes, reservations are absolutely required.

Akti Gennimata, Yialos, 85600 Simi. www.symi-hotel-aliki.gr. ℂ **22460/71-665.** 15 units. 120€–150€ double; 150€–180€ suite. Rates include breakfast. AE, MC, V. Parking on adjacent streets. Closed mid-Nov to Mar. *In room:* A/C, fridge.

Hotel Nireus ★   This beautifully maintained hotel right on the waterfront is gracious and inviting, with its own shaded seafront cafe and restaurant, sunning dock, and swimming area. Its location, amenities, and price make it a favorite on Simi for foreigners and vacationing Greeks alike. The traditional Simiot-style facade has been preserved, while the spacious guest rooms are contemporary and comfortable. Ask for one of the 18 units that face the sea and offer stunning views; if you're fortunate, you might get one with a balcony. All four suites front the sea.

Akti Gennimata, Yialos, 85600 Simi. www.nireus-hotel.gr. ✆ **22460/72-400.** 35 units. 90€ double; 120€ suite. Rates include buffet breakfast. MC, V. Parking on adjacent streets. Closed Nov–Easter. **Amenities:** Restaurant; bar. *In room:* A/C, TV, fridge.

Hotel Niriides   If you crave tranquil seclusion, this small cluster of apartments, on a rise overlooking Nimborios Bay and only minutes on foot from the one-taverna town of Nimborios, may be exactly what you're seeking. It's about 35 minutes from Yialos on foot and appreciably less by land or sea taxi. Each attractive and spotless apartment sleeps four (two in beds and two on couches) and has a bedroom, bathroom, salon, and kitchenette. Seven apartments have balconies, three have terraces, and all face the sea. The Niriides has its own small bar and rents bicycles for excursions to town or beyond. There's a small beach with pristine water just a few minutes down the hill.

Nimborios Bay, 85600 Simi. www.niriideshotel.com. ✆/fax **22460/71-784.** 11 units. 65€–90€ double. Rates include breakfast. MC, V. Parking on adjacent streets. Closed Nov–Mar. **Amenities:** Cafe/bar; bike rental. *In room:* A/C, TV, fridge, kitchenette.

Where to Eat

In Yialos, for traditional home cooking and a respite from the crowds, look for the **Family Taverna Meraklis** (✆ **22410/71-003**), at the top of Menoilkidi Street (the first right after the statue of the little fisher boy across the harbor inlet).

Hellenikon (The Wine Restaurant of Simi) ★ GREEK/MEDITERRANEAN   If you have the impression that the Greek culinary imagination spins on a predictable wheel, you need a night at the Hellenikon. In addition to spectacular fare, this tiny open-air restaurant on the Yialos town square often provides, by virtue of its location, free evening concerts, compliments of the Simi Festival. Start with one of the imaginative appetizers. The chef's fish soup is spectacular, as are the grilled vegetables. In addition to a piquant array of traditional Greek entrees, you can select one of seven homemade pastas and combine it with one of numerous sauces. Host Nikos Psarros is a wine master, who has over 150 Greek wines in his cellar, all from small independent wineries, and he will help you select the perfect wine to complement your meal.

Yialos. ✆ **22410/72-455.** psarrosn@otenet.gr. Main courses 12€–24€. MC, V. May–Oct daily 8pm–midnight.

La Vaporetta (The Steam Cloud) ★ GREEK/ITALIAN   This 2007 addition to Simi's fine dining scene is the offspring of the adjacent Hotel Aliki (see above) and equals it in its high standards. Located in an old mansion right on the harbor, its proprietors are in fact a mix of Greeks and Italians so the dishes are authentic on both sides of the menu. You can sit right on the water's edge or if it's too hot (or windy) inside to partake of any number of well prepared meals, from familiar Italian foods—various pasta dishes, of course—or traditional Greek foods, fresh seafood among them. Congenial, informal service makes for a most pleasant dining experience.

Akti Gemminati, Yialos. ✆ **22460/71-665.** www.symi-hotel-aliki.gr. Main courses 10€–20€. AE, MC, V. May–Nov daily noon–4pm and 7pm–midnight.

Nireus Restaurant ★ GREEK   Michalis, the chef of this superior restaurant in the Nireus Hotel, has gained quite a reputation in recent years. Kudos to his *frito misto,* a mixed seafood plate with tiny, naturally sweet Simi shrimp and other local delicacies. The savory filet of beef served with a Madeira sauce is also recommended. They say you can't eat the scenery, but the view from here is delicious all the same.

Yialos. ✆ **22410/72-400.** www.nireus-hotel.gr. Main courses 8€–22€. MC, V. Easter–Oct daily 11am–11pm.

Taverna Neraida 🐟 SEAFOOD   Proving the rule that fish is cheaper far from the port, this homey taverna on the town square has among the best fresh-fish prices on the island, as well as a wonderful range of *mezedes*. Try the black-eyed-pea salad and *skordalia* (garlic sauce). The grilled daily fish is delicious; the ambience is a treat.

Yialos. ℂ **22410/71-841.** Main courses 7€–24€. No credit cards. Daily 11am–midnight.

KOS

370km (230 miles) E of Piraeus

Kos today is identified with and, at times, nearly consumed by tourism; but the island and its people have endured, and so will you, with a little initiative and independence. Almost three-quarters of the island's working people are directly engaged in tourism, and that tells you something about Kos's beauty and attractions.

Kos has been inhabited for roughly 10,000 years, and, for a significant portion of that time, has been both an important center of commerce and a line of defense. Its population in ancient times may have reached 100,000, but today it is less than a third of that number. Across the millennia, the unchallenged favorite son of the island has been Hippocrates, the father of Western medicine, who has left his mark not only on Kos but also on the world.

The principal attractions of Kos are its **antiquities**—most notably the Asklepion— and its **beaches.** You can guess which are more swamped in summer. But the taste of most tour groups is thankfully predictable and limited so the congestion can be evaded, if that's your preference.

Kos town is still quite vital. Because the island is small, you can base yourself in the town, in an authentic neighborhood if possible, and venture out from there. You'll get the most out of Kos by following the locals—especially to restaurants. If you think you're in a village and see no schools or churches, and no old people, chances are you're not in a village, but in a resort. Kos has many, especially along its coasts.

Essentials

GETTING THERE   By Plane   Kos is serviced by both **Olympic Airways,** with a Kos town office at 22 Vas. Pavlou (ℂ **22420/28-331**), and **Aegean Airlines** (ℂ **22420/51-654**). Although Olympic has experimented with expanded service and may do so again, at present its only direct flights to Kos are from Athens and Rhodes. From **Hippocrates Airport** (ℂ **22420/51-229**), a public bus will take you the 26km (16 miles) to the town center for 8€, or you can take a taxi for about 25€.

By Boat   As a transportation hub of the Dodecanese, Kos offers (weather permitting) a full menu of options: car ferries, passenger ferries, hydrofoils (Flying Dolphins), excursion boats, and caiques. Though most schedules and routes are always in flux, the good news is that, with more or less patience, you can make your way to Kos from virtually anywhere in the Aegean. Currently, the only ports linked to Kos with year-round nonstop and at least daily ferry service are Piraeus, Rhodes, Kalimnos, and Bodrum. Leros and Patmos enjoy the same frequency but with a stop or two along the way. The Kos harbor is strewn with travel agents, who can assist you; or check current schedules with the Municipal Tourism Office (see below).

VISITOR INFORMATION   The **Municipal Tourism Office** (ℂ **22420/24-460;** fax 22420/21-111), on Vas. Yioryiou, facing the harbor near the hydrofoil pier, is your one-stop source of information in Kos. It's open May through October Monday to Friday 8am to 2:30pm and 5 to 8pm, Saturday and Sunday 9am to 2pm;

November through April, hours are Monday to Friday 8am to 2:30pm. Hotel and pension owners keep the office informed of what rooms are available in the town and environs; however, you must book your room directly with the hotel. Be sure to pick up a free map of Kos. For a more extensive and detailed guide to Kos—beaches, archaeological sites, birds, wildflowers, tavernas, and much more—pick up a copy of *Where and How in Kos,* available at most news kiosks for 4€.

GETTING AROUND   By Bus   The **Kos town (DEAS) buses** offer service within roughly 6.4km (4 miles) of the town center, whereas the **Kos island (KTEL) buses** will get you nearly everywhere else. For the latest schedules, consult the **town bus office,** on the harbor at 7 Akti Kountourioti (☎ **22420/26-276**), or the **island bus station,** at 7 Kleopatras (☎ **22420/22-292**), around the corner from the Olympic Airways office. The majority of DEAS town buses leave from the central bus stop on the south side of the harbor.

By Bicycle   This is a congenial island for cyclists. Much of Kos is quite flat, and the main road from Kos town to Kefalos has all but emptied the older competing routes of traffic. As bike trails extend well beyond Kos town, you can avoid the congested east-end beach roads. But don't expect to pedal one-way and then hoist your bike onto a bus, because that won't work here. Rentals are available throughout Kos town and can be arranged through your hotel. Prices range from 10€ to 25€ per day.

By Moped & Motorcycle   It's easy to rent a moped through your hotel or a travel agent. Or, as with bicycles, you can walk toward the harbor and look for an agency. Rentals range from 25€ to 40€. You can also call **Motoway,** 9 Vas. Yioryiou (☎ **22420/20-031**), for mopeds and motorcycles.

By Car   It's unlikely that you'd need to rent a car for more than 1 or 2 days on Kos, even if you wanted to see all its sights and never lift a foot. Numerous companies, including **Avis** (☎ **22420/24-272**), **Europcar** (☎ **22420/24-070**), and **Hertz** (☎ **22420/28-002**), rent cars and all-terrain vehicles. Expect to pay as much as 95€ per day, including insurance and fuel. Gas stations are open Monday through Saturday from 7am to 7pm; there are also several stations open (in rotation) in Kos town on Sunday; ask your hotelier or the tourist office for directions.

By Taxi   For a taxi, drop by or call the **harbor taxi stand** beneath the minaret and across from the castle (☎ **22420/23-333** or 22420/27-777). All Kos drivers are required to know English—but then again, you were once required to know trigonometry.

ORIENTATION   Kos town is built around the harbor from which the town fans out. In the center are an **ancient city** *(polis),* consisting of ruins; an old city, limited mostly to pedestrians; and the new city, with wide, tree-lined streets. Most of the town's hotels are near the water, either on the road north to Lambi or on the road south and east to Psalidi. If you stand facing the harbor, with the castle on your right, **Lambi** is to your left and **Psalidi** on your right. In general, the neighborhoods to your right are less overrun and defined by tourists; this area, although quite central, is overall more residential and pleasant. The relatively uncontrolled area to your left (except for the occasional calm oasis, such as that occupied by the Pension Alexis) has been largely given over to tourism. Knowing this will help you find most of the tourist-oriented services by day and action by night, as well as where to find a bit of calm when you want to call it quits. Most recommended places to stay lie to your left, east of the castle.

FAST FACTS   Any of the major banks can exchange currency, but most people now use the ATMs at the banks' exteriors. The **hospital** is at 32 Hippokratous

(📞 **22420/22-300**). **Del Mare Internet Cafe,** 4a Megalo Alexandrou (📞 **22420/24-244;** www.cybercafe.gr), is open daily from 9am to 2am. A laundromat, **Happy Wash,** 20 Mitropoleos, across from Ayios Nikolaos (📞 **22420/23-424**), is open May through October daily from 8am to 9pm, and November through April daily from 9am to 1:30pm and 4 to 9pm. The **post office,** on Vas. Pavlou (at El. Venizelou), is open Monday through Friday from 7:30am to 2:30pm. Across from the castle, the **tourist police** (📞 **22420/22-444**) are available 24 hours to address any outstanding need or emergency, even trouble finding a room.

What to See & Do

ATTRACTIONS IN KOS TOWN

Dominating the harbor, the **Castle of the Knights** stands in and atop a long line of fortresses defending Kos since ancient times. What you see today was constructed by the Knights of St. John in the 15th century and fell to the Turks in 1522. Satisfying your curiosity is perhaps the only compelling reason to pay the 4€ admission fee. The castle is a hollow shell, with nothing of interest inside that you can't imagine from the outside, except when it serves as a venue for concerts. Best to stand back and admire from a distance this massive reminder of the vigilance that has been a part of life in Kos from prehistory to the present.

At the edge of town, at the intersection of Vas. Pavlou and E. Grigoriou, stands the **Casa Romana** (📞 **22420/23-234**), a Roman villa that straddles what appears to have been an earlier Hellenistic residence. The largest Roman villa in Greece (with 37 rooms), it was actually built and rebuilt over the centuries, and what you see today is the villa of the 3rd century A.D., one with lavish mosaics, marble paving, and fountains. It was closed to the public in 2005 for major restoration but reopened in 2009 (and there has been talk of using the villa's upper story as a museum for the villa's finds, now in Kos town's Archeological Museum). The villa is open Tuesday through Sunday from 8:30am to 3pm and costs 3€ for adults. To the east and west of the Casa Romana are a number of interesting open sites, comprising what is, in effect, a small archaeological park. Entrance is free. To the east lie the remains of a **Hellenistic temple** and the **Altar of Dionysos,** and to the west and south a number of impressive excavations and remains; the jewel is the **Roman Odeon,** with 18 intact levels of seats. The other extensive area of ruins is in the agora of the **ancient town,** just in from Akti Miaouli. Kos town is strewn with archaeological sites, opening like fissures and interrupting the flow of pedestrian traffic. Rarely is anything identified for passersby, so they seem like mere barriers or building sites, which is precisely what they were.

The rich architectural tradition of Kos did not cease with the eclipse of antiquity— Kos is adorned with a surprising number of striking and significant structures, sacred

---

 The Oldest Tree in Europe?

From the Kos Museum, you might want to walk directly across to the **Municipal Fruit Market,** and then have a picnic at the foot of the oldest tree in Europe, only a short walk toward the harbor, at the entrance bridge to the castle. The bizarre-looking tree standing with extensive support is said to be the **Tree of Hippocrates** ★, where he once instructed his students in the arts of empirical medicine and its attending moral responsibilities. Botanists may not endorse this claim, but why not enjoy the legend!

and secular, enfolded unself-consciously into the modern town. While you're strolling about town, note the **sculptures** by Alexandros Alwyn, in the Garden of Hippocrates, opposite Dolphins Square, down along the Old Harbor. An English painter and sculptor with something of an international reputation, Alwyn long maintained a studio in the village of Evangelistra, on Kos.

Asklepeion ★   Unless you have only beaches on the brain, Asklepeion is reason enough to come to Kos. On an elevated site with grand views of Kos town, the sea, and the Turkish coastline, this is the mecca of modern Western medicine, where Hippocrates—said to have lived to the age of 104—founded the first medical school in the late 5th century B.C. (In case your mythology is a bit rusty, Asclepius was the Greek god of healing.) For nearly 1,000 years after his death, this was a place of healing, where physicians were consulted and gods invoked in equal measure. The ruins date from the 4th century B.C. to the 2nd century A.D. Systematic excavation of the site was not begun until 1902. Truth be told, this is one of those archaeological sites that work best for those who bring something to them—namely some associations, some knowledge, some respect for the history behind the ruins . . . in this case, a sense of the role of Hippocrates in our own lives.

Located 4km (2½ miles) southwest of Kos town. ✆ **22420/28-763.** Admission 4€ adults, 2€ E.U. seniors and students, free for children 16 and under. Oct to mid-June Tues–Sun 8:30am–3pm; late June to Sept Tues–Fri 8:30am–7pm, Sat 8:30am–3pm.

Kos Archaeological Museum   For a town the size of Kos, this is an impressive archaeological museum, built by the Italians in the 1930s to display mostly Hellenistic and Roman sculptures and mosaics uncovered on the island. Although there is nothing startling or enduringly memorable in the collection, it will remind visitors of the former greatness of this now quite modest port town. Look in the museum's atrium for the lovely 3rd-century mosaic showing how Hippocrates and Pan once welcomed Asclepius, the god of healing, to this, the birthplace of Western medicine.

Plateia Eleftherias (across from the municipal market). ✆ **22420/28-326.** Admission 3€ adults, 2€ seniors and students, free for children 16 and under. Tues–Sun 8:30am–3pm.

SHOPPING

Kos town is compact, and the central shopping area all but fits in the palm of your hand, so you can explore every lane and see what strikes you. If you've grown attached to the traditional music you've been hearing since your arrival in Greece and want some help in making the right selection, stop by either of the **Ti Amo Music Stores,** 11 El. Venizelou and 4 Ipsilandou, where Giorgos Hatzidimitris will help you find traditional or modern Greek music. At either shop you may sit and listen before making a purchase.

Even if you're unwilling to pack another thing, you won't notice the weight of the unique handmade gold medallions at the jewelry shop of **N. Reissi,** opposite the museum at 1 Plateia Kazouli (✆ **22420/28-229**). Especially striking are the Kos medallions, designed and crafted by Ms. Reissi's father (60€–125€). Handcrafted rings, charms, and earrings are also on display. For unusual ceramic pieces, visit the shop of **Lambis Pittas,** at 6 Kanari (leading away from the inner harbor), or his factory at G. Papendreou (on the coast, leaving town for the southeast).

Another sort of treasure to bring home is a hand-painted Greek icon. **Panajiotis Katapodis** has been painting icons for over 40 years, both for churches and for individuals. His studio and home are on a lovely hillside little more than a mile west of Kos center, at Ayios Nektarios, and visitors are welcome April through October, Monday through Saturday from 9am to 1pm and 4 to 9pm. The way is signposted from just east of the Casa Romana.

BEACHES & OUTDOOR PURSUITS

The beaches of Kos are no secret. Every foot of the 290km (180 miles) of mostly sandy coastline has been discovered. Even so, for some reason, people pack themselves together in tight spaces. You can spot the package-tour sites from afar by their umbrellas, dividing the beach into plots measured in centimeters. **Tigaki** and **Kardamena** epitomize this avoidable phenomenon. Following are a few guidelines to help you in your quest for uncolonized sand.

The beaches 3 to 5km (2–3 miles) east of Kos town are among the least congested on the island, probably because they're pebbled rather than sandy. Even so, the view is splendid, and the nearby hot springs are worth a good soak. In summer, the water on the northern coast of the island is warmer and shallower than that on the south, though less clear due to stronger winds. If you walk down from the resorts and umbrellas, you'll find some relatively open stretches between **Tigaki** and **Mastihari.** The north side of the island is also best for **windsurfing;** try Tigaki and Marmara, where everything you need can be rented on the beach. A perfect day at the northwestern tip of the island would consist of a swim at **Limnionas Bay,** followed by grilled red mullet at Taverna Miltos.

Opposite, on the southern coast, **Kamel beach** and **Magic beach** are less congested than **Paradise beach,** which lies between them. Either can be reached on foot from Paradise beach, a stop for the Kefalos bus. The southwestern waters are cooler yet calmer than those along the northern shore; and apart from Kardamena and Kefalos Bay, the beaches on this side of the island are less dominated by package tour groups. Note that practically every sort of watersport, including jet-skiing, can be found at **Kardamena.** The extreme southwestern tip of the island, on the **Kefalos peninsula,** near Ayios Theologos, offers remote shoreline ideal for surfing. You can end the day watching the sunset at **Sunset Wave beach,** where you can also enjoy a not-soon-forgotten family-cooked feast at **Agios Theologos Restaurant,** which rents molded plastic surfboards as well.

For yachting and sailing, call the **Yachting Club of Kos** (© 22420/20-055) or **Istion Sailing Holidays** (© 22420/22-195;** fax 22420/26-777). For diving, contact **Kos Diving Centre,** 5 Plateia Koritsas (© 22420/20-269** or 22420/22-782); **Dolphin Divers** (© 29405/48-149);** or **Waterhoppers** (© 22420/27-815;** mobile 69444/27-308).

If horseback riding is your thing, you can arrange guided excursions through the **Marmari Riding Centre** (© 22420/41-783),** which offers 1-hour beach rides and 4-hour mountain trail rides. **Bird-watchers** will be interested in the wild peacocks in the forests at Skala, and the migrating flamingos that frequent the salt-lake preserve just west of Tingaki.

EXPLORING THE HINTERLANDS

The most remote and authentic region of the island is comprised of the forests and mountains stretching roughly from beyond Platani all the way to Plaka in the south. The highest point is Mount Dikeos, reaching nearly 900m (3,000 ft.). The mountain villages of this region were once the true center of the island. Only in the last 30 years or so have they been all but abandoned for the lure of more level, fertile land and, since the 1970s, the cash crop of tourism.

There are many ways to explore this region, which begins little more than a mile beyond the center of Kos town. Trekkers will not find this daunting, and by car or motorbike it's a cinch, but peddling a mountain bike over the ups and downs may be a challenge. Regardless of which way you go, the point is to take your time. You could take a bus from Kos to Zia and walk from Zia to Pili, returning then from Pili to Kos town by bus. The 5km (3-mile) walk from Zia to Pili will take you through a number of traditional island villages.(Pili, by the way, celebrates April 23 with horse racing and traditional foods.) Along the way you'll pass the ruins of **old Pili,** a mountaintop castle growing so organically out of the rock that you might miss it. As your reward at day's end, have dinner in **Zia** at **Sunset Taverna,** where at dusk the view of Kos island and the sea is magnificent. Zia also has a ceramics shop and a Greek art shop to occupy you as you wait for your taxi. For those looking to get away from the crowds, an hour's drive from Kos town all the way to the southwest coast leads to **Sunset Wave beach,** below Ayios Theologos. There the Vavithis family, including some repatriated from North America, maintain a restaurant that makes for a most enjoyable setting and meal.

VENTURING OFFSHORE

Two interesting offshore options lie within easy reach of Kos. Hop one of the daily ferries from Kardamena and Kefalos to the small island of **Nissiros.** Nissiros, while not especially attractive, has at its center an active volcano, which blew the top off the island in 600 B.C. and last erupted in 1873. There are also daily ferries from Kos harbor to **Bodrum, Turkey** (ancient Halikarnassos). Note that you must bring your passport to the boat an hour before sailing so that the captain can draw up the necessary documents for the Turkish port police.

Where to Stay

Plan ahead and make a reservation well in advance. Most places are booked solid in summer and closed tight in winter.

EXPENSIVE

Kipriotis Village Resort ★ ☺   Here's a resort hotel that will appeal to families willing to spend at least part of a vacation amid loads of fun-seeking Europeans with all the possible vacation facilities. Only 4km (2½ miles) from Kos town and right on the beach, it is constructed as a village of sorts, with its two-story bungalows and apartments surrounding its outdoor sports facilities (volleyball, basketball, tennis, minigolf). The attractive rooms vaguely suggest an Ikea-modern style with a Greek touch. Kids can take part in a full day of supervised activities. If you're here to soak up the sun, you'll never have to leave the premises; meals, however, as might be predicted for such a large institution, are not especially imaginative, but there is public transportation every 15 minutes into Kos town. While this place is relatively classy, it does tend to be booked by groups, so don't expect a cozy atmosphere.

P.O. Box 206, Psalidi beach, 85200 Kos (4km/2½ miles south of Kos town). www.kipriotis.gr. ✆ **22420/ 27-640.** 512 units. 175€ double; 200€ bungalow for 2 (including breakfast). AE, MC, V. Parking on premises. Closed mid-Oct to mid-Apr. **Amenities:** 5 restaurants; 4 bars; babysitting; children's center; health center w/sauna; 2 pools (1 indoor heated); tennis; watersports equipment/rentals. *In room:* A/C (July–Aug only), TV, fridge, hair dryer, Internet.

MODERATE

Hotel Astron ★   This is the most attractive hotel directly on Kos town's harbor, yet only some 360m (1,180 ft.) from a swimming beach—although the hotel does have its own generous-size pool and pleasant patio. The entrance and lobby are quite striking and suggest an elegance that, in fact, does not extend to the rooms and suites. However, all units are tasteful and clean, with firm beds and balconies. The pricier rooms include extras such as harbor views and Jacuzzis. In the larger and more expensive suites, the extra space is designed to accommodate a third person and is wasted if you intend to use it as a sitting area. One extra that might be worth the money is a harbor view; but remember, by nighttime, you are facing the action. In summer, about 65% of the rooms in town are allotted to package-tour groups who come to live it up.

31 Akti Kountourioti, 85300 Kos. www.astron-hotel-kos.gr. © **22420/23-703.** 80 units. 125€ double; 150€ suite. Rates include breakfast. AE, MC, V. Parking on adjacent streets. **Amenities:** Restaurant; bar; Internet room; Jacuzzi; 2 pools (1 children's); room service. *In room:* A/C, TV, fridge, hair dryer, minibar.

INEXPENSIVE

Hotel Afendoulis ✦   Nowhere in Kos do you receive so much for so little. Nestled in a gracious residential neighborhood a few hundred yards from the water and less than 10 minutes on foot from the very center of Kos, Afendoulis offers the combination of convenience and calm. The rooms are clean and altogether welcoming, with firm beds. Nearly all units have private balconies, and most have views of the sea. Whatever room you have, you can't go wrong. Note that the hotel has an elevator. This is a long-established family run place, and the Zikas family spares nothing to create a special vacation community in which guests enjoy and respect one another. If you are coming to Kos to bask in luxury or raise hell, go elsewhere.

Although this is likely to be many people's first choice in Kos, the family also owns the **Pension Alexis** (see below) several blocks away and can usually accommodate someone who shows up at the last minute.

1 Evrepilou, 85300 Kos. www.afendoulishotel.com. © **22420/25-321.** Fax 22420/25-797. 23 units. 60€–75€ double. MC, V. Parking on adjacent streets. Closed mid-Oct to mid-Apr.

Hotel Yiorgos   This inviting, family run hotel is a block from the sea and no more than a 15-minute walk from the center of Kos town. Although the immediate neighborhood is not residential, the hotel enjoys relative quiet year-round. Guest rooms are modest and very clean. All units have balconies, most with pleasant but not spectacular views of either sea or mountains. Individually controlled central heating makes this an exceptionally cozy small hotel at the chilly edges of the tourist season. Convenience, hospitality, and affordability have created a place to which guests happily return.

9 Harmilou, 85300 Kos. www.yiorgoshotel.com. © **22420/23-297.** 35 units. 40€–65€ double. Rates include breakfast. No credit cards. Parking on adjacent streets. **Amenities:** Breakfast room; bar; Wi-Fi. *In room:* A/C, TV, fridge.

Pension Alexis   Ensconced in a quiet residential neighborhood close to the harbor, Pension Alexis feels like a home because it is one—or was, until it opened as a guesthouse. This is a gracious dwelling, with parquet floors and many tasteful architectural touches. The expansive rooms have high ceilings and open onto shared balconies. Most have sweeping views of the harbor and the Castle of the Knights. Individual rooms are separated from the halls by sliding doors, and share three large bathrooms. Room no. 4 is a truly grand corner space with knockout views. In summer, the heart of the pension is the covered veranda that faces private gardens, where, in the morning, guests can enjoy breakfast and, at dusk, can share stories late into the night. But no doubt a drawback for some is the fact that you have to share the hallway bathrooms with two or three other rooms.

9 Irodotou, 85300 Kos. © **22420/28-798** or 22420/25-594. Fax 22420/25-797. 14 units. 40€–50€ double. Breakfast extra 7€. No credit cards. Parking on adjacent streets. Closed mid-Oct to mid-Apr. **Amenities:** Bar; Internet. *In room:* A/C or fans.

Where to Eat

In Kos, as at all popular Greek tourist destinations these days, there's a lot of routine food and even fast food. But there's no need to make eating on Kos a Greek tragedy;

the key is to eat where the locals do. Along with your meals, you may want to try some of the local wines: dry **Glafkos,** red **Appelis,** or crisp **Theokritos** retsina.

EXPENSIVE

Petrino ★ GREEK   When royalty come to Kos, this is where they dine—so why not live the fantasy yourself? Housed in an exquisitely restored, century-old, two-story stone *(petrino)* private residence, this is hands-down the most elegant taverna in Kos, with food to match. In summer, sit outside on the spacious three-level terrace overlooking the ancient agora; but be sure to take a look at the splendid architecture inside, especially upstairs.

Although the menu focuses on Greek specialties, it is vast enough to include lobster, filet mignon, and other Western staples. But don't waste this opportunity to experience Greek traditional cuisine at its best (and not necessarily all that expensive). The stuffed peppers, grilled octopus, and *beki meze* (marinated pork) are perfection. More than 50 carefully selected wines, all Greek, line the cellar. The dry red kalliga from Kefalonia is exceptional.

1 Plateia Theologou (abutting agora's east extremity). ✆ **22420/27-251.** Reservations recommended. Main courses 10€–55€. AE, DC, MC, V. Mid-Dec to Nov daily 5pm–midnight.

Platanos Restaurant ★ GREEK/INTERNATIONAL   Not only is Platanos in one of Kos's best locations, overlooking the Hippocrates Tree, it is in a handsome building, a former Italian officers' club replete with arches and the original tile floor. Try reserving a place on the upstairs balcony, with its impressive vista. Among the creatively prepared appetizers is chicken stuffed with dates in a spicy sauce. If you're tired of Greek salads, try the mixed vegetable salad. For a main course, try the souvlaki, a combination of chicken, lamb, and beef; or the duck Dijonnaise, served with a tasty sauce and a selection of seasonable vegetables. A generous selection of choice wines, live music, and gracious service makes for a splendid evening.

Plateia Platanos. ✆ **22420/28-991.** Main courses 12€–32€. AE, MC, V. Apr–Oct daily noon–11:30pm.

MODERATE

Taverna Mavromatis ★ GREEK   One of the best choices in town is this 40-year-old vine- and geranium-covered beachside taverna run by the Mavromati brothers. Their food is what you came to Greece for: melt-in-your-mouth *saganaki,* mint- and garlic-spiced *sousoutakia* (meatballs in red sauce), tender grilled lamb chops, moist beef souvlaki, and perfectly grilled fresh fish. In summer, the taverna spills out along the beach; you'll find yourself sitting only feet from the water watching the sunset and gazing at the nearby Turkish coast. A dinner here can be quite magical, something locals know very well, so arrive early to ensure a spot by the water.

Psalidi beach. ✆ **22420/22-433.** Main courses 6€–20€. AE, MC, V. Wed–Sun 11am–11pm. A 20-min. walk southeast of the ferry port, or accessible by the local Psalidi Beach bus.

INEXPENSIVE

Arap (Platanio) Taverna GREEK/TURKISH   Although it requires a short walk or a taxi ride, it is well worth the effort. Like the population of Platinos, the food here is a splendid mix of Greek and Turkish. The spirit of this unpretentious family restaurant is contagious. Whatever you order from the extensive menu, it's impossible for you to choose wrong. Although there are many meat dishes, vegetarians will have a feast. The roasted red peppers stuffed with feta and the zucchini flowers stuffed with rice are splendid, as is the *bourekakia* (a kind of fried pastry roll stuffed with cheese). For a really top-notch meal, put yourself in the hands of the Memis brothers and let them order for you. Afterward, you can walk across the street for the best homemade ice cream on Kos, an island legend since 1955.

Platinos-Kermetes. ✆ **22420/28-442.** Main courses 6€–16€. No credit cards. Apr–Oct daily 10am–midnight. Located 2km (1¼ miles) south of town on the road to the Asklepion.

Taverna Ampavris ★ GREEK This is undoubtedly one of the best tavernas on Kos. It's just outside the bustling town center on the way to the Asklepion, down a quiet village lane. In the courtyard of this 130-year-old house, you can feast on local dishes from Kos island. The *salamura,* from Kefalos, is mouthwatering pork stewed with onions and coriander; the *lahano dolmades* (stuffed cabbage with rice, minced meat, and herbs) is delicate, light, and not at all oily. The *faskebab* (veal stew on rice) is tender and lean, while the vegetable dishes, such as the broad string beans cooked and served cold in garlic and olive-oil dressing, are out of this world.

Ampavris. ✆ **22420/25-696.** Main courses 8€–18€. No credit cards. Apr–Oct daily 5:30pm–1am. Take a taxi.

Taverna Ampeli ★ GREEK This is as close as you come in Kos to authentic Greek home cooking. Facing the sea and ensconced in its own vineyard, Ampeli is delightful even before you taste the food. The interior is unusually tasteful, with high-beamed ceilings, and the outside setting is even better. The dolmades rate with the best in Greece. Other excellent specialties are *pliogouri* (gruel), *giouvetsi* (casserole), and *revithokefteves* (meatballs). Even the fried potatoes set a new standard. The house retsina is unusually sweet, almost like a sherry; the house white wine, made from the grapes before your eyes, is dry and light and quite pleasing—the red, however, is less memorable. If you're here on Saturday or midday on Sunday, the Easter-style goat, baked overnight in a low oven, is not to be missed.

Tzitzifies, Zipari village (8km/5 miles from Kos town). ✆ **22420/69-682.** Main courses 7€–20€. MC, V. Apr–Oct daily 10am–midnight; Nov–Mar daily 6–11pm. Closed Easter week and 10 days in early Nov. Off the beach road, 1km (½ mile) east of Tingaki. Take a bus to Tingaki and walk, or take a taxi.

Taverna Nikolas 🐟 GREEK/SEAFOOD Known on the street as Nick the Fisherman's, this is one taverna in Kos that wasn't designed with tourists in mind. Off season, it's a favorite haunt for locals, with whom you'll have to compete for one of eight tables. In summer, however, seating spills freely onto the street. Although you can order anything from filet mignon to goulash, the point of coming here is the seafood. If the Aegean has it, you'll find it here: grilled octopus, shrimp in vinegar and lemon, calamari stuffed with cheese, and mussels souvlaki, for example. The menu is extensive, so come with an appetite.

21 G. Averof. ✆ **22420/23-098.** Main courses 6€–20€; fixed-price dinners 12€–20€; 2-person seafood dinner 40€. No credit cards. Daily noon–midnight.

Kos After Dark

Kos nightlife is no more difficult to find than your own ears. Go to the harbor and follow the noise. The **portside cafes,** opposite the daily excursion boats to Kalimnos, are best in the early morning. **Apoplous** (on Psalidhi St., near Market) has live Greek music; **Platanos,** across from the Hippocrates Tree, has live music, often jazz; and just across from Platanos is the beginning of **Bar Street,** which needs no further introduction. The lively **Fashion Club,** Kanari 2 Dolphins Sq., has the most impressive light-and-laser show. On Akti Zouroudi there are two popular discos, **Heaven** and **Calua** (with a swimming pool). If you want to hit the bar scene, try **Hamam Club,** on Akti Kountourioti, or **Beach Boys,** at 57 Kanari. Another option is an old-fashioned outdoor movie theater, Kos style, at **Open Cine Orfeas,** 10 Vasileos Yioryiou. Relatively recent films, often in English, cost 6€.

PATMOS ★

302km (187 miles) E of Piraeus

If a musician were to compose and dedicate a piece to Patmos, it might be a suite for rooster, moped, and bells (church *and* goat), for these are the sounds that fill the air. But just because Patmos is wonderfully unspoiled, don't imagine that it's primitive. In fact, in recent years, it has developed quite sophisticated tourist facilities and attracted a large following. The saving grace for those who come seeking a bit of quiet is that most visitors either come for a day or settle in a couple of beach resorts.

Architects sometimes speak of "charged sites," places where something so powerful happened that its memory must always be preserved. Patmos is such a place. It is where **St. John the Divine ★**, traditionally identified with the Apostle John, spent several years in exile, dwelling in a cave and composing the Book of Revelation, also known as the Apocalypse. From that time on, the island has been regarded as hallowed ground, reconsecrated through the centuries by the erection of more than 300 churches, one for every 10 residents.

Neither the people of Patmos nor their visitors are expected to spend their days in prayer, but the Patmians expect—and deserve—a heavy dose of respect for their traditions. Patmos is a place for those seeking a "retreat," and by that, we do not mean a religious calling, but a more subdued, civilized alternative to major tourist destinations. Some guidebooks highlight the island's prohibitions on nude bathing and how to get around them—but if this is a priority for you, then you've stumbled onto the wrong island. Enjoy your stay on Patmos, but don't expect raucous nightlife.

Essentials

GETTING THERE   By Plane   Patmos has no airport, but it is convenient (especially by hydrofoil and catamaran in spring and summer) to three islands that do: Samos, Kos, and Leros. Rather than endure the all-but-interminable ferry ride from Piraeus, fly from Athens to one of these, then hop a boat or hydrofoil the rest of the way to Patmos. Samos is your best bet; with the right schedule, you can get from the Athens airport to Patmos in 3 hours via Samos.

By Boat   Patmos, the northernmost of the Dodecanese Islands, is on the daily ferry line from Piraeus to Rhodes—confirm schedules with **Piraeus Port Authority** (② **210/417-2657** or 210/451-1310) or **Rhodes Port Authority** (② **22410/23-693** or 22410/27-695). Patmos has numerous sea links with the larger islands of the Dodecanese, as well as with the islands of the northeast Aegean. Options are limited from late fall to early spring, but Easter through September, sea connections with most of the islands of the eastern Aegean are numerous and convenient. With **Blue Star Line's** (www.bluestarferries.com) new high-speed ferries, the travel time from Piraeus has been reduced to about 7 hours.

VISITOR INFORMATION   The **tourism office** (② **22470/31-666**) in the port town of Skala is directly in front of you as you disembark from your ship; it's open June through August daily from 9am to 10pm. It shares the Italianate "municipal palace" with the post office and the **tourist police** (② **22470/31-303**), who take over when the tourism office is closed. The **port police** (② **22470/31-231**), in the first building on your left on the main ferry pier, are very helpful for boat schedules and whatever else ails or concerns you; the building is open year-round, 24 hours a day. There is also a host of helpful information about Patmos at **www.patmos-island.com** or **www.travel-to-patmos.com**.

Apollon Tourist and Shipping Agency, on the harbor near the central square (Ⓒ **22470/31-724;** fax 22470/31-819), can book excursion boats and hydrofoils and arrange lodging in hotels, rental houses, and apartments throughout the island. It's open year-round from 8am to noon and 4 to 6pm, with extended summer hours.

GETTING AROUND   By Moped & Bicycle   Mopeds are definitely the vehicle of choice on the island, provided you have a proper license. At the shops that line the harbor, 1-day rentals start at around 25€ and go up to 50€. **Australis Motor Rent** (Ⓒ **22470/32-723**), in Skala's new port, is a first-rate shop; and you can usually rent at a discounted rate for rentals lasting less than a full day. You can also contact **Billis** (Ⓒ **22470/32-218**), on the harbor in Skala. Bicycles are hard to come by on the island, but **Theo & Georgio's** (Ⓒ **22470/32-066**) has 18-speed mountain bikes for 15€ per day.

By Car   Two convenient car-rental offices, both in Skala, are **Patmos Rent-a-Car,** just behind the police station (Ⓒ **22470/32-203**), and **Avis,** on the new port (Ⓒ **22470/33-095**). Daily rentals in high season start about 50€. The island does not have many gas stations, so be sure you watch your gas tank gauge.

By Taxi   The island's main taxi stand is on the pier in Skala Harbor, right before your eyes as you get off the boat. From anywhere on the island, you can request a taxi by calling Ⓒ **22470/31-225.** As the island is quite small, it's much cheaper to hire a taxi than to rent a car.

By Bus   The entire island has a single bus, whose current schedule is available at the tourist office and is posted at locations around the island. Needless to say, it provides limited service—to Skala, Hora, Grikos, and Kambos—so it's best to use another method to get around.

ORIENTATION   Patmos lies along a north-south axis; were it not for a narrow central isthmus, it would be two islands, north and south. **Skala,** the island's only town of any size, is situated near that isthmus joining the north island to the south.

Above Skala looms the hilltop capital of **Hora,** comprising a mazelike medieval village and the fortified monastery of St. John the Divine. There are really only two other towns on Patmos: **Kambos,** to the north, is a real village of roughly 500 inhabitants; **Grikou,** to the south, is mostly a resort, a creation of the tourist industry.

> **For Your Health**
>
> One essential you need to know about Patmos from the outset is that tap water is not for drinking. *Drink only bottled water.*

Most independent visitors to Patmos, especially first-timers, will choose to stay in Skala (Hora has no hotels) and explore the north and south from there. Patmos is genuinely addicting, an island to which visitors, Greek and foreign, return year after year. So while it makes sense on your first visit to Patmos to be centrally located, you may wish to stay elsewhere during future visits.

FAST FACTS   Commercial Bank of Greece, on the Skala harbor, and **National Bank of Greece,** on the central square, offer exchange services and ATMs. Both are open Monday through Thursday from 8am to 2pm and Friday from

8am to 1:30pm. You will also find an ATM where ferries and cruises dock at the main pier. For **dental or medical emergencies,** call ℂ **22470/31-211;** for special **pharmaceutical needs,** call ℂ **22470/31-500.** The **hospital** (ℂ **22470/31-211**) is on the road to Hora. The **post office** on the harbor is open Monday through Friday 8am to 1:30pm. The **tourist police** (ℂ **22470/31-303**) are directly across from the port.

For **Internet access,** the **Internet Cafe at Blue Bay** (Blue Bay Hotel) is open April through October daily, from 8am to 8pm. **Millennium Internet Cafe,** on the lane to Horio, near the OTE office, is open year-round daily, from 9am to 10pm. A short walk down toward the new port will bring you to **Just Like Home** (ℂ **22470/33-170**), where a load of laundry costs 15€. It's open daily until 9pm September through June, and until 10pm in July and August.

What to See & Do
THE TOP ATTRACTIONS

What Patmos lacks in quantity, it makes up for in quality. Apart from its natural beauty and its 300-plus churches, there are several extraordinary sights: the **Monastery of St. John ★★, Cave of the Apocalypse ★★,** and the medieval town of **Hora ★.** The latter is a labyrinthine maze of whitewashed stone homes, shops, and churches in which getting lost is the whole point. By the way, if you are so inclined, put off your visit till the end of September—beginning of October when there is a **Religious Music Festival** with concerts close to the Cave of the Apocalypse—a unique and moving experience. Another such experience is the Easter-time Holy Thursday **Service of the Washing of the Disciples' Feet** in the Monastery.

Off-season, the opening days and times for the **cave** and the **monastery** are unpredictable, as they are designed to accommodate groups of pilgrims and cruise-ship tours rather than individual visitors. Neither place is public. The cave is enclosed within a convent, and the monastery is just that. It's best to consult the tourist office or travel agent above for the open hours on the day of your visit (the times given below are for the peak season May–Aug). To visit both places, appropriate attire is required, which means that women must wear full-length skirts or dresses and have covered shoulders, while men must wear long pants.

The road to Hora is well marked from Skala, but if you're walking, take the narrow lane to the left just past the central square. Once outside the town, you can mostly avoid the main road by following the uneven stone-paved donkey path, which is the traditional pilgrims' route to the sanctuaries above. And if you have taken this much trouble to get to Hora, hang around awhile—it is really quite a delightful old town with many mansions from the 17th and 18th centuries.

Cave of the Apocalypse ★★   Exiled to Patmos by the Roman emperor Domitian in A.D. 95, St. John the Divine is said to have made his home in this cave, though Patmians insist quite reasonably that he walked every inch of the small island, talking with its people. The cave is said to be the epicenter of his earth-shaking dreams, which he dictated to his disciple Prochoros and which has come down to present believers as the Book of the Apocalypse, or Revelation, the last book of the Christian Bible. The cave is now encased within a sanctuary, which, in turn, is encircled by a convent. A stirring brochure, written by Archimandrite Koutsanellos, superior of the cave, provides an excellent description of the religious significance of each niche in the rocks, as well as the many icons in the cave. Other guides are available in local tourist shops. The best preparation, of course, is to bone up on the Book of Revelation.

Even non-Christians are at least vaguely aware that the fourth Gospel, or life of Christ, is attributed to a John; because of its literary associations, they may also be aware that the Book of Revelation is attributed to John; and well-informed Christians may also know that a John wrote the first three Epistles of the New Testament. Oh, yes—and there was a John who was among the 12 disciples. So how many Johns were there? Well, it is agreed that John the disciple was present at the trial and Crucifixion of Jesus, and it is also widely believed that this John wrote the fourth Gospel and those first three Epistles to the early Christian communities. But there is not solid agreement among scholars that this was the same John who wrote the Book of Revelation. Nevertheless, the religious community of Patmos does believe that the John who dictated the book in the cave here was the same as the other John and thus flatly proclaims their institution and site as that of St. John the Divine.

On the road to Hora. 📞 **22470/31-234.** Free admission. May–Aug Sun 8am–1pm and 2–6pm; Mon 8am–1:30pm; Tues–Wed 8am–1:30pm and 2–6pm; Thurs–Sat 8am–1:30pm. Otherwise, hours vary (as described above).

Monastery of St. John ★★   Towering over Skala and, for that matter, over the south island is the medieval Monastery of St. John, which looks far more like a fortress than a house of prayer. Built to withstand pirates, it is certainly up to the task of deterring runaway tourism. The monastery virtually controls the south island, where the mayor wears a hat but the monastic authority wears a miter. In 1088, with a hand-signed document from the Byzantine emperor Alexis I Comnenus ceding the entire island to the future monastery, Blessed Christodoulos arrived on Patmos to establish what was to become an independent monastic state. The monastery chapel is stunning, as is the adjoining **Chapel of the Theotokos,** whose frescoes date from the 12th century. On display in the treasury is a fraction of the monastery's exquisite Byzantine treasures—icons, vestments, rare books—which are second only to those of Mount Athos, a monastic state. One of the icons, by the way, is claimed to be by El Greco.

Hora. 📞 **22470/31-234.** Free admission to monastery; 4€ to treasury. May–Aug Sun 8am–1pm and 2–6pm; Mon–Sat 8am–1:30pm; Tues–Wed also 2–6pm.

OUTDOOR PURSUITS

The principal outdoor activities on Patmos are walking and swimming. The best **beaches** are highlighted (see "Exploring the Island," below) and the best **walking trails** are the unmarked donkey paths which crisscross the island. You won't find jet-skis or surfboards on Patmos, although limited **watersports** are available. Paddle-boats and canoes can be rented and water-skiing arranged at Helen's Place, on Agriolivada beach, while Elisabeth, on Kampos Beach, offers a variety of watersports (water-skiing, tubes, boards). Those intent on scuba diving should start at the Bluefin Center in Skala (📞 **22470/31-251;** www.bluefincenterpatmos.com).

SHOPPING

Patmians are quick to lament and apologize for the fact that just about everything, from gas to toothpaste, is a bit more expensive here. Patmos doesn't even have its own drinking water, and import costs inevitably get passed along to the customer. Having said that, the price differences are much more evident to the locals than to tourists.

There are several excellent jewelry shops, such as **Iphigenia** (© **22470/31-814**) and **Midas** (© **22470/31-800**), on the harbor; though **Filoxenia** (© **22470/31-667**) and **Art Spot** (© **22470/32-243**), both behind the main square, in the direction of Hora, have more interesting contemporary designs, often influenced by ancient motifs. The Art Spot also sells ceramics and small sculptures, and is well worth seeking out. Farther down the same lane is **Parousia** (© **22470/32-549**), the best single stop for hand-painted icons and a wide range of books on Byzantine subjects. The proprietor, Mr. Alafakis, is quite learned in the history and craft of icon painting and can tell you a great deal about the icons in his shop and the diverse traditions they represent.

The most fascinating shop on Patmos may be **Selene** (© **22470/31-742**), directly across from the port authority office. The highly selective array of Greek handmade art and crafts here is extraordinary, from ceramics to hand-painted Russian and Greek icons to marionettes, some as tall as 1m (3 ft.). And be sure to notice Selene's structure, also a work of art. Built in 1835, it was once a storage space for sails and later a boat-building workshop. Look down at the shop's extraordinary floor, made of hand-made stamped and scored bricks, quite special and traditional to Patmos.

Where to Stay in Skala

There are no hotels, only pensions in Hora, but you will find many in Skala and elsewhere around the island. Unless you plan to visit Patmos during Greek or Christian Easter or late July through August, you should not have difficulty finding a room upon arrival, though it's always safer to book ahead. Residents offering private accommodations usually meet ferries at the harbor. If you're interested in renting a kitchenette apartment or villa, contact the **Apollon Agency** (© **22470/31-724;** fax 22470/31-819).

EXPENSIVE

Porto Scoutari (Romantic) Hotel and Spa ★ High on a bluff overlooking Meloï Bay, this luxury hotel is seductively gracious, with the largest rooms and pool on the island. Ground-level suites are designed with families in mind, whereas upper-level suites, with four-poster beds and bathtubs, have "honeymoon" written all over them. Each bungalow-style studio has a kitchenette, year-round climate control, and a private balcony. The common areas—breakfast room, lounge, piano bar, and pool—are simultaneously informal and refined. This is the most ambitious "full-service" hotel on the island. If your stay on Patmos is brief, you probably wouldn't want to stay here, only because you're paying for facilities that you might not have time to use.

Scoutari, 85500 Patmos. www.portoscoutari.com. © **22470/33-123.** 30 units. 120€–280€ double; 260€–520€ studio or suite. Rates include full breakfast buffet. Cheaper rates for paying in advance or booking for a week. MC, V. Parking on premises. Closed Nov–Easter. Note that this hotel overlooks, but is not in, Meloï Bay—so follow the signs to Kambos, not to Meloï Bay. It's less than 3km (2 miles) from the center of Skala. **Amenities:** Restaurant; bar; Internet and fax facilities; pool; room service; smoke-free rooms; spa. *In room:* A/C, TV, fridge, hair dryer.

MODERATE

Blue Bay Hotel ★ Two unique features distinguish this hotel (operated by a Greek-Australian couple): First, its stellar location on the southwest side of the harbor offers a rare fusion of convenience and quiet; second, guests are requested not to smoke anywhere in the hotel except on the private balconies. The bedrooms are spacious, immaculate, and comfortable. Room nos. 114 and 115 share a terrace the size of a tennis court overlooking the sea. The hotel emphasizes service and gracious hospitality. The new Blue Bay Internet Cafe offers Internet access at a reasonable rate.

Skala, 85500 Patmos. www.bluebay.50g.com. ℂ **22470/31-165.** 27 units. 110€ double; 150€–170€ suite. Rates include buffet breakfast. MC, V. Parking on adjacent streets. Closed Nov–Mar. **Amenities:** Breakfast room; bar; Internet. *In room:* A/C, minibar.

Casteli Hotel 🏊 Nothing fancy and with minimal amenities, this hotel's location and rates are what make it attractive. Perched on a hillside overlooking the sea, all rooms have balconies with a view. The hotel's striking sea vista can be enjoyed from cushioned wrought-iron chairs on each room's balcony or from a pleasant covered terrace/bar. The large, spotless rooms have white walls and beige tile floors, and the balconies are covered. The common lounge and lobby areas are filled with photographs, flower-print sofas, seashells, fresh-cut flowers from the surrounding gardens, and other knickknacks of seaside life. The price you pay for the view is a mildly challenging 5-minute climb from the harbor.

Skala, 85500 Patmos. www.casteli.gr. ℂ **22470/31-361.** Fax 22470/31-656. 45 units. 85€–95€ double. Rates include breakfast. No credit cards. Parking on adjacent streets. **Amenities:** Breakfast room; bar. *In room:* A/C, TV, fridge.

Romeos Hotel Of Skala's newer lodgings, this one, run by a Greek-American family from Virginia, is especially commodious, with a large pool and a quiet garden. The simply decorated, spotless rooms are built like semiattached bungalows on a series of tiers, with balconies offering views across the countryside to Mount Kastelli. Large honeymoon suites, with double beds, full bathtubs, and small lounges, are available. One downside to its otherwise attractive location is that the bungalows are on a fairly steep slope; for some, this might present a challenge.

Skala (in the back streets, behind the OTE), 85500 Patmos. romeos@greekhotel.com. ℂ **22470/31-962.** 60 units. 80€–95€ double; 110€ suite. Rates include breakfast. MC, V. Parking on adjacent streets. Closed Nov–Mar. Pets accepted. **Amenities:** Breakfast room; bar; 2 pools (1 large, 1 children's). *In room:* A/C, TV, hair dryer, minibar.

Skala Hotel Tranquilly but conveniently situated well off the main harbor road, behind a lush garden overflowing with arresting pink bougainvillea, this comfortable hotel has become an established Skala favorite. Attractive features include a large pool with an inviting sun deck and bar, a large breakfast buffet, and personalized service. The three views to choose from are the sea, the western mountains, and the Monastery of St. John—and all are striking. If you want to stay here at Easter or in late July and August, you'll need advance reservations. The hotel describes itself as handicap accessible, but this might be a shade optimistic.

Skala, 85500 Patmos. skalahtl@12net.gr. ℂ **22470/31-343.** Fax 22470/31-747. 78 units. 90€ double. Rates include breakfast. MC, V. Parking on adjacent streets. Closed Nov–Mar. **Amenities:** Restaurant; 2 bars; babysitting; pool; room service. *In room:* A/C, TV, minibar, Wi-Fi.

INEXPENSIVE

Australis Hotel and Apartments ★ On the approach, you may have misgivings regarding this hotel's location, down a less-than-charming lane off the new port area. Your doubts will vanish when you enter the hotel compound, a blooming hillside oasis run by the hospitable Fokas family. The pleasant communal porch, where breakfast is served, offers delightful views of the open harbor. The guest rooms are bright, tasteful, and impeccably clean (and with firm beds). Within the same compound and enjoying the same floral and sea vistas, four apartments offer spacious homes away from home for families or groups of four to six people; these are fully equipped with kitchenettes, TVs, and heat for the winter months. In addition to these apartments, the Fokas family has three handsome studios over a house on the old road to Hora; each has a well-stocked kitchen and goes for 45€ to 65€ per day.

Skala (a 5-min. walk from the center), 85500 Patmos. ✆ **22470/32-562.** Fax 22470/32-284. 29 units. 75€ double; 165€ apt., depending on size and season. Rates include breakfast. No credit cards. Parking on adjacent streets. Closed Nov–Mar. *In room:* TV, fridge (in some).

Villa Knossos 🍃   This small, white villa off the new port is set within an abundant garden of palms, purple and pink bougainvillea, potted geraniums, and hibiscus. The tasteful, spacious guest rooms have high ceilings (making them cool even in the summer's heat). All rooms but one have private balconies. The two units facing the back garden are the quietest, while room no. 7, in front, has a private veranda. Guests can use a comfortable sitting room.

Skala, 85500 Patmos. ✆ **22470/32-189.** Fax 22470/32-284. 7 units. 50€–75€ double. No credit cards. Parking on adjacent streets. Closed Nov–Mar. *In room:* Fridge.

Where to Eat in Skala & Hora

The culinary scene in Skala and Hora may not have any true standout restaurants, but there are many that will not disappoint. In Hora, on the path to the Monastery of St. John, you'll find **Pirgos; Balkoni** (with grand view of Skala Harbor); **Patmian House;** and (following signs from the monastery) **Vagelis,** in the central square (Vagelis enjoys views of the south island). Two favorites in Skala are recommended below, but you will want to browse for yourself. Alternatively, venture out to the north and south islands, which serve up some of Patmos's most enticing food. In particular, the restaurant at the Petra Hotel and Apartments (see "Exploring the Island," below) stands out.

Grigoris Grill GREEK   One of Skala's better-known eateries, this place was formerly the center of Patmian chic. Any of the grilled fish or meat dishes are recommended, particularly in the slow season, when more time and attention are lavished on the preparation. Well-cooked veal cutlets, tender lamb chops, and the swordfish souvlaki are favorites. Grigoris also offers several vegetarian specials. Both curbside seating and a more removed and quiet roof garden are available.

Opposite Skala car ferry pier. ✆ **22470/31-515.** Main courses 7€–16€. No credit cards. Easter–June and Sept–Oct 6pm–midnight; July–Aug 11am–midnight.

Pantelis Restaurant GREEK   Pantelis is a proven local favorite for no-frills Greek home cooking. The food here is consistently fresh and wholesome—the basics prepared so well that they surprise you. Daily specials augment the standard menu. Portions are generous, so pace yourself; and if you're not yet a convert to the Greek cult of olive oil, order something grilled. The lightly fried calamari, chickpea soup, swordfish kabob, and roasted lamb meet all expectations. In winter, the spacious dining hall with high ceilings makes this a relatively benign environment for nonsmokers.

Skala (1 lane back from the port). ✆ **22470/31-922.** Main courses 6€–19€. No credit cards. Daily 11am–11pm.

Vegghera Restaurant ★★ GREEK/MEDITERRANEAN   Vegghera has become the premier restaurant of Skala and deserves this status for its food, service, and ambience. Located in a handsome mansion, overlooking the marina where yachts from distant ports dock, Vegghera carries this international flavor into its menu. George Grillis, proprietor and chef, combines traditional Greek fare with French-influenced Mediterranean cuisine, such as salmon smoked with rose sticks or lobster with tagliatelle. Not unexpectedly, its specialties feature seafood from various parts, but the vegetables, pork, and rabbit are all raised by Grillis himself. The wine list is equally selective and desserts are to die for. It's not cheap, but once in awhile, when you've come this far, you should just splurge. And you get a choice of eating on the shaded terrace or inside.

Nea Marina, Skala. ✆ **22470/32-988.** Main courses 9€–34€. MC, V. Easter–Oct daily 7:30pm–1am.

Patmos After Dark

The nightlife scene on Patmos, while not ecclesiastical, is a bit subdued compared to some Greek islands. Clubs tend to open for a few weeks in season, then close like flowers. Up in Hora at Plateia Agia Lesvias, there's **Kafe 1673,** locally known as **Astivi,** where you can dance to whatever the DJ spins. In Skala, a sturdy standby— never fully "in" and never fully "out"—that survives each year's fads is **Consolato Music Club,** to the left of the quay. Skala also has the **Kahlua Club,** at the far end of the new port; and **Sui Generis,** behind the police station. Others recommended by visitors are **Pyrgos Bar, Kafe Aman, Café Arion, Isalos,** and **Celine.** On a more traditional note, **Aloni Restaurant,** in Hora, offers Greek music and dance performances in traditional costume a few nights each week in summer. Most clubs charge a modest admission and tend to stay open into the early hours of the morning. And for those who do come for a more "ecclesiastical" experience, Patmost hosts an annual **Festival of Religious Music** in early September, featuring music from the Balkans, Russia, and Turkey as well as Greece.

Exploring the Island

Apart from the seductive contours of the Patmian landscape, the myriad seascapes, and the seemingly countless churches, the **beaches** of Patmos draw most visitors beyond the island's core. Don't be tempted to think of the strand between the old and new ports in Skala as a beach. It's better and safer to take a shower in your bathroom. Most beaches have tavernas on or near them, as well as rooms to rent by the day or week. They're too numerous and similar to list here.

THE NORTH ISLAND

The nicest beaches in the north lie along the northeastern coastline from Lambi Bay to Meloï Bay. The northwestern coastline from Merika Bay to Lambi is too rocky, inaccessible, and exposed. The most desirable northern beaches are in the following bays (proceeding up the coast from south to north): **Meloï, Agriolivada,** and **Lambi.** Meloï has some shade and good snorkeling. **Kambos Bay** is particularly suitable for children and families, offering calm, shallow waters, rental umbrellas, and some tree cover, as well as a lively seaside scene with opportunities for windsurfing, paragliding, sailing, and canoeing. East of Kambos Bay, at Livada, it's possible to swim or sometimes to walk across to **Ayiou Yioryiou Isle;** be sure to bring shoes or sandals, or the rocks will do a number on your feet. The stretch of shoreline from **Thermia to Lambi** is gorgeous, with crystalline waters and rocks from which you can safely dive. The drawback here is that access is only by caique from Skala. Also, avoid the north coast when the *meltemi* (severe north summer winds) are blowing.

Where to Stay & Eat

Aspri GREEK   Poised on a north island headland just minutes by taxi from Skala, this dramatically situated restaurant enjoys splendid views of Meloï Bay, Aspris Bay, and Skala and Hora from its multiple terraces. In addition to the standard taverna fare offered throughout the islands, which Aspris prepares with great skill, the menu has unusual, enticing items such as cuttlefish with Patmian rice. The portions are generous and attention is paid to presentation in this quite stylish and widely recommended spot.

Geranos Cape. ✆ **22470/32-240.** Main courses 8€–22€. MC, V. June–Sept daily 7pm–midnight.

Patmos Paradise   Perched high above Kambos Bay, this is one of several upscale hotels on the island. The rooms are spacious and inviting, with private balconies that enjoy spectacular sea vistas (although in some cases broken by a power line)—room rates depend on the nature of your view. This unpretentious place is exceptionally pleasant and quite chic. Down below, Kambos Bay has a modest strand, a handful of shops and tavernas, and rental outlets for windsurfing boards, paddleboats, and canoes. A hotel minibus transports you to and from Skala Harbor when you arrive at or depart from Patmos. Highly recommended if you want to stay close to Skala.

Kambos Bay, 85500 Patmos. www.patmosparadise.com. © **22470/32-624.** 37 units. 110€–220€ double; 190€–375€ suite. Rates include buffet breakfast. MC, V. Parking on adjacent streets. Closed Nov–Easter. **Amenities:** Restaurant; 2 bars; large saltwater terrace pool; room service; sauna; indoor squash court; tennis court; Wi-Fi. *In room:* A/C, TV, fridge, hair dryer.

Taverna Leonida ★ GREEK   At least one Patmian in the know claims "the best *saganaki* in the world" is served here. A taxi driver went further, calling this the "number-one taverna," as he dropped off his passengers on Leonida's pebble beach. The restaurant enjoys a dramatic location; at high tide, it's just a few yards from the clear water of Lambi Bay. If the wind is high, the waves come pounding in. The drama continues with the arrival of your flaming *saganaki*. Your next course should be the fresh catch of the day. But you can also order a steak, and there is a good selection of the standard Greek dishes.

Lambi Bay. © **22470/31-490.** Main courses 8€–18€. No credit cards. Easter–Oct daily noon–11pm.

Taverna Panagos & Sarandin GREEK   Eating here is an experience that goes beyond merely consuming food. Just above Kambos Bay sits the sleepy village of Kambos, and squarely on its pulse, directly across from the village church, sits the cafe-estiatorion-taverna Panagos. In this local hangout for everyone from children to cats to timeless, bent figures in black, the sea vistas are replaced by myriad glimpses into Patmian village life. The food is the same fare villagers eat at home, and the origins of the succulent daily specials are visible on the nearby hillsides: capons in wine, kid in tomato sauce, lamb in lemon sauce, Patmian goat cheese.

Kambos. © **22470/31-570.** Main courses 7€–30€. No credit cards. Daily noon–midnight.

THE SOUTH ISLAND

The island's south end has two beaches, one at **Grikou Bay** and the other at **Psili Ammos.** Grikou Bay, only 4km (2½ miles) from Skala, is the most developed locale on Patmos and home to most of the package-tour groups on the island. Psili Ammos is another story, an extraordinary isolated fine-sand cove bordered by cliffs. Most people arrive by one of the caiques leaving Skala Harbor at 10am, and, on arrival (at 10:45am), do battle for the very limited shade offered by some obliging tamarisks. The only way to ensure yourself of a place in the shade is to arrive before 10:30am; the best way to do that is to take a taxi to Diakofti for about 25€ and ask the driver to point the way to Psili Ammos, which is about a 30-minute trek on goat paths (wear real shoes). The caiques returning to Skala leave Psili Ammos around 4 to 5pm. At any given time, a range of caiques provide this service. Round-trip fare is about 30€, 20€ one-way.

Another reason to head south is to eat at Benetos (see below), only a short taxi ride from Skala and known as the finest restaurant on the island.

Where to Stay & Eat

Benetos Restaurant ★ MEDITERRANEAN   For fashionable, unpretentious, fine dining on Patmos, this Tuscan villa at the sea's edge is the place. Where else could you find light jazz filling the air, a fresh arugula salad with shaved Parmesan, shrimp baked in phyllo, and filet mignon, all accompanied by an exclusively Greek wine list? Nowhere but Benetos, where the owners, Benetos and his American wife, Susan Matthaiou, have made it their goal to give Greeks and their visitors "a night out" from what they will find elsewhere on these islands. Their winning recipe begins with the freshest and finest local ingredients, mostly from their own organic garden and from nearby waters. The regular menu strikes primarily Greek notes with its appetizers, and the occasional Asian note with its entrees; daily specials reflect the best fresh materials available. With only 12 tables available, you must reserve yours several days in advance during high season.

Sapsila. ✆ **22470/33-089.** Reservations necessary in high season. Main courses 9€–26€. No credit cards. June–Sept Tues–Sun 7:30pm–1am.

Joanna Hotel-Apartments   These comfortable, relatively spacious, and fully equipped apartments are just a few minutes on foot from the beach. Each has a balcony. Rooms with air-conditioning cost extra. The layout and feel of the one-bedroom apartments is better than that of the two-bedroom apartments, which have very limited kitchen space. Room no. 15 has a large private deck with a sea view, but it is usually reserved for friends, clients, and guests staying 2 to 3 weeks—still, there's no harm in asking. A special feature is the attractive air-conditioned lounge with satellite TV and bar.

Grikos, 85500 Patmos. ✆ **22470/31-031.** Fax 22470/32-031, or 210/981-2246 in Athens. 17 units. 65€–85€ double. Full hot breakfast 8€ extra. V. Parking on adjacent streets. Closed mid-Oct to Easter. **Amenities:** Bar. *In room:* A/C (5€ per day), fan, kitchenette.

Petra Hotel and Apartments ★★   Petra Hotel, true to its name, has long been a rock-solid sure thing, and with a series of major renovations since 2002, it has bolstered its position as one of the finest boutique hotels in Greece. The Stergiou family lavishes care on their stylish, spacious apartments. These one- and two-bedroom apartments come with handsome bathrooms. All except one unit have balconies that enjoy splendid views of Grikos Bay. It's a perfect family place, just a 2-minute walk from the beach. It's also ideal for couples, who can enjoy a drink on Petra's elegant, romantic main veranda. The Stergious provide an intimate dining experience as well, with a menu that includes both Greek standards and gourmet offerings. Advance reservations are advised, especially in August. And now they offer an elegant villa in Horio itself—it requires a short walk from your car and it is not cheap (975€–1,570€ per night) but it has four bedrooms (each with bathroom) so that four couples would find it quite reasonable for such a splendid locale.

Grikos, 85500 Patmos. www.petrahotel-patmos.com. ✆ **22470/34-020.** Off-season ✆/fax 210/806-2697 in Athens. 13 units. 175€–275€ double; 265€–580€ suite. Rates include breakfast. AE, MC, V. Parking on-site. Closed Oct–May. **Amenities:** Restaurant; bar; room service; smoke-free rooms; Wi-Fi. *In room:* A/C, TV, hair dryer, Internet, kitchenette.

Stamatis Restaurant GREEK   Stamatis, serving consistently reliable taverna fare since 1965, is a landmark in Grikou. On its covered terrace, which is practically at water's edge, diners enjoy drinks and consume prodigious amounts of fresh mullet, while watching yachts and windsurfers. This is a pleasant spot to unwind for the evening, while you savor delicious island dishes.

Grikos beach. ✆ **22470/31-302.** Main courses 6€–18€. No credit cards. Easter–Oct daily 10am–11pm.

THE NORTHEASTERN AEGEAN ISLANDS

by John S. Bowman

Looking for a new or different experience with Greek islands, one that gives a sense that this is how Greeks live? The three covered in this chapter—Samos, Hios (Chios), and Lesvos (Mitilini)—might be the destination for you. Far removed from the Greek mainland and dispersed along the coast of Turkey, these islands are still relatively untouched by tourism. Vacationers here tend to be concentrated in a few resorts, leaving the interiors and much of the coast open to exploration. Along their coasts, you'll find some of the finest beaches in the Aegean, and within the interiors richly forested valleys, precipitous mountain slopes, and exquisite mountain villages. These agricultural islands produce olives, grapes, and honey in abundance, providing the basis for excellent local cuisine.

The influence of Asia Minor is not as evident as you might expect, given the proximity of the Turkish coast. What you may notice is the sizable Greek military presence—certain areas of each island are occupied by the military and are strictly off limits, which shouldn't bother you unless you're hiking or biking in the area. Travel between Greece and Turkey is unrestricted, and relations between the two countries on a personal level seem amicable. Many travelers use the Northeastern Aegean islands as jumping-off points for Turkey; in particular, Samos (only 3km/2 miles away at the closest point) offers easy access to **Ephesus.**

Strategies for Seeing the Islands

Because the distances between islands are substantial, island-hopping by boat can be costly and time-consuming. Add to that the fact that each island is quite large, and it becomes clear that you're best off choosing one or two islands to explore in depth rather than attempting a grand tour. Both **Olympic Air** and **Aegean Airlines** offer some interisland flights that are relatively inexpensive, frequent, and fast. If you travel by ferry, you'll find that departure times are more reasonable for travel from north to south, whereas traveling in the opposite direction usually involves departures in the middle of the night. Fly to Lesvos (Mitilini) if you insist on seeing all three. The islands are too large and the roads often too rough

If you visit these islands during the summer, check to see when sites and museums are open before setting out.	The officially posted hours are not always maintained and most are closed 1 day a week.

for mopeds to be a safe option; because the bus routes and schedules are highly restricting, you'll find that if you want to get around it's necessary to rent a car.

SAMOS

322km (174 nautical miles) NE of Piraeus

The most mountainous and densely forested of the Northeastern Aegean isles, Samos appears wild and mysterious as you approach its north coast by ferry. The hills plunging to the sea are jagged with cypresses, and craggy peaks hide among the clouds. Samos experienced a series of wildfires during the summer of 2000, which briefly brought the island to the attention of the international press, but effects of that event have faded.

In recent years, Samos has played host to that highly impersonal form of mass tourism involving "package" groups from Europe. This is mostly confined to the eastern coastal resorts—Vathi, Pithagorio, and Kokkari—all of which have developed a generic waterfront of hotels, cafes, and souvenir shops. The rugged splendor of the island's interior continues to hide the most interesting and beautiful villages. Difficult terrain and a remote location made these villages an apt refuge from pirates in medieval times; the same qualities spare them now from tourism's worst excesses.

Although Samos has several fine archaeological sites, the island is most noted for its excellent beaches and abundant opportunities for hiking, cycling, and windsurfing. Those who remember nothing from studying geometry except the Pythagorean Theorem may be pleased to know that Pythagoas was born on Samos, about 580 B.C. Also, Samos is the best crossover point for those who want to visit **Ephesus ★★,** one of the most important archaeological sites in Asia Minor.

Getting There

Although ferries connect Piraeus to Samos, the trip is long. The best way to get here is to fly.

BY PLANE   Both **Olympic Air** (✆ **210/966-6666;** www.olympicair.com) and **Aegean Airlines** (✆ **801/112-0000;** www.aegeanair.com) offer several flights daily between Athens and Samos. **Athens Airways** (www.athensairways.com) has also been listing some flights to Samos. The Samos airport is 3km (2 miles) from Pithagorio, on the road to Ireon; from the airport, you can take a taxi to Vathi (30€) or Pithagorio (20€).

BY BOAT   The principal port of Samos is **Vathi,** also called Samos; the other two ports are **Karlovasi** and **Pithagorio.** Ferries from the Cyclades usually stop at both Vathi and Karlovasi: Take care not to get off at the wrong port! There are daily boats (sometimes two) from Piraeus to Karlovasi (11–14 hr.) and Vathi (8–14 hr.); in the opposite direction, ferries travel daily or nearly daily from Samos to Mykonos (5½ hr.). Boats to Hios from Vathi via Karlovasi (5 hr.) travel three times per week; there is also

The Northeastern Aegean Islands

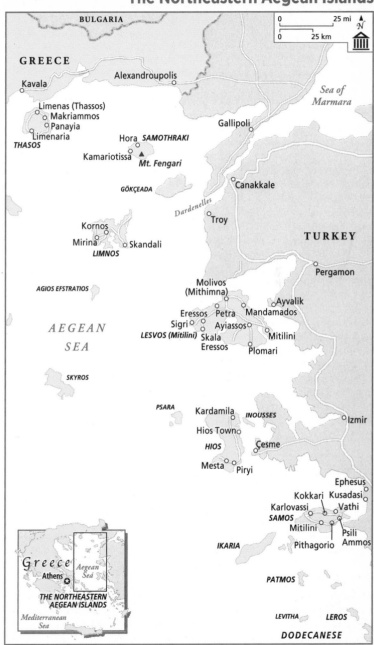

BULGARIA

0 25 mi
0 25 km

N

GREECE

Kavala

Alexandroupolis

Sea of
Marmara

Limenas (Thassos)
Makriammos
Panayia
Limenaria
THASSOS

Hora SAMOTHRAKI

Gallipoli

Kamariotissa ▲ Mt. Fengari

GÖKÇEADA

Canakkale

Dardenelles

Kornos

Troy

TURKEY

Mirina
Skandali
LIMNOS

Pergamon

AGIOS EFSTRATIOS

Molivos
(Mithimna)

10

Eressos
Petra
Ayvalik
Mandamados

AEGEAN
SEA

Sigri
Ayiassos
LESVOS (Mitilini)
Skala
Eressos
Plomari

Mitilini

SKYROS

THE NORTHEASTERN AEGEAN ISLANDS

PSARA

Kardamila
INOUSSES
Izmir

Hios Town

HIOS
Çesme

Mesta
Piryi

Ephesus

Kokkari Kusadasi
Karlovassi
Vathi
SAMOS
Mitilini
Psili
Ammos
IKARIA
Pithagorio

Samos

Greece
Aegean
Sea

Athens

THE NORTHEASTERN
AEGEAN ISLANDS

Mediterranean
Sea

PATMOS

LEVITHA
LEROS

DODECANESE

379

a once-weekly Rhodes-Vathi-Lesvos-Alexandroupoli run. Boats (mostly hydrofoils) to the Dodecanese islands depart regularly from Vathi and Pithagorio. If you want to travel one-way to Turkey, Turkish ferries depart daily (Apr–Oct; less regular off-season); a visa is required for all American, Canadian, British, and Irish citizens who intend to stay for more than 1 day. Be sure to inquire in advance about current visa regulations with a local travel agency. For more information on visas, see "A Side Trip to Turkey: Kusadasi & Ephesus," below.

Vathi, Karlovasi & the Northern Coast

Vathi (aka Samos town), on the northeast coast, and Karlovasi, to the northwest, are the two principal ports of Samos and the island's largest towns. Neither is particularly exciting, and we recommend both as convenient bases rather than as destinations in themselves.

Vathi becomes a slightly overextended resort town in high season but is beautifully situated in a fine natural harbor. An extensive development project in Pithagora Square and along the *paralia* (beachfront road) allows visitors to walk on a widened pedestrian pathway along the water and take in open-air concerts at the large bandstand. The old town, **Ano Vathi,** rises to the hilltops in steep, narrow streets that hide a few small tavernas and cafes.

Karlovasi is even less interesting as a town. Although it's adjacent to several of the best beaches on the island, the town is spread out and offers fewer amenities than Vathi, although nearby is the recently opened, luxurious **Marnei Mare ★★** "retreat" (www.marneimare.gr)—three villas set in a natural and secluded estate. Most tourist facilities are clustered along the water at the west end of town, forming a tiny beach resort with several hotels, restaurants, grocery stores, and souvenir shops. The old town hovers above the lower town on the slopes of a near-vertical pillar of rock; the lovely small chapel of **Ayia Triada** is at the rock's summit.

The **north coast** of the island is wild and steep, with mountains rising abruptly from the water's edge. One of the most interesting areas to explore is the **Platanakia** region, known for its rushing streams, lush valleys, and picturesque mountain villages. A sequence of excellent **beaches** between Kokkari and Karlovasi includes the two finest beaches on the island, **Micro Seitani** and **Megalo Seitani;** you can reach them via a short boat ride or a somewhat long hike to the west of Karlovasi.

ESSENTIALS

VISITOR INFORMATION   There is an official **tourist office** at 107 Themistioklis Sofouli (✆ **22730/28-582**), but it is easier to go directly to private travel agencies for information. Try one of the major travel agencies in Samos: **Rhenia Tours,** 15 Themistoklis Sofouli (✆ **22730/88-800;** www.diavlos.gr/rhenia); and **Samina Tours,** 67 Themistoklis Sofouli (✆ **22730/87-000;** www.samina.gr). Here you can make arrangements for accommodations and excursions (including excursions to Turkey, Patmos, and Fourni, as well as tours of Samos), rent cars, and so on. The **Diavlos** website (www.diavlos.gr) has information on ferries, attractions, and accommodations. Another website with useful information is www.samos-travel.com.

GETTING AROUND   By Bus   There's good public bus service on Samos throughout the year, with significantly expanded summer schedules. The **Vathi bus terminal** (✆ **22730/27-262**) is a block inland from the south end of the port on Kanari. The bus makes the 20-minute trip between Vathi and Pithagorio frequently. Buses also travel to Kokkari, the inland village of Mitilini, Pirgos, Marathokambos, Votsalakia beach, and Karlovasi. Schedules are posted in English at the bus terminal.

HOTELS ■
Hotel Paradissos **6**
Pension Avli **3**
Pythagoras Hotel **1**
Samos Hotel **2**

RESTAURANTS ◆
Christos Taverna **4**
Ta Kotopoula **5**

By Boat From Karlovasi, there are daily excursion boats to **Megalo Seitani,** the best fine-sand beach on the island. A once-weekly around-the-island tour aboard the *Samos Star* is a great way to see the island's remarkable coastline, much of it inaccessible by car. The excursion boat departs from Pithagorio at 8:30am (a bus from Vathi departs at 7:30am), currently on Tuesday, and returns to Pithagorio at 5:30pm; the fare is 75€. Book with one of the travel agencies listed above. Most excursions depart from Pithagorio, although many offer bus service from Vathi an hour prior to departure; for descriptions, see "Pithagorio & the Southern Coast," later in this chapter.

By Car & Moped **Autoplan,** 17 Themistoklis Sofouli (© **22730/23-555;** autoplan@internet.gr), and **Aramis Rent a Car,** at the pier in Vathi (© **22730/23-253;** www.samos-rentacar.com), offer good prices and selections. The least expensive car in high season is about 70€, including insurance and 100 free kilometers (62 miles). Mopeds go for 20€ to 30€ per day. But there are other agencies, so shop around.

By Taxi The principal taxi stand in Vathi is on Plateia Pithagora, facing the *paralia*. The fare from Vathi to Pithagorio is about 16€. To book by phone, call © **22730/23-777** in Vathi, or 22730/33-300 in Karlovasi.

By Bicycle　For renting a bicycle, go online to www.samos-travel.com, where you will find that InterHermes, in Vathi (☎ **22730/28-833**), and AutoLand, in Kokkari (the beach resort just west of Vathi; ☎ **22730/92-825**), offer this service.

FAST FACTS　The **banks** in Vathi are on the *paralia,* in the vicinity of Plateia Pithagora, and are open Monday through Thursday from 8am to 2pm, Friday from 8am to 1:30pm; most have ATMs. Most travel agents change money, sometimes at bank rates, and they're open later. The island's **hospital** (☎ **22730/83-100**) is in Vathi. **Internet access** has been available at Diavlos Internet Cafe (www.diavlos.gr) on the *paralia,* next to the police station; Diavlos is open daily from 9:30am to 11pm May through October, but mornings only November through April. A **self-service laundry** (☎ **22730/28-833**), behind Aeolis Hotel, on the town's market street, is open daily from 8am to 11pm. The **post office** (☎ **22730/27-304**) is on the same street as the Olympic Air office, 1 block farther in from the *paralia,* and 2 blocks from the bus station. The **telephone office** (**OTE**; ☎ **22730/28-499**) is down the street from the Olympic Air office, in the direction of the archaeological museum. The **tourist police** (☎ **22730/81-000**) are on the *paralia,* by the turn into the bus station.

ATTRACTIONS

Archaeological Museum ★

This fine museum is actually two buildings at the south end of the harbor, near the post office. The newest building houses sculpture—the island's best sculptors traveled all over the Hellenistic world to create their art. The most remarkable work is a massive *kouros* (statue of a boy), which stands 5m (16 ft.) tall. The large and varied collection of bronze votives found at the Heraion is also impressive.

Kapetan Yimnasiarhou Kateveni (near park and behind town hall). ☎ **22730/27-469.** Admission 3€, E.U. seniors 2€. Tues–Sun 8:30am–3pm. No parking.

Moni Vronta

The 15th-century fortified monastery of Moni Vronta is on a high mountain overlooking the sea and the lovely hilltop village of Vourliotes. Few if any monks live there these days, but a caretaker is usually about; if the gate is locked when you arrive, try knocking—one of the soldiers from a nearby surveillance post may be around to let you in. Ask to see the *spileo* (cave), an old chapel, built into the thickness of the outer wall, that holds a collection of ancient objects, some from the time of the monastery's founding.

Vourliotes. No phone. Free admission. Daily 8am–5pm. 23km (15 miles) west of Vathi; continue driving uphill about 2km (1¼ miles) past the village of Vourliotes (see below).

THREE HILL TOWNS ON THE NORTH COAST

Amid the densely wooded valleys, cascading streams, and terraced slopes of Samos's Platanakia region, hide many villages that sought to evade the pirates, who repeatedly ravaged all settlements visible from the sea. Three of the most picturesque of the surviving hill villages in this region are Manolates, Vourliotes, and Stavrinides.

Manolates is a 4km (2½-mile) drive uphill from the coast road. The village, until recently, was inaccessible by car, but once the paved road was built, many more visitors have come here to explore the steep, narrow cobblestone streets. There are several tavernas, numerous shops, and *kafenions* (coffeehouses, where the locals go).

Vourliotes, about 21km (14 miles) west of Vathi, was settled largely by repatriated Greeks from the town of Vourla, in Turkey. It's the largest producer of wine in the region, and the local wine is among the best on the island. Walk from the parking lot at the Moni Vronta turnoff to the charming central square. Try **Manolis Taverna,** on the left as you enter the square (☎ **22730/93-290**), which has good *revidokeftedes,* a

A Side Trip to Turkey: Kusadasi & Ephesus

In high season, two boats a day make the run between Vathi and Kusadasi, Turkey, itself a popular, well-developed resort, but of interest here as the gateway to the magnificent archaeological site at Ephesus ★★. Although located in Turkey, Ephesus was a Greek city, famous, among other things, for its Temple of Artemis, one of the Seven Wonders of the Ancient World. A major commercial city in the eastern Mediterranean, it fell to the Romans, and it was under their rule that an important Christian community and church were established here. Excursion boats depart from Vathi, and on certain days, an excursion also departs from Pithagorio. A round-trip ticket to Kusadasi that includes boat fare, port fees, and guided tour with entrance fee costs about 100€. If you're not returning the same day, you'll need to investigate visa requirements. These are granted without difficulty at time of sailing and cost about $20 for Americans, C$50 for Canadians, £15 for U.K. citizens, 10€ for Irish citizens, and A$25 for Australians; New Zealanders don't need a visa. The travel agencies listed above will help you with arrangements.

---

delicious local dish made with chickpea flour and cheese. Also on the square, across from Manolis, is a small market whose displays seem not to have changed in the past 50 years. Be sure to visit the monastery of **Moni Vronta** (aka Vrontiani), 2km (1¼ miles) above the town (see "Attractions," above).

Stavrinides, perched on the mountainside high above Ayios Konstandinos, is the least touristic of the Platanakia villages. Here the tavernas and the few shops cater primarily to the villagers. **Taverna Irida,** in the first square of the village, offers good, simple food. A walking path between Stavrinides and Manolates makes an exceptional outing; the route out from Stavrinides is signposted.

The easiest way to visit these towns is by car. The island buses are an option, if you don't mind the steep 4- to 6km (2½–3¾-mile) walk from the coastal road to the villages. An abundance of footpaths connect these villages—ask locally for routes. **Ambelos Tours,** in Ayios Konstandinos (☎ **22730/94-442;** folas@otenet.gr), operated by the friendly and knowledgeable Manolis Folas, is a useful resource.

BEACHES

The closest decent beach to Vathi is **Gagou,** 2km (1¼ miles) north of the pier. But the best beaches on Samos are found along the north coast, the most beautiful and rugged part of the island. The busy seaside resort of **Kokkari,** 10km (6 miles) west of Vathi, has several beaches in rock coves as well as the crowded stretch of sand running parallel to the town's main road. To find the smaller cove beaches, head seaward from the main square. Just west of Kokkari is **Tsamadou,** a short walk down from the coast road, which offers sufficient seclusion for nude sunbathing. Continue west past Karlovasi to find **Potami,** an excellent long pebble-and-sand beach with road access.

The two best beaches on the island, **Micro Seitani ★** and **Megalo Seitani ★**, are accessible only by boat or on foot. Boat excursions depart daily from the pier in Karlovasi. To get here on foot, continue past the parking lot, on a dirt road, for the beach at Potami; walking time to the first beach is 45 minutes. After about 5 minutes of uphill walking, the road splits—turn right, continuing to follow the coast. After another 5 minutes of walking, three obvious paths turn off to the right in close succession. Take the third, marked by a cairn, and follow the well-worn path another half-hour to Micro Seitani, a glorious pebble-and-cobble beach in a rocky cove. On the beach's far side, a ladder scales the cliff to the trail, which will take you, after an additional 30 minutes of walking, to Megalo Seitani, as incredible a stretch of sea sand as any in the Aegean. At the far end of Megalo Seitani are a few houses and a taverna.

OUTDOOR PURSUITS

BICYCLING   Samos has many dirt roads and trails perfect for mountain biking. The only obstacles are the size of the island, which limits the number of routes available for day trips, and the fact that much of the backcountry is off limits due to Greek military operations. Bike rentals, information about trails, and guided mountain-bike tours are available in Vathi, at **Bike** (© 22730/24-404). The shop is open daily from 8:30am to 2pm and 5 to 9pm; it's behind the old church, opposite the port, on the market street. The bikes are high quality, and the rental includes helmet, pump, and repair kit; clipless pedals and shoes are also available for an extra charge. A basic aluminum-frame bike is 25€ per day; a full-suspension bike is 35€.

WALKING   Some of the best walking on the island is in and around the Platanakia region of Samos's north coast, where well-marked trails connect several lovely hilltop villages. Manolates and Vourliotes (see above) are among the villages on this network of trails. A trail goes from Manolates to the summit of Mount Ambelos, the second-highest peak on Samos at 1,153m (3,780 ft.); the demanding round-trip takes about 5 hours. Those seeking a more "professional" exploration of the truly natural Samos might try one of the outfits listed under "Tours," in chapter 2.

WHERE TO STAY
Vathi

Hotel Paradissos   Despite a central location just off the *paralia* and a block away from the bus station, the walled garden and pool terrace here seem a world away from the traffic and dust of Vathi. Drinks and simple Greek foods are available all day at the poolside bar. The pool invites lingering, with lounge chairs and umbrellas for sunning, and shaded tables for meals or drinks. All guest rooms have balconies, although the views aren't great. Bathrooms are small, but they do have full tubs. Note that although there is air-conditioning in every room, it isn't turned on until sometime in July (unlike the majority of hotels, which will turn on the air-conditioning in June, if it's needed—and it usually is).

21 Kanari, Vathi, 83100 Samos. © **22730/23-911.** Fax 22730/28-754. 51 units. 95€ double. Rates include continental breakfast. MC, V. Closed Nov–Mar. **Amenities:** Restaurant; bar; pool; room service. *In room:* A/C, TV, hair dryer, minibar.

Pension Avli 🖋   Although you won't find any luxuries here, you may enjoy the most charming and romantic pension on the island. Abundant bougainvillea fills the arcaded courtyard of this former 18th-century convent. Most rooms have been renovated within the last few years, but there is no denying they are spartan, with minimal furnishings. Each tiny bathroom is encased entirely in a plastic shell, making a shower a surreal experience. This is definitely a place for those with big imaginations and small budgets.

2 Areos, Vathi, 83100 Samos. © **22730/22-939.** 20 units. 50€ double. No credit cards. Turn in from the *paralia* at Agrotiki Trapeza (down from Aeolis Hotel), turn left on town's market street, and you'll see the Avli's unassuming sign directly ahead. *In room:* No phone.

Pythagoras Hotel   This plain but comfortable family hotel, on a hill overlooking Vathi Bay, offers the best views in town from its nine seaside units and from the restaurant terrace. Guest rooms facing the road can be noisy—book ahead to ensure a unit on the water. Guest rooms and bathrooms are small, clean, and minimally furnished. The neighborhood cafe/restaurant downstairs serves a good, inexpensive breakfast, light meals, and snacks from early morning to midnight. Hotel staff will meet you at the port or airport at any time, a generous offer given the frequency of early-morning ferry arrivals.

12 Kallistratou, Kalami, Vathi, 83100 Samos. On the coast road, 600m (1,968 ft.) north of the pier. www. pythagorashotel.com. © **22730/28-422.** Fax 22730/28-893. 19 units. From 50€ double. MC, V. **Amenities:** Restaurant; bar. *In room:* TV, Internet.

Samos Hotel For travelers who simply want a modern hotel on the harbor with most amenities, this is *the* place in Vathi. Located right along the *paralia*, the hotel is subject to a certain amount of harbor noise. But the hotel is air-conditioned, making it somewhat insulated. Rooms are nothing special in size or decor, but beds and bathrooms are comfortable; most have balconies overlooking the harbor. Only about a 20-minute walk from Gagou Beach, this hotel is not for those seeking atmosphere.

11 Themistoklis Sofouli, 83100 Vathi. www.hotelsamos.gr. © **22730/28-377.** Fax 22730/23-771. 100 units. High season 90€ double; low season 70€ double. Rates include continental breakfast. MC, V. Parking by hotel. **Amenities:** 2 restaurants; 2 bars; Jacuzzi; pool; room service. *In room:* A/C, TV, fridge, hair dryer.

Ayios Konstandinos

This coastal town in the heart of the Platanakia region is a great base for touring the north coast of Samos. Ask Manolis Folas, of **Ambelos Tours** (© **22730/94-442;** folas@otenet.gr), about traditional houses for rent; each unit sleeps three and costs about 50€ per night.

Daphne Hotel ★ The Daphne is the finest small hotel on the island. Artfully incised into the steep hillside in a series of terraces, the hotel commands a fine view of the stream valley leading to Manolates and a wide sweep of sea. All rooms are moderate in size and have balconies with the same great view; bathrooms have both shower and tub. This is a good location for walkers, with many trails nearby to Manolates and other hill towns. This hotel is filled through much of the summer by European tour groups. There is free transportation to and from the airport or the port; due to the somewhat remote location, you'll probably want a car during your stay here.

Ayios Konstandinos, 83200 Samos. www.daphne-hotel.gr. © **22730/94138.** 35 units. 80€ double. Rates include breakfast. V. Closed Nov–Apr. Take the 1st right after turning onto the Manolates rd., 19km (12 miles) from Vathi. **Amenities:** Restaurant; pool w/bar; TV lounge. *In room:* A/C.

WHERE TO EAT
Vathi

The food along the *paralia* in Vathi is mostly tourist quality and mediocre; you'll find the best restaurants in the small towns away from the harbor. The local wines on Samos have long been known for their excellence. (As Byron exclaimed, "Fill high the bowl with Samian wine!") Samaina is a good, dry white; Selana, a relatively dry rosé. The Greeks here also like sweet wines, with names such as Nectar, Doux, and Anthemis. Almost any restaurant on the island will serve one or all of these choices.

Christos Taverna GREEK This simple little taverna, under a covered alleyway decorated with odd antiques, is to the left off Plateia Pithagora, as you come up from the port. The food is simply prepared and presented; it comes in generous portions and is remarkably good. Try the *revidokeftedes*, a Samian specialty that is made with cheese fried in chickpea batter.

Plateia Ayiou Nikolaou. ☎ **22730/24-792.** Main courses 7€–16€. No credit cards. Daily 11am–11pm. Parking on streets around a square.

Ta Kotopoula GREEK   Ta Kotopoula is located on the outskirts of Vathi, somewhat hard to find but worth the trouble. From the harbor's south end, walk inland past the Olympic Air office and the post office, bearing right with the road as it climbs toward Ano Vathi. Where the road splits around a large tree, about 700m (2,296 ft.) from the harbor, you'll see the vine-sheltered terrace of this taverna on the left. The food is basic Greek fare, but the ingredients are exceptionally fresh—chicken being the specialty, as the name suggests. Local wine is available by the carafe.

Vathi. ☎ **22730/28-415.** Main courses 7€–17€. No credit cards. Daily 11am–11pm. Parking near restaurant.

Ayios Konstandinos

Platanakia Paradisos GREEK   Paradisos is a large garden taverna located at the Manolates turnoff from the coast highway; it has been in the Folas family for nearly 30 years and has been operating as a taverna for more than 100. Manolis Folas, the owner, makes his own wine from the excellent Samian grapes. Mrs. Folas's *tiropita* is made from local goat cheese wrapped in a flaky pastry. Live traditional music is performed Wednesday and Saturday nights in summer.

Ayios Konstandinos. ☎ **22730/94-208.** Main courses 6€–17€. No credit cards. Daily 3–11pm. Parking near restaurant.

VATHI AFTER DARK

"In" places change from year to year, but one of the hottest discos in Vathi has been **Metropolis,** behind the Paradise Hotel. For bouzoukia, there's **Zorba's,** out of town on the road to Mitilini. Various kinds of bars line the lanes just off the port. **Number Nine,** at 9 Kephalopoulou, beyond the jetty on the right, is one of the oldest and best known. For more sedate setting and music, try **Nefeli** bar/cafe along the harbor.

Pithagorio & the Southern Coast

Pithagorio, south across the island from Vathi, is a charming but overcrowded seaside resort built on the site of an ancient village and harbor. Although this is a convenient base for touring the southern half of Samos, the town exists primarily for the tour groups that pack its streets in the summer. We recommend staying only for a day or two to explore the nearby historic sites, then moving on to the more interesting and authentic villages of the north coast.

ESSENTIALS

GETTING THERE   By Plane   The Samos airport is 3km (2 miles) from Pithagorio; from the airport, you can take a taxi into town for 20€.

By Boat   Ferries from the Cyclades typically don't stop at Pithagorio, so you'll need to take a taxi or bus from Vathi. Near-daily hydrofoil service links Pithagorio and Patmos (60–90 min.), Lipsi (1½–3 hr.), Leros (1½–3 hr.), Kalymnos (3–6 hr.), and Kos (3–4 hr.); there are also excursion boats to Patmos four times weekly. Check the most current ferry schedules at the **Pithagorio Municipal Tourist Office** (☎ **22730/61-389** or 22730/61-022; www.gtp.gr), or at **Pithagorio Port Authority** (☎ **22730/61-225**).

By Bus   Buses depart frequently for the 20-minute trip between Vathi and Pithagorio. Contact the **Vathi bus terminal** (☎ **22730/27-262**) for current schedules.

VISITOR INFORMATION   The **Pithagorio Municipal Tourist Office** (☎ **22730/61-389** or 22730/61-022) is on the main street, Likourgou Logotheti, 1 block up from the *paralia;* its hours are daily from 8am to 10pm. Here you can get information on ferries, buses, island excursions, accommodations, car rental, and just about anything else. Pick up the handy *Map of Pithagorion,* which lists accommodations, attractions, and other helpful information.

GETTING AROUND   By Bus   The Pithagorio **bus terminal** is in the center of town, at the corner of Polykrates (the road to Vathi) and Likourgou Logotheti. The bus makes the 20-minute trip between Vathi and Pithagorio frequently. There are also four buses daily from Pithagorio to Ireon (near the Heraion archaeological site).

By Boat   Summertime **excursion boats** from the Pithagorio harbor go to **Psili Ammos beach** (on the east end of the island) daily, and to the island of **Ikaria** three times weekly. A popular day cruise goes to **Samiopoula,** a small island with a single taverna and a long sandy beach. Boats leave daily at 9:15am and return to Pithagorio at 5pm; the fare of 35€ includes lunch. Four times each week, the *Samos Star* sails to **Patmos,** departing from Pithagorio at 8am and returning the same day at 4pm; travel time to Patmos is 2 hours, and the fare is 50€. A Sunday excursion to the tiny isle of **Fourni,** also aboard the *Samos Star,* gives you 6 hours to check out the beaches and sample the island's renowned fish tavernas; the boat leaves Pithagorio at 8:30am and costs 35€ per person. A once-weekly **around-the-island tour** aboard the *Samos Star* offers a great way to see this island's remarkable coastline, much of it inaccessible by road. The excursion boat departs from Pithagorio at 8:30am (a bus from Vathi departs at 7:30am) on Tuesday and returns to Pithagorio at 5:30pm; the fare is 60€.

By Car & Moped   **Aramis Rent a Car** has a branch near the bus station in Pithagorio (*©* **22730/62-267;** www.samos-rentacar.com). It often has the best prices, but shop around.

By Taxi   The taxi stand is on the main street, Likourgou Logotheti, where it meets the harbor. The fare from Vathi to Pithagorio is 25€. To book by phone, call *©* **22730/61-450.**

FAST FACTS   National Bank, opposite the bus stop (*©* **22730/61-234**), has an ATM. A small **clinic** on Plateia Irinis, next to the town hall (*©* **22730/61-111**), is located 1 block in from the beach, near the port police. Access the Internet at **Nefeli** (*©* **22730/61-719**), a cafe on the *paralia*'s north side (left, if you're facing the harbor), open from 11am to 2am daily. The rate is 5€ per hour for use of one of the two computers. A self-service **laundry,** Metamorphosis Sotiros, is off the main street, on the road to the old basilica; it is open daily from 9am to 9pm, in summer until 11pm. The **post office** is several blocks up from the *paralia,* on the main street, past the bus stop. The **telephone office (OTE)** is on the *paralia,* near the pier (*©* **22730/61-399**). The **police** (*©* **22730/61-100**) are a short distance up Polikrates, the main road to Vathi.

ATTRACTIONS

Efpalinion Tunnel ★★   One of the most impressive engineering accomplishments of the ancient world, this 1,000m (3,280-ft.) tunnel through the mountain above Pithagorio was excavated to transport water from mountain streams to ancient Vathi. The great architect Efpalinos directed two teams of workers digging from each side, and after nearly 15 years they met within a few meters of each other. You descend into the tunnel, and then if you can muster the courage to squeeze through the first 20m (66 ft.)—the tunnel is a mere sliver in the rock for this distance—you'll see that it soon widens considerably, and you can comfortably walk another 100m

(328 ft.) into the mountain. Even though a generator supposedly starts up in the event of a power outage, you might be more comfortable carrying a flashlight.

Pithagorio. ☎ **22730/61-400.** Admission 4€ adults, 1.50€ students and E.U. seniors, free for youths 17 and under. Tues–Sun 8:45am–2:45pm. 3km (2 miles) northwest of Pithagorio; signposted off the main road to Vathi.

Heraion   All that survives of the largest of all Greek temples is its massive foundation, a lone reconstructed column, and some copies of the original statuary. A forest of columns once surrounded this temple; rival Ionian cities were so impressed that they rebuilt many of their ancient temples in similar style. The Temple of Artemis, in nearby Ephesus, is a direct imitation of the great Samian structure. The Heraion was rebuilt and greatly expanded under Polycrates, in the 6th century B.C. It was damaged during numerous invasions and finally destroyed by a series of earthquakes.

Ireon. ☎ **22730/95-277** or 22730/27-469 (the Archaeological Museum, in Vathi). Admission 4€ adults, 1.50€ students and E.U. seniors, free for youths 17 and under. Tues–Sun 8am–2:30pm. 9km (5½ miles) southwest of Pithagorio; signposted off the road to Ireon.

BEACHES

In Pithagorio, the local beach stretches from Logotheti Castle, at the west side of town, several kilometers to Potokaki and the airport. Expect this beach to be packed throughout the summer. Excursion boats depart daily in the summer for **Psili Ammos,** 5km (3 miles) to the east. The daily boats also leave Pithagorio for **Samiopoula,** an island off the south coast with two good beaches.

On the south coast of the island, the most popular beaches are on Marathokambos Bay. The once-tiny village of **Ormos Marathokambos** has several tavernas and a growing number of hotels and pensions. Its rock-and-pebble beach is long and narrow, with windsurfing an option. A couple of kilometers farther west of Ormos Marathokambos is **Votsalakia,** a somewhat nicer beach.

WHERE TO STAY

Rooms in Pithagorio are quickly filled by tour groups, so don't count on finding a place here if you haven't booked well in advance. You can find a long listing of hotels in Pithagprio at www.samos-hotels.com but you are advised to check them out on tripadvisor.com as many of the expensive ones are found wanting.

Georgios Sandalis Hotel 🏄   Above Pithagorio, this homey establishment has a front garden bursting with colorful blossoms. The tastefully decorated rooms all have balconies with French doors. Back rooms face quiet hills and another flower garden, while the front units face a busy street and can be noisy. All rooms have kitchenettes, but only some have air-conditioning (extra charge, if used). No meals are served on the premises, but breakfast can be had at reduced rates at family-owned Enplo Café, which is nearby, on the harbor.

Pithagorio, 83103 Samos. ☎ **22730/61-691.** 12 units. 50€ double. No credit cards. Parking on adjacent streets. Head north on Polykrates (the road to Vathi); hotel is on your left, about 100m (328 ft.) from the bus station. *In room:* A/C (in some), TV, kitchenette.

Hotel Zorbas 🏄   This place is more pension than hotel, but the rooms are comfortable. Seven units have great views of Pithagorio Harbor. The atmosphere is decidedly casual and friendly—the hotel lobby doubles as the Mathios family's living room. The hotel is on a steep hill on the north side of town, a healthy climb from the *paralia,* at the port police station. Rooms facing the sea have spacious balconies, with views over the rooftops to fishing boats docked in the harbor, while streetside rooms are a bit noisier and have no views. Breakfast is served on a terrace facing the sea.

Damos, Pithagorio, 83103 Samos. ✆ **22730/61-009.** Fax 22730/61-012. 12 units. 55€ double. Breakfast extra 6€. No credit cards. Parking on adjacent streets.

WHERE TO EAT

Esperides Tavern INTERNATIONAL   This pleasant restaurant with a walled garden is a few blocks inland from the port, and west of the main street. You'll find uniformed waiters and a dressier crowd here. The Continental and Greek dishes are well presented and will appeal to a wide variety of palates—try the baked chicken with any vegetables in season.

Pithagorio. ✆ **22730/61-767.** Reservations recommended in summer. Main courses 7€–20€. No credit cards. Daily 6pm–midnight. No parking.

Varka ★ GREEK/SEAFOOD   This ouzeri/taverna is in a stand of salt pines at the south end of the port. Delicious fresh fish, grilled meats, and a surprising variety of *mezedes* (appetizers) are produced in the small kitchen. The grilled octopus, strung up on a line to dry, and the pink *barbounia* (clear gray mullet), cooked to perfection over a charcoal grill, are the true standouts of a meal here. The cafe pavilion by the water is a cool, breezy location for a drink or dessert.

Paralia, Pithagorio. ✆ **22730/61-088.** Main courses 7€–20€. MC, V. Daily noon–midnight. Closed Nov-Apr. Parking on adjacent streets.

HIOS (CHIOS)

283km (153 nautical miles) NE of Piraeus

"Craggy Hios," as Homer dubbed it—and he should know, as this is said to be his native home—remains relatively unspoiled, and that's why I continue to recommend it. Those seeking just to relax will find the black-pebble beaches on the southeast coast of the island well attended, but white-sand beaches on the west coast see far fewer people. The majestic mountain setting of **Nea Moni**—an 11th-century Byzantine monastery in the center of the island—and the extraordinary mosaics of its chapel make for an unforgettable visit. The mastic villages on the island's south side are among the most unusual medieval towns in Greece; the towns get their names from tree resin used in chewing gum, paints, and perfumes that grow nowhere else in the world.

The *paralia* of **Hios town** is likely to be your first glimpse of the island, and admittedly, it isn't an especially appealing sight—unappealing modern buildings and generic cafes have taken over what must once have been a fine harbor. Thankfully, a few pockets of the original town farther inland have survived earthquakes, wars, and neglect. The kastro, the mosque on the main square, the mansions of Kampos, and the occasional grand gateway (often leading nowhere) are among the signs of a more prosperous and architecturally harmonious past.

Essentials

GETTING THERE   By Plane   Both **Olympic Air** and **Aegean Airlines** offer several flights daily between Athens and Hios. (See "Getting There" under "Samos," earlier in this chapter for contact information.) Olympic also offers flights once or twice a week from Lesvos (Mitilini) and Thessaloniki. If you arrive by plane, count on taking a cab into town at about 15€ for the 7km (4¼-mile) ride.

By Boat   From Piraeus, there's one daily Hios-bound car ferry (8–9 hr.); there's also a daily connection with Lesvos (3 hr.). Three ferries weekly serve Limnos (9 hr.)

Currently, anyone who is not carrying a driver's license from a country in the European Union must have an international driver's license to rent a car in Greece; but in most places, they will accept valid U.S. and other national licenses. On Hios, however, car-rental agencies and the police tend to be strict about enforcing this. If you expect to rent a car during your stay on Hios, get an international driver's license before leaving your home country—for whatever reason, the police here enforce this regulation. Relatively easy and cheap to obtain, it can be issued through national automobile associations.

and Thessaloniki (16–19 hr.), two ferries weekly to Samos (5 hr.), and one weekly to Siros (5 hr.). Check with **Hios Port Authority** (℃ 22710/44-434; www.gtp.gr) for current schedules.

VISITOR INFORMATION   The **Tourist Information Office,** on 18 Kanari (℃ 22710/44-389), stocks free brochures, including maps; it's located on the second street from the north end of the harbor, between the harbor and the Central (Plastira) Square. In summer, it's open Monday to Friday from 7am to 2:30pm and 6:30 to 9:30pm, Saturday and Sunday from 10am to 1pm; the off-season sees reduced hours. Ask here (or at any travel agency) about free guided tours to some of Hios's major sites, sponsored by the island's government.

Another mine of information is **Chios Tours,** 4 Kokkali (℃ 22710/29-444; www.chiostours.gr). The office is open Monday to Saturday from 8:30am to 1:30pm and 5:30 to 8:30pm. The staff will assist you with a room search, often at a discount.

GETTING AROUND   **By Bus**   All buses depart from one of the two bus stations in Hios town. The **blue buses** (℃ 22710/23-086), which leave from the blue bus station, on the north side of the public garden by Plateia Plastira, serve local destinations such as Karfas, to the south, and Daskalopetra, to the north. The **green long-distance KTEL buses** (℃ 22710/27-507) leave from the green bus station, a block south of the park, near the main taxi stand. Six buses a day depart to Mesta, eight a day to Piryi, five to Kardamila, and four to Emborio, but only two buses a week go to Volissos and Nea Moni. Fares are 2€ to 7€.

By Car   Hios is a large island to explore, so I recommend a car. For advance reservations, try **Pangosmio Rent a Car** (℃ 2810/811-750; www.pangosmio.gr). On the scene, try **Vassilakis Rent-A-Car** at 3 Evangelos Chandrs (℃ 22710/29-300).

By Taxi   Taxis are easily found at the port, though the taxi station is beyond the OTE, on the northeast corner of the central square. You can call ℃ 22710/41-111 or 22710/43-312 for a cab. Fares from Hios town run about 25€ to Piryi, 30€ to Mesta, and 40€ round-trip to Nea Moni.

By Bicycle/Moped   Hios is too large, and the hills too big, for most bicyclists; rent a motorbike, and if you're inexperienced with these, you're better off with a car.

FAST FACTS   **Commercial Bank (Emboriki Trapeza)** and **Ergo Bank** are located at the harbor's north end, near the corner of Kanari. Both have ATMs and are open Monday through Thursday from 8am to 2pm, Friday from 8am to 1:30pm. The **hospital** is 7km (4¼ miles) from the center of Hios town (℃ 22710/44-301). **Internet access** is available daily from 9am to midnight at Enter Internet Cafe, 98

Aegeou (✆ **22710/41-058**), at the *paralia*'s south end; 1 hour online costs 5€. There's a full-service **laundry** around the corner from the post office, on Psichari (✆ **22710/44-801**); one load costs 15€, and the turnaround time is about 24 hours. The **post office** is at the corner of Omirou and Rodokanaki (✆ **22710/44-350**). The **telephone office (OTE)** is across the street from the tourist office, on Kanari (✆ **131**). The **tourist police** are headquartered at the harbor's northernmost tip, at Neorion 35 (✆ **22710/44-427**).

Attractions

Argenti Museum and Koraï Library ★

Philip Argenti was the great historian of Hios, a local aristocrat who devoted his life and savings to the recording of island history, costumes, customs, and architecture. The museum consists largely of his personal collection of folk art, costumes, and implements, supplemented with a gallery of family portraits and copies of Eugene Delacroix's *Massacre of Hios,* a masterpiece depicting the Turkish massacre of the local population in 1822. The library is excellent, with much of its collection in English and French. If you're interested in local architecture and village life, ask to see the collection of drawings by Dimitris Pikionis (a renowned 20th-c. Greek architect). The drawings of the Kampos mansions and village houses are beautiful, and have yet to be published.

Koraï, Hios town. ✆ **22710/44-246.** Museum admission 3€; free admission to library. Mon–Fri 8am–2pm; also 5–7:30pm on Fri; Sat 8am–12:30pm. Parking on adjacent streets.

Nea Moni ★★

The 11th-century monastery of Nea Moni is one of the great architectural and artistic treasures of Greece. The monastery is in a spectacular setting high in the mountains overlooking Hios town. Its grounds are extensive—the monastery was once home to 1,000 monks—but the resident population has dwindled to several elderly nuns. The focus of the rambling complex is the *katholikon,* or principal church, whose square nave has eight niches supporting the dome. Within these niches are sequences of extraordinary mosaics, among the finest examples of Byzantine art. You can see the portrayals of the saints in the narthex, and a representation of Christ washing the disciples' feet. The museum contains a collection of gifts to the monastery, including several fine 17th-century icons. Also of interest is the cistern, a cavernous vaulted room with columns (bring a flashlight); and the small Chapel of the Holy Cross at the entrance to the monastery, dedicated to the martyrs of the 1822 massacre by the Turks (the skulls and bones displayed are those of the victims themselves). The long barrel-vaulted refectory is a beautiful space, its curved apse dating from the 11th century.

The bus to Nea Moni is part of an island excursion operated by KTEL, departing from the Hios town bus station Tuesday and Friday at 9am and returning at 4:30pm. The route takes you from Nea Moni to Anavatos to Lithi beach to Armolia and back to Hios town; it costs 25€ per person. A taxi will cost about 40€ round-trip from Hios town, including a half-hour at the monastery.

Nea Moni, 17km (11 miles) west of Hios town. No phone. Free admission to monastery grounds and katholikon; museum admission 3€ adults, 1€ students and E.U. seniors. Monastery grounds and katholikon daily 8am–1pm and 4–8pm; museum Tues–Sun 8am–1pm.

A Day Trip to the Mastic Villages: Piryi, Mesta & Olimbi ★

The most interesting day trip on Hios is the excursion to the mastic villages in the southern part of the island, which offer some of the best examples of medieval town architecture in all of Greece. Mastic is a gum derived from the resin of the mastic tree, used in candies, paints, perfumes, and medicines. It was a source of great wealth for these towns in the Middle Ages, and it is still produced in small quantities. All the towns were originally fortified, with an outer wall formed by an unbroken line of houses with no doors and few windows facing out. You can see this distinctive plan at all three towns, although in Piryi and Olimbi, the original medieval village has been engulfed by more recent construction.

Piryi is known for a rare technique of geometric decoration used on buildings, known as *ksisti*. In the main square, this technique reaches a level of extraordinary virtuosity. The beautiful **Ayioi Apostoli ★** church and every available surface of every building are banded with horizontal decorations in a remarkable variety of motifs. At the town center is the tower for which the village was named, now mostly in ruins. It was originally the heart of the city's defenses, and a final place of refuge during sieges.

Mesta ★ is the best-preserved medieval village on Hios, a maze of narrow streets and dark covered passages. The town has two fine churches, each unique on the island. **Megas Taxiarchis,** built in the 19th century, is one of the largest churches in Greece, and it was clearly built to impress. The arcaded porch, with its fine pebble terrace and bell tower, create a solemn and harmonious transition to the cathedral precinct. The other church in town, **Paleos Taxiarchis,** is located a few blocks below the main square. As the name suggests, this is the older of the two, built in the 14th century. The most notable feature here is the carved wooden iconostasis, whose surface is incised with miniature designs of unbelievable intricacy. If either church is closed, you can ask for the gatekeeper in the central square.

Olimbi is the least well known of the three. Though not as spectacular as Piryi, nor as intact as Mesta, it contains many medieval buildings. It has a central tower similar to that of Piryi, and stone vaults connect the houses.

Piryi is the closest of the three villages to Hios town, at 26km (16 miles); Olimbi and Mesta are within 10km (6 miles) of Piryi. The easiest way to see all three villages is by car. Taxis from Hios to Piryi cost about 25€. KTEL buses travel from Hios to Piryi (6€) eight times a day, and to Mesta (7€) five times a day.

Beaches

There's no question that Hios has the best beaches in the Northeastern Aegean. They're cleaner, less crowded, and more plentiful than those of Samos or Lesvos, and would be the envy of any Cycladic isle.

The fine-sand beach of **Karfas,** 7km (4¼ miles) south of Hios town, is the closest decent beach to the town center; it can be reached by a local (blue) bus. The rapid development of tourism here, however, ensures that the beach will be crowded.

The most popular beach on the south coast is **Mavra Volia (Black Pebbles),** in the town of Emborio. Continue over the rocks to the right from the man-made town beach to find the main beach. Walking on the smooth black rocks feels and sounds like marching through a room filled with marbles. The panorama of the beach, slightly curving coastline, and distant headland is a memorable sight. Buses from Hios town or Piryi (8km/5 miles away) run regularly to Emborio. The south coast's best beach, **Vroulidia ★,** is a 5km (3-mile) drive in from the Emborio road. This white-pebble-and-sand beach, in a rocky cove, offers great views of the craggy coastline.

The west coast of the island has a number of stunning beaches. **Elinda Cove** shelters a long cobbled beach, a 600m (1,968-ft.) drive in from the main road, between

An Epic Experience

Little has been made so far of one of Hios's greatest claims to fame—the birthplace and home of Homer—but knowing he is associated with this island adds a special buzz to your visit. In fact, it is one of several islands or cities around the eastern Mediterranean that lay claim to this honor, but Hios's is probably the oldest and strongest. In any case, Hios has been adopted as the home by a group of modern scholars in Homeric studies, and each year this Academia Homerica holds a weeklong session on Hios, where students and scholars gather to lecture, study, and learn more about Homer. (Best is simply to search online for "academia homerica," and several sites will explain what you need to know.) But because most visitors will not be able to spend a week with Homer, I have a better suggestion: Bring a paperback copy of the *Iliad* or the *Odyssey* to read in your downtime here—on a beach or in a cafe. If you like the classics, it's an experience you will treasure.

Lithi and Volissos. Another excellent beach on this road is **Tigani-Makria Ammos,** about 4km (2½ miles) north of Elinda; turn at a sign for the beach, and drive in 1.5km (1 mile) to this long white-pebble beach. There's also a small, cove-sheltered cobbled beach about 300m (984 ft.) before the main beach. There are three beaches below Volissos, the best of which is Lefkathia, just north of the harbor of Volissos (Limnia).

South of Elinda, the long, safe beach at **Lithi Bay** is popular with families. Of the several tavernas there, I recommend **Ta Tria Adelphia (The Three Brothers;** ✆ **22710/73-208**). It's the last taverna you come to as you're walking along the beach.

The beaches of the north coast are less remarkable. **Nagos** (4km/2½ miles north of Kardamila) is a charming town in a small, spring-fed oasis, with a cobble beach and two tavernas on the water. This beach can get very crowded—the secret is to hike to the two small beaches a little to the east. To find them, take the small road behind the white house near the windmill.

Where to Stay

HIOS TOWN

Chios Chandris Hotel   For those who prefer an in-town modern hotel with resort-type facilities that is also within walking distance of the town's attractions, this is the place to be. Rooms are of standard size and decor, but there are suites and studios for those who want something a bit roomier; almost all units have views overlooking the port of Hios town. During the summer, you can take your meals or drinks at the poolside cafe. There's no need to oversell this hotel—what recommends it is the fact that after a day of enjoying other places in town or around the island, you can stroll back in about 10 minutes and be in the pool.

2 Euyenias Handri (in the port), 82100 Hios. www.chandris.gr. ✆ **22710/44-401.** 139 units. 125€ double; 190€–200€ suite or studio (some with kitchenette). Rates include breakfast. DC, MC, V. Parking adjacent to hotel. **Amenities:** Restaurant; 2 bars; pool; room service; tennis courts nearby; Wi-Fi in public areas. *In room:* A/C, TV, hair dryer, Internet, kitchenette (in some), minibar.

Voulamandis House ★ ☺   Although about 6.4km (4 miles) from the center of Hios Town, this is such a delightful place that many would feel it is well worth the short trip. (Free parking would make it worthwhile to rent a car to take excursions around the island.) It's a mansion on a 4.8-hectare (12-acre) estate—in fact, a working farm that provides many of the ingredients for the breakfasts and meals served here. The Voulamandis family makes you feel like a guest at their country home, not at a hotel. You're less than 4km (2 miles) from the Karfas beach (see below), and boat trips to the beaches on the island's south coast can be arranged. Ideal for a family, and what with free Wi-Fi and free parking, this is a true bargain as well as a most pleasant stay on Hios.

117 Fragovouni, 82100 Kampos. www.chioshotel.gr. ✆ **22710/44-500.** Fax 22710/44-600. 10 units. 60€ double; 70€ apt. Rates include breakfast. AE, DC, MC. **Amenities:** Restaurant; babysitting; room service for breakfast. *In room:* A/C, TV, fridge, hair dryer, Wi-Fi.

KARFAS

Karfas, 7km (4½ miles) south of Hios town, around Cape Ayia Eleni, is a resort area exploding with tourist groups in summer. Its fine-sand beach is lined with resorts.

Golden Sand Hotel ☺   For those who prefer to be on a beach, away from the bustle of a city, Karfas offers numerous accommodations, of which this is the finest. Built in 1989, it's been well maintained and offers many of the activities of the typical Greek resort hotel—Greek music/folk-dancing nights, weekly barbecue, and theme nights. Almost all rooms have views overlooking the sea—just insist on one. Drinks and meals can be enjoyed poolside. As Greek luxury resorts go, this is low key, and all the more enjoyable for being so.

Karfas Beach, 7km (4½ miles) from Hios center, 82100 Hios. www.goldensand.gr. ✆ **22710/32-425.** 108 units. 125€–145€ double. Rates include buffet breakfast. AE, MC, V. Parking on premises. **Amenities:** 2 restaurants; 2 bars; children's playground; pool; room service. *In room:* A/C, TV, hair dryer, Internet, minibar.

KARDAMILA

Kardamila, on the northeastern coast, is our choice among the resort towns because it's prosperous, self-sufficient, and not at all touristy.

Hotel Kardamila ★   This modern, and moderate, resort hotel was built for the guests and business associates of the town's ship owners and officers, and it has its own small cobbled beach. The guest rooms are large and plain, with modern bathrooms and balconies overlooking the beach. Service is good.

Kardamila, 82300 Hios. ✆ **22710/23-353.** Fax 22710/23-354. 32 units. 120€ double. Rates include breakfast. No credit cards. Closed Nov–Apr. *In room:* A/C.

VOLISSOS

This small hilltop village is one of the most beautiful on the island. A fine Byzantine castle overlooks the steep streets of the town, which contain shops, cafes, and tavernas. Volissos is too far north to be a convenient base for touring the whole island, but if you want to get to know part of it, you couldn't choose a better focus for your explorations.

Volissos Traditional Houses ★   The care with which these village houses have been restored is unique on this island, if not in the whole Northeastern Aegean. The beamed ceilings, often supported by forked tree limbs—a method of construction described in the *Odyssey*—are finely crafted and quite beautiful. Built into the stone walls are niches, fireplaces, cupboards, and couches. The houses and apartments are distributed throughout the village of Volissos, so your neighbors are likely to be locals rather than fellow tourists. Each apartment and house has a small kitchen, a spacious bathroom, and one or two bedrooms. The largest units (on two floors of a house) have two bedrooms, sitting rooms, kitchens, and large terraces. Most have views of the sea.

Volissos, Hios. volissos@otenet.gr. ✆ **22740/21-421** or 22740/21-413. 16 units. 60€–100€ double. No credit cards. Closed Nov–Apr. *In room:* A/C (in some), TV (in some), no phone.

MESTA

The best-preserved medieval fortified village on Hios, Mesta is a good base for touring the mastic villages (see above) and the island's south coast.

Pipidis Traditional Houses ★   These four homes, built more than 500 years ago, have been restored and opened by the Greek National Tourism Organization as part of its Traditional Settlements program. The houses have a medieval character, with vaulted ceilings and irregularly sculpted stone walls (covered in plaster and white-wash). One unfortunate aspect of these authentic dwellings is the dearth of natural light: If a room has any windows at all, they're small and high in the wall. Each house comes equipped with a kitchen, a bathroom, and sleeping space for two to six people.

Mesta, Hios. ✆ **22710/76-029.** 4 units. 65€ 2 persons; 90€ 4 persons. No credit cards. Closed Nov–Apr. *In room:* Kitchen; no phone.

Where to Eat

HIOS TOWN

If you're just looking for a cheap midday snack, go to the large Platea Vounakiou, at the far end of the Hios waterfront, where vendors set up tents and sell souvlaki and other finger foods—a most enjoyable (and frugal) way to take a meal in Hios town.

Hios Marine Club GREEK   This simple taverna serves the standard Greek dishes, pasta, grilled meats, and fish—but it's good. Don't be put off by the ugly yellow-and-white concrete facade. It's on the bay at the edge of town, just south of the port, 50m (164 ft.) beyond Hotel Chandris.

1 Nenitousi. ✆ **22710/23-184.** Main courses 6€–19€. MC, V. Daily noon–2am. Park on adjacent streets.

Hotzas Taverna GREEK   Hotzas offers a basic, well-prepared selection. It's the best option in a town not known for its restaurants. The summer dining area is a luxurious garden, with lemon trees and abundant flowers. There's no menu; you choose from a few unsurprising but delicious offerings each night. Many of the dishes are meat based, but some are fish based—and squid is always available. This place isn't easy to find: Take Kountouriotou in from the harbor and look for Kondili, the first right turn after a major road merges at an oblique angle from the right; after this it's another 50m (164 ft.) before the taverna appears on your left.

3 Yioryiou Kondili. ✆ **22710/42-787.** Main courses 6€–20€. No credit cards. Mon–Sat 6–11pm. Park on adjacent street.

LANGADA

Note: There are evening dinner cruises to Langada from Hios; check with Chios Tours (see "Visitor Information," earlier) for details.

Yiorgo Passa's Taverna ★ GREEK/SEAFOOD   Langada is a fishing village with a strip of five or six outdoor fish tavernas lining the harbor. Our favorite of these is Yiorgo Passa's Taverna, the first on the left, as you approach the waterfront. As in most Greek restaurants, fish is priced per kilogram. At first it sounds extremely expensive, but divided among two or four diners, it's about what you'd expect to pay at home. And you can't put a price on the warm and friendly ambience.

Langada. ✆ **22710/74-218.** Fish from 50€ per kilo. No credit cards. Daily 11am–2am. 20km (12 miles) north of Hios town, on the Kardamila road.

MESTA

Messaionas Taverna ★ GREEK   You will almost certainly have come to Mesta to visit the 14th-century Paleos Taxiarchis church, with its remarkable carved wooden iconostasis, so while you're here, take a meal at this homey taverna on the main square, long a favorite with everyone. The menu features a great variety of *mezedes,* many with interesting variations on traditional dishes. The stuffed tomatoes with pine nuts and raisins are delicious, as are the fried dishes such as *domatokeftedes* (tomatoes with herbs) or *tiropitakia* (cheese balls).

Mesta. ✆ **22710/76-050.** Main courses 6€–18€. No credit cards. Daily 11am–midnight. Parking on adjacent streets.

LESVOS (MITILINI)

348km (188 nautical miles) NE of Piraeus

Roughly triangular Lesvos—now called Mitilini in many Greek publications—is the third-largest island in Greece, with a population of some 120,000. As a large, bustling island, it long failed to bother itself with attracting tourists, but in recent years, it has been developing as a destination. In particular, it has been promoting itself as the birthplace of Sappho, the ancient poet.

The three principal towns—**Mitilini, Molivos,** and **Eressos**—are near the corners of the triangle. Mitilini and Molivos are about as different as two towns on the same island could possibly be. Mitilini is a working port town, low on sophistication or pretension, with little organized tourism but lots of local character. Molivos is a picture-postcard seaside village, a truly beautiful place; but in the summer, it exists only for tourism. Due to its remote location, Eressos is a good destination for a day trip, but not a recommended base for touring the island.

Not to be missed are the Archaeological and Theophilos museums, in Mitilini (though at press time, the Theophilos may be closing for renovations); the town of **Mandamados** and its celebrated icon (the east-coast road, between Mandamados and Mitilini, is the most scenic on the island); the remarkable, .6km-long (1-mile) beach of **Eressos;** and the labyrinthine streets of Molivos's castle-crowned hill.

Getting around on Lesvos is somewhat complicated by the presence of two huge tear-shaped bays in the south coast, which split the island at its center. Because bus schedules are not designed for day-trippers, this is one island where you'll definitely want a car to get around.

Getting There

BY PLANE   Both **Olympic Air** and **Aegean Airlines** offer several flights daily between Athens and Lesvos (Mitilini); both also offer occasional flights to Thessaloniki. (See "Getting There" under "Samos," earlier in this chapter for contact information.) **Athens Airways** (www.athensairways.com) has also been listing some flights to Mitilini. The **airport** (✆ **22510/61-490** or 22510/61-590) is 7km (4 miles) south of Mitilini. There's no bus to the town; a taxi will cost about 15€.

BY BOAT   The principal port of Lesvos is Mitilini, from which almost all the ferries arrive and depart, although there is some ferry traffic through the west-coast port of Sigri. There's one ferry daily to Mitilini from Piraeus, stopping at Hios (10–12 hr.); there are also several ferries weekly from Rafina to Sigri (9 hr.). There are daily boats, in both directions, between Mitilini and Hios (3 hr.). Two boats call weekly at Mitilini from Kavala (10 hr.) and Thessaloniki (10–13 hr.), stopping at Limnos on the way. There's also one ferry a week from Siros (9 hr.). Check schedules with a local travel agent, **Greek Travel Pages** (www.gtp.gr), the **Mitilini Port Authority** (✆ **22510/ 28-827**), or **Sigri Port Authority** (✆ **22530/54-433**).

In recent years, Lesvos—because of its associations with the poet Sappho (ca. 612 B.C.–?)—has become a favorite destination of lesbians from many parts of the world. Although very little is known about Sappho's life, it is accepted that she was born here; Eressos, in the far west corner, is now the favored site, and as such, has become a popular destination as well. It is also accepted that she was the leader of some sort of circle of young women; certainly some of her finest verses express warm feelings toward females. But it is not really clear that she was herself a lesbian—she married and had a daughter. Little of her poetry survives, but what there is has retained the admiration of readers and critics across the ages. So by all means, come to Lesvos in tribute to Sappho, but don't make a big deal with the locals out of associating the island with modern lesbians—the locals are not especially pleased about this. And don't forget that the tribute that authors really want is that their works be read.

Once you get to Lesvos, double-check the boat schedule for your departure, as the harbor is extremely busy in the summer, and service is often inexplicably irregular.

Mitilini & Southeast Lesvos

With an ambience more like that of a big mainland city than a Greek island port, Mitilini isn't to everyone's taste. Your first impression is likely to be one of noise and traffic. Commercial development has resulted in a modern generic beachfront; the only signs of a more auspicious past are the cathedral dome and the considerable remains of a hilltop castle. Still, once you leave the *paralia*, there's little or nothing in the way of amenities for tourists, which can be refreshing for those who enjoy seeing how others actually live. In the vicinity of Ermou (the market street), Mitilini's crumbling ocher alleys contain a mix of traditional coffeehouses, artisans' studios, ouzeries, stylish jewelry shops, and stores selling antiques and clothing. Although good restaurants are notably absent in the town center, a few authentic tavernas lie on the outskirts of town.

ESSENTIALS

VISITOR INFORMATION The Greek National Tourism Organization (EOT) has turned its functions over to the **North Aegean Islands Tourism Directorate.** Its office is at 6 James Aristarchou, 81100 Mitilini (© **22510/42-511;** fax 22510/ 27-601). Primarily an administrative center, the office is not especially set up to provide hands-on help for tourists. It's open daily from 8am to 2:30pm, with extended hours in the high season. The **tourist police** (© **22510/22-276**) may also be helpful, but private travel agencies are your best bet for information.

GETTING AROUND **By Bus** There are two bus stations in Mitilini, one for local and the other for round-the-island routes. The **local bus station** (© **22510/28- 725**) is near the harbor's north end, by the (closed) Folklife Museum and across from the Commercial Bank (Emporiki Trapeza). Local buses on Lesvos are frequent, running every hour from 6am to 9pm most of the year. The destinations covered are all within 12km (7½ miles) of Mitilini, and include Thermi, Moria, and Pamfilla to the north, and Varia, Ayia Marina, and Loutra to the south. The most expensive local fare is 6€. The posted schedule is hard to read, but ticket sellers can decipher it. You can catch the **round-the-island KTEL buses** (© **22510/28-873**) in Mitilini, at the port's south end, behind Argo Hotel. There's daily service, in summer, to Kaloni and Molivos (four times), Mandamados (once), Plomari (four times), and Eressos and Sigri (once each).

By Car   Rental prices in Mitilini tend to be high, so be sure to shop around. There are many choices here, but for those more comfortable with a well-known brand, try the **Avis Agency** at the airport, or in town, at 99 Koundouriotou (along the left arm of the harbor; ☎ **22510/42-910**). Summer daily rates start at around 100€, with unlimited mileage.

By Taxi   Lesvos is a big island. The one-way taxi fare from Mitilini to Molivos is about 50€; from Mitilini to Eressos or Sigri, it's about 70€. The main taxi stand in Mitilini is on Plateia Kyprion Patrioton, a long block inland from the port's southern end; there's a smaller taxi stand at the port's north end, near the local bus station.

FAST FACTS   The **area code** for Mitilini is 22510, for Molivos (Mithimna) and Eressos 22530, and for Plomari 22520. There are **ATMs** at several banks on the port, including the Ioniki Trapeza and Agrotiki Trapeza (both south of the local bus station). **Vostani Hospital** (☎ **22510/43-777**), on P. Vostani, southeast of town, will take care of emergencies. **Glaros Laundry** (☎ **22510/27-065**), opposite the tourist police, near the ferry pier, is open from 9am to 2pm and 6 to 8pm; the turnaround time is usually 24 hours. The **post office** and the **telephone office (OTE)** are on Plateia Kyprion Patrioton, 1 block inland from the town hall, at the south end of the port. The principal **taxi stand** is also on Plateia Kyprion Patrioton. The **tourist police** (☎ **22510/22-776**) are located just east of the ferry quay.

ATTRACTIONS

Archaeological Museums of Mitilini ★   The excellent Mitilini archaeological museum has been augmented by a large new museum a short distance up the hill toward the kastro. The museums have the same hours, and the price of admission includes both locations. The new museum presents extensive Roman antiquities of Lesvos and some finds from the early Christian basilica of Ayios Andreas, in Eressos. The highlight of its collection is a reconstructed Roman house, from the 3rd century B.C., whose elaborate mosaic floors depict scenes from comedies of the poet Menander, and from classical mythology. All the exhibits are thoughtfully presented, with plenty of explanatory notes in English. A rear building houses more marble sculpture and inscribed tablets, while the main museum contains figurines, pottery, gold jewelry, and other finds from Thermi, the Mitilini kastro, and other ancient Lesvos sites.

7 Eftaliou, Myrina. ☎ **22510/28-032.** Admission 4€ adults, 1€ students and E.U. seniors. Tues–Sun 8:30am–3pm. A block north of the tourist police station, just inland from the ferry pier.

Kastro   Perched on a steep hill north of the city, the extensive ruins of Mitilini's castle are fun to explore and offer fine views of city and sea from the ramparts. The kastro was founded by Justinian, in the 6th century A.D., and was restored and enlarged, in 1737, by the Genoese. The Turks also renovated and built extensive additions to the castle during their occupation. In several places, you can see fragments of marble columns embedded in the castle walls—these are blocks from a 7th-century-B.C. Temple of Apollo, taken by the Genoese. Look for the underground cistern at the north end of the castle precinct: This echoing chamber is a beautiful place, with domed vaults reflected in the pool below. In summer, the castle is sometimes used as a performing-arts center.

8th Noemvriou, Mitilini. ✆ **22510/27-297.** Admission 3€ adults, 1€ students and E.U. seniors. Tues–Sun 8am–2:30pm. Just past the new Archaeological Museum, turn right on the path to the kastro.

Theophilos Museum ★ One of the most interesting sights near Mitilini is this small museum in the former house of folk artist Hatzimichalis Theophilos (1868–1934). Most of Theophilos's works adorned the walls of tavernas and ouzeries, often painted in exchange for food. Theophilos died in poverty, and none of his work would have survived if it weren't for the efforts of art critic Theriade (see below), who commissioned the paintings on display here during the last years of the painter's life. These primitive water-colors depicting ordinary people, daily life, and local landscapes are now widely cele-brated and have been exhibited at the Museum of Folk Art, in Athens. Be sure to see the curious photographs showing the artist dressed as Alexander the Great. As the museum may be closed for renovations, you should call before setting out to visit it.

Varia. ✆ **22510/41-644.** Admission 3€. Tues–Sun 9am–1pm and 4:30–8pm. 3km (2 miles) south of Mitilini, on airport road, next to Theriade Museum.

Theriade Library and Museum of Modern Art The Theriade Library and Museum of Modern Art is in the home of Stratis Eleftheriadis, a native of Lesvos who emigrated to Paris and became a prominent art critic and publisher. (Theriade is the Gallicized version of his surname.) On display are copies of his published works, including *Minotaure* and *Verve* magazines, as well as his personal collection of works by Picasso, Matisse, Miró, Chagall, and other modern artists.

Varia. ✆ **22510/23-372.** Admission 3€. Tues–Sun 9am–1pm and 5–8pm. 3km (2 miles) south of Mitilini, on airport road, next to Theophilos Museum.

WHERE TO STAY
Moderate
Theofilos Paradise Boutique Hotel ★★ A bit pricey and showy for this corner of the Aegean but not when compared to such hostelries elsewhere, and for some who have come this far, it would be a welcomed bargain. Originally an early-1900s man-sion, it has now expanded to include two adjacent buildings—if you can reserve early enough, insist on the mansion. Furnishings are more decorator's bourgeois than tradi-tional Greek, but all kinds of creature comforts are provided— flatscreen TV in rooms, spa, hydromassage shower, pool with its bar, underground parking. It has rooms and facilities for travelers with disabilities and also makes a point of welcoming gays. (And pets are accepted on prior request.) It's located in the neighborhood of Kioski, with its many traditional and fine old homes and away from the town's hustle and bustle.

7 Skra, Mitilini, 81000 Lesvos. www.theofilosparadise.gr. ✆ **22510/43-300.** 24 units. 85€–110€ double. Rates include breakfast. MC, V. **Amenities:** Restaurant; bar; pool; sauna; Wi-Fi. *In room:* A/C, TV, hair dryer, minibar.

 Excursion to a Mountain Village

An enjoyable destination for a day trip is the rural hamlet of **Ayiassos**, 23km (14 miles) west of Mitilini. The town, built on the foothills of Mount Olympos, consists of traditional gray-stone houses (with wooden "Turkish" balco-nies, often covered in flowering vines), narrow cobblestone lanes, and fine small churches. Here, local craftspeople still turn out their ceramic wares by hand. Excursion buses can bring you from Mitilini, or you can share a taxi (about 70€ for the ride and a reason-ably moderate wait).

A Side Trip to Pergamum in Turkey

From Mitilini, there's a direct connection to Turkey via its port of Ayvalik, a densely wooded fishing village that makes a refreshing base camp from which to tour the ancient Greek site of Pergamum. The acropolis of Pergamum is sited on a dramatic hilltop, with substantial remains of the town on the surrounding slopes. The complex dates back to at least the 4th century B.C., and there are significant remains from this period through Roman and Byzantine times. It is one of Turkey's most important archaeological sites. All-inclusive 1-day tours to Pergamum—including round-trip boat fare, bus ride to the site, and guided tour—cost about 100€; inquire at Mitilini travel agencies such as **Dimakis Tours,** 73 Koundouriotou (© **22510/27-865**), or **Aeolic Cruises Travel Agency,** 47A Koutouriotou (© **22510/46-601**). Ships to Turkey usually sail three times a week, more often in high season, if the demand is there. A passport is required, but no visa is required for a 1-day visit. However, U.S., British, Irish, Canadians, and Australians need a visa for even an overnight; it costs between 45€ and 55€, but is good for 90 days in Turkey. Your visa is issued at the Customs House upon your arrival in Ayvalik.

Inexpensive

Hotel Erato   On a busy street leading away from the port, this hotel offers convenience, cleanliness, a friendly and helpful staff, and a noise level marginally below that in many portside hotels. Most of the small, bright rooms have balconies facing the street, some with a view over the traffic to Mitilini Bay; there is also a fine park in front of the hotel. The four-story hotel was converted from a medical clinic and retains an atmosphere of institutional anonymity; on the positive side, it's well maintained. *Note:* If you intend to pay by credit card, inform the desk well in advance of your planned departure.

2 P. Vostani, Mitilini, 81000 Lesvos. © **22510/41-160.** 22 units. 90€ double. MC, V. Free parking. **Amenities:** Bar. *In room:* A/C, TV, minibar.

Hotel Sappho   This no-nonsense, convenient hotel offers simple accommodations at moderate rates. Nine rooms have balconies facing the port (and can be a bit noisy in the morning); the rest have no balconies and face a sunny rear courtyard. All units have wall-to-wall carpets, white walls, minimal furnishings, and tiny bathrooms with showers. A breakfast room, on the second floor, has a terrace with a fine port view.

31 Palou Kountourioti, Mitilini, 81000 Lesvos. © **22510/28-415.** 29 units. 70€ double. Continental breakfast 7€. No credit cards. **Amenities:** Restaurant; bar; Internet; room service. *In room:* A/C.

WHERE TO EAT

Mitilini has more portside cafes than your average bustling harbor town. A cluster of chairs around the small lighthouse at the point heralds the most scenic (as well as the windiest) of the many small ouzeries that specialize in grilled octopus, squid, shrimp, and local fish. Some of the best restaurants are a short taxi ride outside the city.

Averof 1841 Grill GREEK   This taverna, located midport, near the Sappho Hotel, is one of the better grills around, and one of the only restaurants in Mitilini center worth trying. Its beef dishes are particularly good. Try any of the tender souvlaki dishes or the lamb with potatoes.

Port, Mitilini. © **22510/22-180.** Main courses 6€–19€. No credit cards. Daily 7am–5pm and 7–11pm.

O Rembetis GREEK   Kato Halikas is a hilltop village on the outskirts of Mitilini, and although this simple taverna might be hard to find, it's well worth the effort. At the south end of the terrace you can sit beneath the branches of a high sycamore and enjoy a panoramic view of the port. The food isn't sophisticated or surprising, but it's very Greek, and the clientele is primarily local. There's no menu, so listen to the waiter's descriptions or take a look in the kitchen—there's usually fresh fish, in addition to the taverna standards. The wind can be brisk on this hilly site, so bring a jacket, if the night is cool. The best way to get here is by taxi; the fare is about 10€ each way.

Kato Halikas, Mitilini. ✆ **22510/27-150.** Main courses 6€–18€. No credit cards. Daily 8pm–midnight.

Salavos GREEK   Despite its location on the busy airport road, this small taverna is one of the best in Mitilini. A garden terrace in back offers partial shelter from road noise. The seafood is fresh and delicious; try the calamari stuffed with feta, vegetables, and herbs. The restaurant is popular with locals, who fill the place on summer nights. As you travel south from Mitilini toward the airport, it's about 3km (2 miles) from town, on the right. Taxi fare is about 8€ each way.

Mitilini. ✆ **22510/22-237.** Main courses 5€–18€. No credit cards. Daily noon–1am.

MITILINI AFTER DARK

In Mitilini, there's plenty of nightlife action at both ends of the harbor. Several of the cheaper and more informal such as **La Notte** and **Hott Spott** are found on Koundouriotou, the street facing the harbor at the east side (left looking seaward). The more sophisticated places are off the harbor's south end. Outdoor **Park Cinema,** on the road immediately below the stadium, and **Pallas,** on Vournazo (by the post office), are both open May through September. Summer occasionally brings professional entertainment to the Kastro.

Molivos & Northeast Lesvos

Molivos (aka Mithimna) is at the northern tip of the island's triangle. It's a highly picturesque, castle-crowned village, where mansions of stone and pink-pastel stucco are capped by red-tile roofs. Balconies and windowsills are decorated with geraniums and roses. The town has long been popular with package-tour groups, especially during the summer months. Souvenir shops, car-rental agencies, and travel agents outnumber local merchants, and the restaurants are geared toward tourists. Despite this, it is a beautiful place to visit and a convenient base for touring the island.

ESSENTIALS

GETTING THERE   By Bus   KTEL buses (✆ **22510/28-873**) connect Molivos with Mitilini four times daily in the high season. The Molivos bus stop is just past the Municipal Tourist Office, on the road to Mitilini.

By Taxi   The one-way taxi fare from Mitilini to Molivos is about 50€.

VISITOR INFORMATION   The **Municipal Tourist Office,** 6 J. Aristarchou, on the road heading down to the sea (✆ **22530/71-347**), is housed in a tiny building next to the National Bank. It's open Monday through Friday. **Panatella Holidays,** 2 Possidons (✆ **22530/71-520;** www.panatella-holidays.com) can book car rentals, accommodations, and excursions. Both the tourist office and Panatella are open daily in summer from 8:30am to 9:30pm.

GETTING AROUND   By Car   There are numerous rental agencies in Molivos, and rates are comparable to those in Mitilini.

By Boat   Boat taxis to neighboring beaches can be arranged at the port or in a travel agency (see Panatella Holidays, above).

By Bus   Tickets for day excursions by bus can be bought in any of the local travel agencies. The destinations include Thermi/Ayiassos (60€), Mitilini town (35€), Sigri/Eressos (60€), and Plomari (65€); the excursions are offered once or twice each week in the summer.

FAST FACTS   An ATM can be found at the **National Bank,** next to the Municipal Tourist Office, on the Mitilini road. The **Internet** can be accessed at **Communication and Travel** (✆ 22530/71-900), on the main road to the port. The **police** (✆ 22530/71-222) are up from the port, on the road to the town cemetery; the **port police** (✆ 22530/71-307) are—where else?—on the port. The **post office** (✆ 22530/71-246) is on the path circling up to the castle—turn right (up), past the National Bank.

ATTRACTIONS

Kastro   The hilltop Genoese castle is better preserved than Mitilini town, but it's much less extensive and not as interesting to explore. There is, however, a great view from the walls, worth the price of admission in itself. There's a stage in the southwest corner of the courtyard, often used for theatrical performances in the summer. To get here by car, turn uphill at the bus stop and follow signs to the castle parking lot. On foot, the castle is most easily approached from the town, a steep climb no matter which of the many labyrinthine streets you choose.

Molivos. No phone. Admission 3€ adults, 1€ students and E.U. seniors. Tues–Sun 8:30am–3pm.

Mandamados Monastery ★   Mandamados is a lovely village on a high inland plateau, renowned primarily for the remarkable icon of the Archangel Michael housed in the local monastery. A powerful story is associated with the creation of the icon: It is said that during a certain pirate raid, all but one of the monks were slaughtered. This one survivor, emerging from hiding to find the bloody corpses of his dead companions, responded to the horror of the moment with an extraordinary act. Gathering the blood-soaked earth, he fashioned it into the face of a man, an icon in relief of the Archangel Michael. This simple icon, its lips worn away by the kisses of pilgrims, can be found at the center of the iconostasis, at the back of the main chapel.

Mandamados. Free admission. Daily 6am–10pm. 24km (15 miles) east of Molivos, 36km (23 miles) northwest of Mitilini.

BEACHES

The long, narrow town beach in Molivos is rocky and crowded near the town, but becomes sandier and less populous as you continue south. The beach in **Petra,** 6km (3¾ miles) south of Molivos, is considerably more pleasant. The beach at **Tsonia,** 30km (19 miles) east of Molivos, is only accessible via a difficult rutted road, and isn't particularly attractive. The best beach on the island is 70km (44 miles) southwest of Molivos, in **Skala Eressos,** on southwestern coast.

SHOPPING

Molivos, unfortunately, is dominated by tacky souvenir shops. To find more authentic local wares, you'll have to explore neighboring towns. **Mandamados,** known as a center for pottery, has numerous ceramics studios. **Eleni Lioliou** (✆ 22530/61-170), on the road to the monastery, sells brightly painted bowls, plates, and mugs. **Anna Fonti** (✆ 22530/61-433), on a pedestrian street in the village, produces plates with intricate designs, in brilliant turquoise and blue. Also in Mandamados is the diminutive studio of icon painter **Dimitris Hatzanagnostou** (℡ **22530/61-318**), who produces large-scale icons for churches and portable icons for purchase.

WHERE TO STAY
Moderate
Delfinia Hotel & Bungalows ★ ☺   Often rated the best hotel on Lesvos, one of the major attractions of this white-stucco and gray-stone resort is its panoramic setting above the Aegean, but for families it will be the many activities. A path leads 200m (656 ft.) from the hotel to a fine-sand beach and a recreation complex with saltwater swimming pool, snack bar, and tennis courts (the latter illuminated for night games). The hotel rooms are simple, with small, shower-only bathrooms. The 57 bungalows are more spacious: The living room has a couch that pulls out to provide an extra bed, most bathrooms include a bathtub, and each unit has either a large terrace or a balcony. Breakfast at the hotel is served on a terrace, while the bungalows include free room service for breakfast only. The second-floor rooms in the bungalows are the most spacious, have the best views, and cost a bit more.

Molivos, 81108 Lesvos. www.hoteldelfinia.com. ℡ **22530/71-315.** 125 units. 95€–115€ double; 130€–150€ 2-person bungalow. Rates include buffet breakfast. AE, DC, V. Parking adjacent. 1.6km (1 mile) from town center. **Amenities:** 2 restaurants; 2 bars; babysitting; basketball; children's playground; pool; room service; table tennis; 3 night-lit tennis courts; volleyball; free Wi-Fi in public areas. *In room:* A/C, TV, fridge, hair dryer, minibar.

Hotel Olive Press   This charming hotel is—you guessed it—an old converted olive press and, as such, is not much to look at from the outside. But its great attraction is its location, right on the beach. The rooms are on the small side but are comfortable, with terrazzo floors, handsome furnishings, and bathtubs. Some of the units have windows opening onto great sea views, with waves lapping just beneath. The nice inner courtyard has several gardens. Staff is gracious and friendly. On the downside is that the rear rooms can be noisy in July and August, when young people gather at a popular bar nearby.

Molivos, 81108 Lesvos. www.olivepress-hotel.com. ℡ **22530/71-205.** 50 units. 100€ double; 140€ studio. Rates include buffet breakfast. AE, DC, V. Closed Nov–May. **Amenities:** Restaurant; bar; small pool. *In room:* Kitchenette.

Inexpensive
Sea Horse Hotel   Set among a cluster of relatively new Class C hotels below the old town, right along the port, is this smaller, homier hotel. Rooms are tidy, if fairly basic. All units come with a balcony facing the sea; four also have minimal kitchen facilities. On-site are a restaurant and an in-house travel agency.

Molivos, 81108 Lesvos. www.seahorse-hotel.com. ℡ **22530/71-630.** 16 units. 80€ double. Continental breakfast 7€. No credit cards. **Amenities:** Restaurant; travel agency. *In room:* A/C, TV, fridge (in some), hair dryer.

WHERE TO EAT
Captain's Table ★ SEAFOOD/VEGETARIAN   Located right on harbor at Molivos, this is many visitors' favorite restaurant in the area. It's run by Melinda, an Australian, and her Greek husband, Theo. Although the emphasis is now on fresh grilled fish, the menu still offers some of Melinda's excellent trademark vegetable dishes, or Theo's roast lamb or pork fillets wrapped in bacon. There are even curries, Italian gnocchi, and fresh mussels with house white, if you like some variety. Live bouzouki music is played 3 nights a week. Needless to say, the restaurant is crowded in high season.

The Harbor, Molivos. ℡ **22530/71-241.** www.lesvosvacations.com/captainstable.htm. Main courses 8€–22€. V. Daily 11am–1am.

Octopus SEAFOOD   One of the oldest restaurants on the harbor of Molivos, the Octopus has had to serve tasty food in order to survive the tides of fashion. It specializes in grilled fish and meats but offers a selection of other dishes, such as peppers stuffed with spicy cheese, for instance. And your waiter can not only help you assemble your meal, but he can also advise you about the island's attractions.

The Harbor, Molivos. © **22530/71-317.** Main courses 6€–19€. No credit cards. Daily 11am–1am.

Tropicana ★ CAFE/ICE CREAM   Stroll up into the old town to sip a cappuccino or have a dish of ice cream at this outdoor cafe, which offers soothing classical music and a relaxed ambience. The owner, Hari Procoplou, learned the secrets of ice creamery in Los Angeles.

Molivos. © **22510/71-869.** Snacks/desserts 3€–16€. No credit cards. Daily 8am–1am.

MOLIVOS AFTER DARK

Those seeking a bit of culture should ask at the Tourist Office about the occasional theatrical performances at the kastro looming over the town. Young travelers will have no trouble finding clubs and music to their taste, but those seeking something more indigenous will want to head for **Vangelis Bouzouki** ★, Molivos's top acoustic bouzoukia club. It's located west from Molivos, on the road to Efthalou, past the Sappho Tours office. After about a 10-minute walk outside of town, you'll see a sign that points to an olive grove. Follow it for another 500m (1,640 ft.) through the orchard until you reach a clearing with gnarled olive trees and a few stray sheep. When you see the circular cement dance floor, surrounded by clumps of cafe tables, you've found the club. Have some ouzo and late-night *mezedes,* and sit back to enjoy the show.

THE SPORADES

by John S. Bowman

With their excellent golden sand beaches, fragrant pine trees, and unspoiled villages, you might think that the Sporades ("scattered") islands have always been major tourist magnets. But because these islands lack significant archaeological remains and historical associations, foreigners traditionally headed elsewhere in Greece. These days, however, the Sporades can be crowded in high season—although in spring and fall they can be lovely and relaxing. But even in summer, they are worth a visit by those whose notion of an ideal vacation is a lovely beach, good food, and active nightlife.

These days, however, the Sporades are no longer the natural retreats they once were. **Skiathos** becomes extremely crowded in high season—although in spring and fall it can be lovely and relaxing. **Skopelos** is nearly as bustling as Skiathos in the high season, but isn't quite as sophisticated. Its beaches are fewer and less impressive, but Skopelos town is among the more attractive ports in Greece, and the island offers some pleasant excursions. These two most popular islands also have fine restaurants, fancy hotels, and an international (heavily British) following.

More remote **Skyros** hardly seems a part of the group, especially as its landscape and architecture are more Cycladic. But it has a few excellent beaches and a colorful local culture, and it remains a fine destination for those who want to get away from the crowds. Although space limits do not allow us to describe Alinossos, the fourth of these islands, it might be attractive to those seeking a less popular, more natural island.

Strategies for Seeing the Islands

If you have only 1 to 3 days, plan on seeing just one of the Sporades. (Technically, by the way, these are the Northern Sporades.) If you have a bit more time, you will be able to get a ship directly from various ports (identified later) and a plane in the case of Skiathos and Skyros; if time is a factor, we strongly advise flying to Skiathos or Skyros and staying there. If you have more time, you can continue around the islands via hydrofoils (known as Flying Dolphins) or ferryboats. (**Note:** The frequency of all connections is cut back considerably Sept–May.)

SKIATHOS ★

108km (58 nautical miles) from Ayios Konstandinos, which is 166km (103 miles) from Athens

Skiathos, which remained isolated and agrarian until the early 1970s, has become a "package-tour" island, and during high season, Skiathos town can feel like a shopping mall. By the same token, it has some elegant shops, fine restaurants, and a lively nightlife. If you have the choice, come off-season when both the town and beaches are less crowded.

Essentials

GETTING THERE   By Plane   Olympic Air has service daily (twice daily Apr–May, five times daily June–Sept) from Athens; contact www.olympicair.com or the Athens office (© **210/966-6666**) for information and reservations. At this time, Olympic does not maintain an office in Skiathos town, but can be reached at the nearby **airport** (© **24270/22-049**). Public bus service to and from the airport is so infrequent that everyone takes a taxi; expect to pay about 10€ depending on your destination.

By Boat   Skiathos can be reached by either ferryboat (3 hr.) or hydrofoil (1½ hr.) from Volos or Ayios Konstandinos. (Volos is at least a 4-hr. bus ride from Athens, Ayios Konstandinos a 3-hr. bus ride.) From Kimi on Evvia, there is also hydrofoil service (50 min.) and ferryboat service (4 hr.). In high season, there are frequent hydrofoils daily from Volos and from Ayios Konstandinos, as well as service from Thessaloniki (3 hr.). Hydrofoils also link Skiathos to Skopelos (30–45 min.), Alonissos (60–75 min.), and Skyros (2⅓ hr.).

In Athens, **Alkyon Travel,** 97 Akademias, near Kanigos Square (© **210/383-2545;** www.alkyontravel.com), can arrange bus transportation from Athens to Ayios Konstandinos as well as hydrofoil or ferry tickets. Alkyon does not accept reservations by phone, only in person. The 3-hour bus ride costs about 20€ one-way.

For hydrofoil (Flying Dolphins) schedules and information, contact the **Hellenic Seaways,** Akti Kondyli and 2 Aitolikou, Piraeus (© **210/419-9000;** www.hellenic seaways.gr). For ferryboat information from Piraeus, contact the **G.A. Ferries** line in Piraeus (© **210/458-2640;** www.ferries.gr/gaferries). Ferry tickets can be purchased at travel agencies in Athens or on the islands. During high season, I recommend that you purchase your boat tickets in advance through the boat lines. While you may purchase tickets at Alkyon in person, they will not reserve ferryboat or hydrofoil tickets for you in advance, and these often sell out.

VISITOR INFORMATION   The town maintains an **information booth** at the western corner of the harbor; in summer, at least, it's open daily from about 9am to 8pm. Meanwhile, private travel agencies abound and can help with most of your requests. We highly recommend **Mare Nostrum Holidays,** 21 Papadiamandis (© **24270/21-463;** marenost@otenet.gr), which since 2009 has been part of the Heliotropio Travel Group. It books villas, hotels, and rooms; sells tickets to many around-the-island, hydrofoil, and beach caique (skiff) trips; books Olympic Air flights; exchanges currency; and changes traveler's checks without commission. The staff speak excellent English, are exceedingly well-informed, and have lots of tips on everything from beaches to restaurants. The office is open daily from 8am to 10pm.

Museum & Site Hours Update

If you visit the Sporades during the summer, check to see when museums and sites are open. They do not always maintain the hours that are officially posted, and most will be closed at least 1 day a week.

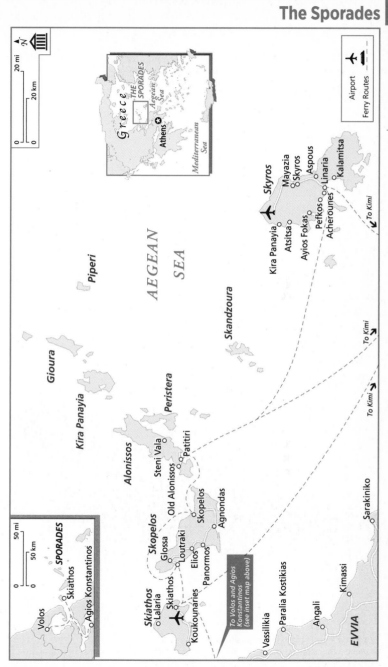

GETTING AROUND   **By Bus**   Skiathos has public bus service along the south coast of the island from the bus station on the harbor to Koukounaries (5€), with stops at the beaches in between. A conductor will ask for your destination and assess the fare after the bus starts moving. Buses run at least six times daily April through November; every hour from 9am to 9pm May through October; every half-hour from 8:30am to 10pm June through September; and every 20 minutes from 8:30am to 2:30pm and 3:30pm to midnight July through August.

By Car & Moped   Reliable car and moped agencies, all on the *paralia* (shore road), include **Avis** (© 24270/21-458), run by the friendly Yannis Theofanidis; **Aivalioti's Rent-A-Car** (© 24270/21-246); and **National-Alamo** (© 24270/23-308). In high season, expect to pay 60€ to 100€ per day; weekly rates are significantly cheaper. Mopeds start at about 35€ per day.

By Boat   The north-coast beaches, adjacent islands, and historic kastro are most easily reached by caique; these smaller vessels, which post their beach and island tour schedules on signs, sail frequently from the fishing harbor west of the Bourtzi fortress. An around-the-island tour that includes stops at Lalaria Beach and the kastro will cost about 50€.

The Flying Dolphins agent, **Skiathos Holidays,** on the *paralia,* is open from 7am to 9:30pm; in high season there are as many as eight high-speed hydrofoils daily to Skopelos and Alonissos. (I feel the extra cost for the hydrofoils is worth it for traveling among the Sporades islands for the time saved.) There are also daily excursions to Skyros in high season. Call © 24270/22-018 for up-to-date schedules. Note that even if you have a ticket, you must appear at the agent's ticket office at least 30 minutes before the scheduled sailing to get your ticket confirmed and seat assigned. **Vasilis Nikolaou** (© 24270/22-209), the travel agent at the corner of the *paralia* and Papadiamandis, sells tickets for the ferryboats to the other islands.

FAST FACTS   The official **American Express** agent is Mare Nostrum Holidays, 21 Papadiamandis (© 24270/21-463; marenost@otenet.gr), open daily from 8am to 10pm. There are many banks in town, such as the **National Bank of Greece,** Papadiamandis, open Monday through Friday from 8am to 2pm and 7 to 9pm, and Sunday from 9am to noon. The **hospital** (© 24270/22-040) is on the coast road at the far-west edge of town. For **Internet access,** try Internet Zone Cafe, 28 Evangelistrias (zonecafe@hotmail.com).

A self-service **laundry** is at 14 Georgios Panora (© 24270/22-341), 85m (279 ft.) up Papadiamandis, the street opposite the National Bank; or you can drop off a load at the **Snow White Laundry** (© 24270/24-256), one street up from the *paralia,* behind the Credit Bank; both are open daily from about 8am to 2pm and 5 to 11pm. The **police station** (© 24270/21-111) is about 250m (820 ft.) from the harbor on Papadiamandis, on the left. The **tourist police** booth is about 15m (49 ft.) farther along on the right. The **post office** (© 24270/22-011) is on Papadiamandis, away from the harbor about 160m (525 ft.) and on the right; it's open Monday through Friday from 7:30am to 2pm. The **telephone office** (**OTE;** © 24270/22-135) is on Papadiamandis, on the right, some 30m (98 ft.) beyond the post office. It's open Monday through Friday from 7:30am to 10pm, Saturday and Sunday from 9am to 2pm and 5 to 10pm.

What to See & Do

Skiathos is a relatively modern town, built in 1930 on two low-lying hills, then reconstructed after heavy German bombardment during World War II. The handsome **Bourtzi Fortress** (originally from the 13th c., but greatly rebuilt across the centuries) jutting into the middle of the harbor is on an islet connected by a broad causeway. Ferries and hydrofoils stop at the port on the right (east) of the fortress, while fishing boats and excursion caiques dock on the left (west). Whitewashed villas with red-tile roofs line both sides of the harbor. The small church of **Ayios Nikolaos** dominates the hill on the east side, as does the larger church of **Trion Ierarchon (Three Archbishops)** on the west side.

The main street leading away from the harbor and up through town is named **Papadiamandis,** after the island's best-known son (see description of the Papadiamandis House, below). Here you'll find numerous restaurants, cafes, and stores, plus services such as Mare Nostrum Holidays, the post office, the telephone office, and the tourist police.

On the west flank of the harbor (the left side as you disembark from the ferry) are numerous outdoor cafes and restaurants, excursion caiques (for the north-coast beaches, adjacent islands, and around-the-island tours) and, at the far corner, the stepped ramp (above the Oasis Café) leading up to the town's next level. Mounting these broad steps will lead you to **Plateia Trion Ierarchon,** a stone-paved square around the town's most important church. The eastern flank, technically the New Paralia, is home to many tourist services as well as a few recommended hotels and many restaurants. At the far end, the harborfront road branches to the right along the yacht harbor—an important nightlife area in summer, and to the left toward the airport and points of interest inland.

The Papadiamandis House   Alexandros Papadiamandis (1851–1911) was born on Skiathos, and after his adult career as a journalist in Athens, he returned in 1908 and died in this very house. His nearly 200 short stories and novellas, mostly about Greek island life, assured him a major reputation in Greece, but his rather idiosyncratic style and vernacular language make his work difficult to translate into foreign languages. His house is less a museum than a shrine containing personal possessions and tools of his writing trade. (A statue of Papadiamandis stands in front of the Bourtzi Fortress on the promontory at the corner of the harbor.) And if you want to read some of his stories, look for *Tales from a Greek Island* (Johns Hopkins University Press).

An alley to right of Papadiamandis (main street), 50m (164 ft.) up from harbor. ☏ **24270/23-843.** Admission 3€. Tues-Sun 9:30am-1pm and 5-8pm.

Skiathos Riding Center ☺   This is the perfect place for at least a half-day excursion and activity, with or without children. It's located just off the road to Koukounaries beach, so could be combined with a visit to that beach. Nikos Drakos started the center in 1990 and continues to breed his own horses here. Anita Reize now operates it with him. The center offers guided walks for small groups (a maximum of four) of different levels of riders on a selection of tours, including an early morning beach walk. The horses, by the way, are not tremendously large, so novices will not feel intimidated. The center provides donkey rides for children and also maintains a small farm/zoo and playground.

En route to Koukounaries beach after crossroad to Ayia Eleni beach. ☏ **24270/49-548.** www.skiathos-horse-riding.gr. Walks 30€–45€; donkey rides 5€; private lessons 25€ for about 40 min.

BEACHES

Skiathos is famous for its beaches, and I'll cover the most important ones briefly, proceeding clockwise from the port. The most popular beaches are west of town along 12km (8 miles) of coastal highway. At most of them, you can rent an umbrella and two chairs for about 15€ per day.

The first, **Megali Ammos,** is the sandy strip below the popular package-tour community of Ftelia. It's so close to town and so packed with groups it probably won't appeal to most. **Vassilias** and **Achladias** are also crowded and developed; **Tzanerias** and **Nostos** are slight improvements. Farther out on the Kalamaki peninsula, south of the highway, **Kanapitsa** is good for fans of watersports; **Kanapitsa Water-Sport Center** (✆ 24270/21-298) has water and jet skis, windsurfing, air chairs, sailing, and speedboat hire. Scuba divers will want to stop at **Dolphin Diving Center** (✆ 24270/21-599) at the big Nostos Hotel.

Across the peninsula, **Vromolimnos (Dirty Lake)** is fairly attractive and relatively uncrowded, perhaps because of its unsavory name and the cloudy (but not polluted) water that inspires it. The beach offers water-skiing and windsurfing. **Koulos** and **Ayia Paraskevi** are fairly well-regarded. **Platanias,** the next major beach, isn't crowded, perhaps because the big resort hotels have their own pools and sun decks. Past the next headland, **Troulos** is one of the prettiest beaches, due to its relative isolation, crescent shape, and the islets that guard the small bay. Nearby is **Victoria Leisure Center** (✆ 24270/49-467), which has rooms to rent, a pool, shops, and two tennis courts.

The last bus stop is at much ballyhooed **Koukounaries ★★**, 16km (10 miles) from Skiathos town. The bus chugs uphill past the Pallas Hotel luxury resort, then descends and winds alongside the inland waterway, Lake Strofilias, stopping at the edge of a fragrant pine forest. *Koukounaries* means "pine cones" in Greek, and behind this grove of trees is a half-mile-long stretch of fine gold sand in a half-moon-shaped cove. Tucked into the evergreen fold are some changing rooms, a small snack bar, and the concessionaires for beach chairs, umbrellas, and windsurfers. The beach can be extremely crowded but with an easy mix of families and singles. (There are several hotels near the beach, but because of the intense mosquito activity and construction, I recommend staying back in town or along the coast road.)

Ayia Eleni, a short but scenic walk from the Koukounaries bus stop (the end of the line) west across the island's tip, is a broad cove popular for windsurfing, as the wind is a bit stronger than at the south-coast beaches but not nearly as gusty as at the north. Across the peninsula, at the far right end of the beach, 15 to 20 minutes of fairly steep grade from the Koukounaries bus stop, is **Banana Beach ★** (sometimes called Krassa). It's slightly less crowded than Koukounaries, but with the same sand and pine trees. There's a snack bar or two, plus chairs, umbrellas, windsurfers, and jet skis for rent. One stretch of Banana Beach is the island's most fashionable nude beach.

Limonki Xerxes, also called Mandraki, north across the island's tip, a 20-minute walk up the path opposite the Lake Strofilias bus stop, is the cove where Xerxes brought in 10 triremes (galleys) to conquer the Hellenic fleet moored at Skiathos during the Persian Wars. It's a pristine and relatively secluded beach for those who crave a quiet spot. **Elia,** east across the little peninsula, is also quite nice. Both beaches have small refreshment kiosks.

Continuing along the northeast coast from Mandraki, you arrive at **Megalos Aselinos,** a windy beach where free camping has taken root. It is linked to the southern coastal highway via the road that leads to the Panagia Kounistria monastery (see below). You must continue north when the main road forks off to the right toward the monastery. There's also an official campsite and a fairly good taverna. **Mikros Aselinos,** farther east, is smaller and quieter, and you can reach it via a dirt road that leads off to the left just before the monastery.

Skiathos's north coast is much more rugged and scenic, with steep cliffs, pine forests, rocky hills, and caves. Most of these beaches are accessible only by boat, and of these, one is well worth the effort: **Lalaria ★**, on the island's northern tip, is one of Greece's most picturesque beaches (although it is a pebble beach). One of its unique qualities is the **Tripia Petra,** perforated rock cliffs that jut into the sea on both sides of the cove. These have been worn through by the wind and the waves to form perfect archways. You can lie on the gleaming white pebbles and admire the neon-blue Aegean and cloudless sky through their rounded openings. The water at Lalaria is an especially vivid shade of aquamarine because of the highly reflective white pebbles and marble and limestone slabs that coat the sea bottom. The swimming here is excellent, but the undertow can be quite strong; inexperienced swimmers should not venture very far. There are several naturally carved caves in the cliff wall that lines the beach, providing privacy or shade for those who have had too much sun. Lalaria is reached by caique excursions from the port; the fare is about 40€ for an around-the-island trip, which usually includes a stop for lunch (not included in the fare) at one of the other beaches along the northwest coast.

Three of the island's most spectacular grottoes—**Skotini, Glazia,** and **Halkini**— are just east of Lalaria. Spilia Skotini is particularly impressive, a fantastic 6m-high (20-ft.) sea cave reached through a narrow crevice in the cliff wall just wide enough for caiques to squeeze through. Seagulls drift above you in the cave's cool darkness, while below, fish swim in the 9m (30-ft.) subsurface area. Erosion has created spectacular scenery and many sandy coves along the north and east coasts, though none are as beautiful or well sheltered from the *meltemi* (high winds) as Lalaria beach.

THE KASTRO & THE MONASTERIES

When you want a change from the beach, I recommend an excursion to the **Kastro ★**, the old fortress-capital on the northernmost point of the island, east of Lalaria beach. The kastro was built in a remote and spectacular site in the 16th century, when the island was overrun by the Turks. It was abandoned after the War of Independence, when such fortifications were no longer necessary. Once joined to firm ground by a drawbridge, it can now be reached by cement stairs. The remains of the more than 300 houses and 22 churches have mostly fallen to the sea, but three of the churches, porcelain plates embedded in their worn stucco facades, still stand, and the original frescoes of one are still visible. From this citadel are excellent views to the **Kastronisia** islet below and the sparkling Aegean. Kastro can be reached by excursion caique (with a fairly demanding climb from the beach), over land by mule or donkey tour (available through most travel agencies), or by car via the road that leads northeast out of town, passing the turnoff to the Moni Evangelistrias (see below), and continuing to the end near the church of Panagia Kardasi. From here it is a mildly demanding 2km (1-mile) walk.

Moni Evangelistrias ★ is the more rewarding of the two monasteries that draw many visitors. Public buses travel here sporadically, but with your own vehicle it can be easily visited in not much more than an hour from Skiathos town. (Driving will also allow you to stop and admire the views.) To get here, take the road out of the northeast end and pass by the turnoff to the airport. After less than a kilometer, take the sharp right turnoff (signed) and climb about 3km (2 miles) to the monastery. Dating from the late 18th century, it has been completely (but authentically) restored; its architecture, icons, and woodcarvings make the trip worthwhile.

The other monastery, **Panagia Kounistria,** is approached from the coastal highway along the beaches (described above); just before Troulos Beach, take the right branch of the road (signed SELINOS) and climb about 4km (2½ miles) to the monastery. The pretty 17th-century structure contains some fine icons (although its most

411

important icon is now displayed in the Tris Ierarches Church in Skiathos town). Nothing spectacular, but a satisfying excursion.

SHOPPING

Skiathos town has no shortage of shops, many offering standard wares but some with distinctive items. The highlight for Greek crafts and folk art is **Archipelago** (℡ **24270/ 22-163**); adjacent to the Papadiamandis House, it offers a world-class assemblage of exquisite objects of art and folklore, both old and new, including textiles, jewelry, and sculpture. **Galerie Varsakis** ★ (℡ **24270/22-255**), on Trion Ierarchon Square above the fishing port, also has a virtually museum-quality collection of folk antiques, embroidered bags and linens, rugs from around the world, and other collectibles. Less stylish but full of curiosities is **Gallery Seraina** (℡ **24270/22-390**), at the first junction of Papadiamandis (opposite the alleyway to the Papadiamandis House); it has a goodly selection of ceramic plates, jewelry, some textiles, and unusual glass lampshades.

Where to Stay

Between July 1 and September 15, it can be very difficult to find accommodations. Try calling ahead from Athens to book a room or, better still, book your accommodations before you leave home. Note that many of the "luxury" hotels were thrown up quickly some years ago, and some have since been managed and maintained poorly— so if you plan an extended stay at a beach resort, we recommend checking into one of the hotels in town and then look over the possibilities before you commit to an extended rental.

If you crave the restaurant/shopping/nightlife scene, or you've arrived without reservations at one of the resort communities, try setting up base in **Skiathos Town.** From here, you can take public buses to the beaches on the south coast or go on caique excursions to the spectacular north coast or other islands.

Families often prefer to stay in two- to four-bedroom villas outside of town or at hotels overlooking a beach, with only an occasional foray into town.

One of the most pleasant parts of Skiathos town is the quiet neighborhood on the hill above the bay at the western end of the port. Numerous **private rooms** to let can be found on and above the winding stairs/street. Take a walk and look for the signs, or ask a travel agent. All over the hillside above the eastern harbor are several unlicensed "hotels," basically rooms to rent. You'll be surprised at which buildings are lodgings.

By the way, the in-town hotels (Alkyon excepted) cannot provide adjacent parking, but there are possibilities at the harbor's far eastern edge.

IN & AROUND SKIATHOS TOWN

In addition to the following options, consider moderately priced **Hotel Athos,** on the "ring road" that skirts Skiathos town (℡/fax **24270/22-4777**), which offers ready access to town without the bustle; and **Hotel Meltemi,** on the *paralia* (℡ **24270/22- 493**), a comfortable, modern place on the east side of the harbor (but avoid the front units, which can be noisy).

Babis Hotel ★ 🗲   A most appealing choice for those who want to stay in town, have a limited budget, and just like to relax at their own pace. There's no bar or restaurant but half of the units have fully equipped kitchenettes (including microwave) and the others have the means for making coffee or tea. There is also a good-size terrace with a barbecue where you can sit and enjoy a fabulous view over the whole harbor and much of the town. It's a homey place, and the proprietors provide free transportation to and from the airport if you've kept them informed of your schedule. There are bicycles available for rent. There is a slight climb up from the harbor so the hotel is not really suitable for anyone with mobility problems. All in all, a true find.

On hill facing New Harbor (approached by steps), 37002 Skiathos. babispension@hotmail.com. *C* **24270/21-968.** 14 units. 65€ double. MC, V. Parking at edge of town. **Amenities:** Wi-Fi. *In room:* A/C, TV, fridge.

Bourtzi Boutique Hotel ★★★ A truly contemporary, luxury hotel in the heart of Skiathos town, and expensive by Greek island in-town standards but not by international standards, and so for some, well worth a few nights here. Quite aside from each room's stylish decor and amenities, the outdoor swimming pool, the furnished balconies, the classy cocktail bar (which serves light snacks), and impeccable staff and service make this a true pleasure to come back to after a day on the island. You're close to everything in town but rooms are soundproofed, but while you're at it, ask for a room that faces the garden in the back.

8 Moraitou (just off and midway up Papadiamandis), 37002 Skiathos. www.hotelbourtzi.gr. *C* **24270/21-304.** 38 units. 145€–175€ double. Rates include breakfast. MC, V. Parking at edge of town. **Amenities:** Bar; pool; free Wi-Fi in public areas. *In room:* A/C, TV, fridge, hair dryer.

Hotel Morfo Looking for a slightly "atmospheric" offbeat hotel and not too fussy about creature comforts? Turn right off the main street opposite the National Bank, then left at the plane tree (there's a sign). You'll find this attractive hotel on your left on a quiet back street in the center of town. You enter through a small garden into a festively decorated lobby. The rooms are comfortable if basic.

23 Anainiou, 37002 Skiathos. *C* **24270/21-737.** Fax 24270/23-222. 17 units. 40€ double. No credit cards. No parking. *In room:* A/C, fridge, hair dryer.

Hotel Orsa ★★ One of the most charming small hotels in town is on the western promontory beyond the fishing harbor. To get here, walk down along the west port all the way past the fish stalls, proceed up two flights of steps, and watch for a recessed courtyard on the left, with handsome wrought-iron details. Rooms are standard in size but tastefully decorated; most have windows or balconies overlooking the harbor and the islands beyond. A lovely garden terrace is a perfect place for a tranquil breakfast. For advance booking, contact **Heliotropio Travel** on the harbor's east end (*C* **24270/22-430;** fax 24270/21-952; info@heliotropio.gr).

Plakes 37002 Skiathos. www.heliotropio.gr. *C* **24270/22-430.** 17 units. 75€ double. Rates include breakfast. Credit cards for reservation only; payment in cash. No parking. **Amenities:** Breakfast terrace. *In room:* A/C, fridge, hair dryer.

ON THE BEACH

Atrium Hotel ★★ This is one of the class acts of Skiathos hotels. Its location (on a pine-clad slope overlooking the sea) plus amenities make the Atrium Hotel a most pleasant place to vacation. Admittedly, the shady beach is some 100m (330 ft.) below and across the road, but the hotel's beautiful pool sits on a plaza high above the Aegean. The rooms have balconies or terraces that offer views over the sea. The hotel has a popular bar and restaurant; if you like, you can enjoy your meal outdoors on the veranda. I've always found the desk personnel and staff most courteous and helpful, but both the staff and guests here do expect a certain level of style in dress and conduct.

Platanias (some 8km/5 miles along the coast road southeast of Skiathos town), 37002 Skiathos. www.atriumhotel.gr. *C* **24270/49-345.** 75 units. 200€–260€ double. Rates include buffet breakfast. MC, V. Parking on grounds. **Amenities:** Restaurant; bar; babysitting; billiards; fitness room; Ping-Pong; pool; watersports equipment. *In room:* A/C, TV, fridge, hair dryer, Wi-Fi.

Troulos Bay Hotel 🏄 ☺   Though it's not exactly luxurious, this would be my first choice among the island's beach hotels for those looking for an unpretentious and laid-back holiday—and especially appealing for families with small children. It's set on handsomely landscaped grounds on one of the south coast's prettiest little beaches. As many of Skiathos's hotels, it's used primarily by groups, but individual rooms are often available. Guest rooms are modest but comfortably furnished; most have a balcony overlooking the beach and the lovely wooded islets beyond it. Some fault the unexciting food, but everyone who stays here reports that they find the staff refreshingly hospitable and helpful.

Troulos (9km/6 miles along the coast road southeast of Skiathos, down from the Alpha Supermarket), 37002 Skiathos. www.troulosbayhotel.gr. ✆ **24270/49-390.** 43 units. 110€ double; 140€ for family of 4. Rates include breakfast. MC, V. Parking on grounds. **Amenities:** Breakfast room; bar. *In room:* A/C (July–Aug only), TV, fridge.

Where to Dine

As in most of Greece's overdeveloped tourist resorts, cafes, fast-food stands, and overpriced restaurants abound, but there are also plenty of good, even excellent, eateries in Skiathos town. Some of the best-regarded restaurants are above the west end of the harbor, around Trion Ierarchon church.

EXPENSIVE

Asprolithos ★ GREEK/INTERNATIONAL   An elegant ambience, friendly and attentive service, and superb meals of light, updated taverna fare make this one of our favorite places to dine on Skiathos. You can get a classic moussaka here if you want to play it safe, or try specialties such as artichokes and prawns smothered in cheese. The excellent snapper baked in wine with wild greens is served with thick french fries that have obviously never seen a freezer. A handsome stone fireplace dominates the main dining room. You can sit at outdoor tables and catch the breeze.

Mavroyiali and Korai (up Papadiamandis a block past the high school, then turn right). ✆ **24270/21-016.** Reservations recommended. Main courses 8€–22€. MC, V. Daily 6pm–midnight. Closed late Oct to mid-Mar.

The Windmill Restaurant ★★ INTERNATIONAL   The town's most special dining experience is at an old windmill visible from the *paralia.* (You can approach it in several ways, but the signed route begins on the street between the back of the Akti and San Remo hotels at the eastern end of the harbor.) It is quite a climb, but well worth it—and reservations are a must in high season. You couldn't ask for a more romantic setting than on one of the terraces, where you can enjoy the sunset and then the lights of the town with your meal. The menu features a stylish version of basic dishes—fish, beef, lamb, pork, as well as vegetarian dishes. The desserts, too, are unusual, and there are many wines to choose from, including the best from Greece. A three-course meal with a modest wine will cost at least 100€, but it's well worth it.

Located on peak east of Ayios Nikolaos church. ✆ **24270/24-550.** www.skiathoswindmill.gr. Reservations strongly recommended. Main courses 12€–25€. MC, V. Daily 7–11pm.

MODERATE

Carnayio Taverna TAVERNA/SEAFOOD   One of the better waterfront tavernas is next to Hotel Alkyon. Favorites over the years have been the fish soup, lamb *you-vetsi* (lamb baked with pasta), and grilled fish. The garden setting is still special. If you're here late, you might be lucky enough to see an authentic round of dancing waiters and diners.

Paralia. ✆ **24270/22-868.** Main courses 6€–18€. AE, V. Daily 8pm–1am.

Taverna Limanakia TAVERNA/SEAFOOD   In the style of its next-door neighbor Carnayio (see above), the Limanakia serves some of the best taverna and seafood dishes on the waterfront. I always vacillate about which of the two neighbors I prefer, but always come away feeling satisfied after a meal at this reliable eatery.

Paralia (at far eastern end, past Hotel Alkyon). © **24270/22-835.** Main courses 6€–18€. MC. Daily 6pm–midnight.

Taverna Mesoyia ★ TAVERNA   You'll have to exert yourself a bit to find some of the best authentic traditional food in town. This little taverna is in the midst of the town's most labyrinthine neighborhood, above the western end of the harbor, but there are signs once you approach it. Try an appetizer such as the fried zucchini balls, enjoy the evening specials, or go for fresh fish in season. You'll feel as though you're at an old-fashioned neighborhood bistro, not a large tourist attraction.

Grigoriou (follow the signs behind Trion Ierarchon, high above the western end of the harbor). © **24270/21-440.** Main courses 8€–20€. No credit cards. Daily 7pm–midnight.

INEXPENSIVE

Kabourelia Ouzeri GREEK   Although it bills itself as an ouzeri—for drinks and snacks—this is really your standard taverna, and one of the most authentic eateries in town. Try the ouzo and octopus (which you can see drying on the front line) combo; or make a meal of the rich supply of cheese pies, fried feta, olives, and other piquant *mezedes*. It's a great place to sit and watch the activity along the waterfront while you linger over a modest but tasty meal.

Paralia (on harbor's western stretch). © **24270/21-112.** Main courses 5€–15€. AE, MC, V. Daily 10am–1am.

Skiathos After Dark

The **Aegean Festival** takes place from late June to early October, offering occasional performances of ancient Greek tragedies and comedies, traditional music and dance, modern dance and theater, and visiting international troupes. Festival events take place in the outdoor theater at the **Bourtzi Cultural Center,** on the promontory on the harbor. (The center itself, open daily 10am–2pm and 5:30–10pm, hosts art exhibits in its interior.) Performances begin at 9:30pm and usually cost about 15€; call © **24270/23-717** for information.

Although many may prefer to pass the evening with a *volta* (stroll) along the harbor or around and above the Plateia Trion Ierarchon, there is no denying that Skiathos town has a lively nightlife scene. I'll do my best to single out some of the more recently popular places, but I cannot be responsible for the frequent changes of names.

The main concentration of **nightclubs** is in the warren of streets west of Papadiamandis (left as you come up from the harbor). On Evangelistrias, opposite the post office, is the **Blue Chips Club;** this street intersects with Polytechniou—also known as "Bar Street": here you'll find **Destiny Bar,** the favorite—and lively—hangout for

---

 A Local Favorite

I think the best-kept secret of Skiathos town is the **little outdoor cafe** at the tip of the promontory with the Bourtzi fortress, a 5-minute stroll from the harbor. Removed from the glitter of the town, | you can sit and enjoy a (cheap) drink in the cool of the evening and watch the ships come and go: This is the Aegean lifestyle at its best.

the gay crowd; the **Admiral Benbow Club,** which offers something a bit quiet; and the flashier **Spartacus.** At the next intersection south, you'll find **Kirki,** a more intimate bar. Wander back down Papadiamandis to find **Kentavros Bar,** on the left beyond the Papadiamandis House, which plays classic rock and jazz.

On the far west end of the harbor, if you want sports with your drinks, try **Oasis Cafe;** if there's a game of any sort going on, it'll be on the tube. Meanwhile, at the far eastern end of the harbor are a few clubs popular with the younger set—among them, **Remezzo** and **Rock 'n' Roll Bar.**

Movie fans might enjoy the open-air showings at **Attikon** (on Papadiamandis, opposite Mare Nostum Holidays) or at **Cinema Paradiso** (up along the "ring road"). Both have two shows nightly, the first around 8:30pm; tickets are 6€.

SKOPELOS

121km (65 nautical miles) from Ayios Konstantinos, which is 166km (103 miles) from Athens

Skopelos is nearly as bustling as Skiathos in the high season, but isn't quite as "sophisticated." Its beaches are fewer and less impressive, but Skopelos town is pleasant enough, and the island offers some pleasant excursions. It was inevitable that handsomely rugged Skopelos would eventually be "discovered," but it has happened at a slower pace and a bit more wisely than on Skiathos. (No coincidence, perhaps, that it was used for most of the Greek scenes in the hit movie *Mamma Mia!*) Skopelos is also known for keeping alive *rembetika* music, the Greek version of American blues, that can be heard in tavernas late in the evening.

Essentials

GETTING THERE   By Plane   Skopelos cannot be reached directly by plane, but you can fly to nearby Skiathos and take a hydrofoil or ferry to the northern port of Loutraki (below Glossa) or to the more popular Skopelos town.

By Boat   If you're in Athens, take a boat or hydrofoil from Ayios Konstantinos to Skopelos (75 min.). **Alkyon Travel,** 97 Akademias, near Kanigos Square (✆ **210/ 383-2545**), can arrange the 3-hour bus ride from Athens to Ayios Konstantinos (about 20€) and hydrofoil or ferry tickets.

Coming from central or northern Greece, depart for Skopelos from Volos (about a 2-hr. trip). For hydrofoil (Flying Dolphins) and ferryboat information, contact **Hellenic Seaways,** Akti Kondyli and 2 Aitolikou, Piraeus (✆ **210/419-9000;** www. hellenicseaways.gr). For ferries from Piraeus, contact the **G.A. Ferries** line in Piraeus (✆ **210/458-2640;** www.ferries.gr/gaferries). Ferry tickets can be purchased at travel agencies in Athens or on the islands. During high season, you should purchase your boat tickets in advance through the boat lines. Although you may purchase tickets at Alkyon in person, they will not reserve ferryboat or hydrofoil tickets for you in advance, and these often sell out.

From Skiathos, the ferry to Skopelos takes 90 minutes if you call at Skopelos town, or 45 minutes if you get off at Glossa/Loutraki; the one-way fare to both is about 12€. Ferry tickets can be purchased at **Vasilis Nikolaou** (✆ **24270/22-209**), the travel agent at the corner of the Paralia and Papadiamandis. The Flying Dolphin hydrofoil takes 15 minutes to Glossa/Loutraki (four to five times daily; 15€), and 45 minutes to Skopelos (six to eight times daily; 17€). If you're on Skiathos, you can also take one of the many daily excursion boats to Skopelos.

There are infrequent ferryboat connections from Kimi (on Evvia) to Skopelos. Check with **Skopelos Port Authority** (© **24240/22-180**) for current schedules, as they change frequently. As stated previously, I think hydrofoils are worth the extra expense for hopping around the Sporades.

In the port of Skopelos town, hydrofoil tickets can be purchased at the Hellenic Seaways agent, **Madro Travel,** immediately opposite the dock where ferries tie up. It also serves as the Olympic Air representative.

VISITOR INFORMATION The **Municipal Tourist Office** of Skopelos is on the waterfront, to the left of the pier as you disembark (© **24240/23-231**); it's open daily from 9:30am to 10pm in high season. It provides information, changes money, and reserves rooms. To call ahead and book a room, the **Association of Owners of Rental Accommodation** maintains a small office on the harbor (© **24240/24-567**).

Madro Travel, opposite the ferry dock (© **24240/22-300;** www.madrotravel. com), is open all year; its knowledgeable and helpful staff know the island inside out and can provide information and make any arrangements you need. **Skopelorama Holidays,** about 100m (330 ft.) beyond Hotel Eleni on the left (east) end of the port (© **24240/23-040;** fax 24240/23-243), can also can help you find a room, exchange money, rent a car, or take an excursion. It's open daily from 8am to 10pm.

GETTING AROUND **By Bus** Skopelos is reasonably well served by public bus; the bus stop in Skopelos town is on the east end of the port. There are four routes. Buses run the main route every half-hour in the high season beginning in Skopelos and making stops at Stafilos, Agnondas, Panormos, the Adrina Beach Hotel, Milia, Elios, Klima, Glossa, and Loutraki. The fare from Skopelos to Glossa is 3€.

By Car & Moped The most convenient way to see the island is to rent a car or moped at one of the many shops on the port. A four-wheel-drive vehicle at **Motor Tours** (© **24240/22-986;** motortours@skopelos.travel) runs around 55€, including insurance; expect to pay less for a Fiat Panda. A moped should cost about 20€ per day.

By Taxi The taxi stand is at the far end of the waterfront (left off the dock). Taxis provide service to almost any place on the island. Taxis are not metered—negotiate the fare before accepting a ride. A typical fare, from Skopelos to Glossa, runs 40€.

By Boat To visit the more isolated beaches, take one of the large excursion boats; these cost about 70€ including lunch, and should be booked a day in advance in high season. Excursion boats to Glisteri, Gliphoneri, and Sares beaches operate only in peak season (about 20€). From the port of Agnondas, on the south coast, fishing boats go to Limnonari, one of the island's better beaches.

FAST FACTS There are several **ATMs** at banks around the harbor. The **health center** is on the road leading out of the east end of town (© **24240/22-222**). Plynthria, a self-service **laundry,** is located (in a basement) just past Adonis Hotel on the upper road at the east end of the harbor (© **24240/22-123**). It's open Monday through Saturday from 9:30am to 1:30pm and 6 to 8pm. The **police station** (© **24240/22-235**) is up the narrow road (Parados 1) to the right of the National Bank, along the harbor. For **Internet access,** try Click & Surf (info@skopelosnet cafe.com), just up from the police station—ask for Platanos Square—then proceed up past the supermarket. The **post office,** on the port's far east end (take the stepped road leading away from the last kiosk, opposite the bus/taxi station), is open Monday to Friday from 8am to 2:30pm. The **telephone office (OTE)** is at the top of a narrow road leading away from the center of the harbor; it's open Monday to Saturday from 8am to 5pm.

What to See & Do

The ferries from Alonissos, Skyros, and Kimi, and most of the hydrofoils and other boats from Skiathos, dock at both Glossa/Loutraki and Skopelos town. Most boats stop first at **Loutraki,** a homely little port near the northern end of the west coast, with the more attractive town of **Glossa ★** high above it. Especially if this is your first visit, we suggest you stay onboard for the trip around the island's northern tip and along the east coast to the island's main harbor, Skopelos town. You'll understand the island's name—"cliff" in Greek—when your boat pulls around the last headland into a huge and nearly perfect C-shaped harbor, and you get your first glimpse of Skopelos town rising like a steep amphitheater around the port.

Skopelos town (also called Hora) is one of Greece's most treasured towns, on par with Hydra and Simi. It scales the steep, low hills around the harbor and has the same winding, narrow paths that characterize the more famous Cycladic islands to the south. Scattered on the slopes of the town are just a few of the island's 123 churches, which must be something of a record for such a small locale. The oldest of these is **Ayios Michali,** past the police station. The waterfront is lined with banks, cafes, travel agencies, and the like. Interspersed among these prosaic offerings are truly regal shade trees. Many of the shops and services are up the main street leading away from the center of the *paralia.* The back streets are amazingly convoluted (and unnamed); it's best that you wander around and get to know a few familiar landmarks.

The **Venetian Kastro,** which overlooks the town from a rise on the western corner, has been whitewashed. Built over an archaic Temple of Athena, it proved to be too strong for the Turks to capture during the War of Independence in the 1820s.

At the far eastern end of town is the **Photographic Center of Skopelos** (*© 24240/24-121*), which during the high season sponsors quite classy photography exhibitions in several locales around town.

SHOPPING

Skopelos has a variety of shops selling Greek and local ceramics, weavings, and jewelry. One of the most stylish is **Armoloi,** in the center of the shops along the harbor (*© 24240/22-707*). It sells only Greek jewelry, ceramics, weavings, and silver; some of the objects are old. The owners make the most of the handsome ceramics. Another special store is **Ploumisti,** at a corner of an alley about midway along the paralia (*© 24240/22-059;* kalaph-skp@skt.forthnet.gr). It sells beautiful Greek rugs, blankets, jewelry, pottery, and crafts. Its friendly proprietors, Voula and Kostas Kalafatis, are full of helpful information for visitors, especially the *rembetika* music scene.

 Sporades National Marine Park

One of the more unusual attractions of a stay on Skopelos could be a day's excursion to the National Marine Park off the adjacent island of Alonissos. There you are guaranteed to see some of the many dolphins that frequent this protected area, and if you are lucky you may even see some Mediterranean monk seals, an endangered species protected within the marine park. The trip usually includes a stop at the volcanic islet of Psathoura, with a chance to dive into a sunken city, and a visit into the Blue Grotto of Alonissos. Any travel agency in Skopelos will be able to arrange such an excursion on one of several licensed ships. Meanwhile, check out the site www.goskiathos.com.

Nikos Rodios (© 24240/22-924), whose gallery is between Hotel Eleni and Skopelorama Holidays agency, is from a Skopelos family who have made ceramics for three generations. Nikos makes each piece on a foot-pumped wheel and his elegant vessels, at once classical and modern, are a change from the usual pottery found around Greece.

EXPLORING THE ISLAND

The whole island is sprinkled with monasteries and churches, but five **monasteries** south of town can be visited by following a pleasant path that continues south from the beach hotels. The first, **Evangelistria,** was founded by monks from Mount Athos, but it now serves as a nunnery, and the weavings of its present occupants can be bought at a small shop; it's open daily from 8am to 1pm and 4 to 7pm. The fortified monastery of **Ayia Barbara,** now abandoned, contains 15th-century frescoes. **Metamorphosis,** very nearly abandoned, comes alive on August 6, when the feast of the Metamorphosis is celebrated here. **Ayios Prodromos** is a 30-minute hike farther, but it's the handsomest and contains a particularly beautiful iconostasis. **Taxiarchon,** abandoned and overgrown, is at the summit of Mount Polouki to the southeast, a hike recommended only for the hardiest and most dedicated.

There is basically a single highway on the island, with short spurs at each significant settlement. It runs south from Skopelos town, then cuts north and skirts the west coast northwest, eventually arriving at Glossa; it then runs down to Loutraki. The first spur leads off to the left to **Stafilos,** a popular family beach recommended by locals for a good seafood dinner, which you must order in the morning. About half a kilometer across the headland is **Velanio,** where nude bathing is common.

The next settlement west is **Agnondas,** named for a local athlete who brought home the gold from the 569 B.C. Olympic Games. This small fishing village has become a tourist resort thanks to nearby beaches. **Limnonari,** a 15-minute walk farther west and accessible by caique in summer, has a good fine-sand beach in a rather homely and shadeless setting.

The road then turns inland again, through a pine forest, coming out at the coast at **Panormos.** With its sheltered pebble beach, this has become the island's best resort with a number of taverns, hotels, and rooms to let, as well as watersports facilities. The road then climbs again toward **Milia** ★, which is considered **the island's best beach.** You will have to walk down about half a kilometer from the bus stop, but you'll find a lovely light-gray beach of sand and pebbles, with the island of Dassia opposite and watersports facilities at **Beach Boys Club** (© 24240/23-995).

The next town, **Elios (Neo Klima),** was thrown up to shelter the people displaced by the 1965 earthquake. It's become home to many of the locals who operate the resort facilities on the west coast, as well as something of a resort itself.

The main road proceeds on to **Glossa** ★, which means "tongue," and that's what the hill on which the town was built looks like from the sea. Most of it was spared during the earthquake, so it remains one of the most Greek and charming towns in the Sporades. Those tempted to stay overnight will find a number of rooms for rent, a good hotel, and a very good taverna. (The hotel is the **Avra;** © **24240/33-550;** fax 24240/33-681.)

Most of the coastline here is craggy and has a few hard-to-reach beaches. Among the best places to catch some rays and do a bit of swimming is the small beach below the picturesque chapel of **Ayios Ioannis,** sitting high on a rocky prominence on the coast a few miles to the east of Glossa; it was at this site and chapel that the climax of

Mamma Mia! takes place. (Bring food and water if you plan to swim.) As for the port of **Loutraki,** it's a winding 3km (2 miles) down; we don't recommend a stay there.

That ends the road tour of Skopelos, but other sites can be reached from Skopelos town by caique. Along the east coast north of Skopelos is **Glisteri,** a small, pebbled beach with a nearby olive grove offering respite from the sun. It's a good bet when the other beaches are overrun in summer. You can also go by caique to the grotto at **Tripiti,** for the island's best fishing, or to the little island of **Ayios Yioryios,** which has an abandoned monastery.

The whole of Skopelos's 95 sq. km (38 sq. miles) is prime for **hiking** and **biking,** and the interior is still waiting to be explored. There's also **horseback riding, sailing** (ask at the Skopelos travel agencies), and a number of interesting **excursions** to be taken from and around the island. Both Skopelorama Holidays and Madro Travel (see "Visitor Information" and "Getting There," above) operate a fine series of excursions, such as monasteries by coach, a walking tour of the town, and several cruises. Another possibility (spring or fall only) is a nature (or town) walk led by a longtime English resident, Heather Parsons (✆ **24240/24-022;** www.skopelos-walks.com); if you prefer to go it alone, you can buy her *Skopelos Trails Guide* (3rd edition) in shops around town.

One excursion that should appeal to many is on one of the licensed boats that take you to the waters around nearby Alonissos that make up the **National Marine Park** (p. 418); lucky visitors may spot Mediterranean monk seals, an endangered species protected within the park.

Where to Stay

In high season, Skopelos is becoming nearly as popular as Skiathos. If you've arrived without reservations and need help, talk to the Skopelorama Holidays agency (see "Visitor Information," above) or to the officials at the town hall. Be sure to look at a room and agree on a price before you accept anything, or you may be unpleasantly surprised. To make matters confusing, there are few street names in the main, old section of Skopelos town, so you'll have to ask for directions to find your lodging.

IN SKOPELOS TOWN

Handsome, traditional-style **Hotel Amalia,** along the coast, 500m (1,640 ft.) from the port's center (✆ **24240/22-688;** fax 24240/23-217), is largely occupied by groups but should have spare rooms in spring and fall.

Hotel Denise One of the most appealing hotels in Skopelos thanks to its premier location, clean facilities, and its own pool, the Hotel Denise stands atop the hill overlooking the town and commands spectacular vistas of the harbor and Aegean. A wide balcony rings each of the hotel's four stories. Most of the guest rooms—admittedly, rather small—have views that are among the best in town. The Denise is popular and open only in high season; before hiking up the steep road, call for a pickup and to check for room availability—or better yet, reserve in advance.

Skopelos town 37003. www.denise.gr. ✆ **24240/22-678.** 25 units. 50€ double. Rates include continental breakfast. MC, V accepted for deposit only. Parking on adjacent street. **Amenities:** Restaurant; bar; pool; Wi-Fi. *In room:* A/C, TV, fridge, Internet.

Hotel Eleni Hotel Eleni is a modern hotel that can boast of location and convenience as it is set back from the coast and only 300m (984 ft.) to the left (off the dock) from the harbor's center. After many years spent operating pizzerias in New York, Charlie Hatzidrosos returned from the Bronx to build this establishment. His daughter operates the hotel and provides gracious service. All rooms have balconies.

Skopelos town 37003. ☎ **24240/22-393.** Fax 24240/22-936. 37 units. 75€ double. AE, MC, V. Parking on adjacent street. **Amenities:** Snack bar. *In room:* A/C, TV, fridge.

Skopelos Village ★ ☺ Although Skopelos Village is considerably more expensive than other Skopelos hotels, it offers a lot for the money. Guests here may want to settle in for a while so that they can take advantage of this miniresort's amenities—or just enjoy the aromatic greenery of the surroundings. The buildings are tastefully constructed as "traditional island houses." Each bungalow is equipped with kitchen, private bathroom, and one or two bedrooms, and can sleep from two to six persons. Facilities include a breakfast room and snack bar. In the evening, the restaurant offers Greek meals accompanied by Greek music and dance. The hotel provides free transportation to the island's various beaches, although one is right in front of the hotel.

About 1km (½ mile) southeast of town center, Skopelos 37003. www.skopelosvillage.gr. ☎ **24240/22-517.** 36 units. High season studio or suite for 2 persons, with a kitchen 175€–195€; bungalow for up to 6 persons, 210€. Rates include buffet breakfast. MC, V. Free parking nearby. **Amenities:** 2 restaurants; babysitting; children's playground; pool; room service; tennis nearby; Wi-Fi. *In room:* A/C, TV, hair dryer, minibar.

IN PANORMOS

This pleasant little resort is on a horseshoe-shaped cove along the west coast, about halfway between Skopelos town and Glossa. Here you'll find several cafeteria-style snack bars and minimarkets. We recommend it as a base, especially because one of the best hotels on the island—Adrina Beach Hotel (see below)—is just above it. As for restaurants, a particularly lively taverna, **Dihta,** is right along the beachfront.

Panormos Travel Office (☎ **24240/23-380;** fax 24240/23-748) has decent rooms to let; offers phone and fax services; exchanges money; arranges tours (including night squid fishing); and rents cars, motorbikes, and speedboats.

If you can't get a room at the Adrina, try 38-unit **Afrodite Hotel** (☎ **24240/23-150;** www.afroditehotel.gr), a more modern choice about 100m (328 ft.) across the road from the beach at Panormos.

Adrina Beach Hotel and Resort & Spa ★ ☺ This traditional hotel on the beach outside Panormos has long rated as one of the better ones on the island, and with the opening of its adjacent grand Resort & Spa in 2011 it is now even more impressive. The hotel's guest rooms are large and tastefully furnished in pastels, each with its own balcony or veranda. In addition to the main hotel's rooms, 22 handsome villas are ranked down the steep slope toward the hotel's private beach. The complex has a big saltwater pool with its own bar, a restaurant, a buffet room, a playground, and a minimarket. Conference facilities for 50 to 60 people can be provided. Meanwhile, the new facility offers in addition to 16 more villas a spa, a gym, its own pool and playground, a beach volleyball court—and a monorail that transports guests up and down the slope from the villas and to the restaurant and beach.

About 500m (¼ mile) from Panormos, 37003 Skopelos. www.adrina.gr. ☎ **24240/23-373** or 210/682-6886 in Athens. 52 units. 75€–145€ double at hotel; 150€–250€ for a villa at Resort accommodating up to 3 adults and 3 children. Rates include buffet breakfast. AE, DC, MC, V. **Amenities:** 2 restaurants; bar; children's playground; Jacuzzi; minimarket; pool; spa. *In room:* A/C, TV, hair dryer, fridge.

IN GLOSSA

There are approximately 100 rooms to rent in the small town of Glossa. Expect to pay about 40€ for double occupancy. The best way to find a room is to visit one of the tavernas or shops and inquire about vacancies. You can ask George Antoniou at **Pythari Souvenir Shop** (☎ **24240/33-077**) for advice. If you can't find a room in

Glossa, you can take a bus or taxi down to Loutraki and check into a pension by the water; or you can head back to Panormos.

Where to Dine

IN SKOPELOS TOWN

Finikas Taverna and Ouzeri ★ GREEK   Tucked away in the upper back streets of Skopelos is a picturesque garden taverna/ouzeri dominated by a broadleaf palm. The Finikas offers what might be Skopelos's most romantic setting, thanks to its isolated and lovely garden seating. (You simply have to ask for directions here.) Among the many fine courses are an excellent ratatouille and pork cooked with prunes and apples, a traditional island specialty.

Upper back street of Skopelos town. ✆ **24240/23-247.** Main courses 6€–14€. No credit cards. Daily 7pm–2am.

The Garden Restaurant GREEK   Some locals claim this is the best restaurant in town. Two young brothers operate what most people call simply the Garden, for its setting and casual atmosphere. The food is tasty and often a bit different. We enjoy the mushrooms with garlic (an appetizer), and calamari with cheese (a main course).

At harbor's far eastern end, 1st left at corner of Amalia Hotel. ✆ **24240/22-349.** www.skopelosweb. gr/kipos. Reservations recommended in high season. Main courses 6€–20€. MC, V. Daily 11am–midnight. Closed Oct to mid-June.

Platanos Jazz Bar SNACK/BAR FOOD   For everything from breakfast to a late-night drink, try this pub. Breakfast in the summer starts as early as 5 or 6am for ferry passengers, who can enjoy coffee, fruit salad with nuts and yogurt, and fresh-squeezed orange juice for about 8€. Platanos is equally pleasant for evening and late-night drinks. Music from the proprietors' phenomenal collection of jazz records will accompany your meal.

Beneath the enormous plane tree just to the left of the ferry dock. ✆ **24240/23-661.** Main courses 5€–12€. No credit cards. Daily 5am–2am.

IN GLOSSA

Taverna Agnanti ★ TRADITIONAL SKOPELITIAN   Highly praised by numerous international travel magazines, this is the place to meet, greet, and eat in Glossa. The food is inexpensive, the staff friendly, and the view spectacular. The menu is standard taverna style, but the proprietors make a point of using the finest fresh products and wines. Specialties include herb fritters, fish *stifado* (rabbit and onions) with prunes, pork with prunes, and almond pie. Traditional music is occasionally played. The Stamataki family runs this and the nearby souvenir shop Pythari.

Glossa (about 200m/656 ft. up from the bus stop). ✆ **24240/33-076.** agnanti-rest@agnanti-rest.gr. Main courses 6€–22€. No credit cards. Daily 11am–midnight.

Skopelos After Dark

The nightlife scene on Skopelos isn't nearly as active as on neighboring Skiathos, but there are still plenty of bars, late-night cafes, and discos. Most of the coolest bars are on the far (east) side of town, but you can wander the scene around Platanos Square, beyond and along the paralia: **Anemos, Karavia, Ntokos, Ionas, Mythos**—one of these places should satisfy. The best place for bouzouki music is **Metro,** and for *rembetika* try the **Kastro.** For live music with a spectacular view of the town, ask for directions to the **Anatoli Ouzeri.**

SKYROS (SKIROS) ★

47km (25 nautical miles) from Kimi; 182km (113 miles) from Athens

Fairly remote **Skyros** hardly seems a part of the Sporades group, especially as its land-scape and architecture are more Cycladic. But it has several excellent beaches, as well as a colorful local culture, and it remains the perfect destination for those who want to get away from the crowds. Some of us, in fact, think Skyros's more meager tourist facilities and the stark contrast between the sea, sky, and rugged terrain make it all the more inviting. Also it can be the base for a day's excursion to Alinossos, the fourth of the Sporades, less popular than the other three but that much more natural.

Essentials

GETTING THERE   By Plane   In summer, **Olympic Air** has about three flights a week between Athens and Skyros and Thessaloniki and Skyros. Call the Olympic office in Athens (☎ **210/966-6666**) for information and reservations; the local Olympic representative is **Skyros Travel and Tourism** (☎ **22220/91-123**). A bus meets most flights and goes to Skyros town, Magazia, and sometimes Molos; the fare is 6€. A taxi from the airport is about 18€, but expect to share a cab.

By Boat   Skyros Shipping Company (www.sne.gr) offers the only ferry service to Skyros; it's operated by a company whose stockholders are all citizens of the island. In summer, it runs twice daily (usually early afternoon and early evening) from Kimi (on the east coast of Evvia) to Skyros, and twice daily (usually early morning and mid-afternoon) from Skyros to Kimi; the trip takes a little over 2 hours. Off season, there's one ferry each way, leaving Skyros early in the morning and Kimi in late afternoon. The fare is 12€ to 20€. For information, call the company's office in either Kimi (☎ **22220/22-020**) or Skyros (☎ **22220/91-790**). The Skyros Shipping Company's offices also sell connecting bus tickets to Athens; the fare for the 3-hour ride is about 15€. In Athens, **Alkyon Travel,** 97 Akademia, near Kanigos Square (☎ **210/383-2545**), arranges bus transportation to Kimi and sells ferry tickets to the Sporades.

In the summer occasional ferries and hydrofoils link Skyros to the other Sporades as well as to ports on the mainland, but these links are either fairly infrequent or involve land transportation to ports that are not on most tourists' itineraries. If you're trying to "do" the Sporades and want to make connections at Kimi, the tricky part can be the connection with ferries or hydrofoils from the other Sporades islands. When they don't hold to schedule, it's not uncommon to see the Skyros ferry disappearing on the horizon as your ship pulls into Kimi. You might have to make the best of the 24-hour layover and get a room in Paralia Kimi. (We recommend **Hotel Korali,** at ☎ **22220/22-212;** or the older **Hotel Krineion,** at ☎ **22220/22-287.**)

From Athens, buses to Kimi and Ayios Konstandinos leave the Terminal B, 260 Lission, six times a day, though you should depart no later than 1:30pm; the fare for the 3½-hour trip is about 20€. At Kimi, you transfer to a local bus to the dock; ask the bus driver if you're uncertain of the connection.

On Skyros, the ferries and hydrofoils dock at **Linaria,** on the opposite side of the island from Skyros town. The island's only public bus will meet the boat and take you over winding, curving roads to Skyros town for 2€. On request, the bus will also stop at Magazia beach, immediately north below the town, next to Xenia Hotel.

VISITOR INFORMATION   The largest tourist office is **Skyros Travel and Tourism** (☎ **22220/91-123;** www.skyrostravel.com), next to Skyros Pizza Restaurant in the main market. It's open daily from 8am to 2:30pm and 6:30 to 10:30pm.

English-speaking Lefteris Trakos offers assistance with accommodations, currency exchange, Olympic Air flights (he's the local ticket agent), phone calls, interesting bus and boat tours, and Hellenic Seaways Flying Dolphin tickets.

GETTING AROUND   By Bus   The only scheduled service is the Skyros-Linaria shuttle that runs four to five times daily and costs 3€. Skyros Travel (see above) offers a twice-daily beach-excursion bus in high season and daylong island excursions in a small bus with an English-speaking guide (50€); for many, this may be the best way to get an overview of the island.

By Car & Moped   A small car rents for about 70€ per day, including insurance. Mopeds and motorcycles are available near the police station or the taxi station for about 25€ per day. The island has a relatively well-developed network of roads.

By Taxi   Taxis can take you just about anyplace on the island at the standard Greek rates, but discuss the price before setting off; service between Linaria and Skyros costs about 20€.

On Foot   Skyros is a fine place to hike. The island map, published by Skyros Travel and Tourism, will show you a number of good routes, and it is pretty accurate.

FAST FACTS   The most convenient ATM on Skyros is at the **National Bank of Greece** in the main square of Skyros town. (Because Skyros's tourist services are relatively limited, we recommend bringing cash and/or traveler's checks for emergencies.) The **clinic** is near the main square (✆ **22220/92-222**). The **police station** (✆ **22220/91-274**) is on the street behind the Skyros Travel Center. The **post office** is near the bus square in Skyros town; it's open Monday through Friday from 8am to 2pm. The **telephone office (OTE)** is opposite the police station. It's open Friday only, from 7:30am to 3pm, but there are card phones in town.

What to See & Do

The Faltaits Historical and Folklore Museum   This is one of the best island folk-art museums in Greece. Located in an old house belonging to the Faltaits family, the private collection of Manos Faltaits contains a large and varied selection of plates, embroidery, weaving, woodworking, and clothing, as well as many rare books and photographs, including some of local men in traditional costumes for Carnival. Attached to the museum is a workshop where young artisans make lovely objects using traditional patterns and materials. The proceeds from the sale of workshop items go to the upkeep of the museum. The museum also has a shop, **Argo**, on the main street of town (✆ **22220/92-158**). It's open daily from 10am to 1pm and 6:30 to 11pm.

Plateia Rupert Brooke on the northeast edge of Skyros Town. ✆ **22220/91-327.** www.faltaits.gr. Admission 2€. Summer Tues–Sun 8:30am–3pm; off season, ring the bell and someone will probably let you in.

EXPLORING THE ISLAND

All boats dock at **Linaria,** a plain, mostly modern fishing village on the west coast, pleasant enough but not recommended for a stay. Catch the bus waiting on the quay to take you across the narrow middle of the island to the west-coast capital, Skyros town, which is built on a rocky bluff overlooking the sea. (The airport is near the northern tip of the island.) **Skyros town,** which is known on the island as Horio or Hora, looks much like a typical Cycladic hill town, with whitewashed houses built on top of one another. The winding streets and paths are too narrow for cars and mopeds, so most of the traffic is by foot and hoof. After you alight at the bus stop square, continue on up toward the center of town and the main tourist services.

Near the market, signs point to the town's **kastro.** The climb takes 15 minutes, but the view is worth it. On the way you'll pass the church of **Ayia Triada,** which contains interesting frescoes, and the monastery of **Ayios Yioryios Skyrianos.** The monastery was founded in 962 and contains a famous black-faced icon of St. George brought from Constantinople during the Iconoclastic controversy. From one side of the citadel, the view is over the rooftops of the town, and from the other the cliff drops precipitously to the sea. According to one myth, King Lykomides pushed Theseus to his death from here. (Skyros also happens to be where Neoptolemis, the son of Achilles, was living when he was sent for to revenge his father' death at Troy.)

The terrace at the far (northern) end of the town is **Plateia Rupert Brooke,** where the English poet, who is buried on the southern tip of the island, is honored by a nude statue, *Immortal Poetry.* (Brooke died on a hospital ship off Skyros in 1915 while en route to the Dardanelles as an army officer.) The statue is said to have greatly offended the local people when it was installed, but you're more likely to be amused (or annoyed) when you see how pranksters have chosen to deface the hapless bronze figure. The Faltaits Historical and Folklore Museum (see above) is near this site, as is the not especially distinguished—and thus not recommended—archaeological museum.

Local customs and dress are currently better preserved on Skyros than in all but a few locales in Greece. Older men can still be seen in baggy blue pants, black caps, and leather sandals with numerous straps, and older women still wear long head scarves. The **embroidery** you will often see women busily working at is famous for its vibrant colors and interesting motifs—such as people dancing hand in hand with flowers twining around their limbs and hoopoes with fanciful crests.

Peek into the doorway of many a Skyrian home and you're likely to see what looks like a room from a dollhouse with a miniature table and chairs, as well as **colorful plates**—loads of them—hanging on the wall. These displays are said to date from the Byzantine era, when the head clerics from Epirus sent 10 families to Skyros to serve as governors. They were given control of all the land not owned by Mount Athos and the Monastery of St. George. For hundreds of years, these 10 families dominated the affairs of Skyros. With Kalamitsa as a safe harbor, the island prospered, and consulates opened from countries near and far. The merchant ships were soon followed by pirates, with whom the ruling families went into business. The families knew what boats were expected and what they were carrying, and the pirates had the ships and bravado to steal the cargo—and then share with their informants. The pirates, of course, soon took to plundering the islanders as well, but the aristocrats managed to hold onto much of their wealth.

Greek independence reduced the influence of these ruling families, and during the hard times brought by World War I, they were reduced to trading their possessions to the peasant farmers for food. Chief among these bartered items were sets of dinnerware. Plates from China, Italy, Turkey, Egypt, and other exotic places became a sign of wealth, and Skyrian families made elaborate displays of their newly acquired trophies. Whole walls were covered, and by the 1920s local Skyrian craftsmen began making their own plates for the poorer families who couldn't afford the originals. This, at least, is the story they tell.

Skyros is also the home of a unique breed of **wild pygmy ponies,** often compared to the horses depicted on the frieze of the Parthenon and thought to be similar to

THE FAMOUS carnival OF SKYROS

The 21-day Carnival celebration is highlighted by a 4-day period leading up to Lent and the day known throughout Greece as *Kathari Deftera* (Clean Monday). On this day, Skyros residents don traditional costumes and perform dances on the town square. *Lagana* (unleavened bread) is served with *taramosalata* (fish roe spread) and other meatless specialties. (Traditionally, vegetarian food is eaten for 40 days leading up to Easter.) Much of this is traditional throughout Greece, but Skyros adds its own distinctive element. Culminating on midafternoon of the Sunday before Clean Monday is a series of ritual dances and events performed by a group of weirdly costumed men. Some dress as old shepherds in animal skins with belts of sheep bells and masks made of goatskin. Other men dress as women and flirt outrageously. (Skyros seems to have an age-old association with cross-dressing: It was here that Achilles successfully beat the draft during the Trojan War by dressing as a woman, until shrewd Odysseus tricked him into revealing his true gender.) Other celebrants caricature Europeans. All behave outlandishly, reciting ribald poetry and poking fun at bystanders. This ritual is thought to be pagan in origin, and what you see has deep roots. Some of the antic elements might seem similar to parts from ancient Greek comedies, and the word "tragedy" means "goat song," so the goat-costume ceremonies may go way back also.

Shetland ponies. Most of these rare animals have been moved to the nearby island of Skyropoula, though tame ones can still be seen grazing outside the town. Ask around and you might be able to find a local who will let you ride one.

Every July 15, the ponies of Skyros are assembled and rated as to their characteristics, and then young boys race some of the ponies around a small track.

BEACHES & OUTDOOR PURSUITS

The island is divided almost evenly by its narrow waist; the northern half is fertile and covered with pine forest, while the southern half is barren and quite rugged. Both halves have their attractions, though the most scenic area of the island is probably to the south toward **Tris Boukes,** where Rupert Brooke is buried. The better beaches, however, are in the north.

To get to the beach at **Magazia,** continue down from Plateia Rupert Brooke. (If your load is heavy, take a taxi to Magazia, as it is a hike.) From Magazia, once the site of the town's storehouses (magazines), it's about 1km (½ mile) to **Molos,** a fishing village, though the two villages are quickly becoming indistinguishable because of development. There's windsurfing along this beach and, beyond Molos, windsurfing at fairly isolated beaches with nudist sections.

South of town, the beaches are less enticing until you reach **Aspous,** which has a couple of tavernas and rooms to let. **Ahili,** a bit farther south, is where you'll find the big new **marina,** so it's no longer much of a place for swimming. Farther south, the coast gets increasingly rugged and has no roadway.

If you head back across the narrow waist of the island to **Kalamitsa,** the old safe harbor, 3km (2 miles) south of Linaria, you'll find a good clean beach. Buses run here in summer.

North of Linaria, **Acherounes** is a very pretty beach. Beyond it, **Pefkos,** where marble was once quarried, is better sheltered and has a taverna that's open in summer.

The next beach north, **Ayios Fokas,** is probably the best on the island, with a lovely white pebble beach and a taverna open in summer. Locals call it paradise, and like all such places it's very difficult to reach. Most Skyrians will suggest walking, but the hike is long and hilly. To get here from Skyros town, take the bus back to Linaria, tell the driver where you're going, get off at the crossroads with Pefkos, and begin your hike west from there.

North of Ayios Fokas is **Atsitsa,** another beach with pine trees, but it's a bit too rocky. It can be reached by road across the Olympos mountains in the center of the island, and has a few rooms to let. It is also the location of a **holistic health-and-fitness holiday community,** which offers "personal growth" vacations, with courses in fitness, holistic health, creative writing, and handicrafts. For information on its activities, contact the **Skyros Centre** in the U.K. at 9 Eastcliff Rd., Shanklin, Isle of Wight PO37 6AA (© **01983/865566;** www.skyros.com). This same outfit runs the **Skyros Centre** at the edge of Skyros town; it differs from the one at Atsitsa in that it offers a somewhat more conventional touristic experience. A 15-minute walk farther north from Atsitsa, **Kira Panagia** is a sandy beach that's a bit better.

The northwest of the island is covered in dense pine forests, spreading down to the Aegean. The rocky shore opens onto gentle bays and coves. This area provides wonderful **hiking** for the fit. Take a taxi (40€ to **Atsitsa**), and arrange for it to return in 5 or 6 hours. Explore the ruins of the ancient mining operation at Atsitsa, then head south for about 7km (4½ miles) to **Ayios Fokas ★**, a small bay with a tiny taverna perched right on the water where you can expect the meal of your trip: fresh fish caught that morning in the waters before you, vegetables plucked from the garden for your salad, and the house feta cheese and wine. Relax, swim in the bay, and then hike back to your taxi. The ambitious may continue south for 11 or 12km (7–8 miles) to the main road and catch the bus or hail a taxi. Note that this part of the road is mainly uphill. In case you tire or can't pry yourself away from the secluded paradise of Ayios Fokas, Kali offers two extremely primitive rooms with the view of your dreams, but without electricity or toilets.

SHOPPING

Skyros is a good place to buy local crafts, especially embroidery and ceramics. **Ergastiri,** on the main street, is noted for its wood furniture. **Yiannis Nicholau,** whose studio is next to Xenia Hotel, is known for his handmade plates. You can find good hand-carved wooden chests and chairs made from beech (in the old days it was blackberry wood) from **Lefteris Avgoklouris;** his studio (© **22220/91-106**) is on Konthili, around the corner from the post office. Another fine carver is **Manolios,** in the main market.

Where to Stay

The island has relatively few hotels, so most visitors to Skyros take private rooms. The best are in the upper part of Skyros town, away from the bus stop, where women in black dresses accost you with cries of "Room! Room!" If you are determined to make arrangements before arriving, you could phone or fax the **Skyros Association of Hotels and Rooms** (© **22220/92-095;** fax 22290/92-770). It is better to wait until you are on the scene and contact **Skyros Travel and Tourism** (see "Visitor Information," above). The island of Skyros is somewhat more primitive in its facilities than the other Sporades, so before agreeing to anything, check out the room to ensure that it's what you want.

IN SKYROS TOWN

Hotel Nefeli ★   The most ambitious—and arguably the best—in-town option is the Nefeli, designed and furnished in traditional Skyrian style. It is actually composed of three buildings, each with various room arrangements and amenities; there are even some with kitchenettes. The bedrooms and bathrooms are decent in size and well appointed; many units have fine views. The large downstairs lobby is a welcoming space. Reserve in advance, as the Nefeli is one of the favorite choices on Skyros.

Skyros town center, 34007 Skyros. www.skyros-nefeli.gr. ✆ **22220/91-964.** 16 units. 100€ double; 120€–180€ for larger units. Breakfast 6€ extra. AE, MC, V. Parking on premises. **Amenities:** Restaurant; bar; children's play area; Internet access; 2 pools (1 children's); smoke-free rooms. *In room:* A/C, TV, hair dryer, minibar.

IN MAGAZIA BEACH & MOLOS

Hotel Angela ⚑   This is among the most attractive and well-kept abodes in the Molos/Magazia beach area, located near the sprawling Paradise Hotel complex. All rooms are clean and tidy with balconies, but because the hotel is set back about 150m (500 ft.) from the beach, it has only partial sea views. Nevertheless, the facilities and hospitality of the young couple running the Angela make up for its just-off-the-beach location, and it's your best bet for the money.

Molos, 34007 Skyros. www.angelahotelskyros.com. ✆ **22220/91-764.** Fax 22220/92-030. 14 units. 90€ double. No credit cards. **Amenities:** Pool. *In room:* A/C.

Pension Galeni ⚑   The small but pleasant Pension Galeni offers modest rooms, all with private bathrooms. Ask for one of the front, sea-facing rooms on the top floor for their (currently) unobstructed views. The Galeni overlooks one of the cleanest parts of Magazia beach.

Magazia beach, 34007 Skyros. ✆ **22220/91-379.** 13 units. 70€ double. No credit cards.

Xenia   With the best location on the beach at Magazia, the Xenia offers some of the nicest (if not cheapest) accommodations on Skyros. The guest rooms have handsome 1950s-style furniture and big bathrooms with tubs, as well as wonderful balconies and sea views. You can get all your meals here if you want. Perhaps the hotel's greatest drawback is the unsightly concrete breakwater that's supposed to protect the beach from erosion.

Magazia Beach, 34007 Skyros. ✆ **22220/92-063.** Fax 22220/92-062. 22 units. 115€ double. Rates include buffet breakfast. V.

IN ACHEROUNES BEACH

Pegasus Apartments   Nothing spectacular, these fully equipped studios and apartments were built by the resourceful Lefteris Trakos (owner of Skyros Travel). They are at Acherounes, the beach just south of the port of Linaria, on the east coast. One of the pluses of staying here is the chance to see (and ride, if you're 14 or under) Katerina, a Skyrian pony.

Acherounes Beach, 34007 Skyros. ✆ **22220/91-552.** 8 units. 60€ studio for 2 persons; 130€ apt. for 3–5 persons. MC, V. *In room:* Minibar.

IN YIRISMATA

Skiros Palace Hotel ★   If you want to get away from it all and enjoy upscale amenities to boot, this is the place for you. This out-of-the-way resort—about 1.6km (1 mile) north of Molos, and 3km (2 miles) north of Skyros town—has some of the most ambitious facilities on the island. The plainly furnished but comfortable guest rooms come with large balconies. The beach across the road is sandy and inviting, but it can be windy and rocky—be very careful in the sea here. Facilities include a lovely (saltwater) pool and adjacent bar, tennis and basketball courts, and a well-planted garden—not to mention a soundproof disco, the island's most sophisticated. A minibus heads into town twice a day.

Yirismata, 34007 Skyros. www.skiros-palace.gr. © **22220/91-994.** 80 units. 110€ double. Rates include breakfast. AE, DC, MC, V. Parking at hotel. **Amenities:** 2 restaurants; bar; basketball court; minibus to town; outdoor pool; sailboat for excursions; tennis; TV in lobby. *In room:* A/C and TV in some rooms.

Where to Dine

The food in Skyros town is generally pretty good and reasonably priced. **Anemos,** on the main drag (© **22220/92-155**), is a nice spot for breakfast, with filtered coffee, omelets, and freshly squeezed juice. Nearby **Skyros Pizza Restaurant** (© **22220/ 91-684**) serves tasty pies as well as other Greek specialties. For dessert, head to **Zaccharoplasteio** (the Greek word for sweet shop/bakery) in the center of town.

Linaria offers three decent tavernas to choose from—**Almyria, Filippeos,** and **Psariotos.**

Kristina's/Pegasus Restaurant ★ INTERNATIONAL   Come here if you need a break from standard Greek fare. Kristina's has been an institution in Skyros town for some years, but in 2000 it moved to the locale of the former Pegasus Restaurant, a neoclassical building (ca. 1890) in the center of town. The Australian proprietor/chef, Kristina, brings a light touch to everything she cooks. Her fricasseed chicken is excellent, her herb bread is tasty, and her desserts, such as cheesecake, are exceptional.

Skyros town. © **2222091-123.** Reservations recommended in summer. Main courses 7€–20€. No credit cards. Mon–Sat 7am–4pm and 7pm–1am. No parking.

Maryetes Grill GRILL   One of the oldest and best places in town, the Maryetes is a second-generation-run grill that's equally popular with locals and travelers. Go for the food, not the dining room, which is as simple as can be. We recommend anything grilled—fish, chicken, or meat. And sample one of the salads.

Skyros town. © **22220/91-311.** Main courses 6€–12€. No credit cards. Daily 1–3pm and 6pm–midnight. No parking.

Restaurant Kabanero ♦ GREEK   One of the best dining values in town, this perpetually busy eatery serves the usual Greek menu: moussaka, stuffed peppers and tomatoes, fava, a variety of stewed vegetables, and several kinds of meat. The dishes are tasty and the prices somewhat lower than those at most other places in town.

Skyros town. © **22220/91-240.** Main courses 6€–14€. No credit cards. Daily 1–3pm and 6pm–midnight. No parking.

Skyros After Dark

Skyros is not the island for you if you've come to Greece looking for a lively bar and club scene. During high season, there is enough of the same to satisfy most people. As usual in such locales, names and atmospheres can change from year to year. But at last checking, the **Kastro Club,** in Linaria, was for dancing. **Skyropoula** on the way from Plateia Rupert Brooke to Magazia, and Linaria's **O Kavos** are other popular hangouts. Aside from these, you'll find few evening diversions other than barhopping on the main street of Skyros town. **Apocalypsis** draws a younger crowd. **Kalypso** attracts a more upscale set of drinkers. **Renaissance** is lively but can be loud. **Rodon** is best for actually listening to music, while **Kata Lathos (By Mistake)** has also gained a following.

THE IONIAN ISLANDS

by John S. Bowman

12

The Ionian Islands (which the Greeks know as the Heptanissi, or "seven islands") include Corfu (Kerkira), Paxos (Paxoi), Levkas (Lefkas, Lefkada), Ithaka (Ithaki), Kefalonia (Kefallinia, Cephalonia), Zakinthos (Zakynthos, Zante), and Kithira (Cythera, Cerigo). Located off Greece's northwest coast (except for Kithera), the Ionians offer some of the country's loveliest natural settings, including beaches, fine hotels and restaurants, a distinctive history and lore, and some unusual architectural and archaeological remains.

Strategies for Seeing the Islands

The Ionian Islands are rainier, greener, and more temperate than other Greek islands, so the high season lasts a little longer, from late June to early September. In this chapter, we single out **Corfu** and **Kefalonia,** with a side trip to **Ithaka.** With a couple of weeks to spare, you can take a ship or plane to either Corfu, in the north, or **Zakinthos,** in the south; and then make your way by ship to several of the other Ionians (although outside high season, you will have to do considerable backtracking). If you have only a week, you should get to one of the larger islands the fastest way possible, and then use ships to get to, at most, a couple of the others. If it comes down to visiting only one, Corfu is a prime candidate, but if you want to get off the beaten track, consider Kefalonia or Ithaka. All the Ionians, especially Corfu, are overrun in July and August; aim for June or September, if you can.

CORFU (KERKIRA) ★★

32km (20 nautical miles) W of mainland; another 558km (342 miles) NW of Athens

Cast aside the Corfu package tour and you will find Homer's "rich and beautiful land" of hazy olive groves and rugged mountains, 20 miles off the west coast of Greece. The sunny beaches and ouzo-fueled revelry are there if you want them, but this island has a unique history and culture that rewards even the casual visitor. Wander Venetian Corfu town as the grand fortress lights up in the evening, visit the beach associated with Odysseus, or just relax while reading the works of British brothers-writers Lawrence and Gerald Durrell to get a feel for the real Corfu.

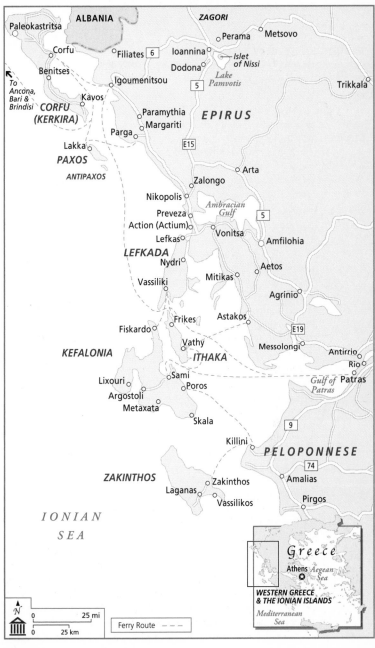

Western Greece & the Ionian Islands

Paleokastritsa

ALBANIA   ZAGORI

Corfu

Filiates 6   Ioannina   Perama   Metsovo

Benitses

To
Ancona,
Bari &
Brindisi

Igoumenitsou   5   Dodona   Islet
of Nissi

Lake
Pamvotis

Trikkala

Kavos

CORFU
(KERKIRA)

Paramythia   EPIRUS
Margariti

Parga

Lakka   E15

PAXOS

ANTIPAXOS

Arta

Zalongo

Nikopolis   Ambracian
Gulf

Preveza   5

Action (Actium)   Vonitsa

Lefkas   Amfilohia

LEFKADA

Nydri   Aetos

Vassiliki   Mitikas

Agrinio

Fiskardo   Frikes   Astakos

E19

Vathy

KEFALONIA   ITHAKA   Messolongi

Antirrio

Rio

Lixouri   Sami   Gulf of   Patras
Patras

Argostoli   Poros

Metaxata

Skala

Killini   9

PELOPONNESE

74

ZAKINTHOS   Zakinthos   Amalias

Laganas   Pirgos

Vassilikos

IONIAN
SEA

Greece

Athens   Aegean
Sea

WESTERN GREECE
& THE IONIAN ISLANDS

Mediterranean
Sea

N

0   25 mi

0   25 km

Ferry Route   - - -

BEACHES **Paleokastritsa** on the northwest coast deserves its reputation, what with its several bays flanked by cave-riddled cliffs and bluer-than-blue sea. Moving south along that coast, **Liapades** has a sublime backdrop, while secluded **Myrtiotissa** attracts nudists. Families especially like **Sidari,** up on the north coast with its sandstone formations, and **Ayios Georgios,** with its fine sand and shallow water. On the northeast coast, nestling amid cypress and olive trees, is crescent-shaped **Kalami Bay,** where the Durrells spent their childhood. For those who enjoy a combination of watersports and partying, there's **Kavos** on the southern tip.

THINGS TO DO With its Italianate buildings, its French arcade, and English remains, **Corfu town** provides a history lesson even to strollers. Visit one or both of the two great **fortresses** to be reminded that the island was long fought over, visit the **Archaelogical Museum** to realize it was once important to Greek sculpture. A more recent footnote to history is the **Achilleon,** the Empress Elizabeth of Austria-Hungary and Kaiser Wilhelm II, outside Corfu town. Up in the northeast is the deserted Byzantine town **Old Perithia,** on the slopes of the nearly 900m (3,000-ft.) summit of **Mt. Pantocrator** from which **Albania** can be viewed. And don't forget to leave time for shopping for the island's **fine handicrafts** such as olive wood and needlework.

EATING & DRINKING Authentic Greek food, English breakfasts, gyros to go, fine Italian cuisine—you'll find it all in Corfu town. In tavernas throughout the island, you'll have your choice of local favorites such as **bourdetto,** spicy fish in a tomato sauce, or **pastitsada,** beef stewed in tomato sauce. And along the water's edge around the island, family-run tavernas serve simple but delicious **fresh fish.** So-called house wines are never that great in Greece, but Corfiots are particularly proud of their island wines. Among the best are wines such as **Robola, Liapaditiko,** and **Theotaki** (this last preferred by James Bond).

NIGHTLIFE & ENTERTAINMENT Do as the Corfiots do and begin your evening with a *volta* (stroll) under the **Liston**'s elegant arcades in Corfu town. The younger set may prefer to join the revelers at one of the many lounge bars and clubs lining **Ethnikis Antistaseos** past the New Port. Elsewhere on the island, at seaside towns such as **Ipsos, Roda,** and **Sidari,** you can find English pubs, karaoke bars, and "Greek nights" with fast-paced sirtaki dancing. And yes, those whose holidays include some serious partying will want to try **Kavos,** appropriately at the island's lowest tip.

Essentials

GETTING THERE **By Plane** **Olympic Air** provides at least three flights daily from and to Athens, and three flights weekly from and to Thessaloniki (via Athens). The Olympic Air office in Corfu town (*C* **26610/38-694**) is at 11 Polila, down from the Ionian Islands Tourism Office, but agents all over town sell tickets. **Aegean Airlines** also offers occasional flights (*C* **210/626-1000** in Athens, or 26610/27-100 in Corfu).

Kerkira = Corfu

Kerkira is the modern Greek name for Corfu. Look for it on many schedules, maps, brochures, and other publications.

Corfu airport is about 4km (2½ miles) south of the center of Corfu town. Fortunately, the flight patterns of most planes do not bring them over the city. Everyone takes taxis into town; the standard fare should be 12€ but may fluctuate with destination, amount of luggage, and time of day.

Information (i)

0   300 m
0   300 y
N

NEW PORT

OLD PORT

Arseniou 2

NEW FORTRESS (NEO FROURIO)

OLD VENETIAN QUARTER 3

Xenofondos Stratigou
Donzelot
Zavitsianou
Solomou
Velissariou
Paleologou
G. Martora
G. Theotoki
Pandova

Bus Station

N. Theotoki

Avramiou

Avrami Hill

I. Theotikos

Mandraki Harbor

Ayios Spyridon Cathedral 4

Voulgareos 5

Eleftherias

Plateia

Guilford

Kapodistriou

Esplanade

OLD FORT (PALEO FROURIO)

Polichroni Konstanda

San Rocco Square
Local Bus Station

Mitropoliti Methodiou
Desila

N. Zambeli

Garitsa Bay

Rizospaston Voulefton
Alexandros

Vraila

6

Demokratias

7

Corfu Town

Greece

Athens

Aegean Sea

Mediterranean Sea

Archaeological Museum **7**
Ayios Spyridon Cathedral **4**
Byzantine Museum **2**
Ionian Academy **6**
Museum of Asian Art **3**
Palace of St. Michael &
   St. George **3**
Synagogue **1**
Town Hall **5**

By Boat   Many lines and ships link Corfu to both Greek and foreign ports. Ferries run almost hourly between Corfu and Igoumenitsou, directly across on the mainland (1–2 hr.), and several go weekly to and from Patras (about 7 hr.). At least during high season, there is now a twice-daily hydrofoil express (about 30 min.) between Corfu and Igoumenitsou. Also in high season are daily ships linking Corfu to ports in Italy—Ancona, Bari, Brindisi, Trieste, Venice—or to Piraeus and/or Patras. The schedules and fares vary so much from year to year that it would be misleading to provide details here; work with a travel agent in your homeland or Greece; or check **www.ferries. gr**. The ship lines are: **Adriatica** (© 210/429-0487 in Piraeus), **ANEK Lines** (© 210/323-3481 in Athens), **Fragline** (© 210/821-4171 in Athens), **Hellenic Mediterranean Line** (**HML;** © 210/422-5341 in Piraeus), **Minoan Lines** (© 210/414-5700 in Piraeus), **Strintzis Lines** (© 210/422-5015 in Piraeus), and **Ventouris Line** (© 210/988-9280 in Piraeus). In high season, the typical one-way cost from Brindisi to Corfu is about 320€ to 380€, for two people in a double cabin with a private bathroom, and with a standard-size vehicle.

By Bus   KTEL offers service from Athens or Thessaloniki; its ferry carries you between Corfu and Igoumenitsou, on the mainland opposite. Buses allow you to get on or off at main points along the way, such as Ioannina. The buses are comfortable enough, but be prepared for many hours of winding roads. The **KTEL office** (℃ **26610/39-627**) is located along Leoforos Avramiou, up from the new port.

VISITOR INFORMATION   In previous years there have been municipal tourist information stations on the Esplanade and down at the new port but you cannot count on these to be there in any given year. The best sources of information are in fact the private travel agencies such as **Corfu Holidays Travel Agency,** at 12 Mantzarou, near the Municipal Theater in New Town (℃ **26610/23-523;** www.corfu holidays.com).

GETTING AROUND   **By Bus**   The dark-blue public buses service Corfu town, its suburbs, and nearby destinations. The semiprivate green-and-cream KTEL buses offer frequent service to points all over the island—Paleokastritsa, Glifada, Sidari, and more. The **KTEL office** (℃ **26610/39-627**) is located along Leoforos Avramiou, up from the new port.

By Taxi   Taxis are of no use inside Corfu town—distances are short and streets clogged—but are handy for getting to and from the harbor and the airport. Although taxi drivers are supposed to use their meters, many don't, so you should agree on the fare before setting out. You may also decide to use a taxi to visit some of the sites outside Corfu town; again, be sure to agree on the fare beforehand.

By Car   You'll find car-rental agencies all over Corfu. Even so, in high season it can be very difficult to get a vehicle at the spur of the moment. If you're sure of your plans on Corfu, make arrangements with an established international agency before departing home. Otherwise, try **Corfu Holidays Travel Agency** (see "Visitor Information," above); or **Avanti Rent A Car,** 12A Ethnikis Antistasseos, along the new port (℃ **26610/42-028**).

By Moped   It's easy to rent mopeds, scooters, and motorcycles, but the roads are so curving, narrow, and steep that you should be very experienced before taking on such a vehicle. And insist on a helmet.

FAST FACTS   The official **American Express** agent for Corfu is Greek Skies Travel Agency, 20A Kapodistriou (℃ **26610/33-410;** fax 26610/36-161). There are numerous **banks** in both the old town and new town; you'll find ATMs at most of them. The **British Consul** is at 1 Menekrates (℃ **26610/30-055**), at the south end of the town, near the Menekrates monument. There is no U.S. consulate in Corfu. The **hospital** is out on Julius Andreatti, and directions are signposted around town.

There are several **Internet cafes:** I've always used the Online Cafe, 28 Kapodistriou, along the Esplanade (café_online1@yahoo.com); there's also the Cyber Café Corfu, 3 Gardikioti, down by New Port (cybercafecorfu@hotmail.com). Both are open daily from late morning to late evening. You can count on quick, careful, and fair-priced **laundry** or **dry cleaning** at the Peristeri, 42 Ioannis Theotikos (leading from San Rocco Sq., on the way to the KTEL Bus Terminal). It's open Monday through Saturday from 8am to 2pm, with additional hours on Tuesday, Thursday, and Friday from 6 to 8pm. The **police station** (℃ **26610/39-575**) is at 19 Leoforos Alexandros (near the post office). The **post office** (℃ **26610/25-544**) is at 26 Leoforos Alexandros. It's open Monday through Friday from 7:30am to 8pm; in July and August, it's also open for a few hours on Saturday. The main **telephone office** (**OTE**) is at 9 Mantzarou; it's open Monday through Friday from 7am to midnight, and 7am to 10pm on Saturday and holidays.

What to See & Do

THE TOP ATTRACTIONS

Archaeological Museum ★ Even if you're not a devotee of ancient history or museums, you should take an hour to visit this small museum. On your way to see its master work, you'll pass a **stone lion** dating from around 575 B.C. (found in the nearby Menekrates tomb, along the waterfront by the museum). Go around and behind it to the large room with arguably the finest example of Archaic temple sculpture extant, the **pediment from the Temple of Artemis.** (The temple itself was south of Corfu town and dates from about 590 B.C.; the remains do not interest most people.) The pediment features the **Gorgon Medusa,** attended by two pantherlike animals. You don't have to be an art historian to note how this predates the great classical works, such as the Elgin marbles—not only in the naiveté of its sculpture but also in the emphasis on the monstrous, with the humans so much smaller in scale.

Interesting for comparison is the fragment from another Archaic pediment found at Figare, Corfu. In an adjoining room, it shows Dionysos and a youth reclining on a couch. Only a century younger than the Gorgon pediment, here the humans have reduced the animal in size and placed it under the couch.

1 P. Armeni-Vraila (on the corner of Demokratias, the road along the waterfront). © **26610/30-680.** Admission 4€; free Sun. Tues–Sun 8:30am–2:30pm. Wheelchair accessible. Parking on adjacent streets.

Kalypso Star ☺ This glass-bottomed boat takes small groups offshore and provides fascinating views of marine life and undersea formations.

Old port, Corfu town. © **26610/46-525.** Admission 15€ adults, 8€ children. In high season, trips leave daily on the hour 10am–6pm, and at 10pm. Call for off-season schedule. Parking along waterfront.

Museum of Asian Art The building itself, an impressive example of neoclassical architecture, was constructed between 1819 and 1824 for several reasons: to serve as the residence of the Lord High Commissioner, the British ruler of the Ionian Islands; to house the headquarters of the Order of St. Michael and St. George; and to provide the assembly room for the Ionian senate. When the British turned the Ionian Islands over to Greece, they gave this building to the king of Greece. As the king seldom spent much time here, it fell into disrepair until after World War II, when it was restored and turned into a museum.

The centerpiece of the museum is the collection of Chinese porcelains, bronzes, and other works from the Shang Dynasty (1500 B.C.) to the Ching Dynasty (19th c.). Go, too, to see the impressive Japanese works: woodblock prints, ceramics, sculpture, watercolors, and *netsuke* (carved sash fasteners). You may not have come to Greece to appreciate Asian art, but this is one of Corfu's several unexpected delights.

The Palace of St. Michael and St. George, north end of Esplanade. © **26610/38-124.** protocol@hepka. culture.gr. Admission 4€. Tues–Sun 8am–2:30pm. No parking.

Old Fort (Paleo Frourio) Originally a promontory attached to the mainland, now separated by a moat, this area is known for its two peaks (*koryphi,* in Greek), which gave the town and the island their modern names. A castle crowns each peak; you can get fine views of Albania to the east and Corfu, town and island, to the west. The promontory itself, for a long time, was the main town, and it appears as such in many old engravings. The Venetians dug the moat in the 16th century; it successfully held off several attempts by the Turks to conquer this outpost of Christianity. What looks like a Greek temple at the south side is in fact a British church (ca. 1830).

An Excursion to Albania

During high season, several travel agencies and ship lines offer 1-day excursions to Albania. The excursion to Albania is becoming popular even though it doesn't go to the capital; the fare for a day trip to Albania now costs about 80€, which should include visas, port fees, and a midday meal. Most interesting is a brief visit to the major archaeological site of Butrint, a UNESCO World Heritage Site. Travel agents in Corfu or at the Albanian port of Saranda, where you land, will set you up with a guide; prices vary, but in general, Albania is still cheap. Ship lines we recommend are **Corfu Holidays** (✆ 26610/23-523; www.corfuholidays. com) and **Ionian Cruises** (✆ 26610/31-649; www.ionian-cruises.com).

In summer, a **sound-and-light** show is held several nights a week (in different languages, so be sure to check the schedule).

The Esplanade (opposite the Liston). Admission 4€ adults, 2€ students and E.U. seniors over 60. Tues–Fri 8am–8pm; Sat–Sun and holidays 8:30am–3pm.

A STROLL AROUND CORFU TOWN ★

This is definitely a browser's town, where as you're strolling in search of a snack or souvenir, you may serendipitously discover an old church or monument. To orient yourself, start with the **Esplanade area** bounded by the Old Fort (see above) and the sea on one side. The small haven below and to the north of the Old Fort is **Mandraki Harbor,** while the shore to the south is home port to the **Corfu Yacht Club.**

Dousmani bisects the Esplanade; at the far side is the circular monument that honors the union of the Ionian Islands with Greece. You might catch a cricket game at the **Plateia,** the northern part of the field. At the far north side of the Esplanade, the Palace of St. Michael and St. George is the home of the **Museum of Asian Art** (see above). If you proceed along the northwest corner of the palace, you'll come out above the coast and can make your way around Arseniou above the *mourayia* (medieval sea walls). On your left is the house of Dionysos Solomos, the 19th-centry poet laureate of Greece.

On your way, you will pass (on the left, up a flight of stairs) the **Byzantine Museum** in the **Church of Antivouniotissa.** Even if you're not a particular fan of Byzantine art, you should enjoy the small but elegant selection of icons from around Corfu; of particular interest are works by Cretan artists who came to Corfu, some of whom went on to Venice. The museum is open Monday from 12:30 to 7pm, Tuesday through Saturday from 8am to 7pm, and Sunday and holidays from 8:30am to 3pm. Admission is 3€.

Proceed along the coast road and descend to the square at the old port. Above its far side rises the **New Fortress,** and beyond this is the new port. Off to the left of the square is a large gateway, what remains of the 16th-century Porta Spilia. Go through it to get to the Plateia Solomou.

If you go left from Plateia Solomou along Velissariou, look on the right for the green doors of the 300-year-old **synagogue,** with its collection of torah crowns. It's open on Saturday from 9am until early evening. To gain entry during the week, call the Jewish Community Center at ✆ 26610/38-802.

Continue on to the part of old Corfu known as **Campiello ★**, with its stepped streets and narrow alleys. You may feel as if you are in a labyrinth—and you will be—but sooner or later you'll emerge onto one or another busy commercial street that will bring you down to the Esplanade.

Heading south on the Esplanade, you'll see a bandstand and, at its far end, the **Maitland Rotunda,** which honors Sir Thomas Maitland, the first British lord high commissioner of the Ionian Islands. Past this is the statue of Count Ioannis Kapodistrias (1776–1836), the first president of independent Greece.

Head south along the shore road from this end of the Esplanade, and you'll pass the Corfu Palace Hotel (see below) on your right; then the **Archaeological Museum** (see above), up Vraila on the right. After 2 more blocks, off to the right on the corner of Marasli, you'll see the **Tomb of Menekrates,** a circular tomb of a notable who drowned about 600 B.C. Proceeding to the right here onto Leoforos Alexandros will bring you into the heart of new Corfu town.

Back at the Esplanade, the western side of the north half is lined by a wide tree-shaded strip filled with cafe tables and chairs, then a street reserved for pedestrians, and then arcaded buildings patterned after Paris's Rue de Rivoli. Begun by the French and finished by the British, these arcaded buildings, known as the **Liston ★★**, provide a great backdrop for a cup of coffee or a dish of ice cream.

At the back of the Liston is **Kapodistriou;** perpendicular from this extend several streets that lead into the heart of old Corfu—a mélange of fine shops, old churches, souvenir stands, and other stores in a maze of streets, alleys, and squares that seem like Venice without the water. The broadest and most stylish is **Nikiforio Theotoki**. At the northern end of Kapodistriou, turn left onto Ayios Spiridon and come to the corner of Filellinon and the **Ayios Spiridon Cathedral,** dedicated to Spiridon, the patron saint of Corfu. Locals credit Spiridon, a 4th-century bishop of Cyprus, with saving Corfu from famine, plagues, and a Turkish siege. Inside the church is the saint's embalmed body in a silver casket, as well as precious gold and silver votive offerings and many fine old icons. Four times a year, the faithful parade the remains of St. Spiridon through the streets of old Corfu: Palm Sunday, Holy Saturday, August 1, and the first Sunday in November.

Proceeding up Voulgareos, behind the southern end of the Liston, you'll come to the back of the **Town Hall,** built in 1663 as a Venetian loggia; it later served as a theater. Turn into the square it faces and enter what seems like a Roman piazza ★, with steps and terraces, a Roman Catholic cathedral on the left, and, reigning over the top, the restored Catholic archbishop's residence (now the Bank of Greece).

 Sitting Still

Probably no one needs to be told that one of the great pleasures of traveling about Greece is just occasionally to sit still—that is, to plunk yourself down on a cafe chair and enjoy a drink, while you observe the passing scene. And arguably no more ideal place to do just that on Corfu is at one of the cafes that set out their tables and chairs between the Liston and the Esplanade. The Liston, the impressive arcade, is a Greek version of "the List," referring to a list of upper-class and privileged individuals who were the only ones allowed to frequent this site after it was erected in the early 1800s. Today we can all sit here and enjoy such pleasures as watching a game of cricket being played on the Esplanade (Spianada, in Greek), the large greensward. Cricket is a vestige of the island's years under British rule, as is ginger beer, which you might consider sipping while you sit there.

From here, finish your walk by wandering up and down and in and out the various streets of old Corfu.

SHOPPING

Corfu town has so many shops selling jewelry, leather goods, olive wood objects, and handmade needlework that it is impossible to single out one or another. If you're looking for needlework, the stores along Filarmonikis (off N. Teotoki) may have something that pleases you; prices are generally fair and uniform.

I would never recommend a trip to Corfu *just* for the kumquat liqueur, but this Chinese fruit has been cultivated on the island since the late 1800s, and the liqueur makes a unique treat—or gift, if it doesn't appeal to you.

Standing out from the many standard souvenir-gift shops, **Antica,** 25 Ayios Spiridon, leading away from the north end of Liston (© **26610/32-401**), offers unusual older jewelry, plates, textiles, brass, and icons. **Gravures,** 64 Ev. Voulgareos, where the street emerges from the old town to join the new town (© **26610/41-721**), has a fine selection of engravings and prints of scenes from Corfu, all nicely matted. Originals (taken from old books or magazines) can cost 150€, reproductions as little as 10€. And for something quite special, visit the **Patounis Soap-Making Factory** on I. Theotaki (© **26610/39-860**) and try some of its hypoallergenic olive oil soap.

There's no dearth of ceramics in Corfu, but I favor the **Pottery Workshop,** 15km (10 miles) north of Corfu on the right of the road to Paleokastritsa (© **26610/90-704**), where you get to observe Sofoklis Ikonomides and Sissy Moskidou making and decorating all the pottery on sale here. Two kilometers (1¼ miles) farther along the road, on the left, is the **Wood's Nest,** offering a large selection of olive wood objects just slightly cheaper than in town

Where to Stay

The island of Corfu has an apparently inexhaustible choice of accommodations, but in high season (July–Aug), package groups from Europe will book many rooms. Reservations are recommended if you have specific preferences for that time, especially for Corfu town. And those considering renting a villa or apartment for a more extended stay should contact **Corfu Holidays Travel Agency** (see "Visitor Information," earlier in this section).

IN TOWN

Very Expensive

Corfu Palace Hotel ★★   This grand hotel combines the most up-to-date features of an international enterprise (it is owned by the Aquis Hotel Group) with Greek hospitality. In addition to its splendid surroundings, superb service, and grand meals, the hotel provides restful isolation above the bay, even though it is near the city center. The comfortable guest rooms, while not exceptionally large, are well appointed; the marbled bathrooms are large. Every balconied room enjoys views of the sea—insist on one. The hotel's two restaurants, the Scheria (a grill room on the poolside terrace) and the Panorama (with a view of the bay), serve Greek and international menus; both vie to claim the finest cuisine on Corfu. Guests can use the facilities of the nearby (night-lit) Corfu Tennis Club and Yacht Club and the Corfu Golf Club, 14km (9 miles) away.

2 Leoforos Demokratias, 49100 Corfu. www.corfupalace.com. © **26610/39-485.** Fax 26610/31-749. 115 units. High season 210€–320€ double; low season 170€–225€ double. Children 12 and under stay free in parent's room (without meals). Rates include buffet breakfast; half board available. AE, DC, MC, V. Free parking. A 5-min. walk from Esplanade, along Garitsa Bay, just south of town center. **Amenities:** 2

restaurants; 3 bars; babysitting; Internet; 3 pools (1 for children); room service; smoke-free rooms. *In room:* A/C, TV, hair dryer, minibar, Wi-Fi.

Moderate

If you prefer old-fashioned period hotels to shiny new accommodations, consider **Astron Hotel,** 15 Donzelot (waterfront road down to old harbor), 49100 Corfu (⟨ⓒ **26610/39-505**). It offers up-to-date bathrooms and other facilities while retaining touches of its original charm.

Arcadion Hotel ★ If you like to be at the center of a city, you can't get much closer than this: When you step out the door, the Esplanade and the Liston are only 15m (50 ft.) away. Admittedly, this also means that on pleasant evenings there will be crowds in front of the hotel, but ask for a room off the front. (All windows are double-glazed for sound control.) It's hard to beat for location and comfort. In the evening, you can sit in the roof garden and enjoy a cool drink with a fabulous view.

44 Kapodistriou, 49100 Corfu. www.arcadionhotel.com. ⓒ **26610/30-104.** Fax 26610/45-087. 33 units. 120€ double. Rates include buffet breakfast. AE, MC, V. Free public parking nearby. Diagonally across from south end of Liston, facing the Esplanade. **Amenities:** Restaurant; bar; health club; room service; Wi-Fi. *In room:* A/C, TV, hair dryer, Internet, minibar.

Bella Venezia ★ 🍴 Like the gold-medal winner of the decathlon, this hotel may not win in any single category, but its combined virtues make it the first choice of many. The building is a restored neoclassical mansion (and a major updating in 2006), with character, if not major distinction. The location is just a bit off center and lacks fine views, but it's quiet and close enough to anyplace you'd want to walk to; a decent beach is 300m (1,000 ft.) away. Although not luxurious or large, the guest rooms have some old-world touches; the showers, however, are undeniably cramped. There is no restaurant, but there's a colorful patio-garden for breakfast and an enclosed kiosk for light snacks.

4 N. Zambeli (approached from far south end of Esplanade), 49100 Corfu. www.bellaveneziahotel.com. ⓒ **26610/46-500.** Fax 26610/20-708. 31 units. High season 200€ double; low season 115€ double. Rates include buffet breakfast. AE, DC, MC, V. Parking on adjacent streets. Within walking distance of old and new towns. **Amenities:** Patio for breakfast and snacks; bar; babysitting; Internet. *In room:* A/C, TV, hair dryer, Internet, minibar.

Cavalieri ★ If you like your hotels in the discreet old European style, this place is for you. For glitz, look elsewhere—the main lounge is done in "Italian velvet." The Cavalieri is in an old building with a small elevator. Service is low key, rooms are spare, and bathrooms standard. Ask for one of the front rooms on the upper floors, which boast great views of the Old Fort. Another draw is the rooftop garden, which, after 6:30pm, offers drinks, sweets, and light meals along with a spectacular view; even if you don't stay here, it's a grand place to pass an hour in the evening. Because of the hotel's appealing location, advance reservations are required much of the year.

4 Kapodistriou, 49100 Corfu. www.cavalieri-hotel.com. ⓒ **26610/39-041.** Fax 26610/39-283. 50 units. High season 142€ double; low season 110€ double. Rates include buffet breakfast. AE, DC, MC, V. Parking on adjacent streets. Within easy walking distance of old and new towns, at far south end of Esplanade. **Amenities:** Breakfast room; bar; room service. *In room:* A/C, TV, hair dryer, minibar.

OUTSIDE TOWN
Expensive

Corfu Holiday Palace ★★ Formerly the Hilton (now in the Aquis chain), this is a grand hotel in the contemporary manner—more like a resort, if you consider the range of its facilities. It boasts of all the celebrities it's hosted, but I've always found the staff friendly. Guest rooms are standard Greek hotel size, with comfortable beds and state-of-the-art bathrooms. The grounds create a semitropical ambience. In addition to the pools, a lovely private beach below beckons. Kanoni, an island landmark, is nearby (see below). The island's airport is off in the middle distance—not a major problem unless your windows are open, but I advise you to ask for a room facing the sea. Patrons get a generous discount at Corfu Golf Club (18km/12 miles away). Perhaps the biggest surprise of all: One of Greece's major casinos is on the premises.

P.O. Box 124, Nausicaa, Kanoni, 49100 Corfu. www.corfuholidaypalace.gr. ℂ **26610/36-540.** Fax 26610/36-551. 266 units. High season 170€–220€ double; low season 100€–125€ double. Rates include buffet breakfast. Half board includes a fixed-price menu. Special packages available for extended stays. AE, DC, MC, V. Free parking on grounds. About 5km (3 miles) south of Corfu town. **Amenities:** 2 restaurants; 2 bars; babysitting; billiards; bowling; casino; health club; Internet; jogging track; 2 pools; room service; shuttle bus to town; table tennis; lit tennis courts; watersports equipment/rentals; Wi-Fi. *In room:* A/C, TV, hair dryer, minibar.

Inexpensive

Fundana Villas ★★ ☺ I predict this will be greatly appreciated by some as a delightful alternative to all the other hostelries listed for Corfu—bungalows off in a completely natural setting. The 12 bungalows vary in size, accommodating from two to seven people, but all have kitchenettes. You are surrounded by fruit trees and the sounds of the Greek countryside, and you can imbibe the pure spring water. Twice a week, the proprietors prepare traditional Corfiot dinners; for other meals, you have to drive into Corfu town or Paleokastritsa, but this gives you a chance to sample our several recommendations. You will also have your choice of beaches, none of which are much more than about 15km (9 miles) away; the island's golf course, horseback riding, and a water park are also within a few miles. Some may recognize the main house as the residence in the BBC-TV version of Gerald Durrell's *My Family and Other Animals.*

1 Odysseos, 49100 Corfu. www.fundanavillas.com. ℂ **26630/22-532.** Fax 26630/22-453. 15 units. High season 80€ per couple. Self-catering breakfast 8€. MC, V. Parking on grounds. 17km (11 miles) from Corfu center, about same to Paleokastritsa. Pets accepted. **Amenities:** Bar; Internet; 2 pools; table tennis. *In room:* A/C, TV, hair dryer, kitchenette.

Where to Dine

IN TOWN
Expensive

Venetian Well ★ MIDDLE EASTERN/INTERNATIONAL/GREEK   For a special dining experience, this remains my top pick in Corfu town. Diners sit at a candlelit table, in a rather austere little square, with a Venetian wellhead (ca. 1699) and a church opposite. When the weather changes, guests sit in a stately room adorned with a mural. There is no printed menu—you learn what's available from a chalkboard or from your waiter—and there's no predicting what the kitchen will offer on any given evening. To some degree, then, the fare can be uneven. Main courses may range from standard Greek dishes such as beef *giouvetsi* (cooked in a pot) to chicken prepared with exotic ingredients. Because the chef uses seasonal vegetables, salads vary from month to month. The wine list is more extensive than in most Greek restaurants.

Plateia Kremasti (on the small square, up from old harbor, behind Greek Orthodox cathedral). ℂ **26610/44-761.** Reservations recommended in high season. Main courses 10€–26€. No credit cards. Mon–Sat noon–midnight.

Moderate

If you want to dine in town yet along the coast, consider **Antranik,** 19 Arseniou (ℂ **26610/22-301**), located under the awnings on the sea side of the road leading

from north of the Esplanade down to the new port. **Faliraki,** at the corner of Kapodistrias and Arseniou, down below the wall (© **26610/30-392**), also has a wonderful location right on the water, although the food is standard Greek fare.

Aegli Garden Restaurant ★ GREEK/CONTINENTAL   The tasty and varied
menu of this longtime favorite attracts both residents and travelers to its several dining areas—indoors, in the Liston arcade, under awnings across from the arcade, or
along the pedestrian mall of Kapodistriou. Try the selection of *orektika* (appetizers)
with the wine or beer on tap. The staff takes special pride in their Corfiote specialties,
several of which are traditional Greek foods with rather spicy sauces: filet of fish,
octopus, *pastitsada* (baked veal), *baccala* (salted codfish), and *sofrito* (veal). If spici-
ness isn't your thing, try the swordfish or prawns. Everything is done with great care.

23 Kapodistriou. Also entered from Liston Arcade. © **26610/31-949.** Fax 26610/45-488. Main courses
8€–20€. AE, DC, MC, V. Daily 9am–1am. No parking.

Bellissimo GREEK/INTERNATIONAL   This restaurant has lived up to its promise of being a welcome addition to Corfu—unpretentious, and tasty food. Located on
a central and lovely town square, it offers a standard Greek menu with some "exotics,"
including hamburgers and chicken curry. Especially welcome is a modestly priced
"Greek sampling plate"—*tzatziki* (yogurt-cucumber salad), tomatoes-and-cucumber
salad, *keftedes* (meatballs), fried potatoes, grilled lamb, and pork souvlaki.

Plateia Lemonia (just off N. Theotoki). © **26610/41-112.** Main courses 6€–18€. No credit cards. Daily
10:30am–11pm. No parking.

Corfu Town After Dark

Corfu town definitely has a nightlife scene, though many people are content to linger
over dinner and then, after a promenade, repair to one of the cafes at the Liston, such
as the **Capri, Liston, Europa,** or **Aegli**—all of which have similar selections of light
refreshments and drinks. (Treat yourself to the fresh fruit salad at the Aegli!) Others
are drawn to the cafes at the north end of the Esplanade, just outside the Liston—
Cafe Bar 92, Magnet, or **Cool Down.** For a special treat, ascend to the rooftop
cafe/bar at **Cavalieri** hotel (see "Where to Stay," above). Another choice is **Lindos
Cafe,** overlooking the beach and facilities of the Nautical Club of Corfu. It's
approached by steps leading off Leoforos Demokratias, just south and outside the
Esplanade. And one of the best-kept secrets of Corfu town is the little **Art Cafe,** to
the right and behind the Museum of Asian Art; its garden provides a wonderful, cool,
quiet retreat from the hustle and bustle of the rest of the town.

If you enjoy more action—loud music and dancing—several nightspots are along
the coast to the north, between Corfu town and the beach resort of Gouvia. They
include **Ekati,** a typical Greek nightclub; **Esperides,** featuring Greek music; and
Corfu by Night, definitely touristy. Be prepared to drop money at these places.

The youngest night crawlers find places that go in and out of favor (and business)
from year to year. Among the more enduring, up around the Esplanade, are the relatively sedate **Aktaion,** just to the right of the Old Fort, and clubs featuring the latest
music, such as **Hook** and **Base,** along Kapodistriou (before the Cavialieri Hotel).
Young people seeking more excitement go down past the new port to a strip of flashy
discos. These clubs charge a cover (about 10€, including one drink).

In summer, frequent **concerts** by orchestras and bands are held on the Esplanade;
most of them are free. Corfu town boasts the oldest band in Greece. The **sound-
and-light** performances are described in the listing for the Old Fort (see "What to
See & Do," earlier in this chapter). September brings **Corfu Festival,** with concerts,

ballet, opera, and theater performances, by a mix of Greek and international companies. **Carnival** is celebrated on the last Sunday before Lent, with a parade and the burning of an effigy representing the spirit of Carnival.

For those who like to gamble, the **casino** at the **Corfu Holiday Palace** (see above) is a few miles outside of town. Open nightly (8pm–3am) to individuals 23 years or older (ID required), it may not have the glamour of Monte Carlo, but it attracts an international set during the high season.

Side Trips from Corfu Town
KANONI, PONDIKONISI & ACHILLEION

Although these sites and destinations are not next door to one another and have little in common, they are grouped here because they all lie south of Corfu town and all could be combined in less than a full day's outing. Everyone who comes to Corfu town will want to visit these places, even if you go nowhere else on the island.

Kanoni is approached south of Corfu town via the village Analepsis; it's well signed. Ascending most of the way, you arrive after about 4km (2½ miles) at the circular terrace (on the right). The area is known as Kanoni (after the cannon once sited here). Make your way to the edge and enjoy a wonderful view. Directly below in the inlet are two islets. If you want to visit one or both, you can take a 10-minute walk down a not-that-difficult path from Kanoni; with a vehicle you must retrace the road back from Kanoni a few hundred yards to a signed turnoff (on the left coming back).

One islet is linked to the land by a causeway; here you'll find the **Monastery of Vlakherna.** To get to the other islet, **Pondikonisi (Mouse Island),** you must go by small boat, which is always available (3€ round-trip). Legend has it that this rocky islet is a Phaeacian ship that turned to stone after taking Odysseus back to Ithaka.

A Villa with Many Tales to Tell

The Achilleion has enough back stories to support a TV miniseries. To begin with, the personal life of the Empress Elizabeth who built it is one of extravagant eccentricities; all I can say here is to look her up in an encyclopedia or online. But aside from this, it was as the mother of Rudolf that she would acquire legendary fame. He was the young prince who in 1889 was found dead at his hunting lodge at Mayerling, Austria, along with his mistress; although generally assumed to have been a double suicide, many questions about their deaths were never satisfied. In any case, Elizabeth identified Rudolf with Achilles, and so the villa is really a memorial to him—thus the many statues and motifs associated with Achilles (including the dolphins, for Achilles' mother was the water nymph Thetis).

Then, in 1898 Elizabeth was assassinated by an anarchist—for no other reason than she was a royal. The villa sat unused until 1907, when Kaiser Wilhelm II of Germany bought it as a summer home. It was appropriated by the Greek government after World War I and used for various government agencies; the Germans used it during their World War II occupation of the island; it then reverted to the Greek National Tourist Organization, which, starting in 1962, allowed the top floor to be used as a casino (seen in the 1981 James Bond film *For Your Eyes Only*). This closed in 1992, when the casino was moved to the Corfu Holiday Palace (see above). Now it remains a major destination for tourists, with more than its share of tales to tell.

The chapel here dates from the 13th century, and its setting among the cypress trees makes it most picturesque. Many Corfiotes make a pilgrimage here, in small boats on August 6, for the Feast of the Transfiguration. It's also the inspiration for the Swiss painter Arnold Boecklin's well-known work *Isle of the Dead,* which, in turn, inspired Rachmaninoff's music of the same name.

A causeway across the little inlet to Perama, on the main body of the island (the Kanoni road is on a peninsula) is for pedestrians only. So to continue to your next destination, a villa known as **Achilleion ★**, you must drive back to the edge of Corfu town and then take another road about 8km (5 miles) to the south, signed to Gastouri and the villa of Achilleion. The villa is open daily 9am to 4pm. Admission is 6€. Bus no. 10, from Plateia San Rocco, runs directly to the Achilleion several times daily.

Empress Elizabeth of Austria-Hungary built this villa between 1890 and 1891. Approaching the villa from the entrance gate, you will see a slightly Teutonic version of a neoclassical summer palace. Take a walk through at least some of the eclectic rooms. Among the curiosities is the small saddle-seat on which Kaiser Wilhelm II of Germany sat while performing his imperial chores.

The terraced gardens that surround the villa are now lush. Be sure to go all the way around and out to the back terraces to see the most famous of the statues Elizabeth commissioned, *The Dying Achilles,* by the German sculptor Herter; also, you cannot miss the 4.5m-tall (15-ft.) Achilles that the Kaiser had inscribed, TO THE GREATEST GREEK FROM THE GREATEST GERMAN, a sentiment removed after World War II. But for a truly impressive sight, step to the edge of the terrace and enjoy a spectacular view of Corfu town and much of the eastern coast to the south.

If you have your own car, you can continue on past the Achilleion and descend to the coast between **Benitses** and **Perama;** the first, to the south, has become a popular beach resort. Proceeding north along the coast from Benitses, you come to Perama (another popular beach resort), where a turnoff onto a promontory brings you to the pedestrian causeway opposite Pondikonisi (see above). The main road brings you back to the edge of Corfu town.

PALEOKASTRITSA ★

If you can make only one excursion on the island, this is certainly a top competitor with Kanoni and the Achilleion. The drive here is northwest out of Corfu town via well-marked roads. Follow the coast for about 8km (5½ miles) to Gouvia, then turn inland. (It is on this next stretch that you pass the **Pottery Workshop** and the **Wood's Nest;** see "Shopping," earlier.) The road eventually narrows but is asphalt all the way as you gradually descend to the west coast and **Paleokastritsa** (25km/16 miles). There's no missing it: It's been taken over by hotels and restaurants, although some of the bays and coves that make up Paleokastritsa are less developed than others. Tradition claims it as the site of **Scheria,** the capital of the Phaeacians—so one of these beaches should be where Nausicaa found Odysseus, though no remains have been found to substantiate this.

Continue on past the beaches to climb a narrow, winding road to the **Monastery of the Panagia** at the edge of a promontory. (The monastery is about 1.6km/1 mile from the beach, and many prefer to go by foot, as parking is next to impossible once you get there.) Although founded in the 13th century, the monastery has no remains that old. It's worth a brief visit, especially at sunset. The monastery is open daily April through October from 7am to 1pm and 3 to 8pm.

Taking a Dive

All of the bays and coves that make up Paleokastritsa boast clear, sparkling turquoise waters. Both **Korfu Diving** (✆ **26630/41-604;** www.dive-centers. net) and **Achilleion Diving Centre** (✆ **69327/29-011;** www.diving-corfu. com) offer courses for beginners, as well as day excursions for advanced divers.

More interesting in some ways, and certainly more challenging, is a visit to the **Angelokastro,** the medieval castle that sits high on a pinnacle overlooking all of Paleokastritsa. Only the hardiest will choose to walk all the way up from the shore, a taxing hour at least. The rest of us will drive back out of Paleokastritsa (2.5km/1½ miles) to a turnoff to the left, signed for Lakones. *Warning:* Don't attempt to drive this road unless you are comfortable pulling over to the very edge of narrow roads—with sheer drops—to let trucks and buses by, something you will have to do on your way down. There commences an endless winding ascent that eventually levels out and provides spectacular views of the coast as the road passes through the villages of Lakones and Krini. Keep going until the road takes a sharp turn to the right and down, and you'll come to a little parking area. From here, walk up to the castle, only 200m (656 ft.) away but seemingly farther because of the trail's poor condition. What you are rewarded with, though, is one of the most spectacularly sited medieval castles you'll ever visit, some 300m (1,000 ft.) above sea level.

If you've come this far, reward yourself with a meal and the spectacular view at one of the restaurants or cafes on the road outside Lakones: **Bella Vista, Colombo,** or **Casteltron.** At mealtimes in high season, these places are taken over by busloads of tour groups. If you have your own transport, try to eat a bit earlier or later.

On your way back to Corfu town from Paleokastritsa, you can vary your route by heading south through **Ropa Valley,** the agricultural heartland of Corfu. Follow the signs indicating Liapades and Tembloni, but don't bother going into either of these towns. If you have time for a beach stop, consider going over to **Ermones Beach** (the island's only golf club is located above it—an 18-hole course) or **Glifada Beach.**

Where to Stay & Dine

If you want to spend some time at Paleokastritsa, it's good to get away from the main beach. I've enjoyed the unpretentious 70-unit family-run **Hotel Odysseus** (✆ **26630/ 41-209;** www.odysseushotel.gr), high above the largely undeveloped cove before the main beach. A double in high season goes for 75€; in low season, the rate is 55€. Rates include buffet breakfast, and the hotel has a pool. The Odysseus is open May to mid-October.

On its own peninsula and both fancier and pricier is the 127-unit **Akrotiri Beach Hotel ★** (✆ **26630/41-237;** www.akrotiri-beach.com)—completely renovated between 2008 and 2010; an air-conditioned double in high season goes for 120€ to 150€, including buffet breakfast. Half board can also be arranged. All rooms have balconies and sea views. In addition to the adjacent beaches, it has two pools and a tennis court and offers Wi-Fi in the lobby. It's open May through October.

The restaurants on the main beach in Paleokastritsa are definitely touristy. The **Vrahos** is probably the most stylish. However, if you like to eat where the action is, the best value and most fun at the main beach can be had at the **Apollon Restaurant,** in Hotel Apollon-Ermis (✆ **26630/41-211**). Main courses are 6€ to 16€.

I prefer someplace a bit removed, such as **Belvedere Restaurant** (© 26630/41-583), just below Hotel Odysseus, which serves solid Greek dishes at reasonable prices. Main courses range from 5€ to 16€. The restaurant is open mid-April to late October from 9am to midnight.

KEFALONIA (CEPHALONIA) ★

Here is a Greek island the way they used to be: It pretty much goes its own (Greek) way, while you (foreigner) travel around and through it. That said, Kefalonia does have a full-service tourist industry, with fine hotels, restaurants, travel agencies, car-rental agencies along with its natural wonders, a few historical buildings, archaeological sites, and many fine beaches. Because Kefalonia was virtually demolished by the earthquake of 1953, most structures on this island are fairly new. And it has long been one of the more prosperous and cosmopolitan parts of Greece, thanks to its islanders' tradition of sailing and trading in the world at large. The filming of the 2001 movie *Captain Corelli's Mandolin* also gave a temporary boost to tourism here, but don't come to Kefalonia for glamour. Come to spend time in a relaxing environment, and to enjoy handsome vistas and a lovely countryside.

Essentials

GETTING THERE **By Plane** From Athens, there are usually two flights daily on **Olympic Air;** fares in high season can vary from 60€ to 110€. The Argostoli office is at 1 Rokkou Vergoti, the street between the harbor and the square of the Archaeological Museum (© 26710/28-808). **Kefalonia Airport** is 8km (5 miles) outside Argostoli. As there is no public bus, everyone goes to Argostoli by taxi, which costs about 15€.

By Boat As with most Greek islands, it's easier to get to Kefalonia in summer than in the off-season, when weather and reduced tourism eliminate the smaller boats. Ferries to Kefalonia are operated by at least four lines: **Strintzis, Agoudimos, Endeavour,** and **Ionian;** check out their schedules at www.gtp.gr or www.ferries.gr. If you don't make arrangements with a travel agent, you can buy tickets dockside. Throughout the year, a car-passenger ferry leaves daily from Patras to Sami (about 2½ hr.). There is also at least one car-passenger ferry daily (1½ hr.) from Killini (on the northwest tip of the Peloponnese) to one of several ports of Kefalonia—Argostoli, Sami Lixouri, or Poros. To give some idea of the cost, a round-trip Patras-Kefallonia-Patras trip for a couple with their own cabin would be about 150€.

Beyond these fairly dependable services, during the high-season months of July and August, there are alternatives—ships to and from Corfu, Ithaka, Levkas, Brindisi (Italy), or other ports—but they do not always hold to the same schedules every year.

VISITOR INFORMATION **Argostoli Tourism Office,** in Argostoli, is at the Port Authority Building, on Ioannis Metaxa, along the harbor (© 26710/22-248). It's open in high season daily from 7:30am to 2:30pm and 5 to 10pm; in low season, hours are reduced to Monday through Friday from 8am to 3pm.

GETTING AROUND **By Bus** You can get to almost any point on Kefalonia—even remote beaches, villages, and monasteries—by **KTEL bus** (© 26710/22-276 in Argostoli). Schedules, however, are restrictive and may cut deeply into your preferred arrival at any given destination. KTEL also operates special tours to major destinations around the island. The **KTEL station** is on Leoforos A. Tritsi, at the far end of the harbor road, 200m (656 ft.) past Trapano Bridge.

By Taxi   If you don't enjoy driving on twisting mountain roads, taxis are the best alternative. In Argostoli, go to Vallianou (Central) Square and work out an acceptable fare. A trip to Fiskardo, with the driver waiting for 3 to 4 hours, might run to 200€— with several passengers splitting the fare, this isn't unreasonable for a day's excursion. Everyone uses taxis on Kefalonia, and although drivers are supposed to use their meters, many don't; settle the fare before you set off.

By Car   There are literally dozens of car-rental firms, from the well-known international companies to hole-in-the-wall outfits. In Argostoli, I've found **Auto Europe,** 3 Lassis (✆ 26710/24-078), and **Euro Dollar,** 3A R. Vergoti (✆ 26710/23-613), to be reliable. In high season, rental cars are scarce, so don't expect to haggle. A compact will come to at least 75€ per day (gas extra); better rates are usually offered for rentals of 3 or more days.

By Moped & Motorcycle   The roads on Kefalonia are asphalt and in decent condition but are often narrow, lack shoulders, and twist around mountain ravines or wind along the edges of sheer drops to the sea. However, many travelers choose to get around Kefalonia this way. Two-seater mopeds and motorcycles rent for about 30€ to 40€ per day.

FAST FACTS   There are several **banks** with ATMs in the center of Argostoli. The **hospital** (✆ 26710/22-434) is on Souidias (the upper road, above the Trapano Bridge). **Internet access** is available at **Internet Point,** 8 A. Metaxa (✆ 26710/22-227; www.f2d.gr) or at **Excelixis Computers,** 3 Minoos (✆ 26710/25-530; xlixis@otenet.gr). **Express Laundry,** 46B Lassi, the upper road that leads to the airport, is open Monday through Saturday from 9:30am to 9pm. A load costs 5€. Argostoli's **tourist police** (✆ 26710/22-200) are on Ioannis Metaxa, on the waterfront across from the port authority. The **post office** is in Argostoli on Lithostrato, opposite no. 18 (✆ 26710/22-124); its hours are Monday through Saturday from 7:30am to 2pm. The main **telephone office (OTE)** is at 8 G. Vergoti. It's open daily, April through September, from 7am to midnight, and October through March, from 7am to 10pm.

What to See & Do

Staying in Kefalonia's capital and largest city, **Argostoli,** allows you to go off on daily excursions to beaches and mountains, yet return to the comforts of a city. It has the island's most diverse offering of hotels and restaurants, and it feels urban. For those who find that Argostoli doesn't offer enough in the way of old-world charm or diversions, we point out some of the other possibilities on Kefalonia.

Argostoli's appeal does not depend on any archaeological, historical, architectural, or artistic particulars. It's a city for observers—travelers who are content strolling or sitting and observing the passing scene: ships coming and going along the waterfront, locals shopping in the market, children playing in the squares. Head to **Vallianou (Central) Square ★** or the **waterfront** to find a cafe for coffee or ice cream. **Premier Cafe,** on the former, and **Hotel Olga,** on the latter, are as nice as any.

The best nearby **beaches** are just south of the city in **Lassi,** which now has numerous hotels, pensions, cafes, and restaurants much loved by package groups.

Historical and Folklore Museum of the Corgialenos Library ★   I recommend this museum over the nearby, rather dry archaeological museum. Many so-called folklore museums, little more than typical rooms, have sprung up in Greece in recent years, but this is one of the most authentic and satisfying. Meticulously

maintained and well-labeled displays showcase traditional clothing, tools, handicrafts, and objects used in daily life across the centuries. Somewhat unexpected are the displays revealing a stylish upper-middle-class life. Also engaging is a large collection of photographs of pre- and post-1953 earthquake Kefalonia. The gift shop has an especially fine selection of items, including handmade lace.

Ilia Zervou. ℂ **26710/28-835.** Admission 3€. Apr–Oct Mon–Sat 9am–2pm; off season by arrangement. 2 blocks up the hill, behind public theater and Archaeological Museum square.

SHOPPING

Interesting ceramics are for sale at **Hephaestus,** on the waterfront, at 21 May; **Alexander's,** on the corner of Plateia Museio (the square 1 block back from the waterfront); and **the Mistral,** 6 Vironis, up the hill opposite the post office, offering the work of the potter/owner.

For a taste of the local cuisine, consider Kefalonia's prized Golden Honey, tart quince preserve, or almond pralines. Another possibility is a bottle of one of Kefalonia's highly praised wines. You can visit **Calliga Vineyard** (selling white Robola and red Calliga Cava) or **Gentilini Vineyard** (with more expensive wines), both near Argostoli; or **Metaxas Wine Estate,** south of Argostoli. The tourist office (see "Visitor Information," above) on the waterfront will tell you how to arrange a tour.

> ### The Home of Odysseus?
>
> Every schoolchild knows (or at least used to) that Odysseus, the hero of Homer's epic, came from the island of Ithaka. Over the centuries, a few scholars debated which island this was—some even arguing that, in any case, it was all a fiction—but in general, it came to be accepted that Odysseus's island was the same as the one we know today by that name. In 2005, however, several Englishmen announced that they had established that the true Ithaka of Homer's Odysseus is the **Paliki** peninsula, which hangs down along the northwestern coast of Kefalonia. As to the objection that Homer's Ithaka was an island, these men claimed that Paliki had been an island but that seismic forces had since joined it to Kefalonia. As of this writing, there is little archaeological evidence to support this claim—and no remains to visit. But for those who relish Homer, it might be worth the few hours it would take to drive over to Paliki and just check out the land. (There is also a frequent ferry that cuts down the travel time; but when you disembark, you would need to get wheels to explore the peninsula.) In any case, you might consider packing a paperback translation of the *Odyssey.*

Where to Stay

Accommodations on Kefalonia range from luxury hotels to basic rooms. During peak times, I strongly recommend reservations. **Ainos Travel, 14 G. Vergoti** (✆ **26710/22-333;** www.ainostravel.gr) can help.

EXPENSIVE

White Rocks Hotel & Bungalows ★★ This low-key place is where travelers catch up on the reading they've meant to do all year. Although not the most elaborate, it is probably the most elegant hotel on Kefalonia. On arriving, you descend a few steps from the main road to enter an almost tropical setting. The lobby is subdued and stylish, a decor that extends to the hotel's guest rooms, which are modest in size but have first-rate bathrooms. Pay the extra for the sea-view rooms; they're well worth it. Guests have use of their own small beach, as well as a larger one that is open to the public. White Rocks is a couple of miles south of Argostoli, just above the two beaches. A quiet retreat that may appeal more to the older set.

Platys Yialos, 28100 Argostoli. At the beach at Lassi, outside Argostoli. www.whiterocks.gr. ✆ **26710/28-332.** Fax 26710/28-755. 162 units (102 rooms, 60 bungalows). 190€ double; 200€ bungalow for 2. Rates include breakfast and dinner. AE, DC, V. Private parking. Closed Nov–Apr. Occasional public buses go from the center of town to and from Yialos, but most people take taxis. **Amenities:** 2 restaurants; 2 bars; pool; room service; Wi-Fi. *In room:* A/C, TV, hair dryer, minibar.

MODERATE

In addition to the following options, you might consider the 60-unit **Hotel Miramare,** 2 I. Metaxa, at the far end of shore road (✆ **26710/25-511;** fax 26710/25-512); it's slightly removed from the town's bustle, yet within walking distance of any place you'd want to go.

Cephalonia Star I don't want to oversell this hotel, but it's just the place for those travelers who are never happier than when they are on the waterfront. For such, its location along the bay and the balconied front rooms with fine views compensate for its rather undistinguished accommodations. The white-walled rooms are a bit austere—along the lines of American motel rooms—but perfectly adequate. Bathrooms are standard issue, clean, and well serviced. There's a cafeteria-restaurant on the premises, but except for breakfast, you'll probably want to try Argostoli's many fine eateries, all within a few minutes' walk. In August, a mobile amusement park has been known to set up on the quay just opposite, but then August all over Greece is a carnival.

60 l. Metaxa, 28100 Argostoli. ℂ **26710/23-181.** Fax 26710/23-180. 40 units, some with shower or tub. High season 90€ double; low season 70€ double. Rates include breakfast. MC, V. Street parking. Along waterfront, across from the port authority. **Amenities:** Restaurant; bar. *In room:* A/C, TV.

Hotel Ionian Plaza ★   Although it doesn't quite qualify as a grand hotel, this is the class act of "downtown" Argostoli, and it's also a fine deal. The lobby, public areas, and guest rooms share a tasteful, comfortable, natural tone. Individual details in the furnishings and decor convey the sense of visiting a fine mansion rather than a commercial hotel. Guest rooms are larger than most, while bathrooms are modern if not mammoth. Breakfast takes place under the awning, and the evening meal could well be at the hotel's adjacent **Il Palazzino** restaurant, where the menu has a strong Italian flavor and prices are surprisingly modest. Stay here if you like to be in the heart of a city; the front rooms overlook the Central Square, but because no vehicles are allowed there, most of the noise comes from children playing in the square.

Vallianou Sq. (Central Sq.), 28100 Argostoli. www.ionianplaza.gr. ℂ **26710/25-581.** Fax 26710/25-585. 43 units. High season 120€) double; low season 90€ double. Rates include buffet breakfast. AE, MC, V. Street parking nearby. **Amenities:** Restaurant; bar; room service. *In room:* A/C, TV, fridge, hair dryer, Wi-Fi.

INEXPENSIVE

Mouikis Hotel   Completely upgraded, this once bare-bones hotel now offers many of the amenities of more expensive hotels and could make a decent choice for those with limited budgets. The rooms and bathrooms are standard for the class. It's on a quiet side street and close to all points in town. It's popular with groups but usually has a few rooms available for individual travelers. One unusual service: A minibus takes patrons to a swimming pool that belongs to a nearby resort, also owned by Mouikis's owners.

3 Vironis, 28100 Argostoli. www.mouikis.kefalonia-gr.com. ℂ **26710/23-281.** 39 units. High season 75€ double; low season 65€ double. Rates include buffet breakfast. AE, MC, V. Street parking. **Amenities:** Bar. *In room:* A/C, TV, fridge.

Where to Dine

Try the two local specialties: *kreatopita* (meat pie, with rice and a tomato sauce under a crust) and *crasato* (pork cooked in wine). The island's prized wines include the Robola, Muscat, and Mavrodaphne.

EXPENSIVE

Captain's Table ★ GREEK/INTERNATIONAL   Generally conceded to be the best restaurant in Argostoli, especially for seafood—but be sure you go to the original just off the Central Square. Some guests dress up a bit, and there's definitely a touch of celebration to meals at this slightly upscale restaurant. Specialties include the Captain's Soup (fish, lobster, mussels, shrimp, and vegetables), filets of beef, delicate squid, and fried *courgette* (small eggplants). Go early; it can get crowded in high season.

Leoforos Rizopaston. ℂ **26710/23-896.** Main courses 8€–20€. MC, V. Daily 6pm–midnight. Just around corner from Central Sq.; identifiable by its boat-model display case.

MODERATE

Consider local favorite **Old Plaka Taverna,** 1 I. Metaxa, at the far end of the waterfront (☎ **26710/24-849**), for modest prices and tasty Greek dishes.

La Gondola GREEK/ITALIAN   Everyone should take at least one meal on the main square to experience the "dinner theater," with Argostoli's citizens providing the action. Frankly, all of the restaurants on the square are about the same in quality and menu, but I've enjoyed some special treats at this one. It offers a house wine, literally made by the house, and serves a special pizza-dough garlic bread, zesty chicken with lemon sauce, and cannelloni that stands out with its rich texture and distinctive flavor. Staff and diners always seem to enjoy themselves here, so we think you will, too.

Central Sq. ☎ **26710/23-658.** Main courses 6€–18€. AE, MC, V. Daily 6pm–2am.

Patsouras ★ GREEK   Patsouras continues to live up to its reputation as the favorite of travelers seeking authentic Greek taverna food and ambience. Dine under the awnings on the terrace, across from the waterfront, and try either of the local specialties, *kreatopita* (meat pie) or *crasto* (pork in wine). Such standards as the *tzatziki* and moussaka have a special zest. Greeks love unpretentious tavernas, and you'll see why if you eat at Patsouras.

32 I. Metaxa. ☎ **26710/22-779.** Main courses 5€–16€. V. Daily noon–midnight. A 5-min. walk from Central Sq., along the waterfront.

INEXPENSIVE

Portside Restaurant GREEK   This unpretentious taverna is what the Greeks call a *phisteria*, a restaurant specializing in meats and fish cooked on the grill or spit. Run by a native of Argostoli and his Greek-American wife, it offers hearty breakfasts, regular plates with side portions of salads and potatoes, and a full selection of Greek favorites. On special nights outside the high season, the restaurant roasts a suckling pig. It's popular with Greeks as well as foreigners, and you've got a front-row seat for harborside activities.

58 I. Metaxa. ☎ **26710/24-130.** Main courses 6€–17€. MC, V. Apr–Oct daily 10am–midnight. Along the waterfront, opposite the port authority.

Argostoli After Dark

Free outdoor concerts are occasionally given in the Central Square. At the end of August, the **Choral Music Festival** hosts choirs from all over Greece and Europe. The grand new **Kefalos Public Theater** stages plays, almost always in Greek and seldom in high season. Young people looking for a bit more action can find a number of cafes, bars, and discos on and around the Central Square; they change names from year to year, but **Cinema Music Club, Rumours, Prive, Stavento, Daccapo,** and **Traffic** have been fairly steady. **Bass,** up by the museum, is a favorite club. If your style runs more to lounging with classic rock, try the **Pub Old House,** off Rizopaston, the palm-tree lined avenue leading away from the main square. At the beach resort of Lassi, **So Simple Bar** is popular.

Side Trips from Argostoli

FISKARDO, ASSOS & MYRTOS BEACH ★

I'd advise this excursion if you only had 1 day for a trip outside Argostoli. The end destination is **Fiskardo** ★★, a picturesque port village that is the only major locale on Kefalonia to have survived the 1953 earthquake. Its charm comes from its many surviving 18th-century structures and its intimate harbor, which attracts an international flotilla of yachts.

You can make a round-trip from Argostoli to Fiskardo in a day on a **KTEL** bus (10€). But with a rental car, on the way there you can detour off the main road to the even more picturesque port and village of **Assos** (it adds about 10km/7 miles), and then reward yourself with another short detour down to **Myrtos beach,** one of Greece's great beaches.

Plenty of restaurants dot Fiskardo's harbor. I can recommend **Tassia's, Vassos, Nicholas Taverna** (up on the hillside), and **Panormos** (around the bend). The latter two offer rooms as well. For advance arrangements, contact **Fiskardo Travel** (© **26740/41-315;** ftravel@kef.forthnet.gr). If you think you might like to stay for as long as a week and can afford something a bit special, contact the (British) **Greek Islands Club,** which specializes in waterfront apartments and houses (www.gic thevillacollection.com).

SAMI, MELISSANI GROTTO & DROGARATI CAVE

When you arrive in Kefalonia, you may come first to Sami, an unexceptional town on the east coast and the island's principal point of entry before tourism put Argostoli in the lead. Sami is still a busy port. Besides the unusual white cliffs seen from the harbor, travelers are drawn by **two caves** to the north of Sami, both of which can be visited on a half-day excursion from Argostoli. Of the two, the Drogarati is the more rewarding.

Spili Melissani, about 5km (3 miles) north of Sami, is well signposted. Once you're inside, you will be taken by a guide in a small rowboat around a relatively small, partially exposed, partially enclosed lake, whose most spectacular feature is the play of the sun's rays striking the water, which creates a kaleidoscope of colors. It's open daily from 9am to 6pm. Admission is 6€.

On the road that leads west to Argostoli (4km/2 miles from Sami), there's a well-signposted turnoff to **Drogarati Cave ★**. Known for its unusual stalagmites, its large chamber has been used for concerts (once by Maria Callas). You walk through it on your own; the cave is well illuminated but can be slippery. It's open daily from 9am to 6pm, with an admission of 4€.

ITHAKA

Despite the recent claims that Oysseus's Ithaka is now a peninsula off Kefalonia, Ithaka continues to attract those who simply are willing to go along with the traditional linkage of several sites to Homer's epic. Such associations aside, Ithaka appeals to many visitors: It may be small and not easily approached, but its rugged terrain and laid-back villages reward those who enjoy driving through unspoiled Greek countryside.

Although there are (infrequent) ferry connections to Ithaka from Patras (Peloponnese), Astakos (mainland, opposite Ithaka), and Kefalonia (Fiscardo), I'd strongly recommend that you approach Ithaka with a rented car from Argostoli (Kefalonia). The boat connecting Kefalonia to Ithaka (its little port shows up as Pissaetos on websites) sails not from Argostoli but from Sami, the port on the east coast of Kefalonia; to make a bus connection with that boat, and then to take a taxi from the tiny isolated port where you disembark on Ithaka, costs far too much time. Rather, in your rented car, drive the 40 minutes from Argostoli to Sami; the boat fare for the car is 12€, for each individual 3€. Once on Ithaka, you can drive to **Vathy,** the main town, in about 10 minutes, and you'll have wheels with which to explore Ithaka and return to Argostoli, all within a day. Most visitors will be able to see what they want of Ithaka in 1 day before driving back to the little port where the last ferryboat to Kefalonia leaves, usually at 5pm—but ask!

Vathy itself is a small port, a miniversion of bigger Greek ports, with their bustling tourist-oriented facilities. For help in making any arrangements, try **Polyctor Tours,** on the main square (© **26740/33-120;** www.ithakiholidays.com). You might enjoy a cold drink or coffee and admire the bay stretching before you, but otherwise there's not much to do or see here. Instead, drive 16km (10 miles) north to **Moni Katheron;** the 17th-century monastery itself is nothing special, but the bell tower offers a spectacular view over much of Ithaka. For a more ambitious drive, head north via the village of **Anogi,** stopping in its town square to view the little church with centuries-old frescoes and the Venetian bell tower opposite it. Proceed on via Stavros, and then down to the northeast coast to **Frikes,** a small fishing village. Finally, take a winding road along the coast to **Kioni,** arranged like an amphitheater around its harbor; this is the place to stay if you want to give some time to Ithaka.

As for the sites associated with the *Odyssey,* what little there is to be seen is questioned by many scholars, but that shouldn't stop you; after all, it's your imagination that makes the Homeric world come alive. From the outskirts of Vathy, you'll see signs for the four principal sites. Three kilometers (1¾ miles) northwest of Vathy is the so-called **Cave of the Nymphs,** where Odysseus is said to have hidden the Phaeacians' gifts after he had been brought back (supposedly to the little **Bay of Dexia,** north of the cave). Known locally as Marmarospilia, the small cave is about a half-hour's climb up a slope.

The **Fountain of Arethusa,** where Eumaios is said to have watered his swine, is about 7km (4 miles) south of Vathy; it is known today as the spring of Perapigadi. The **Bay of Ayios Andreas** is claimed to be the spot where Odysseus landed in order to evade Penelope's suitors. To get to the fountain, drive the first 3km (2 miles) by following the signposted road to the south of Vathy as far as it goes; continue on foot another 3km (2 miles) along the path.

About 8km (5 miles) west of Vathy is the site of **Alalkomenai,** claimed by Schliemann, among others, to be the site of Odysseus's capital; in fact, the remains date from several centuries later than the official dates of the Trojan War. Finally, a road out of Stavros leads down to the **Bay of Polis,** again claimed by some as the port of Odysseus's capital; in the nearby cave of Louizou, an ancient pottery shard was found with the inscription "my vow to Odysseus," but its age suggests that this was the site of a hero-cult.

For lunch back in Vathy, although there are several fine restaurants around the main harbor, I would recommend **Gregory's Taverna** (aka Paliocaravo) on the far northeast corner of Vathy's bay (keep driving, with the bay on your left, even after you think the road may give out). Ideally, you will find a table right on the water, where you can look back at Vathy, while enjoying a fresh fish dinner (not cheap, but fresh fish never is in Greece). And if you are so enamored of Ithaka and its Homeric associations, you could not do better than to spend a night or two at the **Perantzada 1811 Hotel ★★**, in Vathy (www.arthotel.gr/perantzada). As its name indicates, it is a converted early-19th-century mansion, but the amenities (and price) are both luxurious and the most up-to-date (including A/C and Internet access). A more moderately priced choice would be the **Hotel Mentor** (www.hotelmentor.gr), right on the harbor.

PLANNING YOUR TRIP TO GREECE

Greece remains one of the world's oldest and premier destinations for travelers and a visit there should be an occasion for sheer enjoyment—even exultation. There is no denying, however, that as this guidebook goes to press, the news and images coming out of Greece have been unsettling. Greece's finances, economy, government, and society all appear to be in turmoil.

Some of what appears on the news and in the newspapers may not directly affect visitors. For example, the demonstrations are largely confined to a few squares in Athens and a couple of other major cities and have not been directed at foreigners. But there have been strikes that have shut down various means of transportation, and although usually restricted to a few hours, if these were to continue they could interrupt closely scheduled travel plans.

Most museums and archaeological sites have remained open, but often with reduced hours (and even days of closure). If Greece's economic difficulties were to continue, it is possible that some stores, restaurants, and hotels may change the times that they are open, or even close, before you go to Greece. Not to worry: There are more than enough other hotels, restaurants, and shops that we recommend to help you have a great trip. Assuming that Greeks adopt the necessary reforms by the time you use this guide, we believe that most visitors will be able to go about their travels without being unduly inconvenienced. Our best advice is to go to **www.frommers.com** and check for updates online.

Planning ahead has always been advisable for any trip, but with the economic crisis that Greece has been experiencing since 2009, a new layer of warnings comes into play: Many prices of hotels in particular and hours of admission to museums and archaeological sites have been in more than usual flux. Although we have tried to account for these changes, we are not oracles (so to speak).

Still, as with any destination, the ease, comfort, and pleasure of your time in Greece will be greatly improved with some planning. This chapter provides a variety of planning tools, including information on how to get there; tips on accommodations; and quick, on-the-ground resources. One constant we cannot stress enough: If you are planning to visit Greece during the peak season—from July through August, and even from mid-May to mid-September—you are advised to make reservations for airline flights, hotels, and even major cultural events well in advance.

GETTING THERE

By Plane

The vast majority of travelers reach Greece by plane, and most arrive at the Athens airport—officially **Eleftherios Venizelos International Airport (ATH),** sometimes referred to by its new location as "the Spata airport." **Thessaloniki (SKG)** in northeastern Greece is an alternative for those who might like to make their way south but it has far fewer connecting flights to foreign cities.

Four airlines offer direct flights from North America to Athens: Continental, Delta, Olympic Air, and USAir. (Many airlines these days belong to an "alliance" or code-sharing group, so you might be able to use or earn frequent-flier miles with one of the other members.) All the other airlines make stops at some major European airport, where a change of planes is usually required. Once on the continent, nearly all the major European airlines fly to Greece. There are also countless airlines from countries all over the world that provide direct or indirect connections. For example, Ryanair, the bargain airline based in Dublin, makes some flights to Greece, as does Belleair, with its home base in Tirana, Albania.

By Car

It is unlikely that you will find it worthwhile to bring your own car all the way from North America *just* to drive around Greece, but many Europeans do drive down into Greece—and some North Americans may wish to bring their rented cars in. (But make sure a car rented in another country is allowed to be taken to Greece.) Drivers often come from Italy via ferry, usually disembarking at Patras; the drive to Athens is about 210km (130 miles). Others enter from the Former Yugoslavian Republic of Macedonia, or FYROM. (The road from Albania, although passable, doesn't attract many tourists.) There are no particular problems or delays at the border crossings, providing all your papers are in order.

If you come through Skopje, FYROM, the road via Titov Veles to the southeast leads to the border, where it picks up an expressway down to the edge of Thessaloniki (242km/150 miles). Over to the west, there is a decent-enough road via Vitola, FYROM, that leads to Florina, Greece (290km/180 miles); that road then continues east to Thessaloniki (another 161km/100 miles) or south to Kosani (another 89km/55 miles). A long day's drive!

DRIVING YOUR OWN VEHICLE To bring your own vehicle into Greece, valid registration papers, an international third-party insurance certificate, and a driver's license are required. Make sure you have adequate insurance, because many Greek drivers do not. Valid E.U. drivers' licenses are accepted in Greece, as are most U.S. and Canadian licenses, but technically you should have an International Driver's License and you are advised to get one so as to forestall any problems at the border. (National automobile associations issue them.) A free entry card allows you to keep your car in the country up to 4 months, after which another 8 months can be arranged without you paying import duty. Check with your own car insurance company to make sure you are fully covered.

In any case, arm yourself with a good up-to-date map such as the ones published by Baedeker, Hallwag, Michelin, or Freytag & Berndt.

For information on car rentals, prices of gasoline (petrol), unusual conditions, and other matters peculiar to driving in Greece, see "Getting Around: By Car," below.

By Train

There is train service to Greece from virtually all major points in Europe, although the trains tend to be slow and uncomfortable in the summer. A Eurailpass is valid for connections all the way to Athens or Istanbul and includes the ferry service from Italy. Endless types of passes are now offered—long stays, short stays, and combinations with airlines, among others. Note that North Americans must purchase their Eurailpass before arriving in Europe. For information, see **www.raileurope.com**.

By Ship

Probably most people traveling to Greece from foreign ports these days are on cruise ships, but there are still many who come on other ships—mainly from Italy. There is also occasional service from Cyprus, Egypt, Israel, and Turkey. Brindisi, Italy, to Patras is the most common ferry crossing, about a 10-hour voyage, with as many as seven departures a day in summer. There is also regular service, twice a day in summer, from Ancona and Bari, once daily from Otranto, and two or three times a week from Trieste or Venice. Most ferries stop at Corfu or Igoumenitsa, often at both; in summer, an occasional ship will also stop at Kefalonia.

If you want to learn more about the ferry services between Greece and foreign ports, the best website is Paleologos Agency's **www.ferries.gr**. Britons might try the London-based agency **Viamare Travel,** Graphic House, 2 Sumatra Rd., London NW6 1PU (✆ **0870/410-6040;** www.viamare.com). The **Superfast Ferries Line,** 157 Leoforos Alkyonidon, 16673 Athens (✆ **210/969-1100;** www.superfast.com), offers service between Ancona and Patras (17 hr.), or between Ancona and Igoumenitsa (15 hr.); also between Bari and Patras (12 hr.) or between Bari and Igoumenitsa (8 hr.). Not all these so-called superfast ferries actually save that much time if you take into consideration boarding and debarking. In addition, their fares are almost twice as much as those of regular ferries.

On the regular ferries, one-way fares during high season from Brindisi to Patras at press time cost from about 75€ for a tourist-class deck chair to about 135€ per person to share an inside double cabin. Vehicles cost at least another 75€ to 150€ **Note:** The lines usually offer considerable discounts on round-trip/return tickets. Fares to Igoumenitsa are considerably cheaper, but are by no means a better value unless your destination is nearby. Because of the number of shipping lines involved and the variations in schedules, we're not able to provide more concrete details. Consult a travel agent about the possibilities, book well ahead of time in summer, and reconfirm with the shipping line on the day of departure.

GETTING AROUND
By Plane

Compared to the cheaper fare classes on ships and ferries, air travel within Greece can be expensive, but we recommend it for those pressed for time and/or heading for more distant destinations (even if the planes don't always hold strictly to their schedules). Until the late 1990s, **Olympic Air** maintained a monopoly on domestic air travel and thus had little incentive to improve service. In the end, it declared bankruptcy, and it was not until 2009 that it was finally purchased by the Greek-based Marfin Investment Group, which is proceeding with a major overhaul and improvement of services—better computerized booking, reducing delayed flights, more hospitable flight attendants, and such. And it should be said that Olympic has had one of the best safety records of any major airline.

Book as far ahead of time as possible (especially in summer), reconfirm your booking before leaving for the airport, and arrive at the airport at least an hour before departure; the scene at a check-in counter can be quite hectic.

Olympic Air has a number of offices in Athens, though most travel agents sell tickets as well. (For online booking, go to **www.olympicair.com**.) It offers **island** service to Astipalea; Corfu (aka Kerkira); Iraklion, Chania, and Sitia, Crete; Hios (aka Chios); Ikaria; Karpathos; Kassos; Kastellorizo; Kefalonia; Kos; Kithira; Leros; Limnos; Milos; Mykonos; Mitilini (aka Lesvos); Naxos; Paros; Rhodes; Samos; Santorini (aka Thira); Skiathos; Skyros; Siros; and Zakinthos.

All of Olympic's domestic flights leave from the new international airport at Spata. Most flights are to or from Athens, although during the summer there may be some inter-island service. The baggage allowance is 15kg (33 lb.) per passenger, except with a connecting international flight; even the domestic flights generally ignore the weight limit unless you are way over. Smoking is prohibited on all domestic flights.

A round-trip ticket simply costs double the one-way fare. To most destinations within Greece from Athens, round-trip fares (including taxes) at this writing have been about 180€. From Athens to the nearer destinations, fares drop to about 130€. As you can see, such fares are not especially cheap, but there's no denying that for those with limited time, air travel is the best way to go. Ask, too, if Olympic still offers reduced fares for trips Monday through Thursday and trips that include a Saturday-night stay.

Over the years, several private airlines have tried to compete with Olympic, but only one has survived to provide a real alternative: **Aegean Airlines.** Check **www.aegeanair.com**, which allows you to order e-tickets online. Its prices now pretty much match those of Olympic but are sometimes significantly cheaper. Their service is limited, but includes Chania, Chios, Corfu, Iraklion, Kos, Mitilini, Mykonos, Patras, Rhodes, Samos, and Santorini. They also offer direct flights to London, Paris, Rome, Brussels, Barcelona, Madrid, Milan, Moscow, Bologna, Cyprus, and several major German cities. Foreign travel agents and travel booking websites may not be aware of Aegean Airlines, so visit the airline's actual website. People who have been flying Aegean for several years now find the airline reliable, safe, and hospitable.

In recent years, two other airlines have appeared on the scene: **Athens Airways** (www.athensairways.com) and **Sky Express** (www.skyexpress.gr). Both offer limited service between Athens and various major cites and islands. Sky Express actually seems to be more like a charter airline. You are invited to look into their respective websites, but we must state that we cannot yet recommend these airlines based on either our own or friends' personal experience.

Note: *Most Greek domestic tickets are nonrefundable, and changing your flight can cost you up to 30% within 24 hours of departure and 50% within 12 hours.*

By Car

Driving in Greece is a bit of an adventure, but there's no denying that it's the best way to see the country at your own pace. By and large, the public transportation system outside of the main cities simply doesn't arrange its schedules for the convenience of tourists. *Note:* Greece has one of the highest accident rates in Europe, probably due somewhat to treacherous roads, mountain terrain, and poor maintenance of older cars as much as to reckless driving—although Greeks are certainly aggressive drivers. Athens is a particularly intimidating place in which to drive at first, and parking spaces are practically nonexistent in the center of town. (Main routes in and out of cities are sometimes signed by white arrows on blue markers.) A few of the major cities are linked to Athens by modern expressways with tolls; as these highways are currently being upgraded—and sections are to be privatized—it is difficult to tell the exact toll charges, but the toll for Athens to Thessaloniki, for instance, has been about 5€ and may well go up. Accidents must be reported to the police for insurance claims.

If you do intend to do a fair amount of driving, acquire a good up-to-date map before you set off. The best source is a British shop that allows for online ordering, **www.themapstore.com.**

The **Greek Automobile Touring Club (ELPA),** 395 Mesoyion, 11343 Athens (② **210/606-8800**), with offices in most cities, can help you with all matters relating to your car, issue **International Driver's Licenses,** and provide **maps and information** (② **174,** 24 hr. daily). ELPA's emergency road service number is ② **104.** Though the service provided by the able ELPA mechanics is free for light repairs, definitely give a generous tip.

The price of gasoline fluctuates considerably from week to week and from service station to service station, but as of the time this guide went to press it was about 1.75€ per liter—which works out to about US$9.75 for an American gallon. There is no shortage of gasoline stations in all cities, good-size towns, and major tourist centers, but if you are setting off for an excursion into one of the more remote mountain areas or to an isolated beach, fill up on gas before setting out.

CAR RENTALS You will find no end of car-rental agencies throughout Greece, both the familiar international ones and many Greek firms. There is considerable variation in prices, although rates in high season are shockingly high. But we'd be wary of renting from some local agency just because it seems a bit cheaper: if anything goes wrong with your car while out in the countryside, they will probably not be able to do much to help you.

Many cars have a standard shift; if you must have an automatic, make sure in advance that one is available (and be prepared to pay extra). In high season you are

---

Warning on Car Rentals & Licenses

Legally, all non-E.U. drivers in Greece are required to carry an International Driver's License. In practice, most car-rental agencies will rent to Americans and other non-E.U. drivers with their national driver's licenses, although they usually have to have been licensed for at least 1 year. (One major exception is on the island of Hios, where the International Driver's License is usually required.) This is fine as long as you don't get involved in an accident—especially one involving personal injury. Then you could discover that your insurance is voided on a technicality. Meanwhile, you run the risk of an individual policeman insisting that you must have the international license. Best, then, is to obtain one before leaving home (from your national automobile association) or from the **Greek Automobile Touring Club** (see above).

Certainly in Athens and several other large cities, travelers may need or want to resort to a taxi. Here are some tips that will help you understand and navigate the taxi system as you travel in Greece:

○ Taxi rates are in constant (upward) flux, so the rates you see her are the ones in effect as we go to press. First, though (if it's before midnight), check to see that the little window next to the euro display on the meter is **"1"** and not **"2"**—the latter is the setting for midnight-to-5am or outside-the-city-limits rates (which are about double the regular rate). If that's not the case, reach over and indicate that you notice.

○ All fares are subject to change (by law, that is), but at the time this guide went to press, the meter is allowed to start at the basic 1.20€ as you set off—check to see if this is the case. Drivers have been known to start with a much higher number already registered; or they leave the meter off, and then try to extort a much larger fare from you. Even if you don't speak a word

of Greek besides "taxi," point at the meter and say "meter." The basic rate per kilometer is higher between midnight and 5am.

○ The fare from and to the airport in Athens has been fixed at 35€ except between midnight and 5am when it is 50€. (Not to be too technical, but the fare depends on the *arrival* time at the destination.) The minimum fare for any trip in and around Athens and Piraeus is 3.10€ and 4€ for the rest of the country. But you shouldn't pay much more than 15€ for a trip within Athens itself.

○ At least in the major cities you should be able to ask for a receipt from the meter—if not printed, you can ask the driver to write one out. By the way, the taxi should also have the A/C on when the weather calls for it—and do not let the driver charge you extra for it.

○ For a group, a driver may insist that each person pay the full metered fare. Pay only your proportion of the fare if all of you have the same destination. Pairs or groups of tourists should have

strongly advised to make your reservation before leaving home and well in advance. Always ask if the quoted price includes insurance; many credit cards make the collision-damage waiver unnecessary, but you will find that most rental agencies automatically include this in their rates. You can sometimes save by booking at home before you leave; this is especially advisable in summer. If you are shopping around, let the agents see the number of competitors' brochures you're carrying.

Most companies require that the renter be at least 21 years old (25 for some car models). There are occasional reports that some car-rental agencies will not rent to drivers 75 or over—or even 70—but this does not seem to be an issue in Greece. If in doubt, inquire beforehand of the rental company. Technically you should possess an International Driver's License, but many car-rental agencies accept a valid Australian, Canadian, E.U. nation, or U.S. driver's license. You must also have a major credit card (or be prepared to leave a *very* large cash deposit).

a designated arguer; the others can write down names and numbers, stick with the luggage, or look for help—from a policeman, maitre d', or desk clerk.

o Late at night, especially at airports, ferry stops, and bus and railroad stations, a driver may refuse to use his meter and demand an exorbitant fare. Smile, shake your head, and look for another cab; if none are available, start writing down the driver's license number and he will probably relent.

o Again, these may change, but at press time, legal surcharges include: 2.80€ for the Thessaloniki airport, and 2.30€ for other major airports; .95€ pickup at ports, bus terminals, or train terminals; .35€ per piece of luggage over 10kg (22 lb.). (Road tolls are charged to the passengers—for example, you will pay 2€ for the new road from the airport to Athens.) Radio taxis (called from hotels, for instance) get a 2.50€ surcharge, 5€ for a fixed appointment.

o A driver may say that your hotel is full, but that he knows a better and cheaper one. Laugh, and insist you'll take your chances at your hotel.

o A driver may want to let you off where it's most convenient for him. Be cooperative if it's easier and quicker for you to cross a busy avenue than for him to get you to the other side, but you don't have to get out until you're ready.

If things are obviously not going well for you, conspicuously write down the driver's name and number and report him to the **tourist police** (℗ **171**) if he has the nerve to call your bluff. One of the best countertactics is to simply open the door slightly; he won't want to risk damaging it. (Two passengers can each open a door.)

Our final advice: Don't sweat the small change. So the driver is charging you 12€ for a ride you have been told should be about 10€; are you prepared to go to court for 2€? Any difference above 5€ probably should be questioned—but it may have to do with traffic delays when the meter ticks at the rate of 9.60€ per hour. Most cabbies are honest—just be aware of the possibilities. And be sure to reward good service with a tip.

The major car-rental companies in Athens are **Avis** (℗ 210/322-4951), **Budget** (℗ 210/349-8700), **Hertz** (℗ 210/922-0102), **National** (℗ 210/349-3400), and **AutoEurope** (℗ 00800/11574-0300); all have offices in major cities, at most airports, and on most islands. Smaller local companies usually have lower rates, but their vehicles are often older and not as well maintained. If you prefer to combine your car rental with your other travel arrangements, we recommend **Galaxy Travel,** 35 Voulis, near Syntagma Square (℗ **210/322-2091;** www.galaxytravel.gr). It's open Monday through Saturday during the tourist season.

Rental rates vary widely—definitely ask around. In high season, daily rates with unlimited mileage will be about 65€ for a compact and 135€ for a full-size car; weekly rates with unlimited mileage might run 240€ for a compact and 300€ for a full size. In low season, rates are often negotiable in Greece when you show up in person. The prices quoted should include the various taxes (although there may be a surcharge for pickup and drop-off at airports in high season).

Note: If you intend to take your car on a ferry or into a foreign country, you must have written permission from the car-rental agency.

DRIVING RULES In Greece, you drive on the right, pass on the left, and yield right of way to vehicles approaching from the right except where otherwise posted. Greece has adopted international road signs, although many Greeks apparently haven't learned what they mean yet. The maximum speed limit is 100kmph (62 mph) on open roads, and 50kmph (30 mph) in town, unless otherwise posted. Seat belts are required. The police have become stricter in recent years, especially with foreigners in rental cars; alcohol tests can be given and fines imposed on the spot. (If you feel you have been stopped or treated unfairly, get the officer's name and report him at the nearest tourist police station.) Honking is illegal in Athens, but you can hear that law broken at any odd moment.

PARKING Parking a car has become a serious challenge in the cities and towns of Greece. The better hotels provide parking, either on their premises or by arrangement with a nearby lot (our hotel reviews include information on where to park). Greece has few public parking garages or lots; follow the blue signs with the white P and you may be lucky enough to find a space. Most city streets have restricted parking of one kind or another. In some cities, signs—usually yellow, and with the directions in English as well as in Greek—will indicate that you can park along the street but must purchase a ticket from the nearest kiosk. Otherwise, be prepared to park fairly far from your base or destination. If you lock the car and remove valuables from sight, you should not have to worry about a break-in.

By Boat

Ferries are the most common, cheapest, and generally most "authentic" way to visit the islands, though the slow roll of a ferry can be stomach-churning. A wide variety of vessels sail Greek waters—some huge, sleek, and new, with TV lounges, discos, and good restaurants; some old and ill-kept, but pleasant enough if you stay on deck.

Ferry service (often accommodating vehicles) is available between Athens (Piraeus) and several other Greek ports. There's regular service from Piraeus to Aegina and to Poros in the Saronic Gulf; most of the Cyclades; Chania and Iraklion on Crete; Hios; Kos; Lesvos; Rhodes; and Samos. For the Cyclades, crossing is shorter and less expensive from Rafina, an hour east of Athens. From Patras, there's daily service to Corfu, Ithaka, and Kefalonia. The Sporades have service from Ayios Konstandinos, Kimi, and Volos (and then among the several islands). There's also service between many of the islands, even between Crete and Rhodes, as well as car-crossing to and from Turkey between Hios and Çesme; Lesvos and Dikeli; and Samos and Kusadasi.

There is also frequent ferry service (often also for cars) between several Italian ports (Ancona, Bari, Brindisi, Venice) and Patras (with stops at several major islands en route). But if you intend to continue on with your vehicle into Turkey or Italy or plan to enter Greece from Turkey, or Italy, you should inquire long before setting off for either country, and make sure that you have all the necessary paperwork.

The map of Greece offered by the Greek National Tourism Organization (EOT), which indicates the common boat routes, is useful in planning your sea travels. Once you've learned what is *possible,* you can turn your attention to what is *available.* Remember that the summer schedule is the fullest, spring and fall bring reduced service, and winter schedules are skeletal.

There are dozens of shipping companies, each with its own schedule—which, by the way, are regulated by the government. Your travel agent might have a copy of the monthly schedule, *Greek Travel Pages,* or you can search online at **www.gtp.gr** or **www.ferries.gr**. When in Greece, it's best to go straight to an official information office, a travel agency, or the port authority as soon as you arrive at the place that you intend to leave via ferry.

Photos can give you some idea of the ships, but remember that any photo displayed was probably taken when the ship was new, and it is unlikely that anyone will be able (or willing) to tell you its actual age. The bigger ferries offer greater stability during rough weather. Except in summer, you can usually depend on getting aboard a ferry by showing up about an hour before scheduled departure—inter-island boats sometimes depart before their scheduled times—and purchasing a ticket from a dockside agent or aboard the ship itself, though this is often more expensive.

Your best bet is to buy a ticket from an agent ahead of time. In Athens, we recommend **Galaxy Travel,** 35 Voulis, near Syntagma Square (© **210/322-2091;** www. galaxytravel.gr); and **Alkyon Travel,** 97 Akademias, near Kanigos Square (© **210/ 383-2545**). During the high season, both agencies keep long hours Monday through Saturday.

Note: Different travel agencies sell tickets to different lines—this is usually the policy of the line itself—and one agent might not know or bother to find out what

In the early and late weeks of the tourist season—from April to early May, and September to November—boat service can be unpredictable. Boat schedules, at the best of times, are tentative—but during this time, they are wish lists, little more. Our best advice is that you wait until you get to Greece, then go to a major travel agency and ask for help.

13

Getting Around

PLANNING YOUR TRIP TO GREECE

else is offered. However, if you press reputable agencies like those above, they will at least tell you the options. The port authority is the most reliable source of information, and the shipping company itself or its agents usually offer better prices and may have tickets when other agents have exhausted their allotment. It often pays to compare vessels and prices.

First class usually means roomy air-conditioned cabins and its own lounge; on some routes it costs almost as much as flying. However, on longer overnight hauls, you're on a comfortable floating hotel and thus save the cost of lodging. Second class means smaller cabins (which you will probably have to share with strangers) and its own lounge. The tourist-class fare entitles you to a seat on the deck or in a lounge. (Tourists usually head for the deck, while Greeks stay inside and watch TV.) Hold onto your ticket; crews conduct ticket-control sweeps.

Note: Those taking a ferry to Turkey from one of the Dodecanese islands must submit passport (or E.U. citizens, an ID) and payment to an agent the day before departure.

We include more details on service and schedules in the relevant chapters to the various destinations, as well as suggested travel agencies and sources of local information. To give you some sense of the fares, here are examples for standard accommodations from Piraeus at press time: to Crete (Iraklion), 80€ to 110€; Kos, 60€; Mitilini (Lesvos), 68€; Mykonos, 60€; Rhodes, 100€; Santorini, 60€. And don't be surprised if small taxes get added on at the very end.

BY HYDROFOIL So-called "Flying Catamarans" and hydrofoils dubbed "Flying Dolphins" also serve many of the major islands. Undoubtedly faster, they cost almost twice as much as regular ferries, and their schedules are often interrupted by weather conditions. (Never rely on a tight connection between a hydrofoil and, say, an airplane flight.)

Hydrofoils have comfortable airline-style seats and are less likely to cause seasickness, but they are noisy—although smoking is prohibited. They are frequently fully booked in summer, can be quite bumpy during rough weather, and give little or no view of the passing scenery. They're also the best choice if your time is limited. Everyone should ride one of these sleek little crafts at least once.

There is regular hydrofoil service to many of the major islands; new routes and new schedules appear often. Longer trips over open sea, such as between Santorini and Iraklion, Crete, may make them well worth the extra expense. A one-way fare from Heraklion to Santorini in high season, for instance, is 40€ to 50€. The forward compartment offers better views but is also bumpy.

The Flying Dolphins are operated by **Hellenic Seaways,** 6 Astiggos, Karaiskaki Square, 18531 Piraeus (© **210/419-9000;** www.hellenicseaways.gr). The service from Zea Marina in Piraeus to the Saronic Gulf islands and throughout the Sporades is recommended for its speed and regularity. There is also service from Rafina, on the east coast of Attika, to several of the Cyclades islands.

BY SAILBOAT & YACHT Many more tourists are choosing to explore Greece by sailboat or yacht. There are numerous facilities and options for both. Experienced sailors interested in renting a boat in Greece can contact the **Hellenic Professional and Bareboat Yacht Owners' Association,** A8–A9 Zea Marina, 18536 Piraeus (© **210/452-6335**). Less experienced sailors should consider signing up for one of the flotillas—a group of 12 or more boats sailing as a group led by a boat crewed by experienced sailors; the largest of such organizations is **Sunsail USA,** 93 North Park Place Blvd., Clearwater FL 33759 (© **888/350-3568;** www.sunsail.com). However, travel agencies should be able to put you in touch with other such outfits.

At the other extreme, those who want to charter a yacht with anything from a basic skipper to a full crew should first contact the Hellenic Professional and Bareboat Yacht Owners' Association (listed above), or **Ghiolman Yachts,** 8 Propileon, 11742 Athens (© **210/325-5000;** www.ghiolman.com). If you feel competent enough to make your own arrangements, contact **Valef Yachts Ltd.** in the U.S. (© **800/223-3845;** www.valefyachts.com). In Greece, you can contact one of these organizations or try a private agency such as **Alpha Yachting,** 67 Leoforos Possidonos, 16674 Glyfada (© **210/968-0486;** www.alphayachting.com).

By Train

Greek trains are generally slow but are inexpensive and fairly pleasant. The **Hellenic State Railway (OSE)** also offers bus service from stations adjacent to major train terminals. (Bus service is faster, but second-class train fare is nearly 50% cheaper, and trains offer more comfortable and scenic rides.) If you are interested in special arrangements involving rail passes for Greece (sometimes in combination with Olympic Air flights within Greece), check out **www.raileurope.com** or call © **800/622-8600** in the U.S., or 800/361-7245 in Canada.

For information and tickets in Athens, visit the **OSE office** at 1–3 Karolou (© **210/522-4563**), or at 6 Sina (© **210/362-4402**), both near Omonia Square. From abroad, visit www.ose.gr.

Purchase your ticket and reserve a seat ahead of time, as a 50% surcharge is added to tickets purchased on the train, and some lines are packed, especially in summer. A first-class ticket may be worth the extra cost, as seats are more comfortable and less crowded. There is sleeper service on the Athens-Thessaloniki run. Though the costly sleepers are a good value, you must be prepared to share a compartment with three to five others. Express service (6 hr.) runs twice a day, at 7am and 1pm.

Trains to northern Greece (Alexandropolis, Florina, Kalambaka, Lamia, Larissa, Thessaloniki, Volos, and other towns) leave from the Larissa station (Stathmos Larissis). **Trains to the Peloponnese** (Argos, Corinth, Patras) leave from the Peloponnese station (Stathmos Peloponnisou). Take trolley no. 1 or 5 from Syntagma Square to either station.

By Bus

Public buses are inexpensive but often overcrowded. Local bus lines vary from place to place, but on most islands the bus stop is in a central location with a posted schedule. Destinations are usually displayed on the front of the bus, but you might have to ask. The conductor will collect your fare after departure.

Note that in Athens and other large cities, a bus ticket *must* be purchased before *and* validated after boarding. Kiosks usually offer bus tickets as well as schedules. The Athens Metro ticket's cost is based on the destination, but usually costs about .70€.

Note: Save your ticket in case an "inspector" comes aboard. If you don't have a ticket, the fine can be at least 30 times the price of the ticket.

Greece has an extensive **long-distance bus service (KTEL),** an association of regional operators with green-and-yellow buses that leave from convenient central stations. For information about the long-distance-bus offices, contact the KTEL office in Athens (© **210/512-4910**).

In Athens, most buses heading to destinations within **Attica** leave from the Mavromate terminal, north of the National Archaeological Museum. Most buses to **Central Greece** leave from 260 Liossion, 5km (3 miles) north of Omonia Square (take local bus no. 024 from Leoforos Amalias in front of the entrance to the National Garden and tell the driver your destination). Most buses to the **Peloponnese,** and **western** and **northern Greece** leave from the long-distance bus terminal at 100 Kifissou, 4km (2½ miles) northeast of Omonia Square. To get to the long-distance bus terminal, take local bus no. 051 from the stop located 2 blocks west of Omonia, near the big church of Ayios Konstandinos, at Zinonos and Menandrou.

Express buses between major cities, usually air-conditioned, can be booked through travel agencies. Make sure that your destination is understood—you wouldn't be the first to see a bit more of Greece than bargained for—and determine the bus's schedule and comforts before purchasing your ticket. Many buses are not air-conditioned, take torturous routes, and make frequent stops. (NO SMOKING signs are generally disregarded by drivers and conductors, as well as by many older male passengers.)

Organized and guided **bus tours** are widely available. Some of them will pick you up at your hotel; ask the hotel staff or any travel agent in Athens. We especially recommend **CHAT Tours,** the oldest and probably most experienced provider of a wide selection of bus tours led by highly articulate guides. Almost any travel agent can book a CHAT tour, but if you want to deal with the company directly, contact them through their website, www.chatours.gr; in Athens, the CHAT office is at 9 Xenofontos, 10557 Athens (© **210/323-0827**).

Note: Readers have complained that some bus groups are so large they feel removed from the leader; inquire about group size if this concerns you.

TIPS ON ACCOMMODATIONS

Greece offers a full spectrum of accommodations ranging from the extravagant to the basic. Within a given locale, of course, not all options are available, but most readers will find something that appeals to them.

Hotels used to be required to publicize a grading system imposed by the Greek government. Classes still exist and are indicated by stars, but these are based more on facilities such as public areas, pools, and in-room amenities than on any comfort or service ratings. (Each room's rate should be posted on the inside of the door.) Basically it is a market economy, for hotels know better than to ask for too much because

 Climate Control

Most of the Greek hotels recommended in this guide now promise air-conditioning in the hot season and heating in the colder months. The equipment is indeed there, but you should be aware that, except in the most expensive hotels, neither will necessarily be as adequate as you might like.

Try to make reservations **by fax** so that you have a written record of the room and the agreed–upon price. Be aware that a double room in Greece does not always mean a room with a double bed, but might be a room with twin beds. Double beds in Greece are called "matrimonial beds," and rooms with such beds are often designated "honeymoon rooms." This can lead to misunderstandings.

Note that in a few instances—usually at the most expensive hotels—the prices quoted are per person. (We indicate this in our recommendations.)

Note, too, that room prices, no matter what people say officially, are often negotiable, especially at the edges of the season. Because of Greek law and EOT regulations, hotel keepers are often reluctant to provide rates far in advance and often quote prices higher than their actual rates. When you bargain, don't cite our prices, which may be too high, but ask instead for the best current rate. Actual off-season prices may be as much as 25% lower than the lowest rate given to us for this book.

competitors will undercut them. Frommer's own rating system of stars and icons for special features takes care of all such differences.

International travelers will be familiar with some of the major chains—the Westin, Hilton, and Best Western, for example. A number of Greek chains, such as Louis and Chandris, also own numerous hotels, while several hotels now belong to the Luxury Collection of Starwood Hotels and Resorts. These latter tend to be extremely upscale hotels. However, most Greek hotels are independent lodgings run by hands-on owners.

RENTALS (APARTMENTS & HOUSES) An increasingly popular way to experience Greece is to rent an apartment or a house; the advantages include freedom from the formalities of a hotel, often a more desirable location, and a kitchen that allows you to avoid the costs and occasional crush of restaurants. Such rentals do not come cheap, but if you calculate what two or more people might pay for a decent hotel, not to mention all the meals eaten out, a rental can turn out to be a good deal. (Cost per person per day in a really nice apartment runs about 100€; a fancier villa with two bedrooms might cost about 200€ per person per day.) Any full-service travel agency in your home country or in Greece should be able to put you in touch with an agency specializing in such rentals.

The fact is that the British dominate this field in Greece, both in terms of experience and sheer numbers of offerings. So via the Internet, anyone can now see what's offered and contact such outfits as **Simply Travel Ltd.,** Columbus House, Westwood Way, Coventry CV4 8TT (© **0871/231-4050;** www.simplytravel.co.uk); or **Pure Crete,** Bolney Place, Cowfold Road, Haywards Heath, West Sussex RH17 5Q7 (© **1444/881-402;** www.purecrete.com). Among those in the United States are **Villas International,** 17 Fox Lane, San Anselmo CA 94960 (© **800/221-2260;** www.villasintl.com); and **Villas and Apartments Abroad,** 183 Madison Ave., Ste. 201, New York, NY 10016 (© **212/213-6435;** www.vaanyc.com). In Canada, try **Grecian Holidays,** 1315 Lawrence Ave. East, Toronto, Ontario M3A 3R3 (© **800/268-6786;** www.grecianholidays.com).

If price is important to you, ask for the cheapest room at hotels and inquire about special offers. Most island hotels offer seriously discounted prices off-season. If tourism continues to decline in Greece, and the Greek economy remains troubled, many hotels may offer seriously discounted prices. That said, expect weekend hotel prices to be much higher than during the week, due to weekend travel by the Greeks themselves. If you made your hotel reservation by e-mail, be sure to arrive with a printout of your reservation confirmation. And keep in mind that strikes can close museums and archaeological sites without warning. Decide what you want most to see, and go there as soon as possible after you arrive. The fact that something is open today says nothing about tomorrow. If possible, phone the site or museum you are about to visit to see if it is open just before you head there; much information given out by hotels, websites, and even Greek National Tourism offices is wrong.

For apartment, farmhouse, or cottage stays of 2 weeks or more, **Idyll Untours** (🕿 **888/868-6871;** www.untours.com) provides exceptional vacation rentals for a reasonable price—which includes air/ground transportation, cooking facilities, and on-call support from a local resident. Best of all: Untours—named the "Most Generous Company in America" by Newman's Own—donates most profits to provide low-interest loans to underprivileged entrepreneurs around the world.

Another option is to rent a traditional house in one of about 12 relatively rural or remote villages or settlements throughout Greece. These small traditional houses have been restored by the Greek National Tourism Organization (GNTO or EOT); to learn more about this possibility, contact the GNTO office nearest you (see "Visitor Information," in "Fast Facts" below).

[FastFACTS] GREECE

Area Codes All phone numbers in Greece are 10 digits long. Area codes range from three digits in Athens (**210**) to as many as five digits in less populated locales; the phone numbers themselves range from five digits to eight but all must add up to a total of ten including the area code. All numbers provided in the text start with the proper area code. Also see "Telephones," later in this section.

Business Hours Greek business and office hours take some getting used to, especially in the afternoon, when most English-speaking people are accustomed to getting things done in high gear. Compounding the problem is that it is nearly impossible to pin down the precise hours of opening. We can start by saying that almost all stores and services are closed on Sunday—except, of course, tourist-oriented shops and services. Supermarkets, department stores, and chain stores are usually open 9am to 9pm, Monday through Saturday. On Monday, Wednesday, and Saturday, smaller retail shops' hours are usually 9am to 3pm; Tuesday, Thursday, and Friday, it's 9am to 2pm and 5 to 7pm. The afternoon siesta is generally observed from 3 to 5pm, though many tourist-oriented businesses have a minimal crew on duty during naptime, and they may keep extended hours, often from 8am to 10pm. (In fact, in tourist centers, shops may be open at all kinds of hours.) Most government offices are open Monday through Friday only, from 8am to 3pm. Call ahead to check the hours of businesses you must deal with, and try not to disturb Greek friends during siesta hours. Final advice: Anything you really need to accomplish in a government office, business, or store should be done on weekdays between about 9am and 1pm.

Banks are open to the public Monday through Thursday from 8am to 2:30pm, Friday from 8am to 2pm. Banks at a few locations may be open for some services such as foreign currency exchange into the evening and on Saturday. All banks are closed on the long list of Greek holidays. (See "When to Go," in chapter 2.)

Cellphones See "Mobile Phones," later in this section.

Crime See "Safety," later in this section.

Customs Passengers from North America arriving in Athens aboard international flights are generally not searched, and if you have nothing to declare, continue through the green lane. (Because of the continuing threat of terrorism, baggage is X-rayed before boarding domestic flights.) However, citizens of the United States, Canada, Australia, New Zealand, and other non-E.U. countries face a few commonsensical restrictions on what you can bring into Greece. Clearly, no narcotics: Greece is *very* tough on drug users. No explosives or weapons—although upon application, a sportsman might be able to bring in a legitimate hunting weapon. Only medications for amounts properly prescribed for your own use are allowed. Plants with soil are not. Dogs and cats can be brought in, but they must have proof of recent rabies and other health shots.

What You Can Take Out of Greece:

(All Nationalities): Exportation of Greek antiquities is strictly protected by law. No genuine antiquities may be taken out of Greece without prior special permission from the **Archaeological Service,** 3 Polignotou, Athens. Also, you must be able to explain how you acquired any genuinely old objects—in particular, icons or religious articles. A dealer or shopkeeper must provide you with an export certificate for any object dating from before 1830.

In general, **keep all receipts** for major purchases in order to clear Customs on your return home. To avoid having to pay duty on foreign-made personal items you owned before you left on your trip, bring along a bill of sale, an insurance policy, a jeweler's appraisal, or purchase receipts. You could register items readily identifiable by a permanently affixed serial number or marking—think laptop computers, cameras, and CD players—with Customs before you leave. Take the items to the nearest Customs office or register them with Customs at the airport from which you're departing. You'll receive, at no cost, a Certificate of Registration, which allows duty-free entry for the life of the item.

For further information on what you're allowed to bring into your country of residence, contact one of the following agencies:

U.S. Citizens: U.S. Customs & Border Protection (CBP), 1300 Pennsylvania Ave. NW, Washington, DC 20229 (✆ **877/227-5511;** www. cbp.gov).

Canadian Citizens: Canada Border Services Agency (✆ **800/461-9999** in Canada, or **204/983-3500;** www.cbsa-asfc.gc.ca).

U.K. Citizens: HM Revenue & Customs ✆ **0845/010-9000** (from outside the U.K., 020/8929-0152), or consult their website at www.hmce.gov.uk.

Australian Citizens: Australian Customs Service at ✆ **1300/363-263,** or log on to www.customs.gov.au.

New Zealand Citizens: New Zealand Customs, the Customhouse, 17–21 Whitmore St., Box 2218, Wellington (✆ **0800/428-786;** www. customs.govt.nz).

Disabled Travelers
Increasingly, people with physical disabilities who travel abroad will find more options and resources out there than ever before. That said, few concessions exist for travelers with disabilities in Greece. Steep steps, uneven pavements, almost no cuts at curbstones, few ramps, narrow walks, slick stone, and traffic congestion can cause problems.

Archaeological sites are, by their very nature, difficult to navigate, and crowded public transportation can be all but impossible.

The new airport and the new Athens Metro system are, however, wheelchair accessible, and thanks to the 2004 Olympics, an elevator now can take wheelchair-bound individuals to the top of the Acropolis; but even this requires that the wheelchair be pushed up a lengthy path. More modern and private facilities are only now beginning to provide ramps, but little else has been done. Increasingly, too, hotels are setting aside rooms that they advertise as "disability-friendly" or "handicap accessible," but some of these may mean nothing more than handrails in the bathtub. Still, foreigners in wheelchairs—accompanied by companions—are becoming a more common sight in Greece. Several travel agencies now offer customized tours and itineraries for travelers with disabilities; one in particular is the British based, **Makin' Tracks: www. makintracks.eu**.

There is now one particular establishment in Greece that should have a special appeal to those with physical disabilities: the **Eria Resort Hotel** on Crete, designed, built, and dedicated to provide as convenient, comfortable, and active a stay in Greece as possible. For a full description, see p.213.

Organizations that offer a vast range of resources and assistance to travelers

with disabilities include **MossRehab** (✆ 800/CALL-MOSS [225-5667]; www. mossresourcenet.org); the **American Foundation for the Blind (AFB;** ✆ **800/ 232-5463;** www.afb.org); and **SATH** (Society for Accessible Travel & Hospitality; ✆ **212/447-7284;** www.sath.org). **AirAmbulanceCard.com** is now partnered with SATH and allows you to preselect top-notch hospitals in case of an emergency.

Many travel agencies offer customized tours and itineraries for travelers with disabilities. Among them are **Flying Wheels Travel** (✆ **877/451-5006;** www. flyingwheelstravel.com) and **Accessible Journeys** (✆ **800/846-4537;** www. disabilitytravel.com).

Also check out the quarterly online magazine *Emerging Horizons* (www. emerginghorizons.com), available by subscription (five issues $16.95; 10 issues $33.90).

The "Accessible Travel" link at **Mobility-Advisor. com** (www.mobility-advisor. com) offers a variety of travel resources to people with disabilities.

British travelers should contact **Holiday Care** (✆ **0845-124-9971** in the U.K. only; www.holidaycare. org.uk) to access a wide range of travel information and resources for elderly people and those with disabilities.

Doctors Any foreign embassy or consulate can provide a list of area doctors who speak English. If in

a town without these offices, ask your hotel management to recommend a local doctor—even his or her own.

Drinking Laws The minimum age for being served alcohol in public locales is 18. Wine and beer are generally available in eating places, but not in all coffeehouses or dessert cafes. Alcoholic beverages are sold in food stores as well as liquor stores.

Although a certain amount of high spirits is appreciated, Greeks do not appreciate public drunkenness. The resort centers where mobs of young foreigners party every night are tolerated as necessary for the tourist trade, but such behavior wins no respect for foreigners. Do not carry open containers of alcohol in your car and don't even think about driving while intoxicated.

Electricity Electric current in Greece is 220 volts AC, alternating at 50 cycles. (Some larger hotels have 110-volt low-wattage outlets for electric shavers, but they aren't good for hair dryers and most other appliances.) Electrical outlets require Continental-type plugs with two round prongs. U.S. travelers will need an adapter plug and a transformer/converter, unless their appliances are dual-voltage. Laptop computer users will want to check their requirements; a transformer may be necessary, and surge protectors are recommended. But more and more appliances—including laptops and hair dryers—allow for a simple switch to the 220 volts.

Embassies & Consulates   The embassies in Athens are as follows: **Australia,** Thon Building, Corner Kifias and Alexandras avenues (© **210/870-4000**); **Canada,** 4 Ioannou Yenadiou (© **210/727-3400**); **Ireland,** 7 Leoforos Vasileus (© **210/723-2771**); **New Zealand,** 268 Leoforos Kifissias, Halandri (© **210/6874-700**); **U.K.,** 1 Ploutarchou (© **210/727-2660**); **U.S.,** 91 Leoforos Vas. Sofias (© **210/721-2951**).

Emergencies   If there is no tourist police officer available (© **171**), contact the local police, © **100.** For fire, call © **199.** For medical emergencies and/or first aid and/or an ambulance, call © **166.** For hospitals, call © **106.** For automobile emergencies, put out a triangular danger sign and call © **10400.** Embassies, consulates, and many hotels can recommend an English-speaking doctor.

Family Travel   If you have enough trouble getting your kids out of the house in the morning, dragging them thousands of miles away may seem an insurmountable challenge. But family travel can be immensely rewarding, giving you new ways of seeing the world through smaller pairs of eyes. Set goals for your family for your travels in Greece. The whole family can head for the beaches. At the other extreme, however, think twice about taking younger

kids along on a full-day exploration of museums and archaeological sites. Travel with infants and very young children—say, up to about age 5—can work; most children ages 6 to 16 become restless at historical sites. If you're lucky, your children may tune into history at some point in their teens.

There are occasional kid-friendly distractions in Greece: playgrounds all over the place, water parks here and there, and zoos. Greeks boys now play pickup basketball even in small towns—if your kids go for that, it's a great way to be quickly accepted.

To make it easy to pick out those accommodations, restaurants, and attractions in Greece that are particularly kid-friendly, we mark them with the "Kids" icon throughout this guide. Most hotels allow children 5 and under a free bed or cot in your room, and reduced prices for children 11 and under. Some museums have children's prices, but by and large Greece is not set up to offer reductions at every turn.

As for passport requirements for children, see "Passports," later in this chapter (or go to the State Department's website, **www.travel.state.gov**). If you are traveling with children other than your own, you must be sure you have full identification as well as notarized authorization from their parents.

Gasoline/Petrol   Please see "Getting Around: By Car," earlier in this chapter.

Health   If you suffer from a chronic illness, consult your doctor about your travel plans before your departure. For conditions like epilepsy, diabetes, or heart problems, wear a **MedicAlert** identification tag, which will immediately alert doctors to your condition and give them access to your records through MedicAlert's 24-hour hot line. But you must join **MedicAlert** before setting off: see their website: **www.medicalert.com**. If you have special concerns, before heading abroad you might check out the United States **Centers for Disease Control and Prevention** (© **800/232-4636;** www.cdc.gov/travel). You can find advice on health and medical situations in foreign lands as well as listings of reliable medical clinics overseas at the **International Society of Travel Medicine** (www.istm.org). You can also contact the **International Association for Medical Assistance to Travelers** (**IAMAT;** www.iamat.org) for tips on travel and health concerns in the countries you're visiting, and for lists of local, English-speaking doctors. **Travel Health Online** (www.tripprep.com), sponsored by a consortium of travel medicine practitioners, may also offer helpful advice on traveling abroad.

Greeks have national medical insurance. Citizens of other E.U. nations should inquire before leaving, but your policies will probably cover treatment in Greece. Non-E.U. travelers should check your health plan to see if it provides appropriate coverage; you may want to buy **travel medical insurance** instead. (See **www.frommers.com/planning**.) Bring your insurance ID card with you when you travel. Although you will receive emergency care with no questions asked, make sure you have coverage at home.

Prescriptions

Pack prescription medications in your carry-on luggage, and carry prescription medications in their original containers, with pharmacy labels—otherwise they might not make it through airport security. (Even pills with codeine—such as those sold over the counter in Canada—might be questioned.) Also, bring along copies of your prescriptions in case you lose your pills or run out. Don't forget an extra pair of contact lenses or prescription glasses. Carry the generic names of prescription medicines, in case a local pharmacist is unfamiliar with the brand name.

Drugstores/Chemists

These are called *pharmikon* in Greek; aside from the obvious indications in windows and interiors, they are identified by a green cross. For minor medical problems, go first to the nearest pharmacy. Pharmacists usually speak English, and many medications can be dispensed without prescription. In the larger cities, if it is closed, there should be a sign in the window directing

you to the nearest open one. Newspapers also list the pharmacies that are open late or all night.

Common Ailments

Diarrhea is no more of a problem in Greece than it might be any time you change diet and water supplies, but occasionally visitors do experience it. Common over-the-counter preventatives and cures are available in Greek pharmacies, but if you are concerned, bring your own.

If you expect to be taking sea trips and are inclined to get seasick, bring a preventative.

Allergy sufferers should carry antihistamines, especially in the spring.

If you have any concern about the latest situation with diseases in Greece, you could contact the U.S. Centers for Disease Control International Traveler's Notices (**www.cdc.gov/travel**).

Sun Exposure

Between mid-June and September, too much exposure to the sun during midday could well lead to sunstroke or heatstroke. Sunscreen and a hat are strongly advised.

Dietary Red Flags

Nothing in the Greek diet requires any special warning. Greece's natural water is excellent, although these days you will usually be served—and charged for—bottled water. (Cola soft drinks are said to help those with digestive difficulties from too much olive oil in their food.) Milk is pasteurized, though

refrigeration is sometimes not the best, especially in out-of-the-way places. It is easy for vegetarians to eat well in Greece, but restaurants are not equipped to serve kosher meals.

Bugs, Bites & Other Wildlife Concerns

There is no particular risk of poisonous bites, although mosquitoes can occasionally be a nuisance: You might well travel with some bug spray.

Hospitals In Greece, modern hospitals, clinics, and pharmacies are found everywhere, and personnel, equipment, and supplies ensure excellent treatment. Dental care is also widely available. Most doctors in Greece can speak English (many having trained in North America or the U.K.).

You can also try the emergency room at a local hospital. In addition, many hospitals have walk-in clinics for emergency cases that are not life threatening; you may not get immediate attention, but you won't pay the high price of an emergency room visit. For major cities in Greece, the phone numbers and addresses for hospitals or medical centers are given in the relevant "Fast Facts" section in each destination chapter. In an emergency, call a **first-aid center** (*☎* **166**), the nearest **hospital** (*☎* **106**), or the **tourist police** (*☎* **171**).

Emergency treatment is usually given free of charge in state hospitals, but be warned that only basic needs are met. The care in outpatient clinics, which are usually open mornings (8am–noon), is often somewhat better; you can find them next to most major hospitals, on some islands, and occasionally in rural areas, usually indicated by prominent signs.

Insurance Given the sometimes unstable conditions in Greece in recent years, some might consider purchasing travel insurance. But it is vital to understand just what you are paying for—that is, exactly what kind of incident or situation would allow you to cancel and collect. Your own last-minute fears about strikes in Greece would not qualify, nor would a canceled flight within Greece.

For information on traveler's insurance, trip cancellation insurance, and medical insurance while traveling, please visit **www.frommers.com/planning**.

Internet & Wi-Fi Internet connection with or without Wi-Fi is now available virtually anywhere a visitor is apt to be. Some hotels do charge for either or both services (if this is important to you, inquire before you book). It is not necessary to travel with your own laptop unless you are on a working holiday; there are usually cyber/Internet cafes (indicated under "Fast Facts" for cities—but they are apt to come and go). To find cybercafes in your destination you might start by checking **www.cyber captive.com** and **www. cybercafe.com**. But frankly

these lists are by no means thorough or up to date when it comes to Greece. All decent-size cities now have Internet cafes in their centers; if you are having trouble finding one, ask a young person or a shop-owner.

If you have Web access while traveling, you might consider a broadband-based telephone service (in technical terms, **Voice-over Internet protocol,** or **VoIP**) such as Skype (www.skype. com) or Vonage (www. vonage.com), which allows you to make international calls if you use their services from your laptop or in a cybercafe. The people you're calling must also use the service for it to be free, although if you pay an extra fee for SkypeOut, you may call any phone number in the world. It is amazingly cheap. Check the sites for details. Skype also allows you to share full-screen real-time videos if both users have the proper hardware and programs on their computers.

Another way to use your computer to stay in touch (as of this writing who knows what else will come along) is **mobility broadband.** Your computer must be able to handle wireless, but it is not the same system as Wi-Fi. Instead, it turns your laptop computer into a sort of cellphone and connects it with the cellular service—in this case, available basically everywhere throughout Greece. You do this by plugging in a special flash-drive-like modem into a USB port on your

computer. Once connected, you can receive and send your e-mail as well as access Internet sites—and at high speeds. You only pay for the time you are online and rates in Greece, although not especially cheap at 25¢ a minute, are reasonable for quick and vital occasions. You can get a cheaper rate if you buy a block of time by prepaying, or you can have your charge card billed as you use the minutes. Several companies in Greece—Cosmote, Vodaphone, Wind—now offer this service, but you might start by checking into **www.mobility pass.com**.

Language Language is usually not a problem for English speakers in Greece, as so many Greeks have studied it and find it necessary to use in their work worlds—most particularly, in the tourist realm that visitors encounter. Many Greeks have also lived abroad where English is the primary language. Young people learn it in school, from Anglo-American-dominated pop culture, and in special classes meant to prepare them for the contemporary world of business. Several television programs are broadcast in their original languages, and American prime-time soaps are very popular, nearly inescapable. Even advertisements have an increasingly high English content. Don't let all this keep you from trying to pick up at least a few words of Greek; your effort will be rewarded by your hosts, who realize how difficult their language is for foreigners and will patiently help you improve your pronunciation and usage.

There are several books and audio courses on learning Greek, including *Berlitz's Greek for Travelers, Passport's Conversational Greek in 7 Days,* and *Teach Yourself Greek Complete Course* (book and CD pack). In recent years, Rosetta Stone has been heavily promoting its courses as the best way to learn a foreign language; based on my own experience, this is not the best way for those who simply want to learn some basic and functional Greek for traveling there. It is, rather, for those who intend to learn the language for long-term usage.

Meanwhile, see "Useful Terms & Phrases" in chapter 14.

Legal Aid If you need legal assistance, contact your own or another English-speaking embassy or consulate; their addresses and phone numbers are provided at "Embassies & Consulates," above, or in the "Fast Facts" sections of major cities. If these institutions cannot themselves be of help, they can direct you to local lawyers who speak English and are willing to help.

LGBT Travelers
Greece—or at least parts of Greece—has a long tradition of being tolerant of homosexual men, and in recent years these locales

have extended this tolerance to lesbians. Bars and such places especially open to and frequented by LBGT travelers are identified in the relevant locales. But it should be said: Although Greeks in Athens, Piraeus, and perhaps a few other major cities may not care one way or the other, Greeks in small towns and villages—indeed, most Greeks—do not appreciate flagrant displays of dress or behavior. Among the best-known hangouts for gays and lesbians are Mykonos, Mitilini (Lesvos), and Chania, Crete, but gays and lesbians travel all over Greece without any particular issues. That said, the age of consent for sexual relations with homosexuals is 17, and this can be strictly enforced against foreigners.

The International Gay and Lesbian Travel Association (IGLTA; ℰ 800/448-8550 or 954/630-1637; www.iglta.org) is the trade association for the gay and lesbian travel industry, and offers an online directory of gay- and lesbian-friendly travel businesses and tour operators.

Mail The mail service of Greece is reliable—but slow. (Postcards usually arrive weeks after you have returned.) You can receive mail addressed to you c/o *Poste Restante,* General Post Office, City (or Town), Island (or Province), Greece. You will need your passport to collect this mail. Many hotels will accept, hold, and even forward mail for you; ask first. American Express

clients can receive mail at any Amex office in Athens, Corfu, Iraklion, Mykonos, Patras, Rhodes, Santorini, Skiathos, and Thessaloniki, for a nominal fee and with proper identification. If you are in a particular hurry, try FedEx or one of the other major international private carriers; travel agencies can direct you to these.

Postage rates have been going up in Greece, as they are elsewhere. At press time, a postcard or a letter under 20 grams (about .7 oz.) to foreign countries costs .75€; 20 to 50 grams (up to 1.75 oz.), 1.30€; 50 to 100 grams (3.5 oz.), 1.75€. Rates for packages depend on size as well as weight, but are reasonable. *Note:* Do not wrap or seal any package—you must be prepared to show the contents to a postal clerk. If you are concerned about some particular item, you might consider using one of the well-known international commercial delivery services. Your hotel or any travel agency can direct you to the nearest local office.

Medical Requirements There are no immunization requirements for getting into Greece, though it's always a good idea to have polio, tetanus, and typhoid covered when traveling anywhere. See "Health," above.

Mobile Phones The three letters that define much of the world's wireless capabilities are **GSM (Global System for Mobile Communications),** a big, seamless network that makes for easy cross-border cellphone use throughout Europe—including Greece—and indeed most countries around the world. In the U.S., T-Mobile, and AT&T Wireless, use this quasi-universal system; in Canada, Microcell and some Rogers customers are GSM, and most Australians use GSM.

GSM phones function with a removable plastic SIM card, encoded with your phone number and account information. But some phones are "locked" and must be unlocked; go to your phone's website and get information as to how to unlock your phone. If your cellphone is on a GSM system, and you have a world-capable multiband phone such as many Sony Ericsson, Motorola, or Samsung models, you can make and receive calls around much of the globe. Just call your wireless operator and ask for "international roaming" to be activated on your account. Unfortunately, per-minute charges can be high—usually $1 to $1.50 in Greece. But the reassuring point is that cellphone services are generally available wherever you go in Greece.

An alternative way if you intend to make many phone calls in Greece is to bring your unlocked cellphone to Greece and buy a SIM card in the national telephone office (OTE) center in major cities or a commercial phone store. These cards—actually a tiny chip inserted into your phone—cost about 20€ and include a Greek phone number and a number of prepaid minutes; when you have used up these minutes, you can purchase a phone card at a kiosk that gives you more minutes. But it must be said that any calls outside of Greece by this system are very expensive.

For many, **renting** a phone in Greece is a good idea. You can rent a phone from any number of places in Greece—including kiosks at major airports, OTE offices, and cellphone stores.

But if you expect to be abroad for more than a brief time, and/or to be visiting more than one country, **buying a phone** can be economically attractive. Numerous companies now sell phones with a SIM card included and with a U.S. or U.K. phone number assigned to it—so-called global roaming services that offer relatively cheap per-minute rates for both outgoing and incoming calls: Typical would be 90¢ from Greece to the U.S. and 25¢ from the U.S. to Greece. (U.K. rates are much cheaper.) Google "global roaming SIM card" to compare various services and charges or look into **www.cellularabroad.com**.

Alternatively, you can buy a phone in Greece in either the national telephone office (OTE) in any decent sized city or a commercial retail electronics store. If you take the cheapest package; you'll probably pay less than $100 for a phone and a starter calling card. Local calls may be as low as 10¢ per minute, and in many countries incoming calls are free.

For information about VoIP, mobility broadband and related alternatives, see "Internet & Wi-Fi," above; for information about telephone calls in general, see "Telephones," later in this section.

Money & Costs Frommer's lists exact prices in the local currency. The currency conversions provided were correct at press time. However, rates fluctuate, so before departing consult a currency exchange website such as **www.oanda.com/currency/converter** to check up-to-the-minute rates. The currency in Greece is the **euro** (pronounced *evro* in Greek), abbreviated "Eu" and symbolized by €. (If you still own the old drachmas, it is no longer possible to exchange them.)

The euro comes in seven paper notes and eight coins. The notes are in different sizes and colors. They are in the following denominations: 5, 10, 20, 50, 100, 200, and 500. (Considering that each euro is worth over $1, those last bills are quite pricey.) Six of the coins are officially "cents"—but in Greece they have become referred to as *lepta,* the old Greek name for sums smaller than the drachma. They come in different sizes and their value is 1, 2, 5, 10, 20, and 50. There are also 1€ and 2€ coins. Although one side of the coins differs in each of the member E.U. nations, all coins and bills are legal tender in all countries using the euro.

Warning: The 1€ and 2€ coins look similar to a 1 lira Turkish coin—worth less than half the 1€, so count your change carefully.

It's a good idea to exchange at least some money—just enough to cover airport incidentals and transportation to your hotel—before you leave home, so you can avoid lines at airport ATMs. You can exchange money at your local American Express or Thomas Cook office or at some banks.

For many decades after World War II, Greece was one of the great bargain destinations for tourists. But since the 1990s, there is no denying that it can no longer be described this way. It may not be in the category of London or New York or Paris or Tokyo, but in the major cities and hot spots, hotels are no longer bargains and the upscale restaurants are comparable to such restaurants in most other developed countries. Admission to major museums and archaeological sites is now comparable to fees in major cities. Flights within Greece are expensive, as are car rentals—especially in high season.

(Gasoline/petrol will seem outrageously expensive only to Americans.) But it is still possible to have a reasonably modest holiday in Greece. You can start by visiting outside the high season—July and August. Pick midprice hotels and restaurants—and make sure breakfast is included in your hotel price. Look around for deals on car rentals. Fly off-peak hours, and avoid expensive services such as spas or purchases such as jewelry.

For help with currency conversions, tip calculations, and more, download Frommer's convenient Travel Tools app for your mobile device. Go to **www.frommers.com/go/mobile** and click on the Travel Tools icon.

ATMs

In commercial centers, airports, all cities and larger towns, and most tourist centers, you will find at least a couple of machines accepting a wide range of cards. Smaller towns will often have only one ATM—and it may not accept your card. **Commercial Bank (Emboriki Trapeza)** services Plus and Visa; **Credit Bank (Trapeza Pisteos)** and **AlphaBank** accept Visa and American Express; **National Bank (Ethniki Trapeza)** takes Cirrus and MasterCard/Access.

But for all the prevalence of ATMs around Greece, you should keep at least one fallback currency for those occasions when even all the ATMs you can locate are out of order or out of cash. Keep enough euros or your own national currency or travelers' checks hidden somewhere to get you through at least 24 hours.

Note: Greek ATMs accept only a four-digit PIN—you must change yours before you go. And since Greek ATMs use only numeric PINs (personal identification numbers), before you set off for Greece be sure you know how to convert letters to numerals as the alphabet will be in Greek.

Debit Cards

The easiest and best way to get cash away from home is from an ATM. **Cirrus** (☎ 800/622-7747; www.mastercard.com) and **PLUS** (☎ 800/843-7587; www.visa.com) networks span the globe; look at the back of your bank card to see which network you're on, then call or check online for ATM locations at your destination. If your bank, credit, or debit card is affiliated with one of the major international credit cards (such as MasterCard or Visa), you should not have any trouble getting money in Greece. However, there are limits to the amount of cash you can

THE VALUE OF THE EURO VS. OTHER POPULAR CURRENCIES

Euro €	Aus$	Can$	NZ$	UK£	US$
1	A$1.35	C$1.34	NZ$1.80	£0.85	$1.45

WHAT THINGS COST IN ATHENS IN EUROS

Taxi from the airport to downtown Athens	35€–50€
Double room, moderate	90€–110€
Double room, inexpensive	65€–85€
Three-course dinner for one without wine, moderate	12€–20€
Bottle of beer	2.50€–4€
Cup of coffee	1.50€–3.50€
1 gallon/1 liter of gas	6.70€/1.75€
Admission to museums and archaeological sites	2€–12€

withdraw in 24 hours—usually about 200€ so plan ahead if you expect to need a large sum.

A new product that has been introduced by **Travelex** is a debit card known as the **Chip and PIN Cash Passport:** In addition to the magnetic strip, it has a microchip and a PIN that allows you to use it in all those situations that require the European-type card, in particular where there is no one present—parking lots, tollbooths, ticketing machines, and so on. It can be used wherever a MasterCard is accepted. There is no fee but of course you must transfer to Travelex the sum of money you expect to draw on; more can be added by phoning or going online (**www.travelex.com**). These cards may be purchased in most major airports in the U.S. and in Travelex offices in major cities with cash or a MasterCard or Visa; online purchases require either of those charge cards.

Credit Cards
Credit cards are another safe way to obtain cash as well as make payments. They provide a convenient record of your expenses, and they generally offer relatively good exchange rates (although often with hefty fees). You can withdraw cash advances from your credit cards at banks or ATMs provided you know your PIN. In Greece, Visa and MasterCard are the most widely accepted cards. Diners Club is less widely accepted. American Express is still less frequently accepted because it charges a higher commission and is more protective of the cardholder in disagreements.

Beware of hidden credit card fees while traveling. Check with your credit or debit card issuer to see what fees, if any, will be charged for overseas transactions. Recent reform legislation in the U.S., for example, has curbed some exploitative lending practices. But many banks have responded by increasing fees in other areas, including fees for customers who use credit and debit cards while out of the country—even if

those charges were made in U.S. dollars. Fees can amount to 3% or more of the purchase price. Check with your bank before departing to avoid any surprise charges on your statement.

Multicultural Travelers
Greece has a long tradition of welcoming people from around the world, and there is no expectation that people of color are treated any differently than other foreigners. However, people of African descent have up to now not made Greece a particular destination, although that may be changing. Likewise, Greeks have not set up any special network of hotels, resorts, or restaurants to cater to individuals of African descent—or for that matter, any people of color. But we would like to believe that all people of color are treated as all other guests in Greece, and in our (albeit limited) encounters with African-Americans in Greece, we have always found this to be true. What people might experience, however, is being stared at

THREE warnings ABOUT DEBIT & CREDIT CARDS

As part of banks' and credit card companies' increasing concern about fraud, it is our experience that they are apt to deny your cards if you go to use them too far out of your normal circuit of use. It's a wise idea to contact your cards' customer service department by phone and inform them of your travel plans.

Meanwhile, perhaps you have been reading about the new Chip-and-PIN (aka "Smart Cards") credit cards that are being introduced throughout much of the world. Unlike the long-standard credit cards that have only a magnetic strip, these have a small chip embedded in them and then require the user to enter a PIN. The European Union has required all its member nations to introduce these, but as of this writing, most American issuers of credit cards have not adopted them. This means that Americans abroad may face a problem when presenting their standard magnetic strip cards: some places may claim that they are no longer acceptable. In

fact, they are: If the individual rejecting your card doesn't already know this, he must punch in your card number manually—but then you must provide him with that card's PIN. So if you do not know your card's PIN, you must call your card issuer and obtain one (for MasterCard, call ℂ 800/622-7747; for Visa, ℂ 800/857-2911). Allow some time for this as it may involve sending mail from and back to the issuer. *Note:* This problem does not arise if you are using a card as a debit card, which already requires a PIN.

Credit cards are accepted in Greece in the better hotels and at most shops. But even many of the better restaurants in major cities do *not* accept credit cards, and certainly most restaurants and many smaller hotels throughout Greece do not. Some hotels that require a credit card number when you make advance reservations demand payment in cash; inquire beforehand if this will be the case.

by some individuals in communities not accustomed to seeing people of color.

As for making any special travel arrangements, again, it must be said that agencies that do specialize in servicing travelers of African descent probably have little experience in making arrangements in Greece. One exception is the African-American–owned agency in Philadelphia, **Rodgers Travel** (ℂ 888/823-1775; www.rodgerstravel.com), which handles clients of all colors. So the best advice is to go

to any travel agency that handles arrangements for Greece and expect to be treated like everyone else.

Newspapers & Magazines All cities, large towns, and major tourist centers have at least one shop or kiosk that carries a selection of foreign-language publications; most of these are flown or shipped in on the very day of publication. English-language readers have a wide selection, including most of the British papers (*Daily Telegraph, Financial Times, Guardian, Independent,*

Times), the *International Herald Tribune* (with its English-language insert of the well-known Athens newspaper, *Kathimerini*), and *USA Today. Kathimerini,* by the way, has an online English edition that is quite adequate for keeping up with Greek news (**www.ekathimerini.com**).

Passports For entry into Greece, citizens of Australia, Canada, New Zealand, South Africa, the United States, and almost all other non-E.U. countries are required to have a **valid passport,** which is stamped upon entry and exit, for stays up to 90 days. All U.S. citizens, even infants, must have a valid passport, but Canadian children under 16 may travel without a passport if accompanied by either parent.

Citizens of the United Kingdom and other members of the European Union are required to present a valid ID (driving licenses do not qualify) for entry into Greece; you may stay an unlimited period (although you should inquire about this at a Greek consulate or at your embassy in Greece). Children under 16 from E.U. countries may travel without an ID if accompanied by either parent. All E.U. citizens are reminded that they should check the requirements for non-E.U. countries through which you might travel to get to Greece.

For stays longer than 90 days, all non-E.U. citizens will require visas from the Greek embassies or consuls in their home countries. If already in Greece, arrangements must be made with the **Bureau of Aliens,** 173 Leoforos Alexandras, 11522 Athens (© **210/770-5711**). See **www.frommers.com/ planning** for information on how to obtain a passport.

For Residents of Australia Contact the **Australian Passport Information Service** at © **131-232,** or visit the government website at www.passports.gov.au.

For Residents of Canada Contact the central **Passport Office,** Department of Foreign Affairs and International Trade, Ottawa, ON K1A 0G3 (© **800/567-6868;** www.ppt.gc.ca).

For Residents of Ireland Contact the **Passport Office,** Setanta Centre, Molesworth Street, Dublin 2 (© **01/671-1633;** www.irlgov.ie/iveagh).

For Residents of New Zealand Contact the **Passports Office** at © **0800/225-050** in New Zealand or 04/474-8100, or log on to www.passports.govt.nz.

For Residents of the United Kingdom Visit your nearest passport office, major post office, or travel agency or contact the **United Kingdom Passport Service** at © **0870/521-0410** or search its website at www.ukpa.gov.uk.

For Residents of the United States To find your regional passport office, either check the U.S. State Department website or call the **National Passport Information Center** toll-free number (© **877/487-2778**) for automated information.

Petrol (Gasoline) See "Getting Around: By Car," earlier in this chapter.

Police To report a crime or medical emergency, or for information or other assistance, first contact the local tourist police (© **171**), where an English-speaking officer is more likely to be found. If there is no tourist police officer available, contact the local police at © **100.** Tourists who report petty thievery to the local police will probably feel that they are not being taken all that seriously, but it is more likely that the Greek police have realized there is little they can do without solid identification of the culprits. As for the other side of the coin—police being exceptionally hard on foreigners, say, when enforcing traffic violations—although there is the rare reported incident, it does not seem to be widespread. Drugs are a different story: Greek authorities and laws are extremely tough when it comes to foreigners with drugs—starting with marijuana. Do *not* attempt to bring any illicit drug into or out of Greece.

Safety Crime directed at tourists was traditionally unheard of in Greece, but in more recent years there are occasional reports of cars broken into, pickpockets, purse snatchers, and the like. (Ask yourself whether it is necessary to travel with irreplaceable valuables such as jewelry.) Normal precautions are called for. For instance, if you have hand luggage containing expensive items, whether jewelry or cameras, never give it to an individual unless you are absolutely sure it will be safe with him or her. Lock the car and don't leave cameras or other such gear visible. Don't leave your luggage unattended when entering or leaving hotels. Also, it is probably safer not to leave valuables unattended at beaches. And young women should observe the obvious precautions in dealing with men in isolated locales.

One other thing that might be of concern to some: Greece is undeniably exposed to earthquakes, but there are almost no known instances in recent decades of tourists being injured or killed in one of these. Of far more potential danger are automobile accidents: Greece has one of the worst vehicle accident rates in Europe. You should exercise great caution when driving over unfamiliar, often winding, and often poorly maintained roads. This holds true especially when you're driving at night. As for those who insist on renting motorbikes or similar vehicles, at the very least wear a helmet.

Senior Travel Greece does not offer many discounts for seniors. Some museums and archaeological sites offer discounts for those 60 and over, but the practice is unpredictable; in almost all cases the discount is restricted to citizens of an E.U. nation.

For general information before you go, visit the U.S. Department of State website at **http://travel.state. gov** for information specifically for older Americans.

Try mentioning that you're a senior when you make your travel reservations. Although almost all major U.S. airlines have canceled their senior discount and coupon-book programs, many hotels continue to offer discounts for seniors.

Members of **AARP,** 601 E St. NW, Washington, DC 20049 (☎ **888/687-2277;** www.aarp.org), get discounts on hotels, airfares, and car rentals. AARP offers members a wide range of benefits, including *AARP The Magazine* and a monthly newsletter. Anyone over 50 can join.

Many reliable agencies and organizations target the 50-plus market. **Road Scholar** (formerly **Elderhostel;** ☎ **800/454-5768;** www.roadscholar.org) arranges study programs for those ages 55 and over (and a spouse or companion of any age) in the U.S. and in more than 80 countries around the world. Most courses last 5 to 7 days in the U.S. (2–4 weeks abroad), and many include airfare, accommodations in university dormitories or modest inns, meals, and tuition. In Greece, groups typically settle in one area for a week or so, with excursions that focus on getting to know the history and culture. Canada-based **ElderTreks** (☎ **800/741-7956;** www.eldertreks.com) offers small-group tours to off-the-beaten-path or adventure-travel locations, restricted to travelers 50 and older. Britons might prefer to deal with **Saga Holidays** (Saga Bldg., Folkestone, Kent CT20 1AZ; ☎ **800/096-0084** in the U.S. and Canada, or 0808/234-1714 in the U.K.; www.saga.co.uk), which offers all-inclusive tours in Greece for those ages 50 and older.

Single Travelers Single travelers are usually hit with a "single supplement" to the base price for package vacations and cruises, while the price of a single room is almost always well over half that for a double. To avoid such charges, you might consider agreeing to room with other single travelers or to find a compatible roommate before you go from one of the many roommate locator agencies.

Travel Buddies Singles Travel Club (☎ **800/998-9099;** www.travelbuddies worldwide.com), based in Canada, runs small, intimate, single-friendly group trips and will match you with a roommate free of charge. **TravelChums** (☎ **212/787-2621;** www. travelchums.com) is an Internet-only travel-companion matching service with elements of an online personals-type site, hosted by the respected New York–based Shaw Guides travel service.

Many tour companies offer singles-only trips. **Singles Travel International** (☎ **877/765-6874;** www. singlestravelintl.com) offers singles-only escorted tours to places such as the Greek Islands. **Backroads** (☎ **800/462-2848;** www.backroads. com) offers "Singles + Solos" active-travel trips to destinations worldwide.

Smoking In recent years the Greeks have imposed no-smoking regulations on airplanes, on areas of ships, and—as of July 1, 2009—all public locations (banks, post offices, and so on);

also small restaurants, tavernas, and cafes must declare whether they allow smoking or not; larger such establishments are supposed to set aside smoking areas. But Greeks continue to be among the most persistent smokers and, except on airplanes, many Greeks—and some foreigners—feel free to puff away at will. Hotels are only beginning to claim that they have set aside rooms or even floors for nonsmokers, so ask about them if it matters to you. If you are really bothered by smoke while eating, about all you can do is position yourself as best as possible—and then be prepared to leave if it gets really bad.

Student Travel   In Greece, students with proper identification (ISIC and IYC cards) are given reduced entrance fees to archaeological sites and museums, as well as discounts on admission to most artistic events, theatrical performances, and festivals. So you'd be wise to arm yourself with an **International Student Identity Card (ISIC),** which offers substantial savings on rail passes, plane tickets, and entrance fees. It also provides you with basic health and life insurance and a 24-hour help line. The card is available for $22 from **STA Travel** (🕾 **800/781-4040;** www.statravel.com), the biggest student travel agency in the world.

The **International Student Travel Confederation (ISTC;** www.istc.org) was formed in 1949 to make travel around the world more affordable for students. Check out its website for comprehensive travel services information for students.

If you're no longer a student but are still under 26, you can get an **International Youth Travel Card (IYTC)** from the same people, entitling you to some discounts. **Travel CUTS** (🕾 **800/592-2887;** www.travelcuts.com) offers similar services for Canadians and U.S. residents. Irish students may prefer **USIT** (🕾 **01/602-1906;** www.usit.ie), an Ireland-based specialist in student, youth, and independent travel.

In the United States, one of the major organizations for arranging overseas study for college-age students is the **Council on International Education Exchange,** or **CIEE** (🕾 **800/407-8839;** www.ciee.org).

A Hostelling International membership can save students money in some 5,000 hostels in 70 countries, where sex-segregated, dormitory-style sleeping quarters cost about $15 to $35 per night. In the United States, membership is available through **Hostelling International–American Youth Hostels,** 8401 Colesville Rd., Silver Spring, MD 20910 (🕾 **301/495-1240;** www.hiayh.org). A 1-year membership is free for ages 17 and under; $28 for ages 18 to 54; $18 for ages 55 and over. In Greece, an International Guest Card can be obtained at the **Greek Association of Youth Hostels (OESE),** in Athens at 75 Dhamereos, Athens 11633 (🕾 **210/751-9530;** www.athens-yhostel.com).

Taxes & Service Charges   The **value added tax** (VAT) has, in response to Greece's economic crisis, been greatly increased—it now stands at 23% for many purchases and services, including restaurants and car rentals; food and medicine and certain other "vital goods" tend to have a VAT of 11% while books and newspapers have 5.5%. You may sometimes be given a printed receipt that shows these percentages but the point to realize is that the taxes have been included in the price quoted and charged. In addition to the VAT, hotel prices usually include a service charge of up to 12% and a "community tax," about 4% to 5%. (By the way, don't confuse any of these charges with many restaurants' "cover charge" that may be .50€ to 2€ per place setting.) Also, see "Tipping," below.

If you have purchased an item that costs 100€ or more and are a citizen of a non–European Union nation, you can get most of the VAT refunded (provided you export it within 90 days of purchase). It's easiest to shop at stores that display the sign tax-free for tourists. However, any store should be able to provide you with a Tax-Free Check Form, which you complete in the store. If you use your charge card, the receipt will list the VAT separately from the cost of the item. As you are leaving the country, present a copy of this form to the refund desk (usually at the Customs office). Be prepared to show both the goods and the receipt as proof of purchase. Also be prepared to wait a fair amount of time before you get the refund. (In fact, the process at the airport seems designed to discourage you from trying to obtain the refund.)

Telephones Until the late 1990s in Greece, most foreigners went to the offices of the Telecommunications Organization of Greece (OTE, pronounced oh-*tay*, or *Organismos Tilepikinonion tis Ellados*) to place most of their phone calls, especially overseas. But because phone cards are now so widespread throughout Greece, this is no longer necessary, once you get the hang of using them. You must first purchase a phone card at an OTE office or at most kiosks. (If you expect to make any phone calls while in Greece, buy one at the airport's OTE office upon arrival.) The cards come in various denominations, from 3€ to 25€: the more costly the card, the cheaper the units. The cost of a call with a phone card varies greatly depending on local, domestic, and international rates. A local call of up to 3 minutes to a fixed phone costs about .10€, which is three units from a phone card; for each minute beyond that, it costs

another .06€, or two units off the card (so that a 10-min. local call costs 17 units, or .52€). All calls, even to the house next door, cost Greeks something, so if you use someone's telephone even for a local call, offer to pay the charges.

In larger cities and larger towns, kiosks have telephones from which you can make local calls for .10€ for 3 minutes. (In remote areas, you can make long-distance calls from these phones.) A few of the older public pay phones that required coins are still around, but it's better to buy a phone card. If you must use an older pay phone, deposit the required coin and listen for a dial tone, an irregular beep. A regular beep indicates that the line is busy.

Note: All phone numbers in Greece are 10 digits long, including the area code; the area code may range from three to five digits, and the number itself may range from five to eight digits, but the total will always be 10. All (except for cellphones— see earlier) also precede the city/area code with a 2 and end that with a 0. For example, since the Athens city code was originally 1, it is now 210, followed by a seven-digit number, but most other numbers in Greece are six digits with a four-digit area code. In all cases, even if you are calling someone in the same building, you must dial all 10 digits. Calling a mobile phone requires substituting

a 6 for the 2 that precedes the area code.

Long-distance calls, both domestic and international, can be quite expensive in Greece, especially at hotels, which may add a surcharge of up to 100%, unless you have a telephone credit card from a major long-distance provider such as AT&T, MCI, or Sprint. But if possible, avoid making long-distance calls from a hotel.

If you prefer to make your call from an OTE office, these are centrally and conveniently located in all decent sized cities. At OTE offices, a clerk will assign you a booth with a metered phone. You can pay with a phone card, international credit card, or cash. Collect calls take much longer.

To Call Greece from the United States, Canada, U.K., Australia, or New Zealand:

1. Dial the international access code: 011 from the U.S or Canada.; 00 from the U.K., Ireland, or New Zealand; or 0011 from Australia
2. Dial the country code: 30
3. Dial the city code (three to five digits) and then the number. **Note:** All numbers in Greece must have 10 digits, including the city code.

To Make International Calls from Within Greece The easiest and cheapest way is to call your long-distance service provider before leaving home to determine the access number that you must dial in Greece. The principal access codes in Greece are: AT&T, ☏ 00800-1311; MCI, ☏ 00800-1211; and Sprint, ☏ 00800-1411. Most companies also offer a voice-mail service in case the number you call is busy or there's no answer.

If you must use the Greek phone system to make a direct call abroad—whether using an OTE office, a phone that takes cards, or a phone that takes coins—dial the country code plus the area code (omitting the initial zero, if any), then dial the number. Some country codes are: Australia, 0061; Canada, 001; Ireland, 00353; New Zealand, 0064; United Kingdom, 0044; and United States, 001. Thus, if you wanted to call the British Embassy in Washington, D.C., you would dial 001-202-588-7800.

Note that if you are going to put all the charges on your phone card (that is, not on your long-distance provider), you will be charged at a high rate per minute (at least 3€ to North America), so you should not make a call unless your phone card's remaining value can cover it.

For Operator Assistance: If you need operator assistance in making a call, dial ☏ **139** if you're trying to make an international call and ☏ **169** if you want to call a number in Greece.

Toll-Free Numbers: Numbers beginning with **080** within Greece are toll-free, but calling a 800 number in the States from Greece is not toll-free. In fact, it costs the same as an overseas call.

Rechargeable Phone Cards: One of the newest, easiest, and cheapest ways to make calls while abroad is to sign on for a phone card that can be used in most countries and can be recharged (that is, money and therefore minutes added from your charge card account). To learn more about this card and its various other feature, see **www.ekit.com**.

Time   The 24-hour clock is used to measure time, so on schedules you'll see noon as 1200, 3:30pm as 1530, and 11pm as 2300. In informal conversation, however, Greeks express time much as we do—though noon may mean anywhere from noon to 3pm, afternoon is 3 to 7pm, and evening is 7pm to midnight.

Greece is 2 hours ahead of Greenwich Mean Time. In reference to North American time zones, it's 7 hours ahead of Eastern Standard Time, 8 hours ahead of Central Standard Time, 9 hours ahead of Mountain Standard Time, and 10 hours ahead of Pacific Standard Time. Note that Greece does observe daylight saving time, although it may not start and stop on the same days as in North America. For help with time translations, download our convenient Travel Tools app for your mobile device. Go to **www.frommers.com/go/ mobile** and click on the Travel Tools icon.

Tipping   Restaurant bills no longer include a service charge or tip and it is customary to leave 10% to 15%; also consider "rounding off" on larger bills; to the nearest 1€. Good taxi service merits a tip of 5% to 10%. (Greeks rarely tip taxi drivers, but tourists are expected to.) Hotel chambermaids should be left about 2€ per night per couple. Bellhops and doormen should be tipped 1€ to 5€, depending on the services they provide.

For help with tip calculations, currency conversions, and more, download our Travel Tools app for your mobile device. Go to **www. frommers.com/go/mobile** and click on the Travel Tools icon.

Toilets   Most Greek establishments—hotels, restaurants, museums, and so on—now provide flush toilets, but especially in villages, you may still be asked to deposit toilet paper in a container beside the toilet. In cheaper and more remote restaurants, however, you may find that there is no water at the hand bowl or a shortage of toilet paper so you might consider keeping some tissues with you.

Public restrooms are generally available in any good-size Greek town, and though they are sometimes rather crude, they usually work. (Old-fashioned stand-up/squat facilities are still found.) If there is an attendant you are expected to leave a small tip.

In an emergency, you can ask to use the facilities of a restaurant or shop;

however, near major attractions, the facilities are denied to all but customers, because traffic is too heavy. If you use any such facilities, respect its sponsor and give an attendant a tip.

VAT See "Taxes & Service Charges," above.

Visas Travelers bearing passports from the European Union countries, the U.S., Canada, Australia, and New Zealand do not need visas, nor do citizens of many other countries. But to be sure, check with the nearest Greek consulate. And allow several weeks to get such a visa.

Visitor Information The **Greek National Tourism Organization** (**GNTO** or **EOT** in Greece—and increasingly referred to as the Hellenic Tourism Organization) has offices throughout the world that can provide you with information concerning all aspects of travel to and in Greece. Look for them at **www.gnto.gr** or contact one of the following GNTO offices:

United States Olympic Tower, 645 Fifth Ave., 5th Floor, New York, NY 10022 (© **212/421-5777;** fax 212/826-6940).

Australia & New Zealand 37–49 Pitt St., Sydney, NSW 2000 (© **29/241-1663;** fax 29/241-2499).

Canada 1500 Don Mills Rd., Toronto, ON M3B 3K4 (© **416/968-2220;** fax 416/968-6533).

United Kingdom & Ireland 4 Conduit St., London W1S 2DJ (© **207/495-9300;** fax 207/495-4057).

Anyone with access to the Web can obtain a fair amount of information about Greece. Remember that these sources cannot necessarily be counted on for the most up-to-date, definitive, or complete information. We advise you to use computer searches as *supplements only,* and then check out specific facts on which you are going to base your travel plans. Websites are continually being changed and added, but among the most useful for broad-based searches are:

- www.mfa.gr (official Greek matters)
- www.gtp.gr (ship and air travel in Greece)
- www.phantis.com (current news about Greece)
- www.culture.gr (official site for Greek's cultural attractions)
- www.perseus.tufts.edu (classical Greek texts)

But probably the best source for up-to-date on-the-ground travel information is on **www.frommers.com**, both its Updates and its Community Forums.

Water The public drinking water in Greece is safe to drink, although it can be slightly brackish in some locales near the sea. For that reason, many people prefer the bottled water commonly available at restaurants, hotels, cafes, food stores, and kiosks. And the days when Greek restaurants automatically served glasses of cold fresh water are gone; you can ask for simply the tap or house water—be sure to do so before the waiter opens bottled water. If you do order bottled water, you will have to choose between natural or carbonated *(metalliko),* and domestic or imported. Cafes, however, tend to provide a glass of natural water.

Wi-Fi See "Internet & Wi-Fi," earlier in this section.

Women Travelers Women traveling in Greece should not run into any situations particularly different from those encountered by men. That said, young women—especially singles or small groups—may well find Greek males coming on to them, especially at beaches, clubs, and other tourist locales in a rather forward manner. But our informants tell us that in general, Greek males (a) do not attempt any physical contact; and (b) sooner or later respect "No." One tactic said to work for women is to say, "I'm a Greek-American." The other advice is not to leave well-attended locales with someone you don't really know. Women should also be aware that some cafes and even restaurants are effectively male-only haunts; the men will not appreciate attempts by foreign women to enter these places.

THE GREEK LANGUAGE

There are many different kinds of Greek—the Greek of conversation in the street, the Greek used at a fashionable dinner party, the Greek used in newspapers, the Greek of a government notice, the Greek used by a novelist or a poet, and more—and they can differ from one another in grammar and in vocabulary much more than the English of, for example, a conversation at the water cooler and that of an editorial in the *New York Times*. Greek, like English, has a written history molded by influential works that continue to be read and studied for centuries—in Greek even for millennia—so that as in English, older words and styles of expression remain available for use even while the spoken language happily evolves on its own.

Also, as in English, Greek has kept the spelling of its words largely unchanged even though their pronunciation has changed. In English, this spelling lag has extended for some 5 centuries, but in Greek it is 25 centuries old. This makes it easier for us to read Shakespeare and for Greeks to read Herodotus than it might otherwise be, but it also means that Greek children, like English-speaking children, have to learn to spell words that they already know to use in conversation.

The dilemma is further complicated because many Greek words and names have entered the English language by way of Latin or French, and so have become familiar to English speakers in forms that owe something to those languages. When these words are directly transliterated from modern Greek (and that means from Greek in its modern pronunciation, not the ancient one that Romans heard), they almost always appear in a form other than the one you may have read about in school. "Perikles" for Pericles or "Delfi" for Delphi are examples; "Thivi" for Thebes or "Omiros" for Homer can give you an idea of the traps often in store for the innocent traveler. The bottom line is that the names of towns, streets, hotels, items on menus, historical figures, archaeological sites—you name it—are likely to have more than one spelling as you come across them in books, on maps, or before your very eyes.

Sometimes the name of a place has changed over the centuries. If you think you've just arrived in Santorini but you see a sign welcoming you to Thira, smile, remember you're in Greece, and take heart. (Santorini is the name the Venetians used, and it became common in Europe for that reason. Thira is the original Greek name.) This short chapter offers you a few aids to help you make your way in Greek. First: Remember that literacy is nearly universal in Greece. The table below will help you move from Greek letters or words to a sense of how they should sound. This transliteration of modern Greek is used throughout this book, except in reference to names that have become household words in English, like Athens, Socrates, Olympus, and so on. Generally, all you have to say is what you are looking for, raising your voice at the end of the word to let your listener know it's a question, and bingo!—someone will help.

Do remember that *óhi*, although it can sound a bit like "okay," in fact means "no," and that *ne*, which can sound like a twangy "nay," means "yes." To complicate matters, some everyday gestures will be different from those you are used to: Greeks nod their heads upward to express an unspoken *óhi* and downward (or downward and to one side) for an unspoken *ne*. When a Greek turns his or her head from side to side at you—and you will see this despite your best efforts—it is a polite way of signaling, "I can't make out what you're saying." And remember: Almost any 40-year-old Greek can read Greek, and most people under 30 can also make out some English. If you find that your attempts at speaking fall on deaf ears, show someone the word for what you want and if you stumble over *efharisto* (thank you) you can place your hand over your heart and bow your head slightly.

Alphabet		Transliteration	Pronunciation
A α	álfa	a	father
B β	víta	v	viper
Γ γ	gámma	g before α, o, ω, and consonants	get
		y before αι, ε, ει, η, ι, οι, υ	yes
		ng before κ, γ, χ, or ξ	singer
Δ δ	thélta	th	the (not as the th- in "thin")
E ε	épsilon	e	set
Z ζ	zíta	z	lazy
H η	íta	i	magazine
Θ θ	thíta	th	thin (not as the th- in "the")
I ι	ióta	i	magazine
		y before a, o	yard, yore
K κ	káppa	k	keep
Λ λ	lámtha	l	leap
M μ	mi	m	marry
N ν	ni	n	never
Ξ ξ	ksi	ks	taxi
O o	ómicron	o	bought
Π π	pi	p	pet
P ρ	ro	r	round
Σ σ/ς	sígma	s before vowels or θ, κ, π, τ, φ, χ, ψ	say
		z before β, γ, δ, ζ,	
		y before λ, μ, ν, ρ	lazy
T τ	taf	t	take
Y υ	ípsilon	i	magazine
Φ φ	fi	f	fee

Alphabet	Transliteration	Pronunciation
Χ χ chi	h	*h*ero (before e and i sounds; like the *ch*- in Scottish "loch" otherwise)
Ψ ψ psi	ps	colla*ps*e
Ω ω ómega	o	bought

Combinations	Transliteration	Pronunciation
αι	e	g*e*t
αϊ	ai	*ai*sle
αυ before vowels or β, γ, δ, ζ, λ, μ, ν, ρ	av	*Av*e Maria
αυ before θ, κ, ξ, π, σ, τ, φ, χ, ψ	af	pil*af*
ει	i	magaz*i*ne
ευ before vowels or β, γ, δ, ζ, λ, μ, ν, ρ	ev	*ev*er
ευ before θ, κ, ξ, π, σ, τ, φ, χ, ψ	ef	l*ef*t
μπ at beginning of word	b	*b*ane
μπ in middle of word	mb	lu*mb*er
ντ at beginning of word	d	*d*umb
ντ in middle of word	nd	sle*nd*er
Οι	i	magaz*i*ne
Οϊ	oi	o*i*l
Ου	ou	s*ou*p
τζ	dz	roa*ds*
τσ	ts	ge*ts*
υι	i	magaz*i*ne

USEFUL TERMS & PHRASES

When you're asking for or about something and have to rely on single words or short phrases, it's an excellent idea to use *"sas parakaló,"* meaning "please" or "you're welcome" to introduce or conclude almost anything you say.

Airport	Aerothrómio
Automobile	Aftokínito
Avenue	Leofóros
Bad	Kakós, -kí, -kó*
Bank	Trápeza
Breakfast	Proinó
Bus	Leoforío
Can you tell me?	Boríte ná moú píte?
Cheap	Ft(h)inó

Church	Ekklissía
Closed	Klistós, stí, stó*
Coffeehouse	Kafenío
Cold	Kríos, -a, -o*
Dinner	Vrathinó
Do you speak English?	Miláte Angliká?
Excuse me.	Signómi(n)
Expensive	Akrivós, -í, -ó*
Farewell!	Stóka-ló! *(to person leaving)*
Glad to meet you.	Chéro polí.**
Good	Kalós, lí, ló*
Goodbye.	Adío *or* chérete.**
Good health (cheers)!	Stín (i)yá sas *or* Yá-mas!
Good morning *or* Good day.	Kaliméra
Good evening.	Kalispéra
Good night.	Kaliníchta**
Hello!	Yássas *or* chérete!**
Here	Ethó
Hot	Zestós, -stí, -stó*
Hotel	Xenothochío**
How are you?	Tí kánete *or* Pós íst(h)e?
How far?	Pósso makriá?
How long?	Póssi óra *or* Pósso(n) keró?
How much does it cost?	Póso káni?
I am a vegetarian.	Íme hortophágos
I am from New York.	Íme apótí(n) Néa(n) Iórki
I am lost *or* I have lost the way.	Écho chathí *or* Écho chási tón drómo(n)**
I don't understand.	Thén katalavéno.
I don't understand, please repeat it.	Thén katalavéno, péste to páli, sás parakaló.
I'm sorry.	Singnómi.
I'm sorry, but I don't speak Greek (well).	Lipoúme, allá thén miláo elliniká (kalá).
I want to go to the airport.	Thélo ná páo stóaerothrómio.
I want a glass of beer.	Thélo éna potíri bíra.
I would like a room.	Tha íthela ena thomátio.
It's (not) all right.	(Dén) íne en dáxi.
Left (direction)	Aristerá
Lunch	Messimerianó
Map	Chártis**

Market (place)	Agorá
Mr.	Kírios
Mrs.	Kiría
My name is . . .	Onomázome . . .
New	Kenoúryos, -ya, -yo*
No	Óchi**
Old	Paleós, -leá, -leó* (*pronounce* palyós, -lyá, -lyó)
Open	Anichtós, -chtí, -chtó*
Patisserie	Zacharoplastío**
Pharmacy	Pharmakío
Please *or* You're welcome.	Parakaló.
Please call a taxi (for me).	Parakaló, fonáxte éna taxi (yá ména).
Point out to me, please . . .	Thíkste mou, sas parakaló . . .
Post office	Tachidromío**
Restaurant	Estiatório
Restroom	Tóméros *or* I toualétta
Right (direction)	Dexiá
Saint	Áyios, ayía, (*plural*) áyi-i (*abbreviated* ay)
Show me on the map.	Díxte mou stó(n) chárti.**
Square	Plateia
Station (bus, train)	Stathmos (leoforíou, trénou)
Stop (bus)	Stási(s) (leoforíou)
Street	Odós
Thank you (very much).	Efcharistó(polí).**
Today	Símera
Tomorrow	Ávrio
Very nice	Polí oréos, -a, -o*
Very well	Polí kalá *or* En dáxi
What?	Tí?
What time is it?	Tí ôra íne?
What's your name?	Pós onomázest(h)e?
Where am I?	Pou íme?
Where is . . . ?	Poú íne . . . ?
Why?	Yatí?

*Masculine ending -os, feminine ending -a or -i, neuter ending -o.

**Remember, *ch* should be pronounced as in Scottish *loch* or German *ich,* not as in the word *church.*

Numbers

0	Midén	**17**	Dekaeftá	**150**	Ekatón penínda
1	Éna	**18**	Dekaoktó	**151**	Ekatón penínda éna
2	Dío	**19**	Dekaenyá	**152**	Ekatón penínda dío
3	Tría	**20**	Íkossi	**200**	Diakóssya
4	Téssera	**21**	Íkossi éna	**300**	Triakóssya
5	Pénde	**22**	Íkossi dío	**400**	Tetrakóssya
6	Éxi	**30**	Triánda	**500**	Pendakóssya
7	Eftá	**40**	Saránda	**600**	Exakóssya
8	Októ	**50**	Penínda	**700**	Eftakóssya
9	Enyá	**60**	Exínda	**800**	Oktakóssya
10	Déka	**70**	Evdomínda	**900**	Enyakóssya
11	Éndeka	**80**	Ogdónda	**1,000**	Chílya*
12	Dódeka	**90**	Enenínda	**2,000**	Dío chilyádes*
13	Dekatría	**100**	Ekató(n)	**3,000**	Trís chilyádes*
14	Dekatéssera	**101**	Ekatón éna	**4,000**	Tésseris chilyádes*
15	Dekapénde	**102**	Ekatón dío	**5,000**	Pénde chilyádes*
16	Dekaéxi				

*Remember, ch should be pronounced as in Scottish *loch* or German *ich,* not as in the word *church.*

Days of the Week

Monday	**Deftéra**
Tuesday	**Tríti**
Wednesday	**Tetárti**
Thursday	**Pémpti**
Friday	**Paraskeví**
Saturday	**Sávvato**
Sunday	**Kiriakí**

Menu Terms

arní avgolémono   lamb with lemon sauce

arní soúvlas   spit-roasted lamb

arní yiouvétsi   baked lamb with orzo

bakaliáro (skordaliá)   cod (with garlic)

barboúnia (skáras)   red mullet (grilled)

briám   vegetable stew

brizóla chiriní   pork steak or chop

brizóla moscharísia   beef or veal steak

choriátiki saláta   "village" salad ("Greek" salad to Americans)

dolmades   stuffed vine leaves

domátes yemistés mé rízi   tomatoes stuffed with rice

eksóhiko   lamb and vegetables wrapped in phyllo

garídes   shrimp

glóssa (tiganití)   sole (fried)

kalamarákia (tiganitá)   squid (fried)

kalamarákia (yemistá)   squid (stuffed)

kaparosaláta   salad of minced caper leaves and onion

karavídes   crayfish

keftedes   fried meatballs

kotópoulo soúvlas   spit-roasted chicken

kotópoulo yemistó   stuffed chicken

kouloúri   pretzel-like roll covered with sesame seeds

loukánika   spiced sausages

loukoumades   round, doughnut center–like pastries deep-fried, then drenched with honey and topped with powdered sugar and cinnamon

melitzanosaláta   eggplant salad

moussaká   meat-and-eggplant casserole

oktapódi   octopus

païdákia   lamb chops

paradisiako   traditional Greek cooking

pastítsio   baked pasta with meat

piláfi rízi   rice pilaf

piperiá yemistá   stuffed green peppers

revídia   chickpeas

saganáki   grilled cheese

skordaliá   hot garlic-and-beet dip

soupiés yemistés   stuffed cuttlefish

souvlaki   lamb (sometimes veal) on the skewer

spanokópita   spinach pie

stifádo   stew, often of rabbit or veal

taramosaláta   fish roe with mayonnaise

tirópita   cheese pie

tsípoura   dorado

tzatzíki   yogurt-cucumber-garlic dip

youvarlákia   boiled meatballs with rice

Index

Accommodations

3/12

3/12

LINDENHURST MEMORIAL LIBRARY

3 1801 00494 9982

LINDENHURST MEMOR[IAL]
LINDENHURST, NEW Y[ORK]